The Ancient Bronze Implements, Weapons, And Ornaments: Of Great Britain And Ireland...

Sir John Evans

THE ANCIENT

BRONZE IMPLEMENTS,

WEAPONS, AND ORNAMENTS,

OF

GREAT BRITAIN AND IRELAND.

THE ANCIENT

BRONZE IMPLEMENTS,

WEAPONS, AND ORNAMENTS,

OF

GREAT BRITAIN

AND

IRELAND.

BY

JOHN EVANS, D.C.L., LL.D., F.R.S.,

F.S.A., F.G.S., Pres. Num. Soc., &c

LONDON:

LONGMANS, GREEN, & CO.

1881.

LONDON
PRINTED BY VIRTUE AND CO., LIMITED
CITY ROAD.

PREFACE.

THE work which is now presented to the public has unfortunately been many years in progress, as owing to various occupations, both private and public, the leisure at my command has been but small, and it has been only from time to time, often at long intervals, that I have been able to devote a few hours to its advancement. During this slow progress the literature of the subject, especially on the Continent, has increased in an unprecedentedly rapid manner, and I have had great difficulty in at all keeping pace with it.

I have, however, done my best, both by reading and travel, to keep myself acquainted with the discoveries that were being made and the theories that were being broached with regard to bronze antiquities, whether abroad or at home, and I hope that so far as facts are concerned, and so far as relates to the present state of information on the subject, I shall not be found materially wanting.

Of course in a work which treats more especially of the bronze antiquities of the British Islands, I have not felt bound to enlarge more than was necessary for the sake of comparison on the corresponding antiquities of other countries. I have, however, in all cases pointed out such analogies in form and character as seemed to me of importance as possibly helping to throw light on the source whence our British bronze civilisation was derived.

It may by some be thought that a vast amount of useless trouble has been bestowed in figuring and describing so many varieties of what were after all in most cases the ordinary tools of the artificer, or the common arms of the warrior or huntsman, which differed from each other only in apparently unimportant particulars. But as in biological studies minute anatomy often affords the most trustworthy evidence as to the descent of any given organism

from some earlier form of life, so these minor details in the form
and character of ordinary implements, which to the cursory
observer appear devoid of meaning, may, to a skilful archæologist,
afford valuable clues by which the march of the bronze civilisation
over Europe may be traced to its original starting-place.

I am far from saying that this has as yet been satisfactorily
accomplished, and to my mind it will only be by accumulating a
far larger mass of facts than we at present possess that comparative archæology will be able to triumph over the difficulties with
which its path is still beset.

Much is, however, being done, and I trust that so far as the
British Isles are concerned, the facts which I have here collected
and the figures which I have caused to be engraved will at all
events form a solid foundation on which others may be able to
build.

So long ago as 1876 I was able to present to the foreign
archæologists assembled at Buda-Pest for the International Congress of Prehistoric Archæology and Anthropology, a short abstract
of this work in the shape of my *Petit Album de l'âge du Bronze
de la Grande Bretagne*, which I have reason to believe has been
found of some service. At that time my friend the late Sir
William Wilde was still alive, and as the bronze antiquities of
Ireland appeared to be especially under his charge, I had not regarded
them as falling within the scope of my book. After his lamented
death there was, however, no possibility of interfering with his
labours, by my including the bronze antiquities of the sister country
with those of England, Wales, and Scotland in the present work,
and I accordingly enlarged my original plan.

In carrying out my undertaking I have followed the same
method as in my work on the "Ancient Stone Implements, &c., of
Great Britain;" and it will be found that what I may term the
dictionary and index of bronze antiquities is printed in smaller
type than the more general descriptive and historical part of the
book. I have in fact offered those who take an ordinary interest
in archæological inquiry without wishing to be burdened with
minute details a broad hint as to what they may advantageously
skip. To the specialist and the local antiquary the portion
printed in smaller type will be found of use, if only as giving
references to other works in which the more detailed accounts of
local discoveries are given. These references, thanks to members
of my own family, have been carefully checked, and the accuracy

of all the original figures for this work, engraved for me with
conscientious care by Mr. Swain, of Bouverie Street, may, I think,
be relied on.

To the councils of several of our learned societies, and especially
to those of the Societies of Antiquaries of London and Edinburgh,
the Royal Irish Academy, the Royal Archæological Institute, and
the Royal Historical and Archæological Association of Ireland, I
am much indebted for the loan of woodcuts and for other assist-
ance. I have also to thank the trustees and curators of many
local museums, as well as the owners of various private collections,
for allowing me to figure specimens, and for valuable information
supplied.

My warmest thanks are, however, due to Mr. Augustus W.
Franks, F.R.S., and Canon Greenwell, F.R.S., not only for assist-
ance in the matter of illustrations, but for most kindly undertaking the task of reading my proofs. I must also thank Mr.
Joseph Anderson, the accomplished keeper of the Antiquarian
Museum at Edinburgh, and Mr. Robert Day, F.S.A., of Cork, for
having revised those portions of the work which relate to Scotland
and Ireland.

The Index has been carefully compiled by my sister, Mrs.
Hubbard. As was the case with those of my " Ancient Stone Implements," and "Ancient British Coins," it is divided into two parts;
the one referring generally to the subject matter of the book, and
the other purely topographical. The advantages of such a division
in a book of this character are obvious.

In conclusion, I venture to prefer the request that any discoveries of new types of instruments or of deposits of bronze
antiquities may be communicated to me.

JOHN EVANS.

NASH MILLS, HEMEL HEMPSTED,
March, 1881.

CONTENTS.

CHAPTER XII.

LEAF-SHAPED SWORDS.

CHAPTER XIII.

SCABBARDS AND CHAPES.

CHAPTER XIV.

SPEAR-HEADS, LANCE-HEADS, ETC.

CHAPTER XV.

SHIELDS, BUCKLERS, AND HELMETS.

CHAPTER XVI.

TRUMPETS AND BELLS.

CHAPTER XVII.

PINS.

CHAPTER XVIII.

TORQUES, BRACELETS, RINGS, EAR-RINGS, AND PERSONAL ORNAMENTS.

CHAPTER XIX.

CLASPS, BUTTONS, BUCKLES, AND MISCELLANEOUS OBJECTS.

CHAPTER XX.

VESSELS, CALDRONS, ETC.

CHAPTER XXI.

METAL, MOULDS, AND THE METHOD OF MANUFACTURE.

CHAPTER XXII.

CHRONOLOGY AND ORIGIN OF BRONZE.

WOODCUT ILLUSTRATIONS.

———

The references are to the original sources of such cuts as have not been engraved expressly for this book.

CHAPTER V.

SOCKETED CELTS.

ERRATA.

Page 117, under fig. 123, *for* "Crishall" *read* "Chrishall."
  „ 143, line 15, *for* "Spain" *read* "Portugal."
  „ 207, „ 34, *for* "St. Genoulph" *read* "St. Genouph."
  „ 215, „ 16, *for* "St. Julien Chateuil" *read* "St. Jullien, Chapeuil."
  „ 314, „ 3 from bottom, *for* "Staffordshire" *read* "Shropshire."
  „ 322, „ 4, *for* "Suffolk" *read* "Sussex."
  „ 336, „ 20, *for* "Staffordshire" *read* "Shropshire."
  „ 452, „ 4 from bottom, *for* "Staffordshire" *read* "Shropshire."

CHAPTER I.

HAVING already in a former work attempted the arrangement and description of the Ancient Stone Implements and Ornaments of Great Britain, I am induced to undertake a similar task in connection with those Bronze Antiquities which belong to the period when Stone was gradually falling into disuse for cutting purposes, and Iron was either practically unknown in this country, or had been but partially adopted for tools and weapons.

The duration and chronological position of this bronze-using period will have to be discussed hereafter, but I must at the outset reiterate what I said some eight or ten years ago, that in this country, at all events, it is impossible to fix any hard and fast limits for the close of the Stone Period, or for the beginning or end of the Bronze Period, or for the commencement of that of Iron. Though the succession of these three stages of civilisation may here be regarded as certain, the transition from one to the other in a country of such an extent as Britain—occupied, moreover, as it probably was, by several tribes of different descent, manners, and customs—must have required a long course of years to become general; and even in any particular district the change cannot have been sudden.

There must of necessity have been a time when in each district the new phase of civilisation was being introduced, and the old conditions had not been entirely changed. So that, as I have elsewhere pointed out, the three stages of progress represented by the Stone, Bronze, and Iron Periods, like the three principal colours of the rainbow, overlap, intermingle, and shade off the one into the other, though their succession, so far as Britain and Western Europe are concerned, appears to be equally well defined with that of the prismatic colours.

B

In thus speaking of a bronze-using period I by no means wish to exclude the possible use of copper unalloyed with tin. There is indeed every ground for believing that in some parts of the world the use of native copper must have continued for a lengthened period before it was discovered that the addition of a small proportion of tin not only rendered it more readily fusible, but added to its elasticity and hardness, and thus made it more serviceable for tools and weapons. Even after the advantages of the alloy over the purer metal were known, the local scarcity of tin may at times have caused so small a quantity of that metal to be employed, that the resulting mixture can hardly be regarded as bronze; or at times this dearth may have necessitated the use of copper alone, either native or as smelted from the ore.

Of this Copper Age, however, there are in Europe but extremely feeble traces, if indeed any can be said to exist. It appears not unlikely that the views which are held by many archæologists as to the Asiatic origin of bronze may prove to be well founded, and that when the use of copper was introduced into Europe, the discovery had already long been made that it was more serviceable when alloyed with tin than when pure. In connection with this it may be observed that the most important discovery of instruments of copper as yet recorded in the Old World is that which was made at Gungeria in Central India.* They consisted of flat celts of what has been regarded as the most primitive type; but with them were found some ornaments of silver, a circumstance which seems to militate against their extreme antiquity, as the production of silver involves a considerable amount of metallurgical skill, and probably an acquaintance with lead and other metals. However this may be, there are reasons for supposing that if a Copper Age existed in the Old World its home was in Asia or the most eastern part of Europe, and not in any western country.

The most instructive instance of a Copper Age, as distinct from one of Bronze, is that afforded by certain districts of North America, in which we find good evidence of a period when, in addition to stone as a material from which tools and weapons were made, copper also was employed, and used in its pure native condition without the addition of any alloy.

The State of Wisconsin† alone has furnished upwards of a hundred axes, spear-heads, and knives formed of copper; and, to judge from some extracts from the writings of the early travellers

* See *postea*, p. 40.   † Butler, "Prehist. Wisconsin."

given by the Rev. E. F. Slafter,* that part of America would seem to have entered on its Copper Age long before it was first brought into contact with European civilisation, towards the middle of the sixteenth century. It has been thought by several American antiquaries that some at least of these tools and weapons were produced by the process of casting, though the preponderance of opinion seems to be in favour of all of them being shaped by the hammer and not cast. Among others I may mention my friend the Hon. Colonel C. C. Jones, who has examined this question for me, and has been unable to discover any instance of one of these copper tools or weapons having been indisputably cast.

That they were originally wrought, and not cast, is à priori in the highest degree probable. On some parts of the shores of Lake Superior native copper occurs in great abundance, and would no doubt attract the attention of the early occupants of the country. Accustomed to the use of stone, they would at first regard the metal as merely a stone of peculiarly heavy nature, and on attempting to chip it or work it into shape would at once discover that it yielded to a blow instead of breaking, and that in fact it was a malleable stone. Of this ductile property the North American savage availed himself largely, and was able to produce spear-heads with sockets adapted for the reception of their shafts by merely hammering out the base of the spear-head and turning it over to form the socket, in the same manner as is so often employed in the making of iron tools. But though the great majority of the instruments hitherto found, if not all, have been hammered and not cast, it would appear that the process of melting copper was not entirely unknown. Squier and Davis have observed,† "that the metal appears to have been worked in all cases in a cold state. This is somewhat remarkable, as the fires upon the altars were sufficiently strong in some instances to melt down the copper implements and ornaments deposited upon them, and the fact that the metal is fusible could hardly have escaped notice." That it did not altogether escape observation is shown by the evidence of De Champlain,‡ the founder of the city of Quebec. In 1610 he was joining a party of Algonquins, one of whom met him on his barque, and after conversation "tira d'un sac une pièce de cuivre de la longueur d'un pied qu'il me donna, le quel

* "Preh. Copper Impl.," Boston, 1879.
† "Anc. Mon. of the Mississ. Valley," p. 202.
‡ "Les Voyages du Sieur de Champlain," Paris, 1613, pp. 246—7, cited by Slafter, op. cit., p. 13.

estoit fort beau et bien franc, me donnant à entendre qu'il en avoit
en quantité là ou il l'avoit pris, qui estoit sur le bort d'une rivière
proche d'un grand lac et qu'ils le prenoient par morceaux, et le
faisant fondre le mettoient en lames, et avec des pierres le ren-
doient uny."

We have here, then, evidence of a Copper Age,* in comparatively
modern times, during most of which period the process of fusing
the metal was unknown.   In course of time, however, this art was
discovered, and had not European influences been brought to bear
upon the country this discovery might, as in other parts of the
world, have led to the knowledge of other fusible metals, and
eventually to the art of manufacturing bronze—an alloy already
known in Mexico and Peru.†

So far as regards the Old World there are some who have supposed that, owing to iron being a simple and not a compound
metal like bronze, and owing to the readiness with which it may
be produced in the metallic condition from some of its ores, iron
must have been in use before copper. Without denying the
abstract possibility of this having been the case in some part of our
globe, I think it will be found that among the nations occupying
the shores of the eastern half of the Mediterranean—a part of the
world which may be regarded as the cradle of European civilisation
—not only are all archæological discoveries in favour of the succession of iron to bronze, but even historical evidence supports
their testimony.

In the Introductory Chapter of my book on Ancient Stone
Implements I have already touched upon this question, on which,
however, it will here be desirable farther to enlarge.

The light thrown upon the subject by the Hebrew Scriptures is
but small.   There is, however, in them frequent mention of most
of the metals now in ordinary use.   But the word נְחֹשֶׁת, which in
our version is translated brass—a compound of copper and zinc—
would be more properly translated copper, as indeed it is in one
instance, though there it would seem erroneously, when two vessels
of fine copper, precious as gold, are mentioned.‡   In some passages,
however, it would appear as if the word would be more correctly

* For notices of American copper instruments see, in addition to the works already
quoted, Wilson, "Prehist. Man," vol. i. p. 205, &c.; Lubbock, "Preh. Times," p. 258,
&c.   See also an interesting article by Dr. Emil Schmidt, in *Archiv. für Anth.*, vol. xi.
p. 65.

† A Peruvian chisel analyzed by Vauquelin gave ·94 of copper and ·06 of tin (Moore's
"Anc. Mineralogy," p. 42).

‡ Ezra, ch. viii. v. 27.

rendered bronze than copper, as, for instance, where Moses* is commanded to cast five sockets of brass for the pillars to carry the hangings at the door of the tabernacle, which could hardly have been done from a metal so difficult to cast as unalloyed copper. Indeed if tin were known, and there appears little doubt that the word בְּדִיל represents that metal, its use as an alloy for copper can hardly have been unknown. It may, then, be regarded as an accepted fact that at the time when the earliest books of the Hebrew Scriptures were reduced to writing, gold,† silver, iron, tin, lead, and brass, or more probably bronze, were known. To what date this reduction to writing is to be assigned is a question into which it would be somewhat out of place here to enter. The results, however, of modern criticism tend to prove that it can hardly be so remote as the fourteenth century before our era.

In the Book of Job, as to the date of which also there is some diversity of opinion, we find evidence of a considerable acquaintance with the metals : "Surely there is a vein for the silver, and a place for gold where they fine it. Iron is taken out of the earth, and brass is molten out of the stone."‡ Lead is also mentioned, but not tin.

Before quitting this part of the subject I ought perhaps to allude to the passage respecting Tubal-Cain,§ the seventh in descent from Adam, who is mentioned as "an instructer of every artificer in brass and iron," or a furbisher|| of every cutting instrument in those metals. This must, however, be regarded as a tradition incorporated in the narrative at the time it was written, and probably with some accessory colouring in connection with the name which Gesenius has suggested may mean *scoriarum faber,* a maker of dross, and which others have connected with that of Vulcan. Sir Gardner Wilkinson¶ has remarked on this subject that whatever may have been the case in earlier times, "no direct mention is made of iron arms or tools till after the Exodus," and that "some are even inclined to doubt the *barzel* (בַּרְזֶל), of the Hebrews being really that metal," iron.

Movers** has observed that in the whole Pentateuch iron is mentioned only thirteen times, while bronze appears no less than forty-four, which he considers to be in favour of the later introduction of iron; as also the fact that bronze, and not iron,

---

* Exod., ch. xxvi. v. 37. † Numbers, ch. xxxi. v. 22.
‡ Ch. xxviii. v. 1, 2. § Genesis, ch. iv. v. 22.
|| Smith's "Dict. of the Bible," *s. v.* ¶ "Anc. Egyptians," vol. iii. p.
** "Phönicier," ii. 3.

was associated with gold and silver in the fittings for the Tabernacle.

For other passages in Scripture relative to the employment of brass or bronze, and iron, among the Jews, the reader may consult an excellent article by the Rev. John Hodgson in the first volume of the *Archæologia Æliana* (1816), "An Inquiry into the Era when Brass was used in purposes to which Iron is now applied." From this paper I have largely borrowed in subsequent pages.

As to the succession of the two metals, bronze and iron, among the ancient Egyptians, there is a considerable diversity of opinion among those who have studied the subject. Sir Gardner Wilkinson,[*] judging mainly from pictorial representations, thinks that the Egyptians of an early Pharaonic age were acquainted with the use of iron, and accounts for the extreme rarity of actual examples by the rapid decomposition of the metal in the nitrous soil of Egypt. M. Chabas,[†] the author of a valuable and interesting work upon primitive history, mainly as exhibited by Egyptian monuments, believes that the people of Egypt were acquainted with the use of iron from the dawn of their historic period, and upwards of 3000 years B.C. made use of it for all the purposes to which we now apply it, and even prescribed its oxide as a medicinal preparation. M. Mariette,[‡] on the contrary, whose personal explorations entitle his opinion to great weight, is of opinion that the early Egyptians never really made use of iron, and seems to think that from some mythological cause that metal was regarded as the bones of Typhon, and was the object of a certain repugnance. M. Chabas himself is, indeed, of opinion that iron was used with extreme reserve, and, so to speak, only in exceptional cases. This he considers to have been partly due to religious motives, and partly to the greater abundance of bronze, which the Egyptians well knew how to mix so as to give it a fine temper. From whatever cause, the discovery of iron or steel instruments among Egyptian antiquities is of extremely rare occurrence; and there are hardly any to which a date can be assigned with any approach to certainty. The most ancient appears to be a curved scimitar-like blade discovered by Belzoni beneath one of the Sphinxes of Karnak, and now in the British

[*] "Anc. Egyptians," vol. iii. pp. 246, 247. See also "The Egyptians in the Time of the Pharaohs," p. 99.
[†] "Etudes sur l'Antiquité Historique d'après les sources Egyptiennes," &c., 1872, p. 69.
[‡] "Catalogue de Boulaq," pp. 247, 248; Chabas, p. 54. See also Emil Soldi, "L'Art Egyptien," 1879, p. 41.

Museum.* Its date is stated to be about 600 B.C.† A wedge of iron appears, however, to have been found in a joint between the stones of the Great Pyramid.‡

Without in any way disputing the occasional use of iron among the ancient Egyptians, nor the interpretation of the colours red and blue on the tomb of Rameses III. as being intended to represent blades of bronze and iron or steel respectively, I may venture to suggest that the round blue bar,§ against which butchers are represented as sharpening their knives in some of the pictures in the sepulchres of Thebes, may have been too hastily regarded as a *steel* instead of as a whetstone of a blue colour. The existence of a *steel* for the purpose of sharpening seems to imply not only the knowledge of the preparation of the metal and its subsequent hardening, but also of files or of other tools to produce the peculiar striated surface to which the sharpening property of a *steel* is due. Had such tools been known, it seems almost impossible that no trace of them should have come down to our times. Moreover, if used for sharpening bronze knives, a steel such as at present used would sooner become clogged and unfit for use than if employed for sharpening steel knives.

Lepsius ‖ has observed that the pictures of the old Empire do not afford an example of arms painted in blue, the metal of weapons being always painted in red or bright brown. Iron was but little used under the old Empire; copper was employed in its stead where the hardness of iron was not indispensable.

However this may be, it seems admitted on all hands that the use of iron in Egypt in early times was much restricted, probably from some religious motive. May not this have arisen from the first iron there known having been, as it appears to have been in some other countries, of meteoric origin? The Coptic name for iron, **BENIПE**, which has been interpreted by Professor Lauth¶ as "the Stone of Heaven," strongly favours such a view. The resemblance of this term to **BAA-N-ПE**, the *baa* of heaven, or celestial iron, has also been pointed out by M. Chabas,** who, however, is inclined to consider that steel was so called on account of its reflecting the colour of the sky. If the iron in use among the

* Catal., No. 5410.   † Day, "Preh. Use of Iron and Steel," page 14.
‡ Day, *op. cit.*, p. 32.   § Wilkinson, *op. cit.*, vol. iii. p. 247.
‖ "Les Métaux dans les Inscrip. Egypt.," 1877, p. 57.
¶ "Zeitsch. f. Ægypt. Sprache," &c., 1870, p. 114.
** *Op. cit.*, p. 67. Dr. Birch translates *ba en pe* "heavenly wood" or "stone" (*Arch.*, vol. xxxviii. p. 377; *Hierog. Dict.*). See also a paper by the Rev. Basil Cooper in *Trans. Devon. Assoc.*, vol. ii. p. 386, and Day, "Preh. Use of Iron and Steel," p. 41.

early Egyptians were meteoric, and its celestial origin acknowledged, both its rarity and its restricted use would be accounted
for. The term "bone of Typhon," as applied to iron, is given by
Plutarch on the authority of Manetho, who wrote in the days of
the first Ptolemy. It appears to be used only in contrast to the
name "bone of Horus," which, according to the same author, was
applied to the loadstone, and it seems difficult to admit any great
antiquity for the appellation, or to connect it with a period when
iron was at all rare, or its use restricted.

Although the use of iron in Egypt was at an early period comparatively unknown, that of bronze was most extensive. The
weapons of war,* the tools for various trades, including those of the
engraver and sculptor, were all made of that metal, which in its
crude form served also as a kind of circulating medium. It
appears to have been mainly imported from Asia, some of the
principal sources of copper being in the peninsula of Sinai. One
of the chief mines was situated at Sarbout-el-Khadem, where
both turquoises and copper ore were extracted, and the latter
smelted at Wady-Nash. The copper mines of Wady-Magarah are
thought to have been worked as early as the second dynasty,
upwards of 3000 years B.C.; and in connection with ancient
Egyptian mining, it is worth while again to cite Agatharchides,[†]
whose testimony I have already adduced in my "Ancient Stone
Implements," and who relates that in his time, *circa* B.C. 100,
there were found buried in some ancient gold-mines in Upper
Egypt the bronze chisels or wedges (λατομίδες χαλκαῖ) of the old
miners, and who accounts for their being of that metal by the fact
that when those mines were wrought, men were in no way acquainted
with the use of iron.

In the seventh century B.C., however, iron must have been in
general use in Egypt, for on the landing of the Carians and Ionians,[‡]
who were armed with bronze, an Egyptian, who had never before
seen men armed with that metal, ran to Psammetichus to inform
him that brazen men had risen from the sea and were wasting the
country. As Psammetichus himself is described as wearing a
brazen helmet, the arms mentioned would seem to have been
offensive rather than defensive.

The source whence the tin, which formed a constituent part of

* Chabas, *op. cit.*, p. 47. Lepsius, *op. cit.*, p. 57.
† "Photii Bibliotheca," ed. 1653, col. 1343.
‡ "Herod.," lib. ii. c. 152.

the bronze, was derived, is much more uncertain. Indeed, to judge from M. Chabas' silence, its name and hieroglyphic are unknown, though from some of the uses to which the metal designated by ⟨ ⟩ was applied, it seems possible that it may have been tin.

On the whole, to judge from documentary evidence alone, the question as to the successive use of the different metals in Egypt seems to be excessively obscure, some of them being almost impossible to identify by name or representative sign. If, however, we turn to the actual relics of the past, we find bronze tools and weapons in abundance, while those of iron are extremely scarce, and are either of late date or at best of uncertain age. So strong, indeed, is the material evidence, that the late Mr. Crawfurd,[*] while disputing any general and universal sequence of iron to bronze, confesses that Ancient Egypt seems to offer a case in which a Bronze Age clearly preceded an Iron one, or at least in which cutting instruments of bronze preceded those of iron.

Among the Assyrians iron seems to have been in considerable use at an early date, and to have been exported from that country to Egypt, but knives and long chisels or hatchets of bronze were among the objects found at Tel Sifr, in Southern Babylonia. The earliest bronze image to which a date can be assigned appears to be that on which M. Oppert has read the name of Koudourmapouk, King of the Soumirs and Accads,[†] who, according to M. Lenormant, lived about 2100 B.C. Dr. S. Birch reads the name as Kudurmabug (about 2200 B.C.). Others in the British Museum are referred to Gudea, who reigned about 1700 B.C.

The mythology and literature of ancient Greece and Rome are so intimately connected, that in discussing the evidence afforded by classical writers it will be needless to separate them, but the testimony of both Greek and Latin authors may be taken indiscriminately, though, of course, the former afford the more ancient evidence. I have already cited much of this evidence in the Introductory Chapter of my book on Ancient Stone Implements, mainly with the view of showing the succession of bronze to stone; on the present occasion I have to re-adduce it, together with what corroborative testimony I am able to procure, in order to show that, along the northern shores of the Mediterranean, philology and history agree as to the priority of the use of bronze for cutting instruments to that of iron.

[*] *Trans. Ethnol. Soc.*, vol. iv. p. 5.   [†] Soldi, "L'Art Egypt.," p. 26.

The Greek language itself bears witness to this fact, for the words significant of working in iron are not derived from the name of that metal, but from that of bronze, and the old forms of χαλκεύς and χαλκεύειν remained in use in connection with the smith and his work long after the blacksmith had to a great extent superseded the bronze-founder and the copper-smith in the fabrication of arms and cutlery.* An analogous transition in the meaning of words has been pointed out by Professor Max Müller. " The Mexicans called their own copper or bronze *tepuztli*, which is said to have meant originally *hatchet*. The same word is now used for iron, with which the Mexicans first became acquainted through their intercourse with the Spaniards. *Tepuztli* then became a general name for metal, and when copper had to be distinguished from iron, the former was called red, the latter black *tepuztli*." † I am not certain whether Professor Max Müller still retains the views which he expressed in 1864. He then pointed out ‡ that "what makes it likely that iron was not known previous to the separation of the Aryan nations is the fact that its names vary in every one of their languages." But there is a " name for copper, which is shared in common by Latin and the Teutonic languages, *œs, œris,* Gothic *ais,* Old High German *ér,* Modern German *Er-z,* Anglo-Saxon *âr,* English *ore.* Like *chalkós,* which originally meant copper, but came to mean metal in general, bronze or brass, the Latin *œs,* too, changed from the former to the latter meaning; and we can watch the same transition in the corresponding words of the Teutonic languages. . . . . . It is all the more curious, therefore, that the Sanskrit *ayas,* which is the same word as *aes* and *aiz,* should in Sanskrit have assumed the almost exclusive meaning of iron. I suspect, however, that in Sanskrit, too, *ayas* meant originally the metal, *i.e.* copper, and that as iron took the place of copper, the meaning of *ayas* was changed and specified. . . . . . . In German, too, the name for iron was derived from the older name of copper. The Gothic *eisarn,* iron, is considered by Grimm as a derivative form of *aiz,* and the same scholar concludes from this that 'in Germany bronze must have been in use before iron.'"

But to return to Greece. It is, of course, somewhat doubtful how far the word χαλκὸς, as used by the earliest Greek authors, was

* Χαλκεύειν δὲ καὶ τὸ σιδηρεύειν ἔλεγον, καὶ χαλκεάς, τοὺς τὸν σίδηρον ἐργαζομένους (Julius Pollux, "Onomasticon," lib. vii. cap. 24).
† " Lectures on the Science of Language," 2nd S., 1864, p. 229 ; Tylor's " Anahuac," 1861, p. 140.
‡ " Lectures on the Science of Language," 2nd S., p. 231.

intended to apply to unalloyed copper, or to that mixture of copper and tin which we now know as bronze. Mr. Gladstone,[*] who on all questions relating to Homer ought to be one of the best living authorities, regards the word as meaning copper: firstly, because it is always spoken of by Homer as a pure metal along with other pure metals; secondly, on account of the epithets ἐρυθρὸς, ἤνοψ, and νώροψ, which mean red, bright, and gleaming, being applied to it, and which Mr. Gladstone considers to be inapplicable to bronze; and thirdly, because Homer does not appear to have known anything at all of the fusion or alloying of metals. The second reason he considers further strengthened by the probability that Homer would not represent the walls of the palace of Alcinous as plated with bronze, nor introduce a heaven of bronze among the imposing imagery of battle (Il., xvii. 424). On the whole he concludes that χαλκὸς was copper hardened by some method, as some think by the agency of water, or else and more probably according to a very simple process, by cooling slowly in the air.[†]

I regret to say that these conclusions appear to me to be founded to some extent on false premises and on more than one misconception. The process of heating copper and then dipping it in water or allowing it slowly to cool, so far from being adapted for hardening that metal, is that which is usually adopted for annealing or softening it. While the plunging into cold water of steel at a red heat has the effect of rendering that metal intensely hard, on copper the reverse is the result; and, as Dr. Percy has observed,[‡] it is immaterial whether the cooling after annealing—or restoring its malleability by means of heat—takes place slowly or rapidly. Indeed, one alloy of copper and tin is rendered most malleable by rapid cooling.

It has been stated[§] that bronze of the ancient composition may by cooling it slowly be rendered as hard as steel, and at the same time less brittle, but this statement seems to require confirmation.

According to some[||] the impossibility of hardening bronze like steel by dipping it into water had passed into a proverb so early as the days of Æschylus, but "χαλκοῦ βαφάς" has by others been

[*] "Studies on Homer and the Homeric Age," vol. iii. pp. 498, 499.
[†] The reference is to Millin, "Minéralogie Homérique," pp. 126, 132.
[‡] "Metallurgy—Fuel, Fireclays, Copper," &c., p. 6.
[§] Moore, "Anc. Mineralogy," p. 57.
[||] Rev. Arch., N.S., vol. iv. p. 97; Æsch. Agamem., v. 612. Professor Rolleston is inclined to refer the expression to the "tempering" of bronze (Trans. Brist. and Glouc. Arch. Soc., 1878).

regarded as referring to the impossibility of dyeing metal.* Some
of the commentators on Hesiod and Homer speak, however, distinctly as to a process of hardening bronze by a dipping or βαφὴ,
and Virgil † represents the Cyclopes as dipping the hissing bronze
in water—

"Alii stridentia tingunt
Æra lacu"—

but the idea of bronze being hardened or tempered by this process
appears to me to have been based on a false analogy between this
metal and steel, or even iron. The French chemist, Geoffroy,
thought he had succeeded in imitating the temper of an ancient
bronze sword, but no details are given as to whether he added
more than the usual proportion of tin to his copper, or whether
he hardened the edge with a hammer.

With regard to the other reasons adduced by Mr. Gladstone,
it is no doubt true that χαλκὸς is occasionally spoken of by Homer
as a pure metal, mainly, however, it may be argued, in consequence of the same name being applied to both copper and bronze,
if not, indeed, like the Latin " æs," to copper, bronze, and brass.
We find, moreover, that tin, for thus we must translate κασσίτερος,
is mentioned by Homer; and as this metal appears in ancient
times to have been mainly, though not exclusively, employed for
the purpose of alloying copper, we must from this fact infer that
the use of bronze was not unknown. In the celebrated description of the fashioning of the shield of Achilles by Vulcan—which
may for the moment be assumed to be of the same age as the
rest of the Iliad—we find the copper and tin mentioned in juxtaposition with each other; and if it had been intended to represent
Hephaistos as engaged in mixing and melting bronze, the description could not have been more complete.‡

Χαλκὸν δ'έν πυρὶ βάλλεν ἀτειρέα, κασσίτερόν τε.

Even the term indomitable may refer to the difficulty of melting
copper in its unalloyed condition.

But tin was also used in the pure condition. In the breast-
plate of Agamemnon § there were ten bands of black κύανος,
twelve of gold, and twenty of tin. In his shield ‖ were twenty
bosses of tin. The cows ¶ on the shield of Achilles were

---

* Rossignol, " Les Métaux dans l'Ant.," p. 238.   † " Æn.," viii. 450.
‡ " Iliad," xviii. 474.   § xi. 24.   ‖ xi. 34.   ¶ xviii. 574.

made of both gold and tin, and his greaves * of soft tin, and the border of the breast-plate of Asteropæus † was formed of glittering tin.

This collocation of various metals, or inlaying them by way of ornament, calls to mind some of the pottery and bronze pins of the Swiss Lake dwellings, which are decorated with inlaid tin, and the remarkable bronze bracelet found at Mœrigen,‡ which is inlaid with iron and a yellow brass by way of ornament.

With regard to the epithets red, bright, and gleaming, they are perfectly applicable to bronze in its polished condition, though they ill assort with the popular idea of bronze, which usually assigns to that metal the brown or greenish hues it acquires by oxidation and exposure to atmospheric influences. As a matter of fact, the red colour § of copper, though certainly rendered more yellow, is not greatly impaired by an admixture of tin within the proportions now used by engineers, viz. up to about two and a half ounces to the pound, or about 15 per cent. As to the bright and shining properties of the metal, Virgil, when no doubt speaking of bronze swords and shields, makes special mention of their glitter— ||

"Æratæque micant peltæ, micat æreus ensis."

Indeed, the mere fact of the swords of Homer being made of χαλκὸς is in favour of that metal being bronze, as pure copper would be singularly inapplicable to such a purpose, and certainly no copper sword would break into three or four pieces at a blow instead of being merely bent.¶

The bending of the points of the spear-heads against the shields of the adversaries is, however, in favour of these weapons having been of copper rather than of bronze.**

As to Homer having been unacquainted with the fusion or alloying of metals, it may fairly be urged that without such knowledge it would have been impossible to work so freely as he has described, in gold, silver, and tin ; and that the only reason for which Vulcan could have thrown the latter metal into the fire must have been in order to melt it.

---

* "Il.," xviii. 612.
† xxiii. 561. For these and other instances see Prof. Phillips in the *Arch. Journ.*, vol. xvi. p. 10.
‡ Desor et Favre, " Bel Age du Bronze," p. 16.
§ Holtzapffel, " Turning and Mechanical Manipulation," vol. i. p. 271.
|| " Æneid," vii. 743.   ¶ " Iliad," iii. 363.
** "Il.," iii. 348, vii. 259.

Whether steel was designated by the term κύανος is a matter of considerable doubt, and certainly in later times that word was applied to a substance occasionally used as a blue pigment, not improbably a dark blue carbonate of copper. Assuming the word to mean a metal, the difficulty in regarding it as significant of steel appears in a great measure due to the colour implied by the adjective form κυάνεος, being a dark blue.[*] If, however, it were the custom even in those days to colour steel blue by exposing it, after it had been polished, to a certain degree of heat—as is usually done with watch and clock springs at the present day—the deep blue colour of the sky or sea might well receive such an epithet. That steel of some kind was known in Homeric days is abundantly evident from the process of hardening an axe by dipping it in cold water while heated, which is so graphically described in the Odyssey.

If κύανος be really steel, we can also understand the epithet black [†] being occasionally applied to it, even though the adjective derived from it had the signification of blue.

According to the Arundelian Marbles, iron was discovered B.C. 1432,[‡] or 248 years before the taking of Troy, but though we have occasional mention of this metal and of steel in the Homeric poems, yet weapons and tools of bronze are far more commonly mentioned and described. Trees, for instance, are cut down and wood carved with tools of bronze ; and the battle-axe of Menelaus[§] is of excellent bronze with an olive-wood handle, long and well polished.

Before noticing further the early use of iron in Greece, it will be well to see what other authors than Homer say as to the origin and ancient use of bronze in that country.

The name of the principal metal of which it is composed, copper, bears witness to one of the chief sources of its supply having been the island of Cyprus. It would appear that Tamassus in this island was in ancient times a noted mart for this metal, as it is according to Nitzsch and other critics the Temese [||] mentioned in Homer as being resorted to in order to exchange iron for χαλκός, which in this as well as some other passages seems to stand for copper and not bronze.

The advantage arising from mixing a proportion of tin with the

---

[*] M. Ch. Houssel in *Rev. Arch.*, N.S., vol. iv. p. 98.   [†] "Il.," xi. 24.
[‡] *Arch. für Anthrop.*, vol. viii. p. 295; Müller, "Fragm. Hist. Græc.," vol. i. p. 549.
[§] "Il.," xiii. 612.   [||] "Odyss.," i. v. 184.

copper, and thus rendering it at the same time more fusible and harder, must have been known before the dawn of Grecian history.

The accounts given by early Greek writers as to the first discoverer of the art of making bronze by an admixture of copper and tin vary considerably, and thus prove that even in the days when these notices were written the art was of ancient date.

Theophrastus makes Delas, a Phrygian, whom Aristotle * regards as a Lydian, to have been the inventor of bronze. Pausanias † ascribes the honour of first casting statues in bronze to Rhœcus and Theodorus the Samians, who appear to have lived about 640 B.C. They are also said to have improved the accuracy of casting, but no doubt the process on a smaller scale was practised long before their time. Rhœcus and his colleague are also reported to have discovered the art of casting iron,‡ but no really ancient objects of cast iron have as yet been discovered.

The invention of the metals gold, silver, and copper is also ascribed to the Idæan Dactyli,§ or the Telchines, who made the sickle of Chronos ‖ and the trident of Poseidon.¶

Though, as has already been observed, iron and even steel were not unknown in the days of Homer, both seem to have been of considerable rarity, and it is by no means improbable that, as appears to have been the case with the Egyptians, the first iron used by the Greeks was of meteoric origin. I have elsewhere ** called attention to the possible connection of the Greek name for iron (σίδηρος) with ἀστήρ, often applied to a shooting-star or meteor, and with the Latin Sidera and the English Star, though it is unsafe to insist too much on mere verbal similarity. In an interesting article on the use of meteoric iron by Dr. L. Beck,†† of Biebrich on the Rhine, the suggestion is made that the final ηρος of σίδηρος is a form of the Aryan ais (conf: as, æris). Dr. Beck, however, inclines to the opinion that the recognition of certain meteorites as iron was first made at a time subsequent to the discovery of the means of smelting iron from its ore.

The self-fused mass or disc of iron,‡‡ σόλον αὐτοχόωνον, which formed one of the prizes at the funeral games of Patroclus, may possibly have been meteoric, but this is very doubtful, as the forging of iron, and the trouble and care it involved, were well

* Plin. "Hist. Nat.," lib. vii. c. lvi. 6.   † Lib. viii. c. 14, § 5.
‡ *Op. cit.*, lib. iii. c. 12, § 8.   § Diodorus Siculus, lib. v. c. 64.
‖ Strabo, "Geog.," lib. xiv. p. 935, ed. 1807.
¶ Callimachus, "Hymn. in Del.," l. 31.   ** "Anc. Stone Imp.," p. 5.
†† *Archiv für Anthrop.*, 1880, vol. xii. p. 293.   ‡‡ "Iliad," lib. xxiii. v. 826.

known in those days, as is evident from the epithet πολύκμητος so often bestowed upon that metal.

For a considerable time after the Homeric period bronze remained in use for offensive weapons, especially for those intended for piercing rather than cutting, such as spears, lances, and arrows, as well as for those which were merely defensive, such as shields, cuirasses, helmets, and greaves. Even swords were also sometimes of bronze, or at all events the tradition of their use was preserved by the poets. Thus we find Euripides [*] speaking of the bronze-speared Trojans, χαλκεγχέων Τρώων, and Virgil [†] describing the glitter of the bronze swords of some of the host of Turnus.

Probably, however, the use of the word χαλκὸς was not restricted to copper or bronze, but also came in time to mean metal in general, and thus extended to iron, a worker in which metal was, as we have already seen, termed a χαλκεύς.

The succession of iron to bronze is fully recognised by both Greek and Latin authors. The passage in Hesiod,[‡] where he speaks of the third generation of men who had arms of bronze and houses of bronze, who ploughed with bronze, for the black iron did not exist, is already hackneyed ; nor is the record of Lucretius [§] less well known :—

> " Arma antiqua, manus, ungues, dentesque fuerunt,
> Et lapides, et item sylvarum fragmina rami, . . .
> Posterius ferri vis est, rorisque reperta,
> Sed prior æris erat quam ferri cognitus usus ; . . .
> Inde minutatim processit ferreus ensis,
> Versaque in opprobrium species est falcis ahenæ,
> Et ferro cœpere solum proscindere terræ."

The difference between the age of Homer and Hesiod in respect to the use of metals is well described by Mr. Gladstone. The former [‖] "lived at a time when the use of iron (in Greece) was just commencing, when the commodity was rare, and when its value was very great ; " but in the days of Hesiod "iron, as compared with copper, had come to be the inferior, that is to say the cheaper metal," and the poet "looks back from his iron age with an admiring envy on the heroic period."

---

[*] "Troad.," 143.   [†] "Æn.," lib. vii. 743.
[‡] "Op. et D.," i. 150. Τοῖς δ' ἦν χάλκεα μὲν τεύχεα χάλκεοι δέ τε οἶκοι
        Χαλκῷ δ' εἰργάζοντο, μέλας δ' οὐκ ἔσχε σίδηρος.
[§] Lib. v. 1282, et seqq.   [‖] "Juv. Mundi," 1869, p. 26.

Hesiod gives to Hercules* a helmet of steel and a sword of iron, and to Saturn † a steel reaping-hook. His remark that at the feast of the gods the withered ‡ part of a five-fingered branch should never be cut from the green part by black iron, shows that this metal was in common use, and that for religious ceremonies the older metal bronze retained its place.

Bronze was, however, a favourite metal with the poet, if not indeed in actual use long after iron was known,§ for Pindar, about B.C. 470, still frequently cites spears and axes made of bronze.

By the time of Herodotus, who wrote before 400 B.C., the use of iron and steel was universal among the Greeks. He instances, as a fact worth recording, that the Massagetæ,∥ a powerful tribe which occupied the steppes on the east of the Caspian, made no use of iron or silver, but had an abundance of χαλκὸς and gold, pointing their spears and arrows and forming the heads of their battle-axes with the former metal. Among the Æthiopians,¶ on the contrary, he states that bronze was rarer and more precious than gold ; nor was it in use among the Scythians.** The Sagartii †† in the army of Xerxes are mentioned as not carrying arms either of bronze or iron except daggers, as if bronze were still of not unfrequent use.

Strabo,‡‡ at a much later date, thinks it worth while to record that among the Lusitanians the spears were tipped with bronze.

But certainly some centuries before the time of Herodotus, and probably as early as that of Homer, the Chalybes on the shores of the Euxine practised the manufacture of iron on a considerable scale, and from them came the Greek name for steel, χάλυψ.§§ Daïmachus, in the fourth century B.C., records that different sorts of steel are produced among the Chalybes in Sinope, Lydia, and Laconia. That of Sinope was used for smiths' and carpenters' tools ; that of Laconia for files, drills for iron, stamps, and masons' tools ; and the Lydian kind for files, swords, razors, and knives. In Laconia iron is said to have formed the only currency in the days of Lycurgus.

Taking all the evidence into consideration, there can be no doubt that iron must have been known in Greece some ten or twelve centuries before our era, though, as already observed, it was at that time an extremely rare metal. It also appears that as

* "Scut. Hercul.," v. 122—138.   † "Theogon.," v. 161.
‡ "Op. et D.," v. 741.   § "Olymp.," od. i. 123; "Nem.," od. x. 113, &c.
∥ Lib. i. c. 215.   ¶ Lib. iii. c. 23.
** Lib. iv. c. 71.   †† Lib. vii. c. 85.   ‡‡ Lib. iii. p. 208, ed. 1707.
§§ Bochart's "Phaleg.," p. 208, cited in *Arch. Æliana*, vol. i. p. 52.

C

early as B.C. 500, or even 600, iron or steel was in common use, though bronze had not been altogether superseded for offensive arms such as spear-heads and battle-axes.

The tradition of the earlier use of bronze still, however, remained even in later times, and the preference shown for its employment in religious rites, which I have mentioned elsewhere,* is a strong witness of this earlier use. It seems needless again to do more than mention the bronze ploughshare used at the foundation of Tuscan cities, the bronze knives and shears of the Sabine and Roman priests, and the bronze sickles of Medea and Elissa. I must, however, again bring forward the speculations of an intelligent Greek traveller, who wrote in the latter half of the second century of our era, as to the existence of what we should now term a Bronze Age in Greece.

Pausanias † relates how Lichas the Lacedæmonian, in the fifth century B.C., discovered the bones of Orestes, which his countrymen had been commanded by an oracle to seek. The Pythia ‡ had described the place as one where two strong winds met, where form was opposed to form, and one evil lay upon another. These Lichas recognised in the two bellows of the smith, the hammer opposed to the anvil, and the iron lying on it. Pausanias on this observes that at that time they had already begun to use iron in war, and that if it had been in the days of the heroes it would have been bronze and not iron designated by the oracle as the evil, for in their days all arms were of bronze. For this he cites Homer as his authority, who speaks of the bronze axe of Pisander, and the arrow of Meriones. A further argument he derives from the spear of Achilles, laid up in the temple of Minerva at Phaselis, and the sword of Memnon in that of Æsculapius at Nicomedia, which is entirely of bronze, while the ferrule and point of his spear are also of that metal.

The spear-head which lay with the bones of Theseus § in the Isle of Scyros was also of bronze, and probably the sword likewise. There are no works of Latin authors of a date nearly so remote as that of the earlier Greek writers, and long before the days of Ennius, iron was in general use in Italy. If the Articles of Peace which " Porsena, King of the Tuscans, tendered unto the people of Rome " were as Pliny ‖ represents them, the Romans

---

* " Anc. Stone Imp.," p. 4.   † " Lacon.," lib. iii. cap. iii.
‡ Herod., lib. i. c. 67.   § Plutarch, " Thes.," p. 17, c.   Ed. 1624.
‖ " Nat. Hist.," lib. xxxiv. cap. 14.

must even in those early days have had iron weapons, for they were forbidden the use of that metal except for tilling the ground. In B.C. 224 the Isumbrian Gauls who fought with Flaminius were already in possession of iron swords, the softness and flexibility of which led to the discomfiture of their owners. The Romans themselves seem but to have been badly armed so far as swords were concerned until the time of the Second Punic War, about B.C. 200, when they adopted the Spanish sword, and learnt the method of preparing it. Whether the modern Toledo and Bilbao blades are legitimate descendants of these old weapons we need not stop to inquire. In whatever manner the metal was prepared, so thoroughly was iron identified with the sword in classical times that *ferrum* and *gladius* were almost synonyms.

Pliny mentions that the best steel used in Rome was imported from China, a country in which copper or bronze swords are said to have been in use in the days of Ki,[*] the son of Yu, B.C. 2197—48, and those of iron under Kung-Kia, B.C. 1897—48, so that there also history points to a Bronze Age. But this by the way.

Looking at the fact that iron and steel were in such general use at Rome during the period of her wars in Western Europe, we may well believe that had any of the tribes with which the Roman forces came in contact been armed with bronze, such an unusual circumstance could hardly have escaped record. In the Augustan age the iron swords of Noricum were in great repute, and farther north in Germany, though iron did not abound, it was, according to Tacitus, used for spears and swords. The Catti had the metal in abundance, but among the Aestii, on the right coast of the Baltic, it was scarce. The Cimbrians in the first century B.C. had, according to Plutarch,[†] iron breast-plates, javelins, and large swords.

The Gauls of the North of France had in the time of Julius Cæsar [‡] large iron mines which they worked by tunnelling; the bolts of their ships were made of that metal, and they had even chain cables of iron. The Britons of the South of England who were in such close communication with the opposite coast of Gaul must have had an equal acquaintance with iron. Cæsar mentions ingots or rings of iron as being used for money, and observes that iron is obtained on the sea-coast, but in small quantities, and adds that bronze was imported.[§] Strabo includes iron, as well as gold, silver, and corn, among the products of Britain. In Spain,

---

[*] See *Zeitsch. für Eth.*," vol. ii., 1870, p. 131.
[‡] "Bell. Gall.," iii. 13 ; vii. 22.
[†] " Vit. Caii Marii," 420, b.
[§] Lib. v. 12.

as already mentioned, iron had long been known, so that from the concurrent testimony of several historians we may safely infer that in the time of Julius Cæsar, when this country was first exposed to Roman influences, it had already, like the neighbouring countries to the south, passed from the Bronze into the Iron Age.

Notwithstanding all this historical testimony in favour of the prior use of bronze to that of iron, there have been not a few authors who have maintained that the idea of a succession of stone, bronze, and iron is delusive when applied to Western Europe. Among these was the late Mr. Thomas Wright, who has gone so far as to express * "a firm conviction that not a bit of bronze which has been found in the British Islands belongs to an older date than that at which Cæsar wrote that the Britons obtained their bronze from abroad, meaning of course from Gaul." "In fact these objects in bronze were Roman in character and in their primary origin." As in the same page he goes on to show that two hundred years before Christ the swords of the Gauls were made of iron, and as his contentions have already been met by Sir John Lubbock,† and will, I think, be effectually disposed of by the facts subsequently to be mentioned in this volume, it seems needless to dwell on Mr. Wright's opinions. I may, however, mention that,‡ while denying the antiquity of British, German, and Scandinavian weapons and tools of bronze, he admits that in Greece and Italy that metal was for a long period the only one employed for cutting instruments, as iron was not known in Greece until a comparatively late date.

About one hundred and thirty years ago,§ in 1751, a discussion as to the date of bronze weapons took place among the members of the Académie des Inscriptions et Belles Lettres of Paris, on the occasion of some bronze swords, a spear-head, and other objects being found near Gannat, in the Bourbonnais. Some antiquaries regarded them as weapons made for use ; others as merely made for show. The Count de Caylus considered that the swords were Roman, though maintaining that copper or bronze must have been in earlier use than iron. Lévesque de la Ravalière maintained, on the contrary, that neither the Greeks, Romans, Gauls, nor Franks had ever made use of copper or bronze in their swords. The Abbé Barthélemy showed from ancient authors that the

* *Trans. Ethnol. Soc.*, vol. iv. p. 190. See also *Anthrop. Rev.*, vol. iv. p. 76.
† *Trans. Eth. Soc.*, vol. v. p. 105; "Preh. Times," 4th ed., p. 18.
‡ *Arch. Assoc. Journ.*, vol. xxii. p. 73.
§ See Rossignol, "Les Métaux dans l'Ant.," p. 205.

earliest arms of the Greeks were of bronze; that iron was only introduced about the time of the siege of Troy; and that in later times among the Romans there was no mention of bronze having been used for weapons of offence, and therefore that these swords were not Roman. Strangely enough, he went on to argue that they were Frankish, and of the time of Childeric. Had he been present at the opening of the tomb of that monarch in 1653 he would, however, have seen that he had an iron sword.*

A still warmer discussion than any which has taken place in England or France, one, in fact, almost amounting to an international war of words, has in more recent times arisen between some of the German antiquaries and those of the Scandinavian kingdoms of Denmark and Sweden.

So early as 1860† my friend Dr. Ludwig Lindenschmit, of Mainz, had commenced his attack on "the so-called Bronze Period," and shown a disposition to regard all bronze antiquities of northern countries as of Italian origin, or, if made in the countries where found, as mere homely imitations of imported articles. Not content with this, he in 1875‡ again mustered his forces and renewed the campaign in even a more formal manner. He found a formidable ally in Dr. Hostmann, whose comments on Dr. Hans Hildebrand's "Heathen Period in Sweden" are well worth the reading, and contain a vast amount of interesting information.

Dr. Hostmann's method of dealing with Dr. Hans Hildebrand brought Dr. Sophus Müller§ to the rescue, with whom Dr. Lindenschmit‖ at once grappled. Shortly after Dr. Hostmann¶ again appears upon the scene, and before engaging with Dr. Sophus Müller goes so far as to argue that while Greek swords of iron are known to belong to the eighth century B.C., no bronze sword of that country can with safety be assigned to an earlier date than the sixth century, and, indeed, these may have been only weapons of parade, or possibly funereal offerings in lieu of efficient swords. Rector Genthe** also engages in the fight upon the same side.

These three antagonists bring Sophus Müller†† again to the front, and as one great argument of his opponents was that bronze objects could not be produced with the finish and ornamentation which is found upon them without the use of iron and

---

* Cochet, "Le Tombeau de Childéric," i. p. 17.
† "Sammlung zu Sigmaringen," p. 153.
‡ *Archiv. für Anthropol.*, vol. viii. p. 161.
§ *Archiv.*, vol. ix. p. 127.   ‖ *Op. cit.*, p. 141.   ¶ *Op. cit.*, p. 185.
** *Arch. für Anthrop.*, vol. ix. p. 181.   †† *A. f. A.*, vol. x. p. 27.

steel tools, he brings forward an official document signed by four authorities in the museum at Copenhagen, and stating that precisely similar ornamentation to the spirals, zigzags, and punched lines which occur on Scandinavian bronze antiquities had been produced in their presence by a workman using bronze tools only on a plate of bronze. Both plate and tools were of the same alloy, viz. 9 of copper to 1 of tin.

On this a final charge is made by Professor Hostmann [*] and Dr. Lindenschmit, the former of whom produces a kind of affidavit from the late director of the Polytechnic School at Hanover and the court medallist of the same town, to the effect that certain kinds of punched work cannot be produced with bronze punches, and the editors of the *Archiv* think it best to close the discussion after Dr. Lindenschmit's final retort.

I have not thought it worth while to enter into all the details of this controversy, as even to summarise them would occupy more room than I could spare. It seems to me, however, that a considerable amount of misconception must have existed in the minds of some of the disputants, both as to the accepted meaning of the term Bronze Age, as applied not chronologically, but to a certain stage of civilisation, and as to the limitation of the objects which can with propriety be referred to that age. No antiquary of experience will deny that many bronze ornaments, and even some bronze weapons, remained in use long after iron and even steel were known, any more than he would deny that the use of stone for certain purposes continued not only after bronze was known, but even after iron and steel were in general use, and, in fact, up to the present time, not only in barbarian but in civilised countries. Our flint strike-a-lights and our burnishers are still of much the same character as they were some thousands of years ago, and afford convincing instances of this persistent use.

The real question at issue is not whether any bronze weapons co-existed with those of iron and steel in Western Europe, but whether any of them were there in use at a period when iron and steel were unknown. Moreover, it is not a question as to whence the knowledge of bronze was derived, nor whether at the time the Scandinavians or Britons were using bronze for their tools and weapons, the inhabitants of Greece and Italy were already acquainted with iron and steel; but it is a question whether in each individual country there arrived a time when bronze came into

* *Arch. f. Anthrop.*, vol. x. pp. 41, 63.

THE SUCCESSION OF IRON TO BRONZE.

use and for certain purposes superseded stone, while iron and steel were practically unknown.

This is a question to be solved by evidence, though in the nature of things that evidence must to some extent be of a negative character. When barrow after barrow is opened, and weapons of bronze and stone only are found accompanying the interments, and not a trace of iron or steel; when hoards of rough metal and broken bronze, together with the moulds of the bronze-founder and some of his stock-in-trade, are disinterred, and there is no trace of an iron tool among them—the presumption is strong that at the time when these men and these hoards were buried iron was not in use. When, moreover, by a careful examination of the forms of bronze instruments we can trace a certain amount of development which is in keeping with the peculiar properties of bronze and not with those of iron, and we can thus to some extent fix a kind of chronological succession in these forms, the inference is that this evolution of form, which must have required a considerable amount of time, took place without its course being affected by any introduction of a fresh and qualifying influence in the shape of iron tools and weapons.

When, however, in various countries we find interments and even cemeteries in which bronze and iron weapons and instruments are intermingled, and the forms of those in bronze are what we have learnt from other sources to regard as the latest, while the forms in iron are not those for which that metal is best adapted, but are almost servile copies of the bronze instruments found with them, the proof of the one having succeeded the other is almost absolutely conclusive.

The lessons taught by such cemeteries as that at Hallstatt, in Austria, and by our own Late Celtic interments, such as those at Arras, in Yorkshire, are of the highest importance in this question.

It is not, however, to be supposed that even in countries by no means geographically remote from each other the introduction either of iron or bronze must of necessity have taken place at one and the same chronological period. Near the shores of the Mediterranean the use of each metal no doubt prevailed far earlier than in any of the northern countries of Europe; and though the knowledge of metals probably spread from certain centres, its progress can have been but slow, for in each part of Europe there appears to have been some special development, particularly in the forms of bronze instruments, and there is no absolute uniformity in their

types extending over any large area.   In each country the process
of manufacture was carried on, and though some commerce in tools
and arms of bronze no doubt took place between neighbouring
tribes, yet as a rule there are local peculiarities characteristic of
special districts.

So marked are these that a practised archæologist can in almost
all cases, on inspection of a group of bronze antiquities, fix with
some degree of confidence the country in which they were found.
To this rule Britain offers no exception, and though some forms of
instruments were no doubt imported, yet, as will subsequently be
seen, our types are for the most part indigenous.

As to the ornamentation of bronze by bronze tools, I have seen
none in this country on objects which I should refer to the Bronze
Age but what could have been effected by means of bronze
punches, of which indeed examples have been discovered in bronze-
founders' hoards in France,* and what are probably such also in
Britain.   Such ornamentation is, however, simple compared with
that on many of the Danish forms, and yet I have seen the complicated Scandinavian ornaments accurately and sharply reproduced by Dr. Otto Tischler, by means of bronze tools only, on
bronze of the ordinary ancient alloy.

But even supposing that iron and steel were known during some
part of the so-called Bronze Age, I do not see in what manner it
would affect the main features of the case or the interest attaching to
the bronze objects which I am about to describe. "De non apparen-
tibus et non existentibus eadem est ratio" is a maxim of some
weight in archæology as well as in law ; and in the absence of iron
and all trace of its influence, it matters but little whether it was
known or not, except in so far as a neglect of its use would argue some
want of intelligence on the part of those who did not avail themselves of so useful a metal.   It will be seen hereafter that some of
the objects described in these pages actually do belong to an Iron
Period, and nothing could better illustrate the transition of one
Period into another, or the overlapping of the Bronze Age upon
that of Iron, than the fact that in these pages devoted to the
Bronze Period I must of necessity describe many objects which
were still in use when iron and steel were superseding bronze, in
the same manner as in my "Ancient Stone Implements" I was forced
to describe many forms, such as battle-axes, arrow-heads, and
bracers, which avowedly belonged to the Bronze Period.

* Mortillet, "Fonderie de Larnaud," 32, 33.

A point which is usually raised by those who maintain the priority of the use of iron to that of bronze is, that inasmuch as it is more readily oxidized and dissolved by acids naturally present in the soil, iron may have disappeared, and indeed has done so, while bronze has been left; so that the absence of iron as an accompaniment to all early interments counts for nothing. Professor Rolleston,[*] in a paper on the three periods known as the Iron, the Bronze, and the Stone Ages, has well dealt with this point; and observes that in some graves of the Bronze Period the objects contained are incrusted with carbonate of lime, which would have protected any iron instrument of the Bronze Period as well as it has done those of Saxon times. Not only are the iron weapons discovered in Saxon cemeteries often in almost perfect preservation, but on the sites of Roman occupation whole hoards of iron tools have been found but little injured by rust. The fact that at Hallstatt and other places in which graves have been examined belonging to the transitional period, when both iron and bronze were in use together, the weapons and tools of iron, though oxidized, still retain their form and character as completely as those in bronze, also affords strong ground for believing that had iron been present with bronze in other early interments it would also have been preserved. The importance attaching to the reputed occurrence of bronze swords with Roman coins as late as the time of Magnentius cannot be better illustrated than by a discovery of my own in the ancient cemetery of Hallstatt. In company with Sir John Lubbock I was engaged in opening a grave in which we had come to an interment of the Early Iron Age, accompanied by a socketed celt and spear-heads of iron, when amidst the bones I caught sight of a thin metallic disc of a yellowish colour which looked like a coin. Up to that time no coin had ever been found in any one of the many hundred graves which had been examined, and I eagerly picked up this disc. It proved to be a "sechser," or six-kreutzer piece, with the date 1826, which by some means had worked its way down among the crevices in the stony ground, and which from its appearance had evidently been buried some years. Had this coin been of Roman date it might have afforded an argument for bringing down the date of the Hallstatt cemetery some centuries in the chronological scale. As it is, it affords a wholesome caution against drawing important inferences from the mere collo-

* *Trans. Brist. and Glouc. Arch. Soc.*, 1878.

cation of objects when there is any possibility of the apparent association being only due to accident.

In further illustration of the succession of the three Ages of Stone, Bronze, and Iron in Western Europe, I might go on to cite cases of the actual superposition of the objects of one age over those of another, such as has been observed in several barrows and in the well-known instance of the cone of La Tinière, in the Lake of Geneva, recorded by Morlot.

It will, however, be thought that enough, if not more than enough, has already been said on the general question of a Bronze Age in a book particularly devoted to the weapons and instruments of bronze found in the British Isles. It is now time to proceed with the examination and description of their various forms ; and in doing this I propose to treat separately, so far as possible, the different classes of instruments intended each for some special purpose, and at the same time to point out their analogies with instruments of the same character found in other parts of Europe. Their chronological sequence so far as it can be ascertained, the position in time of the Bronze Period of Britain and Ireland, and the sources from which our bronze civilisation was derived, will be discussed in a concluding chapter.

I begin with the instrument of the most common occurrence, the so-called celt.

CHAPTER II.

CELTS.

OF all the forms of bronze instruments the hatchet or axe, to which the name of celt has been applied, is perhaps the most common and the best known. It is also probably among the earliest of the instruments fabricated from metal, though in this country it is possible that some of the cutting instruments, such as the knife-daggers, which required a less amount of metal for their formation, are of equal or greater antiquity.

These tools or weapons—for, like the American tomahawk, they seem to have been in use for peaceful as well as warlike purposes—may be divided into several classes. Celts may be described as flat; flanged, or having ribs along the sides; winged, or having the side flanges extended so as almost to form a socket for the handle on either side of the blade, to which variety the name of palstave has been given; and socketed. Of most of these classes there are several varieties, as will be seen farther on.

The name of celt which has been given to these instruments is derived from the doubtful Latin word "celtis" or "celtes," a chisel, which is in its turn said to be derived *à cœlando* (from carving), and to be the equivalent of *cœlum.*

The only author in whose works the word is found is St. Jerome, and it is employed both in his Vulgate translation of the Book of Job[*] and in a quotation from that book in his Epistle to Pammachius. The word also occurs in an inscription recorded by Gruter and Aldus,[†] but as this inscription is a modern forgery, it does not add to the authority of the word "celtis."

Mr. Knight Watson, Sec. S. A., in an interesting paper communicated to the Society of Antiquaries of London,[‡] has given

---

[*] Cap. xix. v. 24.
[†] P. 329, l. 23. NEQVE HIC ATRAMENTVM, VEL PAPYRVS, AVT MEMBRANA VLLA ADHVC, SED MALLEOLO ET CELTE LITERATVS SILEX. This inscription is said to have been found at Pola, in Istria.
[‡] *Proc. Soc. Ant.*, 2nd S., vol. vii. p. 396.

several details as to the origin and use of this word, which he considers to have been founded on a misreading of the word *certe*, and the derivation of which from *cœlo* he regards as impossible. There can be no doubt, as Beger pointed out two centuries ago, that a number of MSS. of the Vulgate read *certe* instead of *celte* in the passage in Job already mentioned, and that in all probability these are the most ancient and the best. But this only adds to the difficulty of understanding how a recently invented and an unknown word, such as *celte* is presumed to be, can have ever supplanted a well-known word like *certe*; and so far as the Burial Service of the Roman Catholic Church is concerned can have maintained its ground for centuries. Nor is this difficulty diminished when we consider that the ordinary and proper translation of the Hebrew לָעַד is either " in æternum " or " in testimonium," according as the word is pointed לָעַד or לְעֵד, and that, so far as I am aware, there is no other instance of its being translated "*certe*." On the other hand, a nearly similar word, בְּעֵט " with a stylus," or, as it is translated, " a pen," occurs in the same passage; and assuming that this was by some accident read for לעד by St. Jerome, he would have thought that the word for stylus was used twice over, and have inserted some word to designate a graving tool, by way of a synonym. The probability of such an error would be increased if his MS. had the lines arranged in couplets in accordance with its poetical character, the passage standing thus when un-pointed :—

בעט ברזל ועפרת
לעד בצור יחצבון:

Very possibly the word used by St. Jerome may not have been *celte* but *cœlo*, and the corruption into *celte* in order to make a distinction between heaven and a chisel would then at all events have been possible.

The other contention involves two extreme improbabilities—the one, that St. Jerome, having in his second revision of the Bible translated the passage as " in testimonium in petris sculpantur," should in the Vulgate have given the inaccurate rendering " certe sculpantur in silice ;" the other and the more extreme of the two, that the well-known word *certe* should have been ousted by a word like *celte* had it been utterly new-fangled.

Under any view of the case there are considerable difficulties, but as the word celt has now obtained a firm hold in our language, it will be convenient to retain it, whatever its origin or derivation.

It has been the fashion among some who are fond of novelties to call these instruments "kelts," possibly from some mental association of the instruments with a Celtic or Keltic population. From some such cause also some of the French antiquaries must have coined the new plural to the word, *Celtæ*. Even in this country it has been said * with regard to "the ancient weapon denominated the celt," "Our antiquarians have commonly ascribed them to the ancient Celtæ, and hence have given them this unmeaning appellation." If any one prefers pronouncing celt as "kelt," or celestial as "kelestial," let him do so ; but at all events let us adhere to the old spelling. How the Romans of the time of St. Jerome would have pronounced the word *cœlum* or *celtis* may be inferred from the punning line of Ausonius with regard to Venus.†

"Orta salo, suscepta solo, patre edita cœlo."

The first author of modern times whose use of the word in connection with Celts I can trace is Beger, who, in his "Thesaurus Brandenburgicus" ‡ (1696), gives an engraving of a celt of the palstave form, under the title Celtes, together with the following dialogue :—

"Et nomen et instrumentum mihi obscurum est, infit AR-CHÆOPHILUS ; Instrumentum Statuariorum est, respondit DULO-DORUS, qui simulacra ex Cera, Alabastro, aliisque lapidum generibus cædunt et poliunt. Græcis dicitur 'Εγκοπεὺς, quâ voce Lucianus usus est in Somnio, ubi cum lusum non insuavem dixisset, Deos sculpere, et parva quædam simulacra adornare, addit ἐγκοπέα γὰρ τινά μοι δοὺς, scilicet avunculus, id quod Joh. Benedictus vertit, *Celte datâ*. Celte? excepit ARCHÆOPHILUS ; at nisi fallor hæc vox Latinis incognita est ? Habetur, inquit DULO-DORUS, in versione vulgatâ Libri Hiob c. 19 quamvis alii non *Celte*, sed *Certe* ibi legant, quod tamen minus quadrat. Quicquid sit, instrumentum Statuariorum hoc esse, ex formâ patet, figuris incidendis aptissima ; neque enim opinio Molineti videtur admittenda, qui *Securim* appellat, cum nullus aptandi manubrii locus huic faveat. Metallum reposuit ARCHÆOPHILUS, minus videtur convenire. Instrumentum hoc ex ære est, quod duritiem lapidum nescio an superare potuerit ? Uti lapides diversi sunt, regessit DULODORUS, ita diversa fuisse etiam metalla instrumentorum iis

* Rev. John Dow in *Archæol. Scot.*, vol. ii. p. 199. See also Pegge in the *Arch.*, vol. ix. p. 88, and Whitaker's "Hist. of Manchester," vol. i. p. 24.
† Epig. xxxiii. l. 1. ‡ Vol. iii. p. 418.

cædendis destinatorum, facilè cesserim. Vet. Gloss. Celtem *instrumentum ferreum* dicit proculdubio quòd durioribus lapidibus ferreum chalybe munitum servierit. Hoc autem non obstat, ut æreum vel ceris, vel terris, vel lapidibus mollioribus fuerit adhibitum. Si tamen res Tibi minus probetur, me non contradicente, molliori vocabulo γλυφεῖον *cælum* poteris et appellare et credere. Γλυφεῖα etiam Statuariorum instrumenta fuisse, ex allegato modò Luciano planum est, ubi Humanitas, *si me relinquis*, inquit, σχῆμα δουλοπρεπὲς ἀναλήψῃ, καὶ μοχλία, καὶ γλυφεῖα, καὶ κοπέας, καὶ κολαπτῆρας ἐν ταῖν χεροῖν ἕξεις, *habitum servilem assumes*, Vectes, COELA, CELTES, *Scalpra præ manibus habebis.*"

The idea of a bronze celt being a statuary's chisel for carving in wax, alabaster, and the softer kinds of stone will seem the less absurd if we remember that, at the time when Beger wrote, the manner in which such instruments were hafted was unknown, and that all antiquities of bronze were generally regarded as being of Roman or Greek origin.

Dr. Olaf Worm, a Danish antiquary of the seventeenth century, was more enlightened than Beger, for in his "Museum Wormianum,"* published in 1655, he states his belief that bronze weapons had formerly been in use in Denmark, and cites two flat or flanged celts, or *cunei*, as he calls them, found in Jutland, which he regards as hand weapons for close encounters. He also was, nevertheless, at a loss to know how they were hafted, for he adds that had they but been provided with shaft-holes he should have considered them to have been axes.

In a work treating of the bronze antiquities of Britain we must, however, first consider the opinion of British antiquaries, by whom the word celt had been completely adopted as the name for bronze hatchets and axes by the middle of the last century. Borlase,† in his "Antiquities of Cornwall," 1754, speaking of some "spearheads" of copper mentioned by Leland, says that by the spearheads he certainly meant those which we (from Begerus) now call Celts. Leland's words are as follows : ‡—"There was found of late Yeres syns Spere Heddes, Axis for Warre, and Swerdes of coper wrapped up in lynid scant perished nere the Mount in S. Hilaries Paroch in Tynne Works;" so that it by no means follows but that he was right in speaking of spear-heads, for if there were any celts among the objects discovered they were probably termed battle-axes by Leland.

* P. 354. † P. 265. ‡ "Itin.," vol. iii. p. 7.

Camden makes mention of the same find : * " At the foote of this mountaine (St. Michael's Mount), within the memorie of our Fathers, whiles men were digging up of tin, they found Spearheads, axes, and swordes of brasse wrapped in linnen, such as were sometimes found within the forrest of Hercinia in Germanie, and not long since in our Wales. For evident it is by the monuments of ancient Writers that the Greeks, the Cimbrians, and the Britans used brazen weapons, although the wounds given with brasse bee lesse hurtfull, as in which mettall there is a medicinable vertue to heale, according as *Macrobius* reporteth out of Aristotle. But happily that age was not so cunning in devising meanes to mischiefe and murthers as ours is."

Hearne, the editor of Leland's "Itinerary," took a less philosophical view of these instruments. Writing to Thoresby † in 1709, he maintains that some old instruments of bronze found near Bramham Moor, Yorkshire, are not the heads of British spears ; on the contrary, they are Roman, not axes used in their sacrifices, nor the heads of spears and javelins, but chisels which were used to cut and polish the stones in their tents. Such instruments were also used in making the Roman highways and in draining their fens.

Plot ‡ also, at a somewhat earlier date, asserted a Roman origin for bronze celts, which he regarded as the heads of bolts, founding his opinion mainly on two, which are engraved in the Museum Moscardi. These, which are reproduced in the *Archæologia*, vol. v. Pl. VIII. 18 and 19, are of the palstave form, and were regarded by Moscardo § as the heads of great darts to be thrown from a catapult. A flat celt found in Staffordshire,|| Plot takes to be the head of a Roman *securis* with which the *Popæ* slew their sacrifices.

Rowland,¶ in his " Mona Antiqua Restaurata," 1723, suggested that looped palstaves fastened by a thong to a staff might be used as war flails.

The imaginative Dr. Stukeley, in the year 1724, communicated to the Society of Antiquaries a discourse on the use of celts, which is to be found in the Minute Book of the Society. An abstract of it is given by Mr. Lort ** in his paper subsequently men-

* " Britannia," ed. 1637, p. 188.
† " Thoresby's Correspondence." vol. ii. p. 211.
‡ " Nat. Hist. of Staffordshire," 1686, p. 403.
§ " Mus. Lud. Moscard." Padua, 1656, fol. 305, lib. iii. c. 174.
|| " Nat. Hist. of Staff.," p. 403. ¶ P. 86. ** *Arch.*, vol. v. p. 110.

tioned. Dr. Stukeley undertook to show that celts were British
and appertaining to the Druids, who, when not using them to cut
off the boughs of oak and mistletoe, put them in their pouches,
or hung them to their girdles by the little ring or loop at the
side. In a more sensible manner he divided them into two
classes, the recipient and the received; that is to say, the socketed,
in which the handle was received, and the flat and palstave forms,
which entered into a notch in the handle.

Borlase,* notwithstanding that he was under the impression
that a number of socketed celts found at Karnbrê in 1744 were
accompanied by Roman coins, one of them at least as late as
the time of Constantius I., did "not take them to be purely
Roman, foreign, or of Italian invention and workmanship."

He argues that the Romans of Italy would not have made such
instruments of brass after Julius Cæsar's time, when the superior
hardness of iron was so well understood, and that metal was so
easily to be procured. Farther, that no representations of such
weapons occur on the Trajan or Antonine Columns, that few
specimens exist in the cabinets of the curious in Italy, where they
are regarded as Transalpine antiquities, and that none have
been found among the ruins of Herculaneum; † nor are any published in the Museum Romanum or the Museum Kircherianum.
He concludes that they were made and used in Britain, but that
though they were originally of British invention and fabric, they
were for the most part made when the Britons had improved their
arts under their Roman masters, as most of them seem too correct
and shapely for the Britons before the Julian conquest.

As to the uses of celts, Borlase cites the various opinions of the
learned, and observes that if they had not been advanced by men
of learning it would be scarce excusable to mention some of them,
much less to refute them. They had been taken for heads of
walking staffs, for chisels to cut stone withal (as such instruments
must have been absolutely necessary in making the great Roman
roads), as tools with which to engrave letters and inscriptions, as
the sickles with which the Druids cut the sacred mistletoe, and as
rests to support the *lituus* of the Roman augurs. After all, however, Borlase himself comes to the somewhat lame conclusion that
they formed the head or arming of the spear, the javelin, or the

---

* " Ants. of Cornwall," p. 263.

† Count de Caylus has, however, engraved two which are said to have been found at
Herculaneum. He thought that they were chisels (*Rec. d'Ant.*, vol. ii. pl. xciii.
fig. 2; xciv. fig. 1).

arrow, and thinks that Mr. Rowland comes the nearest to the truth of any author he has read, when he says that they might be used with a string to draw them back, and something like a feather to guide them in flying towards the enemy, and calls them sling-hatchets. He concedes, however, that for such weighty heads there was no occasion for feathers, and as for slinging of hatchets against an enemy, he does not remember any instance, ancient or modern. Some of the celts, moreover, are too light to do any execution if thrown from the hand.

The Rev. Mr. Lort,* who communicated some observations on celts to the Society of Antiquaries in 1776, differed from Dr. Borlase, and regarded a large flat celt found in the Lower Furness as manifestly designed to be held in the hand only, and much better adapted to the chipping of stone than to any other use which has hitherto been found out for it. He will not, how-ever, take upon himself to assert that some socketed celts, which he also describes, were designed for the same purpose. Appended to the paper by Mr. Lort are notices of several bronze celts, which at different times had been brought under the notice of the Society of Antiquaries. Some which had been exhibited in 1735 were regarded by Mr. Benjamin Cooke and Mr. Collinson as Gaulish weapons used by the Roman auxiliaries at the time of Claudius. Mr. Cooke, however, took them to be axes, and mounted one of them on a shaft, citing Homer as his authority for doing so, and speaking of the ἀξίνην ἔυχαλκον.

The Rev. Samuel Pegge in 1787 makes some pertinent remarks respecting celts in a letter to Mr. Lort, which is published in the *Archæologia*.† He points out that from some of them having been found in barrows associated with spear-heads of flint, it is probable that some at least were military weapons. He also maintains that though the use of bronze originally preceded that of iron, yet that regard must be had to the circumstances of each country, so that it would not follow that a bronze celt found in Ireland was prior in age to the invention of iron. All that could be said was that it was older than the introduction of iron into Ireland, and when that was, no one could pretend to say. Mr. Pegge did not approve of the derivation of the name of celt from *celtis* or *cœlare*, but thought it derived from the name of the Celtic people who used the instruments. In his opinion the instruments were not Roman, especially as they were frequent in

* *Arch.*, vol. v. p. 106.   † Vol. ix. p. 84.

D

Ireland and in places where the Romans never were settled. The specimen on which he comments is of the palstave form, and, though it might be mounted as a tool, he thinks it could never have served as an axe, but it might have tipped a dart or javelin.

Douglas[*] was of opinion that the bronze arms found in this country were not Roman, but that it was more reasonable to refer them to the early inhabitants, of probably not less than two centuries B.C.

Mr. C. J. Harford, F.S.A.,[†] writing in 1801, expressed his opinion that a clue as to the uses of celts might be obtained from a consideration of similar instruments which had been brought from the South Sea Islands. "Our rude forefathers doubtless attached the celt by thongs to the handle, in the same manner as modern savages do; and, like them, formed a most useful implement or destructive weapon from these simple materials." He thought that the metal celts might have been fabricated abroad and exported to this country, just as we have sent to the South Sea Islands an imitation in iron of the stone hatchet there in use.

Coming down to later times, we find Sir Richard Colt Hoare,[‡] who discovered a few flat and flanged celts in the Wiltshire barrows, regarding them as for domestic, and not for military, architectural, or religious purposes. He thought that the flat form must be the most ancient, from which the pattern of that with the socket for the insertion of a handle was taken; for among the numerous specimens described by Mr. Lort in the *Archæologia*, not one of the latter pattern is mentioned as having been discovered in a barrow. As many were found in Gaul, he rather supposed that they were imported from the Continent; or, perhaps, the art of making them might have been introduced from Gaul. From the method of hafting of one of those he found (see Fig. 189), he seems to have regarded the whole of them as chisels rather than hatchets.

Sir Joseph Banks,[§] in some observations communicated to the Society of Antiquaries in 1818, on an ancient celt found near Boston, Lincolnshire, pointed out the manner in which looped palstaves could be hafted so as to serve either as axes, adzes, or chisels. He thought that they were ill adapted for any warlike purposes, and regarded them as tools such as might be used in hollowing out the trunks of trees to form canoes, and suggested that they were secured to their handles by strings tied round them in the

* "Nænia Britannica" (1793), p. 153.   † *Arch.*, vol. xiv. p. 98.
‡ "Ancient Wilts," vol. i. 1812, p. 203.   § *Arch.*, vol. xix. p. 102.

same manner as the stone axes used in the South Sea Islands were fastened to theirs.

About the year 1816 the Rev. John Dow,* in some remarks on the ancient weapon denominated the celt, advocated the opinion that it was an axe, and probably a weapon of war. He also traces its connection with the stone celt, from which he considered it to have been developed.

About the same year the Rev. John Hodgson, secretary of the Society of Antiquaries of Newcastle-on-Tyne, communicated to that society a valuable memoir in the shape of †"An Enquiry into the Æra when Brass was used in purposes to which Iron is now applied," of which mention has already been made in the Introductory Chapter. He thought that celts were tools which were well adapted for use as wedges for splitting wood, or that with wooden hafts they might be used as chisels for hollowing canoes and for similar purposes, some instruments found with them being undoubtedly gouges. As to their date, he thought that bronze began to give way to iron in Britain nearly as soon as it did in Greece, and that consequently the celts, &c., found in this island belonged to an era 500, or at least 400 years, B.C.

In 1839 Mr. Rickman ‡ communicated to the Society of Antiquaries a paper on the Antiquity of Abury and Stonehenge, in the notes to which he propounds the theory that the socketed celts were used merely as chisels, with hafts of wood inserted in the socket. They could be then either held in the hand or by means of a withe, like a blacksmith's chisel, while they were struck with a stone hammer.

Among writers of comparatively modern times, the first whom I have to mention is the late Mr. G. V. Du Noyer,§ who in 1847 communicated to the Archæological Institute two papers on the classification of bronze celts, which are still of great value and interest. He traces the gradual development in form from the bronze celt shaped like a wedge to that which is socketed, and shows that an important element in the transition from one form to the other has been the method of hafting. He also enters into the subjects of the casting and ornamentation of celts ; and as in subsequent pages I shall have to refer to these as well as to the methods of hafting, I content myself here with citing Mr. Du Noyer's papers as being worthy of all credit.

* *Archæol. Scot.*, vol. ii. p. 199.   † *Archæol. Æliana*, vol. i. p. 17.
‡ *Arch.*, vol. xxviii. p. 418.   § *Arch. Journ.*, vol. iv. pp. 1 and 327.

In 1849 Mr. James Yates communicated a paper to the Archæological Institute of a far more speculative kind than those of Mr.
Du Noyer, his object being to prove that among the various uses
of bronze celts one of the most important was the application of
them in destroying fortifications and entrenchments, in making
roads and earthworks, and in similar military operations.   He
confines his inquiry, however, to those which were adapted to be
fitted to straight wooden handles.   Following in the steps of some
of the older antiquaries, he appears to regard them as of Roman
origin, and identifies them with the Roman *dolabra*, an instrument
which he thinks was used as a chisel or a crowbar.   In fact, he was
persuaded that the celt was commonly used not as a hatchet, but
as a spud or a crowbar.   Had he but been acquainted with the
ancient handles, such as have been discovered in the Austrian
salt-mines and elsewhere, he would probably have come round to
another opinion as to the ordinary method of hafting, though it is
of course possible that in some instances these instruments may
have been mounted and used as spuds.   Had he practically tried
mounting them and using them as crowbars, he would have found
that with but slight strain the shafts would break or the celts
become loosened upon them.   And had he been better versed in
archæology, he would have known that whatever was the form of
the Roman *dolabra*, or whatever the uses for which it served, it
can hardly have differed from their other implements in being
made of bronze and not of iron ; and he would have thought twice
before engraving bronze celts from Cornwall and Furness as illustrations of the Roman *dolabra* in Smith's "Dictionary of Greek
and Roman Antiquities."

The ring or loop, which so often is found on the side of celts of
the palstave and socketed forms, was thought by Mr. Yates to have
been principally of use to assist in carrying them, a dozen or
twenty perhaps being strung together, or a much smaller number
tied to the soldier's belt or girdle.   He also thought that they
might serve for the attachment of a thong or chain to draw the
instrument out of a wall, should it become wedged among the stones
in the process of destruction.

The next essay on celts and their classification which I must
adduce was written by the late Rev. Thomas Hugo, F.S.A.,[*] who
followed much the same system as Mr. Du Noyer, so far as the
development of the socketed celt was concerned, though he differed

---

[*] *Arch. Assoc. Journ.*, 1853, vol. ix. p. 63.

from him with regard to the method of hafting, as he was persuaded that, in general, celts were mounted with a straight shaft, like spuds. He considered that the loop was not used for securing the celt to its haft, but for hanging it up at home when not in use, or for suspending it from the soldier's girdle whilst on the march.

Mr. Hugo's paper was followed by some supplementary remarks from Mr. Syer Cuming, who suggests that a thong may have passed through the loop by which the weapon might be propelled, and contends that socketed celts are neither chisels nor axe-blades, but the ferrules of spear-shafts, which might be fixed in the ground, or even used at times as offensive weapons.

The name of the late Mr. Thomas Wright [*] has already been mentioned. In his various works and papers he claims a Roman origin for bronze celts and swords, though admitting that they may occasionally have been made in the countries in which they are found.

Among other modern writers who have touched upon the subject of celts, I may mention that accomplished antiquary, the late Mr. Albert Way, F.S.A., whose remarks in connection with an exhibition of bronze antiquities at a meeting of the Archæological Institute in 1861[†] are well worth reading. I may also refer to the late Sir W. R. Wilde, in his "Catalogue of the Copper and Bronze Antiquities in the Museum of the Royal Irish Academy," published in the same year; to Mr. Franks, in the "Horæ Ferales;" to Sir John Lubbock, in his "Prehistoric Times;" and to General A. Lane Fox (now Pitt-Rivers), in his excellent lecture on Primitive Warfare, section iii.[‡]

Canon Greenwell, in his "British Barrows,"[§] has also devoted a few pages to the consideration of bronze celts and axe-heads, more especially in connection with interments in sepulchral mounds.

Foreign writers I need hardly cite, but I may mention a remarkable idea that has been promulgated by Professor Stefano de Rossi[||] as to celts having served as money, which has, however, been shown by Count Gozzadini to be unfounded.

In conclusion, I may also venture to refer to an address[¶] which

---

[*] *Arch. Assoc. Journ.*, vol. xxii. p. 64.
[†] *Arch. Journ.*, vol. xviii. p. 148, *et seq.*
[‡] *Jour. Roy. Un. Service Inst.*, vol. xiii., 1869.
[§] P. 43, *et seqq.* 188.
[||] See *Revue de la Numis. Belge*, 5th Ser., vol. vi. p. 299.
[¶] *Proc. Soc. Ant.*, 2nd S., vol. v. p. 392.

I delivered to the Society of Antiquaries on the occasion of an exhibition of bronze antiquities in their apartments in January, 1873.

In treating of the different forms of celts on the present occasion, I shall divide them into the following classes :—

Flat celts.

Flanged celts.

Winged celts and palstaves, with and without loops.

Socketed celts.

What are known as tanged celts may perhaps be more properly included under the head of chisels, to which class of tools it is not unlikely that some of the narrow celts of the other forms should be referred.

It is difficult to draw a hard and fast line between the flat celts and the flanged, and between these latter and the so-called palstaves. I propose, therefore, to include the flanged celts, which are not provided with a stop-ridge to prevent their being driven into their haft, in the same chapter with the flat celts, and to treat of those which have a stop-ridge in the same chapter as the palstaves, with and without a loop. In a subsequent chapter I shall speak as to the manner in which these instruments were probably hafted.

CHAPTER III.

FLAT AND FLANGED CELTS.

FLAT celts, or those of simple form with the faces somewhat convex, and approximating in shape to the polished stone celts of the Neolithic Period, have been regarded by several antiquaries as being probably the earliest bronze implements or weapons. Such a view has much to commend it, but, as already observed, it may be doubted whether in the earliest times, when metal was scarce, it would be so readily applied to purposes for which much of the precious material was required, as to the manufacture of weapons or tools of a lighter kind, such as daggers or knives.

Among celts, however, the simple form, and that most nearly approaching in character to the stone hatchet, was probably the earliest, though it may have been continued in use after the introduction of the side flanges, the stop-ridge, and even the socket. Some celts of the simplest form found in Ireland are of copper, and have been thought to belong to the period when the use of stone for cutting purposes was dying out and that of metal coming in ; but the mere fact of their being of copper is by no means conclusive on this point.

A copper celt of the precise shape of an ordinary stone celt, 6 inches long and 2½ inches wide, which was found in an Etruscan tomb, and is preserved in the Museum at Berlin, appears to have been cast in a mould formed upon a stone implement of the same class. It has been figured and described by Sir William Wilde.[*] I have not seen the implement, nor am I aware of the exact circumstances of the finding. Celts may, however, like the flint arrow-heads inserted in Etruscan[†] necklaces of gold, have been regarded with superstitious reverence, and it does not appear to me quite certain that this specimen was ever in actual use as an

---

[*] "Catal. Mus. R.I.A.," pp. 367, 395 (Etruscan Coll., Berlin, No. 3244).
[†] "Horæ Ferales," p. 136 ; *Arch. Journ.*, vol. xi. p. 169.

implement, and was not placed in the grave as a substitute for a
stone hatchet or *Ceraunius.*

However this may be, some of the earliest bronze or, possibly,
copper celts with which we are acquainted, those from the excavations
of General di Cesnola in Cyprus, and of Dr. Schliemann at Hissarlik, are of the simple flat form, and justify Sir W. Wilde[*] in his
supposition that the first makers of these instruments, having
once obtained a better material than stone, repeated the form
with which they were best acquainted, though they economized

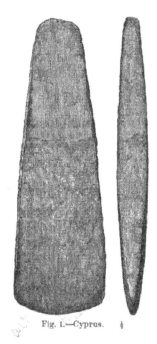

Fig. 1.—Cyprus.

the metal and lessened the bulk by
flattening the sides.   The annexed
cut, Fig. 1, shows a celt from Cyprus
in my own collection, which in form
might be matched by celts of flint,
though it must be acknowledged that
the type in stone is rather that of
Scandinavia than of Eastern Europe
or the Levant.   A slight ridge in
the oxide upon it seems to mark the
distance that the narrow end penetrated the handle.   Numerous tools
or weapons of the same form were
found by Dr. Schliemann [†] in his
excavations in search of Troy.   They
were at first thought to be of copper,
but subsequently proved to have a
small per-centage of tin in them.   A
number of flat celts, some short and
broad, and others long and narrow,
were found at Gungeria,[‡] in the Mhow
Talook, about forty miles north of Boorha, in Central India, many
of which are now in the British Museum.   On analysis Dr. Percy
found them to be of pure copper.   The same form was found at Tel
Sifr, in Southern Babylonia.   Some from that place, and from the
island of Thermia,[§] in the Greek Archipelago, are also in the British
Museum.   Nearly similar instruments, said to be made of copper,
have been found in Austria,[||] Denmark,[¶] Sweden,[**] Hungary,[††]

[*] "Catal. M. R.I.A.," p. 366.   [†] "Troy and its Remains," p. 330, &c.
[‡] "Cong. préh.," Stockholm vol. i. p. 346.   *Proc. As. Soc. Bengal,* May, 1870.
[§] *Proc. Soc. Ant.,* 2nd S., vol. iii. p. 437.   [||] Kenner, "Arch. Funde," 1867, p. 29.
[¶] Worsaae, "Nord. Olds.," fig. 178.   [**] "Cong. préh.," Bologna vol. p. 292.
[††] "Cong. préh.," Buda Pest vol. i. p. 227.

France,* and Italy.† I have one 3¾ inches long, from Royat, Puy de Dôme. A large and thicker specimen is in the Museum at Toulouse. They have usually a small per-centage, 0·15 to 2·08 of tin in them.‡

I have already, in the Introductory Chapter, made some remarks on the probability of a copper age having, in some part of the world, preceded that of bronze, and need here only repeat that the occurrence of implements in copper, of the forms usually occurring in bronze, does not of necessity imply a want of acquaintance with the tin necessary to mix with copper to form bronze, but may only be significant of a temporary or local scarcity of the former metal. I may also add that without actual analysis, it is unsafe, from appearance only, to judge whether copper is pure, or whether it has not an appreciable per-centage of tin in it.

In treating of the different forms and characters of bronze celts, and of the places and circumstances of finding, I think it will be best first to take those from England and Wales, then those from Scotland, and lastly those from Ireland. I begin with those which have been found in barrows in England.

Fig. 2 represents a flat celt found in a barrow in the parish of Butterwick, in the East Riding of Yorkshire, by the Rev. Canon Greenwell, F.R.S., F.S.A.§ It lay at the hips of the body of a young man, at whose right hand the knife-dagger (Fig. 279) and the bronze drill or pricker (Fig. 225) were found, accompanied by a flint knife formed from a broad external flake. In front of the chest were six buttons, five of jet and one of sandstone, two of which are figured in my "Ancient Stone Implements." ‖ The handle of the celt or axe-head could be plainly traced by means of a dark line of decayed wood, and to all appearance the weapon had been worn slung from the waist. "The blade is of the simplest form, modelled on the pattern of the stone axe, and may, it is probable, be regarded as the earliest type of bronze axe antecedently to the appearance of either flanges or socket. It is 4 inches long, 2⅜ inches wide at the cutting edge, and 1¼ inches at the smaller end. It had evidently been fixed into a solid handle to a depth of 2 inches."

Fig. 2.—Butterwick.

* *Bull. Soc. de Borda, Dax*, 1878, p. 57.
† "Cong. préh.," Copenhagen vol. p. 484.
‡ Morlot, *Mém. Soc. Ant. du Nord*, 1866—71, p. 25.
§ "British Barrows," p. 188. The cut is Fig. 38.
‖ Figs. 369 and 370, p. 407.

A very similar discovery to that at Butterwick was made by the late Mr. Thomas Bateman in a barrow upon Parwich Moor, Derbyshire,[*] called Shuttlestone, opened by him in June, 1848. In this case a man of fine proportions and in the prime of life had been interred, surrounded by fern-leaves and enveloped in a hide with the hair inwards. Close to the head were a small flat bead of jet and a circular flint (probably a "scraper"). In contact with the left arm lay a bronze dagger, much like Fig. 279, with two rivets for the attachment of the handle, which had been of horn. About the middle of the left thigh was a bronze celt of the plainest axe-shaped type. The cutting edge was turned towards the upper part of the person, and the instrument itself had been inserted into a wooden shaft for about 2 inches at the narrow end. The celt and dagger are engraved in the *Archæological Association Journal*,[†] and the former in the *Archæologia*.[‡] It is about 5½ inches long, and in form much like Fig. 19.

In a small barrow named Borther Low,[§] about two miles south of Middleton by Youlgrave, Mr. William Bateman discovered a skeleton with the remains of a plain coarse urn on the left side, a flint arrow-head much burnt, a pair of canine teeth of either a fox, or a dog of the same size, and a diminutive bronze celt. In the catalogue of the Bateman Museum [‖] this is described as "of the most primitive type, closely resembling the stone celts in form," and 2 inches only in length. It is there stated to have been found with a flint spear, but this seems to be a mistake for an arrow-head.[¶]

Dr. Samuel Pegge,[**] in his letter to Mr. Lort already cited, mentions that "Mr. Adam Wolsey the younger, of Matlock in Derbyshire, has a celt found near the same place A.D. 1787, at Blakelow in the parish of Ashover, with a spear-head of flint, a military weapon also." Not improbably this was an axe-head of the same class.

A celt of much the same character as Fig. 2, but in outline more nearly resembling Fig. 19, 4⅜ inches long and 2⅜ broad at the cutting edge, was found in company with two diadems or lunettes of gold such as the Irish antiquaries call "Minds," at Harlyn, in the parish of Merryn, near Padstow, Cornwall, and is engraved in the *Archæological Journal*.[††] The objects were found at a depth of about six feet from the surface, and with them was another bronze article, which was unfortunately thrown away. This was described by the man at work on the spot as "like a bit of a buckle." The discovery was quite accidental, and no notice seems to have been taken as to whether there were any traces of an interment at the spot, though the earth in contact with the articles is described as having been "of an artificial character."

It is a celt of this kind which is engraved by Plot [‡‡] as found near St. Bertram's Well, Ilam, Staffordshire. He describes it as "somewhat like, only larger than, a lath-hammer at the edge end, but not so on the other," and regards it as a Roman sacrificial axe.

One (4⅛ inches) was found on Bevere Island, Worcestershire.[§§]

* "Ten Years' Diggings," p. 34. "Catalogue," p. 75. *Arch. Assoc. Journ.*, vol. vii. p. 217.
† Vol. vii. p. 217, pl. xix.
‡ Vol. xliii. p. 445.
§ "Vest. of the Ants. of Derb.," p. 48.
‖ P. 74, No. 11.
¶ See "Catal.," p. 32, No. 29.
** *Arch.*, vol. ix. p. 85.
†† Vol. xxii. p. 277.
‡‡ "Nat. Hist. of Staffordshire," tab. xxiii. p. 403
§§ Allies, p. 151, pl. iv. 11.

Others of the same kind have been found near Duxford, Cambs,* near Grappenhall, Cheshire ;† the Beacon Hill, Charnwood Forest, Leicester-shire ;‡ and, near Battlefield, Shrewsbury,§ in company with a palstave without loop, some sickle-like objects, and other articles. One, 9 inches long and 5 inches broad at the cutting edge, found in the ruins of Gleas-ton Castle, Lower Furness, Lancashire, is engraved in the *Archæologia*.‖

The celts found on Baddow Hall Common,¶ near Danbury, Essex, one of which was 6 inches long and 3¼ inches broad at the edge, seem to have been of this character.

I have seen specimens of the same type from Taxley Fen, Hunting-donshire (4¾ inches long), in the collection of Mr. S. Sharp, F.S.A.; and from Raisthorp, near Fimber, Yorkshire, in that of Messrs. Mortimer.

In Canon Greenwell's collection are three (about 4¼ inches) found at Newbiggin, Northumberland, and others (about 5¼ inches) from Alnwick and Wallsend. A specimen in the same collection (5¼ inches), found at Knapton, Yorkshire (E. R.), has a slight ridge along the centre of the sides, which, as well as the angles between the faces and the sides, is indented with a series of slight hammer marks at regular intervals.

Mr. Wallace of Distington, Whitehaven, has one (6½ inches) from Hango Hill, Castleton, Isle of Man.

I have myself celts of the same class from the Cambridge Fens (4⅝ inches); Sherburn Carr, Yorkshire (5⅝ inches), found with another nearly similar; Swansea (4¼ inches, much decayed); and near Pont Caradog, Brithder, Glamorganshire (6¼ inches), found with three others, and given to me by Canon Greenwell, F.R.S., in whose collection the others are preserved.

A few of these flat plain celts have been found in France. Some from the departments of Doubs and Jura are engraved by Chantre.** One from Normandy,†† figured by the Abbé Cochet, seems to show some trace of a transverse ridge. One from the Seine is engraved in the "Dictionnaire Archéologique de la Gaule." Another was found in Finistère.‡‡ Others are in the Museum at Narbonne§§ and elsewhere. The form is also found in Spain, both in bronze and what is apparently copper. I have specimens from the Ciudad Real district.

The plain flat form like Fig. 2 is also occasionally found in Germany. One from Ackenbach, near Homberg, is figured by Schreiber.‖‖

With nearly straight sides like Fig. 27, the form is not uncommon in Hungary. Some of these are very thin.

Others of nearly the same form, but thicker, have been found on the other side of the Atlantic in Mexico, and many of the copper celts of North America are also of the plain flat type with an oblong section. This circumstance to my mind rather proves that the form is the simplest, and therefore that most naturally adopted for hatchets, than that there was of necessity any intercourse between the countries in which it has prevailed.

Many of the flat celts are ornamented in a more or less artistic

* *Arch. Journ.*, vol. vii. p. 179. † *Op. cit.*, vol. xviii. p. 158.
‡ *Proc. Soc. Ant.*, 2nd S., vol. i. p. 44. § *P. S. A.*, 2nd S., vol. ii. p. 251.
‖ Vol. v. pl. vii. i. p. 106. ¶ *Arch.*, vol. ix. p. 378.
** Pl. ii. 1, 2, 3. †† "La Seine Inf.," p. 552.
‡‡ "Matériaux," vol. iv. p. 525. §§ "Matériaux," vol. v. pl. ii. 2, 3.
‖‖ "Die ehernen Streitkeile" (1842), Taf. i. 1.

manner on the faces, or the sides, or on both; but before proceeding to notice any of them, it will be well to mention another variety of the plain celt, in which the faces, instead of being nearly flat or uniformly convex, slope towards either end from a transverse ridge near the middle of the blade. This ridge is never very strongly defined, as the total thickness of the blade from ridge to ridge is rarely more than half an inch. The plain variety is somewhat rare in Britain, but one ornamented on both faces will be described, under Fig. 5, and an Irish example is shown in Fig. 35.

A large doubly tapering celt (8 inches) was found at East Surby, Rushen,[*] Isle of Man. Some of those already mentioned partake of this character. In Hoare's great work a specimen from the Bush Barrow, Normanton,[†] is engraved as being of this plain doubly tapering type; but from the more accurate engraving given by Dr. Thurnam [‡] it appears that this instrument has flanges at the side, like Fig. 8, and must therefore be spoken of later on.

I now proceed to consider some of the flat celts ornamented with patterns probably produced by punches, as will subsequently be mentioned. The first which I adduce was found with an interment, and the ornamentation is so slight that it is a question whether the celt ought not to rank among those of the plain kind.

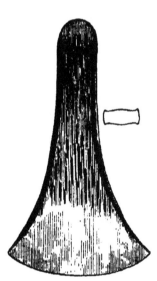

Fig. 3.—Moot Low. ½

The late Mr. Thomas Bateman in 1845 found what he described as "a fine bronze celt of novel form" and "of elegant outline" near the head of a contracted skeleton in a barrow called Moot Low,[§] about half-way between Alsop Moor and Dovedale, Derbyshire. "It was placed in a line with the body, with its edge upwards." By the kindness of Mr. Llewellynn Jewitt, F.S.A.,[||] I am enabled to give a figure of this instrument in Fig. 3. As will be seen, it has slight flanges along the sides, and the upper part is ornamented with short vertical lines punched in.

That shown in Fig. 4 was found in Yorkshire, and is now in the British Museum. The patina upon it has been somewhat injured, but

* "First Rep. Arch. Comm. I. of Man," pl. iv. 2.
† "Ancient Wilts," vol. i. p. 202, pl. xxvi.   ‡ Arch., vol. xliii. p. 444.
§ "Vest. Ant. Derb.," p. 68. "Catal.," p. 75, No. 18.
|| "Grave-mounds," fig. 187.

the ornamentation upon the faces is in places very well preserved. It consists of numerous parallel lines, each made up of short diagonal indentations in the metal, and together forming the pattern which will be better understood from the figure than from any description. The sides are ornamented by having two low pyramidal bosses drawn out upon them, leaving a long concave hexagonal space in the middle between

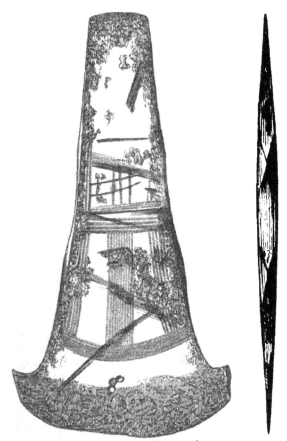

Fig. 4.—Yorkshire. ½

them. This celt has already been figured, but on a much smaller scale, in the "Horæ Ferales." *

This style of ornamentation on the sides is more common on Irish than on English or Scottish celts. One, however, 5¼ inches long, of the doubly tapering form with lunate edge, having the central portion of the blade ornamented with a series of lines in a chevron pattern, and having the sides worked into three facets of a pointed oval form, was found at Whittington,† Gloucestershire, and was presented by Mr. W. L. Lawrence, F.S.A., to the Society of Antiquaries. The ornamentation is much

* Pl. iv. No. 4.　　　　† *Proc. Soc. Ant.*, 2nd S., vol. i. pp. 235, 250.

like that on Fig. 7, but between the ornamented portion of the blade and the edge there is a curved hollow facet, the ridge below which runs nearly parallel with the edge.

The celt shown in Fig. 5 might perhaps be more properly placed among the flanged celts, as, without having well-developed flanges along the sides, there is a projecting ridge running along either margin of the faces, in consequence of the sides having been somewhat chamfered, or having had their angles beaten down by hammering. It was found on Preston Down, near Weymouth, Dorsetshire; but I do not know under what circumstances. It has become thickly coated with a dark sage-green patina, which has in places been unfortunately knocked off. The beautiful original ornamentation of the celt has been admirably preserved by the patina. The greater part of the surface has been figured with a sort of grained pattern like morocco leather, probably by means of a punch in form like a narrow blunt chisel. The faces of the blade are not flat, but taper in both directions from a ridge rather more than half-way up the blade. Along the lower side of this somewhat curved ridge, and again about an inch above the cutting edge, a belt of chevrons has been punched in, having the appearance of a plaited band. Below the lower band the surface has been left smooth and unornamented, so that grind-

Fig. 5.—Weymouth.   ⅓

ing the edge would not in any way injure the pattern. The upper part of the blade has at the present time exactly the appearance of dark green morocco with "blind-tooling" upon it. No doubt many blades which were originally ornamented after the same fashion as this specimen have now, through oxidation or the accidental destruction of the patina, lost all traces of their original decoration. On this, where the patina has been destroyed, nothing can be seen of the graining.

I have a flat celt from Mildenhall, Suffolk (6 inches), in form like Fig. 6, the greater part of the surface of which has been grained in a similar manner, though the graining is now almost obliterated.

In the collection of the Duke of Northumberland[*] is a large celt which appears to be of the flat kind, with the side edges "slightly recurved," and with the surface "elaborately worked with chevrony lines and ornaments which may have been partly produced by hammering." It was found in Northumberland.

Another belonging to James Kendrick, Esq., M.D., found at Risdon,[†] near Warrington, is described as being "ornamented with punched lines in a very unusual manner." Another, of which a bad representation from one of Dr. Stukeley's drawings is given in the *Archæologia*, is said

---

[*] *Arch. Journ.*, vol. xix. p. 363.   [†] *Arch. Journ.*, vol. xviii. p. 159.

to have been found in the long barrow at Stonehenge.* One 4½ inches long, the faces ornamented with a number of longitudinal cuts, was found near Sidmouth.†

In some instances the faces of the celts have been wrought into a series of slightly hollowed facets. One such from Read, Lancashire, is in the British Museum, and is engraved as Fig. 6. The central space between the two series of ridges and also the margins of the faces are ornamented with shallow chevrons punched in. The sides have been hammered into

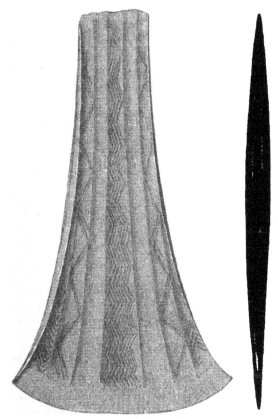

Fig. 6.—Read. ½

three facets, and this has produced slight flanges at the margins of the faces. These facets are ornamented with diagonal lines. This celt was found with two others, apparently of the same kind, and is described and engraved in Whitaker's "History of the Original Parish of Whalley."‡ The author says that these instruments were from 9 to 12 inches long, and had a broad and narrow end, but had neither loops, grooves, nor any other contrivance by which they could be fixed in a shaft, or indeed applied to any known use. That in the British Museum was obtained

* *Arch.*, vol. v. p. 135, pl. viii. 14.　　† *Trans. Devon Assoc.*, vol. v. p. 82.
‡ 3rd edit., 4to, 1818, pl. ii.

by the late Mr. Charles Towneley. The two others were formerly in the collections of the Rev. Dr. Milles, P.S.A., and of Dr. Whitaker.

I now come to the flanged celts, or those which have projecting ledges along the greater part of each side of the faces, produced either by hammering the metal at the sides of the blades, or in the original casting. As has already been observed, some of the celts which have been described as belonging to the flat variety might, with almost equal propriety, have been classed as flanged celts, as the mere hammering of the sides with a view to render them smooth or to produce an ornament upon them "upsets" the metal, and produces a thickening along the margin which almost amounts to a flange.

In the celt shown in Fig. 7 the flanges are very slight, and are in all probability merely due to the hammering necessary to produce the kind of cable pattern or spiral fluting which is seen in the side view. The faces taper in each direction from a transverse ridge, and the blade for some distance below this is ornamented with an incuse chevron pattern. The blade towards the edge and above the ridge is left plain. This specimen was found in Suffolk, but I do not know the exact locality. It is in my own collection.

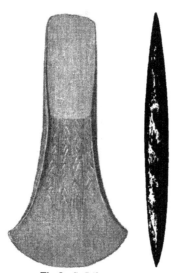

Fig. 7.—Suffolk.

Among nineteen bronze celts discovered about the year 1845 on the property of Mr. Samuel Ware, F.S.A., at Postlingford Hall,* near Clare, Suffolk, were several of this class, two of which (6¼ and 5¼ inches), now in the British Museum, are figured in the *Archæologia*. One of them is ornamented with a chevron pattern, covering the part of the blade usually decorated, and having vertical lines running through the centres of the chevrons, and through the junction of their bases. The other is ornamented with a series of curved parallel lines running across the blade, as on Fig. 16. They have a slight projection or ridge at the thickest part of the blade, as have also two that are not ornamented, which likewise were presented by Mr. Ware to the British Museum.

Another celt of this kind (4⅞ inches) was found with a bronze spear-head having loops at the lower part of the blade in the Kilcot Wood,† near Newent, Gloucestershire. The faces are ornamented with parallel rows

* *Proc. Soc. Ant.*, 1st S., vol. i. p. 83; *Arch.*, vol. xxxi. p. 496; *Proc. Bury and West Suff. Arch. Inst.*, vol. i. p. 26.
† *Proc. Soc. Ant.*, 2nd S., vol. i. p. 369.

of short diagonal lines, bounded at the lower end by a double series of
dots, and a transverse row of diagonal lines.

In the remarkable hoard of bronze instruments discovered on Arreton
Down, in the Isle of Wight, about the year 1735, were, besides the spear-
heads and dagger blades, of which mention will be made in subsequent
chapters, four of these flanged celts.   Of these one (6⅞ inches) was ornamented both on the face and sides, but is at present only known from a
drawing in an album belonging to the Society of Antiquaries.

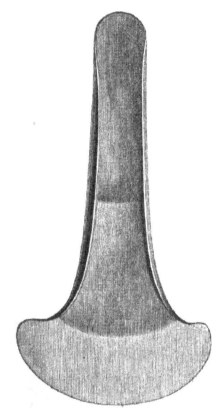

Fig. 8.—Arreton Down.   ½

The others were plain, and of one of them a woodcut is given in the
Archæologia, * which by the permission of the Council of the Society of
Antiquaries is here reproduced as Fig. 8.   It is 8 inches in length, and is
one of the largest of its class in the British Museum.   As will be seen, the
blade itself is of the doubly tapering kind.   The others are 4½ and 4¾
inches long.   They are said to have been found arranged in regular
order,† and, as Mr. Franks has suggested, may possibly have been the
store deposited by some ancient founder, which he was unable to reclaim
from its hiding-place.

* Vol. xxxvi. p. 329.   † *Arch.*, vol. v. p. 113.

E

In Figs. 9 and 10* are shown two more of these doubly tapering flanged celts, which were found in the parish of Plymstock,† Devonshire, about a mile east of Preston. They lay beneath a flat stone at a depth of about two feet below the surface, together with fourteen other celts, three daggers, one of which is given as Fig. 301, a spear-head or dagger, shown in Fig. 327, and a narrow chisel (Fig. 190). All the sixteen

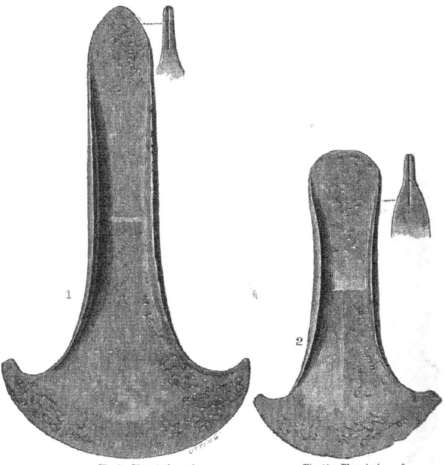

Fig. 9.—Plymstock.   ½   Fig. 10.—Plymstock.   ½

celts are of the same general type, but vary in length from 3¾ inches to 6¾ inches. The extent of the flanges or wings also varies, and in some they project considerably, and are brought with great precision to a sharp edge. At the narrow or butt end, the late Mr. Albert Way, who described the hoard, noticed a peculiar slight groove extending only as far as the

* For the loan of these cuts I am indebted to Mr. A. W. Franks, F.R.S.
† *Arch. Journ.*, vol. xxvi. p. 346. The scale of the cuts is there erroneously stated to be ½.

commencement of the lateral flanges. The character of the groove is shown in the portion of the side view given with each figure. Mr. Way and Mr. Franks thought that the narrow end of the celt, when produced from the mould, had been slightly bifid, and that the little cleft had been closed by the hammer. My own impression is that these marks are merely the result of "drawing down" the narrow ends with the hammer after their sides had been somewhat "upset" or expanded by hammering out the side flanges.

The sides of some of these celts have been hammered so as to present three longitudinal facets; others have the sides simply rounded. One of the most interesting features of this discovery is its analogy with that already mentioned as having been made at Arreton Down. The greater number of the objects found at Plymstock were given by the Duke of Bedford to the British Museum, and the remainder to the Exeter Museum.

Four or five celts with slight side flanges were found in the Wiltshire barrows by Sir R. Colt Hoare. The largest of these (6¼ inches long and 2¼ inches broad) was found in 1808, in a tumulus known as the Bush Barrow, near Normanton.* The following are the particulars of this discovery:—On the floor of the barrow was the skeleton of a tall man lying from south to north. Near his shoulders lay the celt, which owes its great preservation to having been inserted in a handle of wood. About eighteen inches south of the head were several bronze rivets, intermixed with wood and thin pieces of bronze, which were regarded as the remains of a shield. Near the right arm were a large dagger of bronze and a spear-head of the same metal, fully 13 inches long. The handle of this dagger, marvellously inlaid with pins of gold, will be described in a subsequent chapter. On the breast of the skeleton was a large lozenge-shaped plate of gold, ornamented with zigzag and other patterns, and near it were some other gold ornaments, some bone rings, and an oval perforated stone mace, the representation of which I have reproduced in my "Ancient Stone Implements."

We have here an instance of bronze weapons occurring associated with those of stone and with gold ornaments. Sir R. Colt Hoare has recorded some other cases. In a bell-shaped barrow near Wilsford,† at the feet of the skeleton of a tall man, he found a massive hammer of a dark-coloured stone, some objects of bone, a whetstone with a groove in the centre, and a bronze celt with small lateral flanges 3¼ inches long. These were accompanied by a very curious object of twisted bronze, apparently a ring about 4½ inches in diameter, having a tang pierced with four rivet holes for fixing in a handle. In the ring itself, opposite the tang, is a long oval hole, through which passes one of three circular links forming a short chain.

In a barrow on Overton Hill,‡ Sir R. Colt Hoare found a contracted skeleton buried either in the trunk of a tree or on a plank of wood. Near the head were a small celt of this kind, an awl with a handle (Fig. 227), and a small dagger, or, as he terms it, a "lance-head."

The occurrence of celts of this character is not limited to interments by inhumation. In another barrow of the Wilsford group Sir R. C. Hoare found, in a cist 2 feet deep, a pile of burnt bones, an ivory (?) pin, a rude

---

* "Anc. Wilts," vol. i. p. 202, pl. xxvi; *Arch.*, vol. xliii. p. 444.
† "Anc. Wilts," vol. i. p. 209, pl. xxix.
‡ "Anc. Wilts," vol. ii. 90; *Cran. Brit.*, xi. 7, where these objects are figured.

ring of bone, and a small bronze celt, also with side flanges, and only
2½ inches long.

Among other specimens of this form of celt may be cited one found on
Plumpton Plain,* near Lewes, Sussex, now in the British Museum ; one
(4 inches) found near Dover in 1856 ; and one (6½ inches) from Wye
Down, Kent, both in the Mayer collection at Liverpool. Canon Greenwell, F.R.S., has one (3½ inches) from March, Cambridgeshire.

Flanged celts much like Fig. 9 have been found in France. Some
from Haute-Saône,† Rhône, and Compiègne ‡ (Oise) have been figured. I
have specimens from Evreux (Eure), Amiens (Somme), and Lyons.
The type also occurs in Italy§ in some abundance; it is found more rarely
in Germany. ‖   Examples from Denmark are figured by Schreiber,¶
Segested,** and Madsen.††   The form also occurs in Sweden.‡‡

A peculiar form of flanged celt is shown in Fig. 11. The flanges
extend as usual nearly to the edge, but at the upper part of the blade are

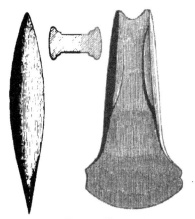

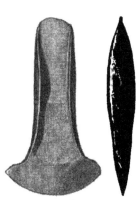

Fig. 11.—Thames.   ¼   Fig. 12.—Norfolk.   ½

set down so as to project still farther over the faces, though at a lower
level. The original was found in the Thames,§§ and is the property of
Mr. T. Layton, F.S.A.

A small example, ornamented with a fluted pattern on the sides and with
the blade slightly tapering in each direction from a central ridge, is shown
in Fig. 12. The original was found in Norfolk, and is in the collection of
Mr. R. Fitch, F.S.A.

Another, decorated with a fluted chevron pattern on the sides, and with
indented herring-bone and chevron patterns on the faces, is given in
Fig. 13. This example was found in Dorsetshire, and is now in the
British Museum. In the same collection is a beautiful celt with side

* *Suss. Arch. Coll.*, vol. ii. p. 268.
† Chantre, "Album," pl. iv. 2, 3. "Cong. préh.," Bologna vol. p. 352.
‡ *Dict. Arch. de la Gaule. Rev. Arch.*, N.S., vol. xiii. Pl. i. fig. H.
§ *Arch. Journ.*, vol. xxi. 100. Lubbock's "Preh. Times," p. 28, fig. 17.
‖ Lisch, "Fred. Francisc.," tab. xiii. 7.   ¶ Die ehernen Streitkeile, Taf. i. 5.
** "Oldsag. fra Broholm," pl. xxiii. 6.   †† "Afbild.," vol. ii. pl. xxi. 6.
‡‡ Montelius, "La Suède préh.," fig. 42. "Cong. préh.," Bologna vol. p. 292.
§§ *Proc. Soc. Ant.*, 2nd S., vol. v. p. 428, pl. i. fig. 1.

flanges found near Brough, Westmoreland (6¾ inches), which has the

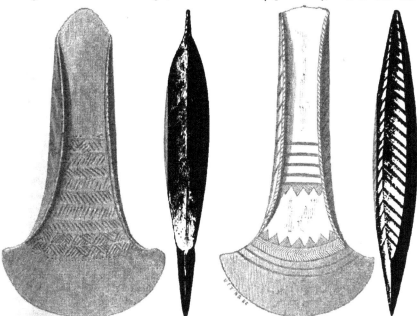

Fig. 13.—Dorsetshire.   ¼   Fig. 14.—Lewes.   ¼

portion of the blade below the thickest part ornamented with a lozengy matted pattern much like that on Fig. 51, but with the alternate lozenges plain and hatched. The hatching on some of the lozenges is from left to right, on others the reverse.

A flanged celt of unusual type, the sides curiously wrought and engraved or punched, and the faces exhibiting a pattern of chevrony lines, is shown in Fig. 14. It was found near Lewes,* Sussex, and is the property of Sir H. Shiffner, Bart.

An example of nearly the same kind is shown in Fig. 15, from a celt found in the Fens near Ely, and now in the museum of Mr. Marshall Fisher, of that city. Both faces are ornamented below the thickest part with broad indented lines, vertical and transverse, as will be best seen in the figure.

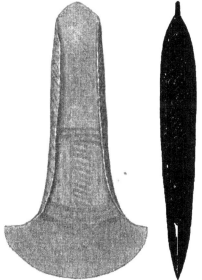

Fig. 15.—Ely.   ¼

* *Arch. Journ.*, vol. xviii. p. 167. Chichester vol. of *Arch Inst.*, p. 62, whence this cut is taken.

The sides are hammered into three facets, each having a series of diagonal grooves wrought in them. The two left-hand facets on each side have the grooves running upwards from left to right; on the third facet they run downwards, but at a much less inclination. The punch with which the grooves and ornaments were produced has also been employed along the inner angle of the flanges.

A pretty little celt, ornamented with transverse ridges in the lower part, is shown in Fig. 16. The original was found at Barrow, Suffolk.

The Rev. Canon Greenwell, F.R.S., possesses one (4⅜ inches) found at Horncastle, Lincolnshire, the faces of which are decorated in a nearly

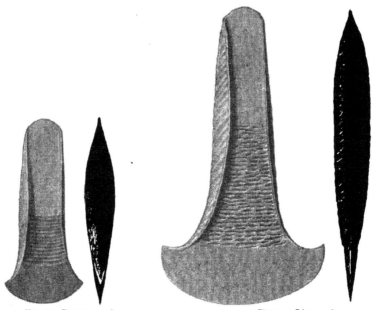

Fig. 16.—Barrow.   ⅓   Fig. 17.—Liss.   ⅓

similar manner; but the sides show a cable pattern, and there is a slight central ridge on the faces.

A much larger specimen (6¼ inches), found near the Menai Bridge,[*] Anglesea, has also cabled sides, but the grooves on the faces are straighter and wider apart.

A Danish celt, ornamented in a similar manner, is engraved by Madsen.[†]

The celt shown in Fig. 17 is of somewhat the same character, but the transverse lines are closer and not continuous. They have evidently been produced by means of a small blunt punch, with the aid of a hammer. The original was found at Liss,[‡] near Petersfield, Hants, and is now in the British Museum.

Flanged celts decorated on the faces are of rare occurrence in France. One of narrow proportions, and ornamented with lozenges and zigzags, was found at Mareuil-sur-Ourcq § (Oise).

* *Arch. Camb.*, 4th S., vol. viii. p. 207.   † " Afbild.," vol. ii. pl. xxi. 2.
‡ *Arch. Journ.*, vol. xii. p. 278, xviii. p. 167.   § *Dict. Arch. de la Gaule.*

The only instance known to me in which the rough castings destined to be wrought into this form of celt have been found in Britain is one recorded in the *Archæologia Cambrensis* * by the Rev. E. L. Barnwell. At the meeting of the Cambrian Archæological Association at Wrexham, Sir R. A. Cunliffe, Bart., exhibited what had evidently been the stock in trade of an ancient bronze-founder or merchant. It had been found at Rhosnesney, near Wrexham, and consisted of six palstaves, all from the same mould, another somewhat slighter and broken in two, the blade of a small dagger, three castings for flanged celts, and the shank of a fourth—all of them rough as they came from the mould. The cut given of one of the last-mentioned castings is here reproduced on a smaller scale as Fig. 18. It will be seen that a broad runner is left at the butt end, which was probably destined to be broken off; the sides would also be hammered, so as to increase the prominence of the flanges; and the whole would be planished by hammering and grinding. All the specimens have the appearance of having been washed over with tin, but this deposit of tin upon the surface may, I think, be due to some chemical action which has gone on since the bronze was buried in the ground, and may not have been intentionally produced.

Fig. 18.—Rhosnesney. ½

A casting for a longer flanged celt found at Vienne (Isère) has been figured by Chantre.†

Turning now to the flat and flanged celts discovered in Scotland, I may remark that the instruments of the flat form appear to be comparatively more abundant in that country than in England and Wales.

In Fig. 19 is shown a remarkably well-preserved specimen in my own collection, which is said to have been found near Drumlanrig, Dumfriesshire. The sides present two longitudinal facets at a low angle to each other. In hammering these the margin of the faces has been somewhat raised; they are otherwise smooth and devoid of ornament. Other specimens have three facets on the sides. Instruments of much the same character have been found near Biggar‡ (6½ inches), Culter§ (5¼ inches),

---

both in Lanarkshire ; on the farm of Colleonard,* near Banff (found with three which were ornamented) ; at Sluie on the Findhorn,† Morayshire (two, 6 inches) ; near Abernethy,‡ Perthshire (4 inches across face) ; near Ardgour House, § Inverness-shire (5¾ inches) ; the Hill of Fortrie of Balnoon,‖ Inverkeithney, Banffshire (5¾ inches long) ; Ravelston,¶ near Edinburgh (7 inches) ; Cobbinshaw, Midcalder, Edinburgh (4¾ inches), in my own collection. One found in the Moss of Cree,** near Wigton in Galloway, has been mentioned by Wilson, and is engraved in the *Ayr and Wigton Collections.*†† Others from Inch and Leswalt, Wigtonshire, have also been figured.‡‡

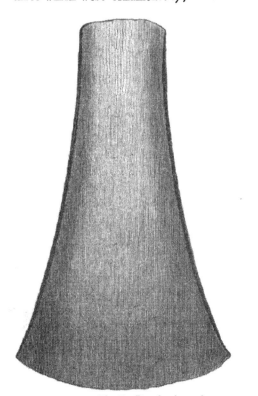

Fig. 19.—Drumlanrig.   ⅓

Some of these blades, and notably the celts from Sluie, the Hill of Fortrie of Balnoon, and Ravelston, have been thought to be tinned. An interesting paper on the subject has been written by Dr. J. Alexander Smith and Dr. Stevenson Macadam.§§ Their conclusion is rather in favour of the celts having been intentionally tinned, so as to protect them from oxidation and the influence of the weather. I think, however, that the tinned appearance of the castings for celts from Rhosnesney affords a strong argument against this feature being the result of intentional tinning ; for, if so, that metal would

---

* *Proc. Soc. Ant. Scot.*, vol. iii. p. 245.   † *P. S. A. S.*, vol. iv. p. 187, and ix. p. 431.
‡ *P. S. A. S.*, vol. iv. p. 380.   § *P. S. A. S.*, vol. ix. p. 182.
‖ *P. S. A. S.*, vol. ix. p. 430.
¶ *Arch. Scot.*, vol. iii. App. II. p. 32 ; *P. S. A. S.*, vol. ix. p. 431.
** " Preh. Ann. of Scot.," 2nd ed., vol. i. p. 381.
†† Vol. ii. p. 6.   ‡‡ *Op. cit.*, p. 7.
§§ *P. S. A. S.*, vol. ix. p. 428.

have been applied to the blades after they had been wrought and ground into shape, and not to the rough castings, from the surface of which the tin would be certainly removed in the process of finishing the blades. A bronze hammer from France in my collection has all the appearance of having been intentionally tinned, even partly within the socket; but in this case the bronze appears unusually rich in tin, which was probably added in order to increase the hardness of the metal, and some considerable alteration of structure has taken place within the body of the metal, as the surface is fissured in all directions, something like "crackle china."

In the Antiquarian Museum at Edinburgh are other flat celts, some of them with slight flanges at the edge, from Eildon, Roxburghshire; Inchnadamff, Sutherlandshire; Dunino, Fifeshire; Vogrie and Ratho, Midlothian; Kintore and Tarland, Aberdeenshire; and other places.

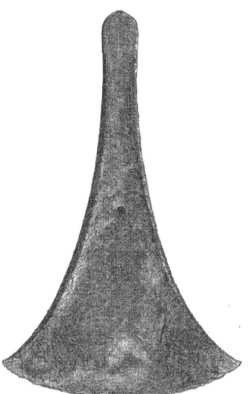

Some celts of this form, but with slight side flanges, have been found in the South of France.*

A celt of this class, also in the Museum at Edinburgh, is probably the largest ever found in the United Kingdom. It is 13⅜ inches in length, 9 inches in its greatest breadth, but only 1⅜ inch at the narrow end. Its thickness is about ⅜ inch in the middle of the blade, and its weight is 5 lbs. 7 ozs. It is shown on a scale of rather more than one-fourth in Fig. 20, for the use of the woodcut of which I am indebted to the Society of Antiquaries of Scotland. It was found in digging a drain on the farm of Lawhead,† on the south side of the Pentland Hills, near Edinburgh.

Fig. 20.—Lawhead. ⅛

Some of the Scottish celts, both flat and doubly tapering, are ornamented on the faces. One with four raised longitudinal ribs, and two with a

* "Matériaux," vol. v. pl. ii. 6, 7.   † *Proc. Soc. Ant. Scot.*, vol. vii. p. 105.

series of short incised or punched lines upon their faces, were among those found on the farm of Colleonard,* Banff; another has shallow flutings on the blade; another, E 22, in the Catalogue of the Antiquarian Museum at Edinburgh, is also ornamented with incised lines. One of those from Sluie,† Morayshire, is cited by Wilson.

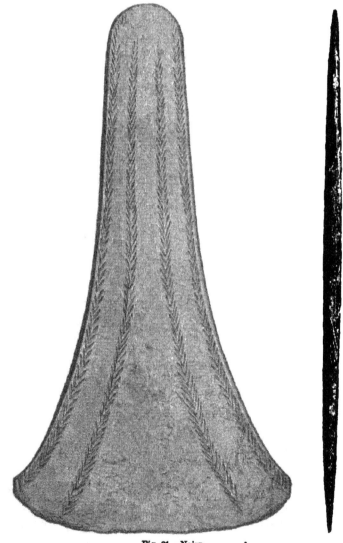

Fig. 21.—Nairn.

The tastefully ornamented celt shown in Fig. 21 was found near Nairn, and is now in the Museum of the Society of Antiquaries of

---

* P. S. A. S., vol. iii. p. 245.
† "Preh. Ann.," 2nd ed., vol. i. p. 381.

Scotland, to the Council of which I am indebted for the use of the cut. The wreathed lines appear to have been produced by a chisel-like punch. The ornamentation of both faces is almost exactly similar.

I have two flat celts, both said to have been found near Falkland, Fifeshire, one of which (6¾ inches) has had grooves about half an inch apart worked in the faces parallel to the sides, so as to form very pointed chevrons down the centre of the blade. The other (5 inches long) has had broad shallow dents about ½ inch long and ⅛ inch apart made in its faces, so as to form a herring-bone pattern.

The doubly tapering celt shown in Fig. 22 is also said to have been found near Falkland. Below the ridge the face has been ornamented

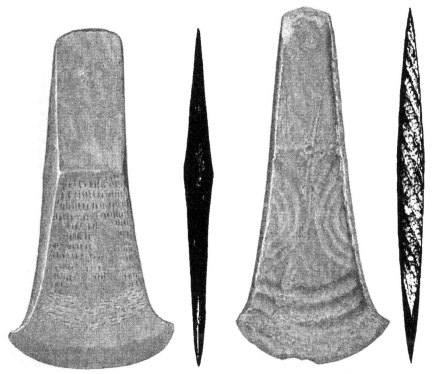

Fig. 22.—Falkland.　⅓　　　　　Fig. 23.—Greenlees.　⅓

with parallel belts of short, narrow indentations arranged longitudinally for about half the length of the lower face, but nearer the edge transversely. The sides are worked into three longitudinal facets.

Of Scottish flanged celts resembling Fig. 9, the following may be mentioned. One found in Peeblesshire * (5¾ inches long, with a circular depression on one face); one from Longman,† Macduff, Banffshire (3¾ inches long).

Another of the same class, having a round hole at the upper part of the blade, is said to have been found in Scotland, and is engraved by Gordon.‡

* Engraved in *Arch. Assoc. Journ.*, vol. xvii. pl. vi. 4, p. 21.
† *P. S. A. S.*, vol. vi. p. 41.　　　‡ "Itin. Septent.," p. 116, pl. l. No. 1.

A celt with but slightly raised flanges and peculiar ornamentation is shown in Fig. 23. It was found at Greenlees,* near Spottiswoode, Berwickshire, and is in the collection of Lady John Scott. There is a faintly marked stop-ridge, above which the blade has been ornamented by thickly set parallel hammer or punch marks. The sides are fluted in a cable pattern. Parallel to the cutting edge are three slight fluted hollows, and on the blade above are segments of concentric hollows of the same kind, forming what heralds would term "flanches" on the blade. Whether in this ornament we are to see a representation of the "flanches" of the winged palstave like Fig. 85, such as is so common on socketed celts, or whether it is of independent origin, I will not attempt to determine.

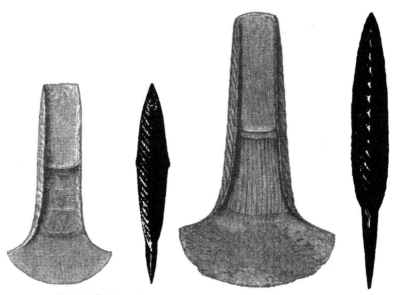

Fig. 24.—Perth.   Fig. 25.—Applegarth.

A flanged celt with a slight stop-ridge, having the sides ornamented with a cable pattern and the faces with rows of triangles alternately hatched and plain, is shown in Fig. 24. The original was found near Perth,† and is in the collection of the Rev. James Beck, F.S.A. A celt with five hatched bands surmounted by triangles, and with the sides cable moulded, though found in Denmark,‡ much resembles this Scottish specimen and some of those from Ireland. Another with similar sides, but with the lower part of the faces ornamented with narrow vertical grooves, was found at Applegarth,§ Dumfriesshire, and is now in the Antiquarian Museum at Edinburgh. It is represented in Fig. 25.

* Proc. Soc. Ant. Scot., vol. xii. p. 601. I am indebted to the Council for the use of this cut.
† Proc. Soc. Ant., 2nd S., vol. viii. p. 5.
‡ Madsen, "Afbild.," vol. ii. pl. xxi. 7. See also "Ant. Tidsk.," 1861—3, p. 24.
§ Proc. Soc. Ant. Scot., vol. xii. p. 602.

Another decorated celt of the same character, though with different ornamentation, is shown in Fig. 26. The curved bands on the faces are formed of lines with dots between, and the sides have a kind of fern-leaf pattern upon them, like that on the winged celt from Trillick, Fig. 98. The original was found at Dams, Balbirnie,* Fifeshire.

A very large number of flat celts of the simplest form have been found in Ireland. So numerous are they that it would only encumber these pages were I to attempt to give a detailed account of all the varieties, and of all the localities at which they have been found. Sir William Wilde, in his most valuable "Catalogue of the Museum of the Royal Irish Academy," has placed on record a

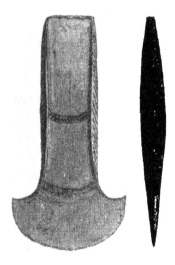

Fig. 26.—Dams. ⅓   Fig. 27.—Ballinamallard. ⅓

large amount of information upon this subject, from which some of the facts hereafter mentioned are borrowed, and to which the reader is referred for farther information. Some of those of the rudest manufacture are formed "of red, almost unalloyed copper."† These vary in length from about 2½ inches to 6½ inches, and are never ornamented.

In Fig. 27 is shown a small example of a celt apparently of pure copper, which was found at Ballinamallard, Co. Fermanagh, and was kindly added to my collection by the Earl of Enniskillen. I have another, more like Fig. 28, from Ballybawn, Co. Cork, presented to me by Mr. Robert Day, F.S.A.

A small celt of this character, from King's County, now in the British Museum, is only 2½ inches in length.

* *Proc. Soc. Ant. Scot.*, vol. xiii. p. 120. I am indebted to the Council for the loan of this cut.   † Wilde, p. 361.

Fig. 28 shows a very common form of Irish celt, in this instance made of bronze. The instruments of this type are in general nearly flat, and

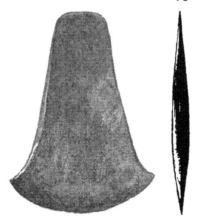 

Fig. 28.—North of Ireland.   ½   Fig. 29.—Ireland.   ½

without any marked central ridge, such as is to be observed more

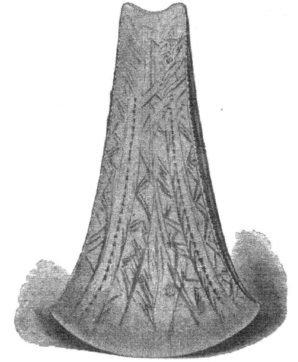

Fig. 30.—Tipperary.   ½

frequently on the longer and narrower form, of which a remarkably small specimen from the collection of Mr. R. Day, F.S.A., is shown in Fig. 29. In this case it will be seen that the blade tapers both ways from a low central ridge. Others of these flat celts are in outline more like Fig. 20. One such, in the museum of the Royal Irish Academy, is 12¼ inches long by 8¼ inches broad, and weighs nearly 5 lbs. One in the British Museum, which, unfortunately, is somewhat imperfect, must have been of nearly the same size. The usual length of the celts like Fig. 28 is from 4 to 6 inches. One from Greenmount, Castle Bellingham, Co. Louth, is engraved in the *Archæological Journal.*＊

Occasionally the flat surface is ornamented. An example of this kind (7½ inches) is given in Fig. 30, from a specimen found in the county of Tipperary,† and now in the British Museum. The surface has the patterns punched in, and the angles between the faces and the sides are slightly serrated. Some few Irish celts are slightly fluted on the face, like the English specimen, Fig. 6.

Another ornamented celt of this class, from my own collection, is shown in Fig. 31. On this the roughly worked pattern has been produced

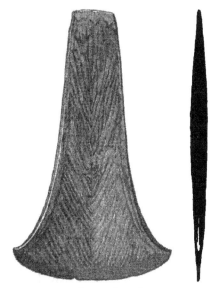

Fig. 31.—Ireland. ⅜

by means of a long blunt punch, or possibly by the pane or narrow end of a hammer; but it is far more probable that the former tool was used than the latter. The two faces are nearly alike, and the sides have been hammered so as to produce a central ridge along them.

A large and highly ornamented flat celt in the collection of Canon Greenwell, F.R.S., is shown in Fig. 32. The ornamentation on each face is the same, and the sides have been hammered so as to produce a succession of flat lozenges upon them. It was found near Connor, Co. Antrim, with two others of nearly the same size, one of which was

＊ Vol. xxvii. p. 308.
† *Arch. Journ.*, vol. vi. p. 410. For the use of this cut I am indebted to Mr. A. W. Franks, F.R.S.

scraped by the finder.   The other is ornamented with a cross-hatched
border along the margins, and three narrow bands across the blade, one
cross-hatched, one of triangles alternately hatched and plain, and one with
vertical lines.   Parallel with the cutting edge, which, however, has been
broken off in old times, is a curved band of alternate triangles, like that
across the centre of the blade.   Much of the surface is grained by vertical
indentations, and the sides are ornamented like those of Fig. 4.

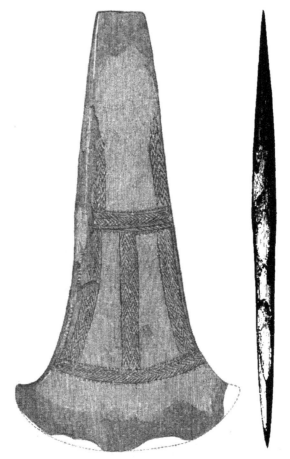

Fig. 32.—Connor.   ½

In the celts tapering in both directions from a slight transverse ridge,
the sides have often been "upset" by hammering, so as to produce a
thickening of the blade at the margins almost amounting to a flange.
Not unfrequently a pattern is produced upon the sides, as in Fig. 33,
where it will be seen that the median ridge along the sides is interrupted
at intervals by a series of flat lozenges.   The faces of this instrument
below the ridge have been neatly hammered, so as to produce a kind of
grained surface not unlike that of French morocco leather.   This speci-

men, which is unusually large, was found near Clontarf, Co. Dublin. The same kind of decoration occurs on the sides of many specimens in the museum of the Royal Irish Academy.*

The decoration of the faces often extends over the upper part of the blade, though, when hafted, much of this was probably hidden. In Fig. 34, borrowed from Wilde (Fig. 248), this peculiarity is well exhibited. The sides have the long lozenges upon them, like those on the celt last described.

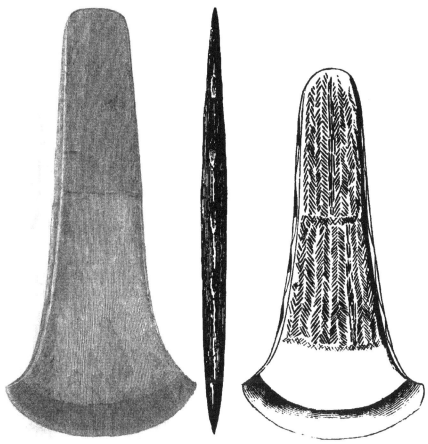

Fig. 33.—Clontarf.   ½   Fig. 34.—Ireland.   ½

The beautiful specimen shown in Fig. 35 was presented to me by Mr. Robert Day, F.S.A. The sides have in this case a kind of cable pattern worked upon them. The ornamentation of the faces is remarkable as having so many curved lines brought into it. The lower part of the blade has two shallow flutings upon it, approximately parallel to the edge.

In the case of a celt of much the same form and size (7¼ inches), which belonged to the late Rev. Thomas Hugo, F.S.A., and was at one time

* See Wilde, Fig. 249. 266.

F

thought to have been found in the Thames,* it is the upper part of the

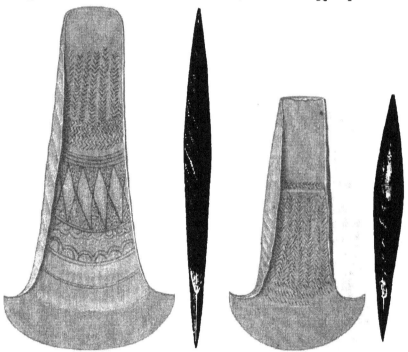

Fig. 35.—Ireland.   ½   Fig. 36.—Trim.   ½

blade that is decorated, and not the lower, which is left smooth.   There
is no central ridge, but the upper part has a coarse lozenge pattern

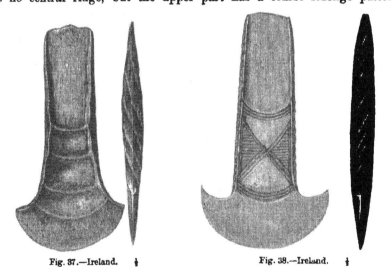

Fig. 37.—Ireland.   ½   Fig. 38.—Ireland.   ½

hammered upon it, the centres of the lozenges being roughly hatched with

* *Arch. Journ.*, vol. xi. p. 295.

transverse lines. Possibly this roughening may have assisted to keep the blade fast in the handle, though in producing it some artistic feeling was brought to bear. There is little doubt of this instrument being of Irish origin.

Other celts, like Fig. 36, have the upper part of the blade plain and the lower ornamented. This specimen was found at Trim, Co. Meath, and is in the collection of Canon Greenwell, F.R.S. It will be observed that even the cabled fluting of the sides ceases opposite the transverse ridge.

In Figs. 37 and 38 are shown two more of these slightly flanged ornamented celts. The first is in the museum of the Royal Irish Academy, and has already been figured by Wilde (Fig. 298). The lower part of the blade is fluted transversely with chevron patterns punched in along the curved ridges. In the second, which was presented to me by Dr. Aquilla Smith, M.R.I.A., there is a fairly well defined though but slightly projecting curved stop-ridge, and the blade is decorated by boldly punched lines, forming a pattern which a herald might describe as "per saltire argent and azure." The cable fluting on the sides is beautifully regular. The Rev. G. W. Brackenridge, of Clevedon, possesses a longer specimen (5⅜ inches), found at Tullygowan, near Gracehill, Co. Antrim, the faces of which are ornamented with a nearly similar design. Canon Greenwell has another example found at Carrickfergus, Co. Antrim.

The patterns punched upon the celts of this type show a great variety of form, and not a little fertility of design in the ancient artificers.* Various combinations of chevron patterns are the most frequent, though grained surfaces and straight lines like those on Fig. 17 also frequently occur. Sir William Wilde describes them as hammered, punched, engraved, or cast. Most of the patterns were, however, produced by means of punches, though it is possible that in some instances the other processes may have been used.

Figs. 39 to 43, borrowed from Wilde (Figs. 286 to 290), show some of the patterns full size. The punch most commonly

Fig. 39.   Fig. 40.   Fig. 41.   Fig. 42.   Fig 43.

employed must have resembled a narrow and blunt chisel; but a kind of centre-punch, producing a shallow round indentation, was also employed, and possibly a somewhat curved punch like a blunt gouge. In some cases the lines between the punched marks are, according to Wilde, engraved. It is, however, a question whether even the finest lines might not have been produced by a chisel used after the manner of a punch. What were probably punches for

* See Wilde, "Catal. Mus. R. I. A.," p. 389 et seq.; "Vallancey," vol. iv. pl. x. 9.

producing such patterns have been found in some English hoards, as will subsequently be mentioned ; and in the Fonderie de Larnaud, Jura,* was a punch with an engrailed end for producing a kind of "milled" mark, either in the mould or on the casting. Another, with concentric circles, seems best adapted for impressing the loam of the mould.

Some few of the Irish ornamented celts have well-defined stopridges like the English example, Fig. 51 ; but these will be more in their place in the following chapter. One or two other forms may, however, be here mentioned, though they approximate closely to the chisels described in subsequent pages.

One of these is shown in Fig. 44, the upper part of the blade of which is, as will be seen, so narrow, and the instrument itself so small and light,

Fig. 44.—Armoy.   ⅓   Fig. 45.—Ireland.   ⅓

that it is a question whether it should not be regarded as a chisel or paring-tool rather than as a hatchet. The blade tapers both ways, and the incipient flange is more fully developed above the ridge than below. The original was found at Armoy, Co. Antrim. It is much broader at the cutting edge than the blade from Culham, Fig. 55, to which it is somewhat allied.

Another Irish form of celt, or possibly chisel, tapers in both directions from a central transverse ridge, near which there are lateral projections on the blade, as if to prevent its being driven into the handle. An example of this kind, from the museum of the Royal Irish Academy. is given in Fig. 45. There are nine or ten in that collection, and they vary in length from about 3¾ to 8 inches. Others are in the British Museum, one of which is more distinctly tanged than the figure, and the stops are formed by the gradual widening out of the blade, which again contracts with a similar curve, and once more widens out at the edge. This type is also known in France. Other varieties of this form are described in Chapter VII.

* Chantre, " Album," pl. l. 9, 10.

A doubly tapering blade in the museum of the Royal Irish Academy, shown in Fig. 46, has a slight stop-ridge on the face, and also expands at the sides, though not to the same extent as the plain specimens just mentioned. It is ornamented with straight and curved bands formed of chevron patterns.

A double-edged instrument, also in the museum of the Royal Irish Academy, has a stop-ridge on one of the faces only, as shown in Fig. 47.

An instrument of the same form, but with stops at the sides instead of on the face, 4⅞ inches long, ⅝ inch broad at the edges, and about ¼ inch thick, was found at Farley Heath, Surrey, and is now in the British Museum.

A Danish instrument of the same kind is figured by Worsaae.[*]

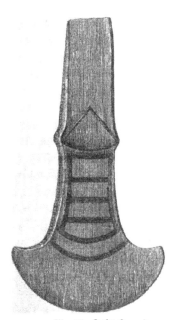

Fig. 46.—Ireland.　½　　　　Fig. 47.—Ireland.　½

Flat celts of iron with lateral stops have been found in the cemetery at Hallstatt, Austria, as well as winged palstaves and socketed celts of the same metal.

Some of the thin votive hatchets found at Dodona[†] are of the same form, and are significant of such blades having been in actual use in Greece.

In the next chapter are described the celts in which the side flanges have become more fully developed, so as to form wings to embrace and steady the handle, and the central ridge has grown into a well-marked shoulder against which the end of the haft could rest.

* *Nord. Oldsager*, No. 176.　　　　† Carapanos, " Dodone," pl. liv. 7.

CHAPTER IV.

WINGED CELTS AND PALSTAVES.

To any one who has examined an extensive collection of the bronze instruments found in this country it will at once be apparent that in the class of celts designed to be fixed in some sort of haft, and not themselves socketed for the reception of a handle, there is a wide range of form. Any attempt, however, to divide them into well-marked classes is soon seen to be futile, as there is found to be a gradual transition from what at first sight appears to be a well-marked form into some other which presents different characteristics. If, for instance, we take the side flanges as a criterion, we find them ranging from a mere thickening on the margins of the flat celts to well-developed flanges, extending along nearly the whole blade; we then find them confined to the upper part of the instrument, and in some cases of great lateral extent, so as to be capable of being hammered over to form a kind of semicircular socket on each side of the blade. In other cases we find that the flanges have some part of their apparent projection due to a diminution in the thickness of the portion of the blade which lies between them. If we take as a criterion the stop-ridge, as it has been termed, a projecting ridge for the purpose of preventing the blade being driven too far into its wooden handle, we find the ridge in a rudimentary form in the blades which taper both ways; next as a slightly raised ridge or bead running across the blade; then as a better-defined ridge, to which, at last, greater development is given by a reduction in the thickness of the blade above it. The presence or absence of a loop at the side is, no doubt, a good differentiation, but as this is a mere minor accessory, and two celts may be identical in other respects with the exception of one being provided with a loop and the other being without it, it does not materially assist in the classification of this group of instruments, although for convenience' sake it is best to treat of the two varieties of form separately. An additional reason for this may be found in the possibility that the loop was a comparatively late invention, so that the palstaves provided with it may be in some cases of later date than those without it, though the identity in the ornamentation of some of the instruments of the two classes, and the fact of their being occasionally found together, are almost conclusive as to their contemporaneity.

In the present chapter I propose to treat of the celts with a stop-ridge, of the winged celts, and of those of the palstave form.

The winged celts may be generally described as those in which the flanges are short and have a great amount of lateral extension. When these wings are hammered over so as to form a kind of socket on each side of the blade, one of the varieties of the palstave form is the result. The other and more common variety of the palstave form has the portion of the blade which lies between the wings or side flanges and above the stop-ridge cast thinner than the rest of the blade, thus leaving a recess or groove on each side into which the handle fitted.

I have already made frequent use of the term palstave, and it will be well here to make a few remarks as to the origin and meaning of the word. The term palstave, or more properly paalstab, comes to us from the Scandinavian antiquaries. Their

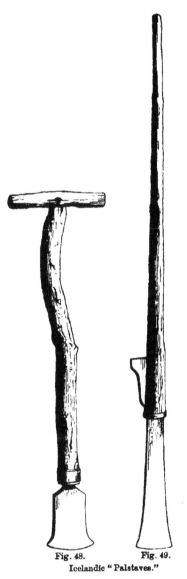

Fig. 48.   Fig. 49.
Icelandic " Palstaves."

reason for adopting the term was that there is still in use in Iceland a kind of narrow spade or spud, which is known by the name of paalstab, and which somewhat resembles these bronze instruments. Woodcuts of two of these Icelandic palstaves are given in the *Archæological Journal*,[*] from drawings communicated to Mr. Yates by Councillor Thomsen, of Copenhagen. They are here by permission reproduced. The derivation of the term suggested in a note to the Journal is that *paal* comes from the Icelandic verb *pula*, or *pala*, to labour, so that the word means the "labouring staff." But this appears to me erroneous. *Pul*, indeed, signifies hard, laborious work; but *pæli* (*at pæla*) means to dig, and *pall* (*conf.* Latin *pala* and French *pelle*) means a kind of spade or shovel. The word, indeed, survives in the English language as *peel*, the name of a kind of wooden shovel used by bakers for placing loaves in the oven. The meaning of the term would appear, then, to be rather "spade staff" than "labouring staff," unless the word labouring be used in the sense of the French *labourer*.

Mr. Thoms, in a note to his "Translation of Worsaae's Primeval Antiquities of Denmark,"[†] says that the "term Paalstab was formerly applied in Scandinavia and Iceland to a weapon used for battering the shields of the enemy, as is shewn by passages in the Sagas. Although not strictly applicable to the (bronze) instruments in question, this designation is now so generally used by the antiquaries of Scandinavia and Germany, that it seems desirable, with the view of securing a fixed terminology, that it should be introduced into the archæology of England." The term had already been used in 1848 in the "Guide to Northern Archæology,"[‡] edited by the Earl of Ellesmere, and has now, like celt, become adopted into the English language.

I have not been able to refer to the passage in the Sagas mentioned as above by Mr. Thoms, but whatever may be the original meaning of the word palstave, it is applied by northern antiquaries to all the forms of celts with the exception of those of the socketed type.[§]

Among English antiquaries it has, I think, been used in a more restricted sense. Professor Daniel Wilson[‖] defines palstaves as "wedges, more or less axe-shaped, having a groove on each side terminating in a stop-ridge, and with lateral flanges destined to secure a hold on the handle. The typical example, however, which he engraves has neither groove nor stop-ridge, but is what I should term a winged celt, like Fig. 56.

[*] Vol. vii. p. 74.   [†] London, 1849, p. 25.   [‡] P. 59.
[§] See Nilsson, "Skandinaviska Nordens Ur-Invånare," p. 92.
[‖] "Preh. Ann.," 2nd ed., vol. i. p. 382.

In the present work I propose confining the term palstave to the two varieties of form already mentioned ; viz. the winged celts which have their wings hammered over so as to form what may be termed external sockets to the blade ; and those with the portion of the blade which lies between the side flanges and above the stop thinner than that which is below.

The first form, however, of which I have to treat is that of the celts provided with a stop-ridge on each face. These are almost always flanged celts.

A fine specimen, with the stop-ridge consisting of a straight narrow raised band across each face, and with a second curved band at some distance below, is shown in Fig. 50. It was found at Wigton, Cumberland,

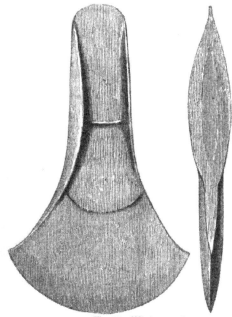

Fig. 50.—Wigton. ½

and is in the collection of Canon Greenwell, F.R.S. The face between the two bands has a grained appearance given it by hammering. The wings or side flanges are also faceted by the same process. In the same collection is another blade (5¾ inches) of this form, with a small stop-ridge, and having the lower part ornamented with vertical punched lines. The sides have three facets, that in the centre ornamented in a similar manner. This celt was found at Rougham, Norfolk. I have a sketch of another (6¼ inches) found near Longtown, Cumberland, in 1860.

I have a nearly similar specimen, but only 4⅞ inches long, from Stanton, Forest of Dean, Gloucestershire. Another (5¾ inches) with only a slight stop-ridge was found at Aynhoe,* Northamptonshire, and is in the collec-

* Baker's "Hist. of North.," p. 558.

tion of Sir Henry Dryden.   Fig. 51 shows a beautifully wrought and
highly decorated flanged celt, provided with a somewhat curved stop-ridge
connecting the two flanges.   The two faces of the celt are ornamented
with an interlaced pattern produced by narrow dents, with a border of
chevrons along each margin punched into the metal.   The flanges are
worked into three facets ornamented with diagonal grooves, and the
lower side of the stop-ridge has a moulding worked on it.   This fine
example of an ornamented celt was found near Chollerford Bridge,
Northumberland, and is in the collection of Canon Greenwell, F.R.S.

A somewhat similar but unornamented variety of instrument, partaking
more of the palstave character, is shown in Fig. 52.   The original was

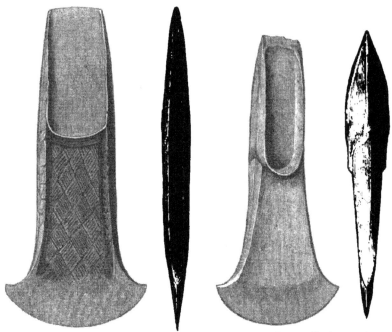

Fig. 51.—Chollerford Bridge.   ½   Fig. 52.—Chatham.   ½

found in excavations at Chatham Dockyard, and is now in the British
Museum.   As will be seen, the recess for the haft ends in a semicircular
stop-ridge.

In Fig. 53 is shown a winged celt without stop-ridge found in Burwell
Fen, Cambridgeshire, and now in my own collection.   The side flanges
or wings have been hammered into three facets, and are well developed.
The form of the blade is otherwise that of a flat celt, except that there is
a slight irregularity in the sweep of the sides, which results from the
hammering of the flanges.   The form occurs occasionally in Ireland, and
one (4¼ inches) is figured by Wilde.*   Winged celts of nearly the same
form, but provided with a stop-ridge, are occasionally found.   One of
these in the British Museum, found at Bucknell, Herefordshire, is shown
in Fig. 54.   The blade below the stop-ridge is $\frac{2}{8}$ inch thick; above it

* "Catal. Mus. R. I. A.," p. 373, fig. 258.

only ⅜ inch. A celt of much the same character (7¼ inches), found at Wolvey, Warwickshire, is in the collection of Mr. M. H. Bloxam, F.S.A.

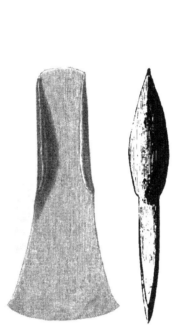

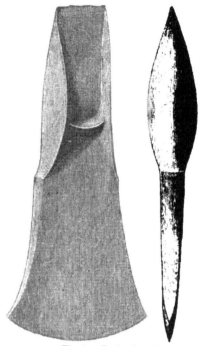

Fig. 53.—Burwell Fen. ½   Fig. 54.—Bucknell. ½

The double curvature of the sides may be noticed in the narrow chisel-like celt shown in Fig. 55. The blade in this instance tapers both ways from a line just below the wings, but without there being any actual stop-ridge; a third slope is produced by the lower part of the blade having been drawn down by hammering to form the edge. The original was found at Culham, near Abingdon, Oxfordshire, and is in my own collection.

I have another specimen, 4¼ inches long, and half as wide again as the Culham chisel, which was found near Dorchester, Oxon. The blade at the lower end of the wings is an inch wide, but in the straight part between that point and the edge only a little more than ¾ inch wide.

Although these instruments are so narrow that they may be regarded as chisels rather than axes, yet from their general character so closely resembling that of Fig. 53, I have thought it best to insert them here.

A Scotch example will be subsequently cited.

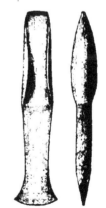

Fig. 55.—Culham. ½

Another form of winged celt without stop-ridge is shown in Fig. 56. In this the blade is flat, and the wings, which form triangular projections,

stand at right angles to it.   Had they been hammered over to form
semicircular receptacles on each side of the blade the instrument would
have been more properly described as a palstave.   It was found with
others near Reeth, in the North Riding of Yorkshire, and is in the collection of Canon Greenwell, F.R.S., where are also other specimens of this
type from Linden, Northumberland (5¼ inches); Brompton, N.R., Yorkshire (5¼ inches); and Wolsingham, Durham (5⅜ inches).

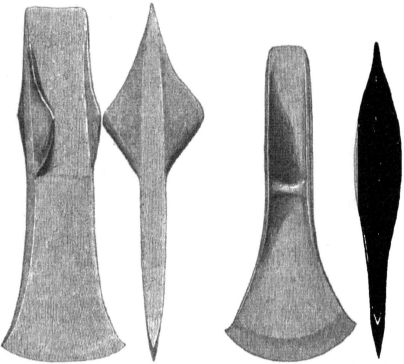

Fig. 56.—Reeth.   ½   Fig. 57.—Dorchester.   ½

Fig. 57 shows a winged celt with a broad low stop-ridge.   The part of
the blade above this is about ½ inch thinner than the part below, so that
though transitional in character it belongs to one of the classes to which
I would wish to restrict the term palstave.   This specimen was found
near Dorchester, Oxfordshire, and is in my own collection.

I have a nearly similar palstave (6 inches long) found in Wicken Fen,
Cambridgeshire.   In this the blade below the stop-ridge is ½ inch thick,
and above it ₁⁴₆ inch.   In this as well as in that from Dorchester the stop-
ridge is well below the level of the side flanges.   In one found on
Hollingbury Hill,* near Brighton, and now in the British Museum, the
stop-ridge is nearly on the same level as the side flanges.   It was found
in the year 1825, together with four looped armillæ, a torque, and three
spiral rings, which are said to have been arranged in a symmetrical
manner in a depression dug in the chalk.   Both the torque and the

* *Arch. Journ.*, vol. v. p. 324.

palstave were broken; and it is thought that this was done intentionally, at the time of the interment.

A similar discovery is recorded as having been made in 1794 on the Quantock Hills, when two large torques were found, within each of which was placed a palstave. In this case, however, these instruments were of the looped kind.

Winged celts of the type of Fig. 57 are of not unfrequent occurrence in Ireland, though the stop-ridge is usually less fully developed.

They also occur in France. One from Jonquières* (Oise) has been figured. I have a good specimen (6¼ inches) from the Seine at Paris. The wings are rather wider and the stop-ridge better defined than in the figure. One from Gasny is in the Museum at Evreux.

There are several in the Göttingen Museum, from a hoard found in that neighbourhood.

Usually the stop-ridge is nearly on the same level as the part of the side flanges on which it abuts, as will be seen in Fig. 58. This specimen was found in the gravel of the Trent at Colwick, near Nottingham, and is in my own collection. The blade immediately below the stop is fluted, and the bottom of this fluting tapers somewhat in the contrary direction to the tapering of the blade. The junction of the fluting and the face produces an elliptic ridge of elegant outline. The blade is ⅝ inch thick at this ridge, but above the stop-ridge barely ⅜ inch. It is rather thinner near the stop-ridge than somewhat higher up, so that the blade would be as it were dovetailed into the handle, if tightly tied to it. I have specimens of much the same type from Attleborough, Nor-

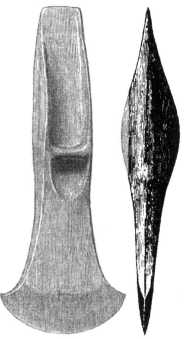

Fig. 58.—Colwick. ½

folk (6⅞ inches), Newbury, Berks (6¼ inches), and Hay, Brecknockshire (7⅛ inches). A curious variety of this type found at Monach-ty-gwyn,† near Aberdovey, has on the bottom of one of the recesses for the handle a number of sunk diagonal lines crossing each other so as to form a kind of lattice pattern. It seems to me that though this cross-hatching occurs on only one face of the palstave, it was intended rather as a means of giving it a grip on the handle than as an ornament, for when hafted this part of the instrument must have been concealed by the wood. Mr. Barnwell, however, regards it in the light of an ornament.

Plain palstaves of this character are of not unfrequent occurrence in the North of France. I have one from a hoard found at Bernay, near Abbeville. With it were palstaves of different varieties, but none of them provided with loops. The form also occurs occasionally in Holland.

---

* *Dict. Arch. de la Gaule.*   † *Arch. Camb.*, 4th S., vol. ii. p. 21.

In the palstave engraved as Fig. 59, the half-oval ornament below the stop-ridge is preserved, but there is a raised bead round it. There is also a slight median ridge running down the blade. The joint of the two moulds in which it was cast can be traced upon the sides of the instrument, and it appears as if one of the moulds had been somewhat deeper than the other. The original was found at Barrington, near Cambridge, and is in my own collection. I have other specimens of the same type, and of nearly the same size, from Swaffham Fen, Cambridge; and from Dorchester, Oxfordshire. The semi-elliptical ridge on the latter is larger and flatter than in that figured. The same is the case in a large specimen (6¼ inches long) from Weston, near Ross, also in my own collection.

I have seen others from the Fens, near Ely (6¾ inches), and from Mildenhall (6¼ inches), in the collections of Mr. Marshall Fisher, of Ely, and the Rev. S. Banks, of Cottenham, near Cambridge. Another (5½ inches) from the Carlton Rode find is in the Museum at Norwich.

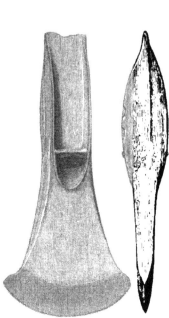

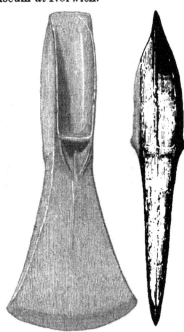

Fig. 59.—Barrington.   ⅟   Fig. 60.—Harston.   ⅟

One from North Wales * (7¼ inches), in an unfinished state, is in the British Museum. Another (6¾ inches) from Llanfyllin,† Montgomeryshire, is also of nearly this type. One from North Tyne (6¼ inches), in the Newcastle Museum, has two of the looped ridges one below the other on each face. In this type and in that subsequently described the ridge at the sides of the semi-elliptical ornament sometimes dies into the upper part of the blade. The variety like Fig. 59 is also abundant in the North of France. There were two or three in the hoard from Bernay, near Abbeville, and I have one from the neighbourhood of Lille.

In Fig. 60 the same general type is preserved, but there is a vertical

* "Horæ Ferales," pl. iv. 25.   † *Arch. Camb.*, 4th S., vol. viii. p. 209.

rib running down the middle of the semi-elliptical ornament below the stop; and the median ridge along the upper part of the blade is more fully developed. In this specimen, which is in my own collection, and was found at Harston, near Cambridge, there is an attempt at ornamentation along the sides, the angles of the blade having been hammered in such a manner as to produce a series of small pointed oval facets along them.

I have other specimens of the same type, but without the ornamentation on the sides, from Burwell, Quy, and Reach Fens, near Cambridge, 6 inches, 5⅞ inches, and 6¾ inches long respectively. In that from Burwell there is no median ridge below the ornament. Canon Greenwell has one which was found with three others, one of them with a loop, near Wantage, Berks.

A rather peculiar variety of this type (6¾ inches), found in Anglesea,[*] has been figured, as well as another from Pendinas Hill,[†] near Aberystwith.

In palstaves of this class there is often a slight projection on each of the sides a little below the level of the stop-ridge. Below this projection the sides are usually more carefully hammered and planished than above it.

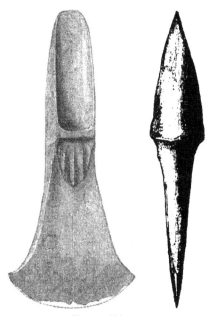

Fig. 61.—Shippey.

In a narrow palstave of this class, found at Freeland, near Witney, Oxfordshire, there are three short ridges at the bottom of each of the recesses for the handle, like those in a palstave from Newbury, subsequently described. These were probably designed to assist in steadying the handle.

A palstave (7¼ inches) from Cynwyd,[‡] Merionethshire, appears to be of this type.

An instrument of this type from Les Andelys§ (Eure) has been figured. Another, with the vertical rib in the shield, from a hoard found in Normandy, has been engraved by the Abbé Cochet.|| Some from the Bernay hoard have a similar ornament.

On some palstaves of this class there is a series of vertical ribs within the semi-elliptical loop, as will be seen in Fig. 61. This is taken from a specimen found at Shippey, near Ely, which is in the collection of Mr. Marshall Fisher of Ely, who has kindly allowed me to engrave it. I have one from Bottisham, near Cambridge (6¾ inches), on which there is a smaller vertical ridge, on each side of the central ridge, within the ornament. One from Snettisham, Norfolk (6¼ inches), like that from Shippey,

* *Arch. Camb.*, 4th S., vol. v. p. 13.
† Meyrick's "Cardigansh." and "Ancient Arm.," by Skelton, pl. xlvii. 1.
‡ *Arch. Assoc. Journ.*, vol. xxxiii. p. 118.   § *Dict. Arch. de la Gaule.*
|| "La Seine Inf.," p. 272.

is in the Norwich Museum.   Another from Lakenheath, Suffolk (5¾ inches), is in the collection of Mr. James Carter of Cambridge.

A palstave with this ornament is in the Museum at Soissons.

The type is also found in Northern Germany.[*]

In some cases these vertical lines below the stop-ridge are not enclosed in any loop. In Fig. 62 is shown an example of the kind from a specimen in my own collection found in the Severn, near Wainlodes Hill, Gloucester. It has a slight rib down the middle of the blade. One of the same class (6¼ inches), with four vertical stripes, found on Clayton Hill, Sussex, is in the collection of Mrs. Dickinson of Hurstpierpoint;

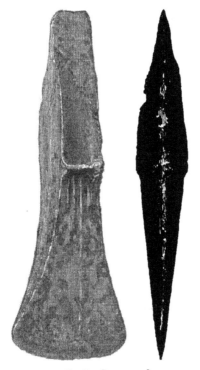 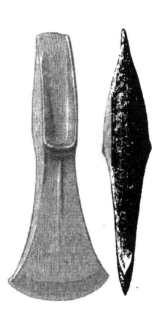

Fig. 62.—Severn.   ⅓   Fig. 63.—Sunningwell.   ⅓

four others (about 6¼ inches long), with five short vertical ridges, were found with two of the type of Fig. 63 in making the railway near Bognor, and are now in the Blackmore Museum at Salisbury.

Another, apparently of the same type, found near Brighton, is engraved in the *Sussex Archæological Collections*.[†]

Another variety, having nearly the same general form, but no elliptical ridge below the stop, is shown in Fig. 63, engraved from a specimen in my own collection, found at Sunningwell, near Abingdon. The end of the recess for the handle is somewhat rounded, and there is a well-marked central rib running down the blade. At the upper part, near the stop

* Lindenschmit, "Alt. uns. heidn. Vorz.," vol. i. Heft. i. Taf. iv. 43.
† Vol. ii. p. 268, No. 11.

ridge, there are also slight side flanges. The metal in the recess for the handle is thinnest near the stop, so as to be somewhat dovetailing.

This is markedly the case in a fine example of the same type (6¼ inches) with the *provenance* of which I am unacquainted. In another, also in my own collection, found at Newbury, Berks, the side flanges of the blade are continued almost down to the edge, and the bottom as well as the end of the recess for the handle is rounded. Near the end of the recess are some slight longitudinal ribs, one on one face and two on the other, perhaps designed to assist in steadying the handle. The mouldings along the sides of the blade are often much more fully developed, like those on Fig. 77.

Palstaves of this type have been obtained from the following localities: from South Cerney,* near Cirencester; from the mouth of the River Wandle,† in Surrey, now preserved in the British Museum; from Bucks‡ (6 inches long), also in the British Museum; from Chichester; § Astley,‖ Worcestershire; Llangwyllog, ¶ Anglesea (6¼ inches); from near Bognor,** Billingshurst,†† and Iford,‡‡ Sussex; and Lovehayne,§§ near Broad Down, Devon (5½ inches); where several appear to have been found in the rough state in which they came from the mould. I have an example from the neighbourhood of Penzance.

One (6¾ inches) found near Ashford, Kent, is in the Mayer Collection at Liverpool. One of the same kind was found with a hammer, a tanged chisel, broken spear-heads, and rough metal, in Burgesses' Meadow, Oxford. The hoard is now in the Ashmolean Museum. In three palstaves of this kind found in the parishes of Llandrinio,‖‖ and Caersws, Montgomeryshire, and St. Harmon, Radnorshire, there is a hole in the metal between the two recesses for the handle just above the stop-ridge. It has been thought by Professor Westwood that these holes were connected with the manner of fastening the instrument to its haft, but it appears to me much more likely that they arise from accidental defects in casting. This is certainly the case with two specimens of my own, which also have holes through the same part of the instrument, where the metal is thin.

One (5 inches), rather narrower in the blade than the figure, found near Longford, Ireland, is in the Blackmore Museum at Salisbury.

Palstaves with a central and two lateral ribs on the blade are of not unfrequent occurrence on the Continent, especially in the North of France. I have examples much like the figure found in the hoard at Bernay, near Abbeville. Others, much narrower in the blade, have been discovered in large numbers in the North-west of France.

German examples have been figured by Lindenschmit.¶¶

In another variety the blade is nearly flat, having only a broad protuberant ridge extending along the upper part to the stop. A palstave of this kind, found near Winfrith, Weymouth, Dorset, is shown in Fig. 64. In this, the metal between the side flanges tapers towards the top of the

* *Arch.*, vol. x. pl. x. 2, p. 132.
† *Arch. Journ.*, vol. ix. p. 8.
‡ "Horæ Ferales," pl. iv. 26.
§ *Proc. Soc. Ant.*, 2nd S., vol. v. p. 38.
‖ Allies, "Worc.," p. 112, pl. iv. 4.
¶ *Arch. Journ.*, vol. xxvii. pl. x. No. 3, p. 163.
** *Suss. Arch. Coll.*, vol. xvii. p. 255.
†† *Suss. Arch. Coll.*, vol. xxvii. p. 183.
‡‡ *S. A. C.*, vol. xxix. p. 134.
§§ *Trans. Dev. Assoc.*, vol. ii. p. 647.
‖‖ "Montgom. Collections," vol. iii. p. 435.
¶¶ "Alt. u. h. Vorz.," vol. i. Heft i. Taf. iv.

instrument, instead of being of nearly even thickness, as is often the case, or thinnest near the stop-ridge, as it is sometimes. Close to the stop the metal is ⅓ inch thick, while at the top of the recess it comes to a nearly sharp edge. A palstave of this character was found on Kingston Hill,* Surrey, near Cæsar's Camp.

In a specimen found at Winwick,† Lancashire, the blade below the stop-ridge appears to be nearly flat. A broad flat ring of bronze, 1¾ inch in diameter (Fig. 188), was found at the same time. It has been thought that this was attached to the shaft to prevent its splitting. A palstave much like that from Winwick was found at Chagford, Devon, and is in

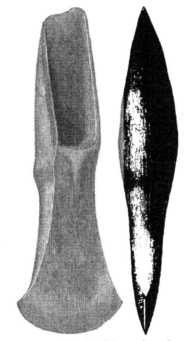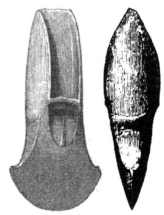

Fig. 64.—Weymouth.   ½   Fig. 65.—Burwell Fen.   ½

the possession of Mr. G. W. Ormerod, F.G.S. Another (6½ inches), from Ashford, Kent, is in the Mayer Collection at Liverpool. Another of these plain palstaves, found near Llanidan,‡ Anglesea, with one of the looped kind somewhat like Fig. 76, is engraved in the *Archæologia Cambrensis*.

I have a palstave of nearly the same form, but with a more clearly defined semi-conical bracket below the stop, which was found at Masseyck, on the frontiers of Belgium and Holland.

A short and thick form of palstave is shown in Fig. 65, engraved from a specimen found in Burwell Fen, Cambridge. On one of its faces

* *Proc. Soc. Ant.*, 2nd S., vol. i. p. 82.
† *Arch. Assoc. Journ.*, vol. xv. pl. xxv. p. 236; vol. xiv. p. 269.
‡ 3rd Series, vol. xiii. p. 283.

it has the semi-elliptical ornament, with one vertical rib in it, below the stop-ridge. On the other there are five ribs instead of one within the ornament.

I have another from Bottisham Fen (4⅜ inches), not quite so heavy in its make, and perfectly flat below the stop-ridge. The ends of the recess for the handle are somewhat undercut, so as to keep the wood close to the blade when a blow was struck.

The shortened proportions of these instruments are probably due to wear. In this instance it is not improbable that the cutting end of the original palstave has been broken off, and the blunt end that was left has been again drawn to an edge by hammering.

A form of palstave without any ornament below the stop-ridge is shown in Fig. 66. This specimen was found in 1846 at East Harnham, near

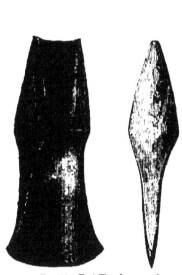
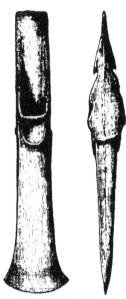

Fig. 66.—East Harnham. ⅓   Fig. 67.—Burwell Fen. ⅓

Salisbury, and is now in my own collection. The thickness of the blade below the stop is nearly ½ inch, above it but little more than ⅛ inch. The sides are remarkably flat.

One, only 2½ inches long, merely recessed for the handle, found at Chatham Hill, Kent, is in the Mayer Collection at Liverpool.

This plain form with a square stop-ridge is found in France and in Western Germany.

A long chisel-like form of palstave is shown in Fig. 67, engraved from a specimen in my own collection found in Burwell Fen, Cambridge. It is ornamented with a semi-elliptical projecting ridge below the stop. The flanges at the sides of the recess have some notches running diagonally into them, so as to form a kind of barb, such as would prevent the blade from being drawn away from the handle when bound to it by a cord.

I have another nearly similar tool, also from the Cambridge Fens, but without any barbs. In a third, from the neighbourhood of Dorchester,

Oxon, there are neither barbs at the sides nor any ornament below the

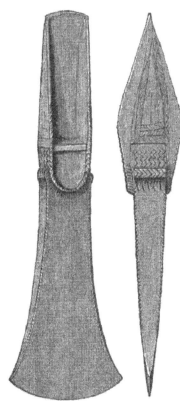

Fig. 68.—Thames.   ½

stop-ridge. I have seen another of the same character (4½ inches) which was found at Wolsonbury, Sussex, and is in the collection of Mrs. Dickinson. Another (4¾ inches), found in the Thames at Kingston, Surrey, is in the Museum of the Society of Antiquaries. I have seen another (6⅝ inches), found at Sutton, near Woodbridge, Suffolk, in which there was a tongue-shaped groove below the stop-ridge, like that on the socketed celt, Fig. 148, but single instead of double.

The Rev. James Beck, F.S.A.,[*] has a palstave of this kind 6 inches long and 1¼ inch wide at the edge, with a projecting rib below the stop-ridge and also in the recess above. It was found at Westburton Hill, near Bignor, Sussex. There are depressions on each side of the rib below the stop, forming an ornament like that on Fig. 81.

A narrow palstave, apparently of the same character, found at Windsor,[†] is engraved by Stukeley.

A very beautiful narrow palstave, found in the Thames, and now in the collection of General A. Pitt Rivers, F.R.S., is shown in Fig. 68. As will be seen, the angles are ornamented with a kind of milling, and the sides are also decorated with zigzag and chevron patterns.

In Fig. 69 is shown an unfinished casting for a palstave of unusually small size, which formed part of the great hoard found at Stibbard,[‡] Norfolk. About seventy such castings were found, and about ten castings for spear-heads (see Fig. 407).

The form of palstave with the side wings or flanges hammered over so as to form a kind of semi-circular socket on either side of the blade, is of rare occurrence in Britain, and is usually provided with a loop. In Canon Greenwell's collection is one (7 inches) without any ornament below the square stop-ridge, with the side wings slightly hammered over. It was found with others (with and without loops), together with a mould for palstaves (Fig. 527), at Hotham Carr, Yorkshire, E. R.

Fig. 69.—Stibbard.   ½

* *Proc. Soc. Ant.*, N.S., vol. iv. p. 442.   † "Itin. Cur." Cent., ii. pl. xcvi.
‡ *Arch. Inst.*, Norwich vol. p. xxvi.

In a hoard of about sixty bronze objects found at Westow,* about
twelve miles from York on the Scarborough Road, was one palstave of
this kind, like Fig. 85, but without a loop, and about thirty socketed celts,
six gouges, a socketed chisel, two tanged chisels, and
numerous fragments of metal, including some jets or
runners broken off castings.

The type is of common occurrence in Austria, South Germany, and the South of France.

Palstaves of the adze form, or having the blade at right
angles to the septum between the flanges, are but very
seldom found in Britain. A small specimen from the
collection of Canon Greenwell, F.R.S., is shown in Fig. 70.
It was found at Irthington, Cumberland.

Another, from North Owersby, Lincolnshire, in the same
collection, is shown in Fig. 71. It has a remarkably narrow
chisel-like blade.

Irish examples will be subsequently cited.

I have, in Fig. 72, engraved for comparison a larger
specimen in my own collection, which came from the Valley
of the Rhine, near Bonn. One from Baden† is figured by Lindenschmit.

Others have been found near Landshut,‡ Bavaria, and in the Rhine
district. § One with a loop, from Hesse,|| is engraved by Lindenschmit.

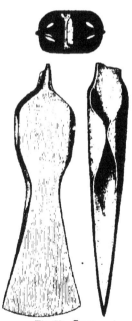

Fig. 70.
Irthington. ½

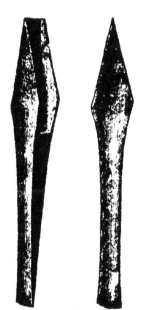

Fig. 71.—North Owersby. ½   Fig. 72.—Bonn. ½

* Arch. Assoc. Journ., vol. iii. p. 58 ; Arch. Journ., vol. vi. p. 381.
† "Alt. u. h. Vorz.," vol. i. Heft i. Taf. iv. 48.
‡ Von Braunmühl, "Alt. Deutschen Grabmäler" (1826), pl. i. 3 ; Schreiber, "Die
ehern. Streitkeile," Taf. i. 13, Taf. ii. 14.   § Dict. Arch. de la Gaule.
|| "Alt. u. h. Vorz.," vol. i. Heft i. Taf. iv. 49.

A long and narrow example of this type * was found at Villeder, near
Ploërmel, Morbihan, and has been figured by Simonin. There are specimens in the museums at Rouen and Tours. Some have a loop on one
face. A specimen from Escoville is in the museum at Caen. Several with
and without loops have been found in the Swiss lake-dwellings,† the
type being termed the Hache Troyon by Desor.‡

A beautiful palstave of the same character is preserved in the Antiken
Cabinet at Vienna. Its sides are ornamented with four small sets of concentric circles and a pattern of dotted lines, punched in after the instrument was fashioned. The form has also been found in Italy.§

Palstaves without loops, but of which no detailed description is given,
are recorded to have been found at the following places:—The Thames,‖
near Kingston; Drewsteignton,¶ Devonshire; Cundall Manor,** North
Riding, Yorkshire; Aspatria,†† Cumberland; Ackers Common,‡‡ near
Warrington, Lancashire; Bushbury, §§ Brewood, Handsworth, and a
barrow on Morridge, Staffordshire; near Llanvair Station, ‖‖ Rhos-y-gad,
Anglesea.

Palstaves of which it is not specified whether they were provided with
a loop or no, have been found in the Thames,¶¶ near London; the old
River, Sleaford,*** Lincolnshire; Canada Wharf,††† Rotherhithe; Wolvey,‡‡‡ Warwickshire; and near Corbridge, §§§ Glamorganshire (?)

Plain palstaves without loops have frequently occurred with other forms
of instruments in hoards of bronze objects. The following instances may
be cited. Several were found with unfinished socketed celts, fragments of
swords and spears, a socketed chisel, and lumps of metal, at Romford,‖‖‖
Essex. At Nettleham,¶¶¶ near Lincoln, one was found with looped palstaves, socketed celts, spear-heads, and a tube, most of which will be mentioned in subsequent pages. In the hoard at Battlefield,**** near Shrewsbury, a palstave without loop, a flat wedge-shaped celt, and three curious
curved objects were found together. Other instances are given in
Chapter XXII.

The palstaves which are provided with a loop on one side
present as many varieties as those without the loop. The same
character of ornamentation occurs on the instruments of both
classes. Indeed, for some length of time both forms appear to
have been contemporaneous and in use together.

Some of them are, however, entirely devoid of ornament, as will be
seen from Fig. 73. This represents a palstave in my own collection
found near Dorchester, Oxfordshire. The loop has unfortunately been
broken off. At the stop the metal is 1¼ inch thick, but the diaphragm

* "La Vie Souterraine," "Matériaux," vol. iii. p. 100.
† Keller, 6ter Bericht, Taf. vii. 30; 7ter Ber., Taf. ix. 30.
‡ "Les Palafittes," fig. 40.
§ *Bull. di Palet. Ital.*, vol. i. p. 10, Tav. I. 9.
‖ *Arch. Journ.*, vol. v. p. 327.   ¶ *Arch. Journ.*, vol. xxix. p. 96.
** *Arch. Assoc. Journ.*, vol. xiv. p. 346.   †† *Arch. Journ.*, vol. xvii. p. 164.
‡‡ *Arch. Journ.*, vol. xviii. p. 158.   §§ Plot's " Nat. Hist. of Staffordsh.," p. 403.
‖‖ *Arch. Journ.*, vol. xiii. p. 85.   ¶¶ *Arch. Journ.*, vol. x. p. 63.
*** *Arch. Journ.*, vol. x. p. 73.   ††† *Proc. Soc. Ant.*, 2nd S., vol. ii. p. 412.
‡‡‡ *Proc. Soc. Ant.*, 2nd S., vol. iii. p. 129.
§§§ *Arch. Journ.*, vol. x. p. 248.   ‖‖‖ *Arch. Journ.*, vol. ix. p. 302.
¶¶¶ *Arch. Journ.*, vol. xviii. p. 159.   **** *Proc. Soc. Ant.*, 2nd S., vol. ii. p. 251.

between the two recesses for the haft is only ⅜ inch thick. This specimen is shorter than usual in the blade, which not improbably has been considerably worn away by use.

A somewhat larger instrument, but of precisely the same type, found at Ramsbury,[*] Wilts, is engraved in the Salisbury volume of the Archæological Institute. The Rev. James Beck, F.S.A., has one (6¼ inches) of narrower proportions, found at Pulborough,[†] Sussex. I have seen another from near Wallingford, Berks. Stukeley has engraved a somewhat similar palstave found near Windsor.[‡]

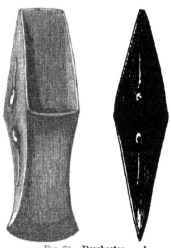

Fig. 73.—Dorchester. ⅓

In some the bottom of the recesses, instead of being square, is rounded more or less like Fig. 52, and there is a projecting bead round its margin. I have a narrow specimen of this kind 5⅜ inches long and 1⅛ inch broad at the edge, found in the neighbourhood of Dorchester, Oxon.

A number of palstaves of this kind were discovered in 1861 at Wilmington,[§] Sussex, in company with socketed celts, fragments of two daggers, and a mould for socketed celts. The whole of these are now in the Lewes Museum.

In the hoard found near Guilsfield,[‖] Montgomeryshire, were some instruments of this kind, associated with socketed celts, gouges, swords, scabbards, spear-heads, &c. Others from Stretton,[¶] Staffordshire (5¼ inches), and Lancashire [**] (5¼ inches) are engraved, though badly, in the *Archæologia*. Two others of this character (5 inches) were found on Hangleton Down,[††] near Brighton, and another at Glangwnny,[‡‡] near Caernarvon.

I have seen others found at Sutton, near Woodbridge, Suffolk.

A larger example of the same type, found near Wallingford, and communicated to me by Mr. H. A. Davy, is shown in Fig. 74. In this the blade is flat and without ornament. The short specimen shown in Fig. 73 may originally have resembled this; as such instruments must have been liable to break, and would then have been drawn out and sharpened in a curtailed condition; or if not broken would become eventually "stumped up" by wear. In the British Museum and elsewhere are many palstaves and celts which have been worn almost to the stump by re-sharpening.

Nearly thirty palstaves, mostly, I believe, of this type, were found with about twelve socketed celts, like Fig. 116, and lumps of rough metal, near Worthing, in 1877. The whole had been packed in an urn, of coarse earthenware.

[*] P. 112, fig. 37.   [†] *Proc. Soc. Ant.*, N.S., vol. iv. p. 442.
[‡] "It. Cur." Cent., ii. pl. xcvi.
[§] *Suss. Arch. Coll.*, vol. xiv. p. 171; *Arch. Journ.*, vol. xx. p. 192.
[‖] *Proc. Soc. Ant.*, 2nd S., vol. ii. p. 251; *Arch. Camb.*, 3rd S., vol. x. p. 214; "Montgom. Coll.," vol. iii. p. 437.
[¶] Vol. v. p. 113.   [**] Ibid.
[††] *Suss. Arch. Coll.*, vol. viii. p. 268. [‡‡] *Arch.*, vol. vii. p. 417.

Looped palstaves of the type of Fig. 74 are occasionally found in Ireland. One with a small bead running down the centre of the blade found in West Meath is engraved in the *Archæologia.**

One from Grenoble,† Isère, is engraved by Chantre.

Some palstaves of much the same general character have a median ridge, occasionally almost amounting to a rib, running down the blade below the stop. One of this kind from Stanton Harcourt, Oxfordshire, is shown in Fig. 75. On the face of the recess there are some slightly raised ribs running down to the stop, which are not shown in the cut.

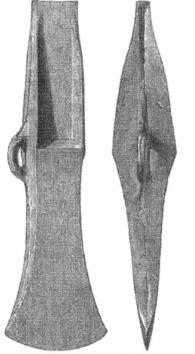
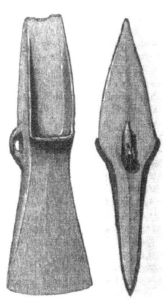

Fig. 74.—Wallingford.   ½   Fig. 75.—Stanton Harcourt.   ½

Two (6¾ inches) were found near Bolton Percy, Yorkshire, one of which is in Canon Greenwell's collection, and the other in the British Museum.

Mr. John Brent, F.S.A., has an example of nearly the same type from Blean, near Canterbury. Another from Buckland, near Dover (6¼ inches), is in the Mayer Collection at Liverpool. One from Ombersley,‡ Worcestershire, appears to be of the same kind. I have also a large specimen (6⅞ inches) from Bottisham, Cambridge.

In the palstave engraved as Fig. 76, the central rib down the blade is much more fully developed. It was found at Brassington, near Wirksworth, Derbyshire, and is in my own collection. It is considerably undercut at the stop, so as to keep the handle pressed against the central diaphragm of metal.

* Vol. ix. p. 84, pl. iii. 1.   † "Album," pl. ix. 4.   ‡ Allies, p. 108, pl. iv. 3.

A palstave of the same character from Llanidan,* Anglesea, has been figured. It is said to have been found with another without a loop. Another from Boston,†* Lincolnshire, is engraved in the *Archæologia.* Others with the ribs very distinct were found in a hoard at Wallington, Northumberland, and are in the possession of Sir Charles Trevelyan.

I have seen others of the same general character which were found at Downton, near Salisbury (5¾ inches), and at Aston le Walls, Northamptonshire.

One with a narrower and more distinct midrib, found at Nymegen, Guelderland, Holland, is in the museum at Leyden.

In Fig. 77 is shown another variety which has two beads running down the sides of the blade, in addition to the central rib. I bought this specimen

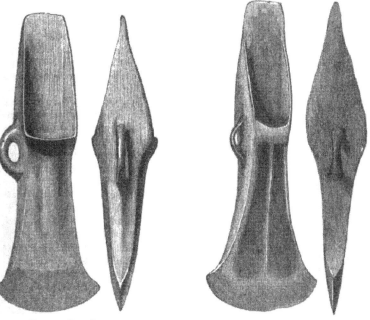

Fig. 76.—Brassington. ¼   Fig. 77.—Bath. ¼

at Bath, but I do not know where it was discovered. It is much like one which was found on the Quantock Hills,‡ in Somersetshire, and is engraved in the *Archæologia.* The side flanges are, however, in that case more lozenge shaped, and project to obtuse points about half an inch above the stop. Two palstaves and two torques were on that occasion found buried together, as has already been mentioned. One of the same type (5¾ inches) from Elsham, Lincolnshire, is in the British Museum.

One of narrower form (6½ inches) but of the same character, found with socketed celts (some of them octagonal at the neck) at Haxey, Lincolnshire, is in the collection of Canon Greenwell, F.R.S.

* *Arch. Camb.*, 3rd S., vol. xiii. p. 283.   † Vol. xix. pl. viii. p. 102.
‡ *Arch.*, vol. xiv. p. 94.

I have another of the same type, but imperfect, which was found with a plain bronze bracelet, and what from the description must have been a small ribbon-like gold torque, at Winterhay Green, near Ilminster. I have a smaller specimen (5 inches) from the Cambridge Fens.

The unfinished casting for a palstave of the type Fig. 77 (5¼ inches) was found with four looped palstaves, and one without a loop, and a spear-head like Fig. 409 at Sherford,* near Taunton, in 1879. Some of the palstaves have a raised inverted chevron below the stop-ridge by way of ornament.

Palstaves of the same character, but without the loop, have already been described under Fig. 63. The looped type, like Fig. 77, occurs also in Ireland.†

In the Museum of the Society of Antiquaries of London is a heavy narrow looped palstave (8 inches by 2 inches) with this ornamentation, found in Spain.

The central rib running down the blade is in many cases connected with some ornament below the stop-ridge. The ornament consists usually of raised ribs, either straight and converging, as on Fig. 78, or curved so as to form a semi-elliptical or shield-shaped loop, as on Fig. 79.

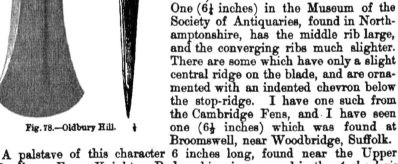

Fig. 78.—Oldbury Hill.   ½

The original of Fig. 78 was found on Oldbury Hill, Much Marcle, Herefordshire, and is in my own collection. I have a smaller example of the same type (5¾ inches) found at Hammerton, Huntingdonshire, as well as one from the Cambridge Fens (6 inches).

One (6¾ inches) found at Danesfield,‡ near Bangor, has been figured. I have seen one found near Chelmsford (6¾ inches) with much the same ornament. One (6¼ inches) in the Museum of the Society of Antiquaries, found in Northamptonshire, has the middle rib large, and the converging ribs much slighter. There are some which have only a slight central ridge on the blade, and are ornamented with an indented chevron below the stop-ridge. I have one such from the Cambridge Fens, and I have seen one (6½ inches) which was found at Broomswell, near Woodbridge, Suffolk.

A palstave of this character 6 inches long, found near the Upper Woodhouse Farm, Knighton, Radnorshire, is engraved in the *Archæologia Cambrensis*.§ The loop, owing to a defect in casting, is filled with metal. Six others (6 inches long), apparently of the same character, were found with some rough castings of flanged celts at Rhosnesney,‖ near Wrexham.

Two others (6 inches) were found with a chisel and a spear-head, like

---

* Pring, "The Brit. and Rom. on the site of Taunton," p. 76, pl. iii.
† Wilde, "Catal. Mus. R. I. A.," p. 381, fig. 273.
‡ *Arch. Camb.*, 3rd S., vol. ii. p. 130.   § 4th Ser., vol. vi. p. 20.   ‖ Ibid., p. 71.

Fig. 407, at Broxton, Cheshire, and are in the collection of Sir P. de M. Grey Egerton, Bart.

The type is found upon the continent. One from Normandy* has been engraved by the Abbé Cochet. I have an example from the neighbourhood of Abbeville.

One from near Giessen, in the museum at Darmstadt, is figured by Lindenschmit.†

That with the shield-shaped ornament below the stop-ridge, shown in Fig. 79, is in my own collection, and was found near Ross. The central rib runs only part of the way up the shield. In a specimen from the

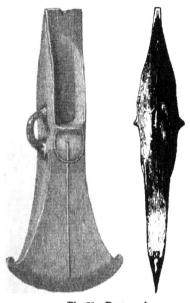
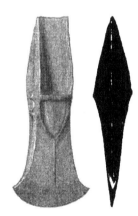

Fig. 79.—Ross. ¼   Fig. 80.—Honington. ¼

Cambridge Fens (5¾ inches) it stops short on joining the ridge forming the shield.

In others it forms a heraldic pale running through the shield, as in five found at Waldron,‡ Sussex.

A smaller variety, in which the vertical rib does not extend into the shield, is shown in Fig. 80. This specimen was found at Honington, Suffolk.

In some the shield-shaped ornament consists of merely two triangular depressions. A palstave of this class, rather narrow at the stop-ridge, and with almost triangular blade, is shown in Fig. 81. The original, which is of more yellow metal than ordinary, was found in the neighbourhood of Ely, and is in the collection of Mr. Marshall Fisher, who has kindly allowed me to figure it. In one such from Downton, near Salisbury, in the Blackmore Museum, the faces of the diaphragm between the recesses for the handle have raised ridges or ribs running along nearly the whole

* "La Seine Inf.," p. 14.   † "A. u. h. V.," vol. i. Heft i. Taf. iv. 44.
‡ *Suss. Arch. Coll.*, vol. ix. p. 366.

length, five on one face and six on the other. These are longer than in the Nottingham specimen shortly to be mentioned.

In one found at Hotham Carr (5¾ inches), Yorkshire, and now in Canon Greenwell's collection, there is a bead running down the blade between the two depressions.

This shield-shaped ornament below the stop-ridge is well shown in a palstave from Bottisham Lode, Cambridge, engraved as Fig. 82. What may be called the field of the shield is on one face nearly flat; on the other there are indentations on either side of the central ridge. As will be seen, the extremities of the cutting edge are recurved, both in this and the specimen from Ross shown in Fig. 79. It does not, however, appear that the instruments were originally cast in this form, but the wide segmental

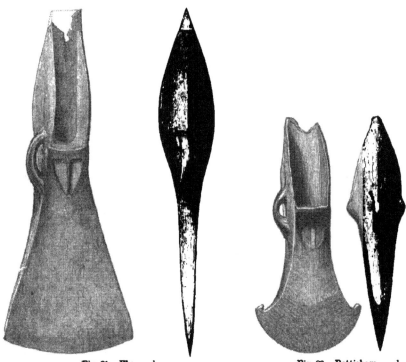

Fig. 81.—Ely.   ⅓   Fig. 82.—Bottisham.   ⅓

edge, together with the recurved ends, seem to be the result of a constant hammering out of the blade, in order to renew or harden the edge. Though the hammer was thus freely used, the whetstone was employed both to polish the sides of the blade and to perfect the cutting edge.

I have a French palstave found near Abbeville, almost identical with this in size and form. The shield ornament is, however, replaced by two triangular depressions with a rib left between them, like that on Fig. 81.

In some specimens the ornamentation consists of a greater or less number of parallel ribs below the stop-ridge, as in that from Nettleham,* Lincolnshire, shown in Fig. 83. With this were found two others and

* *Arch. Journ.*, vol. xviii. p. 160, whence this cut is reproduced.

a fourth without loop, two peculiar socketed celts, two spear-heads, and a ferrule, which will be subsequently mentioned. They are now in the British Museum.

A nearly similar discovery was made in 1860 near Nottingham,* where a palstave was found similarly ornamented, but also having three ribs on the diaphragm above the stop-ridge. It was accompanied by sixteen socketed celts, four spear-heads, a tanged knife, fragments of swords, a ferrule, &c.

In Mr. Brackstone's collection was a palstave of the same type, found near Ulleskelf,† Yorkshire, in 1849, with two socketed celts, one of them of the peculiar type shown in Fig. 158.

I have a palstave found near Dorchester, Oxfordshire, of the same kind as Fig. 83, with three ribs below the stop-ridge. There are also side

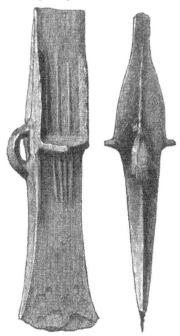

Fig. 83.—Nettleham.   ½   Fig. 84.—Cambridge.   ½

flanges at that part of the blade of the same length and character as the ribs in the middle of the blade, so as virtually to make five ribs.

Canon Greenwell has specimens of this type (6¼ inches) from Llandysilio, Denbighshire, and (6 inches) from Ubbeston, Suffolk. One (6¼ inches) from Keswick, Cumberland, in the same collection has the ribs 1¾ inches long. Another (6⅜ inches) was found at Vronheulog,‡ Merionethshire.

I have a very fine and perfect specimen (6¾ inches) from the Cambridge Fens, on which the three ribs stand out in high relief and converge so as to form a triangle below the stop-ridge something like that on Fig. 78.

* Proc. Soc. Ant., 2nd. S., vol. i. p. 332.
† Arch. Journ., vol. viii. p. 99, and Private Plate.
‡ Arch. Camb., 4th S., vol. viii. p. 209.

A palstave, having a series of ribs upon the diaphragm as well as below the stop-ridge, is shown in Fig. 84. In this instance the upper series of ribs extends nearly to the top of the instrument. It was probably thought that they assisted in making the haft firm to the blade. This specimen, which has been much cleaned, is in the British Museum, and as it formed part of the late Mr. Lichfield's collection it was probably found in the neighbourhood of Cambridge.

The form of palstave, so common in France and Germany, without stop-ridge, and with the side wings hammered over so as to form a kind of semi-cylindrical socket on either side of the blade, is rare in England. A specimen from the great find of Carlton Rode,* Norfolk, is shown in Fig. 85. There is usually at the top of the blade a sort of dovetailed notch, which may possibly have been made of service in hafting the tool. It originates, however, in there having been two runners by which the metal was conducted into the mould, which when broken off left two projections at the top of the blade. These being hammered so as to round the external angles and flatten the ends have come over towards each other, and made what was a notch with parallel sides into one which is dovetailed.

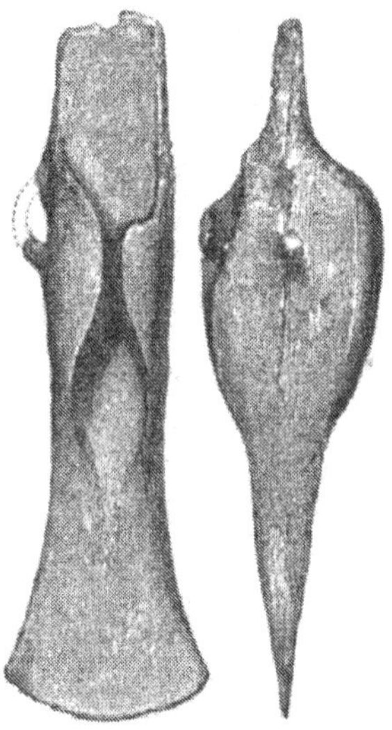

Fig. 85.—Carlton Rode. ½

In this hoard were found numerous socketed celts, gouges, chisels, hammers, pieces of metal, &c. It seems to have been the stock in trade of a bronze-founder. Some other specimens from the same hoard will subsequently be described.

Another palstave of the same character was found, with many socketed celts, fragments of swords and daggers, and rough metal, at Cumberlow,† near Baldock, Herts.

Three others were found in 1806, with two socketed celts, a fragment of a sword, three lumps of raw copper, and four gold armlets, on the beach near Eastbourne,‡ immediately under Beachy Head. They passed with the Payne Knight collection into the British Museum.

That found "in an old wall, in Purbeck," § with the socket "*double or divided by a partition*," as described by Mr. Hutchins in a letter to Bishop Lyttelton in 1768, must probably have been of this kind.

A good specimen of the same character but bent (5⅝ inches), as well

* *Arch.*, vol. xxxi. p. 494; *Arch. Journ.*, vol. ii. p. 80; *Arch. Assoc. Journ.*, vol. i. p. 51; Smith's "Coll. Ant.," vol. i. p. 105; "Catal. Norwich Mus.," No. 9.

† *Journ. Anthrop. Inst.*, vol. vi. p. 195. ‡ *Arch.*, vol. xvi. p. 363, pl. lxviii.

§ *Arch.*, vol. v. p. 117. See Borlase, "Ant. of Cornw.," pl. xx. 6.

as part of another, was found at Wickham Park, Croydon, together with several socketed celts.   They are now in the British Museum.

The upper part of a palstave of this character was found with socketed celts, gouges, &c., in the Hundred of Hoo,* Kent.   It has been thought that this was cast hollow to receive a central prong, but the cavity is probably due to defective casting.   A broken instrument of this kind was found with socketed celts and metal on Kenidjack Cliff,† Cornwall.

Palstaves of this type, both with and without loops, are much more abundant on the Continent than in Britain.   Numerous examples have been found in France, in Rhenish Prussia, and in the Lake habitations of Savoy and Switzerland.

A Danish example is engraved by Worsaae,‡ and several from Germany§ by Lindenschmit.

Iron palstaves with and without loops, some of them closely approximating to the form of Fig. 85, but others more like the ordinary Italian form of palstave, with a broad chisel-like blade, have been found in the cemetery of Hallstatt.∥   In a specimen in my own collection the side flanges are ornamented with transverse ribs, precisely like those on some of the bronze palstaves from the same locality.   In one instance the upper part with the flanges is of bronze, and the lower part of the blade of iron or steel.

This form of instrument, with a section in the form of the letter H above, though easily cast, must have been extremely difficult to forge ; and though we can readily trace its evolution in cast bronze, it so ill accorded with the necessary conditions for the profitable working of malleable iron that it seems soon to have disappeared when iron came into general use.   The fact of the form occurring at all in iron shows that the iron instruments were made in imitation of those in bronze, and not the bronze in imitation of the iron.   The same observation holds good with the iron socketed celts, spear-heads, and swords from the same cemetery.

Looped palstaves, without sufficient details being given of their types, are recorded to have been found in Harewood Square, London,¶ Oxford,** Devonshire,†† and with socketed celts, near Kidwelly,‡‡ Caermarthen.

A looped palstave rather like Fig. 75 is said to have been found in a barrow near St. Austell,§§ Cornwall, in 1791, but no details are given.

Palstaves provided with a loop on either side are of rare occurrence in the British Islands.

A specimen found in 1871 at Penvores,∥∥ near Mawgan-in-Meneage,

* *Arch. Cant.*, vol. xi. p. 123.   † *Journ. Roy. Inst. of Cornw.*, No. 21.
‡ Oldsager, fig. 184.   § " Alt. u. h. V.," vol. i. Heft i. Taf. iv.
∥ Von Sacken, " Das. Grab. v. Hallst.," Taf. vii.
¶ *Arch. Journ.*, vol. vi. p. 188.   ** *Arch. Assoc. Journ.*, vol. ix. p. 186.
†† *Arch. Journ.*, vol. xiii. p. 85.   ‡‡ *Arch. Assoc. Journ.*, vol. xii. p. 96.
§§ Borlase, " Næn. Corn.," p. 188.   ∥∥ *Proc. Soc. Ant.*, 2nd S., vol. v. p. 398.

Cornwall, is engraved as Fig. 86. In character it closely resembles that from Brassington, Fig. 76, the main difference consisting in its second

Fig. 86.—Penvorcs.   ⅓   Fig. 87.—West Buckland.   ⅓

loop. This specimen, with another from Cornwall and two from Ireland, was exhibited to the Society of Antiquaries in 1873, and is now in the British Museum. In the same collection is another, 6¼ inches long, somewhat lighter below the stop-ridge, and having the central rib less fully developed on the blade. It was found in Somersetshire in 1868, in making the Cheddar Valley line of railway. Another found in 1842, near South Petherton,* in the same county, is in the possession of Mr. Norris at that place.

Another example, shown in Fig. 87 was found at West Buckland,† Somersetshire, and is in the collection of Mr. W. A. Sanford. With it were discovered a torque (Fig. 468,) and a bracelet, (Fig. 481,) and also some charcoal and burnt bones, but there was no sign of any tumulus. Irish specimens will be subsequently mentioned.

Another two-looped instrument of a different character was found at Bryn Crûg,‡ near Carnarvon, in company with a tanged knife and a pin with three holes through its flat head (Fig. 450). It is shown in Fig. 88, copied on a reduced scale from the *Archæological Journal*. It resembles a flanged

Fig. 88.
Bryn Crûg. ⅓

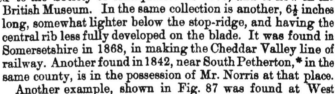

* *Arch. Journ.*, vol. ix. p. 387 ; vol. x. p. 247 ; vol. xxvii. p. 230.
† *Arch. Journ.*, vol. xxxvii. p. 107. For the use of this cut I am indebted to the Council of the Royal Archæological Institute.   ‡ *Arch. Journ.*, vol. xxv. p. 246.

celt except in having that part of the blade which lies between the side
loops raised to the level of the flanges.

In France these double-looped palstaves are of rare occurrence, but I
have seen one much like Fig. 86 which was found in the Department of
Haute Ariège, and is now in the Toulouse Museum. One from Tarbes[*]
was in the Exposition des Sciences Anthropologiques,
at Paris in 1878. Another was found at Langoiran
(Gironde).

The form is much more abundant in Spain, but in
most cases both the blade and the tang are long and
narrow in their proportions. An engraving of one from
Andalusia is given in the *Archæological Journal*,[†] and is
here by permission reproduced as Fig. 89. I have one
like it from a mine in the Asturias. One rather broader
from the Sierra de Baza,[‡] Andalusia, has also been
figured. A broken and unfinished double-looped palstave from Oviedo, now in the British Museum, has a
cup-shaped projection at the butt end which has been
filled with lead, possibly in old times, but for what
purpose it is impossible to say. An engraving of one
much like it has been published.[§] There are several
such in the Museums at Madrid, with the head of metal
left on the castings.

Fig. 89.
Andalusia.

The forms of celts and palstaves treated of in
this chapter are found also in Scotland, though
perhaps less frequently than those of the flat and
flanged forms described in the previous chapter.

Many so closely resemble English specimens
that it is needless to give representations of them,
as a reference to the figures in the preceding pages
will sufficiently indicate their character.

In the Antiquarian Museum at Edinburgh is a winged celt 4½ inches
long much like Fig. 56, which was found on the top of a hill called Lord
Arthur's Cairn, in the parish of Tullynessle,[||] Aberdeenshire. Another,
6 inches long, with the wings somewhat curved inwards, was found at
Kerswell,[¶] in the parish of Carnwath, Lanarkshire. Another winged
celt, 4 inches long, was ploughed up on the estate of Barcaldine,[**] Argyleshire.

In the same Museum are also winged celts (5 inches) from Birrens-
wark, Dumfriesshire, and from the neighbourhood of Peebles, much like
that from Reeth (Fig. 56).

A chisel-shaped celt, in character much like Fig. 55, but having a slight
stop-ridge, was found in Burreldale Moss,[††] Keith Hall, Aberdeenshire,

* "Matériaux," vol. xiv. p. 192.   † Vol. vi. p. 69, 369
‡ Gongora y Martinez, "Ant. preh. de Andal.," p. 110. *Arch. Journ.*, xxvii. p. 237.
§ *Arch. Journ.*, vol. xxvii. p. 230.
|| *Proc. Soc. Ant. Scot.*, vol. v. p. 30; Wilson's "Preh. Ann.," fig. 58.
¶ *Arch. Assoc. Journ.*, vol. xvii. p. 21.   ** *Proc. Soc. Ant. Scot.*, vol. vi. p. 203.
†† *Proc. Soc. Ant. Scot.*, vol. xi. p. 153.

and has been engraved by the Society of Antiquaries of Scotland, to whom I am indebted for the use of Fig. 90.

In a palstave (6¾ inches) from Kilnotrie,* Crossmichael, Kircudbright, the lateral flanges are continued below the stop-ridge, and there is a median ridge down the blade.

In some palstaves in the British Museum, found between Balcarry and Kilfillan, Wigtonshire, the stop-ridges instead of being at right angles to the face of the blade shelve outwards. One of them is engraved as Fig. 91. The sides are hammered into V-shaped depressions forming a kind of fern-leaf pattern along them.

Two of these palstaves are figured on a larger scale in the *Ayr and Wigton Collections.*†

Another palstave from Windshiel, near Dunse, in the Antiquarian Museum at Edinburgh, has also the flanges somewhat hammered over.

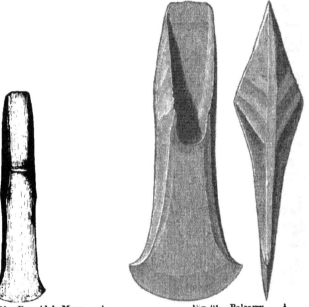

Fig. 90.—Burreldale Moss.   Fig. 91.—Balcarry.

A palstave without loop, and which from the engraving appears to have a well-marked stop-ridge and to have the side flanges much hammered over, is said to have been found near Tintot-top,‡ in Clydesdale. The description, however, says that it has no stop, otherwise the figure would almost justify an attribution of the instrument to Southern Germany rather than to Scotland. Another of much the same character, but without any stop-ridge, has been figured from Baron Clerk's§ collection as having been found in Scotland.

Palstaves with a side loop have been said‖ to be common in Scotland;

* Wilson's " Preh. Ann. of Scot.," vol. i. p. 382, fig. 56; "Cat. Ant. Mus. Ed.," E. 48.   † Vol. ii. pp. 8 and 9.
‡ *Arch.*, vol. v. p. 113, pl. viii. No. 2; Gough's "Camden," vol. i. p. ccvi.
§ Gordon's " Itin. Septent.," p. 116, pl. l. 6.
‖ *Arch. Assoc. Journ.*, vol. xvii. p. 21; Wilson, "Preh. Ann. of Scot.," vol. i. p. 383.

but this can hardly be the case, as in the Museum of the Society of Antiquaries of Scotland there are no authenticated examples.

One from Aikbrae,* Lanarkshire (6¾ inches), like Fig. 77, has been figured. Wilson gives another example like Fig. 78, but does not say where it was found. The "spade" he gives as his Fig. 59 is in all probability Italian.

A palstave rather like that from Balcarry, Fig. 91, but with a loop, is figured by Gordon† as having been found in Scotland.

What may be classed as a celt with two side loops, or possibly as a chisel, is said to have been found in the year 1810 in a barrow near Pettycur,‡ Fifeshire. It is described as very strong, and the bend in the upper part, as seen in Fig. 92, is thought to be accidental. Wilson describes it as a crowbar or lever, but as its total length is only 7¼ inches it can hardly be classed among such instruments.

A somewhat similar tool, but without holes in the side stops (7⅞ inches), is in the Museum of the Royal Irish Academy.§

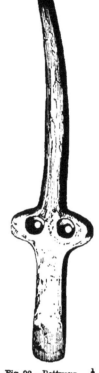

Fig. 92.—Pettycur. ⅓

Turning now to the instruments of this class discovered in Ireland, I may observe that it is so difficult to draw the line between the flanged celts, tapering both ways from a central ridge, and those which have a slight projecting stopridge upon them, that some Irish instruments of the latter class have already been mentioned in the preceding chapter, to which the reader is referred for the more highly ornamented varieties. Other Irish types have also been incidentally cited.

Some of the Irish palstaves much resemble English and Scottish types, but generally speaking there are sufficient peculiarities in their forms to enable a practised observer to recognise their origin. For several other varieties of form, besides those mentioned in the following pages, the reader is referred to Wilde's Catalogue.

Winged celts without a stop-ridge, like Fig. 53, have occasionally been found in Ireland, and one is figured by Wilde. ‖ I have one (5¼ inches) from Armoy, Co. Antrim. The wide-spreading celt with a slight stop-ridge and segmental band upon the blade,

* *Arch. Assoc. Journ.*, vol. xvii. p. 21. † "Itin. Septent.," p. 116, pl. l. 4.
‡ *Arch. Journ.*, vol. vi. p. 377; "Cat. Mus. Arch. Inst. Ed.," p. 27; Wilson, "Preh. Ann. Scot.," vol. i. p. 386.
§ "Catal.," p. 521, fig. 394.   ‖ "Catal. Mus. R. I. A.," p. 373, fig. 258.

like Fig. 50, also occurs. A remarkably fine specimen from West-meath with punctured ornaments on the wings and at the lower margin of the band has been engraved by Wilde.* Some are without the segmental band.

The type of Fig. 54 has also been found. I have a specimen (6 inches) from Ballinamallard, near Enniskillen.

Palstaves without a stop-ridge, and with broad lozenge-shaped wings, like Fig. 56, are of rare occurrence. One of nearly the same type, but having a low projecting ridge between the wings, is shown in Fig. 93.

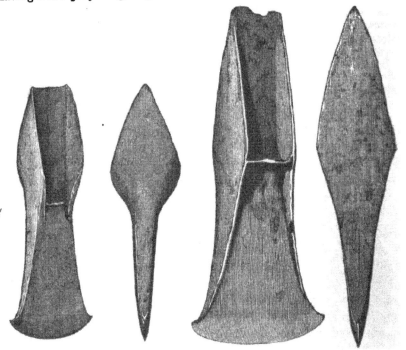

Fig. 93.—Ireland.   ¼   Fig. 94.—Ireland.   ¼

I have another from Armoy, Co. Antrim (6 inches), with a still slighter transverse ridge, which forms the upper boundary to a shield-shaped projection on the blade, on which is a central vertical ridge with two others on each side less definitely marked. The base of the shield is pointed.

A not uncommon type has a very high stop-ridge coming up to the level of the side wings, the blade above the stop-ridge being somewhat thinner than it is below. An example is shown in Fig. 94.

I have another from County Antrim, in which the lower part of the blade has a slight median vertical ridge.

In a palstave in the Museum of the Royal Irish Academy,† with elliptical wings, a long fusiform boss has been cast in the centre of the blade.

* "Catal. Mus. R. I. A.," p. 373, fig. 262.   † Op. cit., p. 373, fig. 259.

In another instrument in the same collection the whole blade is thickened out so as to form the stop-ridge, as will be seen in Fig. 95.

In other cases the ridge of the wings is continued as a moulding on the face of the blade, so as to enclose a space below the stop-ridge. From the base of this there sometimes proceeds a vertical rib, as seen in Fig. 96.

Inverted chevrons by way of ornament below the stop-ridge are not uncommon, sometimes with a vertical rib in addition.

Such compartments are often seen on the winged celts, with only a slight stop-ridge. Fig. 97 shows an example from Lanesborough, Co. Longford, now in the collection of Canon Greenwell, F.R.S. The compartment is ornamented with vertical punch marks. The outside of the wings is faceted after a fashion not unusual in Ireland, but there is here a slight shoulder at the base of the central facet which may have assisted in securing the blade to the handle. On a specimen at Dublin there are on the otherwise flat sides elevated transverse ridges, which, as Sir W. Wilde[*]

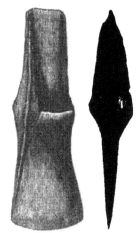

Fig. 95.—Ireland.

has pointed out, may have served "to keep the tying in its place."

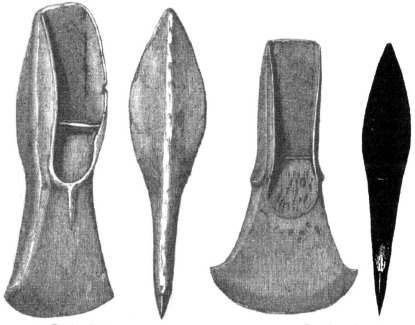

Fig. 96.—North of Ireland.   Fig. 97.—Lanesborough.

[*] "Catal. Mus. R. I. A.," p. 373, fig. 260.

The sides of other specimens of much the same type are otherwise fashioned and ornamented. In Fig. 98 is shown a celt from Trillick, Co.

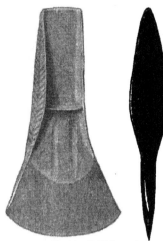

Tyrone, on the sides of which a kind of fern-leaf pattern has been hammered, or rather punched, not unlike the carving on one of the stones in the great chambered tumulus of New Grange. The shield plate has two vertical hollows worked on it.

The side of a celt ornamented in the same manner is engraved by Wilde.*

A small palstave, with two vertical grooves in the blade, is shown in Fig. 99.

Another form of winged celt, with a low stop-ridge and with a vertical rib passing through an inverted chevron on the blade, is shown in Fig. 100. The original is in the collection of Mr. Robert Day, F.S.A.

The same style of ornament occurs on palstaves of other forms.†

Fig. 98.—Trillick.

In some instances, there is in the centre of the stop-ridge a kind of bracket on the blade, and the side wings are hammered over so as to form an imperfect socket. A small example

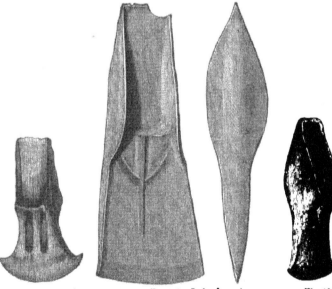

Fig. 99.—Ireland.   Fig. 100.—Ireland.   Fig. 101.—Ireland.

of the kind is shown in Fig. 101. I have a larger specimen (4½ inches) from Trillick, Co. Tyrone. Vallancey‡ engraves a palstave of this type.

* "Catal. Mus. R. I. A.," p. 379, fig. 270.   † Vallancey, vol. iv. pl. x. 7.
‡ Vol. iv. pl. x. 2.

Others with flat blades and no brackets have the side flanges hammered over in the same manner.

A fine example, in which the conical bracket dies into the stop-ridge and side flanges, is in the British Museum.

Palstaves with a loop at the side are not of such frequent occurrence in Ireland as those without. Wilde [*] has engraved a specimen (6⅜ inches) like Fig. 77 as well as that [†] which I have here shown on a larger scale as Fig. 102. This latter has the wings well hammered over at the base, so as to form a kind of socket on each side of the blade. It differs, however, from the English and foreign specimens like Fig. 85 in having a well-marked shoulder or stop on the blade between the wings.

Palstaves of nearly the same character, but without the loop, have already been mentioned as found both in Ireland and Scotland. Others,

Fig. 102.—Ireland.   Fig. 103.—Ireland.   Fig. 104.—Ireland.

with loops like Fig. 103, have a bracket on the blade between the flanges.

A remarkable form with slight side flanges and no stop-ridge, from the Dublin Museum, is shown in Fig. 104. It is No. 630 in Wilde's Catalogue. The sides have deep diagonal notches upon them and the upper part of each face is chequered, perhaps in order to assist in steadying the blade in its handle.

Another noteworthy palstave, found at Miltown, Co. Dublin, is shown in Fig. 105. In this the side wings are not hammered over, and the stop is supported by a conical bracket. The shoulders, instead of being nearly square to the midrib, are inclined upwards at an angle of nearly 45°, so as to form receptacles in which the wedge-shaped ends of the split handle would be held tight against the blade. These inclined stops have been observed in other palstaves of different forms, and Sir W. Wilde [‡] has called attention to them in connection with a palstave much like that now under consideration, but without any projection or loop on the side. The most remarkable feature in the Miltown example is a projecting, slightly

[*] P. 381, fig. 273.   [▲] P. 379, fig. 265.   [‡] "Catal. Mus. R. I. A.," p. 377, fig. 263.

curved spike or neb placed near the top of the blade rather above the position usually occupied by the loop. At first sight it looks like an imperfect loop, but, on examination, it is evident that the casting is perfect; and, on consideration, it seems clear that this projection would serve quite as well as a loop for receiving a cord to hold the blade back upon its haft, while for the actual tying it would be more convenient, as the cord would have merely to be passed over a hook, and not to be threaded through a loop. In a somewhat similar palstave (3⅞ inches) in the Museum of the Royal Irish Academy* there is also a projecting neb, but more semicircular in outline. I am not sure that it was intended for the same purpose. A looped palstave of this type, but with the bottom of the side socket more circular, is engraved by Vallancey.†

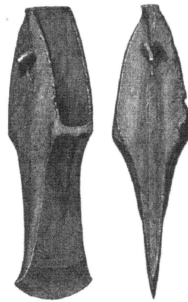

Fig. 105.—Miltown.   ½

Some of the socketed celts from the Bologna hoard have curved nebs on each side instead of rings. Instruments of the same character, also from Italy, have been engraved by De Bonstetten,‡ Schreiber,§ and Caylus.‖

Double-looped palstaves, with a loop on either side, and in character like Fig. 86, are almost or quite as rare in Ireland as in England. The only specimen engraved by Wilde ¶ is in the collection of Lord Talbot de Malahide. It is 6¼ inches long, with the loops not quite symmetrical. It was supposed to be unique. I have, however, another specimen of this type (6⅝ inches) found at Ballincollig,** Co. Cork, in 1854, which was formerly in the collection of the Rev. Thomas Hugo, F.S.A. It so closely resembles Fig. 86 that it is not worth while to engrave it.

Another remarkable and indeed unique instrument, in the Museum of the Royal Irish Academy,†† is shown in Fig. 106. It is like a flat celt, but has grooves and stops at the side like a palstave with a transverse edge. Below the stops are two loops. The sides below the stops are ornamented with transverse lines, and on the face here shown there is a dotted kind of cartouche below the stops, and a square compartment chequered in lozenges above them. This latter is wanting on the other face, but the corresponding cartouche below is divided into small lozenges alternately hatched and plain.

* "Catal.," p. 433, No. 641.   † Vol. iv. pl. x. 1.
‡ "Recueil d'Antiq. Suisses," pl. ii. 6. See also *Arch. Journ.*, vol. vi. p. 377; vol. xxi. p. 100.
§ "Die eher. Streitkeile," Taf. ii. 8.   ‖ "Recueil d'Ant.," pl. xciv. 1.
¶ "Catal. Mus. R. I. A.," p. 382, fig. 274; *Arch. Journ.*, vol. ix. p. 194.
** *Proc. Soc. Ant.*, vol. iii. p. 222.
†† "Catal.," p. 521, fig. 393; *Arch. Journ.*, vol. viii. p. 91, pl. No. 1.

Another Irish instrument of nearly the same form, but without the grooves and stops at the sides, is in the Bell Collection in the Antiquarian

Fig. 106.—Ireland.   ½

Fig. 107.—Ireland.   ½

Museum at Edinburgh; but its exact place of finding is uncertain.   It is shown in Fig. 107, and, like that last described, has each of its faces ornamented in a different manner.

The palstaves with a transverse edge are of more common occurrence in Ireland than in England, but are even there very rare.   That engraved as Fig. 108 was formerly in the collection of the Rev. Thomas Hugo, F.S.A.* A similar tool is figured by Vallancey.†

The smaller specimen shown in Fig. 109 was found near Ballymena, Co. Antrim, and is in the collection of Mr. Robert Day, F.S.A. I have one from the North of Ireland (4 inches) with the stops less distinct.

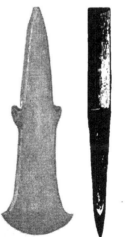

Fig. 108.—Ireland. ½   Fig. 109.—Ballymena. ½

Another Irish specimen (3 inches) is in the British Museum.   In the Museum of the Royal Irish Academy are several varying in length from 2⅝ inches to 5¼ inches. They are classed by Wilde‡ among the chisels.

In describing the various forms illustrated by the figures, I have from time to time called attention to the analogies which they present with other European forms, and it is hardly necessary to make any broad comparison of British palstaves and winged celts with those of other European countries. It would indeed be a difficult task to attempt, as in each country, if not in several districts in each country, the instruments of this kind are characterised by some local peculiarity.

Perhaps it will be more instructive to mention certain continental forms which are conspicuous by their absence in Britain.

We have not, for instance, the southern French form with a kind of contracted waist and broad side flanges or rounded wings in the middle of the blade; nor, again, the long narrow form almost resembling a marrow spoon; nor that with the almost circular blade, much like an ancient mirror. Nor have we the German form, with the V-shaped stop-ridge, nor that in which the stop-ridge forms a circular collar above a blade with beadings along the sides. Nor have we the common Italian form, with the blade like a long spud; nor, again, the narrow Scandinavian form, which is often highly decorated.

And yet, in comparing the instruments described in the present chapter with those of neighbouring countries, and especially of France, it will at once be remarked that, as might have been reasonably expected, the closest analogies are to be observed between some of those of England and France, while in the more peculiarly Scottish and Irish types the resemblances are more remote. It must, however, be borne in mind that there is good evidence in the shape of moulds and bronze-founders' hoards, such as will subsequently be mentioned, to prove that these instruments were cast in various parts of this country; so that, though some palstaves may be of foreign origin, yet, as a rule, it was the fashion of the objects rather than the objects themselves for which the inhabitants of Britain were indebted to foreign intercourse. Even in the area now embraced by France there does not appear to have been any single centre of manufacture, but, taken as a group, the palstaves of the South, the North, and the North-west of France present some distinguishing characteristics. The same is the case with the socketed celts of that country, the English representatives of which will be discussed in the next chapter.

CHAPTER V.

SOCKETED CELTS.

THE class of celts cast in such a manner as to have a socket for receiving the haft is numerously represented in the British Isles. In this form of instrument the haft was actually imbedded in the blade, whereas in the case of the flat and flanged celts, and of the so-called palstaves, the blade was imbedded in the handle, so that the terms, "the recipient" and "the received," originally given to the two classes by Dr. Stukeley, are founded on a well-marked distinction, and are worthy of being rescued from oblivion.

That the recipient class is of later introduction than the received is evident from several considerations. In the first place, a flat blade not only approaches most nearly in form to the stone hatchets or celts which it was destined to supersede, but it also requires much less skill in casting than the blade provided with a socket. For casting the flat celts there was, indeed, no need of a mould formed of two pieces; a simple recess of the proper form cut in a stone, or formed in loam, being sufficient to give the shape to a flat blade of metal, which could be afterwards wrought into the finished form by hammering. And secondly, as will subsequently be seen, a gradual development can be traced from the flat celt, through those with flanges and wings, to the palstave form, with the wings hammered over so as to constitute two semi-circular sockets, one on each side of the blade; while on certain of the socketed celts flanges precisely similar to those of the palstaves have been cast by way of ornament on the sides, and what was thus originally a necessity in construction has survived as a superfluous decoration. There is at least one instance known of the intermediate form between a palstave with pocket-like recesses on each side of a central plate and a celt with a single socket. In the museum at Trent * there is an instrument in which the socket

* "Matériaux," vol. iii. p. 395.

is divided throughout its entire length into two compartments with a plate between, and, as Professor Strobel says, resembling a palstave with the wings on each side united so as to form a socket on each side.   The evolution of the one type from the other is thus doubly apparent, and it is not a little remarkable that though palstaves with the wings bent over are, as has already been stated, of rare occurrence in the British Islands, yet socketed celts, having on their faces the curved wings in a more or less rudimentary condition, are by no means unfrequently found.   The inference which may be drawn from this circumstance is that the discovery of the method of casting socketed celts was not made in Britain but in some other country, where the palstaves with the converging wings were abundant and in general use, and that the first socketed celts employed in this country, or those which served as patterns for the native bronze-founders, were imported from abroad.

Although socketed celts, with distinct curved wings upon their faces, are probably the earliest of their class, yet it is impossible to say to how late a period the curved lines, which eventually became the representatives of the wings, may not have come down.   This form of ornamentation was certainly in use at the same time as other forms, as we know from the hoards in which socketed celts of different patterns have been found together.   As has already been recorded, the socketed form has also been frequently found associated with palstaves, especially with those of the looped variety.

The form of the tapering socket varies considerably, the section being in some instances round or oval, and in other cases presenting every variety of form between these and the square or rectangular.   There is usually some form of moulding or beading round the mouth of the celt, below which the body before expanding to form the edge is usually round, oval, square, rectangular, or more or less regularly hexagonal or octagonal.   The decorations generally consist of lines, pellets, and circles, cast in relief upon the faces, and much more rarely on the sides.   Not unfrequently there is no attempt at decoration beyond the moulding at the top.   The socketed celts are, almost without exception, devoid of ornaments produced by punches or hammer marks, such as are so common on the solid celts and palstaves.   This may be due to their being more liable to injury from blows owing to the thinness of the metal and to their being hollow.   They are nearly always provided with a loop at one side, though some few have been cast without loops. These are usually of small size, and were probably used as chisels rather than as hatchets. A very few have a loop on each side.

The types are so various that it is hard to make any proper classification of them. I shall, therefore, take them to a certain extent at hazard, keeping those, however, together which most nearly approximate to each other. I begin with a specimen showing in a very complete manner the raised wings already mentioned.

This instrument formed part of a hoard of celts and fragments of metal found at High Roding, Essex, and now in the British Museum, and is represented in Fig. 110. With it was one with two raised pellets beneath the moulding round the mouth, and one with three longitudinal ribs. The others were plain.

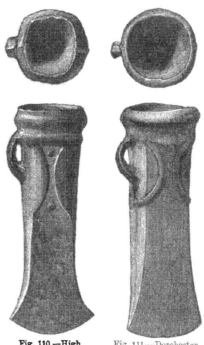

Fig. 110.—High Roding. ⅓.　Fig. 111.—Dorchester, Oxon. ⅓

Another (4 inches), with a treble moulding at the top, from Wateringbury, Kent, was in the Douce and Meyrick Collections, and is now also in the British Museum.

I have a German celt of this type, but without the pellets, found in Thuringia. Others are engraved by Lindenschmit,[*] Montelius,[†] and Chantre.[‡] I have a good example from Lutz (Eure et Loir).

On many French celts the wings are shown by depressed lines or grooves on the faces. I have specimens from a hoard found at Dreuil, near Amiens, and from Lusancy, near Rheims. Others with the curved lines more or less distinct have been found in various parts of France.

There is an example from Maulin in the Museum at Namur, and a Dutch example is in the Museum at Assen.

In Fig. 111 is shown a larger celt in my own collection, found in the neighbourhood of Dorchester, Oxon. The wing ornament no longer consists of a solid plate, but the outlines of the wings of the palstave are shown by two bold projecting beads which extend over the sides of the celt as well as the faces. The socket is circular at the mouth, but the neck of the instrument below the moulding is subquadrate in section. In the socket are two small projecting longitudinal ribs, probably intended

* "Alt. u. h. V.," vol. i. Heft ii. Taf. ii. 5.
† "Cong. préh.," Bologna vol. p. 293.　　　‡ "Age du Br.," ptie. i. p. 59.

to aid in steadying the haft. Such projections are not very uncommon, and are sometimes more than two in number.

A celt ornamented in a similar manner, but with two raised bands near the mouth, was found with several other socketed celts and some palstaves with the wings bent over at Cumberlow,[*] near Baldock, Herts. Some of these are in the British Museum.

Another with two small pellets between the curved lines was found in a hoard at Beddington,[†] Surrey.

Fig. 112 represents another celt of much the same character, but with a bolder moulding at top, and a slight projecting bead all round the instrument just below the two curved lines representing the palstave wings, which on these celts have just the appearance of heraldic "flanches."

Fig. 112.—Wilts.   ⅓   Fig. 113.—Harty.   ⅓

On the face not shown there is a triangular projection at the top like a "pile in chief" between the flanches. Inside the socket there are two longitudinal projections as in the last. The original of this figure, which has been broken and repaired with the edge of another celt, is in the Blackmore Museum at Salisbury, and was probably found in Wilts.

In the British Museum is an example of this type (4 inches) which has on one face only a pellet in the upper part of the compartment between the two "flanches." It was found at Hounslow.

Another (4 inches) from the Heathery Burn Cave, Durham, is now in the collection of Canon Greenwell, F.R.S. I have one with the pattern less distinct from a hoard found in the Barking Marshes, Essex, in 1862. A celt much of the same pattern, but without the transverse line below the flanches, was found on Plumpton Plain,[‡] near Lewes.

The same type occurs in France. I have examples from a hoard found at Dreuil, near Amiens. The same ornament is often seen on Hungarian celts, though usually without the lower band.

In Fig. 113 is shown one of the celts from the hoard discovered in the Isle of Harty,[§] Kent, to which I shall have to make frequent reference. Besides eight more or less perfect unornamented socketed celts, various

* *Journ. Anthrop. Inst.*, vol. vi. p. 195.
† "Surrey Arch. Soc. Coll.," vol. vi. ; Anderson's "Croydon Preh. and Rom.," p. 11, pl. ii. 1.
‡ *Suss. Arch. Coll.*, vol. ii. p. 268, fig. 8.
§ *Proc. Soc. Ant.*, 2nd S., vol. v. p. 408 ; "Cong. Préh." Stockholm vol., 1874, p. 444.

hammers, tools, and moulds, five celts of this type were found. Although so closely resembling each other that they were probably cast in the same mould, in fact in that which was found at the same time, there is a considerable difference observable among them, especially in the upper part above the loop. In the one shown in the figure there are three distinct beaded mouldings above the loop, and above these again is a plain, somewhat expanding tube. In one of the others, however, there are only the two lowest of the beaded mouldings, and the upper half-inch of the celt first mentioned is absolutely wanting. The three others show very little of the plain part above the upper moulding. As will subsequently be explained, the variation in length appears to be connected with the method of casting, and to have arisen from a greater part of the mould having been "stopped off" in one case than another. It will be noticed that the "flanches" on these celts are placed below the loop and not close under the cap-moulding. The beads which form them are continued across the sides. Running part of the way down inside the socket are two longitudinal ridges which are in the same line as the runners by which the metal found its way into the mould. The vertical ridge above the topmost moulding shows where there is a channel in the mould for the metal to pass by. If the celts had been skilfully cast so that their top was level with the upper moulding, no traces of this would have been visible.

Fig. 114.—Harty. ½   Fig. 115.—Dorchester, Oxon.

In Fig. 114 is shown one of the plain socketed celts from the same hoard. The mould in which it was cast was found at the same time, as well as the half of a mould for one of smaller size. The five other plain celts from the same hoard were all rather less than the one which is figured, and appear to have been cast in three different moulds, as the beading round the top varies in character, and in some is double and not single. The two projections within the socket are in these but short, though strongly marked.

In the British Museum is a celt of this kind, 4 inches long, found at Newton, Cambridgeshire, which on its left face, as seen with the loop towards the spectator, has a small projecting boss 1½ inch below the top.

Five socketed celts of this plain character (2½ inches to 3¾ inches) were found together at Lodge Hill, Waddesdon, Bucks, in 1855, and were lithographed on a private plate by Mr. Edward Stone.

The outline and general character of the celt shown in Fig. 115 may be taken as representative of one of the most common forms of English socketed celt. This particular specimen differs, however, from the ordinary form in having a ridge or ill-defined rib on each face which adds materially to the weight and somewhat to the strength of the instrument. It was found near Dorchester, Oxon.

A nearly similar celt found in Mecklenburg has been figured by Lisch.*

A larger celt of the same general character, found with a hoard of bronze objects in Reach Fen, Burwell Fen, Cambridge, is shown in Fig. 116. This may also be regarded as a characteristic specimen

of the socketed celts usually found in England, though the second moulding is often absent, and there is a considerable range in size and in the proportion of the width to the length. No doubt much of this range is due to some instruments having been more shortened by use and wear than others. The edge of a bronze tool must have been constantly liable to become blunted, jagged, or bent, and when thus injured was doubtless, to some extent, restored to its original shape by being hammered out, and then re-ground and sharpened. The repetition of this process would, in the course of time,

Fig. 116.—Reach Fen.   Fig. 117.—Reach Fen.

would, in the course of time, materially diminish the length of the blade, until eventually it would be worn out, or the solid part be broken away from the socketed portion.

Celts of this general character, plain with the exception of a single or double beading at the top, occur of various sizes, and have been found in considerable numbers. In my own collection are specimens (3 inches) from Westwick Row, near Gorhambury, Herts, found with lumps of rough metal; from Burwell Fen, Cambridge (3¼ inches), found also with metal, a spear-head like Fig. 381 and a hollow ring; from Bottisham, Cambridge (3 inches), and other places.

In the Reach Fen hoard already mentioned were some other celts of

* "Pfahlbauten, in M.," 1865, p. 78.

this type. They were associated with gouges, chisels, knives, hammers, and other articles, and also with two socketed celts, one like Fig. 133, and two like Fig. 124, as well as with two of the type shown in Fig. 117, with a small bead at some little distance below the principal moulding round the mouth. One of them has a slightly projecting rib running down each corner of the blade, a peculiarity I have noticed in other specimens. The socket is round rather than square.

I have other examples of this type from a hoard of about sixty celts found on the Manor Farm, Wymington, Bedfordshire (3¾ inches); from Burwell Fen, Cambridge (4 inches); and from the hoard found at Carlton Rode, Norfolk (4 inches). This last has the slightly projecting beads down the angles.

Socketed celts partaking of the character of the three types last described, and from 2 inches to 4 inches in length, are of common occurrence in England. Some with both the single and double mouldings were found in company with others having vertical beads on the face like Fig. 124, and a part of a bronze blade at West Halton,[*] Lincolnshire. I have seen others both with the single and double moulding which were found with some of the ribbed and octagonal varieties, a socketed knife, parts of a sword and of a gouge, and lumps of metal, at Martlesham, Suffolk. These are in the possession of Captain Brooke, of Ufford Hall, near Woodbridge. Another, apparently with the double moulding, was found with others (some of a different type), seven spear-heads, and portions of a sword, near Bilton,[†] Yorkshire. These are now in the Bateman Collection. Another with the single moulding was found near Windsor.[‡] Others with the double moulding, to the number of forty, were found with twenty swords and sixteen spear-heads of different patterns, about the year 1726, near Alnwick Castle,[§] Northumberland. Some also occurred in the deposit of nearly a hundred celts which was found with a quantity of cinders and lumps of rough metal on Earsley Common,[||] about 12 miles N.W. of York, in the year 1735. A socketed celt with the single moulding was found with spear-heads, part of a dagger, and some small whetstones, near Little Wenlock,[¶] Shropshire. Four socketed celts of this class with the double moulding were found, with a socketed gouge and about 30 pounds weight of copper in lumps, at Sittingbourne,[**] Kent, in 1828. They are, I believe, now in the Dover Museum. One (4¾ inches), obtained at Honiton,[††] Devonshire, has a treble moulding at the top, that in the middle being larger than the other two. The socket is square.

A plain socketed celt, 2¼ inches long, was found in digging gravel near Cæsar's Camp,[‡‡] Coombe Wood, Surrey. It is now in the Museum of the Society of Antiquaries. In the collection of Messrs. Mortimer, at Fimber, is a celt with the double moulding (3 inches long), found at Frodingham, near Driffield, which has four small ribs, one in the centre of each side running down the socket. Another, with the double moulding (4 inches), and with a nearly round mouth to the socket, was found at Tun

    * *Arch. Journ.*, vol. x. p. 69.
    † *Arch. Assoc. Journ.*, vol. v. p. 349; Bateman, Catal. M. 60, p. 76.
    ‡ Stukeley, "It. Cur.," pl. xcvi. 2nd.   § *Arch.*, vol. v. p. 113.
    || *Arch.*, vol. v. p. 114.
    ¶ Hartshorne's "Salopia Antiqua," 1841, p. 96, No. 9.
    ** Smith's "Coll. Ant.," vol. i. p. 101.
    †† Engraved in *Arch. Journ.*, vol. xxvi. p. 343.
    ‡‡ *Proc. Soc. Ant.*, vol. i. p. 67; 2nd S., vol. i. p. 83.

Hill, near Devizes, and is in the Blackmore Museum, where is also one found near Bath (3¾ inches) with the mouldings more uniform in size.

A socketed celt without any moulding at the top, which is hollowed and slopes away from the side on which is the loop, is said to have been found in a tumulus near the King Barrow on Stowborough Heath,* near Wareham, Dorset.

Socketed celts of this character occur throughout the whole of France, but are most abundant in the northern parts. They are of rare occurrence in Germany.

The same form is found among the Lake habitations of Switzerland. Dr. Gross has specimens from Auvernier and Mœrigen,† which closely resemble English examples.

A celt of the same general character as Fig. 114, but of peculiar form, narrowing to a central waist, is shown in Fig. 118. The original was found at Canterbury, and was kindly presented to me by Mr. John Brent, F.S.A.

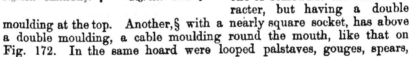

Fig. 118.—Canterbury. ½   Fig. 119.—Usk. ½

Broad socketed celts nearly circular or but slightly oval at the neck, and closely resembling the common Irish type (Fig. 167) in form and character, are occasionally found in England. That shown in Fig. 119 is stated to have been discovered at the Castle Hill, Usk, Monmouthshire.

I have seen another (3¼ inches) in the collection of Mr. R. Fitch, F.S.A., which was found at Hanworth, near Holt, Norfolk.

Among those found at Guilsfield,‡ Montgomeryshire, was one of somewhat the same character, but having a double moulding at the top. Another,§ with a nearly square socket, has above a double moulding, a cable moulding round the mouth, like that on Fig. 172. In the same hoard were looped palstaves, gouges, spears, swords, scabbards, &c.

Another, that, to judge from a bad engraving, had no moulding at the top, which was oval, is said to have been found under a supposed Druid's altar near Keven Hirr Vynidd,‖ on the borders of Brecknockshire.

Another variety, with a nearly square socket and long narrow blade is shown in Fig. 120, the original of which was found at Alfriston, Sussex. The loop is imperfect, owing to defective cast-

* "The Barrow Diggers," p. 74.
† Gross, "Deux Stations, &c.," pl. i. 15, 18.
‡ *Arch. Camb.*, 3rd S., vol. x. p. 214, No. 4; "Montg. Coll.," vol. iii. p. 437.
§ *Arch. Camb., ubi sup.* No. 3.   ‖ *Arch.*, vol. iv. p. 24, pl. i. 6.

ing.   The socket is very deep, and extends to within an inch of
the edge.   Instruments of this type are principally, if not solely,
found in our southern counties.   The type is indeed Gaulish
rather than British, and is very abundant in the north-western
part of France.   It appears probable that not only was the type
originally introduced into this country from France, but that there
was a regular export of such celts to Britain.   For I have in my
collection a celt of this type, 4½ inches long, that was found under
the pebble beach at Portland, and in which
the core over which it was cast still fills the
socket, the clay having by the heat of the
metal been converted into a brick-like terra-
cotta.   It could, therefore, never have been
in use, as no haft could have been inserted.
It is waterworn and corroded by the action
of the sea, the loop having been almost eaten
and worn away, so that it is impossible to
say whether the surface and edge were left
as they came from the mould.   In the large
hoard, however, of bronze celts of this type
which was found at Moussaye, near Plénée-
Jugon, in the Côtes du Nord, the bulk were
left in this condition, and with the burnt
clay cores still in the sockets.

I have another celt of the same size and
form as that from the Portland beach, which
was found near Wareham, Dorset, and appears to have been in use.

Two found with many others in the New
Forest* (3 and 5 inches long) are engraved in
the *Archæologia*.   The larger has a rib 3 inches
long running down the face and terminating in
an annulet.

Fig. 120.—Alfriston.   ½

Others of the same type have been found at Hollingbury Hill,† and
near the church at Brighton,‡ Sussex.

Among the celts found at Karn Brè, Cornwall, in 1744, were some of
this character, but expanding more at the cutting edge.   Others were
more like Fig. 124, though longer in proportion.   With them are said to
have been found several Roman coins, some as late as the time of
Constantius Chlorus.   Others (5 inches long) seem to have formed part

* *Arch.*, vol. v. p. 114, pl. viii. 9, 10 ; Gough's " Camden," vol. i. p. ccvi.
† *Suss. Arch. Coll.*, vol. ii. p. 268, fig. 7.
‡ Ibid., fig. 12.

of the hoard found at Mawgan,* Cornwall, in which there was also
a fine rapier. Another, from Bath,† is in the Duke of Northumberland's
museum at Alnwick. Another has been cited from Cornwall.‡

Celts of this form are of rare occurrence in the North of England,
but one, said to have been disinterred with Roman remains at Chester-
le-Street,§ Durham, is in the Museum of the Society of Antiquaries of
Newcastle-on-Tyne.

Celts like Fig. 120 are of very frequent occurrence in Northern France ;
large hoards, consisting almost entirely of this type, have been found.
A deposit of sixty was discovered near Lamballe ‖ (Côtes du Nord), and
one of more than two hundred at Moussaye, near Plénée-Jugon, in the
same department. Most of the
celts in both these hoards had
never been used, and in a large
number the core of burnt clay was
still in the socket. A hoard of
about fifty is said to have been
found near Bevay,¶ Belgium.

Plain socketed celts nearly square
at the mouth have occasionally
been found in Germany. One from
Pomerania ** is much like Fig. 120
in outline.

Fig. 121.　　　　　Fig. 122.
Cambridge Fens.　 ‡　High Roding.　 ‡

The form of narrow celt, which I
regard as of Gaulish derivation, is
not nearly so elegant as that of a
more purely English type of which
an example is shown in Fig. 121.
The original was found in the Cambridge Fens, and is in my own collection. Within the socket on the
centre of each side is a raised narrow rib running down 2 inches
from the mouth, or to within ¾ inch
of the bottom of the socket.

The type is rare ; but a specimen
(5 inches) of nearly the same form as
the figure was found, with palstaves,
sickles, &c., near Taunton, Somerset.†† There is also a resemblance
to the Barrington celt, Fig. 148.

I have already mentioned a celt with a moulded top, which, on one of
its faces, is ornamented with a small projecting boss. In Fig. 122
is shown an example with two pellets beneath the upper moulding. It
was found with others at High Roding, Essex, and is now in the British
Museum. Another with three such knobs on each face, placed near the

* *Arch.*, vol. xvii. p. 337.　　　　† *Arch. Journ.*, vol. xvii. p. 75.
‡ *Arch. Assoc. Journ.*, vol. vii. p. 172.　§ *Arch. Journ.*, vol. xvii. p. 75.
‖ "Matériaux," vol. i. p. 539.
¶ Lindenschmit, "Alt. u. h. Vorz.," vol. i. Heft ii. Taf. ii. 4.
** "Zeitsch. für Eth.," vol. vii. Taf. ix. 2.
†† *Arch. Journ.*, vol. xxxvii. p. 94. Pring, "Brit. and Rom. on Site of Taunton,"
pl. i. 1.

top of the instrument, is shown in Fig. 123. The original is in the British Museum, and was found at Chrishall,[*] Essex, where also several plain celts with single or double mouldings at the top, some spear-heads, and a portion of a socketed knife were dug up.

A large brass coin of Hadrian, much defaced, is said to have been found at the same time. As in other instances, the evidence on this point is unsatisfactory, and if it could be sifted, would probably carry the case no farther than to prove that the Roman coins and the bronze celts were found near the same spot, and possibly by the same man, on the same day. In illustration of this collection of objects of different dates, I may mention that I lately purchased a fifteenth-century *jeton* as having been found with Merovingian gold ornaments.

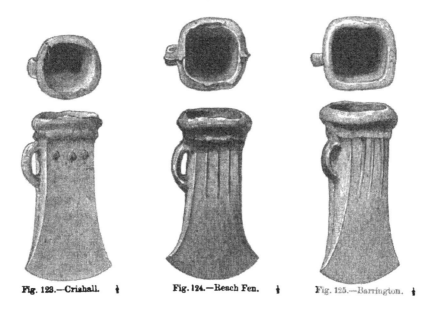

Fig. 123.—Crishall.   Fig. 124.—Reach Fen.   Fig. 125.—Barrington.

Some of the Breton celts, in form like Fig. 120, have two or three knobs on a level with the loop.

Another and common kind of ornament on the faces of socketed celts consists of vertical lines, or ribs, extending from the moulding round the mouth some distance down the faces of the blade. They vary in number, but are rarely less than three. In some instances the ribs are so slight as to be almost imperceptible, a circumstance which suggests the probability of celts in actual use having served as the models or patterns from which the moulds for casting others were made, as in each successive moulding and casting any prominences such as these ribs would be reduced or softened down. On any

* Neville's " Sepulchra Exposita," p. 3.

other supposition it is difficult to conceive how an ornamentation
so indistinct as almost to escape observation could have originated.
There are some celts which on one face are quite smooth and plain,
while on the other some traces of the ribs may just be detected.
The same is the case with some of the celts which have the slightest
possible traces of the "flanches," such as seen on Fig. 111.   The
smearing of metal moulds with clay, to prevent the adhesion of
the castings, would tend to obliterate such ornaments.

A celt with the vertical ribs from the hoard of Reach Fen, Cambridge,
is shown in Fig. 124.   There are slight projecting beads running down
the angles.   The three ribs die into the face of the blade.   Another of
nearly the same type, but with coarse ribs somewhat curved, is shown in
Fig. 125.   It has not the beads at the angles.   This specimen was found
in company with a celt like Fig. 116, and with a gouge like Fig. 204, at
Barrington, Cambridge, and is in my own collection.

Celts of wider proportions, and having the three ribs farther apart,
have been frequently found in the Northern English counties.   I have
one (3¼ inches) from Middleton, on the Yorkshire Wolds, which was
given me by Mr. H. S. Harland; and Canon Greenwell, F.R.S., has
several from Yorkshire.   The celt which was found near Tadcaster,* in
that county, and which has been so often cited, from the fact of its having
a large bronze ring passing through the loop, on which is a jet bead,
is also of this type.   There can be little doubt that the ring and bead,
which not improbably were found at the same time as the celt, were
attached to it subsequently by the finder, in the manner in which they
may now be seen in the British Museum.   A celt with three ribs, from
the hoard found at Westow,† in the North Riding, has been figured, as
has been one from Cuerdale,‡ near Preston, Lancashire, and one (4¼
inches) from Rockbourn Down,§ Wilts, now in the British Museum.
One (3¾ inches long) was found near Hull,‖ in Yorkshire; and five others
at Winmarley,¶ near Garstang, Lancashire, together with two spears,
one of them having crescent-shaped openings in the blade (Fig. 419).

Another was found, with other bronze objects, at Stanhope,** Durham.

The celts found with spear-heads and discs near Newark, and now
in Canon Greenwell's collection, are of this type, but of different sizes.
That found at Cann,†† near Shaftesbury, with, it is said, a human skeleton
and two ancient British silver coins, had three ribs on its face.

Several others were found in the hoard at West Halton,‡‡ Lincolnshire, already mentioned.   Others were discovered in company with a
looped palstave, some spear-heads, ferrules, fragments of swords, and a
tanged knife, near Nottingham,§§ in 1860.   Seven or eight such celts,
and the half of a bronze mould in which to cast them, were found with a
socketed knife, spear-heads, and numerous other objects, in the Heathery

* *Arch.*, vol. xvi. p. 362, pl. liv.; *Arch. Journ.*, vol. iv. p. 6.
† *Arch. Assoc. Journ.*, vol. xx. p. 107, pl. vii. 5; see also vol. iii. p. 58.
‡ *Op. cit.*, vol. viii. p. 332, pl. xxxvii. 1; *Proc. Soc. Ant.*, vol. ii. p. 304.
§ "Horæ Ferales," pl. v. 7.   ‖ *Arch. Assoc. Journ.*, vol. ix. p. 185.
¶ *Op. cit.*, vol. xv. p. 236.   ** *Arch. Æliana*, vol. i. p. 13, pl. ii. 8.
†† Evans' "Anc. Brit. Coins," p. 102.   ‡‡ *Arch. Journ.*, vol. x. pp. 69, 70.
§§ *Proc. Soc. Ant.*, 2nd S., vol. i. p. 332.

Burn Cave,* near Stanhope, Durham, of which further mention will subsequently be made. Many have also been found in Yorkshire and Northumberland.

The type is not confined to the Northern Counties, for specimens occurred in the great find at Carlton Rode,† near Attleborough, Norfolk. I have seen another, 4 inches long, which was found with many other socketed celts and other articles at Martlesham, Suffolk, in the hoard already mentioned (p. 113). I have one (3⅝ inches) from Llandysilio, Denbighshire. Another, with traces of the three ribs, was found at Pulborough,‡ Sussex. This specimen is in outline more like Fig. 130. A socketed celt of this kind (5 inches long), with three parallel ribs on the flat surface, was found near Launceston,§ Cornwall. Some long celts of the same kind were found at Karn Brê, in the same county, as already mentioned.

In some celts with the three ribs on their faces, found in Wales, the moulding at the top is large and heavy, and forms a sort of cornice round the celt, the upper surface of which is flat. That engraved as Fig. 126 was found at Mynydd-y-Glas, near Hensol, Glamorganshire, and is now in the British Museum. In the same collection is another of much the same character, but of ruder fabric, 4¾ inches long, with a square socket, found in 1849 with others similar, in making the South Wales Railway, in Great Wood,‖ St. Fagan's, Glamorganshire. The loop is badly cast, being filled up with metal.

Canon Greenwell has a celt of this type (4 inches), found at Llandysilio, Denbighshire, with two others having three somewhat converging ribs (3¾ inches and 3¼ inches), a socketed knife, and part of a spear-head.

Two others (5⅛ inches and 4⅜ inches) were found with part of a looped palstave ¶ and a waste piece from a casting, and lumps of metal, on Kenidjack Cliff, Cornwall. Another (4 inches) from Cornwall is in the British Museum. One from Sedgemoor, Somersetshire, is in the Taunton Museum.

Fig. 126.—Mynydd-y-Glas. ½

The three-ribbed type occurs occasionally in France. Examples are in the Museums of Amiens, Toulouse, Clermont Ferrand, Poitiers, and other towns. Three vertical ribs are of common occurrence on celts from Hungary and Styria.

In some rare examples the three ribs converge as they go down the blade. One such is shown in Fig. 127. The original is in the possession of Sir A. A. Hood, Bart., and was found with twenty-seven other socketed

* Proc. Soc. Ant., 2nd S., vol. ii. p. 132.   † Arch. Assoc. Journ., vol. i. p. 59.
‡ Suss. Arch. Coll., vol. ix. p. 118, fig. 7.   § Proc. Soc. Ant., 2nd S., vol. ii. p. 31.
‖ "Horæ Ferales," pl. v. 6.   ¶ Journ. Roy. Inst. Corn., No. 206.

celts, some of oval and some of square section, two palstaves, two gouges, two daggers, twelve spear-heads, and numerous fragments of celts and leaf-shaped swords, as well as rough metal and the refuse jets from castings. The whole lay together about two feet below the surface at Wick Park,* Stogursey, Somerset.

In other rare instances there is a transverse bead running across the blade below the three vertical ribs. The celt shown in Fig. 128 was found near Guildford, Surrey, and is in the collection of Mr. R. Fitch, F.S.A.

On other celts the vertical ribs are more or less than three in ·number.

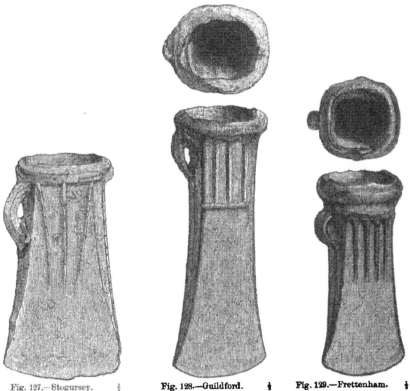

Fig. 127.—Stogursey.   ½   Fig. 128.—Guildford.   ⅓   Fig. 129.—Frettenham.   ⅓

A specimen with four ribs, also in Mr. Fitch's collection, is engraved as Fig. 129. It was found at Frettenham, Norfolk.

Others with four ribs occurred in the find at West Halton,† Lincolnshire, already mentioned. One was also found at the Castle Hill,‡ Worcester, and another at Broust in Andreas,§ Isle of Man. Examples with three and four ribs from Kirk-patrick and Kirk-bride, Isle of Man, are in the collection of Mr. J. R. Wallace of Distington, Whitehaven.

One (4⅛ inches) with five ribs was found in the hoard at Martlesham, Suffolk, also already mentioned.

One (3¾ inches) with six small vertical ribs on the faces, found at Downton, near Salisbury, is in the Blackmore Museum. In a celt with

---

* *Proc. Soc. Ant.*, 2nd S., vol. v. p. 427, pl. i. 3.   † *Arch. Journ.*, vol. x. p. 69.
‡ Allies, " Worc.," p. 18, pl. i. 1.   § " 1st Rep. Arch. Comm. I. of M.," pl. iv. 1.

square socket from the Carlton Rode find there are traces of six ribs on one of the faces only. This specimen, in my own collection, is in good condition, and the probability is in favour of this almost complete obliteration of the pattern being due to a succession of moulds having been formed, each rather more indistinct than the one before it, in which the model that served for the mould was cast.

Celts closely resembling Fig. 129 are in the museums at Nantes and Narbonne.*

As an instance of a celt having only two of these vertical ribs upon it, I may mention a large one in my own collection (4¾ inches) found in the

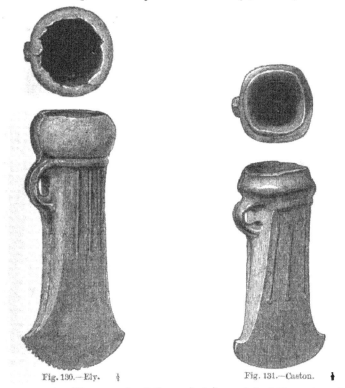

Fig. 130.—Ely. ⅓   Fig. 131.—Caston. ½

Isle of Portland. The mouth of the socket is oval, but the external faces are flat, the sides being rounded. The ribs run about 2½ inches down the faces, but the metal is too much oxidised to see whether they end in pellets or no.

It is not unfrequently the case that the ribs thus terminate in roundels or pellets. That from the Fens, near Ely, which has been kindly lent me by Mr. Marshall Fisher, and is shown in Fig. 130, is of this kind, though the pellets are so indistinct as to have escaped the eye of the engraver. This celt is remarkable for the unusually broad and heavy moulding at the top. The notches in the edge, which the engraver has reproduced, are of modern origin.

The celt from Caston, Norfolk, shown in Fig. 131, has also the three

* "Matériaux," vol. v. pl. ii. 11.

ribs ending in pellets, but there are short diagonal lines branching in each direction from the central rib near the top.

I have another of the same kind, but longer, and without the diagonal lines, from Thetford, Suffolk.

A celt of this type is in the Stockholm Museum.

In Figs. 132 and 133 are shown two celts of this class, one with five short ribs ending in pellets, from the Carlton Rode find, and the other with five longer ribs ending in larger roundels, from Fornham, near Bury St.

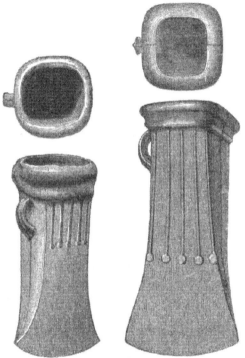

Edmunds. The latter was bequeathed to me by my valued friend, the late Mr. J. W. Flower, F.G.S.

It will be observed that in the Fornham celt the first and last ribs form beadings at the angles of the square shaft. In the other none of the beads come to the edge of the face. I have a celt like Fig. 133, but shorter (4 inches), from the hoard found in Reach Fen, already mentioned. Another (4⅛ inches), in all respects like Fig. 133, except that the outer ribs are not at the angles, was found at Brough,* near Castleton, Derbyshire, and is in the Bateman Collection, where is also another (4¼ inches) from the Peak Forest, Derbyshire. Canon Greenwell, F.R.S., has one (4¼ inches) from Broughton, near Malton, on one face of which there are only four ribs, and in the place where

Fig. 132.—Carlton Rode. ⅜   Fig. 133.—Fornham. ⅜

the central rib would terminate, a ring ornament. The other face of the celt has only four ribs at regular intervals, ending in pellets. Another, similar (5 inches), was found in the Thames, near Erith.† I have seen another rather more hexagonal in section, which was found in the Cambridge Fens.

Celts with vertical ribs ending in pellets are occasionally found in France. One from Lutz (Eure et Loir) is in the museum at Chateaudun; others are in that of Toulouse. Another with four ribs, found at Cascastel, is in the museum at Narbonne. Canon Greenwell has one from l'Orient, Brittany.

I have a small one like Fig. 120 in form, but barely 3 inches long,

* Bateman's "Catalogue," p. 74; Marriott's "Ant. of Lyme" (1810), p. 303.
† *Arch. Journ.*, vol. xviii. p. 157.

found near Saumur (Maine et Loire). It has five ribs, arranged as on Fig. 133.

An example with a far larger array of vertical ribs than usual is shown in Fig. 134. The ribs are arranged in groups of three, and each terminates in a small pellet. The outer lines are so close to the angles of the celt as almost to merge in them. This instrument was found at Fen Ditton, Cambridge, and is now in the collection of Canon Greenwell, F.R.S.

On some celts there is, besides the row of roundels or pellets at the end of the ribs, a second row a little higher up, as is shown in Fig. 135, which represents a specimen in the British Museum, from Bottisham

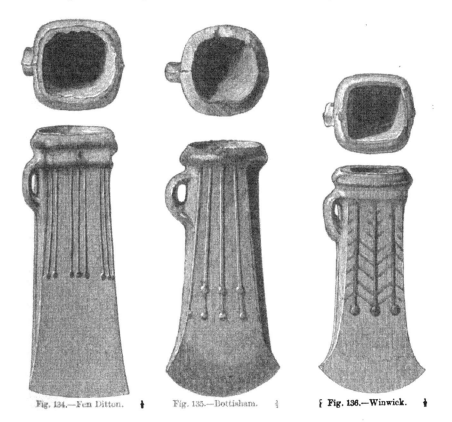

Fig. 134.—Fen Ditton.   Fig. 135.—Bottisham.   Fig. 136.—Winwick.

Lode, Cambridge. The sides of this celt are not flat, but somewhat ridged, so that in its upper part it presents an irregular hexagon in section. There are ribs running down the angles, with indications of terminal pellets.

In the Warrington Museum is a curious variety of the celt with the three vertical ribs ending in pellets, which by the kindness of the trustees of the museum I have engraved as Fig. 136. It will be seen that in addition to the vertical ribs there is a double series of chevrons over the upper part of the blade. The metal is somewhat oxidised, and the pattern is made rather more distinct in the engraving than it is in the original.

This celt has already been figured on a smaller scale, and was found at Winwick,* near Warrington, Lancashire.

An ornamentation of nearly the same character, but without pellets at the end of the ribs, occurs on a socketed celt from Kiew,† Russia.

The vertical ribs or lines occasionally end in ring ornaments or circles with a central pellet, like the astronomical symbol for the sun ⊙. Next to the cross this ornament is, perhaps, the simplest and most easily made, for a notched flint could be used as a pair

of compasses to produce a circle with a well-marked centre on almost any material, however hard. We find these ring ornaments in relief on many of the coins of the Ancient Britons, and in intaglio on numerous articles formed of bone and metal, which belong to the Roman and Saxon periods. On Italian palstaves they are the commonest ornaments. But though so frequent on metallic antiquities of the latter part of the Bronze Age, it is remarkable that the ornament is of very rare occurrence on any of the pottery which is known to belong to that period.

Fig. 137.—Kingston. ⅓   Fig. 138.—Cayton Carr. ⅓

A good example from Kingston, Surrey, of a celt with ring ornaments at the end of the ribs is in the British Museum, and is shown in Fig. 137. Canon Greenwell possesses a nearly similar celt (5 inches) from Seamer Carr, Yorkshire, the angles of which are ribbed or beaded. A socketed celt with the same ornamentation, but with pellets having a central boss instead of the ring ornaments, is in the museum at Nantes.‡ It was found in Brittany.

Some of the Brittany celts like Fig. 120 have one ring-ornament on each face, composed of two concentric circles and a central pellet.

* *Arch. Assoc. Journ.*, vol. xv. pl. xxiv. 7, p. 236; *Arch. Journ.*, vol. xv. p. 158.
† Chantre, " Age du Bronze," 2me partie, p. 284, fig. 81; *Mém. des Ant. du Nord*, 1872—7, p. 115.
‡ Chantre, " Age du Bronze," 2me partie, p. 292, fig. 138.

On a celt found at Cayton Carr, Yorkshire, and in the collection of Canon Greenwell, F.R.S., there is a double row of ring ornaments at the end of the three ribs. Below the principal moulding at the top of the celt is a band of four raised beads by way of additional ornament. It is shown in Fig. 138. A nearly similar specimen is in the Museum of the Society of Antiquaries of Newcastle-on-Tyne.

In a very remarkable specimen from Lakenheath,* Suffolk, preserved in the British Museum and engraved as Fig. 139, there are three lines formed of rather oval pellets, terminating in ring ornaments, and alternating with them two plain beaded ribs ending in small pellets. There are traces of a cable moulding round the neck above.

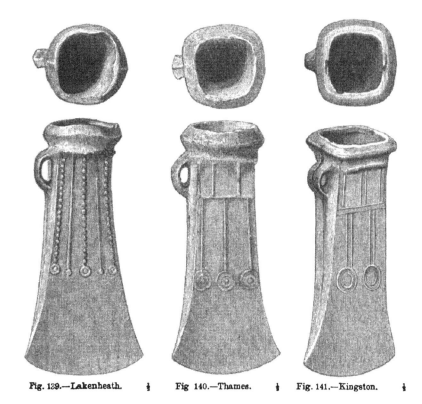

Fig. 139.—Lakenheath.   ½   Fig 140.—Thames.   ½   Fig. 141.—Kingston.   ½

In another variety, also in the British Museum, and shown in Fig. 140, the three ribs ending in ring ornaments spring from a transverse bead, between which and the moulding round the mouth are two other vertical beads, about midway of the spaces between the lower ribs. It is probable that this celt was found in the Thames.

Another of remarkably analogous character was certainly found in the Thames, near Kingston,† and is now in the Museum of the Society of

* *Proc. Soc. Ant.*, 2nd S., vol. i. p. 106.

† *Proc. Soc. Ant.*, vol. ii. p. 101 ; 2nd S., vol. i. p. 83. See also *Arch.*, vol. xxx. p. 491; and *Proc. Soc. Ant.*, vol. i. p. 21.

Antiquaries. It is shown in Fig. 141. On it are only two descending ribs, ending in ring ornaments, the pellets in the centre of which are almost invisible; but above the transverse bead are three ascending ribs, which alternate with those that descend. All these ribs are double instead of single.

In some rare instances there are ring ornaments both at the top and at the bottom of the vertical lines, as is seen on one of the faces of the curious celt shown in Fig. 142, where the usual ribs are replaced by rows of two or three slightly raised lines. On the other face it will be seen that the ornamentation is of a different character, with one ring orna-

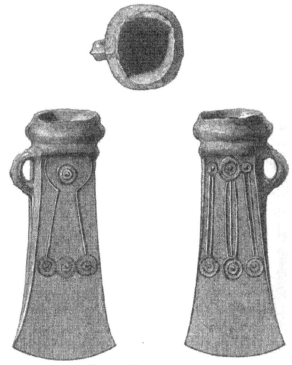

Fig. 142.—Kingston.   ½

ment at top and three below, the two outer of which are connected with ribs diverging from two curved lines above. The original was found, with three others less ornamented, at Kingston,* Surrey, and is in the British Museum.

A nearly similar celt from Scotland is described at page 137.

In another very rare specimen the vertical lines are replaced by two double chevrons of pellets, the upper one reversed. There is still a ring ornament at the base, and lines of pellets running down the margins of the blade. This specimen, shown in Fig. 143, was found in the Thames,† and is in the collection of Mr. T. Layton, F.S.A.

* Engraved also in " Horæ Ferales," pl. v. 5.   † *Proc. Soc. Ant.*, 2nd S., v. p. 428.

In another equally rare form there is a treble ring ornament at the bottom of a single central beaded rib, and at the top two "flanches," represented by double lines, as shown in Fig. 144. The neck of this celt is in section a flattened hexagon. It was found at Givendale, near Pocklington, Yorkshire, E. R., and is now in the British Museum.

In the celt shown in Fig. 145 the central rib terminates in a pellet, and there are three curved ribs on either side. In this case the section of the neck of the blade is nearly circular. The specimen is in the British Museum, and was probably found near Cambridge, as it formed part of the late Mr. Lichfield's collection. A celt ornamented in the same manner, but without the central rib, was found near Mildenhall, Suffolk, and is in the collection of Mr. H. Prigg.

Another (4 inches), also in the British Museum, has two ribs on each

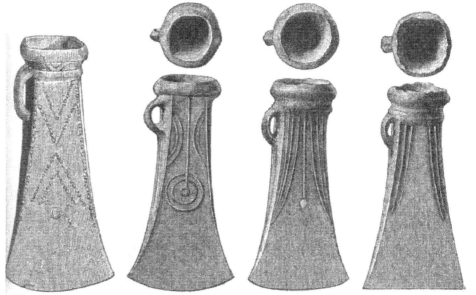

Fig. 143.—Thames.   Fig. 144.—Givendale. ⅓   Fig. 145.—Cambridge. ⅓   Fig. 146.—Blandford. ⅓

margin, parallel to the sides, as seen in Fig. 146. It was found near Blandford, Dorsetshire, in company with unfinished gouges, and is remarkable on account of its having been cast so thin that it seems incapable of standing any hard work.

It seems probable that the instruments from Blandford, now in the British Museum, formed part of a large hoard, for in the collection of the late Mr. Medhurst, of Weymouth, were a dozen or more of much the same outline and character. The section at the neck is a flattened hexagon. Some have a straight rib on each of the sloping sides, as well as two curved lines on the flat face. Others have three lines, one straight and two curved, on the flat face, each ending in a pellet; and others again have merely a central line on the flat face.

A celt of nearly the same outline as Fig. 146 (4¼ inches), found at Gembling, Yorkshire, E. R., has slight flutings down the angles for

about two-thirds of its length.   It is in the collection of Canon Greenwell, F.R.S.

Another of these instruments, ornamented in the same manner, but
having a curved edge, is shown in Fig. 147, from an original in the
British Museum.   It formed part of the Cooke Collection from Parsonstown, King's County, but I doubt its being really Irish.

A rare form of socketed celt is shown in Fig. 148.   The original was
found in the Fens, near Barrington, Cambridge, and is in my own collection.   It has at the top of the blade, below the moulding, a shield-
shaped ornament, of much the same character as that on the palstaves,
like Fig. 60, but in this case formed by indented lines cast in the
metal.

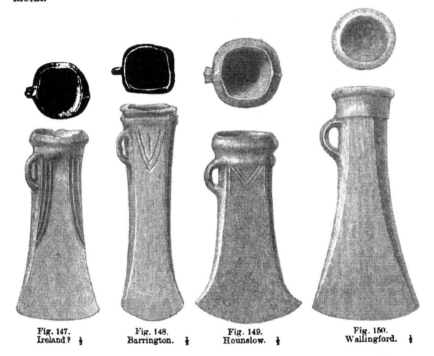

Fig. 147.   Fig. 148.   Fig. 149.   Fig. 150.
Ireland? ⅓   Barrington. ⅓   Hounslow. ⅓   Wallingford. ⅓

Another, of unusually narrow form, found at Thames Ditton,* is in
the Museum of the Society of Antiquaries.

A broader celt, ornamented with a reversed chevron, formed of three
raised ribs, and with short single ribs on each side, is shown in Fig. 149.
It was found at Hounslow, with a flat celt, a palstave, and a socketed
celt like Fig. 112, and is now in the British Museum.

A more common form has a circular socket and moulded top, below
which the neck of the blade is an almost regular octagon.   That shown
in Fig. 150 is in my own collection, and was found at Wallingford.†
Berks, in company with a socketed gouge, a tanged chisel (Fig. 193), a
socketed knife, and a two-edged cutting tool or razor (Fig. 269).

* *Proc. Soc. Ant.*, 2nd S., vol. iii. 398.
† This is possibly the specimen mentioned in *Proc. Soc. Ant.*, vol. iv. 303.

One nearly similar, supposed to have been found in Yorkshire, together with the mould in which it was cast, is engraved in the *Archæologia*.[*] The mould was regarded as a case in which the instrument was kept. Another of the same kind seems to have been found, with other celts and fragments of swords and spears, at Bilton,[†] Yorkshire. I have seen another, 4 inches long, from the hoard found at Martlesham, Suffolk, already mentioned. A broken specimen, found with a socketed gouge and an article like Fig. 493, at Roseberry Topping,[‡] in Cleveland, Yorkshire, appears to be of this kind. Another (5 inches long), found at Minster, Kent, is in the Mayer Collection at Liverpool. I have also one from the Cambridge Fens.

In the collection of Canon Greenwell, F.R.S., are three socketed celts with octagonal necks, which were found with others, both plain and having three ribs on the face, together with a looped palstave, at Haxey, Lincolnshire. Two of these are of the usual type, but the third (3¾ inches) is shorter and broader, resembling in outline the common Irish form, Fig. 167. A celt apparently of the type of Fig. 150, but with a double bead round the top, was found in the Severn, at Holt,[§] Worcestershire. In the Faussett Collection, now at Liverpool, is a celt of this kind, with the angles engrailed or "milled." This was probably found in Kent.

A celt of this type, found at Orgelet, Jura, is figured by Chantre,[||] as well as one from the Lac du Bourget.[¶] They have also been found in the Department of La Manche.[**] I have one from the hoard found at Dreuil, near Amiens, the neck of which is decagonal.

Nearly the same form has been found in Sweden.[††]

Fig. 151.—Newham. ¼

Another example, more trumpet-mouthed, is shown in Fig. 151, from the collection of Canon Greenwell, F.R.S. It was found in 1868 in draining at Newham, Northumberland. I have another of nearly the same form (4¾ inches), from Coveney, in the Isle of Ely. Another, found at Stanhope,[‡‡] Durham, without loop, and with two holes near the top, was regarded as an instrument for sharpening spear-heads.

Occasionally the neck of the blade is hexagonal instead of octagonal. In one found at Ty-Mawr,[§§] on Holyhead Mountain, Anglesea, the hexagonal character is continued to the mouth. The socket is of an irregularly square form. It was found with a socketed knife, a tanged chisel, spear-

[*] Vol. v. 109, pl. vii. 5.
[†] *Arch. Assoc. Journ.*, vol. v. p. 349; Bateman's Catal., p. 76, No. 60.
[‡] *Arch. Scot.*, vol. iv. 65; *Arch. Æliana*, vol. ii. p. 213.
[§] Allies, p. 149, pl. iv. 6.   [||] "Album," pl. x. 4.
[¶] *Op. cit.*, pl. lv. 8.   [**] *Mém. Soc. Ant. Norm.*, 1827—8, pl. xvi. 4.
[††] "Cong. préh.," Bologna vol. p. 293.
[‡‡] *Arch. Æliana*, vol. i. p. 13, pl. ii. 7.
[§§] *Arch. Journ.*, vol. xxiv. 255, pl. fig. 3.

K

heads, &c., which are now in the British Museum. This form occurs more
frequently in Ireland. A nearly similar celt has been found in the Lake
. of Geneva.*

Another celt, with the neck irregularly octagonal, but with a series of
mouldings round the mouth of the socket, is shown in Fig. 152. The
original is in the collection of Canon Greenwell, and formed part of the
hoard found at Westow, in the East Riding of Yorkshire, already mentioned at p. 118.

In Fig. 153 is shown, not on my usual scale of one-half, but of nearly
the actual size, a very remarkable celt, which was found in the bed of the

Fig. 152.—Westow. ½   Fig. 153.—Wandsworth.   Fig. 154.—Whittlesea.   ½

Thames † near Wandsworth, and was presented to the Archæological
Institute. The original is, unfortunately, no longer forthcoming. It was
4¾ inches long, and, besides its general singularity of form, presented the
peculiar feature of having the hole of the loop in the same direction as the
socket of the celt, instead of its being as usual at right angles to the blade.

Socketed celts with a loop on the face instead of on the side are of exceedingly rare occurrence either in Britain or elsewhere. That shown in

* Chantre, "Age du Br.," 1re ptie. p. 59; Desor, "Les Palafittes," fig. 39.
† Arch. Journ., vol. vi. p. 378, whence this cut is borrowed.

Fig. 154 is in the Museum at Wisbech, and was found in company with three socketed celts, two gouges, a hammer, and a leaf-shaped spear-head at Whittlesea. The socket shows within it four vertical ribs at equal distances, with diagonal branches from them. These latter may have been intended to facilitate the escape of air from the mould. I am indebted to the managers of the Museum for the loan of the specimen for engraving.

The type has occasionally been found in the Lake-dwellings of Savoy. In the Museum of Chambéry * there are three examples from the Lac du Bourget, and I possess another specimen from the same locality. Another (about 4 inches), from la Balme,† Isère, is in the Museum at Lyons; it is more spud-shaped than the English example. Another, of different form, was in the Larnaud hoard,‡ Jura. One has also been found at Auvernier,§ in the Lake of Neuchâtel. Another (4 inches), in the late M. Troyon's collection, was found at Echallens, Canton Vaud.

One with curved plates on the sides, like Fig. 155, but having the loop on one face, was found near Avignon, and is now in the British Museum. It has a round neck with a square socket. A smaller one, of nearly the same form, was found in a hoard at Pontpoint, near the River Oise. Another, with curved indentations on the sides, from the department of Jura,‖ is in the museum at Toulouse. Socketed celts with a loop on the face have been found in Siberia.¶

In some socketed celts the reminiscence of the "flanches" or wings upon the palstaves, of which I have spoken in an earlier part of this chapter, has survived in a peculiar manner, there being somewhat hollowed oval projections upon each side of the blade, that give the appearance of the "flanches" on the face, but at the same time produce indentations in the external outline of the instrument.

This will be seen in Fig. 155, which was found with the palstave (Fig. 83), the socketed celt (Fig. 157), and other objects at Nettleham,** near Lincoln, as already described (page 93). Another of the same class is said to have been found in a tumulus on Frettenham Common,†† Norfolk. Another, shown in Fig. 156, was in the Crofton Croker Collection. All these are now in the British Museum. The second celt from Nettleham (Fig. 157) shows only the indented outline without any representation of the oval plates. The nearest approach in form to these celts which I have met with is to be seen in some from the South of France. These are, however, generally without loops. I have two from the departments of Haute Loire and Isère. One from Ribiers, in the department of the Hautes Alpes, is in the museum at St. Omer. Another is in the museum at Metz.

A socketed celt, found at Aninger, and now in the Antiken Cabinet at Vienna, has large oval plates on each of its sides, which nearly meet upon the faces.

In the collection of the late Mr. Brackstone was a remarkable celt, exhibiting a modification of this form. It is said to have been found with a large socketed celt with three mouldings round the mouth, and a looped

* Perrin, "Et. préh. de la Sav.," pl. x. 4, 5; "Exp. Arch. de la Sav.," 1878, pl. vi. 210; Chantre, "Album," pl. lv. 3.
  † Chantre, "Album," pl. x. 2.   ‡ *Op. cit.*, pl. xl. bis. 3.
  § Gross, "Deux Stations," pl. i. 17.
  ‖ "Matériaux," vol. xiv. pl. ix. 10.   ¶ "Matériaux," vol. i. p. 463.
  ** *Arch. Journ.*, vol. xviii. p. 160, whence this and fig. 157 are borrowed.
  †† *Arch. Assoc. Journ.*, vol. iv. 153; Arch. Inst., Norwich vol. p. xxvi.

palstave with three ribs below the stop-ridge, near Ulleskelf, Yorkshire.

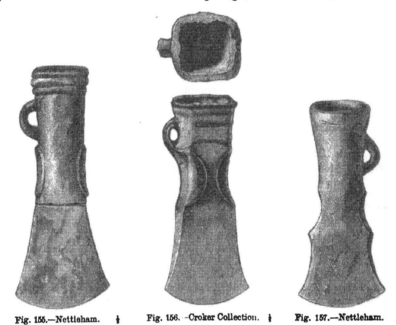

Fig. 155.—Nettleham.   ⅓   Fig. 156.—Croker Collection.   ⅓   Fig. 157.—Nettleham.

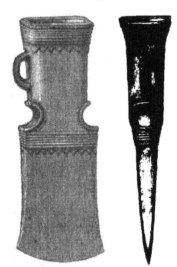

Fig. 158.—Ulleskelf.   ½

Mr. Brackstone printed a lithographic plate of the three, from which and from an engraving in the *Archæological Journal** Fig. 158 is taken. It will be observed that this celt is elaborately ornamented, even on the ring, either by engraving or punching. The original is now in the Blackmore Museum at Salisbury.

A celt of closely allied character, with the lower part of the blade and the C-shaped flanches similar to that from Ulleskelf, with the exception of the chevron ornament, is said to have been also found in Yorkshire. A woodcut, from a drawing by M. Du Noyer, will be found in the *Archæological Journal*.† The upper part is rectangular and plain, without any moulding round the top, and there is no loop. The original is 6 inches long. In general appearance and character this celt approaches those of Etruscan and Italian origin; but I see no reason why it may

* Vol. viii. p. 91. The length is erroneously stated to be about 4 inches in a subsequent volume (vol. xviii. p. 164).
† Vol. viii. 91.

not have been found, as stated, in Britain, though, so far as I know, it is unique of its kind.

The next class of socketed celts which has to be noticed consists of those in which the loop is absent. No doubt, in some cases, this absence arises either from defective casting, or from the loop having been accidentally broken off, and all traces of it removed ; but in many instances it is evident that the tools were cast purposely without a loop. It seems probable that many of them were intended for use as chisels, and not like the looped kinds as axes or hatchets. The similarity between the looped and the loopless varieties is so great that I have thought it best to describe some of the instruments which may be regarded as undoubtedly chisels in this place rather than in the chapter devoted to chisels, in which, however, such of the socketed kinds as are narrow at the edge, and do not expand like the common forms of celt, will be found described.

Fig. 159.
Reach Fen. ½

Fig. 160.
Carlton Rode. ½

The small tool shown in Fig. 159 may safely be regarded as a chisel. It does not show the slightest trace of ever having been intended to have a loop, and is indeed too light for a hatchet. It was found with a tanged chisel, a hammer, numerous socketed celts, and other articles, in the hoard from Reach Fen, Cambridge, already mentioned at p. 112. I have seen another, 2½ inches long, with a somewhat oval socket and no loop, which was found in Mildenhall Fen, and was in the collection of the Rev. S. Banks, of Cottenham.

A longer celt of the same character is engraved by Dr. Plot.[*] It was sent to him by Charles Cotton, Esq., and according to Plot " seems to have been the head of a Roman rest used to support the lituus, the trombe-torte, crooked trumpet, or horne pipe used in the Roman armies." Another of nearly the same form was found on Meon Hill,[†] near Camden, Gloucestershire.

A celt or chisel of this character found at Düren, in North Brabant, is in the museum at Leyden.

Another was found at Zaborowo,[‡] in Posen, in a sepulchral urn.

A celt of the octagonal form of section and without a loop is shown in Fig. 160. It formed part of the great hoard found at Carlton Rode, near Attleborough, Norfolk, of which some particulars have already been given. The joint marks of the moulds are still very distinct upon the

* " Nat. Hist. Staff.," p. 404, pl. xxxiii. 7.   † *Arch.*, vol. v. pl. viii. 23, p. 118.
‡ " Zeitsch. für Eth.," vol. vii. Taf. viii. 4.

sides. This specimen is in the Norwich Museum, and was kindly lent by the trustees for me to have it engraved. A nearly similar Scottish celt is shown in Fig. 165. A celt from the hoard of Cumberlow, near Baldock,[*] has been figured as having no loop, but I believe that this has arisen from an error of the engraver, as in a drawing which I have seen the loop is present.

One of hexagonal section and socket from a hoard found on Earsley Common,[†] Yorkshire, in 1735, is engraved as having no loop.

Celts without loops are not uncommon in France, and are often found of small size in Denmark.[‡]

Socketed celts have rarely if ever been found with interments in barrows in Britain. Sir R. Colt Hoare mentions "a little celt" as having been found with a small lance, and a long pin with a handle, all of bronze, near the head of a skeleton, in a barrow on Overton Hill,[§] near Abury, Wilts. The body had been buried in the contracted attitude, and had, as was thought, been enclosed within the trunk of a tree. It appears, however, from Dr. Thurnam's account,[||] that this was a flat and not a socketed celt. It was a celt like Fig. 116, $3\frac{1}{4}$ inches long, which is reported to have been discovered by the late Rev. R. Kirwan in a barrow on Broad Down, Farway, Devonshire.[¶] It is said to have lain in the midst of an abundant deposit of charcoal which was thought to be the remains of a funeral pyre. Mr. Kirwan informed Dr. Thurnam that there was every reason to believe that the celt was deposited where found at the time of the original interment. No bones, however, were actually with the celt, which lay 18 inches from the central cist.

A socketed celt with three vertical ribs, like Fig. 125, is also

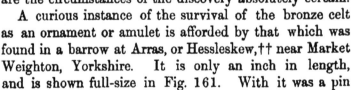

said to have been found with a human skeleton, and two uninscribed ancient British coins of silver, at Cann,[**] near Shaftesbury, in 1849. The celt and coins are now in the collection of Mr. Durden, of Blandford. In neither case are the circumstances of the discovery absolutely certain.

A curious instance of the survival of the bronze celt as an ornament or amulet is afforded by that which was found in a barrow at Arras, or Hessleskew,[††] near Market

Fig. 161.
Arras.

Weighton, Yorkshire. It is only an inch in length, and is shown full-size in Fig. 161. With it was a pin which connected it with a small light-blue glass bead. It accompanied the contracted body of a woman laid in a grave, and

* *Journ. Anth. Inst.*, vol. vi. p. 195.   † *Arch.*, vol. v. pl. viii. 7, p. 114.
‡ Segested, "Oldsag. fra Broholm," pl. xxiii. 8.
§ "Anc. Wilts," vol. ii. p. 90. || *Arch.*, vol. xliii. 443.
¶ *Trans. Dev. Assoc.*, vol. iv. p. 300, pl. ii. 1.
** Evans, "Anc. British Coins," p. 102.
†† *Arch. Journ.*, vol. xviii. p. 156; Arch. Inst., York vol. Catal., p. 27.

having with it a necklace of glass beads, a large amber bead, and a brooch, bracelets, ring, tweezers, and pin, apparently of bronze, some of them ornamented with a kind of paste or enamel. The majority of the objects found in the group of barrows at Arras, of which this was one, seem to belong to what Mr. Franks has termed the "Late-Celtic" period, or approximately to the time of the Roman invasion of this country.

Socketed celts not more than ¾ of an inch in length have been found in Ireland, but with sockets large enough for serviceable handles, so that they might possibly have been used as chisels. The diminutive celts, about 2 inches in length, which have been found in large numbers in Brittany, and have been regarded by French antiquaries as votive offerings, might also by some possibility have served as tools; but this can hardly have been the case with the Arras specimen. A golden celt found in Cornwall is said to have been in the possession of the Earl of Falmouth,* but nothing is known of it by the present Viscount Falmouth, and the statement in the "Barrow Diggers" is probably erroneous.

Fig. 162.
Bell's Mills. ¼

It will be well to postpone the account of the different hoards of bronze objects, in which socketed celts have been found with other tools and weapons, until I come to treat of such ancient deposits, though some of them have already been mentioned.

Turning now to the socketed celts which have been discovered in Scotland, we find them to present a considerable variety of types, though hardly so great as that exhibited by those from England, and the recorded instances of their finding are comparatively few in number.

In Fig. 162 is shown a socketed celt of the plain kind which was found at Bell's Mills,† on the Water of Leith, Edinburgh, in company with those given as Figs. 164 and 165.

A celt found in a bog between Stranraer and Portpatrick, Wigtonshire,‡ like Fig. 162, but with a bead at the level of the top of the loop, has been figured.

The nearly square-necked celt shown in Fig. 163 is of a broader type than usual, and was found at North Knapdale,§ Argyleshire.

* "Barrow Diggers," 1839, p. 72.
† For the use of these cuts I am indebted to the Society of Antiquaries of Scotland.
‡ "Ayr and Wigton Coll.," vol. ii. p. 10.
§ *Proc. Soc. Ant.*, 2nd S., vol. vii. p. 196.

Socketed celts with oval necks, and resembling the common Irish type, Fig. 167, in form, have occasionally been found in Scotland. One (3¼ inches), with a double moulding round the mouth, was found on Arthur's Seat, Edinburgh. Another (3 inches) was found with several other socketed celts and a spear-head near the Loch of Forfar. One of these, like Fig. 150, has a round socket and a twelve-sided neck.

A celt with a long socket and narrow blade was found, with spear-heads, bronze armlets, and some pieces of tin, at Achtertyre,[*] Morayshire.

Another type, which appears to be more especially Scottish, has the ornamented moulding placed on the neck of the blade in such a manner as to run through the loop. One of this character, dug up near Samson's Ribs,[†] Arthur's Seat, Edinburgh, has been figured by Professor Daniel Wilson. A second (2⅞ inches), with three raised bands passing through the loop, was found in the Forest of Birse,[‡] Aberdeenshire.

Fig. 163.—North Knapdale. ½   Fig. 164.—Bell's Mills. ½   Fig. 165.—Bell's Mills. ½

A type which is also common to England is shown in Fig. 164 from another of the Bell's Mills specimens.

Others with raised lines on the sides are preserved in the museum at Edinburgh. One of these was found near the citadel at Leith.[§]

One (3½ inches), ornamented with four longitudinal lines on each face, was found in the parish of Southend,[||] Cantire. Another (4¼ inches), with traces of five ribs, three down the middle and two at the margins of each face, was found at Hangingshaw,[¶] in Culter parish, Lanarkshire.

A third celt from Bell's Mills is shown in Fig. 165. This is of the variety without the loop, and closely resembles that from the Carlton Rode hoard, Fig. 160, the main difference being that the neck is of decagonal instead of octagonal section.

Moulds for celts of other patterns have also been found in Scotland,

* *Proc. Soc. Ant. Scot.*, vol. ix. p. 435.   † "Preh. Ann. Scot.," vol. i. pp. 351, 384.
‡ *P. S. A. S.*, vol. ii. p. 153.   § *P. S. A. S.*, vol. xii. p. 209.
|| *P. S. A. S.*, vol. iv. p. 396.
¶ *Arch. Assoc. Journ.*, vol. xvii. pl. xi. 5, p. 111.

as will subsequently be seen. A modern cast from some moulds found at Rosskeen, Ross-shire, has been engraved by Professor D. Wilson.* It is of hexagonal section, and is ornamented on each face by two diverging ribs starting from an annulet close below the moulding round the mouth, and ending in two annulets about two-thirds of the way down the blade, which expands considerably, and has a nearly flat edge.

For the use of Fig. 166 I am indebted to the Council † of the Ayrshire and Wigtonshire Archæological Association. The original was found in a peat-moss near the farm-house of Knock and Maize, in Leswalt parish, Wigtonshire, and is now in the cabinet of the Earl of Stair. Its

Fig. 166.—Leswalt　½

analogies with that found at Kingston, Surrey (Fig. 142), are very striking, while at the same time it closely resembles the type exhibited by the mould from Ross-shire already mentioned. The occurrence of instruments of so rare a form at such a distance apart is very remarkable; but if, as appears probable, the celts of this type are among the latest which were manufactured, and may possibly belong even to the Late Celtic period, their wide dissemination is the less wonderful.

Socketed celts have been found in very large numbers in Ireland, upwards of two hundred being preserved in the Museum of the

* "Preh. Ann. Scot.," vol. i. p. 384, fig. 61. † "Collections," vol. ii. p. 11.

Royal Irish Academy ; and numerous specimens are to be seen in other collections, both public and private. Mr. R. Day, F.S.A., of Cork, has upwards of forty in his own cabinet. The Irish celts vary much in size, the largest being a little over 5 inches long, and the smallest less than an inch. The most common form is oval at the neck, and expands into a broad cutting edge. There is usually some kind of moulding round the mouth, giving the end of the instrument a trumpet-like appearance. The effect of the

Fig. 167.—Ireland.   ½   Fig. 168.—Ireland.   ½

moulding is not unfrequently exaggerated by a hollow fluting round the neck, as in Fig. 167.

Celts of this and some of the following types have been figured by Vallancey.*

In that shown as Fig. 168 there is a slight shoulder below the trumpet-shaped part of the mouth, and the loop, instead of springing straight out from the neck, has its ends extended into four ridges, running over the neck of the celt like half-buried roots.

An example of a celt with the loop attached in a similar manner has been engraved by Wilde.† Another (3¾ inches) is in the collection of Mr. R. Day, F.S.A.

* Vol. iv. pl. ix. 3, 4, 6.   † "Catal. Mus. R. I. A.," p. 392, fig. 306.

Fig. 169 shows a finely patinated celt, with a triple moulding below the expanding mouth, which was found near Belfast. With it are said to have been found a set of three gold clasps, or so-called fibulæ, with discs at each end of a slug-like half-ring (see Wilde, Figs. 594—598). Curiously enough, I have another set of three of these ornaments, also found together at Craighilly, near Ballymena, Co. Antrim. Mr. Robert Day, F.S.A., has a specimen which also is one of three found together in the Co. Down. It seems,

Fig. 169.—Belfast. ⅓   Fig. 170.—Ireland. ⅓   Fig. 171.—Ireland. ⅓

therefore, probable that, like our modern shirt-studs, these ornaments were worn in sets of three.

A celt with four bands (3½ inches) has been engraved by Wilde.* The middle member of the triple band is often much the largest.

A small example of the same type, but with a single band at the mouth, is shown in Fig. 170. One from Co. Antrim, 1⅝ inch long and 1¼ inch broad at the edge, is in the British Museum.

These oval-necked celts are occasionally, but rarely, decorated with patterns cast in relief upon them. One of them, in the Museum of the Royal Irish Academy,† is shown in Fig. 171.

Inside the sockets of most of the instruments of this class there are near the bottom, where the two sides converge, one, two, or more vertical ridges, probably destined to aid in steadying the haft.

In some instances the upper member of the moulding round the mouth

* P. 385, fig. 279.

† Wilde, " Catal. Mus. R. I. A.," p. 385, fig. 280. This cut is kindly lent by the Council.

is cast in a cable pattern. Fig. 172 shows an example of this kind from Athboy, Co. Meath, in the collection of Canon Greenwell, F.R.S. Others are in the Museum of the Royal Irish Academy.

Socketed celts, with vertical ribs on the faces, are of rare occurrence in Ireland. A specimen from Co. Meath, in Canon Greenwell's collection, is engraved as Fig. 173.

One (2⅝ inches) found near Cork, and now in Mr. Robert Day's collection, has six vertical ribs on each face, three on either margin. They are placed close together, and vary in length, the outer one being about twice as long as that in the middle, which is, however, nearly three times as long as the innermost of the three ribs.

I have an example of the same kind (2¾ inches), from Trillick, Co. Tyrone,*

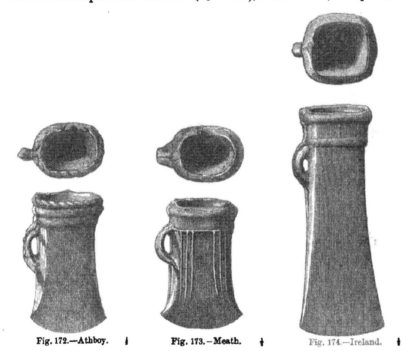

Fig. 172.—Athboy.   ⅓   Fig. 173.—Meath.   ⅓   Fig. 174.—Ireland.   ⅓

in which there are five equidistant vertical ribs on each face. The edge has been much hammered, so as to be considerably recurved at the ends. Wilde† has figured a much larger specimen (4½ inches), with three vertical ribs, which cross a ring, level with the top of the loop, and run up to the lip moulding. Another,‡ with rectangular socket, has the ribs arranged in the usual manner. In a few instances the ribs end in pellets, and in one instance Wilde § describes them as " ending in arrow points."

A short but broad socketed celt in the Petrie Collection has on each face six vertical ribs terminating at each end in annulets.

The socketed celts with an almost square socket and neck are not so common in Ireland as those of the broad type with an oval neck, but are

* Engraved in *Journ. Roy. Hist. and Arch. Assoc. of Ireland*, 4th Ser. vol. v. p. 259.
† Fig. 282.   ‡ Fig. 284.   § P. 429.

yet not absolutely rare. Fig. 174 shows a good specimen of this type. I have another (3½ inches), from the neighbourhood of Belfast, rather wider at the edge, and with three flat vertical ribs below the neck moulding.

Fig. 175 shows a short variety of the same type, from Newtown Crommolin, Co. Antrim. One from Trillick, Co. Tyrone (2½ inches), though nearly rectangular at the neck, has an oval socket.

Mr. Robert Day has an example (3¼ inches), from Dunshaughlin, Co. Meath, with two beads round it, the lower one at the level of the bottom of the loop. This celt is rectangular at the neck, though the socket is oval.

Some few have grooves running down the angles. One from Londonderry (4¼ inches) is in Mr. Day's collection.

The long narrow celt with a rib ending in an annulet on the face, engraved by Wilde as Fig. 283, appears to me to belong to Brittany. rather than to Ireland.

Fig. 175.
Newtown Crommolin. ⅔

Fig. 176.
North of Ireland. ⅔

Fig. 177.
Ireland. ⅔

An elegant type of socketed celt of not uncommon occurrence in Ireland is shown in Fig. 176. The neck is octagonal below the rounded trumpet mouth, which is ornamented with a series of small parallel beads, between which a number of minute conical depressions have been punched, making the beads appear to be corded. Around the loop is an oval of similar punch marks. A nearly similar specimen has been engraved by Wilde (Catal., Fig. 276), who also gives one of the same general type, but with two plain broad beads, alternating with three narrow ones, round the mouth (Catal., Fig. 277). It has a hexagonal neck. A celt (4¼ inches) from Ballina, Co. Mayo, in the collection of Mr. Robert Day, F.S.A., has an octagonal neck, and five grooved lines round its circular mouth.

Canon Greenwell has one of the type of Fig. 176 (3¾ inches), with hexagonal neck and five equal beads round the mouth, from Carlea, Co.

Longford, and another (3¾ inches), with ten small beads round a somewhat oval mouth, from Arboe, Co. Tyrone. The neck of this latter is
nearly rectangular. I have a celt of this type from Balbriggan, Co.
Dublin (3¼ inches), with a hexagonal neck and a plain mouth. The
loop has root-like excrescences from it, as already described.

There is one more Irish type of looped socketed celts which it will be well
to figure, and to which Wilde has given the name of the axe-shaped socketed
celt. As will be seen, the blade is expanded considerably below the
socketed part, and assumes a form not uncommon among iron or steel

axes. I have copied Fig. 177 from Wilde's cut, No.
281, on an enlarged scale.

A socketed celt expanding into a broad axe-like
edge is in the Pesth Museum.

An analogous but narrower form is found in France.
I have seen the drawing of one found at Pontpoint,
Oise (?).

Socketed celts without loops have not unfrequently
been found in Ireland. One of this type has been
figured by Wilde,* whose cut is, by the kindness of
the Council of the Royal Irish Academy, here repro-

Fig. 178.—Ireland. ½

duced as Fig. 178. There are two others in the same
collection. Another of the same length (2⅟₁₆ inches), but wider at the
edge, was found in the Shannon,† at Keelogue Ford. A longer and
narrower instrument (3¾ inches) of the same kind has also been engraved
by Wilde.‡ Another has been engraved by Vallancey.§ Others (2 and
2⅛ inches) from Lisburn and Ballymoney, Co. Antrim, are in the British

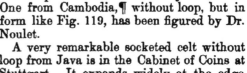

Museum. The former has a small bead on a
level with the base of the socket. The latter
is oval at the neck, but oblong at the mouth.

A bronze instrument of this form, but
wider at the edge, was in common use among
the ancient Egyptians, and has been regarded as a hoe.

A socketed celt without loop, but with two
projections on one side, from the Sanda Valley,‖ Yunan, China, has been figured by
Dr. Anderson. The edge is very oblique.
An example brought from Yunan by the
same expedition is in the Christy Collection.
One from Cambodia,¶ without loop, but in
form like Fig. 119, has been figured by Dr.
Noulet.

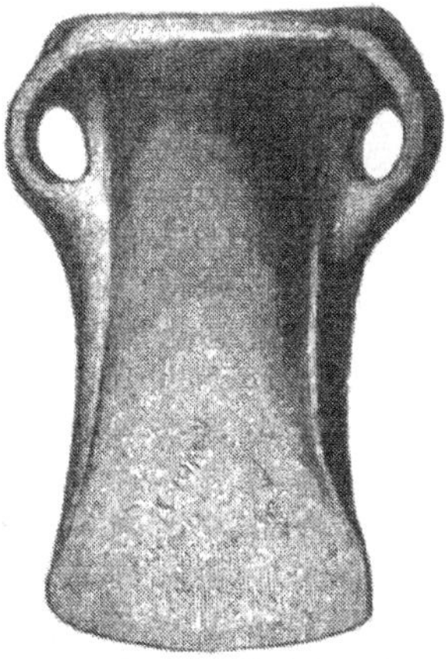

Fig. 179.—Kertch. ½

A very remarkable socketed celt without
loop from Java is in the Cabinet of Coins at
Stuttgart. It expands widely at the edge
and has three facets on one side of the neck, while the other is curved,
so that it was probably mounted as an adze. The surface of the socket
is not flat, but there is a V-shaped depression across it.

* P. 384, fig. 275.   † Proc. Soc. Ant. Scot., vol. xi. p. 170.
‡ P. 521, fig. 398.   § Vol. iv. pl. ix. 7.
‖ Report on "Expedit. to Western Yunan," Calcutta, 1871, p. 414.
¶ "Arch. du Mus. d'Hist. Nat. de Toulouse," vol. i. pl. vi. 6.

Socketed celts with two loops have not as yet been recorded as found within the United Kingdom, though a stone mould for celts of this form was found at Bulford Water, Salisbury. In Eastern Europe the form is more common. The specimen shown as Fig. 179 was found in the neighbourhood of Kertch,[*] and is now in the British Museum. I have seen others ornamented on the faces, brought from Asiatic Siberia by Mr. H. Seebohm. Others from Siberia [†] have been figured. One of these is without loops, and has chevron ornaments in relief below a double moulding.

A socketed celt with two loops, and apparently hexagonal at the neck, found at Ell, near Benfeld, Alsace, is figured by Schneider.[‡]

I have elsewhere described a two-looped socketed celt from Portugal [§] (6¼ inches). It is like Fig. 120, but has a second loop. Another, of gigantic dimensions, 9¼ inches long and 3¼ inches wide, was found in Estremadura, Spain.[||]

A two-looped celt with square socket and the loops at the junction with the flattened blade was in the great hoard found at Bologna. Only one of the loops, however, is perforated.

In the museum at Stockholm are also some socketed celts with two loops.

In looking over these pages, it will have been observed, that though socketed celts occur in numbers throughout the British Isles, yet that those found in England for the most part differ in form from those found in Ireland, and that some few types appear to be peculiar to Scotland. Traces of continental influence are, as might have been expected, most evident in the forms found in the southern counties of England, and are barely, if at all, perceptible in those from Ireland and Scotland. Some few of the socketed celts from both England and Scotland are of the type Fig. 167—a type so common in Ireland as to be characteristic of it—and these appear for the most part, though by no means exclusively, to have been found in western counties. Although, therefore, the first socketed celts in Britain were doubtless of foreign origin, there was no regular importation of them for use over the whole country; but the fashion of making them spread through local foundries, and different varieties of pattern originated in various centres, and were adopted over larger or smaller areas as they happened to commend themselves to the taste of the bronze-using public. The use of socketed celts would, from their abundance, seem to have extended over a considerable period; and from their having apparently been found with objects belonging to the Late

[*] *Arch. Journ.*, vol. xiv. p. 91. For the use of this cut I am indebted to Mr. A. W. Franks, F.R.S.

[†] *Proc. Soc. Ant.*, 2nd S., vol. iv. p. 13; *Arch. Journ.*, vol. xxxi. p. 262; *Mém. des Ant. du Nord*, 1872—7, p. 116, &c.

[‡] "Die ehern. Streitkeile," Taf. ii. 12.   [§] *Trans. Ethn. Soc.*, N. S., vol. vii. p. 45

[||] "Cong. préh." Copenhagen vol. p. 352.

Celtic Period they must have been among the last of the bronze tools or weapons to be superseded by those of iron. A socketed celt, somewhat like Fig. 116 but more trumpet-mouthed, is stated to have been found in company with a looped spear-head, two pins like Figs. 453 and 458, a bronze bridle-bit, and some portions of buckles of a late Celtic character on Hagbourne Hill, Berks. These objects are now in the British Museum, and there seems reason to believe the account of their discovery given in the *Archæologia*.* Some coins of gold and silver are said to have been found with them, but these are not forthcoming. Socketed celts have also been found associated with clasps like Figs. 504 and 505 at Dreuil, near Amiens, while at Abergele such clasps accompanied buckles almost, if not quite, late Celtic in character.

No doubt the final disuse of socketed celts was not contemporaneous throughout the whole of the country, and their employment probably survived in the north and west of Britain and in Ireland to a considerably later date than in the districts more accessible to Gaulish influences. The chronology of our Bronze Period will, however, have to be considered in a subsequent chapter. The transition from bronze to iron cannot so readily be traced in this country as on the Continent; but socketed celts, &c. formed of iron, and made in imitation of those in bronze, have occasionally been found in Britain. One (4 inches) with a side loop, and a part of its wooden handle, was found in Merionethshire, and is now in the British Museum. It has been figured in the Archæologia Cambrensis.† Another of the same type was found in North Wales.‡

I have one (5¼ inches) with a rounded socket and no loop, found at Gray's Thurrock, Essex.

I have another (4 inches) with a square socket, from Pfaffenburg in the Hartz; and others of longer proportions with round sockets from Hallstatt. The metal has been carefully welded together to form the sockets, in which there is no slit like those commonly to be seen in more modern socketed tools of iron. There are ornaments round the mouth of some of the Hallstatt § socketed celts, and both they and the iron palstaves are frequently provided with a side loop, in exact accordance with those on their analogues in bronze. Some of the socketed celts in iron from

* Vol. xvi. p. 348.   † 3rd S., vol. i. p. 250.
‡ *Proc. Soc. Ant.*, 2nd S., vol. iii. p. 518.
§ Von Sacken, "Grabf. v. Hallst.," Taf. vii.

the cemetery of Watsch,* in Carniola, are also provided with a loop.

As an illustration of the view that similar wants, with similar means at command with which to supply them, lead to the production of similar forms of tools and weapons in countries widely remote from each other, I may mention a socketed celt ($10\frac{3}{4}$ inches) found in an ancient grave near Copiapo, Chili.† In general form it is almost identical with some of the Italian bronze celts, but it is of copper, and not bronze; and is not cast, but wrought with the hammer. The socket has, therefore, been formed in the same manner as those of the early iron celts from Hallstatt, with which it also closely corresponds in outline. The surface, however, has been ornamented by engraving; and among the patterns we find bands of chevrons, alternately plain and hatched, closely allied to the common ornament of the European Bronze Age. What is, perhaps, more striking still is that the Greek fret also occurs as an ornament on the faces.

The method in which socketed and other celts were hafted will be discussed in the next chapter.

* Deschmann und Hochstetter, "Präh. Ansied. u. Begr. stätt. in Krain.," 1879, Taf. xvi.
† *Rev. Arch.*, vol. xxiii. p. 257, pl. viii.

CHAPTER VI.

METHODS OF HAFTING CELTS.

ANY account of the various forms of celts and palstaves which have been discovered in this country, such as that attempted in the preceding chapters, would be incomplete without some observations as to the manner in which they were probably hafted or mounted for use, and some account of the discoveries which throw light upon that subject.

In a previous chapter I have cited numerous opinions of the older school of antiquaries as to the nature of these instruments or weapons, and the uses which they were intended to serve. Many of these opinions are so palpably absurd that it is needless again to refer to them. Others which regard the instruments as having been mounted in such a manner as to serve for axes or adzes, for chisels, or for spud-like tools or weapons, have an evident foundation in the necessities of the case. There can, in the first place, be no doubt that celts and palstaves were cutting tools or weapons. There can, in the second place, be but little doubt that they were not destined for direct use in the hand without the addition of any shaft or handle. In fact, with the palstave and socketed forms, it is evident that special provisions are made for a haft of some kind. In the third place, this haft, whether long or short, must either have been straight or crooked. If straight, a kind of chisel or spud must have resulted; if crooked or L-shaped, an axe, hatchet, or adze.

It is possible that the same form of bronze instruments may have been mounted both with straight and with L-shaped handles; but, as will subsequently be seen, the probability, judging from what few ancient handles have been discovered, is that the great majority were mounted with elbowed handles as axes. At the same time, from the form and small size of some celts, especially of some of those of the socketed variety, it is probable that they were used as chisels. Indeed, judging from the analogy of some other forms, and from the discovery at Everley, mentioned at p. 163, this may be regarded as certain.

As the discoveries of the original hafts of bronze celts have principally been made upon the Continent, I shall, in treating of this part of my subject, be compelled to have recourse to foreign rather than British illustrations. It will also, in speaking of the method of hafting, be desirable to make an attempt to trace the successive stages of development of the socketed celts ; and, in connection with this part of the subject also, foreign examples will become of service.

And first, in illustration of the use of bronze blades as axes, rather than as spuds, or chisels of any kind, I may mention an instrument not uncommon in Hungary, and occasionally occurring in other parts of Southern Europe, which is perforated and similar in general form to our modern axe-heads of iron and steel. In Scandinavia also other varieties of these perforated axe-heads have been found. The common axe-like type has also been discovered among Assyrian antiquities. Another and distinct form which has been found in Egypt mounted as an axe or hatchet, with a wooden handle, is a flat blade not unlike the ordinary flat celt, except that instead of tapering at the butt-end it expands so as to have two more or less projecting horns, by which it was bound against the haft in a shallow socket provided for it. Egyptian axes mounted in this manner may be seen in many museums, and have been frequently figured in works on Egyptian antiquities.* The blade of an axe of this kind, formerly in the collection of the Rev. Sparrow Simpson, D.D., F.S.A.,† and by him presented to the British Museum, bears an inscription in hieroglyphics upon it, with cartouches probably containing the name of a shepherd king of the sixteenth or seventeenth dynasty. In my own collection is another bronze blade of the same shape and size, and with the same inscription, except that the names in the cartouches are different. Unfortunately this part of the blade is corroded, but Dr. S. Birch thinks that the cartouches contain the name either of Ramses I. or of a subordinate Ramses of the eighteenth dynasty. The hieroglyphics are the same on both faces of the blade, but on one run from right to left, and on the other from left to right. A hatchet of the same form,

* See "Matériaux," vol. v. p. 376.
† *Arch. Assoc. Journ.*, vol. xxiii. p. 293, pl. xv.

still bound to its haft, was found in the tomb of Queen Aah-Hotep,* of the eighteenth dynasty.

Some of the stone hatchets from Ecuador, in South America, are also provided with projecting ears, and were tied against their helves in the same manner.

The stone axe, said to be that of Montezuma II., preserved in the Ambras Museum at Vienna, and shown in Fig. 180, may also be of this kind. Copper or bronze blades of this crescent or cheese-cutter form, with two projecting lugs at the top of the narrow part of the blade, have been found in Peru.

Fig. 180.—Stone Axe of Montezuma II.

Broad blades of bronze, in form more like the ordinary flat celts, but with the projections at the top, have been found in the same country. I have one about 5 inches long and 3 inches wide, with strong lugs at the top 2 inches long. It came from Eastern Peru.

Some blades of this form were hafted in a rather different manner, as will be seen by means of Fig. 181.

Fig. 181.—Aymara Indian Hatchet.   ⅓

This represents an iron hatchet used by the Aymara Indians, of the province of La Paz, Bolivia, which was brought from that country and presented to me by my friend, the late Mr. David Forbes, F.R.S. In this form the handle is split, and the blade is secured by a leather thong, two turns of which pass under the two lugs of the blade, and thus prevent it from coming forward ; two

* "Matériaux," vol. v. p. 379, pl. xix. 7.

other turns pass over the butt-end, and thus prevent it from being driven backwards by any blow; while all the coils of the thong hold the cleft stick firmly against the two faces of the blade. Although no celts with the T-shaped butt-end have been found in Britain, or, indeed, in Western Europe, I have thought it worth while to engrave this curious example of the method of mounting such blades, especially as the central projections of the Irish form of celt, like Fig. 45, may have been secured by thongs in a somewhat analogous manner.

Turning now to the other British forms of celts, of which, as already observed, the flat and doubly tapering blades, like Fig. 2,

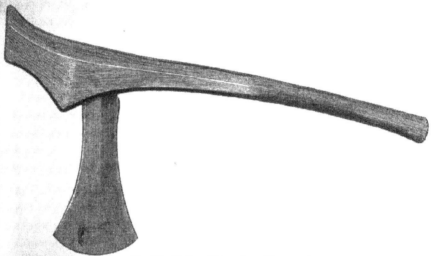

Fig. 182.—Modern African Axe of Iron.   ½

seem to be the most ancient, it is probable that these were hafted by the butt-end being merely driven into a club or handle of wood, in the same manner as many stone celts appear to have been mounted. The modern iron hatchet, from Western Africa, shown in Fig. 182, will give a good idea of the manner in which the bronze celts that are so much like it in form were probably hafted. Another modern African axe has been engraved by Sir John Lubbock.* It is, of course, possible that some of the ancient flat celts were mounted after the manner of spuds, as is, by several German and Danish antiquaries, held to have been the case with those of the palstave form. It must, however, be borne in mind

* "Preh. Times," p. 29. For other examples see Klemm, "Allgem. Culturwiss.," vol. i. p. 100.

that as a rule the stone celts, which the earliest of those in bronze must in all probability have supplanted, were mounted after the manner of hatchets. Moreover, the few stone celts, the axis of the straight handle of which was in the same direction as the blade, appear to have been hafted with short handles as chisels, and not with long shafts as spuds. Among those found still attached to their hafts in the Swiss lake dwellings, some few were mounted in short stag's-horn handles as chisels, but the majority were fitted for use as hatchets, with a club-like handle, in which a short stag's-horn socket was mortised as affording a receptacle for the stone, harder and less liable to split than those of wood. In some cases, however, the handles were made from a bough of a tree with a short projecting branch, which was cleft to receive the stone. One of

Fig. 183.—Stone Axe, Robenhausen.

these, from Robenhausen, is shown in Fig. 183, which is copied from Dr. Keller's work.*

In Britain the traces of the original handles of bronze celts have been not unfrequently found, though the actual wood had perished.

In a barrow in the parish of Butterwick,† Canon Greenwell, F.R.S., found what he describes as "an axe-blade of bronze," engraved as Fig. 2, which lay with a skeleton, and "the handle, which had been under two feet in length, could be plainly traced by means of a dark line of decayed wood extending from the hips towards the heels; moreover, from the presence of decayed wood on the sides of the blade, it would seem as if the axe had been protected by a wooden sheath. To all appearance the weapon had been worn slung from the waist." In this case the blade had been fixed, apparently after the manner of Fig. 182, into a solid handle to the depth of two inches, as is evident from the surface of the metal being oxidized on that part of the blade differently from what it is elsewhere.

* "Lake Dwellings," Eng. ed., p. 110, pl. x. 16. See also xi. 2, and xxviii. 24; and Lindenschmit, "Hohenz. Samml.," Taf. xxix. 4.   † "British Barrows," p. 188.

In a barrow at Shuttlestone,* near Parwich, Derbyshire, Mr. Bateman found about the middle of the left thigh of a skeleton a bronze celt, of "the plainest axe-shaped type. The cutting edge was turned upwards towards the upper part of the person, and the instrument itself has been inserted vertically into a wooden handle by being driven in for about two inches at the narrow end—at least, the grain of the wood runs in the same direction as the longest dimension of the celt." "A fact," adds Mr. Bateman, "not unworthy of the notice of any inclined to explain the precise manner of mounting these curious implements." It may be remarked, however, that no part of the handle itself, beyond this grain upon the bronze, was preserved, and that this direction of the grain of the wood would be quite consistent with the blade having been mounted in a side branch from the shaft, after the manner of the Swiss stone celt shown in Fig. 183.

It appears to me possible that in other cases where the marks of the grain of the wood, or even the traces of the wood itself, have been found upon celts, running along and not across the blade, the somewhat hasty conclusion has been drawn that they were attached to the end of straight shafts instead of into side branches; and that possibly this opinion, when once accepted, may have affected insensibly the reports of the position of the blade of the celts with regard to the bodies with which they were found, and to the traces of their shafts.

The opinion first enounced by J. A. Fabricius that the celt was the ancient German *framea* or spear mentioned by Tacitus, seems also insensibly to have affected observers.

There is an account given by Thorlacius[†] of the discovery in a tumulus near Store-Hedinge, in Denmark, of a palstave with the wooden shaft an ell and a quarter long, into which the blade was inserted; the wood, as might have been expected, running down between the side wings; at the other end of the shaft there was a leather strap wound round for about a quarter of an ell. The whole was so decayed that not the least part of it could be taken out of the ground. Although nothing appears to be said with regard to the position of the palstave with respect to the shaft, this has been cited by Lisch[‡] and others in evidence of this form of instrument having been mounted spud-fashion, as a kind of chisel-

---

* "Ten Years' Diggings," p. 35.
† Cited in Schreiber's "Die ehernen Streitkeile," Freiburg, 1842, p. 4.
‡ See Lisch, "Frederico-Francisceum," p. 38.

ended spear. A more conclusive instance is that adduced by Westendorp,[*] who has figured a socketed celt without a loop, found in a fen in the province of Groningen, Holland, mounted in this manner on a straight shaft. I have, however, already remarked that some of the socketed celts of this character were probably used as chisels.

Whatever reliance may be placed upon the older discoveries, all those of more recent times are in favour of the instruments of the palstave form having been mounted as axes, hatchets, or adzes. In the museum at Salzburg, Austria, there are at least four crooked handles for this kind of blade, found in the salt-mines of Hallein, one of which is shown in the annexed cut. I am not, however,

Fig. 184.—Bronze Axe, Hallein.

sure whether the blade was actually found with the haft in which it is now placed, nor, if so, whether it was originally in its present position with the loop outwards. It looks much more like an Italian than a German specimen, which has been added to the haft in recent times, and it has not the appearance of having been exposed for centuries to the action of salt. It seems more probable that the salt, which has fortunately had the power of preserving the wood, would in course of years have dissolved the whole of the metal, assuming that at the time when the haft was lost, or left in the mine, a blade was still attached to it, than that it should have left the metal, as here, almost uninjured. In this instance, moreover, the haft is perfect, and not, as in some of the other cases, broken, so as to raise an inference of their having been thrown away.

* "Antiquitaiten," iii. Stück, p. 285.

The position of the blade with the loop outwards is also suspicious.

A broken example of the same kind of haft, also from the salt-mines of Hallein, has been figured by Klemm,* and is to be seen in the British Museum. There are others in the museum at Linz.

Handles of the same kind, intended for palstaves, have been found in the Italian lake dwellings. In some discovered in the "palafitta" of Castione,† the notch is in the transverse direction to the shaft, as if the blade had been mounted as an adze, and not as an axe. In others the notch is longitudinal, and not transverse. In one instance the side branch has no notch, but there is a shoulder on it, as if it had served for a socketed celt.

A looped palstave, mounted in a similar branched handle, has been found at the lake dwelling of Mœrigen,‡ on the Lac de Bienne. In this case also the loop is on the farther side of the shaft.

That the flanged and winged celts and palstaves were, as a rule, destined to be mounted in the manner of hatchets or adzes, and not as spuds or spear-heads, is to some extent witnessed by the development of their form; the progressive increase in the size of the wings and flanges, more especially about the middle of the blade, appearing to be intended as a precaution against lateral strains, such as the blade of an axe undergoes, rather than against a mere thrust, such as that to which the head of a spear or lance is subject. Of course the stop-ridge is a preservative against the blade being driven back into its handle, in whatever way it is mounted. But the flanges, at first slight, then expanding at the middle of the blade, then becoming projecting wings, and finally being bent over, so as to form side sockets on each side of the blade, seem rather the result of successive endeavours to steady the blade against a sideways strain.

This development can best be traced in the series of flat celts, flanged and winged celts, and palstaves, discovered in the South of France.

Even the long narrow palstaves, which have so much the appearance of chisels, seem to have been mounted on crooked shafts. There is a long German § form with a narrow butt above the stop-ridge, and with but slight side flanges, which are con-

---

* "Allgemeine Culturwissenschaft," pl. i. fig. 186, p. 105.
† Strobel in *Bull. di Palet. Ital.*, Anno i. (1875), p. 7, Tav. i. ; Anno 4to (1878), p. 46 Tav. ii. ‡ Keller, " 7tor Bericht," Taf. xxiv. 17.
§ See Lindenschmit, " A. u. h. V.," vol. i., Heft. i. Taf. iv. 32.

tinued down along the sides of the blade below the ridge, that seems much more like a chisel than a hatchet. The usual length of this form is about 6 inches, and the width at the edge about 1½ inches, that of the butt-end, including the side flanches, being about ¾ inch. But that palstaves of this kind were mounted as hatchets will be evident from an inspection of Fig. 185, which represents a specimen in my own collection,

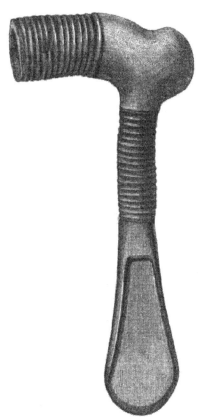

found in the district of Raron, near Brigue, Valais, Switzerland. It is, as will be seen, in fact, a socketed celt, but with the socket at right angles to the axis of the blade. The reason why it should have been cast in this manner is probably to be found in the fact that boughs of trees with a smaller branch at right angles to them are not easily met with, though such boughs are best adapted for conversion into the helves of this kind of hatchet. Some ingenious bronze-founder of old times conceived the idea of producing a hatchet which did not require a crooked helve, but for hafting which any ordinary straight stick would serve; and we have here his new form of axe-head. In practice, however, it was probably found both to balance badly, and to be expensive in metal, and the design appears not to have spread, as up to the present time this specimen seems to be unique. The most remarkable features in it have still to be noticed. The pattern from which it was cast seems to have been a palstave already mounted on its haft, and we have here the smooth and rounded end of the bough, with the smaller side branch running off at right angles, reproduced in bronze. Even the band by which the blade was secured in the cleft part of the handle is reproduced as

Fig. 185.—Raron, Brigue.   ½

a spiral moulding. The banding which extends to the mouth of the socket is also spiral, and probably represents a binding round the original wooden handle at the part where, from experience, it was found most liable to break. The straight haft of this hatchet was secured in its place by a bronze rivet passing through the socket from side to side, which is still in its place, though all trace of the wood has disappeared.

With this singular celt was found a small dagger, 6½ inches long, which had been secured to its hilt by four rivets, and a penannular bracelet decorated with ring ornaments. It is remarkable how well the discovery of this form of celt bears out the theoretical suggestions of Sir Joseph Banks,[*] Sir Samuel Meyrick,[†] Mr. Dunoyer,[‡] and others, including Sir W. Wilde.[§] Indeed, Dr. Richard Richardson[‖] many years ago advanced the same opinion as to the manner in which such celts were hafted.

With regard to the usual manner of mounting those of the socketed form there can be but little doubt, as in some few instances the original handles have been preserved with them.

Fig. 186.—Edenderry.   ⅛

One such, found in the bed of the river Boyne, near Edenderry, King's County, has been figured by Wilde,[¶] whose cut, by the kind permission of the Royal Irish Academy, is here reproduced as Fig. 186. The helve is only 13¾ inches long, but seems well adapted to the size of the blade. So far as I know this is the only instance of such a discovery within the United Kingdom.

In Fig. 187, however, is shown an Italian socketed celt of a common form, with the original handle still attached. This specimen is in my own collection, and was found about the year 1872 in the neighbourhood of Chiusi, Tuscany. With it were another, also retaining its handle, a large *fibula* of silver, a scarabæus, and many small square plates of bronze, each having a fylfot

---

[*] *Arch.*, vol. xix. p. 102, pl. viii. 6.
[†] "Ancient Armour," by Skelton, vol. i. pl. xlvii.
[‡] *Arch. Journ.*, vol. iv. p. 4.   [§] "Catal. Mus. R. I. A.," p. 367.
[‖] Leland's Itin., Hearne's ed., vol. i. p. 145.   [¶] P. 370, fig. 257.

cross upon it, probably the ornaments of a girdle. All these objects had been buried in an urn, which was covered by a slab of stone, and most of them are to be seen in the Etruscan Museum at Florence. With the exception of a fracture not far from the angle, the handle of my specimen is perfect. The preservation is due to its having been entirely coated with thin plates of bronze, the sides of which overlap, and have been secured round the handle by

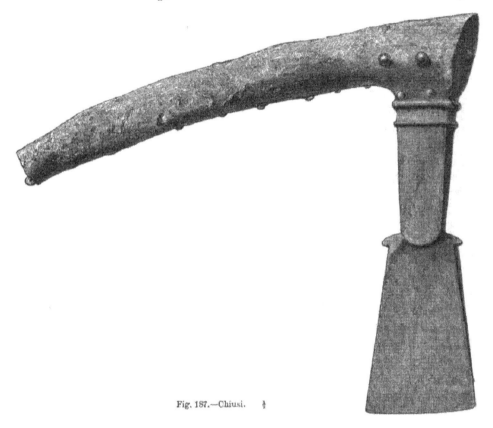

Fig. 187.—Chiusi.   ½

round-headed nails about ¾ inch apart. This plating is turned over square at the end of the handle, where there is a little pro-jecting bronze eye, through which a ring may have passed, so as to serve for its suspension. At the sides above the celt there are some larger round-headed nails, or possibly rivets; and the end of the branch which goes into the socket appears to be secured by a rivet, which passes through from face to face. At the end of the handle itself, above the celt, is a nearly circular flat bronze plate, with a round-headed nail in the middle to attach it to the wood. The fracture exposes the wood inside the plates, which has been preserved by the salts, or oxide, of copper. It has been thought to be oak. On the blade of the celt are some flakes of oxide of iron, as if it had lain in contact with some articles made of that metal. Indeed, from the form, as well as from the objects found with it, the presumption is that this instrument belongs to quite the end of the Bronze Age of Italy, or to the transitional period between bronze and iron.

It may be well here to mention that celts of iron of the flat form, with projections at the sides like Fig. 45; of the palstave kind, with the semicircular side sockets; and of the socketed form, have been found in the cemetery at Hallstatt, in Austria, the researches in which of Herr Ramsauer have been described by Baron Von Sacken.[*] These discoveries seem to show that all three varieties were still in use at the close of the Bronze Period. In the same cemetery celts of the two last-mentioned forms were found in bronze, and palstaves occurred with the wings formed of bronze and the blade of iron.

In 1866 I exhumed from this cemetery with my own hands, when in company with Sir John Lubbock, a socketed celt of iron, with a portion of the haft still in it. The celt is attached to a branch of the main handle, which projects at an angle of about 80°. This has been split off from the handle, only a small part of which remains attached; and it is this portion only of the wood which has been preserved by the infiltration of some salts of iron, while the rest, which was detached from contact with metal, has disappeared. The wood of which the handle was made appears to be fir. On an iron palstave from the same spot it seems to be oak. On two bronze palstaves from France in my own collection, one from Amiens and the other from the Seine, at Paris, the portions of wood which still remain attached to the blades appear also to be oak.

In the Hallstatt specimen the inclination of the blade seems to have been towards the hand, and the part of the handle beyond the branch which enters the socket presents some appearance of having been bound with an iron ferrule, probably with the view of preventing it from splitting. The projection is somewhat longer proportionally than that in Fig. 185, and the end appears to have been truncated, and not rounded.

[*] "Grabfeld von Hallst.," p. 38.

There have been in this country a few instances of the discovery of bronze rings in company with palstaves and socketed celts, and these rings may possibly have served a similar purpose, though it must be confessed that such an use is purely conjectural. That shown in Fig. 188 was found in company with a bronze palstave without a loop, but much like Fig. 74, at Winwick,* near Warring-

Fig. 188.—Winwick. ‡

ton, Lancashire, and was kindly lent me by Dr. James Kendrick, who in 1858 † suggested that it was a "sort of ferrule to put round the handle of the palstave to prevent the wood from splitting when the instrument was struck." The ornament on the ring, somewhat like the "broad arrow" of modern times, is of much the same character as the shield-like pattern below the stop-ridge of some palstaves. In the British Museum is a stone mould from Northumberland for flat rings, 3 inches in diameter, and for flat celts ; but such rings probably served some other purpose.

Another bronze ring, $1\frac{2}{3}$ inches in diameter, was found with a socketed celt in the Thames,‡ opposite Somerset House, but here the actual association of the two is doubtful.

I have already expressed a doubt whether the celt from Tadcaster, Yorkshire, and now in the British Museum, had, when found, the bronze ring with a jet bead upon it passing through the loop. The ring itself is made not of one continuous piece of metal, but of stout wire, with the ends abutting against each other, and nothing would be easier for the workman who found the three objects than to pass the ring through the loop of the celt and the hole of the bead. I have myself received from Hungary two socketed celts, each having imperfect penannular bracelets passed through the loop in the same manner, though they certainly had no original connection with the celts. It is, however, but right to mention that in the British Museum is the upper part of a celt with an octagonal neck, found with other objects near Kensington, on the loop of which is a small ring, barely large enough to encircle the loop. Of what service this could have been it is difficult to imagine.

If the association of the larger rings and the celts must be given up, it is needless to cite the opinions which have been held

---

* *Arch. Assoc. Journ.*, vol. xv. pl. xxv. p. 236 ; *Arch. Journ.*, vol. xviii. p. 159.
† *A. A. J.*, vol. xiv. p. 269.   ‡ *Arch. Journ.*, vol. x. p. 161.

as to the use of the one in connection with the other. Some references are given in the note.[*]

The early Iron Age of Denmark is no doubt considerably later in date than that of Hallstatt, but in several of the discoveries of objects of that period in Denmark socketed celts of iron have been found still attached to their helves. In the Nydam find, described by Mr. Conrad Engelhardt, the majority of the axes were of the ordinary form, with eyes for the shafts; but there were some also of the form of the socketed celt, though without any loops. These were mounted as axes, and not as adzes, on crooked handles about 17 inches long. The helves of axes of the ordinary form were from 23 to 32 inches in length. In the Vimose find [‡] there were several of these iron celts, one of which was thought to have been mounted on a crooked handle, but the others appear to have been mounted as chisels.

The palstaves with the edges transverse to the septum between the side flanges seem to have been mounted in precisely the same manner as those of the ordinary form, except that when attached to their handles they formed adzes, and not axes. It has been suggested [§] that the palstaves of the ordinary form may also have been mounted as adzes, and probably this was so in some exceptional cases. Mention has already been made of some Italian helves with transverse notches for the reception of the blade. Some of the flat celts may have also been mounted as adzes by binding them against the shorter end of an └-shaped handle, in the same manner as the Egyptians fixed their adze blades.

In some palstaves, but more especially in those of the South of Europe, there is at the butt-end of the blade a kind of dovetailed notch, which appears to have been formed by hammering over a part of the jets or runners of the original castings, which were left projecting a short distance instead of being broken off short at the blade. Whether the hammering over was for the purpose of rounding the angles or for that of forming this dovetailed notch is somewhat uncertain; it is, however, possible that one or more pins or rivets may have been driven through the handle, so as to catch the dovetails and retain the blade in its place. It is not often the case that this portion of the blade is so

---

[*] *Arch.*, vol. xvi. p. 362; *Arch. Journ.*, vol. iv. p. 6; Klemm, "Allg. Kult. gesch.," p. 107.

[†] "Nydam Mosefund," 1859—1863. Copenhagen, 1865.

[‡] "Vimose Fundet" af C. Engelhardt, 1869, p. 29.

[§] Westropp in *Proc. Soc. Ant.*, 2nd S., vol. v. p. 335.

long that it would have gone through the handle and have allowed
of a pin beyond it, as suggested by Mr. Dunoyer * in the case of
a long palstave, with a rivet-hole near the butt-end of the blade.
A palstave, found in a tomb in the department of Loir et Cher,†
by my friend the late Abbé Bourgeois, is provided with a rivet-
hole near the top, countersunk on either side so as to guide a
pin into the place intended for it; and it seems probable, as the
Abbé suggests, that this was connected with the securing of the
blade, which is destitute of a loop, to the helve.   Of six thin flat
bronze celts, 7 or 8 inches long, from the Island of Thermia,‡ or
Cythnos, in the Greek Archipelago, which are now in the British
Museum, three that are broad are provided with square or
lozenge-shaped holes towards the upper end of the blade, and
three that are narrower are without.   A flanged celt from Italy,§
6 inches long, has a circular hole in the same position, which
may have received a pin.   Some contrivance for keeping blades
of smooth bronze fast in their handles must have been necessary or desirable from the earliest times.   With stone celts we
often find that the butt-end destined to be let into the wooden
or horn socket was purposely roughened.   With bronze, however, such a process does not seem to have been adopted to
any extent; and probably with blades of bronze, so much less
tapering than those of stone, the difficulty of keeping them in
place was surmounted by attaching them with some sort of
resinous or pitchy cement.   A safe remedy against slipping out
was no doubt found in the addition of the ring or loop to the
side, which there can be but little doubt served for a cord to pass
through, so as to hold the blade back to the handle.   In a socketed
celt, 5¼ inches long, found in the Seine, at Paris, and now in my
own collection, not only is the wood preserved in the socket by
saturation with some salt of copper, but within the upper part of
the loop there are distinct traces of a cord which was apparently
formed of vegetable fibre.   The Irish palstave, Fig. 105, with the
curved projection instead of the usual loop, seems to show that it was
only against the upper part of the loop that the strain came.   No
doubt, however, there was more strength in the loop attached to
the blade at both ends than in the mere neb or projection.   Some
Italian socketed celts have similar projecting nebs, one on either
side.   In the case of the palstaves and celts with two loops, it

* Arch. Journ., vol. iv. p. 4, fig. B.   † Revue Arch., vol. xxix. p. 73, pl. iii. 2.
‡ Proc. Soc. Ant., 2nd S., vol. iii. p. 436.   § Arch. Journ., vol. xxi. p. 100.

seems probable that the handle must have been somewhat prolonged beyond the side branch, which received the palstave or went into the socket of the celt.

It has been stated that some of the Spanish palstaves[*] with two loops were, when first discovered, attached to a straight-handle of wood. But this opinion may have been formed from the grain of the wood impressed on the upper part of the blade running along and not across it. In the first account[†] given of the discovery, these palstaves were regarded as having been used for *picking* out the strata of coal, and one of them is said to have been firmly attached to a wooden handle by means of thongs interlaced and held by notches in the wood. This handle was described as having been straight, so that the instrument was fitted to be used as a crowbar and not as a hatchet. But inasmuch as the groove for the handle is only $2\frac{1}{4}$ inches long and $\frac{1}{2}$ inch wide, while the length of the blade projecting beyond the handle is nearly 5 inches, it is almost impossible for it to have served in this manner.

Axe-heads of bronze of the modern form with an eye through them to receive a straight helve have not been found in this country, though, as already observed, they are not uncommon in Hungary, Southern Germany, and Italy. That the form was already known in Greece in the Homeric Age is evident from the feat of skill in shooting an arrow through the shaft holes of a number of axe-heads, arranged in a row, recorded in the Odyssey.[‡] I have in my collection a fine double-edged axe, or πέλεκυς, from Greece, $8\frac{1}{2}$ inches in length, with a round shaft-hole $\frac{7}{8}$ inch in diameter. I have also two from Salamis.

Looking at the widespread distribution of perforated stone implements, especially battle-axes, throughout Europe, it seems strange that so few bronze weapons of the same class should be found. Possibly, however, these stone weapons may have remained in use even until the latter part of the Bronze Period, as they certainly did through the earlier part of it. In this country it seems doubtful whether any of the perforated battle-axes of stone belong to a time when bronze was absolutely unknown, as bronze knife-daggers, like Fig. 279, have so often been found associated with them in interments. Hungary is the country in which the perforated bronze battle-axes seem to have arrived at

---

* *Arch. Journ.*, vol. vi. p. 369. † *Arch. Journ.*, vol. vi. p. 69.
‡ Lib. xix. v. 573. See also Lib. v. v. 235.

M

their fullest development, many of them being of graceful form and beautiful workmanship. The perforated copper implements of that country were probably used for agricultural purposes, and I see no reason for assigning them to so early a date as the commencement of the Bronze Period of Hungary. They may, indeed, belong to a much later period. It is hard to account for this absence of perforated axes of bronze in Britain, but various causes seem to have conduced to render their introduction difficult. When first bronze came into use it must have been extremely scarce and valuable; and to cast an axe-head in bronze, like one of the perforated axe-hammers of stone, would have required not only a considerably greater amount of the then precious metal than was required for a flat hatchet-head, but would also have involved a far higher skill in the art of casting. Moreover, the flat form of these simple blades rendered them well adapted for being readily drawn out to a sharp cutting edge, and when once they had come into general use they would not have been readily superseded by those of another form, hafted in a different method, even were that method more simple. If the bronze celts were mainly in use for peaceful industries, while the warlike battle-axes were made of stone, the progressive modifications in the shape of the former would be less likely to be affected by the characteristics of the latter. It must also be remembered that in France,* which then as now set the fashion to Britain, perforated axe-heads of stone were very seldom used, and those of bronze were in the north of the country unknown.

But, to return to the celts of the British Islands, there can, I think, be but little doubt that the loop is, as already described, connected with the method of mounting these instruments on their hafts; and is not intended for the attachment of a cord, by which they might be withdrawn and recovered after they had been thrown at the enemy. Like the American tomahawks, they may, no doubt, have occasionally been used as "missile hatchets," the "missiles secures" of Sidonius;† but the days of young Sigimer, whose followers were provided with these weapons, are many centuries more recent than those to which the bronze celts must be referred.

In the same manner, any idea of the loops having merely served

* While speaking of French celts, I may refer to a short Paper on the method in which they were hafted, written by the late M. Penguilly-l'Haridon.—*Rev. Arch.*, 2nd S. vol. iv. p. 329.

† Ep. 20, lib. 4. See *Arch.*, vol. xxx. p. 492.

for hanging these instruments at the girdle may be at once discarded. For such a purpose the projection which we find substituted for the loop would be useless, and the presence of two loops would be superfluous.

On the whole, we may conclude that the majority of these instruments were mounted for use, somewhat in the manner described, so as to serve as axes or adzes. A smaller proportion of them may, however, not improbably have been provided with short straight handles, to serve as chisels, especially the socketed celts of small size and without loops. This is the more probable as several socketed instruments closely resembling them in character cannot be regarded as other than chisels and gouges. No example, however, of a socketed celt provided with a handle of this kind has as yet been found. The little instrument of brass fixed into a handle made of stag's horn, which was found in a cist in a barrow at Everley,[*] Wilts, by Sir R. Colt Hoare, has more the appearance of being a tanged chisel, such as will subsequently be described, than a flat celt. It is shown full size in Fig. 189, which I have copied from Sir R. C. Hoare's plate. There were no bones or ashes found in the cist, but several pointed instruments, and what appears to be a kind of long, flat bead of bone, as well as two whetstones of freestone, and a hone of a blueish colour had been deposited with it.

Fig. 189.—Everley. ¼

Professor Worsaae [†] has published an engraving of a narrow Danish palstave, which was found in a hill in Jutland fastened to its handle by three rings of leather. This handle was straight, but unlike that from Store Hedinage, which was an ell and a quarter long, was not more than about 8 inches in length. In some other instances, he says, the blade has been fastened to the handle by nails or rivets.

I have already mentioned that some of the socketed celts of iron belonging to the early Iron Age of Denmark have been found

* "Anc. Wilts," vol. i. p. 182, pl. xxi.   † "Prim. Ant. of Denmark," p. 26.

mounted as chisels. A good example of one thus hafted has been figured by Engelhardt.* The part of the handle which goes into the socket is tapered to fit it. Above this the handle expands with a shoulder projecting somewhat beyond the outside of the celt. It continues of this size for about 1½ inches, and is then again reduced to the same size as the mouth of the celt. The whole of the handle beyond the metal is about 4 inches in length.

Having said thus much with regard to the early iron chisels, it will, however, now be well to proceed to the consideration of those formed of bronze, and of the other bronze tools found in this country.

* " Vimose Mosefundet," p. 28.

CHAPTER VII.

CHISELS, GOUGES, HAMMERS, AND OTHER TOOLS.

ALTHOUGH, doubtless, many if not most of the instruments of different forms, described in the preceding chapters, were used as tools, and not as weapons, yet in some cases, especially where they have been found in graves, it is more probable that they formed part of the equipment of a warrior than of an artificer. With regard to the various forms of which I intend to treat in the present chapter, there can hardly exist a doubt that they should be regarded as tools, and not as weapons. Already in the Neolithic Period we find many of these forms of tools, such as chisels and gouges, developed; and so far as hammers are concerned, it seems probable that for many purposes a stone held in the hand may have served during the Bronze Period as a hammer or mallet, just as it often does now in the age of steel and steam. I have elsewhere* mentioned a fact communicated to me by the late Mr. David Forbes, F.R.S., that in Peru and Bolivia the masons, skilful in working hard stone with steel chisels, make use of no other mallet or hammer than a stone pebble held in the hand.

The simplest form of chisel is of course a short bar of metal brought to an edge at one end and left blunt at the other where it receives the blows of the hammer or mallet. Such at the present day are the ordinary chisels of the stone-mason, and the " cold chisel " of the engineer.

Most of the Scandinavian chisels of flint are of nearly the same form as the simplest metal chisels, being square in section in the upper part and gradually tapering to an edge at the lower end. Bronze chisels of this form are, however, but rarely met with in any part of Europe. One such, however, was found at Plymstock,†

---

* "Anc. Stone Imp.," p. 207.

† See *Arch. Journ.*, vol. xxvi. p. 346. I am indebted to Mr. A. W. Franks, F.R.S. for the use of this cut.

near Oreston, Devonshire, in company with sixteen flanged celts like Figs. 9 and 10, three daggers, and a tanged spear-head, engraved as Fig. 327. It is shown in Fig. 190. Its length is 4 inches, and the cutting edge is rather more than ¼ inch in width. The late Mr. Albert Way, who describes this specimen in the *Archæological Journal*, regarded it as unique in England; and the form, so far as I am aware, has not again been found in this country. It is now in the British Museum.

I have a large chisel of the same type, but apparently formed of copper, which was found in the neighbourhood of Pressburg, Hungary. It is

Fig. 190. Fig. 191. Fig. 192.
Plymstock. ⅓ Heathery Burn. ⅓ Glenluce. ⅓

7½ inches long, about ⅓ inch square in the middle, and expands in width at the edge, which is lunate. Others of the same form, 4½ inches and 5¾ inches long, also from Hungary, are in the Zurich Museum. Such chisels have also been found in the Swiss Lake-dwellings.

A long chisel, formed from a plain square bar drawn to an edge, was found by Dr. Schliemann[*] in his excavations at Hissarlik.

Bronze chisels of the same form were also in use among the ancient Egyptians.

A smaller chisel, conical at the butt end and possibly intended for insertion into a handle, is shown in Fig. 191. The original is in the collection of Canon Greenwell, F.R.S., and was found with numerous other bronze antiquities in the Heathery Burn Cave, Durham, already so often mentioned. One rather larger, about 3 inches long and ¼ inch broad, probably found in one of the barrows at Lake[†] or Durnford, is in the collection of the Rev. E. Duke, of Lake House, near Salisbury. It may possibly have been a large awl.

An Aztec[‡] chisel of nearly the same form as Fig. 191, and about 4½ inches long, contains 97·87 copper and 2·13 of tin. Another from Lima contains 94 copper and 6 of tin.

The small bronze chisel from Scotland, shown in Fig. 192, exhibits a somewhat different type; the blade tapering evenly away from the edge. The point which was intended to go into the handle appears to have been "drawn down" a little by hammering, which has produced slight flanges

[*] "Troy and its Remains," p. 332. [†] *Arch.*, vol. xliii. p. 467.
[‡] "Anales del Museo de Mexico," vol. i. p. 117.

at the sides. The edge has also been hammered. The original was kindly lent me by the Rev. George Wilson, of Glenluce, Wigtonshire, and was found, with a conical button and a flat plate of cannel-coal or jet, on the Sandhills of Low Torrs, near Glenluce. Numerous arrow-heads and flakes of flint have also been found among the sands at the same place.

A flat chisel (4¼ inches) like Fig. 192, but rather broader at the edge, which is somewhat oblique, was found with two flat sickles on Sparkford Hill,* Somersetshire.

There were some small chisels of this class in the Larnaud hoard† (Jura).

Others have been found in the Swiss Lake-dwellings.‡

Two shorter edged tools, found at Ebnall,§ Salop, which have been described as chisels or hammers, seem rather to have been punches, and will be mentioned subsequently.

As chisels were probably used in ancient times, as at present, not only in conjunction with a mallet, but also in the hand alone with pressure as paring-tools, it would have been found convenient to attach them to wooden or horn handles. Accordingly we find them both provided with a tang or shank for driving into a wooden handle, like the majority of modern chisels, and also, though more rarely, with a socket for the reception of a handle, like the heavy mortising chisels of the present day. Chisels of the tanged variety vary considerably in size and strength, and in the relative width of the blade to the length.

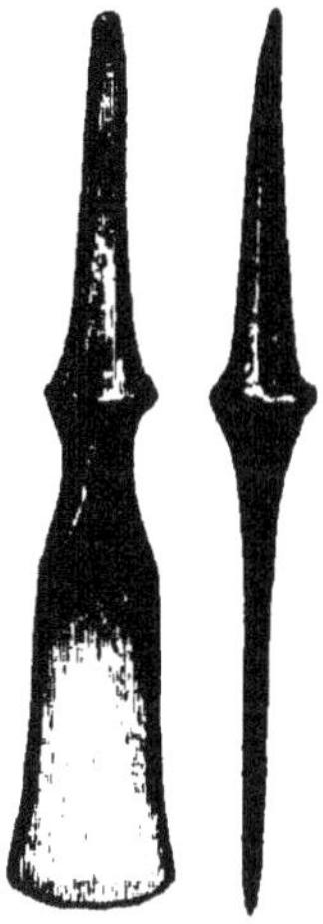

That shown in Fig. 192* is from the great hoard discovered at Carlton Rode,‖ Norfolk, already mentioned, and is preserved in the Norwich Museum. The marks of the joint of the mould are still visible on the tang. It was found with numerous celts and gouges, a hammer, and at least one socketed chisel. Another tanged chisel of nearly the same form and dimensions is

Fig. 192*. Carlton Rode.

also in the Norwich Museum. It formed part of the Woodward Collection, and was probably found in Norfolk.

A chisel much more expanded at the edge, and also of lighter make, was found at Wallingford, Berks, in company with a double-edged knife or razor, and a socketed celt, gouge, and knife, of which notices are given in other parts of this book. It is engraved as Fig. 193, and is in my own collection, as is also the original of Fig. 194. This formed part of the hoard discovered in Reach Fen, Cambridge, and was the only one of the kind there found. A socketed chisel-like celt from the same hoard has been already described and figured at page 133, Fig. 159.

* Somerset Arch. and Nat. Hist. Proc., 1856—7, vol. vii. p. 27.
† Chantre, "Album," pl. xliii. ‡ Keller, 7ter Bericht, Taf. ix. 34, 35.
§ Arch. Journ., vol. xxii. p. 167; Proc. Soc. Ant., 2nd S., vol. iii. p. 66.
‖ Arch. Journ., vol. ii. p. 80; Arch. Assoc. Journ., vol. i. p. 59.

Tanged chisels have also occurred in various other hoards of bronze antiquities. Some were found with numerous celts and other tools at Westow,* on the Derwent, Yorkshire, which from their curved edges and general character the late Mr. James Yates regarded as the σμίλα χαρτο-τόμος, or chisel for cutting paper, mentioned by Philoxenus, and as the currier's chisel, σκυτοτόμος, mentioned by Julius Pollux. If I were to offer an opinion it would be that any cutting tool of the Bronze Period in Britain was more likely to have been used for cutting leather than paper, the latter commodity being, to say the least of it, scarce in Britain at that time; and, moreover, that chisels are generally used for cutting wood and not leather.

In the collection of Canon Greenwell, F.R.S., are two of these tanged chisels from Westow, about 4½ inches long and 1⅛ inch broad at the edge. A small part of the blade below the round collar is cylindrical. In the British Museum is a small specimen of this kind (3¼ inches) from the Thames.

Fig. 193.—Wallingford.   ½   Fig. 194.—Reach Fen.   ½   Fig. 195.—Thixendale.   ½

In the Mayer Collection at Liverpool is a specimen, 4 inches long and ⅞ inch broad at the edge, found near Canterbury in 1761. The collar is flat above and almost hemispherical below. Another, with part of the tang broken off, and the blade 2¼ inches long and 1½ inch wide, was found in the Kirkhead Cave, Ulverstone, Lancashire, and was described to me by Mr. H. Ecroyd Smith.

Another, rather like Fig. 199, but broken at the angles, was found with spear-heads and a socketed celt at Ty Mawr,† Anglesea. What appears to be a chisel of this kind (4¾ inches long) was found near Biggen Grange,‡ Derbyshire, and is in the Bateman Collection. Another was found at Porkington,§ Shropshire.

A fragment of a tanged chisel was found with a large hoard of broad spear-heads, &c., at Broadward, Shropshire.

A remarkably small specimen from Thixendale, in the East Riding of Yorkshire, is in the collection of Canon Greenwell, who has kindly allowed me to engrave it as Fig. 195. The stop, instead of being as usual

* *Arch. Journ.*, vol. vi. p. 381, 408; *Arch. Assoc. Journ.*, vol. iii. p. 58.
† *Arch. Journ.*, vol. xxiv. p. 253.
‡ Bateman's "Catalogue," p. 74, No. 8; "Vest. Ant. Derb.," p. 8.
§ *Arch. Journ.*, vol. vii. p. 195.

a circular collar, consists of a bead on each face, so that in the side view it appears as if an oval pin traversed the blade.

Nearly similar side-stops are to be observed in the chisel represented in Fig. 196, which was found with two others (3¾ inches and 4½ inches) in a hoard of bronze antiquities at Yattendon,* Berks, of which I have given an account elsewhere. With the chisels were instruments of the following forms, some in a fragmentary condition: flat celts, palstaves, socketed celts, gouges, socketed and tanged knives, swords, scabbard

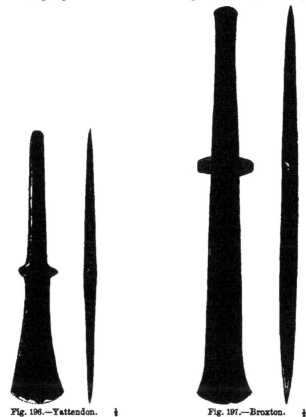

Fig. 196.—Yattendon.   ½   Fig. 197.—Broxton.   ½

ends, spear-heads, and flat, conical, and annular pieces of bronze. The other two chisels from this hoard were more like Fig. 194.

A very large example of a chisel of this kind is shown in Fig. 197, the original of which was kindly lent me by Sir Philip de M. Grey Egerton, F.R.S. It was found in company with two looped palstaves and a spear-head near Broxton, Cheshire, about twelve miles south of Chester.

An instrument of somewhat the same character, from Farley Heath, has already been described at p. 69.

A tanged chisel, 5 inches long, and without any stops or collar, was found with other objects at Burgesses' Meadow, Oxford, in 1830, and is now in the Ashmolean Museum.

* *Proc. Soc. Ant.*, 2nd S., vol. vii. p. 480.

This form of instrument occurs but rarely in Scotland; but what appears to be a chisel of this kind is engraved by Wilson.[*] His figure is, however, a mere diagram, without any scale attached, and the instrument is described as an axe blade with a cross limb, or as a "spiked axe." Whatever its character, the original of the figure is said to have been found with other bronze relics at Strachur, Argyleshire.

An example of a chisel of elongated form is in the Antiquarian Museum[†] at Edinburgh, but it is uncertain in what part of Scotland it was found. By the kindness of the Council of the Society of Antiquaries of Scotland it is shown as Fig. 198.

Fig. 198.—Scotland.   ⅓   Fig. 199.—Ireland.   ⅓

In Ireland they are much more common. There are thirteen specimens in the Museum of the Royal Irish Academy, as catalogued by the late Sir William Wilde,[‡] varying in length from 2⅓ to 6¼ inches. Some of these Irish chisels, which approximate to flat celts in character, have already been described in Chapter III.

That which Wilde has given as his Fig. 395 is almost identical in form with the chisel from Ireland in my own collection which is here engraved as Fig. 199, though considerably longer altogether, and somewhat longer proportionally in the tang.

I have another example from Belaghey, County Antrim, which is 6⅜ inches long, and much stouter in the tang and in the neck of the blade than that here figured. It is only 1⅜ inches wide at the edge.

* "Preh. Ann. of Scot.," vol. i. p. 381, fig. 54.
† *Proc. Soc. Ant. Scot.*, vol. xii. p. 613.   ‡ "Catal. Mus. R. I. A.," p. 520.

Among those in the museum at Dublin is one which is decorated with knobs round the collar. Two others are figured in "Horæ Ferales." * In the British Museum is one (4⅝ inches) with a well-marked collar. Another, with the square tang broken off, has a loop at the side of the round part of the blade, which is 2¼ inches long. This curious specimen was found near Burrisokane, county Tipperary.

Another chisel (4¾ inches) in the same collection has side-projections only, like Fig. 195.

Another (3¼ inches), with a well-developed collar, is engraved in the *Archæological Journal.*† The form shades off into that of the flat celts having projections at the sides.

Others in the collection of Mr. Robert Day, F.S.A., resemble Fig. 196 (4⅛ inches) and Fig. 197 (6 inches). The latter was found at Kanturk, Co. Cork.

Tanged chisels have been found, though not abundantly, in France. One from Beauvais is in the museum at St. Germain.

The socketed form of chisel is by no means common in this country; but some instruments, probably intended for use as chisels, have already been described among the socketed celts not provided with loops. These are all comparatively broad at the cutting edge; but there is another variety, with a narrow end, formed much like the modern engineer's "cross-cut chisel," some specimens of which will be now described.

Fig. 200.
Carlton Rode. ½

That shown in Fig. 200 is from the great find of Carlton Rode,‡ Norfolk (1844), from which several specimens, including a tanged chisel (Fig. 192*) and a socketed celt without loop (Fig. 160), have already been described; and some other forms, such as gouges and hammers, have yet to be mentioned. The edge is only $\frac{3}{16}$ths of an inch in width, and the tool seems well adapted for cutting mortises. The idea of a mortise and tenon must be of very early date, as a mere stake driven into the ground supplies it in a rudimentary form; and tools let into sockets, or having sockets to receive handles, afford instances of connections of the same kind. In our modern mortising chisels the cutting edge, instead of being in the middle of the blade, so as to have a V-shaped section, is usually at the side, and presents an outline like the upper part of a K, V. I have not met with this bevelled edge among bronze chisels.

On the side of this Carlton Rode chisel may be seen the mark of the joint of the mould in which it was cast. The socket, as usual with these tools, is circular.

A bronze chisel of the same form. 3¾ inches long, was found at Romford,[*] Essex, in company with socketed celts, palstaves, fragments of swords, a broken spear-head, and lumps of metal. It has already been figured.

In the hoard found at Westow, Yorkshire, already mentioned, were two or three socketed chisels. One of them, 2¼ inches long, is engraved in the *Archæological Journal*.[†] That which I have here engraved as Fig. 201 is probably the same specimen. It is now in the collection of Canon Greenwell, F.R.S. Tanged chisels, gouges, and socketed celts were found at the same time.

In the same collection is a somewhat smaller chisel, the socket of which is square instead of circular. This was found in the Heathery Burn Cave,

Fig. 201.   Fig. 202.
Westow. ⅓   Heathery Burn. ⅓

Durham, together with a number of objects, belonging to the Bronze Period, of which further mention will be made hereafter. Another, found at Roseberry Topping, Yorkshire, is now in the Bateman Collection, at Sheffield. A small narrow-edged chisel was found in a hoard at Meldreth, Cambridgeshire.

I am not aware of any socketed chisels of the narrow form having been found in Scotland.

In Ireland they are rare, but in the collection of Mr. R. Day, F.S.A., are a few specimens of undoubtedly chisel-like character. The broad celt-like form has been described in a previous chapter.

In France they are also far from common. There are, however, two in the museum at Tours, found at the Chatellier d'Amboise. There is also one in the museum at Narbonne.[‡] They have been found in Savoy,[§] Doubs,[||] and Jura.[¶]

Several have been found in the Lake-dwellings of Switzerland.[**] One with a treble moulding round the mouth and a polygonal neck from Mœrigen[††] exhibits much taste in its manufacture.

A number of chisels both of the tanged and the socketed forms were present in the great hoard of bronze objects discovered at Bologna.

Socketed examples from Italy are in the museum at Copenhagen,[‡‡] and in the British Museum.

* *Arch. Journ.*, vol. ix. p. 303.
† *Arch. Journ.*, vol. vi. p. 382. See also *Arch. Assoc. Journ.*, vol. iii. p. 58, fig. 4.
‡ "Matériaux," vol. v. pl. ii. 12.
§ *Exp. Arch. de Savoie*, 1878, pl. xxi. No. 3; pl. vi. 215, 216 ; Perrin, "Et. Préh. de la Sav.," pl. x. 8.
|| Chantre, "Album," pl. x. 7.   ¶ Ibid. No. 5.
** Keller, 6ter Bericht, Taf. ix. 38; 7ter Ber., Taf. vii. 2, 3, 5, &c.; Desor, "Les Palafittes," fig. 46.
†† Desor and Favre, "Le Bel Age du Br.," pl. i. 7.
‡‡ "Cong. Préh.," Copenhagen vol. p. 485.

I have some from Macarsca, Dalmatia, of which the sockets have been formed by hammering out the metal and turning it over, instead of being produced as usual, by means of a core in the casting.

Socketed chisels from Emmen and Deurne, Holland, are in the museum* at Leyden.

From North Germany I may cite one (6¼ inches) from Schlieben,† which is in the Berlin Museum.

Others are engraved by Lindenschmit,‡ Schreiber,§ and Lisch.‖

One from Kempten, Bavaria, is in the Sigmaringen Collection.¶

GOUGES.

Closely allied to chisels are gouges, in which the edge, instead of being straight, is curved or hollowed, so that it is adapted for working out rounded or oval holes. In some languages, indeed, the name by which these tools are known is that of " hollow chisels." It is an early form of instrument, and a few specimens made of flint have been found in this country, though they are here extremely rare, while, on the contrary, they are very abundant in Denmark and the South of Sweden. In the Scandinavian countries, however, bronze gouges are never found; and though gouges of stone were not unknown in this country during its Stone Period, their successors in bronze do not appear to belong to the early part of the Bronze Period, but, on the contrary, seem to be characteristic of its later phases.

Of bronze gouges there are the same two varieties as of the ordinary chisel, viz. the tanged and the socketed, of which the former is far rarer than the latter. Indeed the only tanged gouge from Britain with which I am acquainted is that from the Carlton Rode** hoard, already so often mentioned, which is shown in Fig. 203. The original is in the Norwich Museum, the trustees of which kindly allowed me to engrave it. As will be seen, it is of remarkably narrow form, especially as contrasted with the socketed gouge from the same hoard shown in Fig. 207. There was a broken tanged gouge in the great hoard of bronze objects found at Bologna.

Fig. 203.
Carlton
Rode. ½

* Jannsen's "Catal.," No. 21.
† Schreiber, "Die ehern. Streitkeile," Taf. ii. 11.
‡ "Alt. u. h. Vorz.," vol. i. Heft v. Taf. iii.   § Taf. ii. 10.
‖ "Freder. Francisc.," Tab. xxxiii. 5.   ¶ Lindenschmit, Taf. xlii. 7.
** Arch. Journ., vol. ii. p. 80; Arch. Assoc. Journ., vol. i. p. 51, 59; " Horæ Ferales," pl. v. 42.

Of English socketed gouges the most common form is that shown in Fig. 204, from an original in the British Museum, which was found with a spear-head (Fig. 391), socketed knife (Fig. 240), hammer (Fig. 210), awl (Fig. 224), and two socketed celts, at Thorndon,[*] in Suffolk. There were six gouges of the same character, but of different sizes, in the hoard found at Westow,[†] Yorkshire, some of which have been figured. Another (3¼ inches) found with socketed celts and some curious ornaments under a large stone at Roseberry Topping,[‡] in Cleveland, has also been figured. Another was found with socketed celts and spear-heads at Exning,[§] in Suffolk. The cutting end of another was associated with socketed celts in the hoard discovered at Martlesham in the same county. Part of another was discovered, with a socketed celt, fragments of blades, and rough copper, at Melbourn,[||] Cambridgeshire. Another was found, with socketed celts, spear-heads, and an armlet, within the encampment on Beacon Hill,[¶] Charnwood Forest, Leicestershire. Another, with

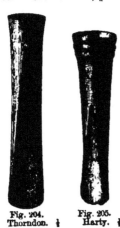

socketed celts, spear-heads, &c., at Ebnall,[**] near Oswestry; and another (2¼ inches), with socketed celts, fragments of knives, a button or stud, and lumps of metal, at Kensington.[††] This hoard is in the British Museum. A gouge was found with four socketed celts and about 30 lbs. of rough copper in an urn at Sittingbourne,[‡‡] Kent. A plain gouge formed part of the hoard found at Stanhope,[§§] Durham. A remarkably fine gouge, 4¼ inches long and nearly 1¼ inch wide at the edge, was found, with spear-heads, socketed celts, part of a celt mould, and lumps of metal, at Beddington,[||||] Surrey. At Porkington,[¶¶] Shropshire, a gouge accompanied the tanged chisel lately mentioned. In the hoard found at Guilsfield,[***] Montgomeryshire, there were two gouges in company with looped palstaves, socketed celts, &c. In my own collection are three socketed gouges, about 3¼ inches long, which form part of the hoard from Reach Fen, Cambridgeshire, in which were socketed celts, socketed and tanged knives, and numerous other objects. In some of the instances cited, as at Guilsfield and Ebnall, the upper part of the socket is beaded instead of plain. One of this kind from the Harty hoard already mentioned is shown in Fig. 205. There were two such in the hoard, which comprised numerous socketed celts and the moulds for them, and various tools of the bronze-founder. There were also the two halves of a bronze mould for such gouges which will subsequently be described. In the Museum of the Cambridge Antiquarian Society is a

Fig. 204.   Fig. 205.
Thorndon. ¼   Harty. ¼

---

* *Arch. Journ.*, vol. x. p. 3; "Horæ. Fer.," pl. v. 36.

† *Arch. Journ.*, vol. vi. p. 381, 408; *Arch. Assoc. Journ.*, vol. iii. p. 58.

‡ *Arch. Scot.*, vol. iv. p. 55, pl. vii. 5; *Arch. Æliana*, vol. ii. p. 213, pl. iv. c.

§ *Arch. Journ.*, vol. x. p. 3. || *Arch. Journ.*, vol. xi. p. 294.

¶ *Proc. Soc. Ant.*, vol. iv. p. 323.

** *Arch. Journ.*, vol. xxii. p. 167; "Horæ Ferales," pl. v. 35.

†† *Proc. Soc. Ant.*, 2nd S., vol. iii. p. 232.

‡‡ Smith's "Coll. Ant.," vol. i. p. 101; *Arch. Journ.*, vol. ii. p. 81.

§§ *Arch. Æliana*, vol. i. p. 13, pl. ii. 12.

|||| "Surrey Arch. Soc. Coll.," vol. vi.   ¶¶ *Arch. Journ.*, vol. vii. p. 195.

*** *Arch. Camb.*, 3rd S., vol. x. p. 214; "Montgom. Coll.," vol. iii. p. 437.

gouge from Bottisham Lode (3 inches) with a slight shoulder about ½ inch from the top of the blade, the upper part of the neck being larger than the lower. One of three found in the Heathery Burn Cave (2¾ inches) is also shouldered. Of the other two (3⅝ inches and 3¼ inches) one is very slightly shouldered. They are in the collection of Canon Greenwell, F.R.S., as is also a plain example (3¾ inches) from Scothorn, Lincolnshire.

In the British Museum are the unfinished castings for two gouges, one 2¾ inches long and fully ½ inch wide, and the other 3 inches long and ⅜ inch wide at the edge, which in both is but slightly hollowed. They were found with a socketed celt (Fig. 146) near Blandford, Dorset. The longer one is of very white and hard bronze.

Two gouges, one 3⅛ inches and the other broader, but only 2 inches long, found with various other objects at Hounslow; as well as one from the Thames at Battersea (4 inches), are in the same collection.

Two gouges (3¼ inches and 5 inches) were found, with a hammer, a spear-head, and a socketed celt with a loop on the face (Fig. 154), near Whittlesea. The whole are in the museum at Wisbech.

Two from Derbyshire are in the Blackmore Museum at Salisbury.

A socketed gouge of unusually long proportions is shown in Fig. 206. It was found at Undley, near Lakenheath, Suffolk, and is in my own collection. In the Carlton Rode hoard were also two long gouges with the hollow extending more nearly to the socket end. They are both rather trumpet-mouthed. One of them is 4½ inches long and ₁₆⁹ inch wide at the edge, the other

Fig. 206. Fig. 207. Fig. 208.
Undley. ⅓ Carlton Rode. ⅓ Tay. ⅓

4¼ inches long and ¾ inch wide. I have not seen the originals, but describe them from a lithographed plate.

The broad short gouge shown in Fig. 207 is also from Carlton Rode. It is broken at the mouth of the socket, but I have, in the figure, restored the part that is wanting. The original was lent me by the trustees of the Norwich Museum. Another* from the same hoard, about 3¼ inches long, has the groove, which is wide and rather flat, extending only an inch upwards from the edge.

Socketed gouges have been found, though very rarely, in Scotland. That shown in Fig. 208, the cut of which has been kindly lent to me by the Society of Antiquaries of Scotland, was dredged up in the river Tay.†   This appears to be almost the only Scottish specimen

---

* "Horæ Ferales," pl. v. 39.   † Proc. Soc. Ant. Scot., vol. v. p. 127.

at present known. Professor Daniel Wilson[*] terms it " one of the rarest of the implements of bronze hitherto found in Scotland ;" but he adds that other specimens have been met with in the Tay.

In Ireland they are considerably more abundant, there being at least twenty specimens in the Museum of the Royal Irish Academy, one of them as much as 4½ inches long.

One, much like Fig. 208, has been engraved by Wilde as Fig. 399. Others are figured in the *Archæological Journal*[†] and "Horæ Ferales."[‡] In one of these, 2½ inches long, the hollow is carried up to the collar round the mouth as a square-ended recess. One gouge appears to have been originally tanged. Several socketed gouges from Ireland are in the British Museum. Mr. R. Day, F.S.A., has examples from Mullingar and Derry, the latter with a collar at the top. They occurred also in the Dowris hoard. A gouge[§] only 2½ inches long and unusually broad has a small loop at the upper end of the concave part. It is here engraved as Fig. 209, from the original in the Museum of the Royal Irish Academy. This may be the specimen figured by Vallancey.[||] I have a specimen like Fig 208.

Fig. 209.—Ireland. ½

Socketed gouges are occasionally found in France. One, 4¼ inches long, with two mouldings round the top, ornamented with faint diagonal lines, was found with socketed celts and other implements in the Commune de Pont-point ¶ (Oise), near the river Oise, and is in the Hotel Cluny, Paris. Others from the Hautes Alpes[**] and from the Fonderie de Larnaud have been figured in Mr. Ernest Chantre's magnificent Album.

There are three with moulded tops, from the hoard of Notre Dame d'Or, in the Poitiers Museum.

A fine gouge (about 5½ inches) with a moulded top is in the museum at Clermont Ferrand (Puy de Dôme). A very fine French gouge of this character is in the British Museum.

I have a specimen much like Fig. 208 found in the Seine at Paris. Others were in the hoard at Dreuil, near Amiens, and in a second hoard also found near that town.

Large gouges with moulded tops, from the Stations of Auvernier,[††] in the Lake of Neuchâtel, and Mœrigen, in the Lake of Bienne, are in Dr. Victor Gross's collection.

There was at least one socketed gouge in the great Bologna hoard.

In Germany they are very rare, but one from the museum at Sigmaringen, with a somewhat decorated socket, is engraved by Lindenschmit. It was found at Kempten, Bavaria.[‡‡] Others, from Düren and Deurne, North Brabant, Holland, are in the museum at Leyden.

* "Preh. Ann. Scot.," vol. i. p. 388.   † Vol. iv. p. 335, pl. iii. 1, 2, 3, 4.
‡ Pl. v. 37, 38, 41.   § "Horæ Ferales," pl. v. 38.
|| Vol. iv. pl. ix. 5.
¶ "Horæ Ferales," pl. v. 34; *Rev. Arch.*, N.S., vol. xiii. pl. ii. x.
** Pl. x. 6, and xl. 5. See also *Mém. Soc. Ant. Norm.*, 1828—9, pl. xvi. 16.
†† "Deux Stations Lacustres," pl. iv. 34. Keller, 7ter Bericht, Taf. vii. 4; Desor and Favre, "Le Bel Age du Br.," pl. i. 5.
‡‡ " Alt. u. h. Vorz.," Heft. v. Taf. iii. 9, 10; "Hohenzoll. Samml.," pl. xlii. 7.

A socketed gouge, with the edge turned to a sweep of about 1 inch radius, is in the museum at Agram, Croatia.

One from Siberia * has been figured by Worsaae.

HAMMERS AND ANVILS.

Another form of tool constructed with a socket to receive the handle in precisely the same manner as the socketed celts and gouges is the hammer. It is worthy of notice that, though perforated hammers formed of stone are comparatively abundant in this country, yet that instruments of the same kind in bronze are unknown. It is true that what looks like a perforated hammer, said to be of bronze, was found in Newport, Lincoln, and is engraved in the *Archæological Journal*,[†] but there is no evidence of its belonging to the same period as the ordinary tools formed of bronze ; and the suggestion that it may have been the extremity of a bell-clapper is, I think, not far from the truth. It is very probable that many of the perforated stone hammers belong to the Bronze Period of this country, as do doubtless most of the perforated stone battle-axes or axe-hammers; for in the early part of the Bronze Period it is likely that metal was far too valuable to be used for heavy tools and weapons, and even towards the close of the period it seems as if it was only the lighter kind of hammers which were formed of bronze. The heaviest I possess weighs only five ounces, and the lightest less than half that weight. As will subsequently be seen, it is possible that some of these instruments were of the nature of anvils rather than of hammers, but for the present it will be most convenient to speak of them under the latter name.

The most common form of hammer is that which is shown in Fig. 210, from an original in the British Museum found at Thorndon,[‡] Suffolk, in company with a spear-head, socketed gouge, socketed knife, and two socketed celts. The two hammer-like instruments engraved as Figs. 211 and 212 were found, with a number of socketed celts, moulds, &c.—in fact the whole stock-in-trade of an ancient bronze-founder—in the Isle of Harty, Sheppey, and are in my own collection. The larger of the two shows a considerable amount of wear at the end, which is somewhat "upset" by constant use. The smaller is more oxidized, so that the marks of use are less easily recognised. The metal of which

* *Mém. Soc. Ant. du Nord*, 1872—7, p. 118.   † Vol. xxvii. p. 142.
‡ *Arch. Journ.*, vol. x. p. 3; *Proc. Soc. Ant.*, 2nd S., vol. iii. p. 66, where it is engraved full size; "Horæ Ferales," pl. v. 33.

they are formed seems to contain a larger admixture of tin than is usual with the cutting tools; and I have noticed the same appearance in some other instances, so that even in early times the

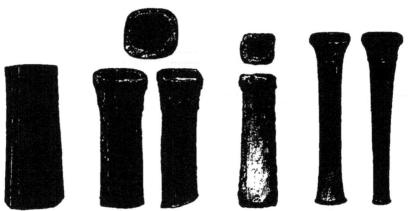

Fig. 210.—Thorndon. ½   Fig. 211.—Harty. ½   Fig. 212.—Harty. ½   Fig. 213.—Carlton Rode. ½

singular fact must have been known that by adding to copper the softer metal, tin, in a larger proportion than the one-tenth usually employed for bronze, a much harder metal resulted. At the present time the extremely hard alloy used for the specula of reflecting telescopes is formed by an admixture of about two parts of copper and one part of tin, the two soft metals mixed in these proportions forming an alloy almost as hard as hardened steel.

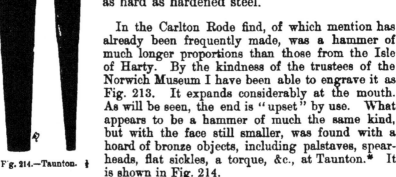

F'g. 214.—Taunton. ½

In the Carlton Rode find, of which mention has already been frequently made, was a hammer of much longer proportions than those from the Isle of Harty. By the kindness of the trustees of the Norwich Museum I have been able to engrave it as Fig. 213. It expands considerably at the mouth. As will be seen, the end is "upset" by use. What appears to be a hammer of much the same kind, but with the face still smaller, was found with a hoard of bronze objects, including palstaves, spear-heads, flat sickles, a torque, &c., at Taunton.* It is shown in Fig. 214.

A hammer somewhat larger in its dimensions than Fig. 211, but in type more resembling Fig. 212, having no shoulder upon its body, was found at Roseberry Topping,† in Cleveland, with a socketed celt, a gouge,

* Arch. Journ., vol. xxxvii. p. 94 ; Pring, "Brit. and Roman Taunton," pl. i. 2.
† Arch. Scot., vol. iv. p. 55, pl. vii. 4 ; Arch. Æliana, vol. ii. p. 213, pl. iv. b.

and other objects. Another broken hammer was found, with a hoard of bronze objects, at Stanhope,* Durham.

A small hammer (2¼ inches), found with gouges and other objects near Whittlesea, is in the Wisbech Museum.

Another with a circular socket was in the hoard found in Burgesses' Meadow, Oxford.

A small one was found at Rugby,† and is in the possession of Mr. M. H. Bloxam, F.S.A. I have one (3 inches) found near Cambridge.

I am not aware of any examples having as yet been found in Scotland.

In Ireland they are rare, but four "round-faced socketed punches," varying from 2 to 4 inches in length, are mentioned in Wilde's Catalogue. These are probably hammers.

In the British Museum are also several Irish hammers, one of which is shown full size in Fig. 215, for the use of which I am indebted to the

Fig. 215.—Ireland.   Fig. 216.—Dowris.

Council of the Society of Antiquaries.‡ It is cylindrical in form, with two rings of projecting knobs around it. The end is circular and slightly convex, and has a ridge across it, due to constant use. Another, found, with trumpets, spear-heads, and numerous other bronze relics, at Dowris,§ King's County, is shown in Fig. 216, also lent me by the same Council. It is of a different type from any of the others, expanding beyond the socket into a large flat blade. It appears never to have been in use. Two other small Irish specimens, one with a long oval face, are in the British Museum. I have a hammer (2½ inches) much like Fig. 210, but

* *Arch. Æliana*, vol. i. p. 13, pl. ii. 13.
† *Proc. Soc. Ant.*, 2nd S., vol. iii. p. 129; "Horæ Fer.," pl. v. 32.
‡ *Proc. Soc. Ant.*, 2nd S., vol. iii. p. 66.   § *Proc. Soc. Ant.*, 2nd S., vol. iii. p. 65.

with the shoulder nearer the top, found with a socketed celt and some perforated and other rings, near Trillick, Co. Tyrone. I have also an imperfect specimen with the end expanded, but not to the same extent as Fig. 216. This was found with a broken sword, spear-heads, and a socketed knife, on Bo Island, Enniskillen, and was kindly procured for me by the Earl of Enniskillen.

Socketed hammers have been found in several European countries. I have two from France. One of them (3¼ inches),¹ like Fig. 212 in form, was found, with a spear-head, a double-edged knife, some curved cutting tools, and an anvil of bronze (Fig. 217), together with a large torque and a plain bracelet of gold, at Fresné la Mère, near Falaise, Calvados. The other (2 inches), stouter in its proportions and more like Fig. 210, was found near Angerville, Seine et Oise. A short thick hammer was found at Briatexte, Tarn.*

An instrument in the British Museum, in form much like Fig. 216, found at Vienne (Isère ?), has only a small square hole in the socket, and may have served as an anvil rather than as a hammer. A hammer also with expanded end was found near Chalon,† and another in the Valley of the Somme.‡

A cylindrical hammer or anvil was found in the hoard of the Jardin des Plantes at Nantes.§

Cylindrical hammers have been found among the Lake-dwellings of the Lac du Bourget,‖ Savoy, one of them provided with a loop. M. Rabut, of Chambéry, has a stone mould from the same lake for casting such hammers. Another hammer-mould of stone was found at the Station of Eaux Vives, near Geneva.

In my own collection is one of these looped socketed hammers, nearly square in section, from Auvernier, in the Lake of Neuchâtel. Others from Swiss Lake-dwellings, both with and without loops, are engraved by Keller. Professor Desor has a hammer expanding towards the end from the Lake of Neuchâtel.¶ A hammer found at Mœrigen ** seems to have been formed from a portion of a looped palstave. The Lake-dwellers frequently utilized such broken instruments. Another hammer, from the Lake of Bienne,†† is hexagonal in section, and ornamented with reversed chevrons on its faces.

They are occasionally found in Hungary. I have seen one ornamented with chevrons in relief upon the sides. One with saltires on the sides, and some fragments of others, were in the Bologna hoard.

The object engraved by Madsen ‡‡ as possibly the ferrule of a lance may be a hammer of this kind.

A solid bronze hammer (4¼ inches), of oblong section, with two projecting lugs on each side for securing the handle, found near Przemysl, Poland, was exhibited at the Prehistoric Congress at Pesth. It was

---

* "Matériaux," vol. xiv. pl. ix. 6.

† Chantre, "Age du Br.," 1ère ptie. p. 38.

‡ "Matériaux," vol. v. p. 452.

§ Parenteau, "Le fondeur du Jard. des Plantes;" "Matériaux," vol. v. p. 190, pl. viii. 10.

‖ "Exp. Arch. de la Sav.," 1878, pl. v.; Chantre, "Album," pl. v. l.; Perrin, " Et. Préh. sur la Sav.," pl. x. 6, 7, xix. 17.

¶ Keller, 7ter Bericht, Taf. vii. 9.

** Desor et Favre, "Le Bel Age du Br.," pl. i. 9; Gross, "Deux Stations," pl. iii. 22.

†† Desor, "Les Palafittes," fig. 47.   ‡‡ "Afbild.," vol. ii. pl. 13, 15.

found with a bronze spear-head, and is in the Museum of the Academy of Sciences at Cracow.

As to the manner in which these socketed hammers were mounted we have no direct evidence. It seems probable, however, that many of them had crooked hafts of the same character as those of the socketed celts. It is worth notice that on some of the coins of Cunobeline * there is a seated figure at work forging a hemispherical vase, and holding in his hand a hammer which in profile is just like a narrow axe, the head not projecting beyond the upper side of the handle. A seated figure on a hitherto unpublished silver coin of Dubnovellaunus, a British prince contemporary with Augustus, holds a similar hammer, or possibly a hatchet, in his hand. But though when in use as hammers they were mounted with crooked shafts, it is quite possible that some of these instruments may have been fitted on to the end of straight stakes and have served as anvils. The Rev. W. C. Lukis, F.S.A., informs me that at the present day the peasants of Brittany make use of iron-tipped stakes, which, when driven into the ground, form convenient anvils on which to hammer out the edges of their sickles, and which have the great advantage of being portable. Though such anvils are not, so far as I am aware, any longer used in this country, traces of their having been formerly employed appear to be preserved in our language, for a small anvil to cut and punch upon, and on which to hammer cold work, is still termed a " stake."

It is worthy of remark that an implement of the same kind as these so-called socketed hammers, and made in the same manner, of a very hard greyish alloy, was found in the cemetery at Hallstatt,† and was regarded by the Baron von Sacken as a small anvil. A bronze file was found with it.

It is also to be observed that of the two hammer-like instruments found together in the Harty hoard one is much larger than the other, and may have formed the head of a · stake or anvil, while the other served as a hammer. Still, as a rule, a flat stone must have served as the anvil in early times, as it does now among the native iron-workers of Africa, and did till quite recently, for many of the country blacksmiths and tinkers of Ireland.‡ Among Danish antiquities some carefully made anvils of stone occur, but

* Evans, " Anc. Brit. Coins," pl. xii. 6.
† " Grabfeld von Hallstatt," pl. xix. 11, p. 89.
‡ Wilde, " Catal. Stone Ant. in R. I. A. Mus.," p. 81.

I am not certain as to the exact age to which they should be assigned.

Bronze anvils of the form now in use are of extremely rare occurrence in any country.   That figured by Sir William Wilde * appears to me to be of more recent date than the Bronze Period, and I am not aware of any other specimen having been found in the British Isles ; but as it is a form of tool which may eventually be discovered, it seems well to call attention to it by engraving a French example. This anvil is shown in two views, in Figs. 217 and 218.   As will be seen, it is adapted for being used in two positions, according as one or the other pointed end is driven into the workman's bench.   In one position it presents at the end two plane-surfaces, the one broad

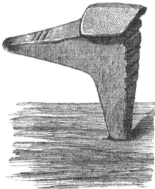 

Fig. 217.—Fresné la Mère.   ½   Fig. 218.—Fresné la Mère.   ½

and the other narrow, inclined to each other at an angle of about 120 degrees, so that their junction forms a ridge.   This part of the anvil has seen much service, as there is a thick burr all round it, caused by the expansion of the metal under repeated blows. On the projecting beak there are three slight grooves gradually increasing in size, and apparently intended for swages in which to draw out pins.   In the other position the anvil presents no smooth surface on which to hammer, but a succession of swages of different forms — some half-round, some V-shaped, and some W-shaped. There are also some oval recesses, as if for the heads of pins.   The metal of which the anvil is made appears to contain more tin than the ordinary bronze, and therefore to be somewhat harder.   On one face is the mark of the runner ⅞ inch in diameter, which was broken off after the tool was cast.

* "Catal. Mus. R. I. A.," fig. 401.

This interesting tool was found with the hammer already mentioned, a spear-head, a double-edged knife or razor, a knife with the end bent round so as to present a gouge-like edge, and a large curved cutting-tool of the same character (Fig. 247), all of bronze, at Fresné la Mère, near Falaise, Calvados. With them was a magnificent gold torque with recurved cylindrical ends, the twisted part being of cruciform section; and a plain penannular ring or bracelet, formed from what was a cylindrical rod. The whole find is now in my own collection. It is not by any means improbable that this anvil was rather the tool of a goldsmith of the Bronze Age than that of a mere bronze-worker.

I have another anvil of about the same size, but thinner, which was found in the Seine at Paris. It also can be mounted two ways, but in each position it presents a nearly flat but somewhat inclined face, and there are no swages in the beaks, one of which is conical and the other nearly rectangular.

M. Ernest Chantre has engraved two other specimens, somewhat differing in form, but of much the same general character. They were found near Chalon-sur-Saône and near Geneva.* The analysis of the metal of one of them gives 16 parts of tin to 84 parts of copper.

Another bronze anvil is in the museum at Amiens, and a fifth, also from France, is in the British Museum. This has a flat projecting ledge at the top, and at right angles a slightly tapering beak. An anvil of the same kind, but without the beak, was found with other objects near Amiens, and is now in the museum of that town.

A small anvil without a beak, found at Auvernier,† in the Lake of Neuchâtel, is in the collection of Dr. Gross. A square flat anvil, somewhat dented on the face, formed part of the Bologna hoard.

In my own collection is what appears to have been a larger anvil of bronze, which was found, with other instruments of the same metal, at Macarsca, Dalmatia. In form it is not unlike an ordinary hammer-head about 5 inches long; but the eye through it appears to be too small for it ever to have served to receive a haft of the ordinary kind, though it probably held a handle by which to steady the tool when in use. One end is nearly square and but slightly convex; the other is oblong and rounded the narrow way. Both ends are much worn. On one face and one side are rounded notches or swages. This tool has been cast in an open mould, as one face presents the rough surface of the molten metal, which contains a large proportion of tin. The other face and the sides are fairly smooth.

SAWS AND FILES.

While speaking of bronze tools, which up to the present time have not been noticed in Britain, but which may probably be some day discovered—if, indeed, they have not already been found—the saw must not be forgotten.

* "Age du Br.," ptie. i. p. 39.
† Keller, 7ter Bericht, Taf. vii. 8 ; Gross, "Deux Stations," pl. iii. 28.

A fragment of what has been regarded as a rudely formed saw of bronze was indeed found, with a sword and several celts, at Mawgan,[*] Cornwall, and is now in the Museum of the Society of Antiquaries. It is 4 inches by ¾ inch, coarsely toothed, and the serrations appear to have been cast. I am, however, rather doubtful whether it was really a saw.

Saws have been found both in Scandinavia and in France, in the latter country in hoards apparently belonging to the later portion of the Bronze Period. One from Ribiers,[†] Hautes Alpes, is about 5¼ inches long and ¾ inch broad, slightly curved, and with a rivet-hole at one end for attachment to the handle. Two from the "Fonderie de Larnaud,"[‡] Jura, are nearly one-half smaller. There were five specimens in that hoard, and M. Chantre enumerates sixteen altogether from various parts of France and Switzerland. A fine specimen, with a rivet-hole for the handle, was found at Mœrigen,[§] in the Lake of Bienne.

The Scandinavian[||] type is of much the same character, though some are more sickle-like in shape, with the teeth on the inner sweep.

A saw, found with celts, spear-heads, diadems, &c., at Lämmersdorf, near Prenzlau, is in the Berlin Museum. A short one, with a rivet-hole for the handle, found at Stade, is in that at Hanover.

A saw of pure copper was found in some excavations of dwellings of remote date at Santorin,[¶] in the Grecian Archipelago, in company with various instruments formed of obsidian. Some fragments of saws occurred in the Bologna hoard. Part of one from Cyprus is in the British Museum. A copper (?) saw from Niebla, Spain, 9 inches long, also in the British Museum, has the teeth arranged to cut as it is drawn towards the workman, and not when pushed away from him.

The file is another tool of exceedingly rare occurrence in bronze, though not absolutely unknown in deposits belonging to the close of the Bronze Period. Sir William Wilde [**] mentions "a bronze circular file, straight, like a modelling tool," as being in the Museum of the Royal Irish Academy, but I have not seen the original and am not confident as to its age. A file [††] was, however, found in the great hoard of the Fonderie de Larnaud, and another from the Lake-dwellings of the Lac du Bourget is in the museum at Chambéry.

The early form of file is indeed much the same as that of a very broad saw, the toothing being coarse and running at right angles across the blade. In the cemetery at Hallstatt,[‡‡] in Upper Austria, files of this character were found, several in bronze and one in iron. The bronze files are from 5 to 10 inches long,

* "Catal. Mus. Soc. Ant.," p. 16; *Arch.*, vol. xvii. p. 337.
† E. Chantre, "Album" pl. xxv. No. 5.
‡ Chantre, "Album," pl. xliii.   § Keller, 7ter Bericht, Taf. vii. 11.
|| Worsaae, "Nord. Olds.," figs. 157, 158; "Cong. préh.," Stockholm vol., 1874, p. 494.
¶ "Comptes Rend. de l'Ac. des Sc.," 1871, vol. ii. p. 476.
** "Catal.," p. 597, No. 96.
†† E. Chantre, "Age du Bronze," 1ère ptie. p. 87.
‡‡ Von Sacken, "Das Grabf. v. Hallst," pl. xix. 12.

and some which are flat for the greater part of their length are drawn down, for about 2 inches at the end, into tapering round files. In the Bologna hoard were several fragments of files, including one of a "half-round" file.

TONGS AND PUNCHES.

From our greater acquaintance with the working of iron than with that of bronze, there seems to us a sort of natural connection between the anvil, hammer, and tongs. It must, however, be borne in mind that bronze is a metal which instead of being, like iron, tough and ductile, becomes "short" and fragile when heated, so that all the hammering to which the tools and weapons of bronze were subjected in order to planish their faces, or to draw out and harden their edges, was probably administered to them when cold. At least one pair of bronze tongs has, however, been found, which is shown in Fig. 219. This instrument was discovered, with numerous other antiquities, in the cave at Heathery Burn,* near Stanhope in Weardale, Durham, and is now in the collection of Canon Greenwell. As half of a mould for socketed celts and some waste runners of bronze were found, it is evident that the practice of casting bronze was carried on in the cave, and these tongs were probably part of the founder's apparatus. Whether they were used merely as fire-tongs, or for the purpose of lifting the crucible or melting-pot, is a question. They appear, however, much too light to be of service for the latter purpose.

In the museum of the Louvre at Paris are some Egyptian tongs of bronze, which are remarkably similar to those from Durham. A workman seated before a small fireplace, holding a blowpipe to his mouth with one hand and with a pair of tongs in the other, is shown in a painting at Thebes, published by Sir Gardner Wilkinson.†

What I have ventured to regard as another of the tools of the

Fig. 219.
Heathery Burn. ‡

* *Proc. Soc. Ant.*, 2nd S., vol. ii. p. 127.
† "Anc. Egyptians," vol. iii. p. 224, fig. 375.

bronze-founder is a kind of pointed punch or pricker, of which an example is given in Fig. 220. This, as well as another which had lost its point, was found, with socketed celts, gouges, moulds, &c., forming the whole stock-in-trade of a bronze-founder, in the Isle of Harty, Kent. It seems to have been furnished with a wooden handle, into which the tang was driven as far as the projecting stop ; and its purpose appears to have been the extraction of the cores of burnt clay from out of the sockets of the celts. That these sockets were formed over a core of clay inserted into the

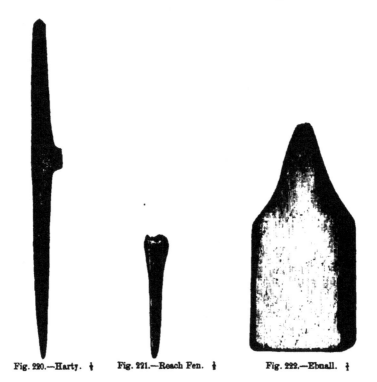

Fig. 220.—Harty. ½   Fig. 221.—Reach Fen. ½   Fig. 222.—Ebnall. ½

mould is proved by numerous celts having been found with the cores still in them. The heat of the melted metal was sufficient to convert the clay into terra-cotta or brick, and in this condition the cores have been preserved. Some force was necessary to extract such hardened cores, and this could be well effected by driving in such a pointed instrument as that here figured. If the two prickers from the Harty hoard were originally of the same length, the broken one has lost a portion from its end exactly corresponding in length with the depth of the socket of the largest celts found with it ; as if it had been driven home through the burnt clay quite to the bottom of the socket, and then had been broken off short at the mouth of the celt in the vain endeavour to extract it.

Some small punches, without any tang for insertion in a handle, were found with socketed celts and numerous other objects in the hoard from Reach Fen, already mentioned. One of these is shown in Fig. 221. No moulds were discovered in this case ; and though the hoard has all the appearance of being the stock of an ancient bronze-founder, it is possible that these shorter punches may here have been used for some other purpose than that of extracting cores. The end of one is sharp, that of the other presents a small oblong face. It is possible that, like the instruments next to be described, these may have been punches used in the decoration of other articles of bronze. Mr. H. Prigg,* in his description of this hoard, has suggested such an use. The large end of the punch shown in the figure bears no mark of having been hammered ; it may, however, have been struck with a wooden mallet. Punches, more chisel-shaped at the point, appear to have been in use for producing the incuse ornaments which occur on so many of the flat and flanged celts. I am not aware of any tools which were undoubtedly used for this purpose having been observed in Britain ; but, as I have already remarked, there were found at Ebnall,† Salop, two short-edged tools, which may possibly be punches, and if so may have been applied to this use. One of these is shown in Fig. 222, the block for which has been kindly lent me by the Council of the Society of Antiquaries. The other is described as of similar form but of rather longer proportions. They were found in company with spear-heads, celts, gouges, and broad dagger-blades ; but it does not appear that any of these were ornamented with punch-marked patterns. The tools may, therefore, have been merely some kind of strong chisels, possibly used for breaking off the jets and superfluous metal from the castings. The thickness of the tool is rather greater than the cut would lead one to imagine, being ½ inch. These two tools have been regarded as hammers, or possibly weights. I have now spoken of them as punches, or possibly chisels, but it may be that after all it was the broad end that was destined for use, in which case they might be regarded as anvils.

* *Arch. Assoc. Journ.*, vol. xxxvi., p. 59.
† *Proc. Soc. Ant.*, 2nd S., vol. iii. p. 66 ; *Arch. Journ.*, vol. xxii. p. 167.

Whatever the purpose of these particular tools, there can be but little doubt that punches were in use for the ornamentation of the flat faces and the sides of celts ; and it will be well to be on the look out for such tools when hoards belonging to the ancient bronze-founders are examined.   For the most part, however, these seem to belong to a period posterior to that of the ornamented flat celts, though decorated spear-heads occur in them.

Some of the punches from the Fonderie de Larnaud and from the Lake-dwellings may have served for decorating other articles in bronze.

Awls, Drills, or Prickers.

Allied to the pointed tools last described, but considerably smaller, are the awls, drills, borers, or prickers of bronze which have so frequently been found accompanying interments in barrows. No doubt such instruments must have been in very extensive and general use ; but it is only under favourable conditions that such small pieces of metal would be preserved, and when preserved it is only under conditions equally favourable that they would attract the attention of an ordinary labourer.   It is, therefore, mainly to the barrow-digger that we are indebted for our knowledge of these little instruments.   Many belong to a very early part of the Bronze Age, but the form continued in use through the whole period.

A somewhat detailed essay upon them has already appeared in the *Archæologia** in the late Dr. Thurnam's admirable and exhaustive paper on " Ancient British Barrows," from which I am tempted largely to borrow.   I am also, through the kindness of the Council of the Society of Antiquaries, enabled to make use of some of the woodcuts which illustrate Dr. Thurnam's paper. He distinguishes three types of these instruments, which, as he points out, correspond to some extent with as many types or varieties of the bronze celt.   They are as follows :—

I. That with a simply flattened end or tang for insertion into its handle.

II. That with a well-marked shoulder, where the stem and tang unite ; the object being to prevent its passing too far into the handle.

III. That with a regular stop-ridge, or waist, almost as marked as that in a carpenter's awl, as distinguished from that of a shoemaker.

* Vol. xliii. p. 464.

One of the first type, from the Golden barrow at Upton Lovel, is engraved by Hoare,[*] and is shown in Fig. 223. With it were two cups, a necklace of amber beads, and a small bronze dagger. It is almost the longest of those found by Sir R. Colt Hoare, which were upwards of thirty in number. The only longer specimen was found in a barrow near Lake,[†] and there also some beads and a bronze dagger accompanied the interment. It is considerably thicker than Fig. 223, and the tang for insertion in the handle is broader and flatter. A smaller awl of the same character was found in a barrow on Upton Lovel Down,[‡] opened by Mr. Cunnington. In this instance there were two interments in the same grave, and several flint celts and a perforated stone battle-axe were found, as well as numerous instruments of bone, and a necklace of beads of jet or lignite.

An awl of this kind ($3\frac{1}{5}$ inches) found, with a spear-head, hammer, knife, and gouge of bronze, at Thorndon, Suffolk,[§] most of them already described, is now in the British Museum, and is shown in Fig. 224.

Fig. 223. Fig. 224. Fig. 225.
Upton   Thorn-   Butter-
Lovel. ¼   don. ½   wick. ¼

Several such instruments, some of them not more than an inch in length, were found by Canon Greenwell[||] in his exploration of the Yorkshire barrows. In nine cases awls or prickers accompanied interments of unburnt bodies, and in three cases they were found among burnt bones. In most instances instruments of flint were found with them. An aged woman in a barrow on Langton Wold[¶] had three bronze awls or prickers, as well as an assemblage of bone instruments, animal teeth, marine shells, and other miscellaneous property, buried with her. Dr. Thurnam regarded these as drills used with a bow, but I think such an use is doubtful. Some of the awls from the Yorkshire barrows, instead of being flattened at one end, are drawn down to a point at both ends, leaving the middle of larger diameter so as to form a kind of shoulder. These, I presume, are included under Dr. Thurnam's Type II. Sometimes this central part of the blade is square and sometimes the tang is square, like that described by Stukeley[**] from a barrow near Stonehenge as "a sharp bodkin round at one end, square at the other where it went into a handle."

An awl, square at the centre, and round at each end in section, is shown in Fig. 225. It was found by Canon Greenwell in a barrow at Butterwick, Yorkshire, in company with the celt (Fig. 2), and other objects. The point has unfortunately been broken off.

A typical example of Dr. Thurnam's second class from a barrow at

[*] Vol. i. p. 99, pl. xi. The cut is from the *Arch.*, vol. xliii. p. 466.
[†] Pl. xxx. 3.   [‡] *Arch.*, vol. xv. p. 122, pl. iv. 5.
[§] *Arch. Journ.*, vol. x. p. 3.   [||] "British Barrows," *passim.*
[¶] *Op. cit.*, p. 138.   [**] "Stonehenge," p. 45, pl. xxxii.

Bulford,* Wilts, is shown in Fig. 226. Another was found at Beckhampton, and a small pricker of the same type was found with a burnt interment at Storrington,† Sussex. Like those found by Sir R. C. Hoare, this was regarded as the pin for fastening the cloth in which the bones were collected from the funeral pyre. The fact of several of them having been found still inserted in their hafts, as will subsequently be seen, will suffice to prove that this view is mistaken.

Several awls pointed at both ends were found by the late Mr. Bateman during his researches in the Derbyshire barrows. In Waggon Low ‡ at the right shoulder of a contracted skeleton were three instruments of flint, and a small bronze awl 1¼ inches long, tapering each way from the middle, which is square. Another, pointed at each end, lay with a drinking cup and a rude spear- or arrow-head of flint near the shoulder of a youthful skeleton in a barrow near Minning Low.§ Another of the same kind was found in a barrow on Ilam Moor,‖ Staffordshire. Another was found with calcined bones in a barrow in Larks-Low,¶ Middleton.

Fig. 226.
Bulford. †

Fig. 227.
Winterbourn
Stoke. ‡

In several instances there were traces of a wooden handle, as was the case with one, upwards of 3 inches long, which was found with a flint spearhead, a double-edged axe of basaltic stone, and objects of bone, among the calcined bones in a sepulchral urn from a barrow at Throwley.**

In a barrow at Haddon Field †† there was a small drinking cup near the back of a contracted skeleton, and beneath this an arrow-head of flint, an instrument of stag's-horn like a netting mesh, and a bronze awl showing traces of its wooden handle.

In another barrow near Gotam, Nottinghamshire,‡‡ there lay near the thigh of a contracted skeleton a neatly chipped spear-head of flint, and a small bronze pin which had been inserted into a wooden handle.

In a barrow near Fimber,§§ Yorkshire, opened by Messrs. Mortimer, there were found near the knee of a contracted female skeleton a knifelike chipped flint and the point of a bronze pricker or awl. With another female interment in the same barrow a bronze pricker was found inserted in a short wooden haft. The Britoness in this instance wore a necklace of jet discs with a triangular pendant of the same material.

A bronze pin, 1¼ inches long, accompanied by a broken flint celt and some arrow-heads and flakes of flint, together with calcined bones, was found in an urn in Ravenshill barrow,‖‖ near Scarborough.

In some of the Wiltshire barrows more perfectly preserved handles have been found. One of these, copied from Hoare's "Ancient Wiltshire,"¶¶ is shown in Fig. 227. It was found in the King barrow with what was probably a male skeleton buried in the hollowed trunk of an

* *Arch.*, vol. xliii. p. 465, fig. 163.
† *Suss. Arch. Coll.*, vol. i. p. 55.
‡ "Ten Years' Dig.," p. 85.
§ "Vest. Ant. of Derb.," p. 41.
‖ "Vest. Ant. of Derb.," p. 82.
¶ Smith's "Coll. Ant.," vol. i. p. 60, pl. xxi. 3.
** "Ten Years' Dig.," p. 155.
†† *Lib. cit.*, p. 106.
‡‡ "Vest. Ant. of Derb.," p. 104.
§§ "Reliquary," vol. ix. p. 67.
‖‖ *Arch. Assoc. Journ.*, vol. vi. p. 3.
¶¶ Vol. i. p. 122, pl. xv. No. 3.

elm tree. With it was a curious urn of burnt clay and two bronze daggers, one near the breast and the other near the thigh. The handle is described as being of ivory, but I think Dr. Thurnam was right in regarding it as of bone. The awl in this instance is of the third type, having a well-marked collar round it. Another of the same character, but retaining only a small part of the haft, so that the shoulder is better shown, was found with burnt bones in an urn deposited in a barrow near Stonehenge.[*] No mention is made as to the nature of the material of which the haft was formed.

In the case of an awl of the first type, engraved by Dr. Thurnam, and here reproduced as Fig. 228, the handle is of wood, but the kind of wood is not mentioned.

One or two bronze or brass awls with square shoulders are in the Museum of the Royal Irish Academy.[†] Several awls with their original wooden handles have been found in the Lake-dwellings of Savoy,[‡] and others in hafts of stag's-horn in the Swiss Lake-dwellings.

Whether the twisted pins from the Wiltshire barrows are of the nature of gimlets, as suggested by Dr. Thurnam, is a difficult question. I shall, however, prefer to treat of them as personal ornaments rather than as tools. It is possible that they may to some extent have combined the two functions. As to the instruments which I have been describing being piercing tools or awls, there seems to be little doubt; and Mr. Bateman can hardly have been far wrong in regarding them as intended to pierce skins or leather. Though not curved like the cobbler's awl of the present day, they are probably early members of the same family. In Scandinavia these instruments are of frequent occurrence, sometimes being provided with ornamental handles also made of bronze.[§] They are

Fig. 228.
Wiltshire. ½

in that part of Europe often found in company with tweezers and small knives of bronze, and all were probably used together in sewing, the hole being bored by the awl and the thread drawn through by the tweezers and, when necessary, cut with the knife. Possibly the use of bristles as substitutes for needles dates back to very early times.

In one instance at least tweezers have been found in Britain in company with objects apparently belonging to the Bronze Age, though no doubt to a very late part of it. Those represented in

---

[*] "Anc. Wilts," vol. i. p. 164, pl. xvii.   [†] Wilde's "Catal.," p. 597.
[‡] Chantre, "Alb.," pl. lxiii.
[§] Worsaae, "Nord. Olds.," figs. 274, 276; Nilsson, "Nordens Ur.-Invånare," figs. 55, 57.

Fig. 229 were discovered near Llangwyllog,[*] Anglesea, together with a two-edged razor, a bracelet, buttons, rings, &c., which are now in the British Museum.

A more highly ornamented pair of tweezers, with a broad end, found with a bone comb, a quern, spindle-whorls, &c., in a Picts' house near Kettleburn,[†] Caithness, belongs to a considerably later period.

The needles of bronze found in the British Isles do not as a rule appear to belong to the Bronze Period, though some of those found on the Continent seem to date back to that age. Two are engraved by Wilde,[‡] and there are altogether eighteen such articles in the Museum of the Royal Irish Academy. A broken specimen (1¼ inch) from the sandhills near Glenluce,[§] Wigtonshire, has been figured.

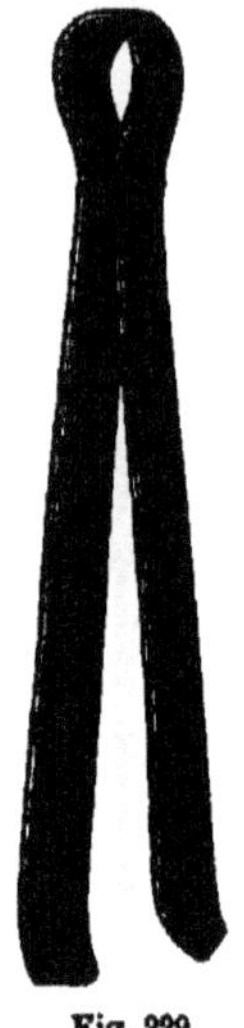

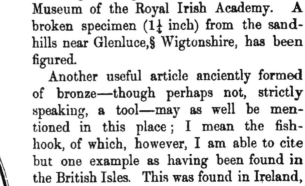

Another useful article anciently formed of bronze—though perhaps not, strictly speaking, a tool—may as well be mentioned in this place; I mean the fish-hook, of which, however, I am able to cite but one example as having been found in the British Isles. This was found in Ireland, and is shown in Fig. 230,[||] kindly lent by the Royal Irish Academy.

Fish-hooks of bronze have been found in considerable abundance on the site of several of the Swiss Lake-dwellings; and it is not a little remarkable that in form many of them are almost identical with the steel fish-hooks of the present day. The barb, to prevent the fish from struggling off the hook, is in most instances present, and double hooks are occasionally found. The attachment to the line was, even in the single hooks, frequently made by a loop or eye, formed by flattening and turning back the upper part of the shank of the hook. Fish-hooks were found in the Fonderie de Larnaud (Jura),[¶] and in the hoard of St. Pierre-en-Châtre (Oise).

Fig. 229.
Llangwyllog.

Fig. 230.
Ireland.

Such are the principal forms of tools and instruments of bronze found in these islands. Some of them, such as the socketed gouges,

* *Arch. Journ.*, vol. xxii. p. 74.
† *Proc. Soc. Ant. Scot.*, vol. i. p. 266; *Arch. Journ.*, vol. x. p. 218.
‡ "Catal. Mus. R. I. A.," p. 547.   § "Ayr and Wigton Coll.," vol. ii. p. 14.
|| Wilde, "Catal. Mus. R. I. A.," fig. 403.   ¶ Chantre, "Age du Br.," 1ère ptie. p. 87.

hammers, and chisels, can only belong to the latter part of the Bronze Period, when the art of using cores in order to produce sockets or other hollow recesses in castings was well known. Others, like the simple awls so frequently found in company with instruments of flint in our barrows, appear to extend from the commencement of the Bronze Age to its close.

There still remains to be described a class of instruments in use by the husbandman, and not by the warrior; and as the present chapter has extended to such a length, it will be well to treat of these under a separate heading.

CHAPTER VIII.

SICKLES.

SICKLES are the only undoubtedly agricultural implements in bronze with which we are acquainted in this country. Already in the Stone Period the cultivation of cereals for food appears to have been practised, and I have elsewhere* pointed out a form of flint instrument which may possibly have supplied the place of sickles or reaping hooks in those early times. The rarity of bronze sickles in this country, as compared with their abundance in some parts of Southern Europe, is, however, somewhat striking, and may, perhaps, point to a considerably less cultivation of grain crops in Britain than in countries with a warmer climate, while the inhabitants were otherwise in much the same stage of civilisation.

The traditions of the use of bronze sickles survived to a comparatively late period in Greece and Italy, and Medea is described by Sophocles† as cutting her magic herbs with such instruments (Χαλκέοισιν ἧμα δρεπάνοις τομάς), and by Ovid ‡ as doing it " curvamine falcis ahenæ." Elissa is by Virgil § represented as using a bronze sickle for similar purposes—

> " Falcibus et messæ ad lunam quæruntur aënis
> Pubentes herbæ nigri cum lacte veneni."

When bronze sickles were used for reaping corn it seems to have been a common custom merely to cut the ears of corn from off the straw, after the manner of the Gaulish reaping machine described by Pliny,‖ and not to cut and carry away straw and ear together from the field. This practice will probably account for the small size of the sickles which have come down to us, unless we are to reverse the argument, and derive the custom of cutting off the

---

* " Anc. Stone Imp.," p. 320. † Macrob. " Saturn.," v. c. 19.
‡ " Met.," vii. 224. § " Æn.," lib. iv. 513.
‖ " Nat. Hist.," xviii. c. 30.

ears only from the diminutive size of the instruments employed for reaping.

Bronze sickles were hafted in different ways, sometimes being fastened to the handle by a pin, either attached to the stem of the blade or passing through a hole in it, combined with some system of binding ; and sometimes being provided with a socket into which the haft was driven, and then secured by a transverse pin or rivet.

The sickles with a socket to receive the handle appear to be peculiar to Britain and the North of France. The other form occurs over the greater part of Europe, including Scandinavia, and the blades, as has been observed by Dr. Keller, are always adapted for use in the right hand. Dr. Gross, of Neuveville, on the Lake of Bienne, has been so fortunate as to discover at Mœrigen, the site of one of the ancient pile-villages on the lake, two or three handles for sickles of this kind. A figure showing three views of one of these handles has been published by the Royal Archæological Institute,* and is here by permission reproduced as Fig. 231. This handle is formed of yew, curiously carved so as to receive the thumb and fingers, and has a flat place at the end against which the blade was fastened. In this place there are two grooves to receive the slightly projecting ribs with which the stem of the sickle-blade is usually strengthened. Dr. Keller† has suggested that the blade of the sickle was made fast to the handle by means of a kind of ferrule which passed over it, and was secured in its place by two pins or nails.

The end of the handle forms a ridge, through which are two holes that would admit a small cord for the suspension of the sickle, and thus prevent its being lost either on land or water. We find this sailor-like habit prevailing among the Lake-dwellers in the case of their flint knives also, the handles of which were often perforated.

There is a remarkable resemblance in character between this handle and some of those in use among the Esquimaux ‡ for their planes and knives, which are recessed in the same manner for the reception of the fingers and the thumb.

Some iron sickles, of nearly the same form as those in bronze with the flat stem, were present in the great Danish find of the Early Iron Age at Vimose,§ described by Mr. C. Engelhardt. The

* *Arch. Journ.*, vol. xxx. p. 192. † Keller, 7ter Bericht, Taf. vii. 1.
‡ See Lubbock's " Preh. Times," p. 513. § " Vimose Fundet," 1869, p. 26.

chord of the curved blades is from 6 to 7 inches in length, and one of the instruments still retained its original wooden handle. This is between 9 and 10 inches long, and is curved at the part intended to receive the hand. The end is conical, like the head

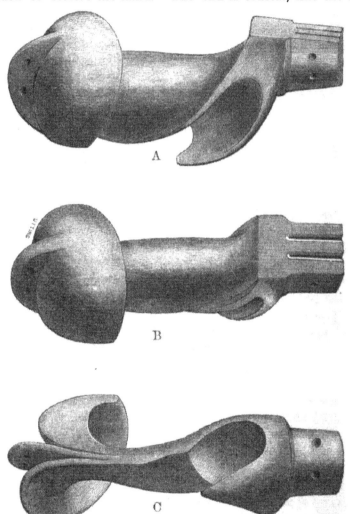

Fig. 231.—Three views of a handle for a sickle, Mœrigen.

of a screw, and is evidently thus made in order to give a secure hold to the reaper when drawing the sickle towards him. Sickles with nearly similar handles were in use in Smaaland,* in the South of Sweden, until recent days.

* "Aarböger for Oldkynd.," 1867, p. 250.

Of sickles without a socket but few have been found in Britain, and those mostly in our Western Counties. In a remarkable hoard found in a turbary at Edington Burtle,* near Glastonbury, Somersetshire, were four of these flat sickles. One of these had never been finished, but had been left rough as it came from the mould, into which the metal had been run through a channel near the point of the sickle. A projection still marks the place where the jet was broken off. As will be seen from Fig. 232, this blade is

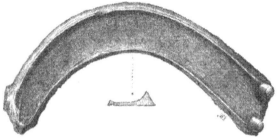

Fig. 232.—Edington Burtle. ¼

provided with two projecting pins for the purpose of attaching it to the handle. In this respect it differs from the sickles of the ordinary continental type, which, when of this character, have usually but a single knob.

Another of the Edington sickles with a single projection is

Fig. 233.—Edington Burtle. ¼

shown in Fig. 233. This blade is more highly ornamented, and has a rib along the middle in addition to that along the back, no doubt for the purpose of increasing stiffness while diminishing weight. Of the other two sickles found at Edington, one is imperfect and the other much worn. Both are provided with the two projecting pins.

Two other sickles found on Sparkford Hill,† also in Somersetshire, present the same peculiarity. One of these much resembles

---

* *Somerset Arch. and Nat. Hist. Proc.*, 1854, vol. v. p. 91.
† *Op. cit.*, 1856—7, vol. vii. p. 27.

Fig. 233, though nearly straight along the back. The other is flat on both faces. Each has lost its point. A chisel-like tool was found with them.

With the Edington sickles were found a broad fluted penannular armlet and what may have been a finger-ring of the same pattern, a plain penannular armlet of square section, part of a light funicular torque like Fig. 467, part of a ribbon torque like Fig. 469, and four penannular rings, some of them apparently made from fragments of torques.

Two other sickles of the same character, each with two projecting pins, were found in Taunton * itself in association with twelve palstaves, a socketed celt, a hammer (Fig. 214), a fragment of a spear-head, a double-edged knife, a funicular torque (Fig. 468), a pin (Fig. 451), some fragments of other pins, and several penannular rings of various sizes.

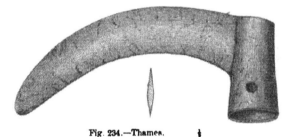

Fig. 234.—Thames.

All the objects found at Edington, Sparkford Hill, and Taunton are now in the museum in Taunton Castle.

A thinner form of flat sickle, if such it be, has been found in Kent. Among a number of bronze objects which were discovered at Marden,† near Staplehurst, there is a slightly curved blade with a rivet at one end, which appears to present a sickle-like character. I have not seen the original, and as it is described as a knife-blade it may prove to have been one, or possibly, what is of far rarer occurrence, a saw.

Of socketed sickles a few have at different times been dredged up from the Thames. One of these, found in 1859, is in my own collection, and is shown in Fig. 234. The blade, which is almost as sharp at the back as at the edge, is not quite central with the

* *Arch. Journ.*, vol. xxxvii. p. 94.   Pring, " Brit. and Roman Taunton," pl. i. 3.
† *Arch. Assoc. Journ.*, vol. xiv. p. 258, pl. 13, No. 1.

socket, but so placed as to make the instrument better adapted for use in the right hand than in the left. The socket tapers considerably, and is closed at the end.

In another sickle found in the Thames, near Bray, Berks* (Fig. 235), the socket dies into the blade instead of forming a distinct feature. A third, found near Windsor, and engraved in the *Proceedings of the Society of Antiquaries*,† closely resembles Fig. 234, but the end of the socket, instead of being closed, is open. The blade of this also is sharp on both edges.

One from Stretham Fen, in the Museum of the Cambridge Antiquarian Society (about 5½ inches), is of the same character. It has two rivet-holes in the socket. Another from Downham Fen (5¾ inches) is sharp on both edges.

In the Norwich Museum is a sickle of somewhat the same character as Fig. 235, but the socket instead of being oval is oblong, and is placed at a less angle to the blade, which in this case also is double-edged. The

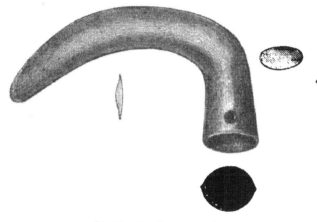

Fig. 235.—Near Bray.

socket is 1½ by 1⁄16 inch, and has one rivet-hole through it. The curved knife from Wicken Fen, to be described in the next chapter, much resembles this Norwich example in outline. Another sickle from Norfolk‡ was exhibited to the Archæological Institute in 1851. Mr. Franks has shown me a sketch of another found at Dereham which has the external edge of the blade extending across the end of the socket. Both edges of the blade are sharp.

But few sickles have been found in Scotland. That shown in Fig. 236 was found in the Tay,§ near Errol, Perthshire, in 1840, and has been described by Dr. J. Alexander Smith. The block, which has been kindly lent me by the Society of Antiquaries of Scotland, is engraved on the scale of two-thirds linear, instead of my usual scale of one-half. The main difference between this specimen and mine from the Thames (Fig.

---

* *Proc. Soc. Ant.*, 2nd S., vol. iv. p. 85.   † 2nd S., vol. v. p. 95.
‡ *Arch. Journ.*, vol. viii. p. 191.   § *Proc. Soc. Ant. Scot.*, vol. vii. p. 378.

234) consists in the blade being fluted. Another more rudely made sickle, found at Edengerach,* Premnay, Aberdeenshire, has also been engraved. This has a single central rib along the blade and no rivet-hole through the socket. Perhaps it is an unfinished casting.

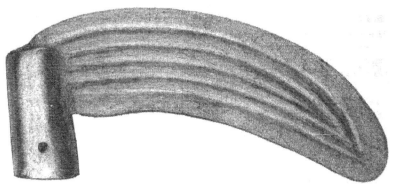

Fig. 236.—Near Errol, Perthshire.

In Sinclair's "Statistical Account of Scotland"† it is stated that an instrument of this class was found at Ledbeg, Sutherlandshire, and was pronounced by the Earl of Bristol, then Bishop of Derry, to whom it was presented, to be a Druidical pruning hook similar to several found in England.

In Ireland these instruments are much more abundant. Eleven specimens are mentioned by Wilde ‡ as being in the Museum of the Royal Irish Academy, and there are three in the British Museum, as well as one in that at Edinburgh.

Fig. 237.—Garvagh, Derry.

That engraved as Fig. 237 is in the collection of Canon Greenwell, F.R.S., and was found at Garvagh, county Derry. The blade is fluted somewhat like that of the Tay specimen. In one of those engraved by Wilde (Fig. 405) it is more highly ornamented. In another the socket is not closed at the end, but resembles that of the Windsor example already mentioned. This appears to be the one engraved by Vallancey§ who observes that it was "called by the Irish a Seare," and that it was used "to cut herbs, acorns, misletoe, &c." In another‖ the blade forms

* *Proc. Soc. Ant. Scot.*, vol. vii. p. 376.
† Vol. xvi. p. 206, cited by Wilson, "Preh. Ann.," vol. i, p. 401.
‡ "Catal.," p. 527.
§ "Coll. de Reb. Hib.," vol. iv. pl. x. 4, p. 60.
‖ Fig. 406. Compare "Horæ Ferales," pl. x. 19.

a direct continuation of the socket as in Fig. 238, which is engraved from a specimen in the British Museum, found near Athlone, county Westmeath.

Vallancey, in his "Collectanea," has figured another. In the collection of Mr. J. Holmes is another example of this type. Another sickle of the same character as Fig. 237, found near Ballygawley,* Tyrone, has also been figured. This specimen is among those in the British Museum.

A socketed sickle, double-edged, and with a concavity on each side at the angle between the blade and the socket so deep as to meet and form a hole, was found in Alderney, and is engraved in the *Archæological Association Journal.*† With it were found socketed celts, spear-heads,

Fig. 238.—Athlone.

and broken swords and daggers. This may be regarded as a French rather than an English example.

In my own collection is another, from the Seine at Paris, about 7 inches in length along the outer edge of the blade, which extends past the end of the socket. This still contains a part of the wooden handle, which has been secured in its place by two rivets, apparently of bronze. In general outline this sickle is much like Fig. 234, but the blade is narrower and more curved and the socket more flattened. In the museum at Amiens

* *Arch. Journ.*, vol. ii. p. 186. See also *Dublin Penny Journ.*, i. p. 108; "Horæ Ferales," pl. x. 18.

† Vol. iii. p. 9.

is another sickle, in form closely resembling Fig. 234, but with a loop at
the back of the socket.   M. Chantre in his magnificent work, "L'Age
du Bronze," does not specify this socketed type, though he divides the
form without socket into five different varieties.   The socketed form
appears to be quite unknown in the South of·France, as it also is in
Switzerland.

These three are the only instances I can cite of socketed sickles
having been found outside the British Isles, so that this type of
instrument appears to be peculiarly our own.   The existence of
a socket shows that the form does not belong to an early period
in the Bronze Age, and the same is to be inferred from the
character of the other bronze objects with which the Alderney
sickle was found associated.

Inasmuch as the continental forms are as a rule different
from the British, and as they are, moreover, well known, it will
suffice to indicate some few of the works in which descriptions of
them will be found.   Some from Camenz, in Saxony, have been
engraved in illustration of a paper by myself in the *Proceedings
of the Society of Antiquaries.*[*]

Others from Germany, some of which are said to have Roman
numerals upon them, have been figured by Lindenschmit.[†]

Examples from Italy have been given by Strobel,[‡] Gastaldi,[§]
Lindenschmit,[‖] and others.

They have been found in great abundance in some of the settle-
ments on the lakes of Switzerland and Savoy.   It has been thought
that the Lake-dwellers did not cut off merely the ears of their corn,[¶]
but "that the straw was taken with it, otherwise there would not
have been the seeds of so many weeds in the corn."   Diodorus Siculus,
however, who wrote in the first century B.C., tells us distinctly
that the Britons gathered in their harvest by cutting off the ears
of corn and storing them in subterraneous repositories.   From
these they picked the oldest day by day for their food.   Whether
for threshing they made use of the *tribulum,*[**] that "sharp
threshing instrument having teeth," before Roman times, is doubtful ; but that so primitive an instrument, armed with flakes of
flint or other stone, should have remained in use in some Mediterranean countries until the present day, is a remarkable instance

---

[*] 2nd S., vol. iii. p. 333.
[†] "Samml. zu Sigmar.," Taf. xli. ; "Alt. u. h. Vorz.," vol. i. Heft xii. Taf. ii.
[‡] "Avanzi Prerom.," 1863, Tav. ii. 6, 7.
[§] "Nuovi Cenni," 1862, Tav. iv. 17, 18.   [‖] "Samml. zu Sigmar.," Taf. xli.
[¶] Stevens, "Flint Chips," p. 157.
[**] See Evans, "Anc. Stone Imp.," p. 256.

of the power of survival of ancient customs. Such an instance of persistence in a primitive form much reduces the extreme improbability of the use of bronze sickles in Germany having lasted until a time when Roman numerals might appear upon them. If every St. Andrew's cross and every straight line found upon ancient instruments is to be regarded as a Roman numeral, and the objects bearing them are to be referred to Roman times as their earliest possible date, the range of Roman antiquities will be much enlarged, and will be found to contain, among other objects, a large number of the bronze knives from the Swiss Lake-dwellings ; for one of the most common ornaments on the backs of these knives consists of a repetition of the pattern **XIIIIIXIIIIIXIIIII**.

Even were it proved that in some part of Europe the use of bronze sickles survived to so late a date as supposed by Dr. Lindenschmit, their great scarcity in the British Isles affords a conclusive argument against their being assigned to the period of the Roman occupation, of which other remains have come down to us in such abundance.

CHAPTER IX.

KNIVES, RAZORS, ETC.

It is a question whether, if in this work strict regard had been paid to the development of different forms of cutting implements, the knife ought not to have occupied the first place, rather than the hatchet or celt; for when bronze was first employed for cutting purposes it was no doubt extremely scarce, and would therefore hardly have been available for any but the smaller kinds of tools and weapons.

Both hatchets and knives, or rather knife-daggers, have been found with interments in barrows; but it seems better to include the majority of the latter class of instruments, which appear to occupy an intermediate place between tools and weapons, in the next chapter, which treats of daggers; rather than in this, which will

Fig. 239.—Wicken Fen.

be devoted to what appear to be forms of tools and implements. Some of these, however, like the celt or hatchet, may have been equally available both for peaceful and warlike uses; and though I have to some extent tried to keep tools and weapons under different headings, it appears impossible completely to carry out any such system of arrangement. Nor in treating of what I have regarded as knives does it seem convenient first to describe what appear to be the simpler and older forms, inasmuch as there are other forms which in all respects except the shape of the blade so closely resemble some of the socketed sickles described in the last chapter, that they seem almost of necessity to follow immediately in order. The first instrument which I shall cite has sometimes indeed been regarded as a sickle, though it is more properly speaking a curved knife.

It was found in Wicken Fen, and is now in the Museum of the Cambridge Antiquarian Society, the Council of which has kindly permitted me to engrave it as Fig. 239. It has already been figured, but not quite accurately, in the *Archæological Journal*,[*] the rib at the back of the blade being omitted. I am not aware of any other example of this form of knife having been found in the United Kingdom, but a double-edged socketed knife with a curved blade, found in Ireland, is in the Bateman Collection.

The ordinary form of socketed knife has a straight double-edged blade, extending from an oval or oblong socket, pierced by one or two holes, through which rivets or pins could pass to secure the haft. These holes are usually at right angles to the axis of the blade, but sometimes in the same plane with it.

Fig. 240 shows a knife with two rivet-holes, which was found at Thorndon, Suffolk, together with socketed celts, a spear-head, hammer, gouge, and an awl, several of which have been figured in preceding pages. Another (9 inches long), much like Fig. 240, but with the sides of the socket flat, and the blade more fluted, was found in the Thames, and is engraved in the *Archæological Journal*.[†] Another, of much the same size and general character, formed part of a hoard of bronze objects found in Reach Fen, near Burwell, of which mention has already frequently been made. It is in my own collection, and is shown in Fig. 241. I have another, 6¼ inches long, found in Edmonton Marsh.

Fig. 240.— Thorndon. ⅓   Fig. 241.— Reach Fen. ⅓

A fine blade of this kind, with two rivet-holes in the hilt (14¼ inches), was found in the New Forest, Glamorganshire, and was formerly in the Meyrick Collection.[‡] It is now in the British Museum. The blade has shallow flutings parallel with the edges.

A socketed knife of this kind (4½ inches) was found by General A. Pitt Rivers, F.R.S., in a pit at the foot of the interior slope of the rampart of Highdown Camp,[§] near Worthing, Sussex. It may possibly have accompanied a funereal deposit.

[*] Vol. vii. p. 302.
[‡] "Anc. Armour," pl. xlvii. 11.
[†] Vol. xxxiv. p. 301.
[§] *Arch.*, vol. xlii. p. 75, pl. viii. 22.

In some instances the two rivet-holes run lengthways of the oval of the socket. One such, discovered with other objects at Lanant, Cornwall (8¼ inches), is engraved in the *Archæologia*.* It is now in the Museum of the Society of Antiquaries. One like it was found on Holyhead Mountain,† Anglesea, and is now in the British Museum.

A fragment of a knife of this kind is in the museum at Amiens, and formed part of a hoard found near that town. It has a beading at the mouth of the socket, and also one about midway between the rivet-holes.

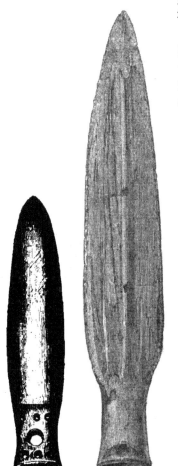

Fig. 242.—Heathery Fig. 243.—Kilgras-
Burn Cave. ⅓   ton, Perthshire. ⅓

Commonly there is but a single hole through the socket, especially in the smaller specimens. That shown in Fig. 242 is of this kind, but presents the remarkable feature of having upon each face of the socket six small projecting bosses simulating rivet-heads. It was found in the Heathery Burn Cave,‡ Durham, with socketed celts, spear-heads, and numerous other articles. Another from the same cave (5⅛ inches) with a plain and rather larger socket is in the collection of Canon Greenwell, F.R.S.

Of other specimens, but without the small bosses, the following may be mentioned :—One (6¼ inches long) found with socketed celts, part of a sword blade, and a gouge, at Martlesham, Suffolk, and in the possession of Captain Brooke, of Ufford Hall. Two found in the Thames near Wallingford.§ Another (5⅜ inches), from the same source, in my own collection. This was found with a socketed celt, gouge, chisel, and razor (Fig. 269). One from Llandysilio, Denbighshire, found with socketed celts and a spear-head, is in Canon Greenwell's collection. A knife of this kind was among the relics found above the stalagmite in Kent's Cavern, near Torquay.

I have a knife of this character (4¾ inches), but with the rivet-hole in a line with the edges of the blade, found in Dorsetshire.

* Vol. xv. p. 118, pl. ii.; "Catal. Mus. Soc. Ant.," p. 16.
† *Arch. Journ.*, vol. xxiv. p. 254.
‡ *Proc. Soc. Ant.*, 2nd S., vol. ii. p. 132; *Arch. Journ.*, vol. xix. p. 359. This cut is lent by the Society.   § *Proc. Soc. Ant.*, vol. iv. p. 303.

In Scotland the socketed form of knife is very rare.

That shown in Fig. 243 was found at Kilgraston, Perthshire, and is in the collection of Canon Greenwell, F.R.S. It has a central rib along the blade and two shorter lateral ribs, and in some respects has more the appearance of being a spear-head than a knife.

Another, with the rivet-hole in the same plane as the blade, was found near Campbelton, Argyleshire, and has been engraved as a spear-head by Professor Daniel Wilson.[*] The discovery of a blade having its original handle, as subsequently mentioned, proves, however, that some of these are rightly regarded as knives, though another form (Fig. 328) has more the appearance of being a spear-head. The curved knife with a socket, figured by the same author,[†] can hardly, I think, be Scottish.

In Ireland the socketed form of knife is more abundant than in either England or Scotland. No less than thirty-three such knives[‡] are recorded by Sir W. Wilde, as preserved in the Museum of the Royal Irish Academy, of five of which he gives figures. Many specimens also exist in private collections.

That shown in Fig. 244 is in the collection of Canon Greenwell, F.R.S., and was found at Kells, Co. Meath. As will be observed, the blade is at the base somewhat wider than the socket. The indented lines upon it appear to have been produced in the casting, and not added by any subsequent process. A knife of the same kind, found in the Bog of Aughrane, near Athleague, Co. Galway, is still attached to the original handle, which, like many of those of the flint knives found in the Swiss Lake-dwellings, is formed of yew. It has been several times figured.[§]

I have a specimen of the same character, but in outline more like Fig. 240, 6 inches long, from the North of Ireland.

A knife of this kind, found in a hoard at St. Genoulph, is in the Tours Museum.

Fig. 244.—Kells. ½

In some instances the junction between the blade and the socket is made to resemble that between the hilt and blade of some of the bronze swords and daggers, such as Figs. 291 and 349.

The example shown in Fig. 245 is in my own collection. I do not, however, know in what part of Ireland it was found. The rivet-hole is at the side, and not on the face, in which, however, there is a slight flaw, which assumes the appearance of a hole in the figure. In Canon Greenwell's collection is a nearly similar specimen (10¾ inches), found at Balteragh, Co. Derry, with two rivet-holes at the side and the socket somewhat ornamented by parallel grooves at the mouth and at the junction with the blade.

* "Preh. Ann. of Scot.," vol. i. p. 390.   † Op. cit., p. 402.   ‡ "Catal.," p. 465.
§ "Catal. Mus. R. I. A.," fig. 350; Arch., vol. xxxvi. p. 330; "Horæ Ferales," pl. x. 29.

One of the socketed knives in the Academy Museum at Dublin has two rivet-holes on the face. Of the others, about two-thirds have a single rivet-hole on the face, and the other third one on the side.

A long blade, somewhat differing in its details from Fig. 245, was found between Lurgan and Moira, Co. Down, and, it is stated, in company with the bronze hilt or pommel shown in Fig. 246. These objects formed part of the Wilshe Collection, and are now in the Museum of the Royal Irish Academy. Two objects, somewhat similar to Fig. 246, found with spear-heads in Cambridgeshire, will subsequently be mentioned. A piece of bronze of much the same form, found with a hoard of bronze objects at Marden,* in Kent, seems to be a jet or waste piece from a casting. It has, however, been regarded as part of a fibula.

The socketed form of knife is hardly known upon the Continent, though, as will have been observed, it has occasionally been found in the North of France. Among the fragments of metal forming part of the deposit of an ancient bronze-founder, and discovered at Dreuil, near Amiens, I have the fragments of two such knives. I have also a fine and entire specimen, 9¼ inches long, from the bed of the Seine at Charenton, near Paris. There is a transverse rib at each end and in the middle of the socket, through the face of which are two rivet-holes. A portion of the original wooden handle is still in the socket, secured in its place by two pins, also apparently of wood, which pass through the rivet-holes. Another knife (6⅝ inches), like Fig. 241, but with only one rivet-hole, was also found in the Seine at Paris, and is now in my collection.

Several socketed knives with curved blades have been found in the Swiss Lake-dwellings, and one such, found with the sickle already mentioned, is in the Amiens Museum.

There is another form of socketed knife which it will be well here to mention. The blade is sharp on both sides, but instead of being flat it is curved into a semicircle. For a typical example I am obliged to have recourse to a French specimen.

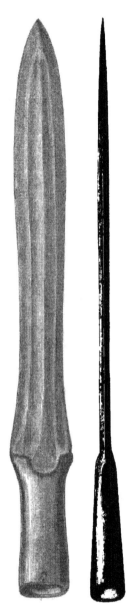

Fig. 245.—Ireland.   ⅓

That shown in Fig. 247 is in my own collection, and was found with a

* *Arch. Assoc. Journ.*, vol. xiv. p. 258.

gold torque and bracelet, a bronze anvil (Fig. 217), and other objects, at Fresné 'la Mère, near Falaise, Calvados. It seems well adapted for working out hollows in wood. With it was found a small, tanged, single-edged knife, the end of which is bent to a smaller curve.

An instrument of much the same character (4 inches) was found, with a bronze sword, spear-heads, &c., in the Island of Skye, and is now

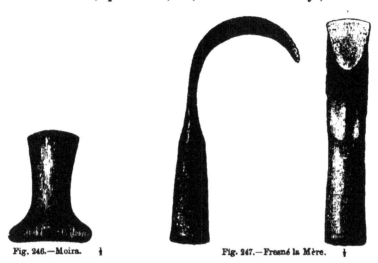

Fig. 246.—Moira. ½   Fig. 247.—Fresné la Mère. ½

in the Antiquarian Museum at Edinburgh. As Professor Daniel Wilson* observes, "in general appearance it resembles a bent spear-head, but it has a raised central ridge on the inside, while it is nearly plain and smooth on the outer side.—The most probable use for which it has been designed would seem to be for scraping out the interior of canoes and other large vessels made from the trunk of the oak." It is shown as Fig. 248. Another instrument of the same kind (4½ inches), found at Wester Ord, Invergordon, Ross-shire, is engraved in the *Proceedings of the*

Fig. 248.—Skye. ½   Fig. 249.—Wester Ord. ½

Society of Antiquaries of Scotland,† and is here by their permission reproduced as Fig. 249.

It seems by no means improbable that such instruments may have been

* "Preh. Ann.," vol. i. p. 400 ; *Proc. Soc. Ant. Scot.*, vol. viii. p. 310. The cut is here reproduced by permission of Messrs. Macmillan.

† Vol. viii. p. 310.

mistaken for bent spear-heads, and that they are not quite so rare as would at present appear.

Two specimens of the socketed form have been found in the Lake settlement of the Eaux Vives, near Geneva, and are now in the museum of that town. Another, with a tang, is in the collection of M. Forel, of Morges, and was found among the pile-dwellings near that place.

A fragment of what appears to have been one of these curved knives, but with a solid handle, and not a socket, was found with gouges and various fragments at Houn-slow, and is now in the British Museum.

What seems to be a tanged curved knife of this kind formed part of the great Bologna hoard.

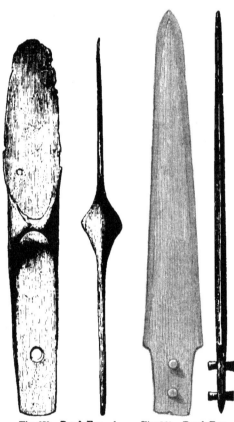

Fig. 250.—Reach Fen. ½   Fig. 251.—Reach Fen. ½

Another form of knife, which appears to be intermediate between those with sockets and those with merely a flat tang, is shown in Fig. 250. In this there are loops extending across the blade on either side, which would receive the ends of the two pieces of wood or horn destined to form the handle, so that a single rivet sufficed to bind them and the blade between them firmly together.

The original was found in Reach Fen, Cambridgeshire, and is now in my own collection. The blade has the appearance of having been originally longer, but of being now worn away by use. I know of no other specimen of the kind. The power to cast such loops upon the blade is a proof of no ordinary skill in the founder.

A palstave with a loop of this kind instead of a stop or side-flanges was found at Donsard,* Haute Savoie.

Another form of knife or dagger has merely a flat tang, in some

* Chantre, "Album," pl. vi. 2.

cases provided with rivets by which it could be fastened to a handle, in others without rivets, as if it had been simply driven into a handle.

The blade shown in Fig. 251 was found in the same hoard as that engraved as Fig. 241. The rivets are fast attached to the blade, and the handle through which they passed was probably of some perishable material, such as wood, horn, or bone.

Another blade (5¼ inches), with a broad tang and two rivet-holes, was found in the Thames.*

In the British Museum is a knife much like the figure, 8 inches long, and showing three facets on the blade, found in the Thames at Kingston.

The knife-blades with broad tangs, which were not riveted to their handles, were in some instances provided with a central ridge upon the tang, which served to steady them in their handles, and in others the stem or tang was left plain.

One of the former class, from the Heathery Burn Cave, is shown in Fig. 252. It is in the collection of Canon Greenwell, F.R.S.

An imperfect knife of the same kind, found in Yorkshire, is in the Scarborough Museum.

Another, with the edges more ogival, like Fig. 241, was found in the neighbourhood of Nottingham,† with socketed celts and numerous other objects in bronze.

Another, broader at the base and more like a dagger in character, was found with various other articles at Marden,‡ Kent.

More leaf-shaped and sharply pointed blades of this kind, probably daggers rather than knives, have been often found in Ireland. One § (10½ inches) has been figured by Wilde. Another was in the Dowris hoard.

In the Isle of Harty hoard, already more than once cited, was a knife with a plain tang, shown in Fig. 253. It has rather the appearance of having been made from the point of a broken sword, as the edges of the tang have been "upset" by hammering. The blade itself is now narrower than the tang, the result probably of much wear and use.

The end of a broken sword in the Dowris hoard has been converted into a knife in a similar manner. In the collection of the late Lord Braybrooke is what appears to be part of a tanged knife, sharpened at the broken end so as to form a chisel.

In the Reach Fen hoard was a knife (4¼ inches) of much the same character, but not so broad in the tang.

A flat blade with a tang for insertion in a haft must have been a very early form of metal tool. Among the Assyrian relics from Tel Sifr, in South Babylonia, such blades were found, of which there are examples in the British Museum.

Canon Greenwell, F.R.S., has two leaf-shaped blades of copper, with tangs set in handles of bone rather longer than the blades, which were lately in use among the Esquimaux. In form they resemble Fig. 257.

* Proc. Soc. Ant., 2nd S., vol. ii. p. 229.   † Proc. Soc. Ant., 2nd S., vol. i. p. 332.
‡ Arch. Assoc. Journ., vol. xiv. p. 258.   § "Catal.," p. 467, fig. 355.

P 2

It will now be well to mention some of the other Irish specimens of this class.

The knives with the projecting rib upon the tang are by no means
uncommon, and there are several in the Museum of the Royal Irish
Academy and elsewhere. Canon Greenwell has one (6⅜ inches) from

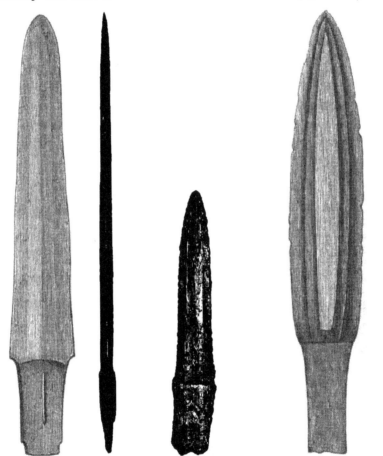

Fig. 252.—Heathery Burn Cave.   ⅓   Fig. 253.—Harty.   ⅓   Fig. 254.—Ireland.   ⅓

Ballynascreen, Co. Tyrone, much like that from the Heathery Burn Cave
(Fig. 252).

The knife or dagger with a plain tang and an ornamented blade
engraved as Fig. 254 is in the Museum of the Royal Irish Academy.
Another, simply ridged and with a single rivet-hole in the tang, found at
Craigs,* Co. Antrim, is in the collection of Mr. R. Day, F.S.A. It is less
round-ended than the blade with a central rib along it and one rivet-hole
in the tang, shown in Fig. 255. This is in my own collection, and was
found at Ballyclare, Co. Antrim.

* *Proc. Soc. Ant.*, 2nd S., vol. v. p. 269 (woodcut).

A mould for blades of this character will subsequently be mentioned.

Another form of knife, unless possibly it was intended for a lance-head, is shown in Fig. 256. This specimen is also from the Reach Fen hoard, but is of yellower metal and differently patinated from the objects found with it. Canon Greenwell has a knife of the same form (4¾ inches), found at Seamer Carr, Yorkshire. Another, smaller (3⅜ inches), is in the British Museum, but its place of finding is not known. A nearly similar blade, found near Ballycastle, Co. Antrim, is shown in Fig. 257.

Another example of this form (5¾ inches) is in the British Museum.

Sir W. Wilde [*] has figured some other examples of the same kind, from 3 to 4 inches long, which he regarded as arrow-heads. They appear to me, however, too large for such a purpose.

In the Museum of the Royal Irish Academy is yet another variety, with the blade pierced in the centre (Fig. 258).

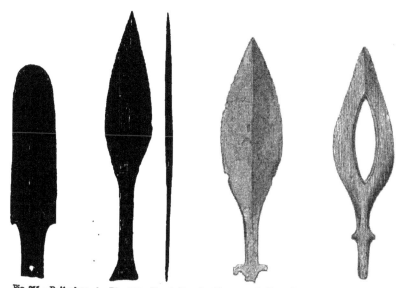

Fig. 255.—Ballyclare. ½   Fig. 256.—Reach Fen. ½   Fig. 257.—Ballycastle. ½   Fig. 258.—Ireland. ½

Before proceeding to describe some other symmetrical double-edged blades, it will be well to notice such few examples as have been found of single-edged blades, like the ordinary knives of the present day. Abundant as these are, not only in the Lake-dwellings of Switzerland, but in France and other continental countries, they are of extremely rare occurrence in the British Isles.

In Fig. 259 I have engraved a small instrument of this kind, found at Wigginton, near Tring, Herts, the handle of which terminates in the head of an animal. It was therefore not intended for insertion into a haft of some other material.

[*] "Catal. Mus. R. I. A.," p. 503, figs. 387, 388, 389.

I have another bronze knife, rather longer and narrower, and with a pointed tang, which is said to have been found in London; but of this I am by no means certain.

The rude knife found with the Isle of Harty hoard, and shown full size

Fig. 259.—Wigginton.   ½

as Fig. 260, is the only other English specimen with which I am acquainted, but no doubt more exist.

The only specimen mentioned in the Catalogue of the Museum of the Society of Antiquaries of Scotland is in all 14 inches long, with a thick back and notched tang, and of this the place of finding is unknown.

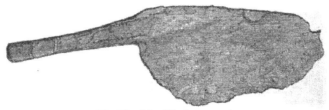

Fig. 260.—Isle of Harty.   ½

Professor Daniel Wilson * speaks of it as having been found in Ayrshire, and regards it as a reaping instrument. He also figures a socketed knife of much the same size from the collection of Sir John Clerk at Penicuick House, in which are also some tanged specimens. I cannot help suspecting that these are of foreign origin.

In Ireland the form appears to be at present unknown.

In Fig. 261 is shown a knife of a form which is of extremely rare occurrence in this country; though, as will be seen, it has frequently been found in France.

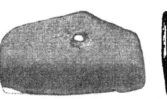

Fig. 261.—Allhallows, Hoo.   ½

The specimen here figured has been kindly lent me by Mr. Humphrey Wickham, of Strood, and was found with a hoard of bronze objects at Allhallows, Hoo,† Kent. The hoard contained socketed celts, gouges, a spear-head, fragments of swords, and the object engraved as Fig. 286. One more crescent-like in form was found with a hoard of bronze objects near Meldreth, Cambridgeshire, and is in the British Museum.

Knives of this kind were associated with celts, gouges, &c., in the hoard

* "Preh. Ann. Scot.," vol. i. p. 402.   † *Arch. Cant.*, vol. xi. p. 125, pl. c. 14.

of Notre-Dame d'Or, now in the museum at Poitiers. Two also were present in the Alderney hoard found near the *Pierre du Villain.**

Some knives of this character were found with a hoard of bronze tools and weapons at Questembert, Brittany, and are now in the museum at Vannes. A broken one was in the hoard of the Jardin des Plantes, Nantes.† One from La Manche is engraved in the *Memoirs of the Society of Antiquaries of Normandy*, 1827—8, pl. xvi. 20. A knife of this character of rectangular form, each side being brought to an edge, was found with other bronze relics at Plonéour, Brittany, and is engraved in the *Archæologia Cambrensis*.‡ In character this knife closely resembles some of those in flint.§ A kind of triangular knife of the same character was found at Briatexte‖ (Tarn). One from the station of Eaux Vives, in the Lake of Geneva, has the face ornamented at the blunt margin with a vandyke of hatched triangles. In some French varieties there are rings at the top of the blade instead of holes through it. In a curious specimen from St. Julien, Chateuil, in the collection of M. Aymard, at Le Puy, the edge is nearly semicircular, and there are eight round holes through the blade as well as two rings at the back. Some of the razors from the Lake-dwellings of Savoy and Switzerland are of much the same character as these knives. I have a knife of this class with a rather large triangular opening in it and two circular loops, found at Bernissart, Hainault.¶ Another somewhat different was found at Lavène** (Tarn).

Fig. 262.—Cottle.

A Danish†† knife of this character has five circular loops along the hollowed back. A Mecklenburg‡‡ knife has three such loops and corded festoons of bronze between.

The bronze knife or razor, shown full size in Fig. 262, was found at Cottle,§§ near Abingdon, and is now in the British Museum. It is of a peculiar and distinct type, but somewhat resembles in character the oblong bronze cutting instrument found at Plonéour, Brittany, already mentioned. It is thinner and flatter than would appear from the figure. A Mecklenburg‖‖ knife or razor figured by Lisch is analogous in form.

I have a rough and imperfect blade of somewhat the same character as that from Cottle, but thinner and more curved. It has no hole through

* *Arch. Assoc. Journ.*, vol. iii. p. 9.   † Parenteau, "Matériaux," vol. v. pl. viii. 16.
‡ 3rd S., vol. vi. p. 138.   § "Anc. Stone Imp.," p. 304, fig. 255.
‖ "Matériaux," vol. xiv. pl. ix. 4.
¶ "Ann. du cercle Arch. de Mons," 1857, pl. i. 6.
** "Matériaux," vol. xiv. p. 489.   †† Worsaae, "Nord. Olds.," fig. 160.
‡‡ Lisch, "Freder. Francisc.," tab. xvii. 10.
§§ *Proc. Soc. Ant.*, 2nd S., vol. ii. p. 301. For the use of this cut I am indebted to the Council of the Society.
‖‖ "Freder. Francisc.," tab. xviii. 14.

it, but thickens out at one end into a short boat-shaped projection about ¼ inch long. It was found near Londonderry.

A diminutive pointed blade which appears to be too small to have been in use as a dagger, and which from the rivet-hole through the tang can hardly have served as an arrow or lance head, is shown in Fig. 263. This specimen formed part of the Reach Fen hoard. A very small example of this kind of blade, from a barrow near Robin Hood's Ball, Wilts, has been figured by the late Dr. Thurnam, F.S.A., in his second exhaustive paper on "Ancient British Barrows," published in the *Archæologia,* [*] from which I have derived much useful information.

A small blade with the sides more curved is shown in Fig. 264, which I have copied from Dr. Thurnam's engraving.[†] The original was found in Lady Low, Staffordshire.

A smaller example, with a longer and imperforated tang, found in an urn at Broughton,[‡] Lincolnshire, and now in the British Museum, has been thought to be an arrow-head; but I agree with Dr. Thurnam in regarding both it and the small blades described by Hoare [§] as arrow-heads, as being more probably small double-edged knives.

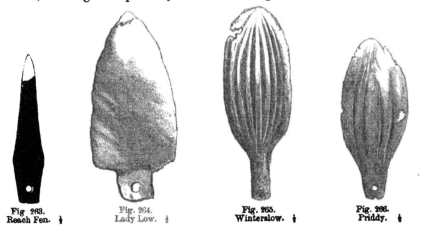

Fig. 263.   Fig. 264.   Fig. 265.   Fig. 266.
Reach Fen. ¼ Lady Low. ¼ Winterslow. ¼ Priddy. ¼

Some remarks as to the almost if not absolutely entire absence of bronze arrow-heads in this country will be found in a subsequent page.

The larger specimens of these tanged blades of somewhat triangular outline I have described as daggers, but I must confess that the distinction between knives and daggers is in such cases purely arbitrary. The more rounded forms which now follow seem rather of the nature of tools or toilet instruments than weapons.

Fig. 265, copied from Dr. Thurnam's plate,‖ represents what has been regarded as a razor blade. It was found in a barrow at Winterslow,

* Vol. xliii. p. 450, pl. xxxii. 5. † *Arch.*, vol. xliii. pl. xxxii. fig. 4.
‡ *Arch. Journ.*, vol. viii. p. 346. § " Anc. Wilts,"vol. i. pp. 67, 176, 238, pl. xxxii. 1.
‖ *Arch.*, vol. xliii. pl. xxxii. fig. 8.

Wilts, and is now in the Ashmolean Museum at Oxford. Its resemblance to the leaf of rib-wort (*Plantago media*) has been pointed out by Dr. Thurnam, who records that it was found in an urn with burnt bones and a set of beautiful amber buttons or studs. He has also figured one of nearly the same size, but with fewer ribs, from a barrow at Priddy, Somerset. This also has been regarded as an arrow-head, though it is 3 inches long and 1½ inches broad. It has a small rivet-hole through the tang. The original is now in the Bristol Museum, and its edge is described as sharp enough to mend a pen.* I have reproduced it in Fig. 266. A blade of much the same kind was found in an urn, with an axe-hammer of stone and a whetstone, at Broughton-in-Craven,† in 1675.

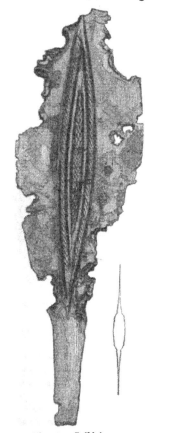

Fig. 267.—Balblair.   Fig. 268.—Rogart.   ½

Canon Greenwell records the finding of an oval knife (2⅞ inches) with burnt bones in an urn at Nether Swell,‡ Gloucestershire.

A flat blade, almost circular, with a somewhat longer tang than any here figured, formed part of the great Bologna hoard.

* *Arch. Journ.*, vol. xvi. p. 152.
† Thoresby's "Catal.," in Whitaker's ed. of "Ducat. Leod.," p. 114.
‡ "British Barrows," p. 446.

These instruments are occasionally found in Scotland. Some of them are of rather larger size, and ornamented in a different manner upon the face.

A small plain oval blade, which has possibly lost its tang, was found in a tumulus at Lieraboll,* Kildonan, Sutherland, and has been figured. Two oval blades were found with burnt bones in urns near St. Andrews.†

Another, found in a large cinerary urn at Balblair,‡ Sutherlandshire, is shown full size in Fig. 267. The edges are very thin and sharp, and the central rib shown in the section is ornamented with incised lines.

Another blade of the same character, but ornamented with a lozenge pattern, and with the midrib less pronounced, is shown in Fig. 268, also of the actual size. It was found in a tumulus at Rogart,§ Sutherland.

Fig. 269.—Wallingford.   ⅟

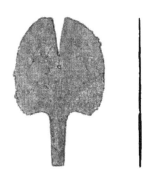

Fig. 270.—Heathery Burn Cave.   ⅟

Another, apparently more perfect, and with many more lozenges in the pattern, is engraved in Gordon's "Itinerarium Septentrionale." ‖ He describes it as "the end of a spear or Hasta Pura of old mixt brass, finely chequered." It was in Baron Clerk's collection.

The only English example which I can adduce was found with some sickles, a torque, and numerous other objects at Taunton. It is of nearly the same size and shape as Fig. 267, but the centre plate is fluted with a slight ridge along the middle and one on either side, and is not ornamented. It is described as a lance-head in the *Archæological Journal*.¶

I am not aware of any such blades having ever been found in Ireland, in which country the plainer forms of oval razors also seem to be extremely rare.

In Canon Greenwell's Collection is an oval blade (4 inches) with a flat central rib, tapering to a point, running along it. It has no tang, but

* *Proc. Soc. Ant. Scot.*, vol. x. p. 434.   † Greenwell, "Brit. Barrows," p. 446.

‡ *Proc. Soc. Ant. Scot.*, vol. vii. p. 476. For the use of this cut, as well as figs. 268, 271, 272, and 273, I am indebted to the Society.

§ *Proc. Soc. Ant. Scot.*, vol. x. p. 431.   ‖ P. 116, pl. 1. 8 (1726).

¶ Vol. xxxvii. p. 95. See also Pring, "Brit. and Rom. Taunton," pl. i. 4.

there is a rivet-hole through the broad end of the rib. It was found in an urn with burnt bones at Killyless, Co. Antrim.

The form most commonly known under the name of razor is that shown in Fig. 269, from a specimen in my own collection, found in the Thames, with a socketed knife and other objects, near Wallingford. One of almost identical character was found at Llangwyllog,* Anglesea.

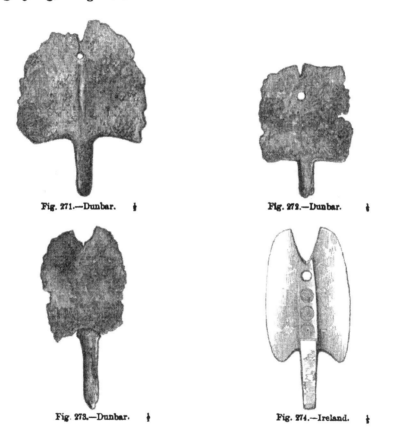

Fig. 271.—Dunbar.   ½   Fig. 272.—Dunbar.   ½

Fig. 273.—Dunbar.   ½   Fig. 274.—Ireland.   ½

Another, without midrib, from the Heathery Burn Cave, is, by the permission of Canon Greenwell, F.R.S., shown as Fig. 270.

An example from Wiltshire† in the Stourhead Museum (now at Devizes) is more barbed at the base and rounded at the top, in which there is neither notch nor perforation.

It is difficult to assign a use for the small hole usually to be seen in

---

* *Arch. Journ.*, vol. xxii. p. 74; *Arch. Camb.*, 3rd S., vol. xii. p. 97; *Arch.*, vol. xliii. pl. xxxii. 7.

† *Arch.*, vol. xliii. pl. xxxii. 6.

these blades. It may possibly be by way of precaution against the fissure in the blade extending too far, though in most cases the notch in the end of the blade does not extend to the hole.

Razors of this character have been discovered in Scotland. Three which are believed to have been found together in a tumulus at Bower-houses, near Dunbar,* Haddingtonshire, about 1825, are shown in Figs. 271, 272, and 273. They are all in the Antiquarian Museum, at Edinburgh, together with a socketed celt found with them.

Razors of the class last described have been found in Ireland, and three are mentioned in Wilde's Catalogue† of the Museum of the Royal

Fig. 275.—Kinleith.   ½

Irish Academy, to the Council of which body I am indebted for the use of Fig. 274. The midrib of the specimen here shown is decorated with ring ornaments formed of incised concentric circles, an ornament of frequent use in early times, though but rarely occurring on objects of bronze in Britain. There is a large razor of this kind in the Museum of Trinity College, Dublin. Several unornamented blades of this character were present in the Dowris hoard. Two which were found in a crannoge‡ in the county of Monaghan were regarded as bifid arrow-heads. One of these (2⅝ inches) is in the British Museum.

* *Proc. Soc. Ant. Scot.*, vol. x. p. 440; "Catal.," p. 83, No. 182.
† P. 549, fig. 433.   ‡ *Arch. Journ.*, vol. iii. p. 47.

A blade of this kind, but with a loop instead of a tang, and a hole at the base of the blade as well as one near the bottom at the notch, was found at Deurne,* Guelderland, and is in the Leyden Museum.

The only remaining form of razor which has to be noticed is that of which a representation is given of the actual size in Fig. 275.

This instrument was found at Kinleith,† near Currie, Edinburgh, and has been described and commented on by Dr. John Alexander Smith. The blade, besides being perforated in an artistic manner and having a ring at the end of the handle, is of larger dimensions than usual with instruments of this kind. The metal of which it is composed consists of copper 92·97 per cent., tin 7·03 (with a trace of lead).

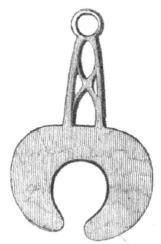

It affords the only instance of a razor of this shape having been found in the British Isles. The form much more nearly approaches one of not uncommon occurrence on the Continent than any other British example, and Dr. Smith has illustrated this by the accompanying figure of a razor from the Steinberg, near Nidau,‡ on the Lake of Bienne (Fig. 276). I have a razor of nearly the same form from the Seine at Paris, and others have been found in various parts of France.§

The nearest in character to Fig. 275 is perhaps one found in the hoard of Notre-Dame d'Or,‖ and preserved in the museum at Poitiers. Instead of the blade being a single crescent, it consists of two penannular concentric blades with a plain midrib connecting them, which has a ring at the external end.

Fig. 276.—Nidau.

An instrument with the blade formed of a single crescent was found at the same time.

A German example is in the Museum of the Deutsche Gesellschaft, at Leipzig.

In the next chapter I shall treat of those blades which appear to be weapons rather than tools.

* Jannsen's " Catal.," No. 209.
† *Proc. Soc. Ant. Scot.*, vol. v. p. 84 ; vol. x. p. 441.   I am indebted to the Society for the use of this and the following cut.
‡ See Keller, 5ter Bericht, Taf. xvi.
§ See Chantre, " Age du Br.," 1ère partie, p. 76.
‖ *Mém. de la Soc. des Ant. de l'Ouest*, 1844, pl. ix. 10.

CHAPTER X.

DAGGERS AND THEIR HILTS.——RAPIER-SHAPED BLADES.

AMONG all uncivilised, if not indeed among all civilised nations, arms of offence take a far higher rank than mere tools and implements; and on the first introduction of the use of metal into any country, there is great antecedent probability that the primary service to which it was applied was for the manufacture of weapons. So far as there are means of judging, a small knife or knife-dagger appears to have been among the earliest objects to which bronze was applied in Britain. Possibly, like the Highland dirk, the early form may have served for both peaceful and warlike purposes; but there are other and apparently later forms made for piercing rather than for cutting, and which are unmistakably weapons. The distinction which can be drawn between knives, such as some of those described in the last chapter, and the daggers to be described in this, is no doubt to a great extent arbitrary, and mainly dependent upon size. In the same way the distinction between a large dagger and a small sword, such as some of those to be described in the next chapter, is one for which no hard and fast rule can be laid down.

Nor in treating of daggers can any trustworthy chronological arrangement be adopted, though it is probable, as already observed, that the thin flat blades are earliest in date. The late Dr. Thurnam, in the paper already frequently cited, has pointed out that of bronze blades without sockets there are two distinct types. These are the tanged, which he regards as perhaps the more modern, and those provided with rivet-holes in the base of the blade, which seem to be the most ancient. I purpose mainly to follow this classification; and, inasmuch as the tanged blades are most closely connected with the smaller examples of the same character, described in the last chapter, I take them first in order, though possibly they are not the earliest in date.

But for its size, the blade shown in Fig. 277 might have been regarded as a knife for ordinary use. The original was found in a barrow at Roundway,* Wilts, covered with a layer of black powder, probably the remains of a wooden sheath and handle, the upper outline of which latter is marked upon the blade. It lay near the left hand of a contracted skeleton, with its point towards the feet. Between the bones of the left fore-arm was a bracer,† or arm-guard, of chlorite slate, and part of the blade and the tang of some small instrument, perhaps a knife. Near the head was a barbed flint arrow-head.

A smaller blade ‡ (5½ inches), of nearly the same shape and character, was found in one of the barrows near Winterslow, Wilts, as well as one more tapering in form.

Another, from Sutton Courtney, Berks (6¼ inches by 1⅜ inches), is in the British Museum.

Another (5¼ inches) was found by Mr. Fenton in a barrow at Mere Down,§ Wilts. In this case also there was a stone bracer near the left side of the contracted skeleton. Another, imperfect, and narrower in the tang, was found at Bryn Crûg,‖ Carnarvon, with interments. The double-looped celt (Fig. 88) was found at the same place.

Canon Greenwell, F.R.S., has what appears to be a tanged dagger (6 inches) from Sherburn Wold, Yorkshire.

A blade of this character (10 inches) was found by M. Cazalis de Fondouce in the cave of Bounias,¶ near Fonvielle (Bouches du Rhône), associated with instruments of flint.

Smaller tanged blades, of which it is hard to say whether they are knives or daggers, are not uncommon in France. · Two are engraved in the "Matériaux."** I have specimens from Lyons, and also from Brittany.

Another form, which appears to be a dagger rather than a knife, has the tang nearly as wide as the blade, and towards its base there is a single rivet-hole. A dagger of this kind was found with a contracted interment in a barrow near Driffield, Yorkshire, and an engraving of it

Fig. 277.—Roundway. ½

* *Arch.*, vol. xliii. p. 450, fig. 154, from which this cut is copied; "Wilts. Arch. Mag.," vol. iii. p. 186; "Cran. Brit.," pl. 42, xxxii. p. 3.
† "Anc. Stone Imp.," p. 381, fig. 355.
‡ *Arch.*, vol. xliii. pl. xxii. 2, 3, p. 449.
§ Hoare's "Anc. Wilts," vol. i. 44, pl. ii.
‖ *Arch. Journ.*, vol. xxv. p. 246.
¶ Chantre, "Age du Br.," 1re partie, p. 91; Cazalis de Fondouce, "Allées couv. de la Provence," pl. iv. 1.
** Vol. xiv. p. 491.

is given in the *Archæologia*,[*] from which Fig. 278 is reproduced.   It had a wooden sheath as well as the wooden handle, of which a part is shown. On the arm of the skeleton was a stone bracer.

Another, rather narrower in the tang and about 4¼ inches long, was found, with a stone axe-hammer, and bones, in an urn within a barrow at Winwick,[†] near Warrington, Lancashire.   One (2¼ inches) with a rivet-hole in its broad tang was found in an urn on Lancaster Moor.[‡]

A dagger of nearly the same form but having two rivet-holes was found by the late Rev. R. Kirwan in a barrow at Upton Pyne,[§] Devon.

One, only 3¼ inches long, and much like Fig. 278 in form, was found in an urn with burnt bones in Moot Low,[||] near Middleton, Derbyshire.

Fig. 278.—Driffield. ⅓

Another was found with burnt bones in a barrow at Lady Low,[¶] near Blore, Staffordshire.   The end of the handle in this instance was straight, and not hollowed.   One (5⅜ inches) with a broad tang, through which passes a single rivet, was found in the Thames.[**] It is now in the British Museum.

What Sir R. C. Hoare terms a lance-head (3 inches), found with amber beads in the Golden Barrow,[††] Upton Lovel, appears to have been a knife-dagger of this character.

A knife, 1 inch wide, which had been fastened to its haft of ox-horn by a single rivet, was found by Canon Greenwell in a barrow at Rudstone, Yorkshire.[‡‡] With the same interment was an axe-hammer of stone and a flint tool.   A blade like Fig. 278 (3 inches), from the sand-hills near Glenluce,[§§] Wigtonshire, has been figured.

Daggers, or possibly spear-heads, with a broad tang, as well as the moulds in which they were cast, were discovered by Dr. Schliemann on the presumed site of Troy.[||||]

The more ordinary form of instrument is that of which the blade was secured to the handle by two or more rivets at its broad base. These may be subdivided into knife-daggers with thin flat blades, and daggers which as a rule have a thick midrib and more or less ornamentation on the surface of the blade.   The former variety is now generally accepted as being the more ancient of the two, and may probably have served as a cutting instrument for all purposes, and not have been intended for a weapon.

Fig. 279, representing a knife-dagger from a barrow at Butterwick,[¶¶] Yorkshire, E.R., explored by Canon Greenwell, will give a good idea of

[*] Vol. xxxiv. pl. xx. 8, p. 255.
[†] *Arch. Assoc. Journ.*, vol. xvi. p. 295, pl. xxv. 9.
[‡] *Arch. Assoc. Journ.*, vol. xxi. p. 160.   [§] *Trans. Devon. Assoc.*, vol. iv. p. 643.
[||] "Vest. Ant. Derb.," p. 51; *Arch. Journ.*, vol. i. p. 247; Bateman's "Catal.," p. 4.
[¶] "Ten Years' Digg.," p. 163; "Catal.," p. 19.
[**] *Proc. Soc. Ant.*, 2nd S., vol. iii. p. 45.   [††] "Anc. Wilts," vol. i. p. 99, pl. xi.
[‡‡] "British Barrows," p. 265.   [§§] "Ayr and Wigton Coll.," vol. ii. p. 12.
[||||] "Troy and its Remains," p. 330.   [¶¶] "British Barrows," p. 186.

the usual form, though these instruments are not unfrequently more acutely pointed. This specimen was found with the body of a young man, and had been encased in a wooden sheath. The haft had been of ox-horn, which has perished, though leaving marks of its texture on the oxidized blade. In the same grave were a flat bronze celt (Fig. 2), a bronze pricker or awl (Fig. 225), a flint knife, and some jet buttons. Another blade of the same character, but rather narrower in its proportions, was found in a barrow at Rudstone,* Yorkshire. The handle had in this instance also been of ox-horn. In the same grave were a whetstone, a ring and an ornamental button of jet, and a half-nodule of pyrites and a flint for striking a light. Of the shape of the handles I shall subsequently speak; I will only here remark that at their upper part, where they clasped the blade, there was usually a semi-circular or horseshoe-shaped notch, in some instances very wide and in others but narrow. This notch is more rarely somewhat V-shaped in form.

A blade of nearly the same form as Fig. 279, but with only two rivet holes, found in a barrow at Blewbury,† Berks, is preserved in the Ashmolean Museum at Oxford. Another, also with two rivets, was found by the late Mr. Bateman in a barrow near Minning Low,‡ Derbyshire. Its handle appears to have been of horn. Its owner, wrapped in a skin, had been buried enveloped in fern-leaves, and with him was also a flat bronze celt, a flat bead of jet, and a flint scraper. Dr. Thurnam mentions eighteen § other blades, varying from 2½ inches to 6¾ inches in length, as having been found during the Bateman excavations, as

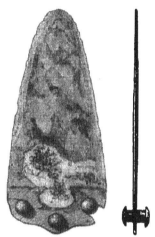

Fig. 279.—Butterwick.   ½

well as one 7¾ inches long and sharply pointed, found at Lett Low,∥ near Warslow, Staffordshire. Of these twenty, sixteen were found with unburnt bodies and four with burnt. Some of these were, however, of the tanged variety, and some fluted or ribbed. At Carder Low a small axe-hammer of basalt, as well as a knife-dagger of this kind, with the edges worn hollow by use, had been placed with the body. The same was the case in a barrow at Parcelly Hay, near Hartington, Derbyshire.

At End Low, near Hartington, there was a rudely formed "spearhead" of flint beside the knife-dagger, and at Thorncliff,¶ on Calton Moor, Staffordshire, "a neat instrument of flint."

In some cases, though there were holes in the blade, there were no rivets ** in them, which led Mr. Bateman to think that they were attached

* "British Barrows," p. 264, fig. 125; "Anc. Stone Imp.," p. 284.
† *Arch. Journ.*, vol. v. p. 282; *Arch. Assoc. Journ.*, vol. xvi. p. 249.
‡ *Arch. Assoc. Journ.*, vol. vii. p. 217; Bateman's "Catal.," p. 15; "Ten Years' Dig.," p. 34.
§ "Vest. Ant. Derb.," pp. 61, 63, 66, 68, 90, 96; "Ten Years' Dig.," pp. 21, 24, 34, 29, 57, 91, 113, 115, 119, 148, 160, 163; "Cran. Brit.," pl. 13, xxii. 2.
∥ "Ten Years' Dig.," p. 245; *Arch. Assoc. Journ.*, vol. xviii. p. 42.
¶ "Ten Years' Dig.," p. 119.   ** *Op. cit.*, pp. 57, 113.

Q

to their handles by ligatures. In a barrow in Yorkshire,[*] Mr. Harland found, with remains of a burnt body, a small bronze knife which still had adhering to it some portions of cord partly charred, apparently the remains of what had formed the attachment to the handle. Pins of wood, bone, or horn were no doubt frequently used instead of metal rivets. Such pins seem to have been commonly employed for securing spearheads to their shafts. "An instrument of brass,[†] formed like a spearhead, but flat and thin," was found in a barrow on Bincombe Down, Dorsetshire. "It had been fixed to a shaft by means of three wooden pegs, one of which remained in the perforation when found, but on being exposed to the air fell immediately into dust." In certain dagger blades with four or more rivet-holes some are devoid of rivets, while there are metal rivets in the others.

A remarkably small blade, only 1¾ inches long, with two rivet-holes, was found in a tumulus in Dorsetshire.[‡] Another (4⅛ inches) lay with burnt bones, in what was regarded as a cleft and hollowed trunk of a tree, in a barrow near Yatesbury,[§] Wilts. Another, more triangular in shape, and also with two rivet-holes, was found in a barrow near Stonehenge.[||]

Another (2⅛ inches) of the same character was found with burnt bones, a needle of wood, and a broken flint pebble, in an urn at Tomen-y-Mur,[¶] near Festiniog, Merionethshire.

Of knife-daggers with three rivet-holes found in our southern counties, may be mentioned one (5¼ inches) found with a drinking cup and a perforated stone axe, accompanying an unburnt interment, in a barrow at East Kennett,[**] Wilts. Another (4¼ inches), also accompanied by a stone axe-hammer, was found in a barrow called Jack's Castle,[††] near Stourton. The body had in this instance been burnt. Another knife-dagger, also with burnt bones, in a barrow at Wilsford,[‡‡] was accompanied by two flint arrow-heads, some whetstones, and some instruments of stag's-horn. Another, protected by a wooden scabbard, was found in a barrow at Brigmilston.[§§]

What appear to have been blades of the same kind were found with burnt bones in the barrows near Priddy,[||||] Somerset, and Ashey Down,[¶¶] Isle of Wight (6 inches). The latter is tapering in form. One (7¾ inches) which shows no rivets was found at Culter,[***] Lanarkshire.

An unfinished blade without rivet-holes was also found, with castings of palstaves and flanged celts, at Rhosnesney,[†††] near Wrexham.

From Derbyshire may be cited that from Carder Low,[‡‡‡] already described, and one from Brier Low.[§§§] Another from Lett Low,[||||||] Staffordshire, has already been mentioned, as have been others described by Bateman.[¶¶¶] One from a barrow at Middleton [****] was regarded by Pegge as a spear-head.

[*] Greenwell, "Brit. Barrows," p. 360, n.
[†] M.S. Minutes of Soc. Ants., 1784, p. 51, cited in Warne's "Celtic Tumuli of Dorset," pt. iii. p. 7.   [‡] Arch. Journ., vol. v. p. 323.
[§] Arch. Inst., Salisb. vol. p. 97.   [||] Stukeley's "Stonehenge," p. 45, pl. xxxii.
[¶] Arch. Journ., vol. xxiv. p. 16; Arch. Camb., 3rd S., vol. xiv. p. 241.
[**] Arch. Inst., Salisb. vol. p. 110; Arch. Journ., vol. xxiv. p. 29.
[††] Hoare's "Anc. Wilts," vol. i. p. 39, pl. i.; Archæol., vol. xliii. p. 452.
[‡‡] "Anc. Wilts," vol. i. p. 209.   [§§] "Anc. Wilts," vol. i. p. 185.
[||||] Arch. Journ., vol. xvi. p. 148, 151.   [¶¶] Arch. Assoc. Journ., vol. x. p. 164.
[***] Arch. Assoc. Journ., vol. xvii. p. 21.   [†††] Arch. Camb., 4th S., vol. vi. p. 71.
[‡‡‡] Archæol., vol. xliii. pl. xxxiii. fig. 4.   [§§§] Ibid., fig. 3.   [||||||] Ibid., fig. 5.
[¶¶¶] "Ten Years' Dig.," pp. 21, 115, 119.   [****] Archæol., vol. ix. p. 94, pl. iii.

From Yorkshire Mr. Bateman describes one (4½ inches) with a crescent-shaped mark showing the form of the handle, found with an extended skeleton at Cawthorn.* Another (6 or 7 inches), from a barrow near Pickering,† had a V-shaped notch in the handle, to which had been attached a small bone pommel. One from Bishop Wilton,‡ belonging to Mr. Mortimer, has been engraved by Dr. Thurnam.

The mention of this pommel suggests that it is time to consider the manner in which these blades were hafted, as to which the discoveries of Sir Richard Colt Hoare in the Wiltshire barrows, and of Canon Greenwell in those of Yorkshire, leave no doubt. The hafts appear in nearly all cases to have consisted of ox-horn, bone, or wood, sometimes in a single piece with a notch for receiving the blade, and sometimes formed of a pair of similar pieces riveted together, one on each side of the blade. The lower end of the haft was often inserted in a hollow pommel usually of bone.

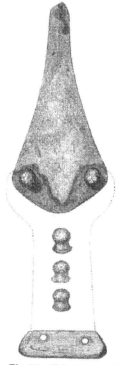

Fig. 280.—Helperthorpe. ⅓

The nature of the arrangement of the haft when formed of two pieces will be readily understood on reference to Fig. 280, in which the presumed outline of the original ox-horn haft is shown by dotted lines, and the rivets by which the two plates of horn were bound together are in the position they originally occupied along the centre of the haft. The outline of the upper part of this handle, where it was secured by two rivets to the blade, is still visible, and is shown by darker shading. The pommel at the lower end was attached by pins of horn or of wood, and not by metal rivets. A separate view and section of the pommel is shown in Fig. 281. The original was found by Canon Greenwell, F.R.S., with a contracted interment in a barrow at Helperthorpe,§ Yorkshire, at the open-

Fig. 281.—Helperthorpe. ⅓

ing of which I was present. As will be seen, the blade has all

* "Ten Years' Dig.," p. 206. † *Op. cit.*, p. 226. ‡ *Arch.*, vol. xliii. pl. xxxiii. 6.
§ "British Barrows," p. 207. This specimen has since been presented, with the rest of the Greenwell Collection, to the British Museum.

the appearance of having been much worn by use and repeated whetting.

Bone pommels of the same kind have been frequently met with in barrows, but their purpose was not known to some of the earlier explorers. One from a barrow on Brassington Moor* is described by Mr. Bateman as a bone stud perforated with six holes, and was thought to have been intended for being sown on to some article of dress or ornament. Another was found in a barrow at Narrow-dale Hill,† near Alstonefield, and is also described as a bone button. In both these instances the dagger itself seems to have entirely perished.

In a barrow subsequently opened by Mr. Ruddock near Pickering,‡ the butt end of a dagger handle was recognised in one of these objects. In this instance the pommel was made of three pieces of bone fastened together by two bronze rivets, and having two holes for the pegs by which it was secured to the handle.

Fig. 282.—Garton.

Fig. 283.—Wilmslow.

Two others in solid bone from barrows at Garton § and Bishop Wilton, Yorkshire, have been figured by Dr. Thurnam. The former is here by permission reproduced. That from the well-known Gristhorpe tumulus,‖ near Scarborough, in which the body lay in the hollowed trunk of an oak-tree, is more neatly made, being of oval outline with a projecting bead round the base. It has holes for three pins.

Another pommel of an ornamental character was found with burnt bones in an urn at Wilmslow, Cheshire, and is engraved in the *Journal of the British Archæological Association*,¶ from which Fig. 283 is here reproduced. The receptacle is so small that the haft to which it was attached probably consisted of but a single piece of ox-horn or wood. It appears as if the mortise had been made by drilling three holes side by side.

A very remarkable and beautiful hilt of a sword or dagger, formed of amber of a rich red colour and inlaid with pins of gold, was found in a barrow on Hammeldon Down,** Devonshire. By the kindness of the Committee of the Plymouth Athenæum I am enabled to give two views

* "Catal.," p. 1; "Vest. Ant. Derb.," p. 39.
† "Catal.," p. 12; "Vest. Ant. Derb.," p. 98.
‡ "Ten Years' Dig.," p. 226.   § *Arch.*, vol. xliii. p. 441.
‖ "Cran. Brit.," 52, 4; "Reliquary," vol. vi. p. 4.
¶ Vol. xvi. pl. 25, fig. 5, p. 288.
** *Trans. Devon. Assoc.*, vol..v. p. 555, pl. ii.

and a section of this unique object in Fig. 284. Instead of a socket or mortise, there is in this instance a tenon, or projection, which entered into a mortise or hole in the handle. On each side of this tenon is a small mortise of the same length, and through the tenon have been drilled two small holes, one from each side, for pins to attach the pommel to the handle. A small part of the pommel which was broken off in old times seems to have been united to the main body by a series of minute gold rivets or clips, but this piece has again been severed, though the pins round the margin of the fracture remain. This pommel seems disproportionately large for the slightly fluted blade, of which a fragment was found in the same barrow.

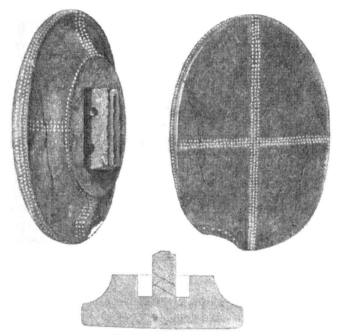

Fig. 284.—Hammeldon Down. ½

A small object of amber, apparently the pommel of a diminutive dagger, was found in a barrow at Winterbourn Stoke,* Wilts. A small knife or scraper, mounted in a handle formed of two pieces of amber, secured by two rivets and bound with four strips of gold, is also preserved at Stourhead.† The blade is at the side like that of a hatchet.

Amber was used for inlaying some of the ivory hilts of iron swords at Hallstatt.

The bronze object shown full size in Fig. 285 may not improbably be the pommel of the hilt of a dagger or sword. The hole through the base is irregular in form, and may be accidental. It was found in the hoard at Reach Fen, Cambridge, in which were also the tip of a scabbard and some fragments of swords, as well as two large double-edged knives.

* "Ancient Wilts," vol. i. p. 124, unpub. pl. xv. B; *Arch.*, vol. xliii. p. 503, fig. 196.
† "Ancient Wilts," vol. i. p. 201, pl. xxv. 4; *Arch.*, vol. xliii. p. 459.

A somewhat similar object is in the Musée de l'Oratoire, at Nantes. Another, found at Grésine,* Savoy, has been regarded as the tip for a scabbard. Another was found in the department of La Manche.†

What appears to be the hilt of either a sword or dagger was found in a hoard of bronze objects at Allhallows,‡ Hoo, Kent. By the kindness of Mr. Humphrey Wickham I am able to engrave it as Fig. 286. It consisted originally of a rectangular socketed ferrule with a rivet-hole through it, and attached to a semicircular end like the half of a grooved pulley. The socket itself extends for some distance into this semicircular part. From portions of a sword having been found with it, Mr. Wickham has regarded it as a kind of pommel. It may, however,

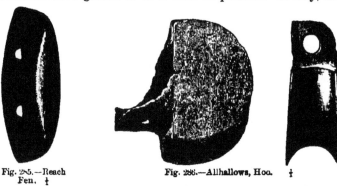

Fig. 285.—Reach Fen. ‡   Fig. 286.—Allhallows, Hoo. ‡

have been the end of a scabbard or a chape, and, if so, should have been described in Chapter XIII. The knife, Fig. 261, was found in the same hoard.

To return, however, to undoubted examples. The most remarkable of all dagger handles discovered in the British Isles are those obtained by Sir R. Colt Hoare from the barrows of Wiltshire.

One of these, from a barrow at Brigmilston,§ is here reproduced in Fig. 287, taken from the engraving in "Ancient Wiltshire." It is thus described by the late Dr. Thurnam: "It is of the thin broad-bladed variety. The handle is of wood, held together by thirty rivets of bronze, and strengthened at the end by an oblong bone pommel fastened with two pegs. It is decorated by dots incised in the surface of the wood, forming a border of double lines and circles between the heads of the rivets." He goes on to say that a similar dagger of the broad variety, having exactly the same number of rivets, was found in one of the Derbyshire‖ barrows. Two buttons of polished shale accompanied this interment. Another, from Garton,¶ Yorkshire, in the collection of Mr. Mortimer, has thirty-seven rivets and two strips of bronze at the sides of the handle, in addition to the four rivets for securing the blade. The bone pommel is shown in Fig. 282.

* "Exp. Arch. de la Sav.," 1878, pl. xii. 357.
† "Mém. Soc. Ant. Norm.," 1827—8, pl. xix. 4, 5.
‡ *Arch. Cant.*, vol. xi. p. 125, pl. c, 18.
§ "Ancient Wilts," vol. i. p. 185, pl. xxiii.; *Arch.*, vol. xliii. p. 458, pl. xxxiv. 2.
‖ Bateman, " Vest. Ant. Derb.," p. 68.   ¶ *Arch.*, vol. xliii. p. 462, pl. xxxiv. 3.

Another dagger, of somewhat the same character, was found at Leicester, and is preserved in the museum of that town. For the sketch from which Fig. 288 is engraved I am indebted to Mr. C. Read. In this instance the pommel consists of two pieces of bone riveted on either side of a bronze plate, which, however, does not appear to have been continuous with the blade. From the length of the rivets remaining

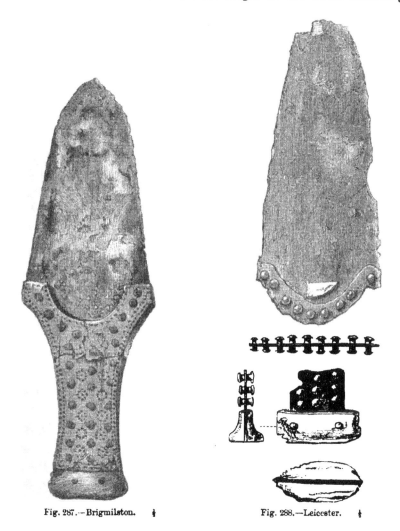

Fig. 287.—Brigmilston.   ½   Fig. 288.—Leicester.   ½

in the blade, the handle appears to have been somewhat thicker in the middle than at the sides.

In the British Museum is a dagger from a barrow at Standlow, Derbyshire, with a bone pommel of nearly the same character as that from Leicester.

Perhaps the most highly ornamented dagger handle ever discovered is that which was found by Sir R. Colt Hoare in the Bush Barrow,* near Normanton, the lower part of which, copied from the engraving in "Ancient Wiltshire," is shown in Fig. 289. A drawing of the whole dagger with its handle restored has been published by Dr. Thurnam.† The blade is 10½ inches long and slightly fluted at the sides, so that it is not, strictly speaking, a knife-dagger such as those hitherto described. It appears, however, best to call attention to it in this place. It lay with a skeleton placed north and south, with which were some rivets and thin plates of bronze, supposed to be traces of a shield. At the shoulders was a flanged bronze celt, like Fig. 9. Near the right arm was the dagger and "a spear-head" of bronze. These were accompanied by a nearly square plate of thin gold, with a projecting flat tongue or hook, which was

Fig. 289.—Normanton.

thought to have decorated the sheath of the dagger. Over the breast lay another lozenge-shaped plate of gold, 7 inches by 6 inches, the edges lapped over a piece of wood. On the right side of the skeleton was a stone hammer,‡ some articles of bone, many small rings of the same material, and another gold lozenge much smaller than that on the breast. As to the handle, I may repeat Sir Richard's words: "It exceeds anything we have yet seen, both in design and execution, and could not be surpassed (if, indeed, equalled) by the most able workman of modern times. By the annexed engraving you will immediately recognise the British zig-zag or the modern Vandyke pattern, which was formed, with a labour and exactness almost unaccountable, by thousands of gold rivets smaller than the smallest pin. The head of the handle, though exhibiting

* "Ancient Wilts," vol. i. p. 202, pl. xxvii. 2.   † *Arch.*, vol. xliii. pl. xxxv. 1.
‡ "Anc. Stone Imp.," p. 203, fig. 154.

no variety of pattern, was also formed by the same kind of studding. So very minute, indeed, were these pins, that our labourers had thrown out thousands of them with their shovels and scattered them in every direction before, by the necessary aid of a magnifying glass, we could discover what they were, but fortunately enough remained attached to the wood to enable us to develop the pattern." Some of the pins are shown in the figure below the hilt.

As Dr. Thurnam has pointed out, the ornamentation on a thin piece of metal (said to have been gilt), which apparently decorated the hilt of a bronze dagger, found in a barrow in Dorsetshire,* is of the same character, though produced in a different manner. This dagger is said by Douglas to have been "incisted" into wood. It is uncertain whether this refers to the hilt or to the sheath; but in several instances remains of sheaths have been found upon the blades of daggers, some of which have been already adduced, and others will hereafter be mentioned. Sir R. Colt Hoare, in a barrow near Amesbury,† found an interment of burnt bones, and with it a bronze dagger which had been "secured by a sheath of wood lined with linen cloth." A small lance-head, a pair of ivory nippers, and an ivory pin accompanied the interment. In one instance the wood of the sheath was "apparently willow."‡

I am unable to guarantee the accuracy of the representation of a large dagger with its handle given in Fig. 290, the original having unfortunately been destroyed in a fire. I have, however, copied it from Dr. Thurnam's § engraving, which was taken from a drawing by the late Mr. S. Solly, F.S.A.‖ It was found in 1845, in a barrow on Roke Down, near Blandford, Dorsetshire, and is thus described by Mr. Shipp: ¶ "The blade is exquisitely finished, and the handle, which is ivory, as perfect and as highly polished as any of more recent date. It was found with two small bronze spear-heads at the bottom of a cist cut in the chalk, and

Fig. 290.—Roke Down. ½

* Douglas, "Nenia," p. 153, pl. xxxiii. fig. 3.
† "Anc. Wilts," vol. i. p. 207.
‡ *Op. cit.*, p. 194.
§ *Arch.*, vol. xliii. pl. xxxiv. 1.
‖ *Proc. Soc. Ant.*, 1st S., vol. i. p. 75.
¶ *Arch. Assoc. Journ.*, vol. ii. p. 98; vol. xv. p. 228.

covered with burnt bones and ashes; and over it was an inverted urn of the coarsest make, unburnt and unornamented." In Mr. Shipp's drawing the handle expands gradually to the base like the mouth of a trumpet. In a subsequent communication * Mr. Shipp describes the two spear-heads as of iron.

Mr. Solly † says that with it was a second small blade, also of bronze, which may have been a knife, and makes no mention of iron spear-heads. He also says that it lay beneath a stone more than a ton in weight. Mr. C. Warne, F.S.A., has informed me that the spear-heads—if, indeed, such they were—were of bronze and not of iron. He has engraved the dagger in his Plate X.,‡ not from the original, but from the figure in the *Journal of the Archæological Association.*

Hilts made of bronze, though of frequent occurrence in Scandinavia, the South of France, and Italy, are rarely discovered in England or Scotland. That said to have been found at Bere Hill, near Andover, cast in one piece with the blade and with a raised rim round the margin, and studs like rivet-heads in the middle, has been kindly submitted to me by Mr. Samuel Shaw, its owner, and I believe it to be of Eastern and probably Chinese origin. Near Little Wenlock,§ however, a portion of a dagger was found with part of the handle, in form like that of the sword from Lincoln (Fig. 350), attached by four rivets. With it were a socketed celt, some spear-heads, and whetstones.

A beautiful Egyptian ‖ bronze dagger from Thebes is in the Berlin Museum. It has a narrow rapier-like blade and a broad flat hilt of ivory. Others of nearly the same character are in the British Museum. The end of the hilt is often hollowed, like that of Fig. 277, and the attachment to the blade is by means of three rivets.

In Ireland a few daggers have been found with bronze hilts still attached.

In the Museum of the Royal Irish Academy is a fine example, which has frequently been published, and which I have here reproduced as Fig. 291, from the engraving given by Wilde,¶ but on the scale of one-half. Both blade and handle are "highly ornamented, both in casting and also by the punch or graver."

A portion of a blade with a bronze hilt still attached was found near Belleek, Co. Fermanagh, and has been engraved in the *Proceedings of the Royal Historical and Archæological Association of Ireland.*** The cut is by their kindness here reproduced as Fig. 292. The handle is hollow, and the blade appears to have been originally attached by four pins or rivets, of which but two now remain. Possibly the other two were of horn.

Another Irish form of hafted dagger has also been frequently published.†† It is shown in Fig. 293. Vallancey describes this specimen as

* *Arch. Assoc. Journ.,* vol. ii. p. 100.   † *Arch.,* vol. xliii. p. 459.
‡ "Celtic Tumuli of Dorset," pl. ii. p. 17.
§ Hartshorne's "Salop. Ant.," p. 96, No. 7.
‖ Bastian und A. Voss, "Die Bronze schwerter des K. Mus.," Taf. xvi. 31; Wilkinson's "Ancient Egyptians," vol. i. p. 320. Another dagger with a hilt is figured at p. 23.
¶ "Catal. Mus. R. I. A.," p. 458, fig. 334; "Horæ Ferales," pl. vii. 14.
** *Proc.,* 4th S., vol. ii. p. 196.
†† Vallancey, "Coll.," vol. iv. p. 61, pl. xi. 4; Gough's "Camden," vol. iv. pl. xviii. 4; Wilde, "Catal. Mus. R. I. A.," p. 467, fig. 354; "Horæ Fer.," pl. vii. 13.

cast in one piece, the rivets being either ornamental or intended to stop against the top of the scabbard. No doubt these imitation rivets are

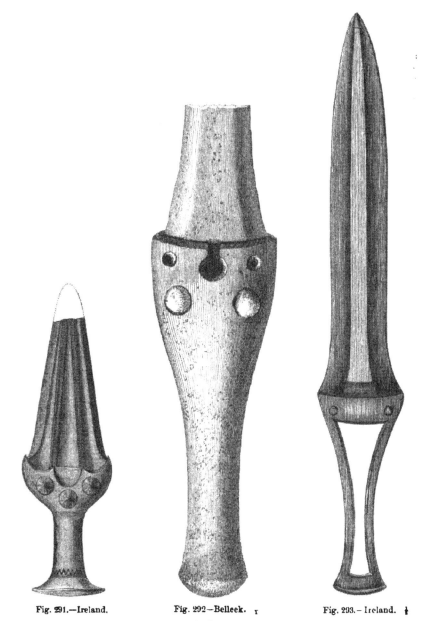

Fig. 291.—Ireland.   Fig. 292—Belleek.   Fig. 293.— Ireland.

mere "survivals" from those of the daggers, which were thus fastened to their handles before it was found that it saved trouble to cast the whole in one piece. The hole in the handle, the sides of which are left rough, was probably filled by two slightly overlapping plates of wood or horn riveted together.

Another * (14½ inches) was thought to have the "loop-fashioned" handle for suspending the weapon to a thong or the belt. I think, however, that when the daggers were in use the handles were to all appearance solid. In one found in Dunshaugh-lin † crannoge, Co. Meath, there is a second oval hole at the end of the hilt, which may have been used for suspension.

There is a good example of this type of dagger in the Blackmore Museum at Salisbury.

A small dagger (7½ inches), found near Balli-namore,‡ Co. Leitrim, has an extension of the blade in the form of a thin plate with a button at the bottom so as to form the body of the handle. In this part are two rivet holes for the attachment of the plates of wood or horn to form the handle.

Some handles of bronze knives found in Scan-dinavia and Switzerland § are formed with similar openings. Daggers with the blade and handle cast in one piece have been found in the Italian *terramare*.‖ I have a dagger of the same kind from Hungary.

I must now return, from this digression as to the hafting of daggers, to the thin blades or knife-daggers of which I was speaking.

Of those with four rivets but few can be cited. One of unusually large size is shown in Fig. 294. The original was found by Sir R. C. Hoare in a barrow at Woodyates.¶ It was protected by a wooden scabbard. A perforated ring and two buttons of jet, four barbed flint arrow-heads, and a bronze pin were found with the same skeleton. This blade, like many others, is described as having been gilt, but this can hardly have been the case. Dr. Thurnam ** has tested such bril-liantly polished surfaces for gold, but found no traces of that metal.

Fig. 294.—Woodyates. ⅔

A blade of this form is engraved in the "Barrow Diggers," †† but is described as a stone celt split in two.

* *Arch. Journ.*, vol. x. p. 161.
† Wilde, "Catal. Mus. R. I. A.," p. 466, fig. 353.
‡ Wilde, "Catal. Mus. R. I. A.," p. 463, fig. 346.
§ "Cong. préh.," Stockholm vol., 1874, p. 521; Keller's "Lake-dwell.," Eng. ed., pl. xli. 5.
‖ Strobel, "Avanzi Preromani," 1863, Tav. ii. 35; Gastaldi, "Nuovi Cenni," 1862, Tav. ii. 7.
¶ "Anc. Wilts," vol. i. p. 239, pl. xxxiv.
** *Arch.*, vol. xliii. p. 455.　　　　†† P. 74, pl. ii. fig. 3.

A nearly similar blade from Oefeli* (Lac de Bienne) is said to be of copper.

In Fig. 295 is shown a blade with five rivets, from an interment at Homington,† near Salisbury, which is now in the British Museum. One side is still highly polished, with an almost mirror-like lustre. The mark of the hilt is very distinct upon it.

One of more pointed form, and with a more V-shaped notch in the hilt, was found with an unburnt body in a cairn at North Charlton,

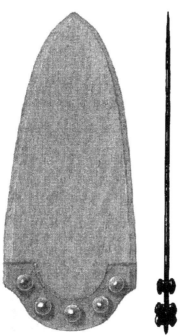

Fig. 295.—Homington. ½   Fig. 296.—Idmiston. ½

Northumberland, and is in the Greenwell Collection in the British Museum. The portion is broken off in which were the rivets.

Occasionally the surface of these thin blades is ornamented by engraved or punched patterns. The decoration usually consists of converging bands of parallel lines. The example given as Fig. 296 was found in a barrow at Idmiston, near Salisbury, and is now preserved in the Blackmore Museum. In one found in Dow Low,‡ Derbyshire, shown in Fig. 297, there are three parallel lines on either side which meet in chevron. This blade has two rivets.

In a barrow near Maiden Castle,§ Dorchester, opened by Mr. Sydenham, there lay in the midst of the ashes two bronze daggers. One

* Gross, " Deux Stations," pl. iv. 3.
† *Proc. Soc. Ant.*, vol. iv. p. 329; "Horæ Ferales," p. 158, pl. vii. 21; *Arch.*, vol. xliii. pl. xxxiii. 1.
‡ "Vest. Ant. Derb.," p. 96; *Arch.*, vol. xliii. p. 461, fig. 161.
§ *Arch.*, vol. xxx. p. 332, pl. xvii. 8; "Celtic Tumuli of Dorset," pt. iii. p. 46 pl. x. d, e.

(4 inches) has two lines engraved on it, forming a chevron parallel with the edges; the other (5½ inches) is described as "curiously wrought, chased, and gilt." This latter, to judge from Mr. Warne's engraving, has a slight projecting rib along the middle of the blade, between two others converging to meet it near the point. The space on each side of the central rib appears to be decorated by small circular indentations.

One from another barrow in Dorsetshire * has a treble chevron on the blade and a straight transverse groove between two ridges just above the hilt.

A small blade found in an urn at Wilmslow,† Cheshire, seems to have a single chevron upon it.

A dagger from a tumulus at Hewelinghen (Pas de Calais), and now in the museum at Boulogne, is of this character. It has double lines to the chevron and four rivet-holes.

Another was found with an interment at Rame‡ (Hautes Alpes) in company with other articles of bronze. It has six rivet-holes. A narrower blade and more of the rapier shape, with four rivet-holes, was found in the Marais de Donges § (Loire Inférieure).

A dagger much like Fig. 296, but with a double row of rivets, has been found at Mœrigen,‖ in the Lac de Bienne.

A dagger with a pointed blade having two parallel grooves just within each edge was found with other dagger blades, flat celts, flint arrow-heads, &c., in the tumulus of Kerhué-Bras, Finistère.¶ It has a plain wooden handle, to which the blade is attached by six rivets. The character of some of the other blades is peculiar.

A beautifully patinated dagger (7¼ inches) from the Seine at Paris, now in my own collection, has six rivet-holes at the base, as in Fig. 296, and is of nearly the same shape, though rather more sharply pointed. One of the rivets which remains is ⅝ inch long. The blade has upon it a small low rib on either side running parallel with the edge. On the inner side of the rib there is a groove, on the outer side the blade is flat. The edge itself is fluted.

I have a small thin blade (4⅜ inches), like Fig. 298, found in the Palatinate, which has four rivet-holes at the base. There is a band of five parallel lines running along each edge, and in the centre of the blade a chevron with the sides slightly curved inwards formed of two similar bands. The lines seem to have been punched in. The mark left by the hilt is like that on Fig. 296.

What appear to be knife-daggers, some of them with notches at the side for the reception of rivets, have been found with interments in Spain, and have been described by Don Gongora y Martinez** as lance-heads.

Knife-daggers of much the same character as the English have occasionally been found in Scotland.

* *Arch. Journ.*, vol. v. p. 322.
† *Arch. Assoc. Journ.*, vol. xvi. p. 288, pl. 25, fig. 6.
‡ "Matériaux," vol. xiii. p. 155.
§ *Rev. Arch.*, vol. xxxiii. p. 231.
‖ Gross, "Deux Stations," pl. iv. 4.
¶ "Matériaux," vol. xv. p. 289.
** "Ant. Preh. de Andalusia," pp. 97, 105.

That shown in Fig. 298 was found in a stone cist in a cairn at Cleigh,* Loch Nell, Argyleshire. Along the margin of the original handle is a line of small indentations made with a pointed punch.

Another (4¼ inches) was found in a cairn at Linlathen,† Forfarshire, together with a "drinking cup." Particulars of the finding of several others, with interments in sepulchral cairns, have been given by

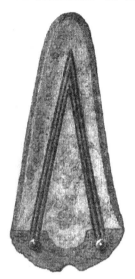

Fig. 297.—Dow Low.   Fig. 298.—Cleigh. ½

Mr. Joseph Anderson‡ in an interesting paper, to which the reader is referred.

Three others, from Drumlanrick,§ near Callander, Perth (4½ inches, two rivets), Crossmichael, Kirkcudbright- shire, and Callachally, Island of Mull, are in the Antiquarian Museum at Edinburgh. Another, apparently of the same type, was found in a cairn at Collessie,‖ Fife, the handle of which appears to have been en- circled by the gold fillet shown in Fig. 299. The sheath seems to have been of wood covered with cow-hide, the hairs on the outside.

Fig. 299.—Collessie. ¼

In Ireland the thin flat blades are of rare occurrence. Canon Greenwell, F.R.S., has one from Co. Antrim (4¾ inches) with three rivet-holes, and with a V-shaped notch in the mark of the handle.

There is a form of blade which appears to be intermediate between the flat knife-daggers and those to which the name of dagger may more

* *Proc. Soc. Ant. Scot.*, vol. x. pp. 84, 459. I am indebted to the Council of the Society for the use of this and the following cut.
† *Proc. Soc. Ant. Scot.*, vol. xii. p. 449.   ‡ *Op. cit.*, vol. xii. p. 439.
§ *P. S. A. S.*, vol. xii. p. 456.   ‖ *Op. cit.*, vol. xii. p. 440.

properly be applied, which are either considerably thicker at the centre than towards the edges, or else have a certain number of strengthening ribs running along the blade. This intermediate form has a single narrow rounded rib running along the centre of the blade. That shown in Fig. 300 is an example of the short and broad variety of this kind. It was found in a barrow at Musdin,* Staffordshire, and has a splendid

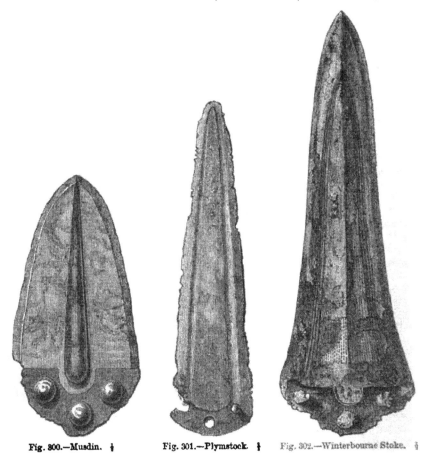

Fig. 800.—Musdin. ⅓   Fig. 301.—Plymstock. ⅓   Fig. 302.—Winterbourne Stoke. ⅓

patina, rivalling malachite in colour. The relation of the dagger to any interment is uncertain.

A dagger of this class, but more pointed and with two parallel lines engraved on each side of the midrib, was found by Canon Greenwell, F.R.S., in one of the barrows called the Three Tremblers,† Yorkshire. It showed traces of both its handle and sheath. With it was a beautifully flaked large flint knife.

A more pointed blade, with the central rib much less pronounced, and

* Bateman's "Ten Years' Diggings," p. 148; engraved in *Arch.*, vol. xliii. p. 461, fig. 162, from which my cut is copied.
† "British Barrows," p. 359; *Arch. Journ.*, vol. xxii. p. 243.

the notch in the hilt more distinct, was found with a skeleton in a cist near Cheswick,[*] Northumberland, and is now in the Greenwell Collection in the British Museum. It has been carefully polished.

Another, with a small, well-defined central midrib and two rivets, was found by Canon Greenwell in a barrow at Aldbourn, Wilts. It accompanied a burnt body.

Some of the Italian dagger blades are provided with similar midribs.

Of the English weapons just described some closely resemble in character the much larger blades of which I shall subsequently have to speak, and which not improbably were those of some form of halberd or battle-axe.

A much longer and narrower form, in which the central rib is partly the result of two long lateral grooves along the sides of the blade, is shown in Fig. 301. This was found with two others at Plymstock,[†] Devon, in company with flanged celts, a chisel, and a tanged spear-head or dagger, Fig. 327, and is now in the British Museum.

I have a much smaller blade, of somewhat the same character (4¾ inches), but imperfect at the base, found in a barrow near Cirencester; and one smaller still (4¼ inches), from a small barrow near Ablington, Cirencester, Gloucestershire. This latter appears to have had two rivet-holes.

A beautiful example of the form of dagger of which Sir Richard C. Hoare found numerous examples in the Wiltshire barrows is shown in Fig. 302. It lay with burnt bones in a wooden cist in a barrow near Winterbourn Stoke.[‡] With it was another, which was, however, broken, an ivory pin and tweezers, and two small pieces of ivory with bronze rivets, which were supposed to have appertained to the tips of a bow. They may more probably have formed part of the hilt of the dagger. The blade is ornamented with parallel lines as usual, but it also has a series of fine dotted lines.

Two other blades (8¼ and 8 inches), less highly ornamented, and one of them straighter at the edges, were found with a skeleton buried in the hollowed trunk of an elm-tree in the King Barrow,[§] Winterbourn Stoke. With one of these at the breast of the skeleton were traces of a wooden scabbard, with indentations which were thought to have been gilt. The handle is described as having been of box-wood, and rounded somewhat like that of a large knife. The other dagger was at the thigh. On the breast was also a bronze awl with what is said to have been an ivory handle (Fig. 227).

Dr. Thurnam[‖] thinks it not improbable that one of the blades may have been a spear-head for use in the chase. In writing of these blades he observes, " Where two are found with the same interment they are not exactly of one type, but one is light and thin and of greater breadth, the other strengthened by a stout midrib relatively heavier and of more pointed or leaf-like form; the rivets also are larger. In such cases the former may, perhaps,

* Raine, " North Durham," p. 235.

+ *Arch. Journ.*, vol. xxvi. p. 346; *Trans. Devon. Assoc.*, vol. iv. p. 304. For the use of this cut I am indebted to Mr. A. W. Franks, F.R.S.

‡ " Anc. Wilts," vol. i. p. 122, pl. xiv.   § Ibid., pl. xv.   ‖ *Arch.*, vol. xliii. p. 456.

be supposed to be the dagger, the latter the spear." Sir Richard Hoare in some cases discriminates between the spear and the dagger when two blades were found; and Mr. Cunnington observed in a barrow at Roundway,* Wilts, that a pointed blade only 3 inches long with three rivets had a wooden shaft about a foot in length, which, as Dr. Thurnam remarks, could not have been the haft of a dagger.

The fact that many of these blades bore traces of having had a sheath is in favour of their being daggers rather than spear-heads, though it must not be forgotten that Homer † describes Achilles as drawing the spear which had belonged to his father from its sheath—

Ἐκ δ'ἄρα σύριγγος πατρώϊον ἐσπάσατ' ἔγχος.

Though Sir Richard Colt Hoare at first regarded all these blades as spear-heads, he observes, about two-thirds of the way through his first volume,‡ "daily experience convinces me that those implements we supposed to be spear-heads, may more properly be denominated daggers, or knives, worn by the side, or in a girdle, and not affixed to long shafts like the modern lance." Further on, however, he mentions a "spear-head" from a barrow near Fovant,§ having the greater part of the wooden handle adhering to it, so that the mode by which it was fastened was clearly seen. From the figure given in the *Archæologia*, and in an unpublished plate of Hoare, this seems, however, to have been a dagger rather than a spear.

Other blades of much the same character, found at Everley and Lake, Wilts, and West Cranmore, Somerset, are figured by Dr. Thurnam.‖ This latter was found by my friend the late Mr. J. W. Flower, F.G.S. It is straight at the bottom of the blade, which went only ¼ inch into the handle at the part where the usual semicircular notch was formed. There was a single rivet on either side. The one preserved is ¼ inch long. Another, from Lake,¶ is given by Hoare. It was found with burnt bones and was accompanied by a whetstone.

Others have been found in a barrow at Ablington,** near Amesbury, Wilts, and at Rowcroft,†† Yattendon, Berks (7¼ inches).

A fine blade of this character (9¼ inches long), with three rivets, was found near Leeds. The midrib ends in a square base. It is not unlike the blade of a halberd.

A hafted blade of the same kind,‡‡ from Bere Regis, Dorsetshire, has already been mentioned; as well as the decoration of the hilt of one of the same form. One (9 inches) was found in a barrow at Came,§§ and

---

* *Wilts Arch. Mag.*, vol. vi. p. 164.   † Iliad, lib. xix. v. 387.
‡ P. 185.   § *Op. cit.*, p. 242.
‖ *Arch.*, vol. xliii. pl. xxxiv. fig. 4 ; xxxv. figs. 2, 4.
¶ "Anc. Wilts," vol. i. p. 211, pl. xxviii.   ** *Arch. Journ.*, vol. x. p. 248.
†† *Arch. Assoc. Journ.*, vol. xvii. p. 334.   ‡‡ *Ante*, p. 233.
§§ *Arch. Journ.*, vol. v. p. 322.

exhibited to the Archæological Institute. Mr. Warne,[*] however, records the finding of two at that place. One seems to have the midrib dotted over with small indentations.

That shown in Fig. 303 (which is copied from Dr. Thurnam's [†] engraving) is from Camerton, Somerset. It is remarkable as having a kind of second midrib beyond the parallel grooves which border the first. As usual it has but two rivets.

A bronze dagger (5½ inches) of the Wiltshire type was found in the well-known barrow at Hove,[‡] near Brighton, in which the interment had been made in an oak coffin. An amber cup, a perforated stone axe-hammer, and a whetstone had also been deposited with the body.

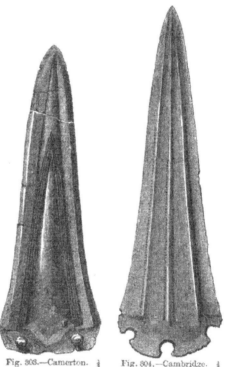

In a blade of this class (7 inches), found with burnt bones and chippings of flint in a barrow at Teddington,[§] the midrib appears to be formed of three beads.

Another (9 inches) formed part of the Arreton Down [||] find, of which more will hereafter be said. The blade is ornamented with delicate flutings and curves, and the midrib ends in a crescented hollow exactly opposite to the usual notch in the handle. This specimen is now in the British Museum.

A bronze dagger (6¾ inches) with three rivets, of which the blade has much suffered from decomposition, was found with a lump of iron pyrites within an urn in a barrow at Angrowse Mul-

Fig. 303.—Camerton. ⅔   Fig. 304.—Cambridge. ⅔

lion,[¶] Cornwall. A dagger blade of nearly the same kind, but with six rivets, found in a barrow at Carnöel,[**] Finistère, is in the museum at the Hôtel Cluny, Paris.

I have a dagger (9 inches) much like Fig. 302, only somewhat more taper, found in the Seine at Paris. It has had three rivet-holes, and on the blade are two bands of four lines parallel with the edge.

The strengthening of the blade is sometimes effected by forming it with three or more projecting ribs instead of a single midrib. In Fig. 304 is shown a dagger blade in my own collection, found not far

[*] "Celtic Tum." pt. i. p. 35, pl. x. E. and G.   [†] *Arch.*, vol. xliii. p. 453, fig. 157.
[‡] *Arch. Journ.*, vol. xiii. p. 184; vol. xv. p. 90; *Suss. Arch. Coll.*, vol. ix. p. 120.
[§] *Surrey Arch. Soc. Trans.*, vol. i. ; *Arch. Journ.*, vol. xiii. p. 305.
[||] *Arch.*, vol. xxxvi. p. 328, pl. xxv. fig. 6; "Horæ Fer.," pl. vii. 18
[¶] Borlase, "Nænia Corn.," p. 236.
[**] Lindenschmit, "Alt. u. h. Vorz.," vol. i. Heft xi. Taf. ii. 1.

from Cambridge. On either side of the central rib and along the outer margin of the two other ribs are lines of minute punctures by way of ornament.

A somewhat larger blade (8¼ inches), from Little Cressingham,* Norfolk, has two deep furrows, one on each side of the broad central midrib, and beyond these again two lateral ribs. This was secured to its hilt by six rivets, three on each side. It was found with a contracted male skeleton, accompanied by a necklace of amber beads and some articles made of thin gold plate.

A dagger with a central rounded midrib, and apparently two lateral ribs like those on Fig. 304, was found in a barrow near Torrington,† Devon. It has three rivets, by which it was attached to a wooden handle, and the blade showed traces of a wooden sheath, which like the handle had perished.

A very small dagger or knife, with apparently a well-marked central rib, found near Magherafelt,‡ Co. Londonderry, is shown in Fig. 305. It has a haft of oak attached, which is thought to be original. Any pins or rivets that may have existed are now lost, and possibly what were used may have been formed of wood or horn. Some thin wedges of oak appear to have been used for steadying the blade in the haft, the upper part of which has somewhat suffered from fire.

One of the daggers from the great find at Arreton Down,§ Isle of Wight (9¼ inches), has the blade strengthened by three raised ribs. It is shown in Fig. 306. It was found with several tanged blades like Fig. 324, some flanged celts, and other objects. In a blade (9 inches) in Canon Greenwell's collection, and found at Ford, Northumberland, there are two slight ribs about ⅛ inch from the edges and parallel to them. There are punctures along the sides of the ribs.

Possibly some of these weapons may have been halberd blades, such as those hereafter described.

Another form of dagger widens out considerably at the base, so as to give the edges an ogival outline, and this form passes into what have been termed rapier-like blades. As is the case with the leaf-shaped blades, which will presently be described, some of these latter are so long that it is hard to say whether they ought to be classed as swords or as daggers.

The example engraved as Fig. 307 is from Scotland, and not England, the original being in the Antiquarian Museum at Edinburgh. It was found in 1828 upon the farm of Kilrie, near Kinghorn, Fifeshire. The blade, as is usually the case, shows a central ridge upon it, but is also ornamented with parallel lines engraved on either side, which is a feature of far less common occurrence.

A plain blade of the same character (7½ inches), but narrower in its proportions, was found at Bracklesham,‖ Sussex. It has as usual two rivets only.

I have another (7¼ inches), showing four facets on the blade, from

* *Proc. Soc. Ant.*, 2nd S., vol. iv. p. 456; *Arch.*, vol. xliii. p. 454, fig. 158.
† *Trans. Devon. Assoc.*, vol. vii. p. 104.
‡ *Journ. Royal Hist. and Arch. Assoc. of Ireland*, 2nd S., vol. i. p. 286, whence this cut has been kindly lent.
§ *Arch.*, vol. xxxvi. p. 328, pl. xxv. 5, from which the cut is copied.
‖ Dixon's "Geol. of Sussex," p. 12; *Arch. Journ.*, vol. viii. p. 112; *Suss. Arch. Coll.*, vol. ii. p. 260.

Soham Fen; the two rivet-holes cut through the margin of the base, as in Fig. 304.

I have seen others from the Cambridge Fens.

Another (13¼ inches) with four rivets, and more nearly approaching the rapier form, was found in the Thames at Ditton,* Surrey, and was presented to the British Museum by the Earl of Lovelace. Another of the

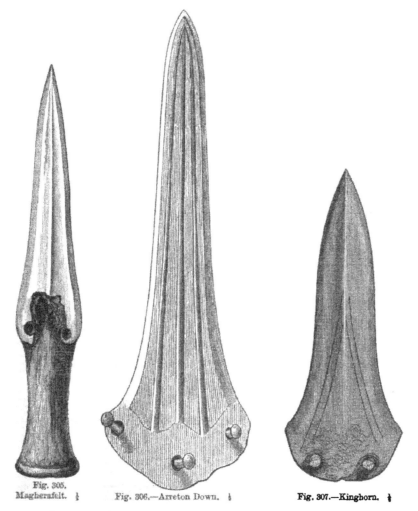

Fig. 305,
Magherafelt. ½   Fig. 306.—Arreton Down. ½   Fig. 307.—Kinghorn. ½

same character (7 inches) was found in the Thames near Maidenhead,† and another (8 inches) at Battersea.‡

One (9¾ inches) with two rivets, and the base forming half a hexagon, was found at New Bilton,§ near Rugby. I have another of nearly the same form (7¾ inches) from Waterbeach Fen, Cambridge.

* Fig. in *Arch. Journ.*, vol. xix. p. 364.   † *Arch. Assoc. Journ.*, vol. i. p. 311.
‡ *A. A. J.*, vol. xiv. p. 329.   § *Proc. Soc. Ant.*, 2nd S., vol. iv. p. 50.

In some the blade is ornamented by ribs cast in relief and by engraving. A good example of the kind from the collection of Mr. Robert Day, F.S.A., is shown in Fig. 308. It was found in the old castle of Colloony,* Co. Sligo. One of much the same form as the Wiltshire dagger (Fig. 302), found in the Thames,† near Richmond (7$\frac{9}{10}$ inches), has at the base a vandyke border and hatched diagonal bands. The blade is slightly ridged but not otherwise ornamented. It is now in the British Museum. One (5$\frac{1}{4}$ inches), ornamented at the base in a similar manner, but with a short

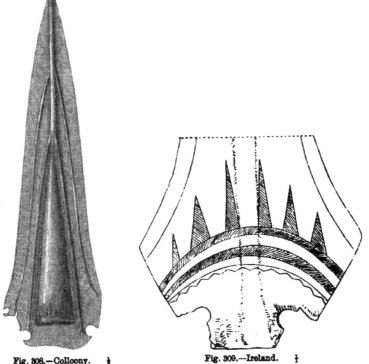

Fig. 308.—Colloony. $\frac{1}{2}$ Fig. 309.—Ireland. $\frac{1}{2}$

broad tang and one rivet-hole, was found on Helsington Peat Moss,‡ Westmoreland.

A blade (7 inches) also ornamented at the base with a vandyke pattern was found at Pitkaithly, Perthshire, and is now in the museum at Edinburgh.

Many blades of daggers from Germany are ornamented. One of the most beautiful that I have seen is that in the museum at Laibach, Carniola. Another (11$\frac{1}{2}$ inches), with the hilt complete, and the blade and pommel-plate beautifully ornamented, was found near Vienna.§ Von Sacken points out that from the shortness of the hilt it is probable that these daggers were held in the same manner as among the Peruvians of

* *Proc. Soc. Ant.*, 2nd S., vol. v. p. 268.
† *Arch. Journ.*, vol. xi. p. 79; "Horæ Ferales," pl. vii. 19.
‡ *Proc. Soc. Ant.*, 2nd S., vol. ii. p. 370.
§ Von Sacken, "Die Funden an der Langen Wand bei Wiener Neustadt," 1865, p. 6.

the present day, with the two first fingers not round the hilt, but stretched along the blade.

In the museum of the Royal Irish Academy* is a broad dagger blade 6⅜ inches long, and engraved with a kind of vandyke pattern at the base. The ornamented portion is shown full size in Fig. 309, kindly lent me by the Academy. It is rather remarkable that the ornaments should extend to so near the base, as they must have been intended to be free of the hilt, in which, in consequence, it would appear that only a small part of the blade can have been inserted. The sides of the socket in the hilt may, however, have extended some distance up the sloping part of the base of the blade.

An ornamented blade of more elongated form (16½ inches) is engraved on the scale of one-fourth in Fig. 310. It was found at Kilrea, Co. Sligo, and is in the collection of Canon Greenwell, F.R.S. There is a vandyke pattern near the base, which is not shown in the cut.

I have a plain blade (14 inches) with merely a central ridge, and with two rivet-holes, which is also from Ireland, and of much the same form.

In a small English blade (5 inches) of the same character there are no rivet-holes at the base.

A blade from the Thames† of an ordinary rapier shape is shown on the scale of one-fourth in Fig. 311. It is provided with two rivets, and there are notches at the side of the base as if to allow of two others being passed through the hilt to steady the blade.

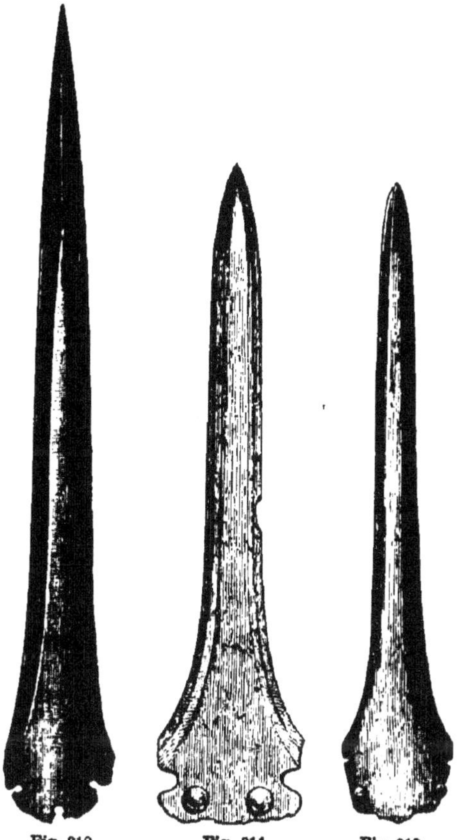

A blade of the same form

Fig. 310.
Kilrea. ¼

Fig. 311.
Thames. ¼

Fig. 312.
Thatcham. ¼

(10 inches), but with only two rivet-holes at the base, was found at the foot of "the Castle Tump," Newchurch,‡ Radnorshire.

Rapier-shaped blades from 8½ inches to 12½ inches long, found at Auchtermuchty, Fife; at Fairholm, Dumfries-shire; and near Ardoch, Perthshire, are preserved in the Antiquarian Museum at Edinburgh.

Fig. 312 represents a small blade of this character dredged up from the Kennet and Avon Canal, between Theale and Thatcham, Berks, and

* Wilde, "Catal.," p. 465, fig. 347.   † *Proc. Soc. Ant.*, 2nd S., vol. v. p. 403, fig. 6.
‡ *Arch. Camb.*, 4th S., vol. vi. p. 19.

given me by Mr. W. Whitaker, F.G.S. The two little notches at the side of the base are peculiar.

A number of blades of this character, but without these small notches, have been found in the Cambridgeshire Fens. Mr. Fisher, of Ely, has four, varying in length from 8 inches to 9 inches, about 2 inches wide at the base and 1 inch in the middle of the blade. They all have two rivet-holes, in some of which are rivets $\frac{5}{8}$ inch long.

Two blades found at South Kyme,* Lincolnshire, seem to have been of this character. Another ($13\frac{1}{4}$ inches) was found at Corbridge,† Northumberland, in company with a leaf-shaped spear-head. One from Burwell Fen, in my own collection, has three rivet-holes, in which are still two of the rivets, of which one is formed from a nearly square piece of metal. A long blade of this kind ($16\frac{1}{4}$ inches), but with the blade tapering more gradually from a rounded base, was dredged from the Thames‡ near Vauxhall. Other rapier-shaped blades ($18\frac{5}{8}$ inches and $14\frac{1}{16}$ inches) have been found in the Thames near Kingston.§

The base of these blades appears sometimes to be disproportionately broad with regard to the blades themselves. An example from Coveney, near Downham Hithe, Cambridgeshire, is in the collection of Mr. Fisher, of Ely, and is shown in Fig. 313. This widening was no doubt intended to aid in steadying the blade in its hilt.

I have a dagger of the same form (8 inches), but with a more tapering blade, found in Waterbeach Fen, Cambridge. Another ($11\frac{1}{4}$ inches), from Harlech, Merionethshire, is even narrower in the blade than the Coveney example, but it has lost its edges by corrosion.

Some blades, from $12\frac{1}{4}$ inches to $15\frac{1}{4}$ inches long, and rapier-like in character, from Maentwrog in the same county, are engraved in the *Archæologia*,‖ and are now in the British Museum. The rivet arrangements vary. A spear-head, with loops attached to the blade, was found with them. One of them has notches at the sides of the base, as in Fig. 311.

One $14\frac{3}{4}$ inches long, and of much the same outline, but flat in the centre instead of ridged, was found at Fisherton,¶ near Salisbury, and is in the Blackmore Museum. Another of the same character, but broad in the blade ($16\frac{1}{4}$ inches), was found in the Thames.**

Canon Greenwell has two rapier-like blades from the Thames, $17\frac{1}{2}$ inches and $15\frac{5}{8}$ inches long, from Sandford. With the latter was found a leaf-shaped blade (19 inches) with two rivet-holes in the base.

Such blades are almost long enough to be regarded as swords.

A weapon of this form ($16\frac{7}{8}$ inches), with the blade reduced in thickness towards the edges, and with two large rivets, one of them still *in situ*, was found in the Thames, and is now in the British Museum. Another in the same collection ($12\frac{7}{8}$ inches), from the Thames at Kingston, is much narrower at the base.

A blade of this character from Blair Drummond Moss was exhibited in the museum at Edinburgh, and is preserved at Blair Drummond House.

The type occurs in France. One found at Auxonne,†† Haute Saône, is in the St. Germain Museum.

---

* *Arch. Journ.*, vol. x. p. 73.
† *Arch. Journ.*, vol. xix. p. 363.
‡ *Arch. Assoc. Journ.*, vol. iii. p. 60.
§ *Proc. Soc. Ant.*, 2nd S., vol. i. p. 83.
‖ Vol. xvi. p. 365, pl. lxx.
¶ *Arch. Journ.*, vol. xviii. p. 160.
** *Op. cit.*, p. 158.
†† Chantre, "Alb.," pl. xvi. 2.

Another, rather shorter and broader, with two rivets and two notches in the sides of the base, was found in the bay of Penhouët* (Loire Inférieure).

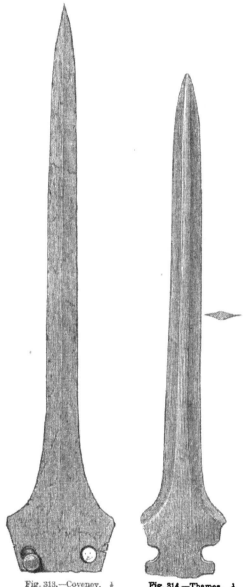

I have examples from the Seine at Paris, and also from the neighbourhood of Amiens.

In some cases the rivet-holes cut through the margin of the metal as in Fig. 304.

Blades appear sometimes to have been cast with deep rounded notches in the base to receive the rivets instead of having holes drilled or cast in them. That shown in Fig. 314 is of this character, and was found in the Thames at London. It was given to me by Mr. C. Roach Smith, F.S.A. Others of the same character have also been found in the Thames. One of these (16⅝ inches), of nearly the same type but more rounded at the lower part of the wings, is in the British Museum.

Canon Greenwell has a blade of this type (8¾ inches), found near Methwold, Norfolk.

A specimen of this form (11 inches) from Edington Burtle, Somerset, is in the Museum at Taunton.

A blade from Inchigeela,† Co. Cork, figured in the *Archæological Journal*, seems to be notched in a similar manner. Another of different form, but apparently notched after the same fashion, is engraved by Vallancey.‡

Fig. 313.—Coveney. ¼   Fig. 314.—Thames. ¼

Some of the rapier-shaped blades, and especially those of larger size, such as seem intermediate between swords and daggers, are ornamented

* *Rev. Arch.*, vol. xxxiii. p. 231.   † Vol. x. p. 73.
‡ "Collect.," vol. iv. pl. xi. 9.

as well as strengthened by a projecting midrib, while their weight is diminished by flutings along either side. A beautiful example of this kind, found at the bottom of an old canoe, between the peat and clay, near Chatteris, Cambs, is shown one-quarter size in Fig. 315. I have another (14 inches) with the midrib not quite so prominent, and with the rivet-holes cutting the margin of the base, found at Aston Ingham, Herefordshire. A portion of another was found near Water-beach,* Cambs.

A broader blade of the same character (12¾ inches), with two very large rivets, was found in the Thames at Kingston, and is now in the British Museum. A narrower blade (12 inches) with the rivet-holes cutting through the base, was found at Cæsar's Camp, Farnham, Surrey, and is in the same collection.

A long blade of this character from the Thames (21 inches long and 2¾ inches wide at the base), with central ridge and slight flutings at the edges, may more properly be regarded as a sword. It is in the British Museum.

Six blades, all of the rapier character, but varying in details, and from 12 inches to 22 inches in length, were found at Talaton, Devonshire.† Some moulds of stone for blades of the same kind were found at Hennock in the same county, and will subsequently be described. Another blade (17 inches) was found at Winkleigh,‡ near Crediton, Devon.

A blade of the same character from Ireland is given by Vallancey.§ A fine specimen from the same country (18 inches) is in the British Museum.‖ What appears to be a part of a blade¶ of the same kind has been regarded as a kind of "steel" for sharpening other blades.

A rapier-shaped blade (21 inches) with two rivet-holes was found, with socketed celts and a palstave, at Mawgan,** Cornwall.

Blades of this character are also found in France. Two from the departments of Aisne and Somme,†† have been figured. One (20 inches long) is in the Museum at Nantes.

A rapier blade from the Chaussée Brunehault, and now in the Boulogne Museum, is almost like a trefoil in outline at the hilt end.

A still longer blade of this character, which perhaps ought with greater propriety to have been classed among swords, is shown in Fig. 316 on the scale of one-fourth. It has unfortunately lost its point, but is still 17¾ inches long. It would appear to have been originally about 20¼ inches long, as shown in the figure. The blade in this case has three projecting ribs between which and again towards the edges it is fluted. It was found in the River Ouse, near Thetford. The imperfect rivet-holes at the base appear to have been cast in the blade, and the means of steadying it in its hilt must have been but inadequate. Such weapons, however, can only have been intended for stabbing, and not for striking.

Another blade of similar form, but with perfect rivet-holes, was found in the fine earthwork of Badbury, Dorsetshire, and is in the collection of Mr. Durden, of Blandford. It is 23½ inches long and 2₁⁶₀ inches wide at the base above the rivet-holes.

Blades of this kind are occasionally found in Ireland. In the British

---

* *Arch. Journ.*, vol. xii. p. 193.   † *Arch. Journ.*, vol. xxiv. p. 110.   ‡ *Op. cit.*, p. 113.
§ "Collect.," vol. iv. pl. xi. 10; Gough's "Camden," vol. iv. pl. xviii. 10.
‖ "Horæ Ferales," pl. vii. 23.   ¶ *Arch. Journ.*, vol. ix. p. 186.
** *Arch.*, vol. xvii. p. 337.   †† *Dict. Arch. de la Gaule.*

Museum is one (9 inches) with deep notches for the rivets, found in Rathkennan Bog, Co. Tipperary.

Nearly all the rapier-shaped blades which have still to be noticed may be regarded as probably those of swords rather than of daggers. That

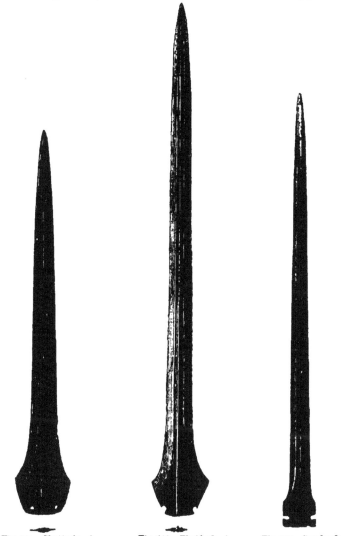

Fig. 315.—Chatteris. ¼   Fig. 316.—Thetford. ¼   Fig. 317.—Londonderry. ¼

shown in Fig. 317 is in my own collection, and was found near London-derry. The method of attachment to the hilt by two rivets fitting into notches at the sides of the base of the blade is the same as in some of the shorter weapons already mentioned.

Another (19 inches), found at Killeshandra,* Co. Cavan, has similar

* Wilde, " Catal.," p. 448, fig. 326.

notches at the sides, but the base is somewhat differently shaped. Many of these rapier-shaped blades have been found in Ireland, and Canon Greenwell has one (27¼ inches) which was bought in Scotland, and probably found in that country.

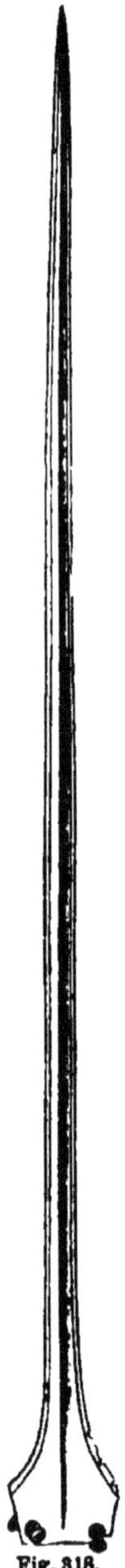

A blade (14 inches) found in the Loire, and now in the Nantes Museum, has side notches of nearly the same character as those in Fig. 317.

The finest example of the rapier kind ever found in Ireland is that shown in Fig. 318, which by the kindness of the Royal Irish Academy I here reproduce from Sir W. Wilde's Catalogue. It is no less than 30¼ inches long, and is only ⅝ inch in width at the centre of the blade, which has a strong midrib. It was found in a bog at Lissane, Co. Derry. I have a blade, found at Noailles, near Beauvais, Oise, France, identical in form and character, but only 23¼ inches long. Were it not that the rivets are wanting, Fig. 318 might have been taken from the French instead of the Irish specimen.

Another narrow blade, with a heavy rounded midrib (22⅝ inches long and 1¾ inch broad at the base), was found in a bog at Galbally, Co. Tyrone, and had at the time of its discovery the original hilt attached. There also appear to have been some remains of a scabbard, but this is uncertain. The hilt has been engraved in the *Proceedings of the Royal Historical and Archæological Society of Ireland*,* and is here by their kindness reproduced as Fig. 319.

Mr. Wakeman, of Enniskillen, in his interesting account of the discovery, describes the material of which the hilt is formed as bone, or rather whalebone. Both blade and haft are, however, now in my own collection, and I think there can be no doubt that the material of the hilt is in reality a dark-coloured ox-horn. On some Danish blades I have seen the fibrous texture of this substance still shown by the oxide or salt of the metal, forming as it were a cast of its surface, which has outlasted the horn against which it was originally formed. There are no traces of the rivets in the Galbally hilt, so that probably pins of hard wood served to secure it to the blade.

Some Scandinavian daggers have been found with their handles of horn still attached. One from a barrow in Hasslöf,† South Halland, Sweden, had its leather sheath with a long rectangular end of bronze still preserved. The length of the sheath is about twice that of the blade of the dagger.

Fig. 318.
Lissane. ¼

* 4th Series, vol. ii. p. 197.
† "Hallands Fornminnes-Förenings Aarskr.," 1869, p. 89.

The bronze hilts for the long rapier-like blades are rare, but not unknown.

One of these blades, found in the Co. Tipperary,* has its hilt still

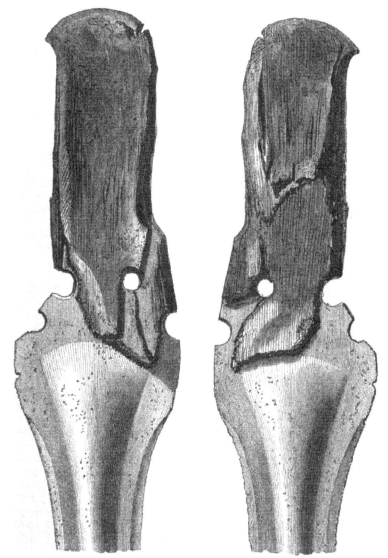

Fig. 319.—Galbally. ⅓

attached by metal rivets, as shown in Fig. 320. The hilt is hollow and is

* Wilde, " Catal.," p. 458, fig. 333, from which the fig. in the text is copied on a somewhat larger scale; " Horæ Ferales," pl. vii. 15.

now open at the end, though probably, as Wilde suggests, originally closed by a bone stud.

The hilt of a sword in the museum at Tours is joined to the blade in much the same fashion, but has a mere indentation instead of the central semicircular notch. The body of the hilt is engraved with bands of triangles and circles.

Fig. 320.—Tipperary.

A rapier-shaped blade, with a bronze hilt of nearly the same form, but with six rivets, is in the museum at Narbonne.* Another nearly similar was found at Cheylounet,† Haute Loire.

Some Egyptian bronze daggers have the hilts formed in the same style.

In another form, the blade of which is more leaf-shaped, like the ordinary bronze sword, the means of attachment to the haft are merely slight notches at the sides. That shown in Fig. 321 is only 11 inches long, but the edge has been removed for about 1½ inch from the base, showing the portion which presumably was inserted in the hilt. The original was found near Ely, and is in the collection of Mr. M. Fisher, of that town.

I have a small specimen of the same kind (6¾ inches) from Fordham, Cambs.

A more leaf-shaped blade (14 inches), with rivet notches at the side of the base, was found, with leaf-shaped spear-heads, at Worth,‡ Washfield, Devon. Possibly this, as suggested by Mr. Tucker, F.S.A., was originally a sword from which the hilt was broken.

A blade more like Fig. 321 (15¼ inches long and 1 inch broad) was found in the Mardyke, near Grays Thurrock,§ Essex. Some of the weapons of this kind, like one from the Thames at Kingston (11¼ inches), appear to have been made from broken sword or rapier-like blades.

A long-tanged form, of which it is sometimes difficult to say whether it is a sword, a knife, or a dagger, is of not unfrequent occurrence in Ireland. That shown in Fig. 322 is in my own collection.

I have another found near Armagh (8¼ inches), which is rather broader in its proportions. It has a diagonal row of circular indentations across each side of the blade just above the shoulders. Not improbably these and other specimens originally existed in a somewhat different form, but having been injured at their base were refitted with a tang for attachment to the haft instead of being secured by rivets at the sides like those last mentioned.

Some Danish daggers are provided with merely a slight tang like that of a modern chisel.

* "Matériaux," vol. v. pl. ii. 1. † "Matériaux," vol. x. p. 370.
‡ Arch. Journ., vol. xxiv. p. 120.
§ Arch. Journ., vol. xxvi. p. 191; Proc. Soc. Ant., 2nd S., vol. iii. p. 406.

Another form of blade is more of the nature of a bayonet than of a

Fig. 321.—Ely.   ⅓   Fig. 322.—North of Ireland. ⅓   Fig. 323.—Raphoe.   ⅓

rapier, yet this would appear to be the proper place in which to notice it.

The example shown in Fig. 323 is in the collection of Canon Greenwell, F.R.S., and was found at Raphoe, Co. Donegal.

The section of the blade is nearly square, and the faces are ornamented with parallel engraved lines. It ends in a tang with a single hole through it, and with it was found a ferrule of bronze for receiving the end of the handle.

In the Royal Irish Academy Museum is another blade of the same character, 33 inches long and nearly square in section, but having the faces fluted. With it was a ferrule, 3¾ inches long, having four ribs at the base, with hollows between. It has one rivet-hole through it. This specimen was found in a bog near Glenarm, Co. Antrim.

From the ferrules and general form of the blades it is probable that they were lance or pike heads rather than of the nature of swords or daggers. The "javelin with loop" found in Monaghan, and engraved in the *Archæological Journal* * seems to be somewhat of the same nature.

It may possibly be the case that some of the other blades described in this chapter have served as the points of spear-like weapons, though, from the hilts being discovered with so many of them, there can be no doubt that the majority must be regarded as having been the blades of daggers or rapiers. Among modern weapons we have, however, some which, like the sword-bayonet, are intended to serve a double purpose; and though there can be little doubt as to the true character of the knife-daggers, it is hardly safe to assert that all the dagger-like blades were without exception mounted with short hilts as poniards, and that none were provided with straight shafts as pikes, or placed transversely on a handle to serve as halberds or battle-axes.

The weapons described in this chapter probably range over the whole of the Bronze Period of Britain. The knife-daggers, which have almost exclusively been found in barrows, often associated with other weapons formed of stone, may be regarded as among the earliest of our bronze antiquities; while the rapier-shaped blades, though of rare occurrence in hoards, appear to belong to a period when socketed celts were already in use. Of the dagger-like blades, in whatever manner they were mounted, a considerable number belong to an early period. The analogies of the different forms with those found upon the Continent have already from time to time been noted in the preceding pages.

* Vol. iii. p. 47.

CHAPTER XI.

TANGED AND SOCKETED DAGGERS, OR SPEAR-HEADS, HALBERDS, AND MACES.

BEFORE passing to the leaf-shaped swords, which would seem naturally to follow in order after the blades last described, it will be well to notice two sets of weapons which, though in many respects identical with daggers, may in the one case have served as spear-heads, and in the other most probably as the blades of battle-axes or halberds. To the first of these two classes the term "Arreton Down type" has been conventionally applied, as it was in the hoard found at that place that the largest proportion of such weapons occurred; and, indeed, until that discovery the type appears to have been unknown.

The tanged blades are still rare, but have now been found in several other places besides the Isle of Wight. The centre of the blade is usually thick and strong, showing a central ridge and having the sides more or less decorated with flutings or lines where the metal is reduced in thickness. The tang, unlike that of the daggers described at the beginning of the last chapter, is long and narrow, and tapers away from the blade. At its end is a hole for a rivet or pin. In one instance a ferrule was found upon the blade, as will be seen in Fig. 324. This figure is copied from that in the *Archæologia*,* which is taken from a drawing made in 1737 by Sir Charles Frederick. Upon the ferrule are a number of raised bosses in imitation of rivets, but there seems to be no rivet-hole in the ferrule itself, though there is one in the end of the tang of the blade with the rivet still in it.

Accounts of the discovery of this and other weapons at Arreton Down, near Newport, in the Isle of Wight, were communicated to the Society of Antiquaries in the years 1735 and 1737, and the latter has been printed by Mr. A. W. Franks, F.R.S.† At least

---

* Vol. xxxvi. pl. xxv. 2. † *Arch.*, vol. xxxvi. p. 326.

S

sixteen articles were found in a marl-pit, and they are said to have been arranged in a regular order. Of these, nine were of this tanged type, but varying in details. One (Fig. 328) was provided

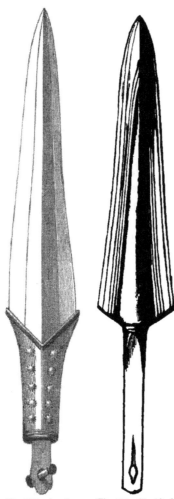

with a socket; two were dagger blades, already mentioned (one of which is given in Fig. 306), and four were flanged celts, like Fig. 8, but varying in size. Six specimens from this hoard are now in the British Museum. Mr. Franks, in the paper already mentioned, regards these tanged weapons as spear-heads, and is I think right in so doing; the blades, however, present such close analogies with the daggers from the Wiltshire barrows, and the socketed variety (Fig. 328) is so dagger-like in character, that it is hard to speak with any degree of confidence upon this point.

In 1855 Mr. Franks observed that the type was quite new to him, but since that time several other specimens have been found besides those from Arreton Down. One of these, discovered in the River Lea at Stratford-le-Bow, Essex, is now in the British Museum, and is shown in Fig. 325. As will be seen, it has a rounded midrib, with several parallel grooves on each side of it engraved or punched on the blade.

Fig. 324.—Arreton Down. ⅓

Fig. 325.—Stratford-le-Bow. ⅓

Some of the weapons from* Arreton Down are of nearly the same description, but the midrib is more ridged, and is ornamented with rows of engraved or punched dots. One has a double crescent-shaped line of dots punched in at the base of the blade.

I have a blade (10 inches) of the same form and character, but without any engraved dots upon it, from Burwell Fen, Cambridge. The parallel flutings on the blade appear to have been produced in the casting, and not by engraving or punching. The hole in the tang was also made in

* *Arch.*, vol. xxxvi. pl. xxv. 1; "Horæ Ferales," pl. vi. 24.

the casting, being irregular in form. It is nowhere less than ¼ inch in diameter. Another weapon (7¼ inches) of the same character, but apparently without any fluting, was found near Newbury,* Berks.

Such blades are of extremely rare occurrence in Ireland, but one (9 inches) closely resembling Fig. 325 was found in the county of West Meath, and is now in the collection of Mr. Robert Day, F.S.A., of Cork.

A slightly different variety of blade is shown in Fig. 326. It is ridged along the centre, and has a groove on each side running parallel to the edge, such as would afford facility for sharpening the edge by hammering it out. The end of the tang has been broken off at the hole. This specimen is said to have been found near Matlock, Derbyshire, and is in my own collection.

One with much broader and deeper grooves on each side of the midrib (10 inches), found in Swaffham Fen, is in the Museum of the Cambridge Antiquarian Society.

A nearly similar blade, but with four slight channels on either side instead of one, is in the museum at Copenhagen, and is said to have been found in Italy. †

Another of these blades, but without any lateral flutings, and in character similar to Fig. 324, was found near Preston,‡ in the parish of Plymstock, Devon, and is shown in Fig. 327. It is now in the British Museum. In this instance, as at Arreton Down, the accompanying articles were flanged celts like Fig. 9, of which there were sixteen, and three dagger blades (see Fig. 301). There was also a narrow chisel (Fig. 190).

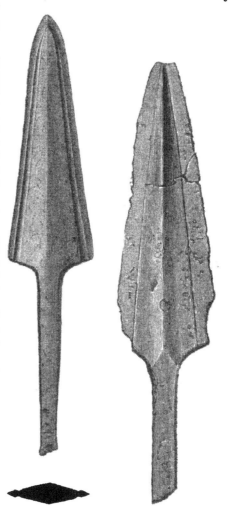

Fig. 326.—Matlock. ½   Fig. 327.—Plymstock. ½

* *Arch. Assoc. Journ.*, vol. xvi. p. 322, pl. 26, No. 1.
† "Cong. préh.," Copenhagen vol., p. 483.
‡ *Arch. Journ.*, vol. xxvi. p. 349. For the use of this cut I am indebted to Mr. A. W. Franks, F.R.S.

Two specimens from Suffolk (8 inches and 10¼ inches), one of them from Hintlesham,* formed part of the collection of the late Mr. Whincopp, and are now in the British Museum.

One of the Arreton Down † specimens, without a ferrule, is also much of this type.

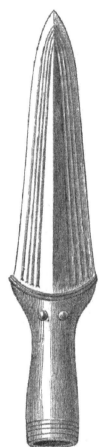

In the Arreton Down hoard there was a single example of a weapon of this kind which was provided with a socket for the insertion of a handle or shaft, instead of having a tang. Fig. 328 is copied from the engraving published in the *Archæologia*.‡ As will be observed, the socket part is made to abut on the blade, much after the manner of a dagger handle, and has cast upon it two bosses in imitation of the heads of rivets for securing the blade. A weapon (8¼ inches), which there can hardly be a doubt is the original from which Sir Charles Frederick made his drawing for the Society of Antiquaries, is now in Canon Greenwell's collection, and I know of no other example. It differs from the socketed knives in the character of the blade, which is thicker and more highly ornamented, like some of the daggers from the Wiltshire barrows. Whether it was itself intended to be a dagger, or whether it was the head of a spear or lance, I will not attempt to determine.

Fig. 328.—Arreton Down. ½

What has somewhat the appearance of being a weapon of the same character was found in a moss near Campbeltown,§ Argyleshire, together with a bronze sword. It may, however, as already suggested, be merely a socketed knife.

A very beautiful weapon of this kind is in the museum at Lausanne. The blade is ornamented somewhat in the same manner as that of Fig. 328. The socket is shorter and ornamented with parallel rings and bands of triangles, alternately hatched and plain. There appear to be six rivets, and what may be termed the hilt has a deep half-oval notch in it, like that which is common on swords and daggers. The margin of this notch is decorated with punctured dots. It was, I believe, found near Sion, Valais, with por-

---

* *Arch. Journ.*, vol. xxvi. p. 349.
† *Arch.*, xxxvi. pl. xxv. 3; "Horæ Ferales," pl. vi. 25.
‡ Vol. xxxvi. p. 328, pl. xxv. 3.
§ Wilson's "Preh. Ann.," vol. i. p. 390; Catal. Mus. Arch. Inst., Edinb., p. 23.

tions of what may have been the ornaments of a sheath, and also with a long narrow celt, flanged at the upper part. The general resemblance between the Swiss and the English specimens is very remarkable.

An Egyptian * blade, with the side edges slightly curved inwards, and with the socket rather shorter than in Fig. 328, is in the museum at Boulaq. It is attached to the socket by three rivets.

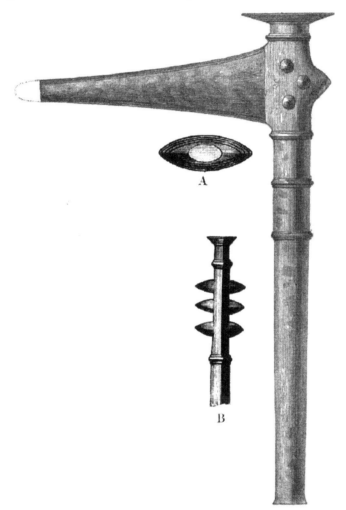

Fig. 329.—Årup.   ⅓

The second series of blades of which it is proposed to treat in this chapter are usually from six to sixteen inches long, rather broad at the base, and not unfrequently curved longitudinally. This

* "Matériaux," vol. v. pl. xix. 11.

latter circumstance, as well as their shape and weight, proves that some of these broad blades were not intended for use as daggers ; and this being admitted, it seems to follow that others, which resemble the curved blades in all respects except their curvature, must be regarded as belonging to the same class of weapons. What these weapons were may I think be best shown by some examples from Scandinavia and Northern Germany, which also show the manner in which similar blades were attached to their shafts so as to form a kind of halberd or battle-axe.

That which I have selected by way of illustration is one that is engraved in Dr. Oscar Montelius' "Sveriges Forntid," * who has kindly lent me the block of Fig. 329. In this instance the scale adopted is one-third linear measure. In A is given a view of the upper end, seen from above, and in B a view from behind the blade, showing the great projection of the

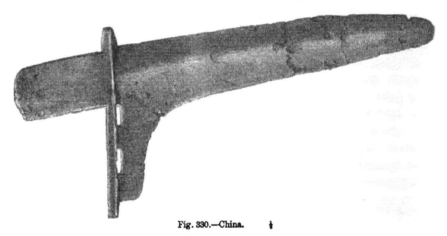

Fig. 330.—China.   ‡

rivet-like knobs. The handle as well as the blade is in bronze. This specimen was found at Årup, in Scania. Another is engraved in Lisch's "Frederico-Francisceum." † It was found, with two others, at Blengow, near Buckow, Mecklenburg Schwerin, and is regarded by Lisch as a kind of battle-axe, or possibly as a "commander's staff" or bâton of honour. Good examples of the same kind are in the museums at Malmoe and Kiel, and others have been described by Klemm.‡ Two have been found near Neu Ruppin. Others are in the Schwerin Museum. Another, with a separate socket, having three rivet-like bosses upon it, is in the Berlin Museum.§ There can be little doubt that this last-mentioned weapon is a representative of an earlier form, when the shaft was merely of wood and the transverse blade was secured in it by means of

* Fig. 131.   † Taf. vii. 1 ; xxxiii. 1 ; "Horæ Ferales," pl. x. 2.
‡ "Handb. der Germ. Alterth.," p. 208. See also Preusker, "Blicke," Taf. iii. 44 f. ; Klemm, "Allg. Culturwiss," p. 112.
§ Bastian und A. Voss, "Die Bronze Schwerter des K. Mus.," Taf. vi. 6.

three rivets. An intermediate form, in which the blade fits into a kind of open-work bronze socket for receiving a shaft, is preserved in the Berlin Museum.*

An instance of the use of an analogous form of weapon in another part of the world is afforded by some bronze blades from China, of which one is represented in Fig. 330. For the loan of the original of this figure I am indebted to Mr. A. W. Franks, F.R.S. As will be readily seen, the blade is adapted for being attached at nearly a right angle to a shaft, into which the flat tang behind the stop-ridge would be inserted, and the blade would then be secured in its position by laces or straps passing through the slots at the base of the blade. The antiquity of such weapons in China it is hard to ascertain, but they probably date back to a period many centuries remote from the present day.

Several of them are engraved in a Chinese work on antiquities, "The Golden Study," to which Mr. H. N. Moseley, F.R.S., has kindly called my attention. What appear to be bronze spear-heads and swords are figured in the same work.

A bronze weapon of the same kind, but with a socket, which, like the blade, is highly ornamented, was found on the Yenissei,† in Siberia. There is the figure of a kind of antelope projecting from the socket opposite the blade. Another, from Viatka, in Russia, has the head of an animal in the same position.

An iron weapon with a socket at right angles to the blade, from the Inwa,‡ Perm, appears to be a halberd of much the same kind.

This form of weapon closely approximates to the Australian "malga" § and to some other wooden weapons in use in New Caledonia.

As it is in Ireland and Scotland that the most characteristic of the halberd blades have been discovered, it will be well to commence with the examples from those countries rather than with those from England.

In Fig. 331 is represented a fine specimen of a form not unusual in Ireland, though the central rib is somewhat more ornamented than is generally the case. The rivets, as usual, are three in number, and are still preserved in the blade. In this case they are about ⅜ inch in diameter and ¾ inch between the heads, which are about ⅝ inch in diameter and have been carefully hammered into an almost hemispherical form. The midrib ends abruptly in a straight line where it abutted on the shaft. The metal appears to have a considerably less proportion of tin to copper than is usual with bronze weapons. It looks in fact almost like pure copper.

This coppery appearance is by no means uncommon in these blades. I have another specimen of the same form (9¾ inches), but without the bead on the midrib. It was found at Letterkenny, Co. Donegal. A specimen much like Fig. 331 is termed by Vallancey,‖ "the brass head of a *Tuagh*

* "Horæ Ferales," pl. x. 3; Von Ledebur, "Königl. Mus.," p. 15.
† "Matériaux," vol. viii. pl. xvi. 14; vol. xiii. p. 232; Chantre, "Age. du Br.," 2me partie, p. 283; *Mém. des Ant. du Nord*, 1872–7, p. 116.
‡ "Zeitsch. für Ethnol.," vol. ix. 1877, Proc., p. 34, Taf. vi. 3.
§ Col. A. Lane Fox, "Prim. Warfare," lect. 2.
‖ "Coll. Hib.," vol. iv. p. 62, pl. xi. 11.

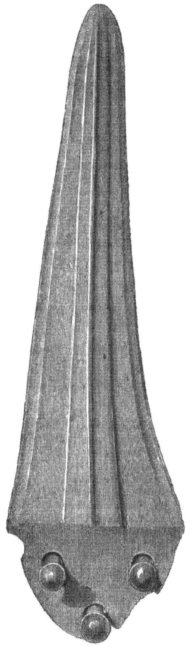

Fig. 331.—Ireland.   ⅓

catha, a general name for the war-axe." "The large rivets of this weapon show it was mounted on a very strong shaft."

Sir W. Wilde has described, under the two distinct headings of "Broad scythe-shaped Swords," and " Battle-axes," the weapons which I have here classed together. Of the former he mentions forty-one specimens in the Museum of the Royal Irish Academy, of the latter but two or three. The "swords"* he describes as thick, heavy, and round-pointed, averaging about 12 inches in length by about 2½ inches in breadth at the base ; twenty-two of the blades being curved. With the strong blades, however, he classes some which are quite thin and flat, and which have more the appearance of having been intended for daggers. The curved shape is much against their having been attached to staves "spear-ways ;" so that Wilde's other suggestion of the scythe-shaped swords having been mounted like axes, or " affixed to long handles like modern halberds," seems much more reasonable. As to the shorter and broader blades, whether curved or not, he appears to have had no doubt of their being a kind of battle-axes.

Wilde has inferred from the large size of the rivets, some being 1½ inches in length and

* " Catal. Mus. R. I. A.," p. 449.

nearly 1 inch across the burr or head, that they must have been attached to massive metal handles, of which, however, no fragments have been preserved. If this view had been correct, the disappearance of the handles would be a remarkable circumstance ; but the large rivets appear rather intended for securing the blades to wooden shafts, the disappearance of which from ordinary decay is exactly what might be expected. In one instance there are large conical washers or broad rings of bronze 1¼ inches in diameter beneath the rivet-heads, and these in the case of a metal handle would have been superfluous.

Wilde appears to me to have fallen into another error with respect to the antiquity of this form of weapon.* Arguing from the fact that many of the specimens are formed either of red bronze or of pure copper, he thinks it probable that, like the celts of that material, they are of immense antiquity. And in another place he says that their antiquity may be gathered from the fact of many being of copper, the use of which metal invariably preceded that of bronze. As I have already had occasion to observe, it is perfectly true that many of these blades have the appearance of being made of copper, but the absence of tin in their composition has not as yet been proved. Even were they of pure copper the form and character of the blades show them to be derivatives from the dagger, as the dagger itself sprang from the simpler knife; and the cause for using a less proportion of tin, or indeed none of that metal in them, appears to me to have been the wish to make them less brittle than if they had been of bronze. A weapon used as a battle-axe would not be less deadly from having a somewhat duller cutting edge than if formed of bronze, and should it get bent in an encounter, the straightening of it might quickly be effected, while the loss of a blade by its breaking would be irreparable. I have elsewhere contended that the Hungarian perforated double-ended axes (like pickaxes) of copper, with but little or no tin in them, were made of this material, not because tin was unknown, but because the ductile and malleable copper was found better adapted for certain purposes than the more fragile bronze. In the same manner copper rather than brass sets or punches are in use among engineers at the present day, when an intermediate piece of metal is required to convey the blows of a hammer to an iron key or other object which would be injured by receiving the blows direct.

Sir William Wilde, in his Fig. 360, has shown a hollow tube of

* P. 449.

---

bronze as forming the handle of a wide halberd blade; but this juxtaposition of the two objects has been questioned. Not only are the projecting spikes upon the tube somewhat inconsistent with its use as a handle, but from a comparison with some similar objects since discovered there can be no doubt of the presumed halberd shaft being in reality a portion of a trumpet.

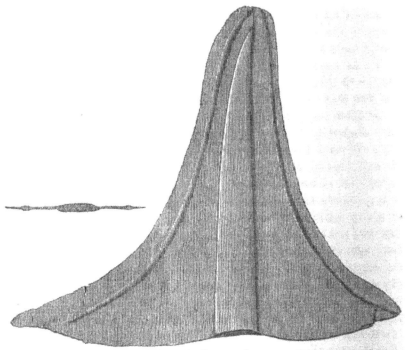

Fig. 332.—Cavan.   ⅓

The blade which is figured in connection with this handle was found near Roscrea, Co. Tipperary, and closely resembles Fig. 332 both in form and size, being 7⅜ inches long and 8⅝ inches wide at the base, in which are two rivet-holes and also two notches in the margin. It has a kind of treble midrib. The blade shown in Fig. 332 has but a single midrib, but near the edges and following the same curve is a minor ridge. A section is given at the side of the figure. The original was found near Cavan, and is in my own collection. From the absence of rivet-holes it seems doubtful whether it was ever mounted on a shaft so as to form a complete weapon, unless, indeed, the sharp base was merely driven into the wood. The metal appears to have a larger admixture of tin in it than is usual in the scythe-like blades. I am not aware of the existence of any other specimens of this very broad form besides the two now mentioned.

A curved blade, of much the same section as Fig. 332, but 15½ inches long and 3¼ inches broad at the base, found at the foot of Slieve Kileta Hill, Co. Wexford, is in the British Museum. It has three stout rivets.

The long and narrow blade shown in Fig. 333 seems also to belong

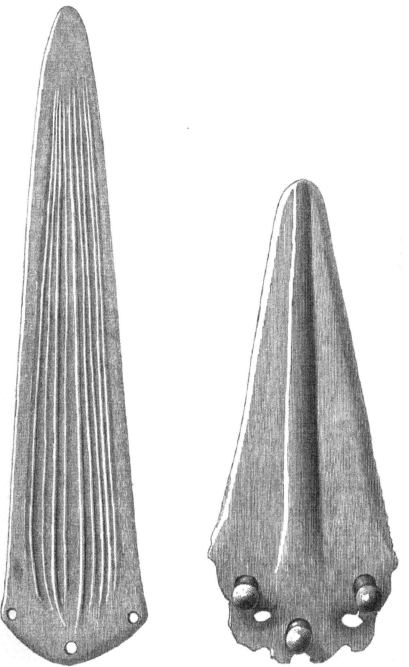

Fig. 333.—Newtown Limavady.   ¼   Fig. 334.—Ballygawley.   ¼

to the category of halberds, though the rivet-holes are smaller than usual, and the blade itself thinner. It is strengthened by a number of small converging ribs formed in the casting, instead of by a broad midrib, and is also straight and not curved. The original was found near Newtown Limavady, Co. Derry, and is in the collection of Canon Greenwell, F.R.S.

The shorter and much more massive blade shown in Fig. 334 is also in Canon Greenwell's collection, and was found at Ballygawley, Co. Tyrone. It has probably seen much service, as what appear to have been the

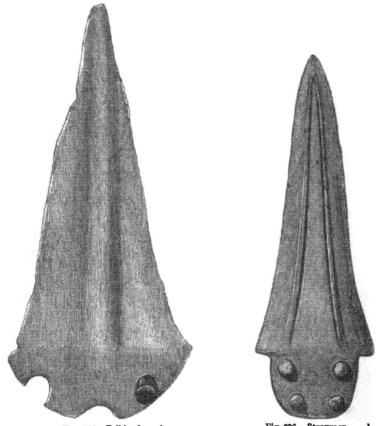

Fig. 335.—Falkland.   ¼   Fig. 336.—Stranraer.   ¼

original three rivet-holes have in two cases been partly closed by hammering, while in the third the base of the blade has broken away. In order to make use of the weapon, three fresh holes have been drilled rather farther from the base, in which the rivets are still preserved.

Some of the Irish * blades are more rounded than this at the point, and have been secured to the shafts by four rivets arranged as in Fig. 336. There is also occasionally a shoulder between the blade and the part let into the handle, as in that from Stranraer.

* Conf. Wilde, *op. cit.*, p. 489, figs. 356 and 357; and "Horæ Fer.," pl. x. 6.

In Fig. 335 is shown another blade much like that from Ballygawley,

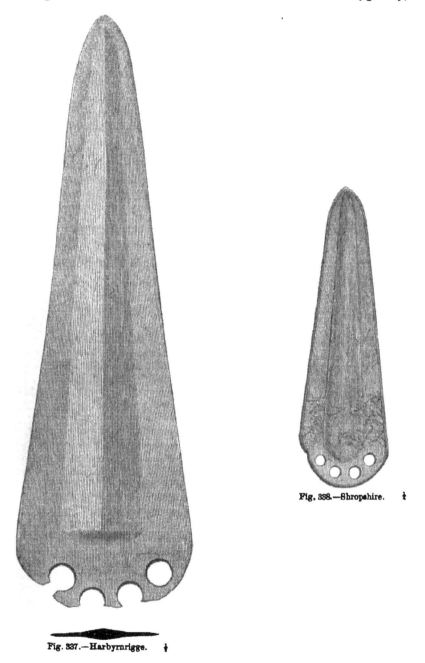

Fig. 337.—Harbyrnrigge.   ¼

Fig. 338.—Shropshire.   ¼

but found near Falkland, Fifeshire. The metal appears to be nearly pure copper, and it is doubtful whether it ever had more than one rivet-hole, though there are notches for the reception of two besides the rivet still left in the blade.   It would, however, be fairly secured in its handle by a second rivet in the notch on the left, while a third at the back of the midrib would prevent the blade from being driven into its handle by a blow.

In the Antiquarian Museum at Edinburgh are several of these halberd-like blades, some of them curved.   One from Sluie,* Edinkillie, Elgin-shire, is 11 by 3¼ inches, and has four rivet-holes arranged in a semi-circle.   It was found with two flat celts.   Three others, from 10 to 13¼ inches by 3 inches, were found together at Kingarth,† Bute.   They are described as of reddish bronze.

The original of Fig. 336 was found near Stranraer,‡ Wigtonshire, and is now in the Antiquarian Museum at Edinburgh.   It is 12½ inches long and 4½ broad, and weighs nearly 1¾ lbs., so that if mounted as a halberd, it must have been a formidable weapon.   The rivets are an inch in length.

In England and Wales the blades which can with any degree of confidence be regarded as those of halberds are by no means common.   I think, however, that the example from Harbyrnrigge,§ Crosby Ravensworth, Westmoreland, shown in Fig. 337, must be looked upon as a halberd rather than as a dagger.   It is in the collection of Canon Greenwell, F.R.S.

Another blade of much the same character is shown on the scale of one-fourth in Fig. 338.   It was found in Shropshire,‖ but the exact locality is not known.   Another (11¼ by 4 inches), bearing much resemblance to that from Shropshire, was found near Manea,¶ Cambridgeshire.   It is provided with four rivets, and has a small rib running down the thickened centre of the blade.   It is now in the Museum of the Cambridge Antiquarian Society.

The late Mr. J. W. Flower, F.G.S., bequeathed to me a blade of this character (9¾ by 3¼ inches) thickened out in the middle like Fig. 334, and with three large rivet-holes in the base, which is somewhat of a trefoil form.   It was found with broken sword-blades and spear-heads at Stoke Ferry, Norfolk, and appears to be formed of copper.

The only Welsh example which I have to mention was found in the parish of Llansanffraid,** Cwm Deuddwr, Radnorshire.   It is 9 inches long and 4 inches wide, and weighs 15 oz.   In form and character it closely resembles the Irish and Scotch specimens (Figs. 334 and 335), having a plain midrib, bevelled edges, and three rivet-holes.

A large blade, with a strong midrib and three rivets, found in Zealand, and engraved by Madsen,†† may have belonged to a halberd of this class.

* *Proc. Soc. Ant. Scot.*, vol. iv. p. 187.   † *Ibid.*, vol. iv. p. 396.
‡ *Ibid.*, vol. vii. p. 423.   I am indebted to the Council for the use of this cut.
§ *Proc. Soc. Ant.*, 2nd S., vol. iii. p. 258.
‖ *Arch. Journ.*, vol. xi. p. 414; vol. xviii. p. 161; *Proc. Soc. Ant.*, 2nd S., vol. v. p. 403.
¶ *Arch. Journ.*, vol. xii. p. 193; "Horæ Fer.," pl. x. 7.
** *Arch. Camb.*, 4th S., vol. vi. p. 20 (figured).
†† "Afbild.," vol. ii. pl. xi. 14.

I have already mentioned the halberd blades from Scandinavia and North Germany, and have seen but one example from any of the western countries of Europe. This is from Spain, and was found near Ciudad Real. It is about 8¼ inches long, and more T-shaped at the base than any British specimen, the blade suddenly expanding from 2 inches in width to 5. In this expanded part are the usual three rivets, each about 1 inch in length. The discovery of a weapon of this type in Spain seems to lend support to those who maintain that there was some connection between the Iberians and the early inhabitants of Ireland. The curious similarity of some of the Portuguese forms of flint arrow- and javelin-heads to those of Ireland is also worthy of notice.

Fig. 339.—Lidgate. ¼   Fig. 340.—Great Bedwin. ¼   Fig. 341.—Ireland. ¼

Besides the battle-axe or halberd there is another form of weapon for hand-to-hand encounters—the mace—of which it will be well to say a few words; for though I do not for a moment believe that the bronze mace-heads so frequently found in this and other European countries belong to the Bronze Age, yet by many they have been classed among the antiquities of that period. These weapons vary considerably in size and weight, but the cuts will show the more common forms.

That shown in Fig. 339 is in the Museum of the Cambridge Antiquarian Society, and is stated to have been found at Lidgate,* Suffolk. In the Meyrick † Collection is one precisely similar, which was brought from Italy. The mace to which these dentated rings were attached is thought to have been a kind of "morning star" or flail. Others from Lanark-

* *Arch. Journ.*, vol. vi. p. 181.   † Skelton's Meyrick, vol. i. pl. xlv.

shire * are of similar character. Professor Daniel Wilson refers these to the time of the Roman occupation.

I have three heavy rings with four long and eight short spikes each, from Hungary.

Another form is provided with a socket, and is evidently intended for mounting on a straight staff. That shown in Fig. 340 was found in a well at Great Bedwin,† Wilts, and is now in the British Museum. Another of the same class, with a longer socket, is in the Museum‡ of the Cambridge Antiquarian Society; and two are in the collection of Mr. M. Fisher, at Ely. Others have been found in London,§ and at Stroud,‖ Gloucestershire.

An Irish example from Wilde ¶ is shown in Fig. 341. There are three such in the Museum of the Academy, varying in length from 2 to 5 inches. One from Tipperary ** (4 inches) is of the same kind.

I have specimens of this kind from Hungary, one (4¾ inches) with three rows of four spikes, and one (4¼ inches) with five rows of five spikes. I have another from the Seine at Paris (4¾ inches) with six longitudinal ribs instead of spikes.

Lindenschmit †† has figured seven examples, from various parts of Germany and Italy, some more or less similar to each of the three figures I have given. Some of these are decorated with spirals in relief. Lisch ‡‡ has also engraved some specimens.

In the British Museum §§ are some foreign specimens decorated with patterns of a decidedly mediæval character.

An instrument of this kind, with eight lateral spikes and a long iron spike coming out from the end, was found with numerous mediæval relics in the ruins of Söborg,‖‖ in North Zealand. Such a discovery seems to me conclusive as to the date to be assigned to this class of weapons.

I must apologise to the reader for this digression, and now proceed to the consideration of the leaf-shaped bronze swords, which are far more closely allied to the arms described in Chapter X. than to the objects which have been discussed in the present chapter.

* *Arch. Assoc. Journ.*, vol. xvii. p. 111.   † *Arch. Journ.*, vol. vi. p. 411.

‡ *Arch. Journ.*, vol. vii. p. 302.

§ *Arch. Assoc. Journ.*, vol. i. p. 249, vol. iii. p. 60.

‖ *Arch. Journ.*, vol. xviii. p. 160.

¶ "Catal. Mus. R. I. A.," p. 493, fig. 361. I am indebted to the Council for this cut.

** *Proc. Soc. Ant.*, 2nd S., vol. v. p. 12.

†† "Alt. u. h. Vorzeit," vol. i. Heft viii. Taf. 2.

‡‡ "Freder. Francisc.," Taf. xxv. 13, 14.   §§ *Proc. Soc. Ant.*, *ubi sup.*

‖‖ Annalen for Nord. Oldkynd., 1851, Taf. v. 1.

CHAPTER XII.

LEAF-SHAPED SWORDS.

AMONG ancient weapons of bronze, perhaps the most remarkable both for elegance of form and for the skill displayed in their casting are the leaf-shaped swords, of which a considerable number have come down to our times. The only other forms that can vie with them in these respects are the spear-heads, of which many are gracefully proportioned, while the coring of their sockets for the reception of the shafts would do credit to the most skilful modern founder. Neither the one nor the other belong to the earliest period[*] when bronze first came into general use for weapons and tools, the flat celts and knife-daggers characteristic of that period being as a rule absent from the hoards in which fragments of swords and spear-heads are present.

There is also this remarkable circumstance attaching to the bronze swords, viz., that there is no well-authenticated instance[†] of their occurrence with any interments in barrows. It is true that Professor Daniel Wilson[‡] speaks of the frequent discovery of broken swords with sepulchral deposits, and mentions one found alongside of a cinerary urn in a tumulus at Memsie, Aberdeenshire, and another which lay beside a human skeleton in a cist under Carlochan Cairn, Carmichael, Galloway. But one of these discoveries took place so long ago as 1776, and in both cases there may, as Canon Greenwell has suggested, either have been some mistake as to the manner of finding, or the connection of the sword with the interment may have been apparent rather than real. A portion of a sword 6½ inches long, said to have been found in a cairn at Ballagan,[§] Strathblane, Stirlingshire, in 1788, is in the Antiquarian Museum at Edinburgh. A "sarcophagus with ashes" is said to have been in the cairn. Another sword, broken in four pieces, is said to

---

[*] Conf. Greenwell, "British Barrows," p. 49.   [†] *Op. cit.*, p. 44.
[‡] "Preh. Ann. of Scot.," vol. i. p. 394.   [§] *Arch. Scot.*, vol. iii. App. p. 67.

have been found in a barrow in Breconshire.* Another, found at Wetheringsett, Suffolk, is said to have lain fourteen feet deep in clay, with a great number of human bones, but no pottery or other remains. In this case, however, there is no mention of a barrow. The sword is elsewhere said to have been found in a sandpit.†

In Scandinavia, however, bronze swords have not unfrequently been found with interments in barrows; and inasmuch as the owners of the bronze swords in Britain were, after death, in all probability interred, either in a burnt or unburnt condition, there appears no reason why in some instances their swords may not have been buried with them, though as yet the evidence of these weapons having been found in tumuli, is far from satisfactory. Possibly at the time when the swords were in use the practice of erecting mounds over graves had ceased, and there are now no external marks upon the ground to indicate the graves of the warriors who wielded the bronze swords, and who have thus escaped disturbance in their "narrow cells" from the hands of treasure-seekers and archæologists; or possibly the custom of burying weapons with the dead may at that time have ceased.

But not only has there been a question, as to what was the method of interment in vogue among the owners of the bronze swords, but, as already mentioned in the Introductory Chapter, serious dispute has arisen whether the swords themselves are not Roman, or at all events of Roman date. The late Mr. Thomas Wright‡ was the most ardent advocate of this latter view, and he has been to some extent supported by Mr. C. Roach Smith.§ The contrary view, that the swords belong to a Bronze Age before the use of that metal was superseded by that of iron, has been ably advocated by the late Mr. A. Henry Rhind, F.S.A.Scot.,‖ and Sir John Lubbock.¶ It seems almost needless for me here to enter further into this controversy, in which, to my mind, as already stated in the Introductory Chapter, the whole weight of the argument is in favour of a pre-Roman origin for these swords in Western and Northern Europe. There was no doubt a time when bronze swords were in use in Greece and Italy, and the substitution of iron or steel for bronze, so far as we can judge from the early iron swords found in the ancient cemetery at Hallstatt and

---

* *Arch. Assoc. Journ.*, vol. iii. p. 60.   † *A. A. J.*, vol. xv. p. 230.
‡ " On the True Assignation of the Bronze Weapons," &c., *Trans. Ethn. Soc.*, N.S., vo'. iv. p. 176. *The Celt, Roman and Saxon*, 2nd Ed. p. 7, *et seqq.*
§ " Catal. Lond. Ant.," p. 80.   ‖ *Proc. Soc. Ant. Scot.*, vol. ii. p. 72.
¶ " Preh. Times," 4th Ed. p. 17; *Trans. Ethn. Soc.*, N.S., vol. v. p. 105.

elsewhere, involved little if any alteration in the form and character of the weapon, which was better adapted for thrusting than for striking. Even here in Britain, by the time when the Roman invasion took place, not only were swords made of iron in use, but the form of what is known as the Late-Celtic* sword was no longer leaf-shaped, but slightly tapering, with the edges nearly straight almost as far as the point. Among the Romans it would seem that more than one change was made in the form of their swords after the introduction of iron as the material from which they were formed. As Mr. Rhind has pointed out, Polybius speaks of the swords wielded by the soldiers of Æmilius at the battle of Telamon, B.C. 225, as made not only to thrust but to give a falling stroke with singular effect. "During the Second Punic War, however, which immediately succeeded the battle of Telamon, the Romans adopted the Spanish sword," the material of which we have no difficulty in definitely ascertaining, as "Diodorus Siculus† particularly mentions the process by which the Celtiberians prepared their iron for the purpose of manufacturing swords so tempered that neither shield, helmet, nor bone could resist them." How far their process of burying iron underground until a part of it had rusted away would, in the case of charcoal iron, leave the remaining portion more of the nature of steel, I am unable to say. Perhaps the amount of manipulation in charcoal necessary to restore the rusted plates to a serviceable condition may have produced this effect of converting the iron into mild steel. The steel of the sabres made in Japan,‡ which will cut through an iron nail without their edge being injured, is said to be prepared in a similar manner from iron long buried underground.

Most of the bronze swords are shorter than those of the present day; but the Roman sword would, in the time of Julius, appear to have been longer than ours. Otherwise Cicero's joke about his son-in-law, Lentulus, would have but little point, however small in person he may have been. Indeed, Macrobius§ expressly says that it was a long sword that Lentulus was wearing when Cicero made the inquiry, Who has tied my son-in-law to a sword?

The swords in use among the Britons at a somewhat later period appear to have been of great size, for Tacitus speaks of them as "ingentes" and "enormes." They were also bluntly pointed, or "sine mucrone." Such a description is entirely inconsistent with

* See "Horæ Ferales," pls. xiv., xv., and xviii.   † Lib. v. c. 33.
‡ Beckman, "History of Inventions," vol. ii. p. 328.   § "Saturn.," lib. ii. cap. 3.

the form and size of our bronze swords, though it might well refer to some of the iron blades of the Late-Celtic Period, which are 3 feet in length.   Others are, however, shorter.

Of the comparative rarity of bronze swords in Italy, and of their abundance in Scandinavia and Ireland, countries never occupied by the Romans, Sir John Lubbock [*] has already spoken ; and he has also summarized the reasons which convince him, as they do me, that our bronze weapons cannot be referred to Roman times. I will only repeat one of the arguments, of which perhaps not sufficient use has been made.   It is that at the time when Julius Cæsar was invading Britain, and its inhabitants were thus for the first time brought in contact with Roman weapons, iron had been so long in use for swords in Italy that the term for the weapon was "ferrum."

Another feature in bronze swords, which has been frequently commented on by archæological writers, is the comparatively small size of the hilt.   "The handles are always very small, a fact which tends to prove that the men who used these swords were but of moderate stature." [†]   "The handles of the bronze swords are very short and could not have been held comfortably by hands as large as ours—a characteristic much relied on by those who attribute the introduction of bronze into Europe to a people of Asiatic origin." [‡]

I must confess that I regard this view of the smallness of the hilts as being somewhat exaggerated.   My own hand is none of the smallest, and yet where the bronze hilts of the Danish and Hungarian swords have been preserved I have no difficulty in finding room to clasp them.   The part of the hilt where it expands to embrace the base of the blade was, I think, probably intended to be within the grasp of the hand, and not to be beyond it as a guard.   In the case of some of the short dagger-like weapons it seems possible that the projecting rim, which forms a kind of pommel at the end of the hilt, was intended to rest between the fourth and the little finger, and thus to assist in its being grasped firmly when in use as a stabbing weapon.   When the plates of horn or wood, which, as we shall subsequently see, once covered the hilt portion of the sword, have perished, it is hard to realise what was the exact form of the hilt ; but it is quite evident that we must not assume that because the bare bronze does not fill the

[*] "Preh. Times," p. 22.   [†] Worsaae's "Prim. Ant. of Denmark," p. 29.
            [‡] Lubbock, "Preh. Times," p. 32.

hand so as to give it a good grip, the same was the case when it had a plate of some other material on each face, which also possibly projected beyond the sides.

There is, moreover, one peculiarity about the hilt-plates of these swords which I have often pointed out by word of mouth, but which I think has not as yet been noticed in print. It is that there is generally, though not universally, a proportion between the length of the blade and the length of the hilt-plate; long sword blades having as a rule long hilt-plates, and short sword blades short hilt-plates. So closely is this kind of proportion preserved, that the outline of a large sword on the scale of one-sixth would in some cases almost absolutely correspond with that of one which was two-thirds of its length, if drawn on the scale of one-fourth.

This relative proportion between the length and size of a blade and its handle is by no means restricted to the swords of the Bronze Period, but prevails also among various tools, such as the saws and chisels of the present day. If, for instance, we were to argue from the saw-handles in a carpenter's shop as to the size of the hands of the carpenters, we should soon find ourselves in difficulties. The handle of an ordinary hand-saw is sufficiently large to admit the hand of any one short of a giant, while the orifice in the handle of a small keyhole-saw will not admit more than a couple of fingers, and the handles of saws of intermediate size range between these two extremes. This fact suffices to inculcate caution in arguing from the hilt-plates of the bronze swords as to the size of the hands of those who used them. It is a question which will be more safely determined on osteological than archæological evidence; but, owing to the remarkable absence of bronze swords from the interments in our barrows, it may be some time before a sword and the bones of the hand that wielded it are found in juxtaposition.

Professor Rolleston* has well said, "I am not quite clear that this bronze sword, leaf-shaped or other, has always a very small hilt." "At any rate, there can be no doubt that in this country the skeletons of the Bronze Period belonged to much larger and stronger and taller men than did the skeletons of the Long Barrow stone-using folk who preceded them. In some parts of England the contrast in this matter of size between the men of the Bronze and those of the Stone Age is as great as that now existing between the Maori and the gentle Hindoo."

* *Trans. Brist. and Glouc. Arch. Soc.*

The stature of several of the men interred in the Yorkshire barrows, examined by Canon Greenwell, was not less than five feet nine inches, and the bones of the hands were proportional to those of the bodies ; but, unfortunately, no bronze swords accompanied them, though many of the interments were of the Bronze Age.

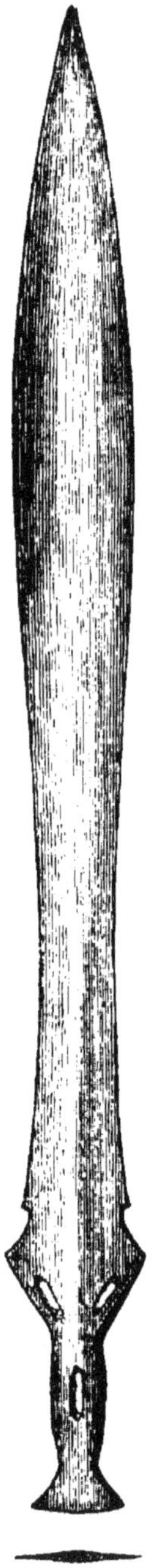

The usual form of sword to which the term "leaf-shaped" has been applied is that shown in Fig. 342. Their total length is generally about 24 inches, though sometimes not more than 16 inches, but they are occasionally as long as 30 inches, or even more. The blades are in most cases uniformly rounded, but with the part next the edge slightly drawn down so as to form a shallow fluting. In some instances, however, there is a more or less bold rounded central rib, or else projecting ridges running along the greater part of the blade near the edges. They differ considerably in the form of the plate for the hilt, and in the number and arrangement of the rivets by which the covering material was attached. This latter, as will subsequently be seen, usually consisted of plates of horn, bone, or wood, riveted on each side of the hilt-plate. In rare instances the outer part of the hilt was of bronze. Of the scabbards of such swords and the chapes attached to them I shall subsequently speak.

The sword shown in Fig. 342 was found about the year 1864 in the Thames, near Battersea Bridge, and is now in my own collection. Its length is 25¼ inches, and the blade is 2¼ inches broad in its broadest part, though at the top of the hilt it is 2⅜ inches in breadth. Just above this point the edge of the blade has been removed so as to form two broad notches, the object being probably to save the hand of the warrior from being cut should the sword be drawn back in his hand, there being apparently no transverse guard. The hilt has been attached by rivets or pins passing through three longitudinal slots, which have been produced in the casting, and not subsequently drilled or made. The hilt-plate expands into a kind of fish-tail termination, which was probably enclosed in a pommel-like end formed by the plates of horn, or other material, of which the hilt was made.

I have another sword, about 21 inches in length, which was found in the year 1851 near the circular encampment

Fig. 342.—Battersea. ¼

at Hawridge, on the south-eastern border of Buckingham-
shire. The hilt-plate is of the same character as that of
Fig. 342, but the lower slot is longer and the upper ones
shorter. In the latter were found the bronze rivets for
fastening on the hilt. This blade is figured on a small scale
in the *Proceedings of the Society of Antiquaries.*[*]

Another sword (22 inches) of the same character, with
three pointed oval slots for the rivets, was found at Washingborough,[†] Lincolnshire. Two other leaf-shaped swords
were found near the same spot. Another (24 inches), found
near Midsummer Norton,[‡] Somerset, has the central slot
nearly rectangular.

The central slot is sometimes accompanied by two or more
rivet-holes in the projecting wings of the hilt-plate. A
sword (24 inches) with two rivets was found between Wood-
lands and Gussage St. Michael,[§] Dorset. Another, broken,
was found, with fragments of others, socketed celts, spear-
heads, a sickle, and other objects, near the Pierre du Villain,
Alderney.[||]

One (24½ inches) from the Thames,[¶] at Battersea, and now
in the Bateman Collection, has a long rectangular slot and
four rivets. One of two (24 inches), found in broken condition, with a spear-head and two ferrules, on Fulbourn Common,[**] near Cambridge, was of this type. Another, from
Aldreth, Cambs. (23½ inches), is in the Museum of the Cambridge Antiquarian Society.

I have an example, originally 26 inches long, found with
a leaf-shaped spear-head near Weymouth.

The type occurs also in France. I have one (18¾ inches),
with a slot and four rivets, from Albert, near Amiens.
Another was found near Argenteuil,[††] Seine et Oise. I
have seen a bronze sword from Spain, also with the three
slots.

In the collection of Canon Greenwell, F.R.S., is a remarkably fine sword (27½ inches) from Barrow, Suffolk, in
which the long slot in the hilt-plate is combined with ten
small rivet-holes. The central ridge on the blade is well
pronounced, as will be seen by Fig. 343. The blunted part
of the blade near the hilt is engraved or milled diagonally.
The number of rivets is here larger than usual; but in a
sword (28½ inches) from the Thames, near Vauxhall,[‡‡] there
are five rivet-holes in the centre of the plate in lieu of the
slot, and four in each of the wings—thirteen in all. In
another (23½ inches) from the same locality there are eleven,

Fig. 343.
Barrow. ⅓

[*] 1st S., vol. ii. p. 215.
[†] *Arch. Assoc. Journ.*, vol. xi. p. 263; vol. xv. 230, pl. 23, 5.
[‡] *Somerset Arch. and N. H. Soc. Proc.*, vol. xxii. p. 70, pl. iii.
[§] *Arch. Assoc. Journ.*, vol. xv. p. 229, pl. 23, 3.
[||] *Op. cit.*, vol. iii. p. 9.
[¶] *Op. cit.*, vol. xiv. p. 328, pl. xxiv. 5.
[**] *Arch.*, vol. xix. p. 56, pl. iv.
[††] *Rev. Arch.*, N.S., vol. v. pl. ix. 1.
[‡‡] *Arch. Assoc. Journ.*, vol. iii. p. 60.

three in each wing and five in the centre. One (27 inches) from the
Thames, in the Museum of the Society of Antiquaries, has ten rivets, of
which four are in the centre.

Another (28½ inches) with ten rivet-holes, four in the hilt-plate and
three in each wing, was found in the Thames * in 1856, and is in the
British Museum.

A sword from the Roach Smith Collection (20⅜ inches) has a well-
marked midrib to the blade, which is somewhat hollowed on either side
of it. The hilt-plate has the central slot and four rivet-holes, in which
two rivets remain.

In the British Museum is another sword (27⅝ inches) of much the same
form at the hilt, but with ten rivet-holes, three in each wing and four in
the central plate, which is prolonged beyond the fishtail-like expansion in
the form of a flat tang, 1 inch by ⅝ inch. It was found in the Lea,† near
London. The lower part of the hilt has been united to the blade by a
subsequent process of burning on, as will shortly be mentioned.

This prolongation of the hilt-plate is not singular. In the Rouen
Museum is a sword with thirteen rivets which exhibits this peculiarity.
The same exists in a Swiss Lake ‡ sword, and is not uncommon in swords
found in Italy.

Another sword from the Thames (23 inches) has five holes in the hilt-
plate and four in each wing. The blade, which expands from 1¼ inch
near the hilt to 2¼ inches at two-thirds of its length, is ornamented with
a single engraved line skirting the edge.

In the British Museum is another remarkably fine sword from the
Thames, ornamented in a similar manner, but with a slot in the hilt-plate
and three rivet-holes in each wing. The blade is 24½ inches long and
from 1⅞ inch to 2⅜ inches wide.

Another, from Battle, Sussex (29½ inches), has eleven rivets, three in
the hilt-plate, which is in form much like that of Fig. 343. The blade is
drawn down towards the edges. The lower end shows where the runner
was broken off after it was cast, and is left quite rough, thus raising the
presumption that it was covered by some kind of pommel. Five rivets
are still preserved.

A sword from the Medway, at Upnor Reach, is 31¼ inches long and
1⅞ inch wide at the broadest part. It has no less than fifteen rivet-holes
for the hilt, in three groups of five each.

One from the Thames (28⅝ inches), with plain blade and thirteen rivet-
holes, has five small rivets still *in situ.*

More commonly the rivet-holes are fewer in number. One (24½ inches)
in Canon Greenwell's Collection, from Broadway Tower, Broadway,
Worcester, has nine rivet-holes, three in the tang and three in each wing.
One from the Thames at Battersea § (26 inches), and one from Ebberston,
Yorkshire, in the Bateman Collection, have the rivets arranged in the
same manner, as has one which was found near Whittingham,|| Northum-
berland, with another sword subsequently to be described, and also with
three spear-heads.

---

* See " Horæ Fer.," pl. ix. 2, p. 161.
† *Proc. Soc. Ant.,* 2nd S., vol. ii. p. 50 ; *Arch. Journ.,* vol. xix. p. 91.
‡ Keller, 8ter Bericht, Taf. iii. 1.
§ *Arch. Assoc. Journ.,* vol. xiv. p. 329 ; *op. cit.,* vol. xxii. p. 244.
|| *Proc. Soc. Ant.,* 2nd S., vol. v. p. 429.

I have one (19 inches) with eight rivet-holes, four in the centre and two in each wing, found near Cambridge. The holes appear to have been either made or enlarged by a punch having been driven through them, the rough burr being left on. On either side of the central ridge of the blade there is a pair of engraved lines parallel to the edges and at about ¼ inch distant from them. The base of the blade next the expansion for the hilt has been neatly serrated or engrailed, like that of the sword from Barrow, but in this case transversely. Unfortunately this blade, which is beautifully patinated, has been broken into three pieces.

French swords of this class, both with a central slot combined with rivets and with rivets only, are by no means uncommon. Specimens of each, from the department of Seine et Oise, are figured in the "Dictionnaire Archéologique de la Gaule." One with a slot and four rivets is in the museum at Nantes. Two with seven rivet-holes were found at St. Nazaire-sur-Loire * (Loire Inférieure).

Seven is, indeed, a more usual number for the rivet-holes than any of these higher numbers. In Fig. 344 is shown a fine example of a sword with seven rivet-holes, found in the Tyne, near Newcastle, and now in the collection of Canon Greenwell, F.R.S. It is 28 inches in length, and has a bead or rib just within the edges, which is somewhat exaggerated in the figure. The hilt-plate is provided with slight flanges for retaining the horn or wood that formed the hilt, and has a semicircular notch at the base, possibly for the reception of a rivet. See Fig. 356.

A sword from the Thames near Battersea (28¾ inches), in the British Museum, is of nearly the same form as Fig. 344, but the end of the hilt-plate has no notch, and there is no midrib running down it. The hilt has been fastened by seven rivets, which fit tightly in the holes and are nearly all in position. Their ends have conical depressions in them, as if a punch had been used as a riveting tool. In some the rivets have been closed by a hollow punch, so as to leave a small stud projecting in the middle of each surrounded by a deep hollow ring. Some French swords present the same peculiarity.

A sword of the same form (23¾ inches), but with a plain blade and only five small rivet-holes, was found in the Medway at Chatham Reach, and is now in the same collection. The hilt seems to have been burnt on.

A sword of this form (25¼ inches), with raised ridges parallel to the edges, has a rounded end to the hilt-plate and holes for six very small pins or rivets at the base and for one large one. The hilt-plate has been much hammered. It was found in the Thames. A second (24¾ inches), almost identical in every respect, has retained five of its pins.

There are two swords in the Norwich Museum, each of them with seven rivet-holes, both 21½ inches long, but the

* *Rev. Arch.*, vol. xxxiii. p. 231.

Fig. 344.—New-
castle. ¼

one found at Woolpit, Suffolk, and the other at Windsor. One of the swords found at Fulbourn,* Cambridge, had its rivets arranged as in Fig. 344. The blade is somewhat fluted between the central ridge and has smaller ridges running parallel to the edges. Another (23¾ inches), found in Glamorganshire,† is of the same character. Another like this was found in the bed of the Lark,‡ at Icklingham, Suffolk.

I have two swords (about 23 inches) with seven rivet-holes, which were found with spear-heads, a halberd, and other objects at Stoke Ferry, Norfolk. They are unfortunately broken. One of them appears to have been a defective casting, and to have wanted a portion of its hilt-plate. This has been subsequently supplied by a second hilt-plate having been cast over the broken end of the original plate, a hole in which has been stopped with a rivet, which has been partly covered over by the metal of the second casting. This is not an unique instance of mending by burning on additional metal. I have a small leaf-shaped sword (17¼ inches), for which I am indebted to the Earl of Enniskillen, found near Thornhill, Killina, Co. Cavan, which has in old times had a new hilt-plate cast on the original blade in this manner.

Other swords with seven rivet-holes arranged as in Fig. 344 have been found near Alton Castle,‖ Staffordshire, and at Billinghay,§ Lincoln.

A sword with six rivet-holes (23 inches) was found near Cranbourne,¶ Dorset. Another of the same length was dug up at Stifford,** near Gray's Thurrock, Essex. Another (20½ inches) was found in the Severn†† at Buildwas, Salop. The rivet-holes are two in the middle and two in each wing.

A leaf-shaped sword, the hilt broken off, but the blade still 22½ inches long, was found with a bronze spear-head, a palstave, and a long pin, in the Thames,‡‡ near the mouth of the Wandle. It is now in the British Museum.

A sword with the hilt-plate like that of Fig. 344 has been found in Rhenish Hesse.§§

Another variety of the sword has a strong central rounded rib along the blade, of which kind a good example is shown in Fig. 345. The original is in the collection of Mr. Robert Fitch, F.S.A., who has kindly lent it to me for engraving. It was found at Wetheringsett,‖‖ Suffolk, and is said to have had remains of a wooden hilt and scabbard attached to it when found. Human bones are also reported to have been found near it. It is 25¼ inches long, with engraved lines on the hilt, and has only two rivet-holes besides the central square-ended slot.

Mr. Fisher, of Ely, has a sword of the same character (25 inches), but with four rivets and a slot, found in the Fens near Ely.

A fragment of what appears to have been a sword of the same character,

* *Arch.*, vol. xix. p. 56, pl. iv.; Skelton's "Meyrick's Anc. Armour," pl. xlvii. 14.
† *Arch. Journ.*, vol. iii. p. 67; *Arch.*, xliii. p. 480.
‡ *Bury and West Suff. Proc.*, i. p. 24.   § "Reliquary," vol. iii. p. 219.
‖ *Arch.*, vol. xi. p. 431, pl. xix. 9.
¶ *Arch. Assoc. Journ.*, vol. xv. p. 229, pl. xxiii. 2.
** *Proc. Soc. Ant.*, 2nd S., vol. iii. p. 406; *Arch. Journ.*, vol. xxvi. p. 191.
†† "Horæ Fer.," pl. ix. 5, p. 162.   ‡‡ *Arch. Journ.*, vol. ix. p. 7.
§§ Lindenschmit, "A. u. h. V.," vol. i. Heft iii. Taf. iii. 5.
‖‖ *Arch. Assoc. Journ.*, vol. iii. p. 264; xv. p. 230, pl. xxiii. No. 4.

but with two rivet-holes instead of the central slot, was found with socketed celts and spear-heads at Bilton,* Yorkshire.

I have a fragment of a blade of this kind in the Reach Fen hoard. Another fragment, from Chrishall, Essex, is in the British Museum, as is also one found under Beachy Head.† It has two rivet-holes in each wing, and three considerably larger in the centre. They appear to be cast, and not drilled. With this fragment were found palstaves, socketed celts, lumps of copper, and gold armlets.

The type also occurs in France. I have a specimen from the Seine at Paris, with the hilt and lower part almost identical with Fig. 345, but the blade does not expand in the same manner, and has two lines engraved on each side of the central rib, the inner pair meeting on the rib some little way from the point, the outer continued to nearly the end of the blade. I have fragments of a sword of similar character from the hoard found at Dreuil, near Amiens. The fragment from Beachy Head already mentioned may possibly be of Gaulish origin.

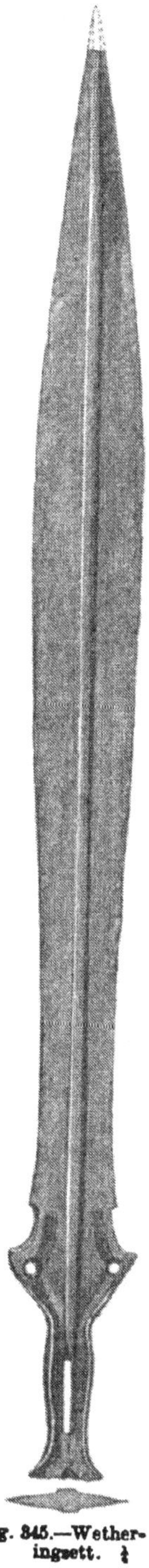

On an Italian oblong bronze coin or *quincussis*, 6⅔ inches by 3½ inches, and weighing about 3½ lbs., is the representation of a leaf-shaped sword with a raised rib along the centre of the blade, and in general character much like Fig. 345. A specimen of this coin is in the British Museum,‡ and bears upon the reverse the figure of a scabbard with parallel sides, and a nearly circular chape. Another coin of the same type, engraved by Carelli,§ has a nearly similar scabbard on the reverse, but the sword on the obverse is either represented as being in its scabbard or is not at all leaf-shaped, the sides of the blade being parallel. The hilt is also curved, and there is a cross-guard. In fact, upon the one coin, the weapon has the appearance of a Roman sword of iron, and on the other that of a leaf-shaped sword of bronze. These pieces were no doubt cast in Umbria, probably in the third century B.C., but their attribution to Ariminum is at best doubtful. From the two varieties of sword appearing on coins of the same type, the inference may be drawn either that

* *Arch. Assoc. Journ.*, vol. v. p. 349.
† *Arch.*, vol. xvi. p. 363.
‡ Catal. of Gr. Coins in Brit. Mus., Italy, p. 28.
§ "Numm. Vet. Ital. descript.," pl. xli.

Fig. 345.—Wetheringsett. ⅓

at the time when they were cast, bronze swords were in Umbria
being superseded by those of iron ; or that the type originally
referred to some sacred weapon of bronze such as is represented
on the coin in the British Museum, but was subsequently made
more conventional so as to represent the sword in ordinary use
at the period.

The sword with a central rib was sometimes attached to the hilt in a different manner from any
of the blades hitherto described, as will be seen
by Fig. 346, copied from the *Archæological Association Journal.** This sword was found at Tiverton, near Bath, and it is provided with four
rivets, a pair on each side of the continuation of
the central rib along the hilt-plate. Human remains and stag's-horns are said to have been
found near it.

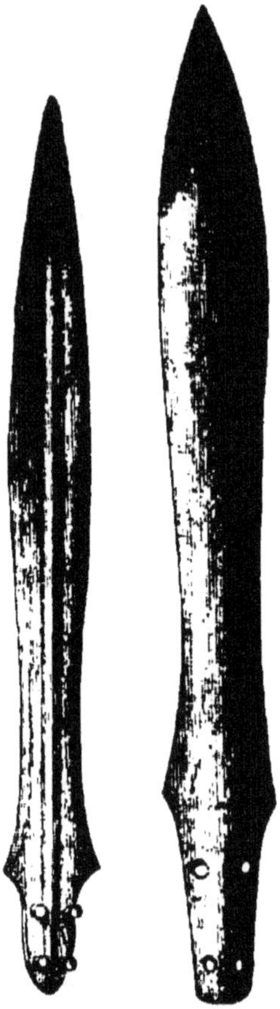

In the British Museum is a blade of the same
kind (19¾ inches), with semicircular notches for
the four rivets. It was found in the Thames at
Kingston. Another from the Thames (21 inches)
has the two upper holes perfect.

Leaf-shaped swords of the ordinary type also
occasionally had their hilts attached in the same
manner. Fig. 347 shows a blade from the
Thames,† near Kingston (16½ inches) with the
rivet-holes thus arranged. I have another, from
the Hugo Collection (18 inches), found in the
Thames about a mile west from Barking Creek,‡
which has had four rivet-holes arranged in the
same manner, though the margins are now broken
away, so that only traces of the holes remain.
Another apparently of this type was found in
Lincolnshire.§

In Canon Greenwell's Collection is a leaf-shaped
blade of the same character (15¾ inches), which,
however, has only two rivet-holes, one on each
side of the hilt-plate. It was found at Sandford,‖ near Oxford, together with a rapier-shaped
blade.

Fig. 346.   Fig. 347.
Tiverton. ¼   Kingston. ¼

Another variety has a narrower tang and rivet
holes in the median line. A blade of this kind,
which is in Mr. Layton's Collection, was found in the Thames at
Greenwich, and is engraved in the *Archæological Journal.*¶

Before proceeding to the consideration of the swords with more perfect
hilts and pommels found in England, it will be well to give references to

* Vol. iv. p. 147 ; vol. iii. p. 334.
† *Arch. Journ.*, vol. v. p. 327 ; *Proc. Soc. Ant.*, 2nd S., vol. i. p. 83, No. 14.
‡ *Proc. Soc. Ant.*, 2nd S., vol. i. p. 44.
§ *Arch. Journ.*, vol. xix. p. 91.   ‖ *Arch. Journ.*, vol. xxxiv. p. 301.
¶ *Anth. Inst. Journ.*, vol. iii. p. 230.

some of the other instances of leaf-shaped swords found in this country and in Wales. Several have been found in the Thames [*] besides those already mentioned. Others have been discovered in the Isle of Portland; [†] at Brixworth,[‡] Northamptonshire; and in the sea-dike bank between Fleet and Gedney,[§] Lincolnshire. Two, one with the chape of the scabbard, of which more hereafter, were found at Ebberston,[‖] Yorkshire.

Two were found at Ewart Park,[¶] near Wooler, Northumberland, one of which is in the Museum of the Society of Antiquaries of Newcastle-on-Tyne.

Some fragments of swords, regarded as being of copper, were found, with spear-heads, celts, and lumps of metal, at Lanant,[**] and also at St. Hilary, Cornwall, about the year 1802.

There were also some fragments in the Broadward find,[††] Shropshire, which consisted principally of spear-heads and ferrules. Occasionally a considerable number of swords are said to have been found together. No less than twenty are reported to have been discovered about the year 1726 near Alnwick Castle,[‡‡] in company with forty-one socketed celts and sixteen spear-heads; and two broad swords, one sharp-pointed sword, a spear-point, and a socketed celt were found "in a bundle together" at Ambleside, Westmoreland,[§§] about 1741.

Two swords, some spear-heads, celts, and other relics were discovered at Shenstone,[‖‖] Staffordshire, in 1824. Near them are said to have been some fragments of human bones. Some swords are reported to have been found in a marsh on the Wrekin Tenement,[¶¶] Shropshire, with a celt and about one hundred and fifty fragments of spear-heads.

Two swords and a fragment of a third were found in the Heathery Burn Cave, in company with numerous bronze and bone instruments and a gold armlet and penannular hollow bead. Most of these objects are now in the collection of Canon Greenwell, F.R.S. Three swords were found at Branton, Northumberland, and are now in the Alnwick Museum; where are also two which had pommels of lead, and were found with two rings near Tosson, parish of Rothbury, in that county. Another, which was also accompanied by two rings, were found near Medomsley, Durham. These rings may in some manner have served to attach the swords to a belt.

Most of the swords found in Wales appear to be in a fragmentary condition. Engravings of some leaf-shaped swords are said to exist on a rock between Barmouth [***] and Dolgellau, North Wales.

A fragment of a sword was found, with a bronze sheath-end, looped palstaves, spear-heads, and a ferrule, near Guilsfield,[†††] Montgomeryshire. Fragments of three swords were found, with lance-heads, ferrules, a chape, and other objects, at Glancych,[‡‡‡] Cardiganshire. They appear to have had six rivets.

[*] *Arch. Journ.*, vol. xviii. p. 158 (24½ inches); *Arch. Assoc. Journ.*, vol. xxii. p. 243; *Arch.*, vol. xxvi. p. 482 (said to have had a bone or wooden hilt when found).
[†] *Arch. Journ.*, vol. xxi. p. 90. [‡] *Arch. Assoc. Journ.*, vol. ii. p. 356.
[§] Stukeley, "It. Cur.," vol. i. p. 14. [‖] *Arch. Assoc. Journ.*, vol. xvii. p. 321.
[¶] *Arch. Æliana*, vol. i. p. 11, pl. iv. 3. [**] *Arch.*, vol. xv. p. 118.
[††] *Arch. Camb.*, 4th S., vol. iii. p. 353. [‡‡] *Arch.*, vol. v. p. 113.
[§§] *Arch.*, vol. v. p. 115. [‖‖] *Arch.*, vol. xxi. p. 548.
[¶¶] *Arch.*, vol. xxvi. p. 464. [***] *Arch. Journ.*, vol. ix. p. 91.
[†††] *Proc. Soc. Ant.*, 2nd S., vol. ii. p. 250; *Arch. Camb.*, 3rd S., vol. x. p. 214.
[‡‡‡] *Arch. Camb.*, 3rd S., vol. x. p. 221.

English swords, with the hilts, or pommels, or both, formed of bronze, are not of common occurrence. The first which I have

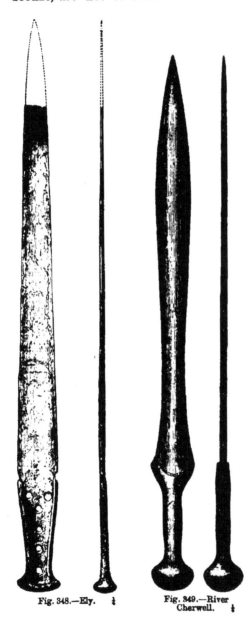

selected for illustration has the side edges so straight that it hardly belongs to the class usually known as leaf-shaped. The hilt-plate is peculiar in having well-developed side flanges which expand at the base so as to form an oval pommel. The hilt has as usual been formed of two plates of bone or wood, which have been secured to the hilt-plate by six rivets. This sword, which was found in the Fens, near Ely, has unfortunately lost its point, but is still 19¼ inches long. It was lent me for engraving (as Fig. 348) by Mr. M. Fisher, of Ely. In some Danish examples the high flanges of the hilt-plates are covered by thin plates of gold, beyond which, of course, the hilt of bone, wood, or horn did not project, and no doubt in this instance also the side flanges were left visible and not in any way covered. They are upwards of 4 inches in length, so that the hilt would fit into a large hand.

Fig. 348.—Ely.   ¼   Fig. 349.—River Cherwell.   ¼

A small but very interesting sword with a perfect bronze hilt and pommel is shown in Fig. 349. It was found in the River

Cherwell,* and is now in the Museum at Oxford. It was kindly
lent me by Professor Rolleston for the purpose of engraving. The
total length of the weapon is 21 inches, of which the pommel and
hilt, which is adapted for a decidedly large hand, occupy about 5
inches. The hilt has the appearance of having been cast upon
the blade, and seems to be formed of bronze of the same
character. There are no rivets visible by which the two
castings are attached the one to the other.

I am of opinion that the same process of attaching
the hilt to the blade by casting the one upon the other
was in use in Scandinavia and Germany. Some of the
bronze daggers from Italy seem also to have had their
hilts cast upon the blades in which the rivets were
already fixed.

Fig. 350.
Lincoln.

In the British Museum is a sword blade with slight ribs
inside the edges, retaining a portion of the hilt, which is cast
in a separate piece and attached to the wings by two rivets.
It is said to have been found in the Thames.† The hilt has
had ribs round it at intervals of about half an inch apart.

On a fragment of a sword blade, ornamented on each side
with five parallel engraved lines, the upper margin of the hilt
is marked out by a raised and engrailed line of the same form
as the upper end of the hilt of Fig. 350. It was found in the
Fen, near Wicken, Cambs, with a part of a scabbard end,
spear-heads, and other objects now in the British Museum.

A remarkably fine sword, found in the River Witham,‡
below Lincoln, in 1826, is shown in Fig. 350, for the use of
which I am indebted to the Council of the Society of Antiquaries. The original is in the museum of the Duke of Northumberland, at Alnwick. It presents the peculiarity of having
two spirals attached to the base of the hilt with a projecting
pin between them, the whole taking the place of the pommel. The blade appears to be engraved with parallel lines
on either side of the midrib. These spirals are of far more
common occurrence on the Continent than in Britain, and this
sword, though found so far north as Lincoln, is not improbably of foreign origin.

Several such have been found in France. One with the
spirals but a different form of hilt was found at Aliès,
Cantal.§

A bronze sword found in the Rhône at Lyons, but now in
the museum at Rennes,‖ Brittany, has a nearly similar hilt and pommel.
It has three raised bands on the hilt, but no pin between the spirals.
Some of the swords from the Swiss Lake-dwellings have similar hilts.

* *Journ. Anthrop. Inst.*, vol. iii. p. 204.   † " Horæ Fer.," pl. ix. 9, p. 162.
‡ *Proc. Soc. Ant.*, vol. ii. p. 199.   § *Rev. Arch.*, N.S., vol. xxiv. pl. xxv. 3.
‖ Chantre, " Alb.," pl. xiv. *bis*, 3 ; *Dict. Arch. de la Gaule.*

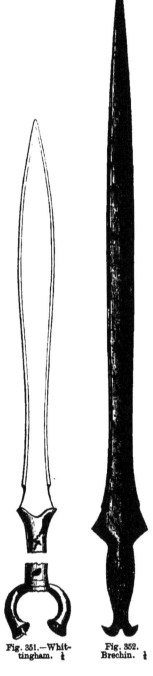

They have been found at Concise,* in the Lake of Neuchâtel, and in the Lac de Luissel.†

Another of the same kind is in the Johanneum at Gratz, Styria. The same form was also found at Hallstatt.‡ Another was found near Stettin.§ Another from Erxleben,‖ Magdeburg, is in the Brunswick Museum.

The hilt of a sword with spirals and a central pin was found in the great Bologna hoard. A perfect example is in the Royal Armoury at Turin.¶

There are several swords with this kind of hilt in the Museum of Northern Antiquities at Copenhagen,** some of which are figured by Madsen.†† The spirals are sometimes found detached. A highly interesting paper by Dr. Oscar Montelius on the different forms of hilts of bronze swords and daggers is published in the Stockholm volume of the Congress for Prehistoric Archæology.‡‡

The remarkable sword with a somewhat analogous termination to the hilt, shown in Fig. 351, was found at Thrunton Farm.§§ in the parish of Whittingham, Northumberland, and is in the collection of Lord Ravensworth. With it was found another sword already mentioned, a spear-head with lunate openings in the blade (Fig. 418), and some smaller leaf-shaped spear-heads. They are said to have been all found sticking in a moss with the points downwards, and arranged in a circle. The pommel end of the hilt is in this instance a distinct casting, and is very remarkable on account of the two curved horns ex-

Fig. 351.—Whittingham. ¼

Fig. 352. Brechin. ¼

* Keller, 7ter Bericht, Taf. iii. 4; 3ter Bericht, Taf. iii. 35; Desor and Favre, "Le Bel Age du Br.," pl. v. 10; Troyon, "Habit. Lacust.," pl. ix. 11.
† Keller, 7ter B., Taf. xxiv. 9.
‡ Von Sacken, "Grabf. v. Hallst.," pl. v. 10.
§ Lindenschmit, "A. u. h. V.," Heft i. Taf. ii. 1.
‖ "Zeitsch. für Ethn.," vol. vii. Taf. x. 2.
¶ "Bull. di Palet. Ital.," anno ii., p. 26.
** "Atlas for Nord. Oldk.," pl. B. iv., 40—42; Worsaae, "Nord. Olds.," figs. 135, 136.
†† "Afbild," vol. ii. pl. v. vi.
‡‡ P. 882.
§§ Proc. Soc. Ant., 2nd S., vol. v. p. 429; "Horæ Fer.," pl. ix. fig. 3, p. 161.

tending from it, which are somewhat trumpet-mouthed, with a projecting cone in the centre of each.

In Scotland a number of bronze swords have been found which bear, as might have been anticipated, a close resemblance to those from England.

That shown in Fig. 352 was found in a moss at Leuchland, Brechin, in Angus, and is now in the collection of Canon Greenwell, F.R.S. Its length is 26¼ inches, and the six rivets for attaching the hilt are still in the hilt-plate, which is doubly hooked at the end. A rib from the thicker part of the blade is prolonged part of the way down the hilt-plate as in Fig. 344. Another sword, broken at the hilt, but still 26¾ inches long, was found on the same farm. A find from Brechin is mentioned further on. A sword with four rivet-holes, like those from Arthur's Seat, found on the borders between England and Scotland, and engraved by Grose,[*] has the same peculiar end to the hilt-plate, as has one with five rivets from Methlick, Aberdeenshire, now in the Antiquarian Museum at Edinburgh. Grose has also engraved two, each with six rivet-holes in the wings and two or three in the hilt-plate, found in Duddingston Loch,[†] near Edinburgh, as well as the hilt-plate of another, found near Peebles, with slots in the wings and a slot and rivet-hole in the tang.

Some fragments of swords from this loch are in the Antiquarian Museum at Edinburgh. Almost directly above Duddingston Loch, on Arthur's Seat,[‡] two other swords were found during the construction of the Queen's Drive. They are 26¼ inches and 24¼ inches long, in outline like Fig. 342, with one rivet-hole in each wing and two in the centre of the hilt-plate.

Two (23¾ inches and 20¼ inches) of the usual character, with nine rivets and hilts much like Fig. 354, have been found in Lanarkshire.[§]

In Gordon's "Itinerarium Septentrionale"[||] a sword (24¼ inches) found near Irvine, Argyleshire, is engraved, as is also one (26 inches) found in Graham's Dyke near Carinn, which is said to be in the Advocates' Library at Edinburgh. The figures do not seem accurate, but show seven rivets in one and three in the other. Gordon makes no doubt that these swords are Roman.

Other specimens have been found at Forse,[¶] Latheron, Caithness (25 inches), near the Point of Sleat,[**] Isle of Skye (22¼ inches), with two spear-heads and a pin. Another was found in Wigtonshire.[††]

In the Antiquarian Museum are specimens from the following counties: Aberdeen, Argyle, Ayr, Edinburgh, Fife, Forfar, Kincardine, and Stirling.

In peat, at Iochdar,[‡‡] South Uist, were found two swords like that from Arthur's Seat, the hilts of which are said to have been formed of wood. A leather sheath is also reported to have been present.

A bronze scabbard tip, such as will subsequently be described, was

---

[*] "Treatise on Anc. Armour," pl. lxi. 1.   [†] *Op. cit.*, pl. lxi. 2, 3, 4.
[‡] Wilson's "Preh. Ann.," vol. i. p. 352, fig. 52.
[§] *Arch. Assoc. Journ.*, vol. xvii. p. 210, pl. xx. 10, 11.   [||] Pl. li. 2, 3, p. 118.
[¶] *Proc. Soc. Ant. Scot.*, vol. ii. p. 33.   [**] *P. S. A. S.*, vol. iii. p. 102.
[††] Ayr and Wigton Coll., vol. ii. p. 14.   [‡‡] *Proc. Soc. Ant. Scot.*, vol. vi. p. 252.

found, with four bronze swords (about 24 inches) and a large spear-head, near Brechin,[*] Forfarshire; and in Corsbie Moss,[†] Legerwood, Berwick, a bronze sword and spear-head were found, the former having, it is said, a scabbard, apparently of metal, but so much corroded as to fall in pieces on removal. This also may have been of leather stained by the metal.

A sword with a large pommel (24 inches), closely resembling Fig. 353,

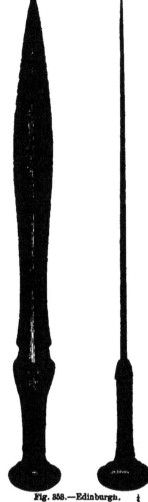

Fig. 353.—Edinburgh.   ⅓

was found, together with two other sword blades (one 25 inches with slots), a scabbard end, and two bronze pins, with large circular flat heads, at Tarves,[‡] Aberdeenshire. Some of these were presented to the British Museum by the Earl of Aberdeen. There is a recess on the hilt-plate for the reception of the horn or bone of the hilt, which was fastened by three rivets still remaining.

Another sword, the blade 22 inches long, the handle, including a round hollow pommel, 5¼ inches, was found in Skye, and is engraved in "Pennant's Tour."[§] It shows four rivet-holes arranged like those in the sword from Arthur's Seat, so that the hilt was probably formed as usual of horn or wood and not of bronze.

A few other swords with pommels to their hilts have been found in Scotland. That shown in Fig. 353 was found in Edinburgh,[||] with, it is said, thirteen or fourteen more, a pin, and ring, and a kind of annular button, of bronze. It is now in the Antiquarian Museum at Edinburgh. The hilt appears to have been added to the hilt-plate by a subsequent process of casting. The pommel has been cast over a core of clay, which it still retains within it. Another of the swords (24¼ inches) has the hilt-plate pierced for six rivets. Two others which have been examined are imperfect.

Mr. Joseph Anderson, who has described this find, points out that this hilt must have "been cast in a matrix modelled from a sword which had the grip made up of

* *Proc. Soc. Ant. Scot.*, vol. i. pp. 181, 224: *Arch. Journ.*, vol. xiii. p. 203.
† *Proc. Soc. Ant.*, vol. iii. p. 121.　　　‡ "Horæ Fer.," pl. ix. 4, p. 161.
§ Vol. ii. p. 334, pl. xliv.　　　|| *Proc. Soc. Ant. Scot.*, vol. xiii. p. 321.

two convex plates attached on either side of the handle plate, and their ends covered by a hollow pommel"—in fact, from such a sword as that from Tarves, already mentioned. He also observes that the holes in the hilt are not rivet-holes, and thinks that they may have been caused by wooden pins used to hold the clay core in position, for the handle as well as the pommel is hollow. I am rather doubtful as to the accuracy of this theory, as such pins would, I think, produce blow-holes in the metal in casting. There may, however, have been clay projections from the inner core which would leave holes such as these, into which studs of wood, bone, or horn might afterwards be inserted by way of ornament and to add firmness to the grip. For details of the finding of from thirty to forty bronze swords in Scotland, the reader is referred to Mr. Anderson's paper.

The bronze leaf-shaped swords from Ireland, of which nearly or quite a hundred, either perfect or fragmentary, are preserved in the Museum of the Royal Irish Academy, have been treated of at some length by the late Sir William Wilde,* whose Catalogue the reader may consult with advantage. In general appearance they closely resemble the swords from the sister countries, and vary in length from about eighteen to thirty inches. The blades are usually rounded on the faces, or have a faintly marked median ridge, and are slightly fluted along the edges. This fluting or bevelling is sometimes bounded by a raised ridge. The form with a rounded rib along the middle of the blade is almost unknown. There is considerable variation in the form of the end of the hilt-plate, in which occasionally there is a deep V-shaped notch, or several smaller notches. The most common termination is that like a fish-tail as seen in Fig. 354. The number of rivet-holes is various, ranging from four to eleven. There are occasionally slots † in the hilt-plate and in the wings at the base of the blade.

They have been found in most parts of the kingdom.

A common type of Irish sword is shown in Fig. 354 from a specimen found at Newtown Limavady, Co. Derry, in 1870. One wing of the fish-tail termination is wanting and has been restored in the sketch. The nine rivet-holes seem to have been cast and not drilled, though they may have been slightly counter-sunk subsequently to the casting. The hilt-plate is slightly fluted, perhaps with the view of steadying the hilt. In a fragment of a sword found with spear-heads, a socketed dagger, and a fragment

* "Catal. Mus. R. I. A.," p. 439.　　　† Op. cit., p. 454.

of a hammer on Bo Island, Enniskillen, there are five deep flutings

Fig. 354.—New-   Fig. 355.—Ireland. ½   Fig. 356.—Ireland. ½   Fig. 357.—Ireland. ½
town Limavady. ½

on each side of the hilt-plate. As is the case with some of the English examples already mentioned, this hilt-plate has been joined to the blade by some process of burning on. One of the four rivet-holes in it has been partially closed by the operation. Sir William Wilde has noticed that several of the leaf-shaped swords under his charge had been broken and subsequently "welded" both by fusion and by the addition of a collar of the metal which encircles the extremities of the fragments. The term "welding" is, however, inappropriate to a metal of the character of bronze.

In the British Museum is a sword of this type with nine rivet-holes (25¼ inches), found near Aghadoe,* Co. Kerry.

In the small Irish blade of much the same type (Fig. 355) there are only three rivet-holes, which have been cast in the blade, a fourth having from some cause been filled up with the metal, though a depression on each face marks the spot where the hole was intended to be.

There were several swords, mostly broken, in the great Dowris hoard. They had a rivet-hole in each wing and two or three in the hilt-plate.

Some of the bronze swords found in Ireland attracted the attention of antiquaries upwards of a century ago. Governor Pownall described two found in a bog at Cullen, Tipperary, which are engraved in the *Archæologia.*† They are 26½ inches and 27 inches long, and one of them is of the same form as the Scotch sword, Fig. 352. Vallancey‡ has also figured one (22 inches) with eight rivets.

From among those in the Museum of the Royal Irish Academy I have selected two for engraving. The first, Fig. 356 (26¼ inches), has had its hilt attached by a number of very small pins instead of rivets of the usual size. The second, Fig. 357, is a short blade about 19½ inches long, with a central rib extending down the hilt-plate, in which there are four rivet-holes, two on each side.

A bronze sword from Polignac, Haute Loire, now in the Museum at Le Puy, Haute Loire, has its hilt-plate like that of Fig. 356, but has only four rivets. Another with seven rivets was found in a dolmen at Miers,§ Lot. Another with six rivets from the Department of Jura‖ is in the museum at St. Germain.

Another from near Besançon,¶ Doubs, has six small rivets. One found at Alise Ste. Reine,** Côte d'Or, has four rivets only.

The type also occurred at Hallstatt,†† and in Germany.‡‡

At least two swords have been found in Ireland still retaining the plates of bone which formed their hilts. By the kindness of Mr. Robert Day, F.S.A., I am able to reproduce full-sized figures of

---

* "Horæ Ferales," pl. ix. 7, p. 162.　　　† Vol. iii. p. 355, pl. xix.
‡ Vol. iv. pl. vii. 1, p. 50.
§ De Bonstetten, "Essai sur les Dolm.," 1865, pl. ii. 2; *Rev. Arch.*, N.S., vol. xiii. p. 183, pl. v. D.
‖ Chantre, "Alb.," pl. xvi. 1.　　　¶ *Dict. Arch. de la Gaule.*
** *Rev. Arch.*, N.S., vol. iv. pl. xiii. 23.　　　†† Von Sacken, Taf. v. 2.
‡‡ Lindenschmit, "A. u. h. V.," vol. i. Heft iii. Taf. iii. 6.

both sides of one of the most perfect specimens, as Figs. 358 and

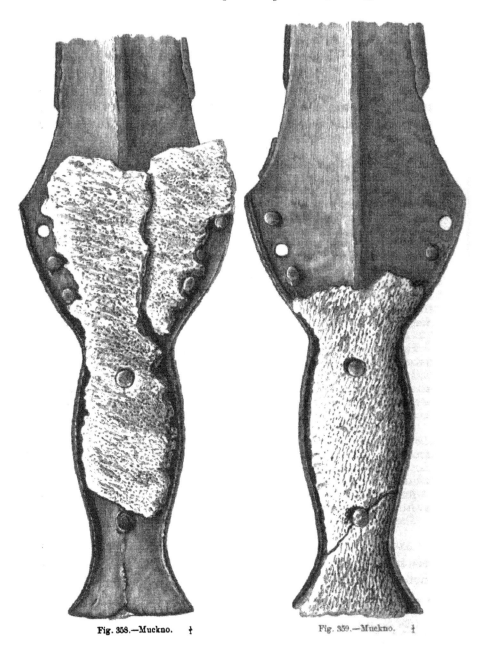

Fig. 358.—Muckno.   ¼   Fig. 359.—Muckno.   ¼

359, which have already appeared in the *Journal of the Royal*

*Historical and Archæological Association of Ireland.** The sword

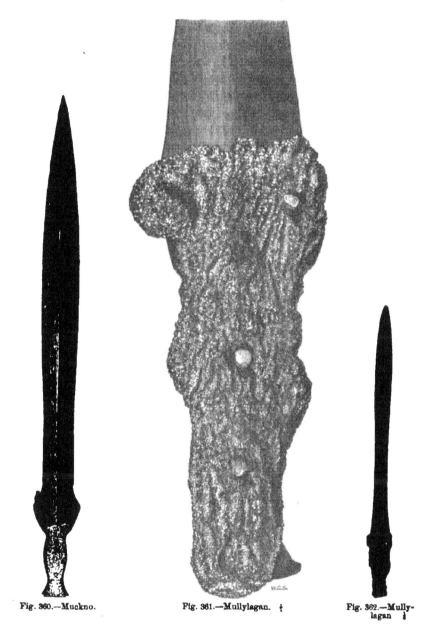

Fig. 360.—Muckno.   Fig. 361.—Mullylagan. ⅓   Fig. 362.—Mully-
                                                                       lagan ⅓

itself, shown on a small scale in Fig. 360, was found in Lisletrim

* 3rd S., vol. i. p. 23; 2nd S vol. vi. p. 72; "Reliquary," vol. x. p. 65

Bog, Muckno, Co. Monaghan. It is $24\frac{1}{2}$ inches long, with a thick midrib running along the blade. The plates of bone which are still attached have been pronounced by Professor Owen to be mammalian, and probably cetacean. It will be observed that at the wings of the hilt-plate the bone projects somewhat beyond the metal. The same peculiarity may be observed in the bone hilt of a sword found at Mullylagan,[*] Co. Armagh, which has somewhat the appearance of having been carved at the end next the blade into a pair of rude volutes. It is shown full-size in Fig. 361. The sword itself, on a small scale, is shown in Fig. 362. In this instance the bone projects beyond the sides of the hilt-plate. I have not seen the specimen, which is preserved in the collection of Mr. A. Knight Young, of Monaghan.[†] A bronze sword with six rivets, found near Kallundborg, Denmark,[‡] had the hilt formed of wood.

Fig. 363.—Ireland.

As is the case with several of the bronze swords discovered in Scandinavia, some of those found in Ireland seem to have been decorated with gold upon their hilts.

On one of the rivets of a sword found in a bog near Cullen,[§] Tipperary, was a thin piece of gold weighing upwards of 12 dwts. Another sword,[‖] found near the same place in 1751, had a plate of gold on one side which covered the hilt; at the end was a small object like a pommel of a sword, with three links of a chain hanging from it. The whole weighed 3 ozs. 3 dwts. 11 grs. In this bog about twenty bronze swords were found at intervals, besides about forty pieces of hilt-plates in which the rivets stood. In one sword[¶] there was a recess near the blade, $\frac{1}{4} \times \frac{1}{4} \times \frac{1}{4}$ inch, in which was "a piece of pewter which just fitted it, with four channels cut in it, in each of which was laid a thin bit of fine copper, so that they resembled four figures of 1."

A fragment of a blade which Wilde [**] considers to be that of a sword, is decorated with raised lines and circles in relief, which were cast with the blade. A portion of it is shown in Fig. 363. As the whole fragment is only $4\frac{1}{4}$ inches long, it may have formed part of a socketed knife or some other instrument, and not of a

---

* *Jour. Royal Hist. & Arch. Assoc. of Ireland*, 4th S., vol. ii. p. 257. I am indebted to the Council for the use of the cuts.
† *Op. cit.*, 4th S., vol. i. p. 505.   ‡ "Aarböger for Nord. Oldk.," 1871, p. 15.
§ *Arch.*, vol. iii. p. 363.   ‖ Ib., p. 364.   ¶ Ib., p. 365.
** "Catal. Mus. R. I. A.," p. 446, fig. 322, here by permission reproduced.

sword. A part of a spear-head, with a series of ring ornaments engraved on the blade, was in the hoard found at Haynes Hill, Kent.[*]

There is considerable general resemblance between the bronze swords found in the British Islands and those of the continental countries of Europe. The similarities with those from France have already been pointed out. Several with ornamented hilts have been figured by Chantre[†] and others. One has a hemi-spherical pommel and a varied design on the hilt.

The bronze swords from the Swiss Lake-dwellings[‡] have frequently bronze hilts, like those of the swords from the South of France. In some instances the hilt-plate has side flanges, with a central slot or line of rivets, and rivets in the wings. In others the broad tang forming the hilt has two or three rivet-holes. In some hilts cast in bronze there is a recess for receiving a piece of horn or wood. The blades have frequently delicate raised ribs, sometimes six on each face, running along them.

The bronze swords of Italy[§] present several varieties not found in Britain. The sides of the blades are more nearly parallel, and many have a slender tang at the hilt, sometimes with two rivet-holes forming loops at the side of the tang, sometimes with one rivet-hole in its centre. In some the blade narrows somewhat for the tang, in each side of which are two semicircular notches for the rivets. In some Italian and French swords the blade is drawn out to a long tapering point, so that its edges present a somewhat ogival curve.

A fragment of a very remarkable Greek sword from Thera[‖] has a series of small broad-edged axes of gold, in shape like conventional battle-axes, inlaid along the middle of the blade between two slightly projecting ribs.

The double-edged bronze swords found by Dr. Schliemann[¶] at Mycenæ are tanged and often provided with pommels made of alabaster. The hilts and scabbards are in some cases decorated with gold. The blades are usually long and narrow, though some widen considerably at the hilt-end, so as to form a broad shoulder

[*] *Arch. Journ.*, vol. xxx. p. 282.
[†] "Age du Br.," 1ère ptie. p. 105 *et seq.*; Alb., pl. xv. *bis*, 2; De Ferry, "Macon préh.," pl. xxxix.
[‡] Keller, *passim*.
[§] See Gastaldi, "Iconografia," 1869, Tav. viii.; Pellegrini, "Sepolchreto Preromano," 1876, Tav. iii., iv. Gozzadini, "Mors de Cheval et l'Épée de Rorzano," 1875.
[‖] "Aarbög. f. Nord. Oldk.," 1879, pl. i.
[¶] "Mycenæ und Tiryns," 1878, pp. 281, 303, &c.

to the tang.   Swords appear to have been much rarer on the presumed site of Troy.

There appear to be doubts whether the beautiful bronze sword
in the Berlin Museum,* reported to have been found at Pella, in
Macedonia, does not belong to the valley of the Rhine.

Bronze swords have but rarely been found in Egypt.   In my own
collection, however, is one which was found at Great Kantara during
the construction of the Suez Canal.   The blade, about 17 inches
long, is leaf-shaped, and much like that of Fig. 360, but more
uniform in width.   Instead of having a hilt-plate it is drawn down
to a small tang about $\frac{3}{16}$ inch square.   This again expands into
an octagonal bar, about $\frac{3}{8}$ inch in diameter, which has been drawn
down to a point, and then turned back to form a hook, probably
for suspending the sword at the belt.   At the base of the blade
are two rivet-holes.   The hilt must have been formed of two
pieces which clasped the tang.   The total length of the sword
from the point to the top of the hook is $22\frac{3}{4}$ inches.   I have
never seen another similar example, but a bronze sword blade,
presumably from Lower Egypt, is in the museum at Berlin.   It has
an engraved line down each side of the blade, and its sides are
more parallel than in mine from Kantara, already mentioned.
The hilt is broken off.   A German sword from the Magdeburg
district, with a tang and two rivet-holes at the base of the blade,
closely resembles mine from Egypt, except that it has no hook to
the tang.

The bronze swords found in Denmark † and Northern Germany ‡
have often side flanges to the hilt-plate, like Fig. 348, occasionally plated with gold ; but the blades are generally more uniform
in width, and have the edges straighter than those from the United
Kingdom.   Some blades have a simple tang.   On a very large
proportion the hilt formed of bronze (or of some more perishable
material alternating with bronze plates) has been preserved.   The
pommels are usually formed of oval or rhomboidal plates with a
central boss, and are generally ornamented below.

Some of the swords found in Sweden and Denmark have been
regarded by Dr. Montelius § and Mr. Worsaae ‖ as of foreign
origin.

---

* Bastian und A. Voss, " Die Bronze Schwerter des K. Mus. zu Berlin," 1878, p. 56.
† " Atlas for Nord. Oldk.," pl. B, ii., iii., iv. ; Worsaae, " Nord. Olds.," figs. 114
to 137.
‡ Lisch, " Freder. Francisc.," Tab. xiv., xv.
§ " Cong. préh.," Stockholm vol. i. p. 506.   ‖ " Cong. préh.," Buda Pest vol., p. 238.

A bronze sword from Finland with a flanged hilt-plate and eight rivet-holes has been * figured.

In Germany † the bronze swords present types which more nearly resemble those of France and Denmark than those of the British Isles. Those with a flanged hilt-plate are found, however, both in Northern and Southern Germany, as well as in Italy, Austria and Hungary. Others have long and narrow tangs, but a large proportion are provided with bronze hilts, usually with disc-like pommels. These hilts conceal the form of the tangs. Some few have spirals at the end of the hilt, as already mentioned, and one from Brandenburg, in the Berlin Museum, has a spheroidal pommel. In some of the bronze hilts there are recesses for the reception of pieces of horn or wood, as on some of the French and Swiss swords.

Iron swords of the same general character as those of bronze have been found in the ancient cemetery at Hallstatt and else-where. Those from Hallstatt ‡ are identical in character with the bronze swords from the same locality. In one instance the hilt and pommel of an iron sword are in bronze; in another the pommel alone; the hilt-plate of iron being flat, and provided with rivets exactly like those of the bronze swords. In others the pommel is wanting. I have a broken iron sword from this cemetery, with the hilt-plate perfect, and having three bronze rivets still in it, and the holes for two others at the pommel end. The blade has a central rounded rib along it like Fig. 345, but with a small bead on either side. I have a beautiful bronze sword from the same locality, on the blade of which are two small raised beads on either side of the central rib, and in the spaces between them a threefold wavy line punched in or engraved. In this instance a tang has passed through the hilt, that was formed of alternate blocks of bronze and of some substance that has now perished, possibly ivory. A magnificent iron sword from Hallstatt, now in the Vienna Museum, has the hilt and pommel formed of ivory inlaid with amber.

The late Celtic iron swords found in Britain have been described by Mr. A. W. Franks, F.R.S., in an exhaustive paper in the *Archæologia*,§ in which also the reader will find many interesting particulars of analogous swords found in continental countries.

Several iron swords have been found in France with flat hilt-

---

* "Cong. préh.," Copenhagen vol., p. 449.
† See Bastian und A. Voss, "Die Bronze Schwerter des K. Mus. zu Berlin," 1878.
‡ Von Sacken, "Grabf. v. Hallst.," Taf. v.; Lindenschmit, "Alt. u. h. Vorz.," vol. ii. Heft i. Taf. v.
§ Vol. xlv. p. 251.

plates and rivets exactly of the same character as those of the bronze swords. Nine have been discovered in tumuli at Cosne, Magny Lambert, and elsewhere in the department of Côte d'Or. Others have been found at Cormoz, Ain; and at Gédinne, in Belgium. There can be but little doubt that M. Alexandre Bertrand[*] is right in assigning the French examples to the fourth or fifth century B.C., and in regarding them as direct descendants from the bronze swords of ordinary type. He adduces, also, the remarkable fragment of an iron sword with a bronze hilt found in the Lac de Bienne, which is in exact imitation of a bronze sword with ribs on the blade, as an additional proof that these early iron swords are the reproductions, pure and simple, of those in bronze, and fabricated from the metal then recently introduced into the West. How far back in time the use of bronze swords in Gaul may have extended it is difficult to say, but the varieties in their types testify to a lengthened use before they began to be superseded by those of iron.

I must, however, now describe the sheaths by which these blades were protected.

* *Rev. Arch.*, N.S., vol. xxvi. p. 321.

CHAPTER XIII.

SCABBARDS AND CHAPES.

ALTHOUGH the sheaths which protected the daggers and swords described in the preceding chapters consisted probably for the most part of wood or leather, yet in many instances some portion of the scabbard and its fittings was made of bronze; and to the description of these objects it seems desirable to devote a separate chapter. It is rarely that the metallic portions of the sheaths have been found in company with the blades; but in one instance at least a portion of a sword blade has been discovered within a surrounding sheath of bronze; which, however, does not extend the full length of the blade, the upper part of the scabbard having probably been formed of wood. This discovery proves that the short bronze sheaths, which are usually from 8 to 12 inches long, belonged to swords, and not, as at first sight might be inferred from their size, to daggers.

In France some much longer bronze sheaths have been found with the swords still in them. The most noteworthy is that from the neighbourhood of Uzés,* Gard, now in the Musée d'Artillerie, at Paris, which is decorated with transverse beaded lines alternating with ornaments of concentric rings. This scabbard is longer by some inches than the blade it contains. In fact, in no instance does the point of the sword appear to have reached so far as the end of the sheath. Another sheath found at Cormoz (Ain)† is in the museum at Lyons.

In a few instances the wooden sheaths of bronze swords have been found entire. The finest is that from the Kongshöi,‡ Vamdrup, Ribe, Denmark. It was found with a body in a tree-coffin

---

* "Horæ Ferales," pl. viii. 7; Chantre, "Age du Br.," 1ère ptie., p. 108; Lindenschmit, "A. u. h. V.," vol. ii. Heft i. Taf. 3.
† Chantre, *op. cit.*, p. 135.
‡ Madsen, "Afb.," vol. ii. pl. vii.; Lindenschmit, "Alt. u. h. Vorz.," vol. ii. Heft i. Taf. iii. 1.

of oak.

This sheath is about a fifth longer than the blade of the sword, and is carved on both faces, though more highly decorated on what must have been the outer face, than on the inner.   There is no metal mounting at either end.   Another scabbard found in the Treenhöi[*] is likewise of wood.   Its chape also is formed of some hard wood.   It has been lined with skin, the hair towards the blade of the sword.   This sheath is about an eighth longer than the blade of the sword.

No doubt many of the British sheaths were made of wood alone.   Others, though partly made of that material, were tipped with bronze, the metal being secured to the wood, or the leather, if that material was used, by a small rivet which passed diagonally through the metal.   As Mr. Franks [†] has pointed out, the presence of this rivet-hole would have been sufficient to show that these objects are not dagger sheaths, as some have thought, for the rivet leaves too small a part of the bronze receptacle available for a blade even as long as that of an ordinary dagger.   The discovery already mentioned places this question beyond doubt.

The bronze sheaths of the iron swords and daggers of the Late Celtic Period are of a different character from those I am about to describe, and are made of sheet bronze, and not cast in a single piece.

In Fig. 364 is shown a portion of a sword blade, with the scabbard end still in position, which was found in the Thames near Isleworth, and is in the collection of Mr. T. Layton, F.S.A.[‡]   This scabbard end has a central rib and two other slight ribs along each margin in order to give it strength, and, as will be seen from the figure, probably extends at least 6 inches beyond the end of the sword, thus giving an opportunity of securing the metal end to the wooden or leather scabbard at a place where the blade would not interfere with the passage of a pin or rivet.

A scabbard end of much the same form (13¼ inches) is shown in Fig. 365.   It was found with fifteen others, some broken, near Guilsfield,[§] Montgomeryshire, together with looped palstaves, spear-heads, &c.   It has a small rivet-hole about half-way along it.   Another,[||] somewhat straighter

Fig. 364.
Isleworth. ¼

* Madsen, *op. cit.*, pl. v.
+ "Horæ Ferales," p. 159.   See also *Arch. Journ.*, vol. xxxiv. p. 301, fig. 3.
‡ *Proc. Soc. Ant.*, 2nd S., vol. v. p. 404.
§ *Proc. Soc. Ant.*, 2nd S., vol. ii. p. 251; *Arch. Camb.*, 3rd S., vol. x. p. 214:
"Montgom. Coll.," vol. iii. p. 437.
|| *Arch. Journ.*, vol. x. p. 259, whence this cut is taken, by permission of Mr. Franks.

(12½ inches), found with a bronze buckler in the River Isis near Dorchester, Oxon,* is shown in Fig. 366. It is now in the British Museum. There is a small rivet-hole passing transversely through it. Several † other sheath ends of the same kind are preserved in the same collection. One, imperfect, from the Thames at Teddington (10 inches), with ribs along the middle and edges, has a hole for a diagonal rivet, and retains a fragment of wood inside, as does also another from the Thames at London, which has a very slightly projecting midrib. A third, of the same

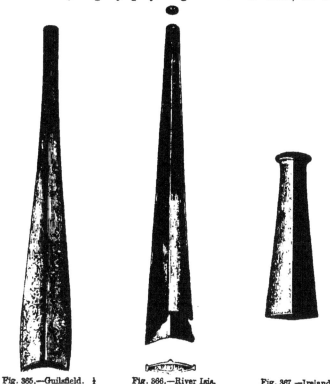

Fig. 365.—Guilsfield. ½   Fig. 366.—River Isis, near Dorchester. ½   Fig. 367.—Ireland. ½

character (10¾ inches), from the Thames at Chelsea, has a small end plate secured by a central rivet. This has traces of either leather or wood inside.‡ In another, also from the Thames (7¾ inches), the end plate has been cast with the sheath, and there is a wooden lining secured by a diagonal rivet. The opening is nearly flat.

In some there is no rib down the middle, but merely a projecting ridge, and in others no rivet-holes are visible.

This straight form of scabbard end has been very rarely found in Ireland. The only specimen mentioned by Wilde is by permission here reproduced as Fig. 367. Another (5½ inches) was in the collection of Mr. Wakeman, of Enniskillen.

* *Proc. Soc. Ant.*, iii. p. 118 ; *Arch.*, vol. xxvii. p. 298.
† *Arch. Journ.*, vol. xii. p. 201. See " Horæ Ferales," pl. ix. No. 10 to 14, and C. R. Smith, " Coll. Ant.," vol. iii. p. 72.
‡ *Proc. Soc. Ant.*, vol. iii. p. 118.

A scabbard end of much the same general character as that from Guilsfield, but shorter and broader, is shown in Fig. 368. It was found at Wick Park, Stogursey, Somerset,* with palstaves, socketed celts, gouges, spear-heads, and fragments of swords, together with jets from castings and rough metal.

Scabbard ends occur also in Scotland, for one nearly similar to these last (5¾ inches) was found with four leaf-shaped swords and a large spear-head, all of bronze, at Cauldhame, near Brechin, Forfarshire.† They are now in the Antiquarian Museum at Edinburgh. The scabbard is by permission of the Society of Antiquaries of Scotland here shown as Fig. 369. Another scabbard tip in the same museum is rather shorter. It was found at Gogar Burn, near Edinburgh, together with a sword and a

Fig. 368.—Stogursey, Somerset. ⅓   Fig. 369.—Brechin. ⅓   Fig. 370.—Pant-y-maen. ⅓

penannular brooch of bronze and a small penannular ornament of gold. A Scotch specimen from the farm of Ythsie, Tarves, Aberdeenshire, is in the British Museum. It is like that from Brechin, and is 5½ inches long.

The straight form of scabbard end has been discovered, though rarely, in Northern France. One from Caix, Somme, is engraved in the Dictionnaire Archéologique de la Gaule. A fragment of another, more like Fig. 365, has been found near Compiègne (Oise).

A still shorter form is shown in Fig. 370, the original of which was found at Pant-y-maen, near Glancych, Cardiganshire, ‡ together with broken swords, spear-heads, and ferrules, as well as some small rings.

* *Proc. Soc. Ant.*, 2nd S., vol. v. p. 427.
† *Proc. Soc. Ant. Scot.*, vol. i. p. 181; *Arch. Journ.*, vol. xiii. p. 203; "Catal. Mus. Arch. Inst. Ed.," p. 24.
‡ *Arch. Camb.*, 3rd S., vol. x. p. 221, whence the figure is copied.

A still more simple form, and one more nearly approaching the modern chape, has occasionally been found. That shown as Fig. 371 formed part of the hoard found in Reach Fen, Cambridgeshire, which comprised also some fragments of swords. It is of especial interest, as the small bronze nail which served to fasten it to the wooden scabbard was found with it. This nail is shown above the chape in the figure.

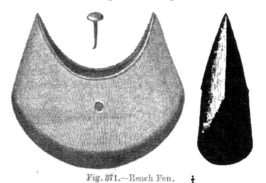

Fig. 371.—Reach Fen.   ‡

Another chape of the same kind, but more like Fig. 372 in form, was found at Haines Hill, near Hythe, Kent,* with a perforated disc of bronze, like Fig. 503, and some other objects.

Fig. 372, kindly lent by the Royal Irish Academy, shows a chape found at Cloonmore, near Templemore, Co. Tipperary.† This form seems to be of very rare occurrence in Ireland.

It has, however, been found in Savoy,‡ and in the Swiss Lake-dwellings.

Fig. 372.—Cloonmore.   ‡   Fig. 373.—Stoke Ferry.   ‡

An English form, which is, I believe, as yet unique, is shown in Fig. 373. It was found, with several broken swords and spear-heads, at Stoke Ferry, Norfolk. It is ornamented with a neat fluting, produced apparently by means of punches. The rivet-holes are at the sides, instead of being, as usual, on the face.

* *Arch. Journ.*, vol. xxx. p. 280.   † Wilde, "Catal. Mus. R. I. A.," p. 461, fig. 336.
‡ "Exp. Arch. de la Sav.," 1878, pl. xii. 354, 356.

X

A curious socketed object in bronze, found near Piltown,* in the barony of Iverk, Co. Kilkenny, has been regarded as the haft of a dagger. It is rectangular in section and expanding at the base which is closed. But from its analogy with some of the scabbard ends lately described it seems possible that it formed part of a sheath. The objection to this view is that the breadth of the socket is much greater than usual with these chapes. The zig-zag and other ornamentation upon it is described as having been engraved with a fine point after the object was cast. The lower face is not ornamented.

The form is not unlike that of the end of the scabbard of some modern African leaf-shaped swords of iron, as to which Mr. Syer Cuming† has remarked, that while the point of the blade is as sharp as a needle, the base of its receptacle measures nearly 3 inches across. It is possible that

Fig. 374.—Keelogue Ford, Ireland.   ⅓   Fig. 375.—Mildenhall.   ⅓

the object engraved as Fig. 286 may be intended for the end of a scabbard, and not for that of a hilt, but this can only be determined by future discoveries.

Another Irish form is shown in Fig. 374, the original of which was found at Keelogue Ford, in the Shannon, and is in the Royal Irish Academy. In this instance the chape has assumed a kind of boat-like form with pointed ends. As Sir W. Wilde‡ has observed, the indentations at the top mark the overlapping of the wooden portion of the scabbard, which was fastened to the bronze by two slender rivets, so that the ends projected about an inch on each side.

Fig. 375 shows an English scabbard tip of the same class, though differing in details, which was found in the neighbourhood of Mildenhall, Suffolk, and is in the collection of Mr. Simeon Fenton, of that town, to whom I am indebted for permission to engrave it. The surface of this chape is beautifully finished, and the raised rib round the semi-circular notch is delicately engrailed or "milled." There is a single minute hole for a pin or rivet on one face only. As will be seen, this English example closely resembles that from Ireland shown in the previous figure.

Such projections as those on the chapes of this form would appear to be inconvenient; but in another variety the projecting

* *Journ. R. H. and A. Assoc. of Ireland*, 4th S., vol. iv. p. 186.
† *Arch. Assoc. Journ.*, vol. xvii. p. 322.   ‡ "Catal. Mus. R. I. A.," p. 461.

ends shoot out into regular spikes, the ends of which are tipped by a small button. In some cases the length from point to point is not less than 8 inches. There are several in the museum of the Royal Irish Academy. Sir W. Wilde considered that the bronze sword was suspended high up on the thigh and not allowed to trail on the ground, so that these projections would be less in the way of the wearer than might at first sight appear. The lengthening of these points may have been the result of a kind of prehistoric dandyism, analogous to that which led to the lengthening of the points of boots and shoes in England at the beginning of the fifteenth century.* Specimens of these still exist in which the points extend 6 inches beyond the foot, and it has been

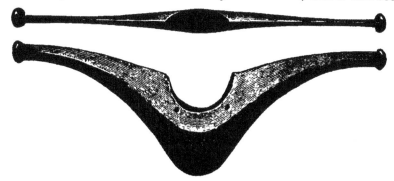

Fig. 376.—Thames. ½

asserted that they had to be chained to the knees of the wearers to give them a chance of walking with freedom.

Though chiefly found in Ireland, this elongated form of scabbard has occasionally been discovered in England. Fig. 376 represents a specimen from the Thames, now preserved in the British Museum.

Another example, but slightly more curved, was found with a bronze sword at Ebberston, Yorkshire, and is in the Bateman Collection.† It has been figured. The rivets for attaching it to the wooden scabbard are still in position.

This type of scabbard end has also been found in France. In the Museum of Bourges is an example about 5½ inches long, much like Fig. 376, but rather more V-shaped. Another, more like the figure, was found with a bronze sword, near Marsanne‡ (Drôme), and a third in the tumulus of Barésia § (Jura). Another was found at the end of an iron sword in a tumulus at Mons ‖ (Auvergne).

* Fairholt's " Costume in England," p. 382.
† Arch. Assoc. Journ., vol. xvii. p. 321, pl. 30, fig. 2.
‡ Chantre, " Age du Br.," 1ère ptie. p. 136. Rev. Arch., N.S., vol. xxxix. p. 306.
§ Dict. Arch. de la Gaule.
‖ " Matériaux," vol. xiii. p. 64. See also a paper by M. Alex. Bertrand, in the Bull.
Soc. Ant. de France, 1878, p. 56. " Matér.," vol. xv. p. 162.

It is to be observed that the ends of some of the knife sheaths of the Early Iron Period* expand in somewhat the same manner, so as to assume an anchor-like appearance.

A bronze bouterolle or scabbard tip of a very peculiar type, the sides being elongated and flattened out so as to form two sickle-shaped wings curving upwards, was exhibited to the Society of Antiquaries in 1867† as having been found in Britain. A figure of it was to have appeared in the *Archæologia*, but has not yet been published. Perhaps there was room to doubt its English origin. Certainly the description, with the exception of the sickle-shaped wings curving upwards, agrees with a form of which several examples have been found in Germany and in France.‡ Some of these are sharp at the end like a socketed celt, with two expanding sickle-like wings, but their purpose as chapes has not always been recognised. One from Hallstatt is described by Von Sacken § as a cutting tool to be attached to a thin shaft. There are two in the Museum at Prague, found at Korno and Brasy.

One from Oberwald-behrungen is in the Museum at Würzburg. Another is at Hanover.

The fact that traces of wooden sheaths to daggers have been found in the Wiltshire and other barrows has already been mentioned, but no

Fig. 377.—Isle of Harty.   ⅓

bronze fittings have been found with them. There are, however, some objects which may have served either as the mouth-pieces of sheaths for daggers or small knives, or as ferrules for their hilts.

One of these from the Harty hoard is shown full size in Fig. 377.

Another of identically the same character, but rather shorter, was found, with a bronze knife or dagger and numerous other articles, at Marden,‖ Kent. It was regarded by Mr. Beale Poste as the mounting of the top of a dagger sheath formed of leather.

Another was found with various other relics near Abergele,¶ Denbighshire.

Some elongated loops formed of jet are of a shape that would have served for the mouth-pieces of sword scabbards, but whether so fragile a substance was used for such a purpose may well be questioned. They may have been merely ornamental. One about 3 inches long, found in Scotland,** has been regarded as a clasp for a belt. Possibly these objects in bronze may, after all, be of the nature of slides or clasps.

Another loop, more rounded at the ends, found in the peat at Newbury,††

* De Bonstetten, "Rec. d'Ant. Suisses," Supp., pl. xxi. 1; Von Sacken, "Grabf. v. Hallstatt," Taf. vi. 11.
† *Proc. Soc. Ant.*, 2nd S., vol. iii. p. 518.   ‡ *Rev. Arch.*, N.S., vol. xxxix. p. 305.
§ "Das Grabfeld von Hallstatt," p. 155, pl. xix. fig. 10.
‖ *Arch. Assoc. Journ.*, vol. xiv. p. 257, pl. xiii. 6; Wilson, "Preh. Ann.," vol. i. p. 441, fig. 82.
¶ *Arch. Scot.*, vol. i. p. 393.   ** *Arch.*, vol. xliii. p. 556, pl. xxxvii. 3.
†† *Arch. Assoc. Journ.*, vol. xvi. p. 323, pl. xxvi. 5; *Proc. Soc. Ant.*, 2nd S., vol. iv. p. 521.

Berks, has been described as a slider for securing some portion of the dress, or for passing over a belt. Not improbably this is their true interpretation. Some other slides are described at p. 404.

Some bronze objects of nearly similar form, but about 3 inches in length, found with late Celtic remains, have been regarded as the cross-guards * of daggers or knives.

In my own collection is a fine bronze sword from Denmark with broad side flanges to the hilt plate, on the blade of which is a bronze loop about ¼ inch wide, rebated for the reception of wood, but without any rivet-holes. Each face presents four parallel beadings. For some time, in common with some Danish antiquaries, I regarded this loop as the mouthpiece of a scabbard, for which it appears well adapted; but I now find that such a view is erroneous, and that this loop is the ferrule for receiving the ends of the plates of wood or horn which formed the hilt. For in the barrow of Lydshöi,† near Blidstrup, Frederiksborg, was a bronze sword with a similar ferrule upon it, and the remains of the plates of horn beneath it still in position. One of these Danish ferrules is of gold.‡ A sheath § from a barrow at Hvidegaard, made of birch wood with an outer and inner casing of leather, has a leather band for the mouthpiece, and a leather eye for receiving the belt. Some small sheaths for bronze knives and for a flint dagger found at the same time are simply of leather.

* Arch. Inst., York vol. p. 33; *Arch.*, vol. xiv. pl. xx. 6.
† "Atlas for Nord. Oldk.," pl. B ii. 2; Worsaae, "Nord. Olds.," fig. 115; Madsen, "Afbild.," vol. ii. pl. xi. 1.
‡ Boye, "Oplys. Fortegnelse over det K. M.," p. 31.
§ "Annalen for Oldk.," 1848, p. 336; "Atlas for Nord. Oldk.," pl. B. ii. 7; Worsaae, "Nord. Olds.," fig. 119; Madsen, "Afbild.," vol. ii. p. 9. pl. iv. 8.

CHAPTER XIV.

SPEAR-HEADS, LANCE-HEADS, ETC.

THERE can be but little doubt that one of the weapons of offence in earliest use among mankind must have been of the nature of a spear—a straight stick or staff, probably pointed and to a certain extent hardened in the fire. The idea of giving to such a staff a still harder and sharper point by attaching to it a head of bone or of stone, such as is still commonly in use among many savage tribes, would come next. And, lastly, these heads or points would be formed of metal, when its use for cutting tools and weapons had become general, and means had been discovered for rendering it available for this particular purpose. In the earlier part of the Bronze Age, when bronze was already in use for knife-daggers and even for daggers, it would appear that the spears and darts, if any such were in use, were in this country still tipped with flint. How long this practice continued it is impossible to say, and it is even doubtful whether any bronze spear-heads were in use before the time when the founders had discovered the art of making sockets by means of cores placed within the moulds. It is, however, not impossible that some of the blades found in the Wiltshire barrows, and the tanged weapons which have already been described in Chapter XI., may have been the heads of spears rather than the blades of daggers; but even at the period to which they belong the art of making cores must have been known, as the ferrule found at Arreton Down, and shown in Fig. 324, will testify, as well as the hollow socket of Fig. 328.

In the South-east of Europe and in Western Asia, as in Cyprus and at Hissarlik, tanged and not socketed spear-heads have been found in considerable numbers; but such a form is of very rare occurrence in Europe, and is unknown in Britain, unless possibly some of the blades already described as knives or daggers, such as Fig. 277, were attached to long rather than short handles, and should, therefore, have been treated of in this chapter rather than in that in which I have placed them. If spears were deposited in the graves with the dead, the shafts must in all probability have been broken, for as a rule the graves for bodies buried in the contracted position are not long enough to receive a spear of ordinary length.

In the case of some few ancient socketed tools of bronze, the socket has not been formed by casting over a core, but a wide plate of metal has been hammered over a conical mandril so as to form a socket like that of many chisels of the present day, and of the iron spear-heads of earlier times. I am not aware of any bronze instruments with the sockets formed in this manner ever having been found in this country. In all cases the sockets have been produced by cores in the casting, and in many spear-heads the adjustment of the core has been effected with such nicety that a conical hollow extends almost to the tip, with the metal around it of uniform substance, and often very thin in proportion to the size of the weapon.

The heads of arrows, bolts, darts, javelins, lances, and spears so nearly resemble one another in character, that it is impossible to draw any absolute line of distinction between them. The larger varieties must, however, have served for weapons retained in the hand as spears, while those of small and moderate size may have been for weapons thrown as lances, or possibly discharged as bolts or arrows. In length these instruments vary from about 2 inches to as much as 36 inches.

Sir W. Wilde * has divided the Irish spear-heads into four varieties, as follows:—

1. The simple leaf-shaped, either long and narrow, or broad, with holes in the socket through which to pass the rivets to fix them to the shaft.

2. The looped, with eyes on each side of the socket below and on the same plane with the blade. These are generally of the long, narrow, straight-edged kind.

3. Those with loops in the angles between the edge of the blade and the socket.

4. Those with side apertures and perforations through the blade. To these four classes may be added—

5. Those in which the base of each side of the blade projects at right angles to the socket, or is prolonged downwards so as to form barbs.

* "Catal. Mus. R. I. A.," p. 495.

A remarkably fine specimen of a broad leaf-shaped spear-head of the first class is shown in Fig. 378.   The original was found in the

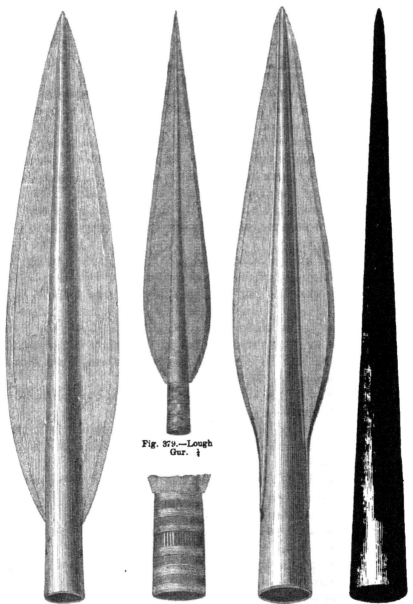

Fig. 379.—Lough Gur. ⅓

Fig. 378.—Thames, London. ⅓   Fig. 380.—Lough Gur. ⅓   Fig. 381.—Heathery Burn Cave. ⅓

Thames at London, and still contains a portion of the wooden shaft smoothly and carefully pointed.   The wood is, I think, ash;

and my opinion is supported by that of Mr. Thiselton Dyer, F.R.S.,
who has kindly examined the shaft for me. There are no traces
of the pin or rivet, which in the spear-heads of this character
appears to have been formed of wood, horn, or bone, rather than
of metal, probably with the view of the head being more readily
detached from the shaft, in case the latter was broken. I have,
however, a leaf-shaped bronze spear-head of this class, found in
the Seine at Paris, in which a metallic rivet is still present. It is
formed of a square rod of bronze, which at each end has been
hammered into a spheroidal button, of at least twice the diameter
of the hole through which the rivet passes. Portions of the
wooden shaft are still adhering to the rivet. The wood in this
instance also appears to be ash.

I have a rather narrower spear-head of the same type as Fig. 378 (10¾
inches), found with a bronze sword near Weymouth; and another identical
in type with that from the Thames, but only 9 inches long, found in the
county of Dublin.

Others of nearly the same form (12¼ inches and 8¾ inches) were found
with a bronze sword in an ancient entrenchment at Worth,* in the parish
of Washfield, Devon.

Another spear-head of this type from the Thames† (13½ inches) is in
the British Museum, as are others (13 inches and 10 inches long).

A remarkably fine bronze spear-head, found in Lough Gur, Co. Limerick, with the lower part of the socket ornamented with gold, is of much
the same form as Fig. 378, and is shown on the scale of one-fourth in
Fig. 379. The ornamented part is shown on the scale of one-half in
Fig. 380. It is in the collection of General A. Pitt Rivers, F.R.S., who
has thus described the socket.‡ Around it, " at top and bottom, are two
ferrules of very thin gold, each ⅜ inch in width. Each ferrule is ornamented
with three bands scored with from four to seven transverse lines, and
separated from each other by two bands scored with incised longitudinal
lines. The two ferrules are separated by a band about ₇⁄₁₆ inch in width,
in which longitudinal lines of gold have been let into grooves in the bronze,
leaving an intervening line between each of the gold lines." Most of
these gold strips have, however, now disappeared. The shaft of this spear
is of bog oak 4 feet 8¼ inches long, but though its authenticity has been
accepted by many good judges, I must confess that I do not regard it
as the original. Some other spear-heads ornamented with engraved lines,
but not with inlaid gold, will be mentioned further on. I may incidentally
recall the fact that the gold ring or ferrule around the spear-head of
Hector is more than once mentioned by Homer.§

πάροιθε δὲ λάμπετο δουρὸς
Αἰχμὴ χαλκείη περὶ δὲ χρύσεος θέε πόρκης.

Another fine specimen of a spear-head with a long oval leaf-shaped
blade in Canon Greenwell's Collection is shown in Fig. 381. It was

* Arch. Journ., vol. xxiv. p. 120.　　† "Horæ Fer.," pl. vi. 29.
‡ Journ. Ethnol. Soc., 1868, N.S., vol. i. p. 36.　§ Iliad, vi. v. 319; viii. v. 494.

found with several others varying in length from 6⅝ inches to 11¼ inches, and numerous other articles of bronze and bone, in the Heathery Burn Cave,* Durham.   As will be seen, the blade is continued as a slight narrow projection along the socket as far as the rivet-hole.   The edges are somewhat fluted.

A spear-head of nearly the same form (10½ inches) was found in a peat moss near the Camp Graves,† Bewcastle, Cumberland.   Another was found in a hoard at Bilton, Yorkshire.‡

A very fine example (about 15 inches), as well as a smaller one of the same type (about 8 inches), and one with lunate openings in the blade (Fig. 418), were found with two swords (see Fig. 351) near Whittingham,§ Northumberland.

I have others (9 inches to 11 inches) found with broken swords at Stoke Ferry, Norfolk, and from the Reach Fen hoard.   The same form occurs in Ireland.   I have a fine specimen (8⅝ inches) from Athlone.   Another (13¼ inches) is engraved by Wilde as his Fig. 362.   A very narrow spear-head, 14¾ inches long, and only 1⅝ inch wide, said to have been found in a barrow near Headford, Co. Galway, is in the British Museum.

A spear-head of this character from the Thames (16¾ inches), not fluted at the edges and quite plain, is in the British Museum.   The blade is only 2¼ inches wide.

One from Stanwick, Yorkshire (8 inches), is in the British Museum, as is one (11 inches) from Bannockburn, Scotland.   An Irish specimen (10 inches) is devoid of rivet-holes.

Another spear-head of nearly the same type, but of smaller dimensions, is given in Fig. 382.   It was found, with some other spear-heads (Fig. 410), socketed celts (Figs. 155 and 157), palstaves (Fig 83), and a ferrule, to be subsequently mentioned, at Nettleham,‖ near Lincoln, in 1860.   They are now in the British Museum.

Fig. 382.
Nettleham. ⅓

Others of the same type have been found at Winmarleigh¶ and Cuerdale,** Lancashire, at Wardlow,†† Derbyshire, Little Wenlock,‡‡ Staffordshire (8 inches), near Windsor §§ (7 inches), at Bottisham,‖‖ Cambridge, and in Herts.¶¶

* Dawkins, "Cave Hunting," p. 143, fig. 34.
† Arch. Journ., vol. xi. p. 231.
‡ Arch. Assoc. Journ., vol. v. p. 349.
§ Proc. Soc. Ant., 2nd S., vol. v. p. 429, pl. iv.
‖ Arch. Journ., vol. xviii. p. 159.   I am indebted to Mr. Franks for the use of this block.
¶ Arch. Assoc. Journ., vol. xv. p. 235, pl. xxiv. 3.
** Op. cit., vol. viii. p. 332.   †† Op. cit., vol. xv. p. 235, pl. xxiv. 4.
‡‡ Hartshorne's "Salop. Ant.," p. 96.   §§ Stukeley's "It. Cur.," pl. 96, vol. ii.
‖‖ Arch. Assoc. Journ., vol. xiv. p. 351.
¶¶ Skelton's "Meyrick's Anc. Arm.," pl. xlvii. 10.

I have one from the River Lea* at St. Margaret's, Herts, and others
from Reach Fen, Cambridge.

Others were in the Guilsfield hoard,† and in that of Pant-y-maen,‡ or
the Glancych hoard. One from the latter hoard is about 11 inches long.
Another, more like Fig. 386, about 4 inches. With them were found
fragments of swords, a scabbard tip, some rings and ferrules. Others
(9 inches and 5 inches) were found, with a socketed
celt and knife, a tanged chisel, and other objects, at
Ty Mawr,§ on Holyhead Mountain.

Five were found in the hoard near Stanhope,‖ Durham,
with socketed celts, a gouge, &c.

Of Scottish specimens the following may be noticed :
one from Lanark¶ (5¾ inches), which has been figured ;
two (7¾ inches) rather long in the socket, found with
a bronze sword and a long pin on the Point of Sleat,**
Isle of Skye ; one (6 inches) from Balmaclellan,†† New
Galloway. One (5⅛ inches) from Duddingston Loch,
Edinburgh, is in the British Museum.

Leaf-shaped spear-heads such as Fig. 382 are of
frequent occurrence in various parts of France. A
number were found at Alise Ste. Reine ‡‡ (Côte d'Or),
several of them ornamented with rings round the
sockets.

They also are found in the Lake-dwellings of Switzerland §§ and Savoy. Many of them have parallel rings
round the mouth of the socket by way of ornament.
They also occur in Germany ‖‖ and Denmark.¶¶ One
from Northern Germany, still containing a part of its
wooden shaft, has been engraved by Von Estorff.***

Those from Italy and Greece have very frequently facets running along the midrib which
contains the socket.

In Fig. 383 is shown a variety (11¼ inches) with a
projecting fillet running down to the rivet-holes as in
Fig. 381, which, however, in this case forms the termination of small beads running along the sides of the

Fig. 383.
Achtertyre. ⅓

central rib. There is also a beading running along the midrib. The
original was found, with another spear-head, plain, a socketed celt, some
bronze rings, and fragments of tin, at Achtertyre,††† Morayshire. Mr. R.
Day, F.S.A., has a nearly similar spear-head (5 inches), found in Dublin.

* *Proc. Soc. Ant.*, vol. iv. p. 279.
† *Proc. Soc. Ant.*, 2nd S., vol. ii. p. 251 ; "Montgom. Coll.," vol. iii. p. 437.
‡ *Arch. Camb.*, 3rd S., vol. x. p. 221.   § *Arch. Journ.*, vol. xxiv. p. 254.
‖ *Arch. Æliana*, vol. i. p. 13, pl. i.   ¶ *Arch. Assoc. Journ.*, vol. xvii. p. 110.
** *Proc. Soc. Ant. Scot.*, vol. iii. p. 102.   †† *Proc. Soc. Ant. Scot.*, vol. iv. p. 417.
‡‡ *Rev. Arch.*, N.S., vol. iv. pl. xiii. 2—14.
§§ Keller, *passim*.
‖‖ Von Braunmühl, "Alt Deutschen Grabmäler ;" Schreiber, "Die ehern. Streit-
keile," Taf. ii. 19 ; Lisch, "Fred. Francisc.," Taf. viii.
¶¶ Worsaae, "Nord. Olds.," fig. 190.   *** "Heidnisch. Alterth.," Taf. viii. fig. 1.
††† *P. S. A. S.*, vol. ix. p. 435. The cut has been kindly lent by the Society.

A more elongated form, with the projecting part of the socket considerably shorter, is shown in Fig. 384, from a specimen found in the North of Ireland. A spear-head (20 inches) of the same form of outline, but with a slight ridge running the whole length of the socket from its mouth to the point, was found at Ditton,* Surrey. It is now in the British Museum, having been presented by the Earl of Lovelace.

Another (14⅜ inches) in the same collection, found in the River Thames,† near the mouth of the Wandle, retains a portion of the original wood in its socket. It was found in company with a bronze sword, a palstave, and a long pin (Fig. 454).

One of much the same form as the figure (11 inches) was found at Teigngrace,‡ Devon. It has a delicate bead running down each side of the midrib, and continued as a square projection below the blade.

Canon Greenwell has a long spear-head (14¼ inches) from Quy Fen, with grooves running up the blade at the side of the socket. The ends of the blade are truncated so as to leave projections on the sides of the socket above the rivet-hole. These are slightly ornamented.

I have seen another spear-head (11½ inches) with the base of the blade slightly truncated in a similar manner. It was found near Eastbourne.

This elongated form is of common occurrence in Denmark and Northern Germany,§ the necks being usually ornamented by delicate punch-marking or possibly engraving.

A broader variety, with the socket considerably enlarged in the part extending below the blade, is shown in Fig. 385. The original was found in company with other spear-heads like Fig. 382 from 5⅜ inches to 10⅜ inches long, two socketed celts with three vertical lines on the face like Fig. 125, and two somewhat conical plates with central holes, near Newark, and is in the collection of Canon Greenwell, F.R.S.

A spear-head (6¼ inches) not quite so broad in its proportions, said to have been found in a tumulus, near Lewes,‖ Sussex, is in the British Museum, as is another (6¼ inches) found near Bakewell, Derbyshire.

* *Arch. Journ.*, vol. xix. p. 364.
† *A. J.*, vol. ix. p. 8. It is there erroneously stated to be 26 inches long.
‡ *Trans. Devon. Assoc.*, vol. vii. p. 199; *Proc. Soc. Ant.*, 2nd S., vol. vii. p. 40.
§ Worsaae, "Nord. Olds.," figs. 185, 186; "Atlas for Nord. Oldk.," pl. B 1, 16.
‖ "Horæ Fer.," pl. vi. 28.

Fig. 384.—North of Ireland. ½

A spear-head of the same general outline as Fig. 385, but with the sides of the socket straighter, was found with others, as well as with 16 socketed celts, a knife, fragments of swords and of a quadrangular tube (qy. a scabbard ?) and a long ferrule, near Nottingham.*

It is often the case that the sides of the upper part of the blade are nearly straight, and the socket itself appears large in proportion to the width of the blade. Such a spear- or lance-head from the Reach Fen hoard is shown in Fig. 386. I have several others from the Fen districts, as well as one of a shorter and broader form (5 inches) with a large

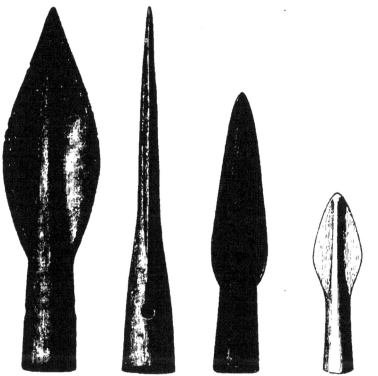

Fig. 385.—Newark. ⅓   Fig. 386.—Reach Fen. ⅓ Fig. 387.—Ireland. ⅓

socket extending only an inch below the blade, found at Walthamstow, Essex.

A spear-head from Unter-Uhldingen† exhibits the same narrowness of blade in proportion to the size of the socket.

In some cases the blade and socket are of nearly equal length.

Fig. 387 is here by permission reproduced from Wilde's Catalogue, Fig. 367. It is only 3½ inches long, and may have been the head of a dart or javelin rather than of a spear. I have an example of nearly the same form and size from Co. Dublin. One in the British Museum is only 2 inches long, though the mouth of the socket is ¾ inch in diameter.

* *Proc. Soc. Ant.*, 2nd S., vol. i. p. 332.   † Keller, 6ter Bericht, Taf. ix. 34.

Some of these very small weapons may possibly have served to point arrows. In the Norwich Museum is a head like Fig. 387, but with the blade shorter in proportion and narrower, the total length of which is only 1½ inch. The blade is ½ inch wide, and the socket is only ⅜ inch in external diameter. A bronze arrow-head is said to have been found in the Isle of Portland,* but particulars are not given. Another small point, in form rather like Fig. 386, and only 3½ inches long, was found at Llan-y-mynech Hill,† Montgomeryshire. Another, 3½ inches, was found near Pyecombe,‡ Sussex.

One 4 inches long is said to have been found in Yorkshire.§

Some double-pointed arrow-heads of bronze are mentioned as having been found in Ireland,‖ but in point of fact these were "razors" like Fig. 274.

In this country,¶ however, and not improbably in others, during the period when bronze was in use for cutting tools and the larger weapons, flint still served as the material from which arrow-heads were usually made. Such a method of taking the census as that devised by the Scythian king Ariantas would in Britain have produced but small results ; at all events, but few of the inhabitants would have been able each to contribute his bronze arrow-head. Many of the bronze arrow-heads found on the Continent appear to belong to the Early Iron Age, but it is mainly in southern countries that they have been found.

In Egypt** and Arabia they have occurred of the leaf-shaped as well as of the three-edged form, which latter is common in Greece.

Some spear-heads appear to have had the form of their point somewhat modified by grinding, as if from time to time they became blunted by use and required to be re-sharpened. A kind of ogival outline such as is shown in Fig. 388 appears, however, to have been intentional. The original was found in the North of Ireland.

This ogival outline is of frequent occurrence among the bronze spear-heads from Hungary.

The lance-head shown in Fig. 389, also from Wilde (Fig. 368), has the blade of a trapezoid rather than of a leaf-shaped form, and in general character more nearly approaches the looped variety, Fig. 397, than those now under consideration. The socket also appears to be quadrangular rather than round.

It will now be well to speak of some of the spear-heads of this

* *Arch. Journ.*, vol. xxi. p. 90.
† "Montgom. Coll.," vol. iii. p. 433; vol. xi. p. 205.
‡ *Suss. Arch. Coll.*, vol. viii. p. 269.
§ *Arch. Assoc. Journ.*, vol. xx. p. 107.
‖ *Arch. Journ.*, vol. iii. p. 47. There is an article by Mr. Du Noyer on the classification of bronze arrow-heads in vol. vii. p. 281.
¶ See "Anc. Stone Imp.," p. 328.
** *Arch. Journ.*, vol. xiii. pp. 20, 27; vol. xxii. p. 68; *Proc. Soc. Ant. Scot.*, vol. v. p. 187; *Proc. Soc. Ant.*, 2nd S., vol. i. p. 222.

class which have either their sockets or their blades ornamented by engraving or punching.

In Fig. 390 is shown a spear-head from the Reach Fen hoard, the nature of the ornamentation on which will be seen from the cut. The five bands, each of four parallel lines around the socket, have the appearance of being engraved; but I think that this is not actually the case, but that the lines have been punched in with a chisel-like punch.

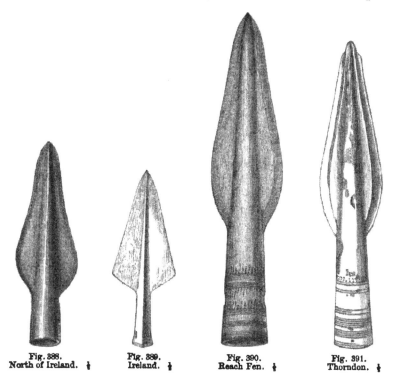

Fig. 388.
North of Ireland. ⅓

Fig. 389.
Ireland. ⅓

Fig. 390.
Reach Fen. ⅓

Fig. 391.
Thorndon. ⅓

The short transverse dotted lines have probably been made with a serrated punch.

Another spear-head, with ornamentation of a nearly similar character, is shown in Fig. 391. This example was found at Thorndon, Suffolk,[*] in company with a hammer (Fig. 210), a knife (Fig. 240), a gouge (Fig. 204), and an awl (Fig. 224), the whole of which are now in the British Museum. Another in the same collection from Thames Ditton (6½ inches) has three sets of three rings each, with short vertical lines above the upper ring.

A small lance-head of this type (4½ inches), found at Ingham, Norfolk, with socketed celts, has one band of four parallel lines round the socket. It is now in the Mayer Collection at Liverpool. Another from the Broadward hoard (Shropshire)[†] has two bands of four, and one of two rings,

* *Arch. Journ.*, vol. x. p. 3; "Hor. Fer.," pl, vi. 27.
† *Arch. Camb.*, 4th S., vol. iii. p. 351.

the latter close to the mouth of the socket. A second in the same hoard shows eight rings near the mouth of the socket, and a line running down each side of the midrib prolonged below the blade as far as the rivet-hole which it encloses. A spear-head from the hoard found at Beddington, near Croydon,* is ornamented in nearly the same manner. It was found with a gouge, socketed celts, a portion of celt mould, &c. That from Culham, near Abingdon, shown in Fig. 392, has three sets of four rings and one of two, as well as some vertical dotted lines above the upper ring. In this case the bands seem to have been punched in with a serrated punch which produced four short lines at each stroke, and by skilful manipulation these short lines were made to join so as to form a continuous ring.

I have a spear-head from Lakenheath, Suffolk (5¾ inches), with a small raised band cast on the socket just below the rivet-hole.

A spear-head (6½ inches) in the Antiquarian Museum at Edinburgh, found near Forfar, is ornamented with two bands of three parallel lines round the socket.

The sockets of some Irish spear-heads are highly decorated. That of a long leaf-shaped specimen from Athenry, Co. Galway, is shown in Fig. 393, kindly lent me by the Royal Irish Academy. It is Fig. 382 in Wilde's Catalogue, in which also some other examples are engraved. The chevron ornament and the alternate direction of the hatching are highly characteristic of the style of the Bronze Period.

A similar decoration is found on English specimens. One found at Bilton, Yorkshire,† with other spear-heads, fragments of swords, and socketed celts, has round

Fig. 392. Culham. ¼

Fig. 393. Athenry.

the socket three bands of triangles alternately hatched and plain, and the blade is ornamented with a single row of the same kind on each side of the central rib. One from Edington Burtle, Somerset (4½ inches), in the Taunton Museum, has a band of hatched triangles above three bands of parallel lines with transverse lines between.

A broken spear-head from the Broadward ‡ find has the blade ornamented in the same way. A row of plain triangles is left on each side of the midrib, while the rest of the blade is hatched, the set of parallel lines in each point between the plain triangles being alternately to the right and to the left.

A fragment of a blade from the Haynes Hill hoard,§ Kent, has ring ornaments engraved along each side of the midrib.

As has already been observed, the edges of this class of spear-heads are not unfrequently fluted, but it occasionally happens that the whole blade is ornamented by minute ribs and flutings. The spear-head (10½ inches) found with two swords and two ferrules at Fulbourn, Cambridge,‖ affords an example of this kind. On each side of the central rib

* Anderson's "Croydon Preh. and Rom.," p. 11, pl. iii. 4.
† *Arch. Assoc. Journ.*, vol. v. p. 349.   ‡ *Arch. Camb.*, 4th S., vol. iii. p. 351.
§ *Arch. Journ.*, vol. xxx. p. 282.   ‖ *Arch.*, vol. xix. p. 56, pl. iv. 5.

containing the socket are two sharp ridges one below the other, next comes a hollow fluting, then a ridge, and then the fluting which forms the edge. To judge from the engraving, another found at Gringley, Nottinghamshire,* must also have been fluted in a somewhat similar manner.

The discovery of other leaf-shaped spear-heads with rivet-holes through the sockets is recorded to have been made at the following places, and many others might no doubt be added to the list: the Thames, near Battersea † (16¾ inches); near Wallingford ‡ (7¼ inches); and Kingston § (6¼ and 7¼ inches); two (7¾ inches and 6 inches) were found near Toddington, Beds; ‖ at Beacon Hill, Charnwood Forest, Leicestershire,¶ two (7¼ inches and 6¼ inches) were found with a socketed celt and gouge. Others were discovered near Yarlet, Staffordshire; ** near Alnwick Castle †† (sixteen with celts and swords); Vronheulog, Merionethshire;‡‡ and Longy Common, Alderney §§ (one with blade ornamented).

Fig. 394.—Thetford. ¼

The spear-heads of the second of the classes into which they are here divided are those with loops at the side of the projecting socket. These loops are usually more elongated than those on socketed celts and palstaves, though they probably served a similar purpose, that of securing the metallic head to the wooden handle. The metal of which the loops are formed has frequently been flattened by hammering, so as to reduce the projection of the loops beyond the socket; the flattened part is often wrought into a lozenge form.

The strings which passed through these loops were probably secured to some stop or collar on the shaft, and may have been arranged in some chevron-like pattern with which these lozenges coincided. There are usually no rivet-holes in the spear-heads of this class.

A specimen exhibiting these lozenges, and with the blade of nearly the same form as those of the spear-heads of the first class, is shown in Fig. 394. The upper part of the midrib containing the socket is ridged, so that the section near the point is almost square. The socket is slightly fluted round the mouth. The original was found at Thetford, Suffolk.

A spear-head of the same type, but with only a single large loop, found

* Arch., vol. xvi. p. 361, pl. lxiv. 1. † Proc. Soc. Ant., vol. iv. p. 244.
‡ P. S. A., 2nd S., vol. iv. p. 280. § P. S. A., 2nd S., vol. i. p. 83.
‖ Arch., vol. xxvii. p. 105. ¶ P. S. A., vol. iv. p. 323.
** Plot's "Stafford.," p. 404, pl. xxxiii. 8. †† Arch., vol. v. p. 113.
‡‡ Arch. Camb., 4th S., vol. viii. p. 210. §§ Arch. Assoc. Journ., vol. iii. p. 9.

Y

in Glen Kenns, Galloway, is engraved in the *Archæologia*,* but it seems probable that the figure is somewhat inaccurate.

Another (5¼ inches) with two loops was found at Hangleton Down, Suffolk.† Another (5¼ inches), rather more elongated than Fig. 394, was found at Trefeglwys, Montgomeryshire.‡ Another from Shirewood Forest is engraved in the *Archæologia*.§ It has a slightly ogival outline on each side, a peculiarity I have noticed in other specimens. An example given in the same plate seems to have lost the flat part of the blade.

I have one (6¼ inches) from Fyfield, near Abingdon.

Mr. M. Fisher has a specimen from the Fens at Ely (5⅝ inches), with the midrib ridged like Fig. 396.

One from Hagbourn Hill, near Chiltern, Berks,‖ is reported to have been found with a socketed celt, a pin like Fig. 458, and another like Fig. 453, together with a bronze bridle-bit, and some portions of buckles like those of the late Celtic Period. These are now in the British Museum. A few coins of gold and silver are said to have been found at the same time.

One (6 inches) was found at Chartham, near Canterbury.¶

One, 5 inches long, from the Thames, is in the British Museum. It has a small ridge or bead along the mid-feather. The loops have a diamond engraved or punched upon them.

In one from Beckhampton, Wilts ** (4¾ inches), the side loops do not appear to be flattened.

The form is of not unfrequent occurrence in Ireland, though perhaps that with the raised ribs on the blade, like Fig. 397, is more common.

In one instance (13¼ inches) †† the loops upon the socket are not opposite each other, though, as usual, in the same plane as the blade.

A small specimen (5¼ inches) from Fairholme, Lockerbie, Dumfriesshire, is in the British Museum.

A small example of this type (about 3¼ inches) is in the collection formed by Sir R. Colt Hoare at Stourhead, and now at Devizes, and in the same case with the dagger blades. It has been figured by the late Dr. Thurnam ‡‡ in his valuable memoir in the *Archæologia*, and is thought by him to have been found in a grave with burnt bones in one of the Wilsford barrows near Stonehenge.

There is a diminutive variety of this class of weapon with two loops, in which the blade is extremely narrow, like that from Lakenheath shown in Fig. 395. I have another, 4⅛ inches, with even a smaller and shorter blade, from Cumberland.

Canon Greenwell has one only 3 inches long, found near Nottingham. It has three parallel grooves round the socket mouth. One, 4¼ inches, from Ashdown, Berks, is in the British Museum.

A fragment of another of very small dimensions was found at Farley Heath, Surrey, and is now in the British Museum.

A lance-head with a more leaf-shaped blade (6¼ inches) is said to have been found in a tumulus at Craigton, near Kinross.§§

* Vol. x. p. 480, pl. xl. 5.   † *Sussex Arch. Coll.*, vol. viii. p. 269.
‡ "Montgom. Coll.," vol. iii. p. 432, and vol. xii. p. 25.
§ Vol. ix. p. 94, pl. iii.   ‖ *Arch.*, vol. xvi. p. 348, pl. l.
¶ *Arch. Assoc. Journ.*, vol. xvii. p. 334.   ** Arch. Inst., Salisb. vol., p. 110.
†† Wilde, "Catal. R. I. A.," p. 496, fig. 363; "Hor. Far.," pl. vi. 15.
‡‡ *Arch.*, vol. xliii. p. 447; "Anc. Wilts," vol. i. p. 208.
§§ *Proc. Soc. Ant. Scot.*, vol. xi. p. 168.

An Irish example, 2⅜ inches long, and comparatively broad in proportion to its length, has been regarded as an arrow-head. It was found at Clonmel, Co. Tipperary.* It has probably been broken and repointed. An example much like Fig. 395 is engraved by Wilde as his Fig. 379.

In some cases there is a ridge running along the whole or a great part of the midrib on the blade so as to make the section near the point almost cruciform. An example of this kind from the neighbourhood of Cambridge is shown in Fig. 396. In this case the side loops are unusually

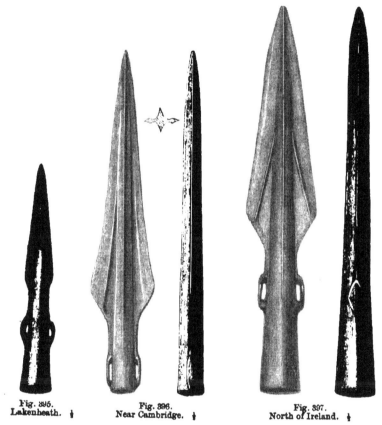

Fig. 395.
Lakenheath. ⅓

Fig. 396.
Near Cambridge. ⅓

Fig. 397.
North of Ireland. ⅓

near the mouth of the socket, the cavity of which extends about half-way along the blade. Canon Greenwell has an example of this type (6½ inches), from Langton, Lincolnshire, with a longer socket, and the loops about half-way along it.

This ribbing along the midrib is of frequent occurrence on Irish spear-heads, and was probably intended to strengthen as well as to decorate the blade. The projecting ribs on the flat part of the blade were also probably added for the same purpose. Fig. 397 shows a spear-head with these ridges, found in the North of Ireland. The blade is carried down

* *Arch. Journ.*, vol. vii. p. 282, and xviii. p. 167.

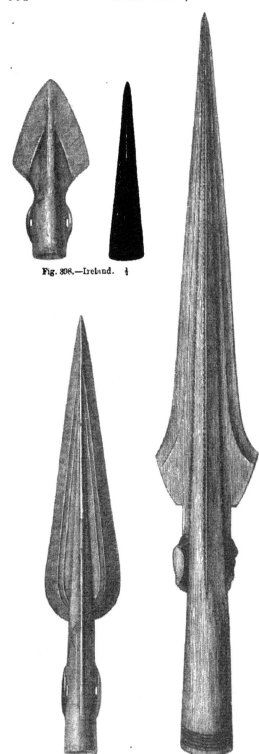

Fig. 398.—Ireland. ¼

Fig. 399.—Thames. ¼   Fig. 400.—Ireland. ¼

as a slight projection along the socket until it meets the side loops, the outer faces of which are expanded into lozenges.

I have a shorter example (5½ inches) from Old Kilpatrick, Dumbartonshire, Scotland; one from Termon, Co. Tyrone, is engraved in the *Archæological Journal*.[*]

In some the blade is proportionally wider and shorter. I have one from near Enniskillen (7¼ inches), in which the blade between the socket and the ribs is so thin that two long holes have been eaten or worn through it, giving it the appearance of belonging to the perforated class to be subsequently described.

An Irish specimen much like Fig. 397 is engraved in " Horæ Ferales." [†]

A small broad-bladed form is of very common occurrence in Ireland. An example is given in Fig. 398. Another is engraved by Wilde (Fig. 369). Some have two diagonal ribs on each side of the blade instead of only one. A rather more pointed form is given by Vallancey.[‡] There are others figured in the " Horæ Ferales." [§]

This type is of rare

[*] Vol. ii. p. 187.
[†] Pl. vi. 17.
[‡] "Coll. Hib.," vol. iv. pl. xi. v.
[§] Pl. vi. 12, 13.

occurrence in England, but one (4½ inches?) much like Fig. 398 was ploughed up at Heage,* in the parish of Duffield, Derbyshire, and another (4⅝ inches) was found near Lincoln.†

A gracefully shaped spear-head, with parallel beadings upon the blade, and having very flat loops with pointed oval faces on the socket, was found in the Thames, and formed part of the Roach Smith Collection, now in the British Museum. It is shown in Fig. 399, and appears to be unique of its kind. A plain spear-head (7 inches) of much the same form, and another of the same length, but wider and flatter, were found at Edington Burtle, Somerset, and are now in the Museum at Taunton.

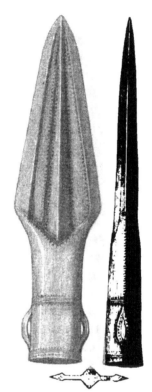

A very remarkable specimen in the Royal Irish Academy is engraved as Fig. 400. It has already been figured on a small scale by Wilde, who thus describes it:‡ "A long narrow spear with concave or recurved sides, and long lozenge-shaped loops on each side of the socket, where the circular form of that portion of the weapon becomes angular. Narrow lateral ridges connect these loops with the base of the blade, which has hollow bevelled edges, and is as sharp as the day it came from the mould. The socket margin is decorated with a fillet of five elevations, and a double linear engraved or punched ornament forming a triangular pattern like that seen in some antique gold ornaments. A sharp ridge extends along the middle of the socket from the loops to the point, on each side of which, as well as in the angles between the blade and the socket, there are lines of small oval punched indentations apparently effected by the hand."

In one of the looped forms both the blade and the socket are often highly ornamented. The socket part is made to appear somewhat like a haft to the blade, as in the Arreton Down specimen (Fig. 328), and the blade itself has ridges running nearly parallel to the edges, the midrib being

Fig. 401.—Near Ballymena. ¼

almost square in section. An example of this kind from Ballymena is, by the kindness of Mr. R. Day, F.S.A., shown in Fig. 401. As will be seen, the socket, blade, and external faces of the loops are all ornamented with engraved and punctured lines. A beautiful example from Ireland (6½ inches), the socket engraved with a double ring of chevrons near the middle, and a single ring near the base, and also ornamented with dotted circles and lines extending down the blade, is in the British Museum. It has two knobs on each side of the socket simulating rivets.

---

* *Arch. Assoc. Journ.*, vol. ii. p. 280; "Vest. Ant. Derb.," p. 9.
† *Arch. Assoc. Journ.*, vol. xv. p. 285.   ‡ "Catal. Mus. R. I. A.," p. 496.

Other varieties with the midrib more rounded are given by Wilde,[*] and two of his figures are, by the kindness of the Council of the Royal Irish Academy, here reproduced as Figs. 402 and 403.[†] The original of Fig. 402 is 5 inches long. It has "a central circular stud opposite the base of the blade, beneath which there are a series of minute continuous lines margined on both sides by a row of elevated dots." The socket and the outer surface of the loops are also highly decorated.

Fig. 403 is 7¼ inches long, and is also artistically ornamented.

Fig. 402.—Ireland. ⅓   Fig. 403.—Ireland. ⅓   Fig. 404.—Ireland.

An example of this kind is given in "Horæ Ferales."[‡]

One (5¼ inches) from the Dean Water, Forfarshire, is in the Antiquarian Museum at Edinburgh. The blade is ornamented by incised lines and punctulations.

Fig. 404, also kindly lent by the Royal Irish Academy (Wilde, Fig. 378), shows a smaller and a plainer type.

An unornamented lance-head of this type (5 inches) was found at Peel,[||] in the Isle of Man. Another, 5⅝ inches, with three bands of parallel lines round the socket, was obtained at Douglas, Lanarkshire.[§]

* "Catal. Mus. R. I. A.," pp. 498, 501.   † Ibid., Figs. 385 and 386, p. 502.
‡ Pl. vi. 19. || Arch. Journ., vol. ii. p. 187.
§ Arch. Assoc. Journ., vol. xvii. p. 111, pl. xi. 4.

The spear-heads of this class with loops at the side of the sockets are almost unknown out of the British Islands. In my own collection, however, is one from the Seine at Paris (6¼ inches), almost identical in form with Fig. 394, but with the lozenge-shaped plates forming the loops somewhat wider.

A highly ornamented spear-head from Hungary,* preserved in the Museum at Buda-Pest, has small semicircular loops at the sides of the socket.

The third class of spear-heads consists of those with loops at the base of the blade connecting it with the socket. There are many varieties of this class, which includes some of the most elegant forms of these ancient weapons. The reason for adopting this particular kind of loop appears to be that they were, when thus attached to the blade, less liable to be broken off or damaged than when they formed isolated projections from the socket. The spear-heads were also more readily polished and furbished when the socket was left as a plain tube.

The loops are very frequently formed by the continuation of two ribs along the margin of the blade, which are curved inwards from the base of the blade until they join the socket.

A good example of this formation of the loop is shown in Fig. 405. The original was found at Elford, Northumberland, and is in the collection of Canon Greenwell, F.R.S.

Another of nearly the same form, but without the ribs on the blade, was found near Lowthorpe, Yorkshire, E.R., and is in the possession of Mr. T. Boynton, of Ulrome Grange.

The very graceful spear-head shown in Fig. 406 was found at Isleham Fen, Cambridge, in 1863, and is a remarkably fine casting, the cavity for the reception of the shaft being no less than 12¼ inches in length, and perfectly central in the blade.

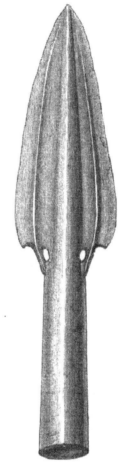

Fig. 405.—Elford. ⅓

I have another spear-head of the same type (18 inches), probably from the Thames, almost as well cast, but rather heavier in proportion to its size. There are traces of wood in the socket, as is also the case in another of the same form (14¼ inches) dredged from the Thames at Battersea,† and now in the Bateman Collection. The wood has been thought to be ash. Another similar, but originally about 20 inches long, was found in the

* Lindenschmit, "Alt. u. h. Vorz.," vol. ii. Heft iv. Taf. i. 9.
† Arch. Assoc. Journ., vol. xiv. p. 329, pl. xxiv. fig. 3.

Thames near Runnymede; * and another in the collection of General A. Pitt Rivers, F.R.S., 17 inches long, was found at Hampton Court.

Another (13¾ inches) from the Thames at Thames Ditton is in the British Museum.

One (15¼ inches) from Bottisham Lode, Cambridge, is in the British Museum; as is another (14¼ inches) from the New River Works, Pentonville. I have seen others from Coveney Fen (16¾ inches, Mr. Fisher), and from Woolpit, near Bury St. Edmunds (8¾ inches). The blade of one (11⅜ inches) without the socket was found at Stanwick, Yorkshire, and is now in the British Museum.

One (13¼ inches) was found with three rapier-shaped blades near Maentwrog, Merionethshire, and is in the same collection.†

Another, broken, in the Museum at Taunton, is said to have been found in the Roman villa at Wadsford, Combe St. Nicholas, near Chard. Its original length must have been about 18 inches.

In the specimen from Stibbard, Norfolk,‡ shown in Fig. 407, the ribs upon the blade are less distinct, and the loops are widened out so as to show a lozenge form when the edge of the blade is seen. This spear-head was found with nine others and about seventy palstaves about 1806, and is in the state in which it left the mould, having never been finished by hammering and grinding, though the core has been extracted. I have seen a specimen in the collection of Mr. J. Holmes, found at Morley, near Leeds, in which the hammering process had been applied to a part only of the blade, which had evidently broken in the operation. The partly finished base and the unfinished point were found together.

An Irish example of this form has been engraved by Vallancey.§

This type is rare in France, but a specimen is in the Museum at Carcassonne (Aude), and another in that at St. Germain.

In some spear-heads of nearly the same form there is a raised bead running down the midrib as in Fig. 408. This beautifully finished weapon was bought in Dublin, but I cannot say in what part of Ireland it was found.

A smaller and broader specimen (7 inches) in my collection was found at Clough, near Antrim.

* *Arch. Assoc. Jour.*, vol. xvi. p. 322.
† *Arch.*, vol. xvi. p. 365, pl. lxx. 3.
‡ Arch. Inst., Norwich vol., p. xxvi. Another from this hoard is in the Brit. Mus., "Hor. Fer.," pl. vi. 22. Mr. Franks thinks that the mould was in four pieces besides the core, but on this point I am rather doubtful.
§ Vol. iv. pl. xi. 6.

Fig. 406.—Isleham Fen.

I have another (10¾ inches) from the north of Ireland in which the midrib half-way along the blade expands to form an edge almost as sharp as that at the sides.   Near the point the section is cruciform, as in Fig. 396.

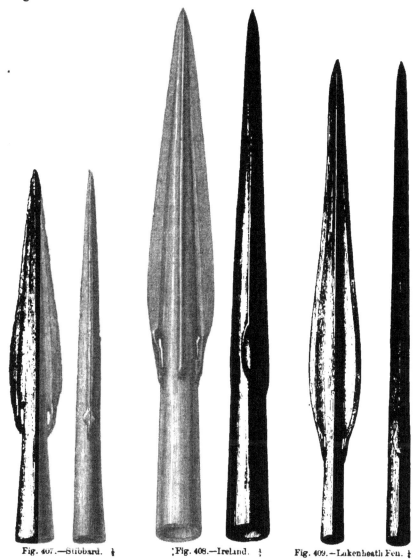

Fig. 407.—Stubbard. ½   ;Fig. 408.—Ireland. ½   Fig. 409.—Lakenheath Fen. ½

A spear-head found near Hay, on the river Wye, and now in the Museum of the Society of Antiquaries of London, presents the same peculiarity as Fig. 408.

Some ancient bronze spear-heads from China * are provided with

* *Arch. Journ.*, vol. xi. p. 415.

central ridges of the same kind on the blades. They have but one loop, and that is on the face, and there is a deep notch at the mouth of the socket.

The long blades are often more leaf-shaped and less truncated at the base than that shown in Fig. 406. A very large specimen of this kind from Lakenheath Fen is shown on the scale of ¼ inch in Fig. 409. The point is unfortunately lost, but is restored in the engraving. The midrib containing the socket is ridged, and the outer faces of the loops expand into the diamond form.

One of nearly the same character (22¼ inches), found in the Thames at Datchet, forms part of the Roach Smith Collection,* now in the British Museum. Another (11¼ inches) was found with palstaves at Sherford,† near Taunton.

A specimen in the British Museum (15¾ inches) has an ornament of hatched chevrons round the base of the socket, and the lozenge-shaped flanges are also ornamented with hatched open mascles.

A spear-head of the same form (15½ inches) from Ireland ‡ has the ridge decorated with lines of dots, and the socket with bands and a chevron pattern. A plain specimen, no less than 26¾ inches long, found at Maghera, Co. Londonderry,§ has been figured by Wilde.

In others the midrib is conical, and the blade nearly flat, or with only a shallow channel along the sides of the midrib. One such from the find at Nettleham, Lincolnshire,‖ now in the British Museum, is, by the kindness of Mr. Franks, shown in Fig. 410. I have one nearly similar (9¼ inches) from Edmonton Marsh. One (7½ inches) from the Thames at Lambeth is in the British Museum, as are others from the same river varying in length from 9 to 15¾ inches.

One from Speen, Berks ¶ (7 inches), is of the same character, as is one (8¼ inches) from Crawford, Lanarkshire.** Another (9 inches) from Horsey, near Peterborough, Hunts, has been engraved by Artis.†† Another (10¼ inches) from the Severn at Kempsey, Worcestershire,‡‡ appears to have been of this type. I have seen others from the Cambridge Fens. One (5¼ inches) from Edington Burtle, Somerset, is in the Taunton Museum.

Fig. 410.
Nettleham. †

A spear-head of this character (10½ inches), with the faces of the loops lozenge-shaped, was found with two looped palstaves and a chisel

* "Catal. Mus. Lond. Ant.," p. 83, No. 370.
† Pring, "Brit. and Rom. Taunton," pl. iii.
‡ "Horæ Fer.," pl. vi. 20.
§ "Catal. Mus. R. I. A.," fig. 366, p. 496; "Hor. Fer.," pl. vi. 18.
‖ Arch. Journ., vol. xviii. p. 160.
¶ Arch. Assoc. Journ., vol. xvi. p. 322, pl. xxvi. 3.
** Op. cit., vol. xvii. p. 110, pl. xi. 3.
†† "Durobrivæ," p. lvi. 4.
‡‡ Arch. Journ., vol. iii. 354; Allies, "Worcester.," p. 60.

(Fig. 197) at Broxton, about twelve miles south of Chester. It is now in the collection of Sir P. de M. G. Egerton, Bart., who has kindly shown it to me.

Spear-heads of this character are occasionally found in Scotland. Two from Wigtonshire * have been figured.

The form is common in Ireland. I have one 12 inches long from one of the northern counties.

A spear-head (6½ inches) with small projecting loops at each side of the blade was found near Hawick, Roxburghshire.†

In Fig. 411 is shown a remarkably fine spear-head in the collection of Canon Greenwell, F.R.S., which exhibits the peculiarity of having the loops formed by the prolongation of small ribs on each side of the midrib, and of having, in addition, a rivet-hole through the socket. It was found at Knockans, Co. Antrim.

An Irish spear-head (14¾ inches) with loops at the lower end of the blade, and the socket pierced for a rivet, was exhibited to the Archæological Institute in 1856.‡

The fourth class of spearheads, those with openings in the blade, may again be subdivided into those in which the openings appear to have served as loops for attaching the blade to the shaft, and those in which these apertures seem to have been mainly intended for ornament, or possibly for diminishing weight.

Of the former kind appear to be those which have merely two small slits in the lower

* Ayr and Wigton Coll., vol. ii. p. 13.
† Proc. Soc. Ant. Scot., vol. v. p. 214.
‡ Arch. Journ., vol. xiii. p. 296.

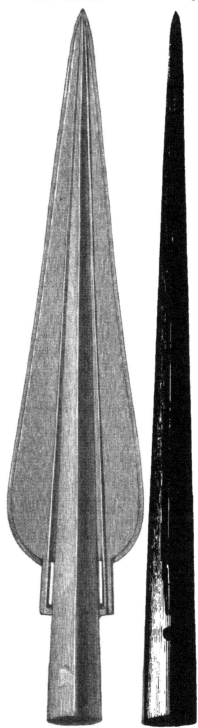

Fig. 411.—Knockans. ⅓

part of the blade, such as would seem adapted for the insertion of a cord. These holes are usually protected by projections rising from the blade on the outer side of the holes.

A fine spear-head in my own collection thus perforated, found near Lurgan, Co. Armagh,[*] is shown in Fig. 412. It is 24 inches in length, and 3¼ inches in extreme breadth.

The openings are about 17 inches from the point. An Irish friend has suggested that they were for the reception of poison, but after the blade had penetrated seventeen inches into the human body such an use of poison would probably be superfluous.

A spear-head of the same form (19½ inches) was found on the hill of Rosele, Duffus, Morayshire,[†] and

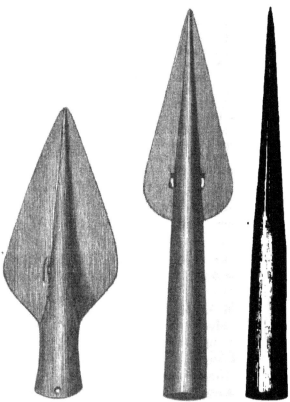

Fig. 412.—Lurgan. ¼   Fig. 413.—Ireland. ¼   Fig. 414.—Antrim. ¼

* Proc. Soc. Ant., 2nd S., vol. ii. p. 65. I am indebted to the Council for the use of this block.
† Arch. Journ., vol. xiii. p. 413; "Hor. Fer.," pl. vi. 21.

is now in the Elgin Museum. Another, broken, but still 10⅜ inches long, was found with a rapier-shaped blade at Corbridge, Northumberland.[*] A broken specimen was found in the Isle of Portland.[†]

A spear-head (10 inches) with small openings in the blade was found, with palstaves, socketed celts, rapiers, bracelets, and a ferrule, at Wallington, Northumber-land, and is in the pos-session of Sir Charles Trevelyan.

An "eyed" spear-head 22 inches long was found in the Thames near Datchet,[‡] but whether it was of this or some other type I cannot say. One (9 inches) with two holes at the base of the leaf above the ferrule was found near Speen, Berks.[§]

A broader form (13¼ inches) from Ireland is engraved by Wilde (Fig. 365), and another broader still is shown in my Fig. 413. This has a rivet-hole on the front of the socket, as well as the holes in the blade.   This is also in the Dublin Museum.

In some instances the blade is very much shorter in proportion to the length of the socket, as will be seen in Fig. 414, the original of which was found in the county of Antrim, and is now in Canon Greenwell's collec-tion.

A remarkably fine Eng-lish example of the same class is shown in Fig. 415. This specimen was found in the Thames, and is now

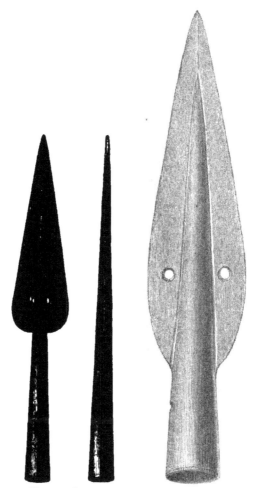

Fig. 415.—Thames. ⅓   Fig. 416.—Naworth Castle. ⅓

in the British Museum. The small projecting flanges at the side of the holes in the blade are very strongly marked, and form circular discs when seen with the edge of the spear-head towards the spectator.

The simplest of the forms, in which the holes in the blade appear to be

* *Arch. Journ.*, vol. xix. p. 363.
† Ibid., vol. xxv. p. 49.
‡ *Arch. Assoc. Journ.*, vol. v. p. 89.
§ Ibid., vol. xvi. p. 250.

for ornament rather than use, is that in which there are two circular or oval holes through the blade, one on either side of the midrib containing the socket.   The spear-head shown in Fig. 416 was found near Naworth Castle, Cumberland, in 1870, and is in the collection of Canon Green-

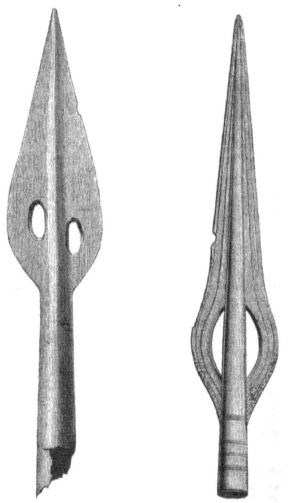

Fig. 417.—Blakehope. ⅓   Fig. 418.—Whittingham. ⅓

well.   In general form it resembles the type, Fig. 381.   It is provided with a rivet-hole through the socket.

Some Italian spear-heads have two circular holes in the blade, but nearer the base.

In the spear-head shown in Fig. 417 there is no trace of a rivet-hole in the socket, the end of which, however, is broken, and the two oval orifices in the blade are placed one somewhat below the other.   This specimen is in Canon Greenwell's collection, and was found at Blakehope, Northumberland.

The more truly characteristic spear-heads of this class have two crescent-shaped or lunate openings, one on each side of the mid-rib containing the socket, which thus is made, as it were, to reappear in the middle of the blade. There is usually a rivet-hole in the projecting part of the socket below the blade, so that these openings must be regarded as ornamental, or else as intended to diminish the weight of the weapon.

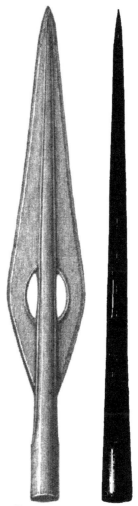

The original of Fig. 418 was found about 1847, near Whittingham, Northumberland,[*] in company with some other spear-heads and two swords, and is now in the possession of Lord Ravensworth. The surface of the blade is ornamented by being worked into steps or terraces, and the socket by bands of parallel lines.

A rather longer specimen was found, together with a plain leaf-shaped spear-head and five socketed celts, at Winmarleigh, near Garstang, Lancashire.[†] By the kindness of the curators of the Warrington Museum I am enabled to give it as Fig. 419. It is 19¼ inches long. There are small ridges by the side of the midrib and round the margin of the openings.

Another like it, but only 15¼ inches long, was found with a socketed celt near Middleham, Yorkshire.

Some fragments of spear-heads of this character were found with other bronze antiquities in Duddingston Loch, Edinburgh.[‡]

The same form has occurred in Ireland.[§] A fine example (14 inches) from a hoard at Dowris, King's County,[||] is in the British Museum.

A spear-head of this type, about 8 inches long, is in the Boucher de Perthes Collection at Abbeville.

Fig. 419.—Winmarleigh. ¼

A spear-head smaller than Fig. 419, but of the same general character, is

* *Proc. Soc. Ant.*, 2nd S., vol. v. p. 429.
† *Arch. Assoc. Journ.*, vol. xv. p. 234; *Arch. Journ.*, vol. xviii. p. 158.
‡ Grose's "Treat. on Anc. Armour," 1786, pl. lxi. 5.
§ Vallancey, "Coll. Hib.," vol. iv. pl. xi. 7.
|| "Horæ Fer.," pl. vi. 16.

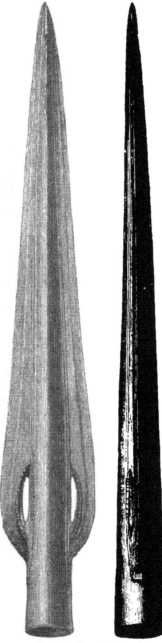

Fig. 420.—Burwell Fen. ¼

shown in Fig. 420. It was found in Burwell Fen, Cambridge, about 1869. There is a double bead along each side of the midrib, and the blade is in two steps or terraces. Around the crescent-shaped opening the beading is grained or milled transversely. A projection is carried down along the socket from the blade, so as to allow the rivet-hole to be made in it. The socket extends to within 1¼ inches of the point.

A spear-head of nearly the same size, with the openings somewhat smaller, but ornamented in a similar manner, was found with celts, palstaves, gouges, swords, scabbards, &c., at Guilsfield, Montgomeryshire,* in 1862. Another, broken, was found at the same time. Another was in the hoard at Little Wenlock, Staffordshire,† but does not appear to have been ornamented. There was a fragment of another, plain, in the Broadward ‡ find.

In the Antiquarian Museum at Edinburgh are some spear-heads of this character, with the openings on the blade rather longer in proportion. One was found in the bottom of a cairn at Highfield, Urray, near Dingwall, Ross-shire.§ Others were found in Roxburghshire and Stirlingshire.

Some of the spear-heads of this type which have been found in Ireland are highly ornamented. A very fine specimen given by Wilde (Fig. 374) has several mouldings with a kind of cable pattern upon them. Others have circular perforations in addition to the lunate openings; and in one instance the socket is decorated with bands and vertical lines (Wilde, Fig. 372).

A small lance-head from Jelabugy, Russia, ‖ with comparatively large crescent-shaped openings in the blade, has been figured by Worsaae.

The cut for Fig. 421 is kindly lent me by the Society of Antiquaries of

* *Arch. Camb.*, 3rd S., vol. x. p. 217, fig. 8 ; *Proc. Soc. Ant.*, 2nd S., vol. ii. p. 251.
† Hartshorne's "Salop. Ant.," p. 96.   ‡ *Arch. Camb.*, 4th S., vol. iii. p. 352.
§ *Proc. Soc. Ant. Scot.*, vol. ii. p. 154.   ‖ *Mém. des Ant. du Nord*, 1872—7, p. 115.

Scotland. The original, 19 inches long, was found with a bronze sword at Denhead, Cupar-Angus, Forfarshire,* and has unfortunately been

somewhat broken. As will be seen, there are ten circular holes, besides two long crescents. The socket is said by Professor Daniel Wilson to contain a thin rod or core of iron, which was inserted in the mould to strengthen this unusually large weapon; but what seemed to Dr. Wilson to be an iron rod is really a piece of wood that has been recently inserted when the spearhead was mended.

In the last class into which these weapons are here divided, are placed those which are barbed at the base of the blade, or in very rare instances are square at that part.

A good typical example ($10\frac{1}{15}$ inches) is shown in Fig. 422, from an original found at Speen, Berks.† It is very heavy, weighing $11\frac{3}{4}$ ozs. troy, or more than $\frac{3}{4}$ lb. avoirdupois.

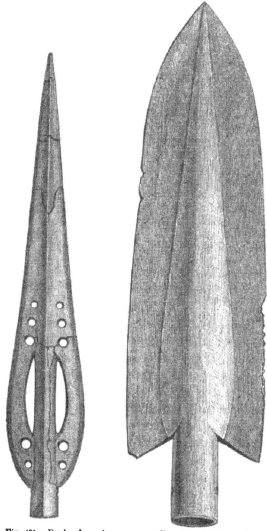

Fig. 421.—Denhead. ¼   Fig. 422.—Speen. ¼

Another of the same size, but lighter (8 ozs.), was found in the Severn, near Worcester.‡

* Wilson's "Preh. Ann.," vol. i. p. 391; "Horæ Fer.," pl. vi. 23; "Catal. Mus. Arch. Inst. Ed.," p. 23.

† *Proc. Soc. Ant.*, 2nd S., vol. v. p. 404, pl. iii. 11; *Arch. Assoc. Journ.*, vol. xvi. p. 322, pl. xxvi. 4.

‡ *Arch. Journ.*, vol. ii. p. 187; vol. iii. p. 354; "Horæ Fer.," pl. vi. 26; Allies, "Worc.," p. 30; "Arch. Inst.," York vol., pl. v. 4.

Another (10¾ inches), found in the Plaistow Marshes, Essex, and now in the British Museum, has a rivet of bronze 2⅜ inches in length still in the rivet-hole. Curiously enough this long rivet appears to be a speciality of this class of weapons. Some of this type, together with some fragments twisted and adhering together as if partially molten, were found in the Thames at Kingston,* and in one of them was the bronze rivet. These are now in the British Museum. Some broken barbed spear-heads of larger size (about 14 inches), also with the rivets still in position, were found with bronze ferrules at a spot called "Bloody Pool," South Brent, Devon.†

Another (7 inches), found at Pendoylan, near Cardiff, Glamorganshire,‡ has an oval socket pierced on one side for a rivet, which, however, is wanting.

Canon Greenwell, F.R.S., possesses an example much like that from Speen (10¾ inches) found in Yorkshire, near the river Humber.

In the Broadward find§ (Shropshire) were several spear-heads of this type, mostly retaining their bronze rivets. One of them, about 6 inches long and 3 inches broad, has the base of the blade at right angles to the socket, and not sloping downwards. Several bronze ferrules were included in the hoard. What appears to have been a discovery of nearly the same character took place in a bog on a farm called the Wrekin Tenement,‖ also in Shropshire, where a celt, a small number of swords, and about one hundred and fifty fragments of spear-heads were found. They are described as being for the most part about 8 inches in length, and having rivets of bronze through the sockets. I have not met with the type in Scotland or Ireland.

It has been suggested that these weapons were fishing spears, and certainly their barbed form, so distinct from that of the more common spear-heads, raises a presumption that they were intended for some special purpose. It appears to me, however, as it already has done to others, that such weapons are too clumsy to have been used for the capture of fish of any ordinary size, and would have made sad havoc even of a forty-pound salmon. If they were used for the chase at all, it is more probable that they were intended for attacking large four-footed game, such as wild oxen, either by thrusting or darting, and that the weapons were left in the wound, the shafts encumbering the animal in its flight. If, as would probably be the case, these got broken by the animal, the long rivets were well adapted for being removed so as to allow of the broken shaft being taken out, and would again serve to retain a new one.

Mention has already been made of ferrules having been frequently

* *Proc. Soc. Ant.*, 2nd S., vol. i. p. 125.
† *Arch. Journ.*, vol. xii. p. 84; vol. xviii. p. 160.
‡ Ibid., vol. xiv. p. 357; vol. xviii. p. 161.
§ *Arch. Camb.*, 4th S., vol. iii. pp. 339, 347.
‖ *Arch.*, vol. xxvi. p. 464.

discovered in company with ordinary spear-heads ; and from this fact, and the size and character of the ferrules, the inference has, with much probability, been drawn that they served to tip the lower ends of the shafts of spears and lances.

The illustrations given in Figs. 423 and 424 will serve to show the usual character of these objects. They vary in length from about 16 inches down to 8 inches, and are about ¾ inch or less in diameter. They are not made from a flat piece of metal turned over, but are cast in one piece, having been very carefully "cored." The metal, especially near the mouth, is very thin, and there is usually a small hole nearer this end than the other to allow of a pin or rivet being inserted to keep the ferrule on the shaft.

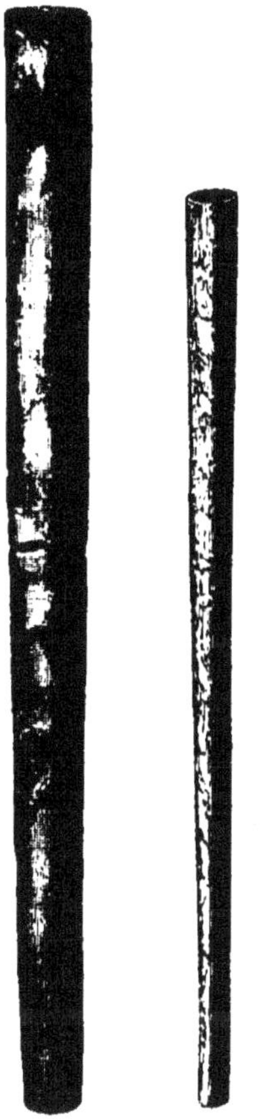

The original of Fig. 423 (8¼ inches) was found with spear-heads and other articles at Nettleham, near Lincoln, and is now in the British Museum.*

One 14 inches long, bluntly pointed at the base, was found in the Thames, near London, and is now in the British Museum. It has a portion of the wooden shaft inside, which appears to be of beech. The hole for the pin is still visible in the wood, but the pin has perished. It may have been made of horn.

Fig. 424 is on the scale of one-fourth, the original being 14 inches long. It was found with eleven others, varying in length from 10 to 16 inches, and with spear-heads and other articles, at Guilsfield, Montgomeryshire.†

Another ferrule (9¼ inches) was found, with spear-heads, socketed celts, &c., near Nottingham.‡

Four such (about 7 inches) were found, with spear-heads, &c., at Bloody Pool, South Brent, Devon.§

Fig. 423. Fig. 424.
Nettleham. ¼ Guilsfield. ¼

Canon Greenwell has a specimen from Antrim (9¼ inches), the end of which is worn obliquely, as if by trailing on the ground. It has a single rivet-hole.

A very long ferrule of this kind (14¼ inches), but with a small disc at the base, is in the Museum at Nantes. It was found in the bed of the Loire.

* *Arch. Journ.*, vol. xviii. p. 160. I am indebted to Mr. Franks for the use of this cut.

† *Proc. Soc. Ant.*, 2nd S., vol. ii. p. 250; vol. v. p. 422; *Arch. Camb.*, 3rd S., vol. x. p. 214; "Montgom. Coll.," vol. iii. p. 437.

‡ *Proc. Soc. Ant.*, 2nd S., vol. i. p. 332. § *Arch. Journ.*, vol. xii. p. 84.

A shorter form, somewhat expanding towards the base, is shown in Fig. 425. This, together with three others, none more than 4¼ inches long, was found, with spear-heads, &c., at Pant-y-maen, near Glancych.*

In the Broadward find† were six tubes, varying in length from 6 to 2 inches, of which one only was of this type. Some were so small that the diameter did not exceed ¼ inch.

A small ferrule of this kind was in the hoard found at Beddington, near Croydon,‡ and part of one in that of Wickham Park. The latter is now in the British Museum.

What appears to be a ferrule of this kind, but more widely expanded at the end, like Fig. 425, is described in Gordon's "Itinerarium Septentrionale"§ as "a Roman tuba, or trumpet."

Another of these expanded ferrules is in the Museum of the Cambridge Antiquarian Society.‖

In the Fulbourn find¶ there were two ferrules expanding at the base to about 2 inches in diameter, which were regarded by Dr. Clarke as having been the feet of two spears. He points out that similar feet for spears may be seen represented on Greek vases.** The οὐρίαχος or σαυρωτήρ of Homer†† appears to have been more susceptible of being driven into the ground. This point at the base was sometimes used for fighting when the spear-head proper was broken.

Among the African tribes on the shores of the Gambia, the spears, as Mr. Syer Cuming‡‡ has pointed out, have a chisel- or celt-like ferrule at the base of their shafts; and this fashion extends all across Africa to Madagascar,§§ and recurs in Borneo.

Some Danish ferrules‖‖ present the same peculiarity of being chisel-like at the base.

Another form, more spherical at the base, is shown in Fig. 427, copied from the *Archæological Journal*.¶¶ The original, with several others, was found at St. Margaret's Park, Hereford. The socket tapers to a point 1⅛ inches from the extremity.

A nearly similar ferrule, but with a slight cylindrical projection beyond the spherical part, was found with other bronze objects at Lanant, Cornwall.*** A kind of pointed ferrule of a nearly square section, with the faces hollowed, which was found near Windsor,††† and is now in the British Museum, not improbably belongs to a later date than the Bronze Period.

In the Museum of the Royal Irish Academy are several ferrules, apparently for the end of spear shafts, some of which are said to have been found with spear-heads. Many of these have ornaments of a late Celtic‡‡‡ character upon them. Others§§§ appear to have been made from plates turned over and soldered, and not to have been cast hollow. Both of these kinds are of more recent date than the Bronze Age.

---

* *Arch. Camb.*, 3rd S., vol. x. p. 221.   † Ibid., 4th S., vol. iii. p. 353.
‡ Anderson's "Croydon Preh. and Rom.," p. 11, pl. iii. 5.
§ P. 116, pl. l. 7.   ‖ *Arch. Journ.*, vol. xii. p. 96.
¶ *Arch.*, vol. xix. p. 56, pl. iv. 10, 11; Skelton's "Meyrick's Anc. Arm.," pl. xlvii. 12.
** *Arch. ubi sup.*, "Millin, Peintures de Vases," tome ii. p. 25.
†† "Iliad.," lib. x. 153; lib. xiii. 443, &c.
‡‡ *Arch. Assoc. Journ.*, vol. xv. p. 235.   §§ "Preh. Cong.," Norwich vol., p. 77.
‖‖ Worsaae, "Nord. Olds.," fig. 191; "Atlas for Nord. Old.," pl. B 1, 22, 23.
¶¶ Vol. xi. p. 55.   *** *Arch.*, vol. xv. p. 118.
††† *Arch.*, vol. v. pl. viii. 15.
‡‡‡ Wilde, "Catal. Mus. R. I. A.," figs. 390, 391.   §§§ *Op. cit.*, p. 517.

Tapering ferrules of bronze occur in Italy, and a pointed iron ferrule, probably belonging to a barbed javelin of Roman age, was found in the river Witham, near Lincoln.*

A ferrule, about 3 inches long, with parallel lines engraved round it, is in the Museum at Clermont Ferrand. Another, more conical, is in that of Narbonne.† Some with expanded button-like ends have been found in the Lake-dwellings of Savoy. Several ferrules, some of them very short, were found with bronze spear-heads at Alise Ste. Reine (Côte d'Or).‡

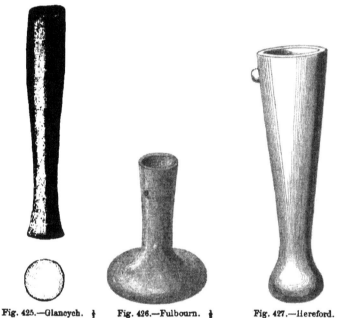

Fig. 425.—Glancych. ‡   Fig. 426.—Fulbourn. ‡   Fig. 427.—Hereford. ‡

Others, some of them ornamented, formed part of the great Bologna hoard.

A ferrule was found with a bronze spear-head, between 23 and 24 inches long, in the Alban Necropolis, and is figured in the *Archæologia.*§ Padre Garrucci regards this spear as neither Greek, nor Etruscan, nor Latin, but Celtic.

Although the simple leaf-shaped spear-heads from the British Isles present close analogies with those from the other parts of Europe, yet for the most part those of the other types, with loops to the sockets, with openings in the blade, or of the barbed class last described, present peculiarities of their own. Several of these types appear, indeed, to have been evolved in Britain or in Ireland, and the differences they exhibit from the ordinary continental types are more marked than in any other class of bronze

* *Proc. Soc. Ant.*, vol. iv. p. 211.   † " Matériaux," vol. v. pl. ii. 25.
‡ *Rev. Arch.*, N.S., vol. iv. pl. xiii.   § Vol. xlv. p. 383.

weapons. Though loops are such a common adjunct to the socketed celts of other countries, yet looped palstaves are comparatively rare abroad.   At the same time, as will have been seen, hardly any examples of looped spear-heads from foreign countries can be cited, while in Britain, and more especially in Ireland, they are very abundant.   This fact, in whatever way it is to be accounted for, affords a most conclusive argument against assigning a Roman origin for our bronze weapons ; a looped spear-head, so far as I am aware, never having been discovered in Italy, and but very rarely even in Gaul.   The spear-heads with the small apertures in the blade appear also to be of an indigenous type.

Some of the iron spear-heads from Hallstatt and elsewhere have been made in imitation of those in bronze, and have been welded along the whole length of their sockets in a manner which displays the highest skill in the smiths.   But, unlike the iron palstaves and socketed celts, none of the spear-heads are provided with a loop.   In later times the sockets of the iron spear-heads were left with an open slit along them, a method of manufacture which produced an equally serviceable weapon, and involved far less trouble.

As to the position in time which spear-heads occupy in the Bronze Age, it is probable that it is towards the close rather than the beginning of that period.   Not only are spear-heads almost, if not quite, absent from our barrows, but the skill involved in producing implements so thin and so truly cored could only have been acquired after long practice in casting.   The objects to be considered in the next chapter are also of comparatively late date.

CHAPTER XV.

SHIELDS, BUCKLERS, AND HELMETS.

HAVING now described the various weapons of offence of which in early times bronze formed the material, it will be well to examine the arms of defence fabricated from the same metal, and presumably of the same or nearly the same age.

The shields first in use in Britain were probably formed of perishable materials, such as wicker-work, wood, or hide, like those of many savage tribes of the present day; and it can only have been after a long acquaintance with the use of bronze that plates could have been produced of such size as those with which some of the ancient shields and bucklers found in this country were covered. They would appear, therefore, to belong to quite the close of the Bronze Age, if not to the transitional period when iron was coming into use. There are, indeed, several bronze coverings of shields of elongated form, such as those from the river Witham* and from the Thames,† with decorations upon them, in which red enamel plays a part, that have been found associated with the iron swords of what Mr. Franks has termed the Late Celtic Period. Those, however, which appear to have a better claim to a place in these pages are of a circular form.

That which I have shown in Fig. 428 is now in the British Museum, and has already been figured in the *Archæologia,*‡ and described by Mr. Gage. It was dredged up from what appears to have been the ancient bed of the river Isis, near Little Wittenham, Berks, not far from the Dyke Hills, near Dorchester, Oxon. It is about 13¼ inches diameter, not quite circular in form, though

---

* "Horæ Fer.," pl. xiv.; *Arch.*, vol. xxiii. p. 97; *Proc. Soc. Ant.*, vol. iv. p. 144; Skelton's "Meyrick's Anc. Arm.," pl. xlvii. 7.

† "Horæ Fer.," pl. xv.; *Arch. Assoc. Journ.*, vol. xiv. p. 330.

‡ Vol. xxvii. pl. xxii. p. 298; "The Barrow Diggers," pl. ii. 1, p. 73; Worsaae, "Prim. Ant. of Denm.," Eng. ed., p. 32. I am indebted to Messrs. James Parker & Co. for the use of this block.

probably intended so to be. The raised bosses have all been
wrought in the metal with the exception of four, two of which
form the rivets for the handle across the umbo, and two others
serve as the rivets or pivots for two small straps or buttons of
bronze on the inner side of the buckler. Such buttons occur on
several other examples, but it is difficult to determine the exact
purpose which they served. From the pains taken in this instance
to conceal the heads of these pivots on the outside, by making
them take the form and place of bosses, it would appear that they
were necessary adjuncts of the shield, and possibly in some way
connected with a lining for it. Such a lining can hardly have

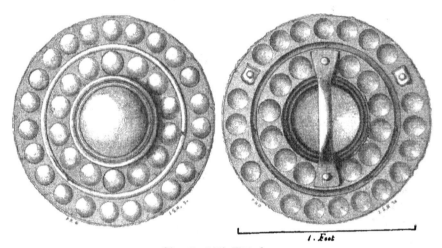

Fig. 428.—Little Wittenham.

been of wood, or many rivet or pin holes would have been necessary
for securing the metal to it. It may be that a lining of hide was
moulded while wet to the form of the shield, and that these
buttons served to keep it in place when dry. In one case * it is
said that some fibrous particles resembling leather still remain
attached to the inside of the shield. In general the metal is so
thin that without some lining these bucklers would have afforded
but a poor defence against the stroke of a sword, spear, or arrow.
In this Little Wittenham example, and possibly in some others, it
is probable that the shield itself was larger than the bronze plate.
Another view is that these buttons fastened a strap for carrying
the shield when either in or out of use.

* *Journ. R. H. and A. Assoc. of Ireland,* 4th S., vol. iv. p. 488.

Another buckler, in Lord Londesborough's collection, 14 inches in diameter, with two circles of small bosses divided by a raised band, is stated to have been found with a large bronze spear-head at Athenry,[*] Co. Galway. Two of the bosses of the inner circle are the heads of rivets for securing the handle. A much smaller buckler, or centre of a buckler, only 9¼ inches in diameter (also with two rings of bosses), presumably found in the Isis,[†] near Eynsham Bridge, is in the Museum of the Society of Antiquaries. It has a slightly conical boss, surrounded by a circle of smaller bosses between two raised ribs. There is also a raised rib round the margin formed by turning over the metal towards the outer face. In the outer ring of bosses two are missing at the places where, no doubt, were formerly the rivets of the buttons or loops.

A shield in the British Museum (21 inches), found in the Thames, has four rows of bosses, about an inch in diameter, and the same number of

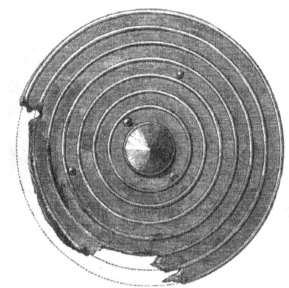

Fig. 429.—Harlech.

raised rings. The inner set of bosses abuts on the umbo. There is a marginal rim about an inch beyond the outer ring. This shield appears to have had two buttons, which as usual are nearly in a line with one of the rivets which fasten the handle. One of these loops remains secured by a large-headed rivet matching the bosses. There is at least one hole through the shield which may have resulted from a spear thrust.

The rivets which secure the handle have heads made in imitation of bosses.

In some the decoration consists of a series of concentric ribs or beads, as in that found in a peat moss near Harlech,[‡] which is shown in Fig. 429. Its diameter is 22 inches. The heads of the four rivets for

[*] "Horæ Fer.," p. 167, pl. xi. 1; *Arch. Journ.*, vol. xiii. p. 187.
[†] *Op. cit.*, p. 167, pl. xi. 3; "Catal. of Ants., &c., of the Soc. Ant.," p. 17.
[‡] *Arch. Journ.*, vol. vii. p. 77, whence the cut is copied; "Hor. Fer.," p. 167, pl. xi. 4.

holding the handle and the two buttons are in this case visible in the spaces between the ribs.

Another of the same pattern was discovered in company with that shown in Fig. 430, in Coveney Fen,* near Ely, and is now in the Museum of the Cambridge Antiquarian Society. The metal of which it is formed has been found on analysis to contain—

Copper	.	.	.	.	87·55
Tin	.	.	.	.	11·72
Nickel	.	.	.	.	0·40
					99·67

The presence of the nickel is probably due to impurities in the ore from which the copper was extracted.

Fig. 430.—Coveney.

The second Coveney shield is shown in Fig. 430.† The ornament in this instance is of a very peculiar character, and appears to represent two snakes, one long and the other short, twisted about into a symmetrical pattern. They are of the *amphisbæna* kind, with a head at each end. The two outermost ribs, one of them at the margin, are continuous. The rivets for holding the handle are visible, as are also three on either side connected with the inner buttons, that in this case have been regarded as

* "Hor. Fer.," p. 167; *Trans. Camb. Ant. Soc.*, vol. ii. p. 12.
† Copied from *Publ. Camb. Ant. Soc.*, vol. ii. Misc. pl. 3.

loops by which the shield was suspended. The buttons have a small
hole through them, as will be seen by Fig.
431. In front of each is a pair of small conical studs, of which the purpose can now
hardly be determined. Mr. Goodwin thought
that they might be intended to prevent a
thong which passed beneath the buttons from
slipping away from them.

Fig. 431.—Coveney. ⅓

The type of shield, of which the largest
number has been found in the British Isles, is that having a

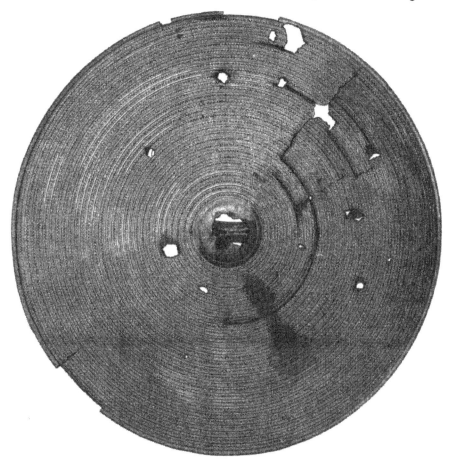

Fig. 432.—Beith. ⅛

series of concentric rings, from about twelve to thirty in number, and between them circles of small studs.

A very fine example of this kind of shield is preserved in the Museum of the Society of Antiquaries of London,* and is shown on the scale of one-sixth, together with some of its details on a larger scale, in Figs. 432,

Fig. 433.—Beith.   ‡

433, and 434, for the use of which I am indebted to the Council of the Ayr-shire and Wigtonshire Archæological Association.†

A figure of the shield has been given by Professor Daniel Wilson,‡ but the illustrations here given will convey a much more accurate impression of its character and details.

Though there is some discrepancy as to measurement, there is little doubt that this is the shield found about the year 1780 in a peat moss on a farm called Luggtonriggc, in the parish of Beith, Ayrshire, and pre-sented to the Society of Antiquaries by Dr. Ferris,§ who was informed

* "Catal. Mus. Soc. Ant.," p. 16.
† See "Ayr. and Wigt. Coll.," vol. i. p. 66, where I have described this shield.
‡ "Preh. Ann. of Scot.," 1st ed., p. 267 ; 2nd ed., vol. i. p. 397.
§ "Minute Book of Soc. Ant.," vol. xxiv. p. 147.

that four or five others of the same kind were discovered at the same time. A portion of the margin of the shield is shown of the full size in Fig. 433, and the handle across the inner side of the boss on the scale of one-half in Fig. 434. These figures give so complete an idea of the original that it seems needless to enter into further details. It is, however, well to call attention to the fact that the handle of the buckler, which is made from a flat piece of bronze, is rendered more convenient to grasp, and at the same time strengthened, by its sides being doubled over, and thus made to present a rounded edge. It is secured to the shield by a rivet at each end. About midway between the edge of the umbo and that of the shield, but placed so that one of the rivets of the handle is in the same line and midway between them, have been two rivets, each fastening a short button like those on the Coveney Fen shield, of which at present only one remains. The rivet-hole for the other has been closed by a short rivet.

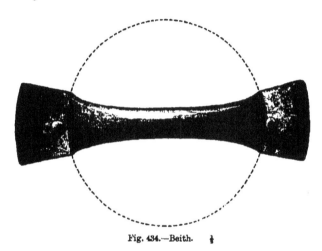

Fig. 434.—Beith. ½

Other shields, almost identical in character, have likewise been found in Scotland, one of which, by the kindness of the Council of the Society of Antiquaries of Scotland, is shown in Fig. 435, on the scale of one-sixth. A portion of the margin is shown full size in Fig. 436, and the interior of the umbo in Fig. 437, on the scale of one-fourth. It was found in 1837, together with another, in a marshy field near Yetholm, Roxburghshire. These shields have been described in a paper by the late Mr. W. T. M°Culloch,* of some of whose references I have here made use.

One of these Yetholm shields is 23½ inches in diameter, and has thirty concentric rings of convex knobs alternating with projecting circular ribs or beads; the other measures 24 inches across, and has twenty-four rings of both knobs and ribs. In the centre of each is a hollow circular umbo 4 inches in diameter, with a handle riveted across it.

Another shield of the same character was found at Yetholm † in 1870, near the place where the two others were discovered. It is 22½ inches in

* *Proc. Soc. Ant. Scot.*, vol. v. p. 165. See also *Tr. R. Hist. and Arch. Assoc. of Ireland*, 4th S., vol. iv. p. 487.
† *Proc. Soc. Ant. Scot.*, vol. viii. p. 393.

diameter, with twenty-nine concentric rings alternating with the usual small knobs. The boss is 3½ inches in diameter.

Fig. 435.—Yetholm.   ⅛

Fig. 436.—Yetholm.   ¼

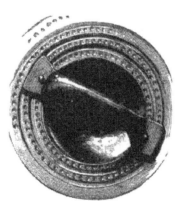

Fig. 437.—Yetholm.   ¼

At the back of each of these shields, about midway between the centre and the rim, are the usual small movable tongues of bronze, which have been supposed to serve for the attachment of a leather strap by which the shield might be slung round the body. Mr. Jeffrey, F.S.A. Scotland, of Jedburgh, who described this third shield, has pointed out that there is too little room beneath the tongues for a strap of any kind.

So far as at present known these are the only instances of bucklers of this kind having been discovered in Scotland.

In England and Wales several such have been found. One was in the Meyrick Collection * at Goodrich Court, and is now in the British Museum. It is about 26¼ inches in diameter, with twenty concentric circles of knobs and ribs between, and is in all respects like those just described. It was found about 1804 in a turbary near Aberystwith, Cardiganshire. It has had the usual buttons, one of which remains.

Another example † of the kind (25¼ inches), with twenty-seven concentric rings, was also in the Meyrick Collection, and is now in the British Museum. It was found in a peat moss at Moel Sinbod, near Capel Curig, Carnarvonshire. It has one of the usual loops and the rivet of the other. Sir Samuel Meyrick had heard of another shield, dug up near Newcastle-on-Tyne, which the owner, wishing to gratify all his friends, cut up like a cake, and sent to each a slice. This may be the shield found at Broomyholme, Chester-le-Street, Durham, of which a fragment is in the Museum of the Society of Antiquaries of Newcastle-on-Tyne.

Another now in the possession of Sir Edward Blackett, Bart., was found near Corbridge, Northumberland.

Fragments ‡ of two other shields of the same character were also found in Northumberland, at Ingoe, in the parish of Stamfordham, about two miles north of the Roman wall. They were originally about 20 inches in diameter, and like so many others were discovered during draining operations.

Another buckler of the same character was found in the Thames § at London, and passed into the British Museum with the Roach Smith Collection. This specimen is 21¼ inches in diameter, and has eleven rings of the small bosses upon it separated by concentric ribs. A curious feature in this shield is that the places to which the usual little buttons were attached have been neatly cut out, leaving triangular holes. There is also a third hole of the same kind. In one place also there is a hole through the shield, such as might have been produced by the thrust of a bronze spear. Close by this hole is a clean cut, such as might have been made by a sword. The plate of bronze has been turned over on to the face, so as to form the outer rim.

A circular shield,‖ with twenty-six concentric rings of studs, was dredged up, together with a leaf-shaped bronze sword, from the bed of the Thames off Woolwich in 1830.

A thin bronze plate from the Thames, 19 inches in diameter, convex, and with small knobs round the margin, is in the Mayer Collection at Liverpool. It has been marked with the hammer, possibly in imitation

* *Arch.*, vol. xxiii. p. 92; "Anc. Arm.," by Skelton, vol. i. pl. xlvii. 4.
† *Arch.*, vol. xxiii. p. 95.   ‡ *Arch. Journ.*, vol. xviii. p. 157.
§ "Hor. Fer.," pl. ix. 168 ; C. Roach Smith, "Catal. of Lond. Ant.," p. 80.
‖ C. Roach Smith, *ubi sup.*

of basket-work, and has been mended in one place in ancient times. It may be the bottom of a caldron, and not a shield.

Another buckler, 26 inches in diameter, having twelve concentric raised rings with the usual knobs between them, is also said to have been found in the Thames * between Hampton and Walton, in September, 1864.

In draining a meadow at Bagley,† about five miles from Ellesmere, in Shropshire, another of these circular bucklers was found. This is 23 inches in diameter, with an umbo of 4 inches, and has twenty-six concentric circles, with the same rings of knobs between them as on the other examples. It has the usual holes for the rivets of the small buttons.

Another, found on Burringham Common,‡ Lincolnshire, in 1843, is 26 inches in diameter, with an umbo of 4½ inches, and only nineteen concentric circles with intermediate rings of knobs. The boss of this shield is conical rather than hemispherical. It is now in the Museum of the Royal Irish Academy. A shield of this kind 20½ inches in diameter, having thirteen concentric circles of small bosses and raised rings between, was found at Sutton St. Michael's, Norfolk.§

In the collection of Canon Greenwell is the bronze boss of a shield nearly 5 inches in diameter, probably intended for the centre of a wooden buckler. It has three small holes for nails or rivets in the rim. In one place there is a square hole, apparently made by a thrust from a spear. This boss was found at Harwood, Northumberland.

Shields like Fig. 435, with several concentric rings alternating with small knobs, are rare, but by no means unknown in Ireland. One (27¾ inches in diameter) was found in a bog near Ballynamona,‖ Co. Limerick, and has been figured. As usual, it has the two movable loops or buttons at the back. There is a little patch of bronze over a small irregular hole in the shield, such as an arrow or a javelin would make. It is soldered on with a metal which is stated to be bronze, but which I imagine must be some more fusible alloy of copper. This shield is now in the Museum of the Royal Irish Academy, and in their *Proceedings* ¶ is stated to have been found in Lough Gur, Co. Limerick, but this must be an error.

The central portion of a bronze shield, including the umbo, was found at Toome Bar, Lough Neagh, and is now in the collection of Mr. William Gray, of Belfast.

A somewhat doubtful instance has been recorded of the remains of a bronze shield having been found with an interment in a barrow. Sir R. Colt Hoare, in his examination of the Bush Barrow, Normanton,** found a skeleton lying from S. to N., and about eighteen inches S. of the head " several brass rivets intermixed with wood, and some thin bits of brass nearly decomposed. These articles covered a space of twelve inches or more; it is probable, therefore, that they are the mouldered remains of a shield." Near the shoulders lay a flanged bronze celt like Fig. 9. A large dagger of bronze, and what Sir Richard calls a spear-head of the same metal, but which was probably a dagger, the inlaid hilt (Fig. 289),

* *Proc. Soc. Ant.*, 2nd S., vol. iii. p. 518; v. p. 363; *Gent. Mag.*, Dec., 1865, p. 771.

† *Proc. Soc. Ant.*, 2nd S., vol. iii. p. 200.

‡ *Arch. Assoc. Journ.*, vol. iv. p. 395; *Proc. Soc. Ant.*, 2nd S., vol. iii. p. 200; *Proc. Roy. Irish Acad.*, 1874, p. 277.   § *Arch. Assoc. Jour.*, vol. xxxvi. p. 165.

‖ *Journ. Royal Hist. and Arch. Assoc. of Ireland*, 4th S., vol. ii. p. 118, and vol. iv. p. 487. See *Arch.*, vol. xliii. p. 480.

¶ Vol. x. p. 155.   ** " Anc. Wilts," vol. i. p. 203.

a stone hammer, and some plates of gold accompanied this interment. It is much to be regretted that more is not known of the real character of the object with the rivets, but their presence shows that it could not have been a shield such as those here described, in which the only rivets are those securing the handle and the movable buttons.

The umbo of a Late-Celtic shield was among the objects found at Polden Hill,[*] Somersetshire.

Some wooden bucklers have been found both in Scotland [†] and Ireland, but it is hard to determine their age.

Mr. Franks [‡] has already remarked that bronze shields are of far less common occurrence on the Continent than in the British Isles. He cites three from the Copenhagen Museum,[§] one of which, about 27 inches in diameter, has five concentric ribs round the boss and ten sets of knobs; these, however, are arranged in such a manner as to leave a star of eight rays of smooth metal radiating from the boss. The other two are less like the British in character. A fine shield in the Stockholm Museum, with swan-like figures upon it, has been thought to have been imported from Italy.[||]

One found near Bingen, on the Rhine,[¶] about 15½ inches in diameter, has merely four raised concentric ribs. There are two small bowed handles secured with two rivets, each in about the same position as the usual button. They seem certainly intended for a strap to pass through them. There are, however, two other rivets in the shield to which movable buttons may possibly have been attached.

The Italian shields mentioned by Mr. Franks are of a different type. One in the British Museum (34 inches in diameter) has a very slight boss, and is ornamented with concentric bands of sphinxes and other designs.

As has already been observed, it is somewhat hard to judge of the date of these bucklers. I am not aware of any portions of them having been found in the hoards of metal in which fragments of swords frequently occur. Still in the case of the shield dredged up off Woolwich the sword which accompanied it was of bronze, though of course there is no evidence of the two having been lost or deposited together. The whole character, however, of the ornamentation and workmanship is, I think, more in accordance with the Bronze Age than with the Late Celtic or Early Iron Period, though the shields probably belong to the close of the Bronze Period.

Circular bucklers, or targets, no doubt remained in use until a considerably later date, but it seems probable that some other material than a thin plate of bronze was used for their manufac-

---

[*] *Arch.*, vol. xiv. p. 90. pl. xviii.   [†] See *Arch. Scot.*, vol. v. p. 217.
[‡] "Hor. Fer.," p. 166.
[§] Madsen, "Afbild.," vol. ii. pl. xvii.; "Atlas for Nord. Oldk.," pl. B, v.; Worsaae "Prim. Ant. of Den.," Thoms' Eng. ed., p. 31.
[||] "Cong. préh.," Bologna vol., p. 294.
[¶] Lindenschmit, "Alt. u. h. Vorzeit," vol. i. Heft xi. Taf. 1, 4, and 5.

ture.   Professor Daniel Wilson* remarks that on the gold coins of
Tasciovanus, Cunobeline, and others of our native rulers contemporary with the first intercourse with Rome, the shields borne by
the warriors are either long and double-pointed, or, if round, large
and disked, and of very different construction from the Luggton-
rigge shield.   On one coin of Cunobeline, however (Evans, pl. xii.
14), the horseman bears a circular buckler, which, so far as can be
judged from so diminutive a representation as that given on the
coin, would be about 2 feet in diameter.   On two small gold coins
of Verica,† recently published, the horseman carries a target of
somewhat larger proportions.   Somewhat smaller circular bucklers
are carried by the horsemen on certain Spanish coins,‡ probably
of the second century B.C.   One of these shields shows four
smaller bosses, arranged in cruciform order around the central
boss ; another seems to be plain except the umbo and a projecting rim.

This buckler is no doubt the Cetra, or Cætra (καίτρεα, Hesych.),
in use among the people of Spain and Mauretania, which was
usually made of hide, among the latter people sometimes of that
of the elephant.   Cæsar§ speaks of the "cetratæ Hispaniæ cohortes,"
and Tacitus ‖ mentions the Britons as armed "ingentibus gladiis
sine mucrone et brevibus cetris."   It does not appear that the
Romans ever carried the cetra, which has been by Livy compared
to the pelta of the Greeks and Macedonians.¶   The clipeus appears
to have been larger in size, and to have been held on the arm
and not by the handle only.

But whatever shields may have been in use in this country at
the time of the Roman invasion, I am inclined to refer these
circular bucklers to a somewhat earlier date, as already in Cæsar's
time iron was fully in use for swords and for cutting purposes
generally ; and, as has already been observed, the shields with
which the early iron swords are found are of a different form
from these.   As is the case with bronze swords, such bucklers are
never found with interments, and those discovered seem to have
been lost in the water, or hidden in bogs, rather than buried as
accessories for the dead.

The skill requisite for the production of such bucklers must

---

* "Preh. Ann. of Scot.," 2nd ed., vol. i. p. 398.
† *Num. Chron.*, N.S., vol. xvii. pl. x. 7 and 8.
‡ See *Arch. Journ.*, vol. xiii. p. 187.
§ "De Bell. Civ.," i. 39, 48.   ‖ "Agric.," 36.
¶ See Smith's "Dict. of Ant.," *s. v.* Cetra.

have been great, and the appliances at command by no means contemptible. The whole of the work is *repoussé* and wrought with the hammer, and not improbably the original sheet of bronze from which a shield was made was considerably less in diameter and also much thicker than the finished shield. To produce so large a casting of such even substance, and yet so thin, would I think be beyond the skill of most modern, and probably most ancient, brass-founders ; and moreover there is no appearance on the shields, of the metal having been cast in the form in which it now appears.

While still upon the subject of defensive armour it will be well to say a few words about bronze helmets, though there is good reason to believe that in this country at all events such objects do not belong to the Bronze Age properly so-called. Indeed the earliest known bronze helmets in some other countries, such as those from Assyria and Etruria, appear to belong to a time when iron was already in use in those countries. The date of an Etruscan helmet of bronze preserved in the British Museum* can be determined with precision, for an inscription upon it proves that it was offered in the Temple of Zeus at Elis, by Hiero, Tyrant of Syracuse, from the spoils of the Etruscans after the naval battle of Cumæ, which took place in B.C. 474. It is of simple form with a brim around it. Those which have been found in Styria and Germany† are in some cases half ovals in form, sometimes with a knob at the top, without any rims round the opening, but with a certain number of small holes for the attachment of cheek-pieces or appendages of other kinds. These may belong to a true Bronze Period. Others, like those from Hallstatt,‡ have rims and even ridges for crests.

In the Salzburg Museum is a fine helmet without a rim, but with an ornamented ridge and cheek-pieces. It was found, with twelve others now at Vienna, at Mattrey,§ between Innsbruck and Brixen. One of these bears an Etruscan inscription upon it. According to Pliny, "the ancient inhabitants of Brixen came from Etruria."

Even in the time of Severus, the Britons, according to Herodian,‖ made no use of helmets or cuirasses, though they wore an iron collar round the neck and an iron belt round the body, and regarded them as ornaments and signs of wealth.

* "Horæ Ferales," p. 168, pl. xii. 1.
† Lindenschmit, "A. u. h. Vorzeit," vol. i. Heft xi. Taf. 1.
‡ Von Sacken, "Grabf. zu Hallst.," Taf. viii. 5, 6.
§ *Proc. Soc. Ant.*, vol. i. p. 167.   ‖ Lib. iii. c. 14.

The following English and French helmets of bronze may just be mentioned.

(1.) A helmet of hemi-spherical form tapering to a projection, pierced above to receive a crest or ornament, the extreme height being about 8¼ inches, and the diameter at the base nearly the same. This was found in Moorgate Street, London.*

(2.) One found in the Thames,† near Waterloo Bridge, with projecting horns and ornamented with scroll-work and red enamel. This is undoubtedly of the Late Celtic Period. Some Etruscan helmets also bear horns, but more curved in form than those on this helmet from the Thames.

(3.) Another, more conical in form, and with a semicircular plate at the back, locality unknown, but probably from a river.‡ This was in the Meyrick Collection, and is now in the British Museum.

The helmets found on Ogmore Down,§ Glamorganshire, appear to be of much later date.

A helmet from Auxonne, Côte d'Or, has been figured by Chantre.‖ Another was found with various bronze antiquities at Theil¶ (Loir et Cher).

* *Proc. Soc. Ant.*, 2nd S., vol. iii. p. 518.
† *Proc. Soc. Ant.*, 2nd S., vol. iii. p. 342; Waring's "Ornaments of Remote Ages," pl. xci. 10.
‡ *Proc. Soc. Ant.*, 2nd S., vol. v. p. 362.
§ *Arch.*, vol. xliii. p. 553, pl. xxxvi.   ‖ "Album," pl. xvi. *bis.*
¶ Chantre, "Age du Br.," 1ère ptie., p. 146.

CHAPTER XVI

TRUMPETS AND BELLS.

ANOTHER instrument probably connected with warfare, though not strictly speaking an arm either of offence or defence, is the trumpet, of which numerous examples in bronze have been found, especially in Ireland. It is very doubtful whether the greater part of them do not belong to the Early Iron Age, rather than to that of Bronze ; but as it seems probable that some at least belong to a transitional period, and it is possible that others are of even earlier date, they could hardly be passed over without notice in these pages.

There are two distinct classes of these instruments, so far as the process of their manufacture is concerned, viz. those which are

Fig. 438.—Limerick. ⅓

cast in one piece, and those which are formed of sheet-metal turned over and riveted to form the tube. There are also two distinct varieties of the instrument, viz. those in which the aperture for blowing is at the end, and those in which it is at the side.

Sir W. Wilde, in his Catalogue* of the Museum of the Royal Irish Academy, has devoted several pages to a detailed description of the trumpets found in Ireland, to which the reader is referred. Those which he figures are all curved, some almost to a semicircle, others to a more irregular sweep. Some straight tubes which were found in company with several curved horns he has regarded, but without sufficient cause, as the portions of a " commander's staff," or of the handle of a halberd. One of these is shown in Fig. 438, borrowed from his Catalogue.† A similar straight tube,

* P. 623 *et seqq.*   † Fig. 360, p. 492.

(23¾ inches,) found with trumpets at Dunmanway, Co. Cork, is now in
the British Museum. The earliest known instance of the discovery
of such instruments is, according to Wilde, that recorded by Sir
Thomas Molyneux,* in 1725, of a "short side-mouthed trumpet"
being found with others in a mound near Carrickfergus, which was
then regarded as of Danish origin. But so early as 1713 Mr. F.
Nevill described eight bronze trumpets found at Dungannon,† Co.
Tyrone. In 1750 thirteen or fourteen more curved bronze horns
were discovered between Cork and Mallow, three of which are
described and figured in the "Vetusta Monumenta."‡

There is a remarkable resemblance between these trumpets and
three of those found near Chute Hall, Tralee, Co. Kerry, and
described by Mr. Robert Day, F.S.A., in the *Journal of the Royal
Historical and Archæological Association of Ireland*.§ By his
kindness I am able here to reproduce his cuts as Figs. 439, 440, and
441. It will be observed that in two of them the ends are open,

Fig. 439.—Tralee.

so as to be adapted for the reception of mouth-pieces, and that the
end of the other is closed. In this there is a lateral opening to
which to apply the mouth. It is on the inner curve of the trumpet,
but in some other cases it is at the side. As Mr. Day has
observed, there are rivet-holes at the wide ends of two of the
horns, as if for securing some more widely expanding end, while
in the more bell-mouthed examples no such rivet-holes are present.
The trumpet shown in Fig. 440 is made of two pieces which fit
exactly into each other, one of them being nearly straight. The
length of this instrument, taken along the external curve, is
50 inches, and its bell-shaped mouth is 4 inches in diameter. It
will be seen that at the mouths, and in other positions on these

* "Discourse concerning Danish Mounds, &c."   † *Phil. Trans.*, vol. xxviii. p. 270.
‡ Vol. ii. pl. xx. 3, 4, 5; Gough's "Camden," vol. iv. pl. xiv.; "Hor. Fer.," pl. xiii. 1.
§ 4th S., vol. iii. p. 422.

three trumpets, there are small conical projections or spikes always in groups of four. Mr. Day has suggested the possibility of these being added to give effect to blows with the trumpets in case it became necessary to use them as weapons of offence. He has also pointed out the remarkable resemblance between the horns with the lateral openings and the war trumpets in use in Central Africa,

Figs. 440 and 441.—Tralee.

which are made from elephants' tusks. One of these is shown in Fig. 442, also kindly lent by Mr. Day. The conch-shell trumpets of Fiji have also lateral openings.

As will subsequently be seen, trumpets of the two types repre-

Fig. 442.—Africa.

sented by Figs. 439 and 440 have been found associated with bronze weapons.

To return to the trumpets from Cork described in the "Vetusta Monumenta." Two of these are formed, like Fig. 440, of two pieces, and are open at the end, which may have been provided with some kind of mouth-piece. The other, like Fig. 439, is cast in a single piece and is closed at the small end, but has a large orifice at the side like the Portglenone specimen Fig. 444. Both are provided with a number of conical projections by way of ornament round the mouth, and one of them has similar small spikes in other positions. With them were found some pieces of straight tubing, which were also decorated in a similar manner. The horn with the side aperture is provided with a ring for suspension, like Fig. 439. Some of the straight tubes have a sliding ferrule upon them also furnished with a ring.

Sir W. Wilde observes of a horn about 24 inches long with the aperture at the end slightly everted, as if for holding the lips, that it requires a great exertion even to produce a dull sound with this instrument. As to those with lateral apertures 2 inches long on the average, and 1¼ inches wide, he says that " it is not possible by any yet discovered method of placing the lips to this mouth-hole to produce a musical sound ; but, as conjectured by Walker in 1786, these instruments might have been used as speaking-trumpets, to convey the voice to a great distance as well as render it much louder."

In one instance of a trumpet, like Fig. 439, being broken across the mouth-piece, it has been repaired by a process of burning

Fig. 443.—Derrynane.

together, like that adopted in the case of broken swords * previously mentioned. The mended portion is shown in Fig. 443,† borrowed from Wilde. This trumpet was found at Derrynane, Co. Kerry.

A trumpet, broken across the middle and mended in a similar manner, formed part of the " Dowris find," from which a number of specimens are preserved in the British Museum,‡ and others are in the Museum of the Royal Irish Academy. The metal of which most of the articles in this hoard are formed has a peculiar golden lustre which is thought to arise from the admixture of a certain proportion of lead. A horn analyzed by Donovan § gave :

Copper	79·34
Tin . . .	10·87
Lead	9·11
	99·32

* P. 282.
† Wilde, fig. 529, p. 592, kindly lent by the Council of the R. I. A. One of Mr. Day's trumpets is also patched.
‡ *Arch. Journ.*, vol. xii. p. 96. There is an article on Irish trumpets by Dr. Petrie in the *Dublin Penny Journal*, vol. ii. See also *Proc. R. I. A.*, vol. iv. pp. 237, 423.
§ Von Bibra, "Die Br. u. Kupf.-leg.," p. 140.

The find took place at Dowris, near Parsonstown, in King's County, and comprised, besides trumpets and socketed celts, a casting for a hammer-head, a socketed knife, tanged knives, razors, a broad rapier-shaped dagger-blade, broken swords, a dagger formed from a part of a sword, spear-heads both leaf-shaped and with openings in the blade, vessels of thin bronze, rough metal, some rattles or crotals, such as will shortly be mentioned, a pin with a hook somewhat like a crochet-needle, and some rubbing stones for grinding and polishing. There may have been other articles, but those here mentioned are represented in the portion of the hoard now in the British Museum. The association of trumpets with such a series raises the presumption that some of them at least belong to the close of the Bronze Age proper.

Some of these Dowris trumpets are engraved in the "Horæ Ferales," [*] and one of them belonging to the Earl of Rosse is peculiar as having two

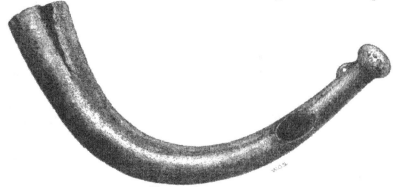

Fig. 444.—Portglenone.

loops opposite each other above and below. A detached portion of another consists of a nearly straight tube, 9 inches long, expanding at each end.

Another slightly differing example with the opening at the side is also figured by Mr. R. Day, and here with his permission reproduced. It was found at Portglenone, Co. Derry, and measures 24½ inches along the convex margin.

The other finds of trumpets have been for the most part isolated. Most of those I am about to cite have already been mentioned by Wilde. A fine specimen, like Fig. 444, is figured by Vallancey [†] and in Gough's "Camden's Britannia." [‡] Three others and a portion of a straight tube were found in the county of Limerick [§] in 1787. Others have been found near Killarney; [||] Cornaconway, Co. Cavan; Kilraughts, Co. Antrim; Diamond Hill, Killeshandra; Crookstown and Dunmanway, Co. Cork.

* Pl. xiii. 3, 4, 5, 6, 9.   † "Coll. Hib.," vol. iv. pl. vii. 2.
‡ Vol. iv. pl. xiii. 2.   § Trans. R. I. A., vol. ii.
|| Wilde's "Catal. Mus. R. I. A.," p. 624 et seqq.; Jour. R. H. and A. A. of Ireland,
4th S., vol. iii. p. 422 et seqq. See also Ulster Journ. of Arch., 1860, vol. viii. p. 99;
and "Horæ Ferales," p. 172.

As the riveted variety of trumpet appears from its ornamentation to belong to the Late Celtic Period, a short mention of it will suffice.   One[*] found near Armagh, and now in the Museum of the Royal Irish Academy. has at the end a disc 7½ inches in diameter, embossed with the peculiar scroll patterns characteristic of that period. Another is no less than 8 feet 5 inches along the convex margin, and consists of two portions made of sheet bronze, each turned over to form a tube, and having the abutting edges riveted to a long strip of metal extending along the interior of the tube.   This strip of bronze is only half an inch in width, and has two rows of minute rivet-holes in it, the rivets being placed alternately.   Their circular heads are on the inside of the tube, and so minute are the rivets, that there are no less than 638 of them along the seam.   It is, indeed, not unlike a modern riveted hose pipe of leather. In what manner such an ingenious and complicated piece of riveting could have been effected is, as Sir W. Wilde remarks, a subject for speculation.

Fig. 445.—The Caprington Horn. [‡]

These riveted trumpets appear to be unknown in Britain, and the cast-bronze variety is extremely scarce.   A fine and perfect specimen found at Caprington, Ayrshire, has been engraved for the Ayrshire and Wigtonshire Archæological Association,[†] and is here, by the kindness of the Council of the Association, reproduced as Fig. 445.   It was found some time before 1654, on the estate of Coilsfield, in the parish of Tarbolton, in Kyle, but is known as the Caprington horn.   According to Mr. R. W. Cochran-Patrick, F.S.A., it has been described by Sir Robert Gordon in Blaeuw's Atlas[‡] and by Defoe.[§]   This horn is 25 inches in length, and is the only specimen recorded to have been found in Scotland. The metal of which it is formed has been analyzed by Professor Stevenson Macadam, and consists of—

* Wilde, 630 et seqq.
† "Collections," vol. i. p. 74; Proc. Soc. Ant. Scot., vol. xii. p. 565.
‡ Vol. vi. p. 50.   § "Tour through Britain," vol. iv. p. 130.

Copper	.	.	.	.	. 90·26
Tin	.	.	.	.	. 9·61
Loss	.	.	.	.	. ·13

100·00

English trumpets of bronze are of extremely rare occurrence. One found in the river Witham, Lincolnshire, has been figured in the *Philosophical Transactions*,[*] and is nearly straight for the greater part of its length (about 28 inches), curving upwards near the end into an irregularly-shaped expanding mouth. It has an ornament or crest like a mane along the exterior curve. In form it is not unlike the *carnyx* which is brandished by the horseman on the coins of the British princes Eppillus and Tasciovanus,[†] and which also appears on some Roman coins and monuments commemorative of Gallic and British victories. The metal on analysis gave copper 88, tin 12, and the tube was formed from a hammered sheet and soldered with tin. It not improbably belongs to a period not far removed from that of the Roman invasion of this country.

Another, with two joints and a perfect mouth-piece, is said to have been found at Battle, Sussex, and has been engraved by Grose.[‡] A bronze horn about 3 feet 7 inches long, found in Mecklenburg,[§] is not unlike the Scotch horn in character, though smaller at the wide end. The curved bronze horns or "lurer," found in Denmark,[‖] have usually broad bossed flanges at the wide end, and most resemble the Irish Late Celtic trumpets.

The use of war trumpets among the Celtic population of Western Europe has been more than once mentioned by classical writers, and passages from them have been cited by Mr. Franks and others. Polybius[¶] speaks of the innumerable trumpeters in the army of the Celts, and Diodorus Siculus[**] says of the Gauls that they have barbaric trumpets of a special nature which emit a hoarse sound well suited to the din of battle. The Roman *lituus* in use for cavalry seems to have been of much the same shape as the *carnyx*, the end of which latter was in some cases made to resemble a fanciful head of an animal. The continuance of the

[*] Vol. lxxxvi. 1796, pl. xi.; "Horæ Fer.," pl. xiii. 2; *Arch. Journ.*, vol. xviii. p. 150.
[†] Evans, "Anc. British Coins," pl. iii. No. 11, and pl. v. No. 10, &c.
[‡] "Anc. Armour," pl. xiii.; Gough's "Camden," vol. iv. p. 231.
[§] Lisch, "Fred. Francisc.," Tab. ix. 3.
[‖] "Atlas for Nord. Oldk.," pl. B, vii.; Worsaae, "Nord. Olds.," figs. 199—201.
[¶] Lib. ii. c. 29.
[**] Lib. v. c. 30. See also Livy, lib. v. 37 and 39.

same character of instrument into the Early Iron Age, and the advanced art shown in producing such castings as the trumpets from Dowris and elsewhere, go to prove that they must belong to the close of the Bronze Period, if, indeed, some may not more probably be placed in a period of transition from Bronze to Iron.

Another form of instrument intended for producing sound, if not indeed deserving to be classed as a musical instrument, is the bell, or rattle, formed of a hollow egg-shaped or pear-shaped piece of bronze, with a pebble or piece of metal inside by way of clapper.

The only examples which I am able to adduce are those which formed part of the Dowris hoard, one of which is represented in

Fig. 446.—Dowris.

Fig. 446.* There are three such in the Museum of the Royal Irish Academy, and four in the British Museum. With the latter is a smaller plain bell of the same character and two unfinished castings. Sir W. Wilde observes that in casting, the metal appears to have been poured into the mould by an aperture at the side, through which the core of clay that contained the metal clapper was broken up. The mould was in two halves, and the rings and staples at the ends were cast together. In the perfect examples at the British Museum, the sides of the holes by which the core was extracted have been hammered together so as in some cases to be almost closed. In one instance there is some appearance of the sides having been brazed together.

The sound emitted by these bells is dull and feeble. Like the modern horse bells, a number of them may have been hung together, and not improbably employed in a similar manner to attract the attention both of the eye and ear.

* Wilde, "Catal. Mus. R. I. A.," p. 612, fig. 523, whence this cut is reproduced. See also *Proc. R. I. A.*, vol. iv. pp. 237, 423.

CHAPTER XVII.

PINS.

PINS for the purpose of fastening the dress or the hair seem to have been in use from very early times. Made of bone,* they have been found associated with polished stone implements, and pins of the same material are of extremely common occurrence with Roman remains, and are not unknown at the present day. In the same manner, pins of bronze or of brass have remained in use ever since their first introduction during the Bronze Period, and it is, therefore, by no means easy, and, indeed, often absolutely impossible, to assign a date with any degree of confidence to such objects when found by themselves, and not in association with other remains of which the antiquity can be more readily determined. In the case of small or imperfect pins there is considerable difficulty in distinguishing them from awls, such as have already been described in Chapter VII. In other cases, it is often difficult to say whether bronze pins, certainly of great antiquity, are to be assigned to the Bronze Period properly so called, or the Late Celtic or Early Iron Period.

Fig. 447.
Heathery
Burn. ½

In describing the objects of this class, it will, perhaps, be best to take first such examples as have been found in the exploration of tumuli or in direct association with bronze weapons or instruments.

Among the numerous relics found in the Heathery Burn Cave, Durham, were a large number of bronze pins, of which one,† 3¼ inches long, is shown in Fig. 447. Canon Greenwell has eleven others from 3 inches to 5⅝ inches long, with flat heads, all from this cave, as well as one which has had its end hammered flat, and then turned over into a loop, so as to

---

* Greenwell, " British Barrows," pp. 16, 31.
† *Proc. Soc. Ant.*, 2nd S., vol. ii. p. 130. I am indebted to the Council of the Society for the use of this cut.

form the head. A socketed knife and many other objects from this cave have been described in previous pages.

Four imperfect bronze pins, without heads, the longest 3⅞ inches long. were found in the hoard at Marden,[*] Kent, with a sickle, dagger, and other objects.

What is termed part of a bronze pin, some chipped flints, and long ribbed beads of pottery, were found in the barrow called Matlow Hill,[†] Cambridgeshire. Another, also fragmentary, was found with a flake of calcined flint, four jet beads, and burnt bones in a barrow on Wykeham Moor,[‡] Yorkshire, by Canon Greenwell. Others are mentioned by Bateman ; [§] but in all these cases, as Canon Greenwell[||] has pointed out, the presumed pins may have been awls or prickers. The little pin found with a lance-head, a small urn, and some gold ornaments at Upton Lovel,[¶] Wilts, may have been of the same character, as also other pins mentioned by Sir R. Colt Hoare.[**] A "fine brass pin " is described as having been found with glass, jet, and amber beads, together with burnt bones, in a barrow near Wilsford.[††] A very fine one in a barrow at Lake,[‡‡] which, from the engraving, was probably an awl. The long pin with a handle found with a bronze celt and lance-head, or dagger, in a barrow at Abury,[§§] may also have been a tool of that kind. The bronze pins recorded to have been found in a barrow at Bulford,[||||] Wilts, likewise seem to come under this category.

Fig. 448.
Brigmilston. ⅓

Fig. 449.
Everley. ⅓

In a barrow at Brigmilston[¶¶] an interment of burnt bones was accompanied by a pin of twisted bronze, 6 inches long, in the form of a crutch, the head perforated (Fig. 448), a small dagger of bronze, and two whetstones.

A smooth pin of the same character and nearly the same size, but broken, was found in a barrow at Normanton,[***] in company with burnt bones, two bronze daggers, a whetstone, and a pipe of bone.

The curious pin, with two rings at the head, in each of which is another ring (Fig. 449), was found by Sir R. Colt Hoare in a barrow near

---

[*] *Arch. Assoc. Journ.*, vol. xiv. p. 259.   [†] *Arch. Journ.*, vol. ix. p. 227.
[‡] *Arch. Journ.*, vol. xxii. p. 247.
[§] " Vest. Ant. Derb.," p. 34 ; "Ten Years' Dig.," p. 130.
[||] " Brit. Barrows," p. 366.   [¶] *Arch.*, xv. p. 129.
[**] " Anc. Wilts," vol. i. pp. 206—208.   [††] *Op. cit.*, p. 207.
[‡‡] *Op. cit.*, p. 210. The references to the plate are somewhat confused or confusing.
[§§] " Anc. Wilts," vol. ii. p. 90.   [||||] *Arch. Journ.*, vol. vi. p. 319.
[¶¶] " Anc. Wilts," vol. i. p. 194, pl. xxiii., here copied. See also *Arch.*, vol. xliii. p. 467.   [***] " Anc. Wilts," vol. i. p. 199, pl. xxiv.

Everley. The interment seems to have been in the hollowed trunk of a tree, but the bones were burnt. With them was a dagger with three rivets, and this instrument, which is described as having been in a sheath of wood lined with cloth. Its purpose is difficult to determine.

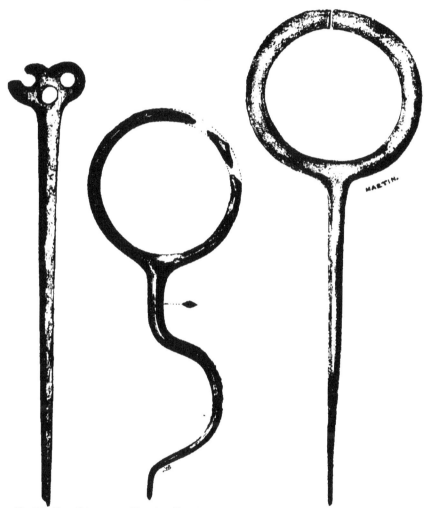

Fig. 450.—Bryn Crûg. ⅓   Fig. 451.—Taunton. ⅓   Fig. 452.—Chilton Bustle. ⅓

Another pin (4¼ inches), with a bi-lobed head and three perforations, was found with a two-looped palstave and a knife with an interment at Bryn Crûg,* near Carnarvon. It is shown in full size in Fig. 450.

Pins with large rings for their heads have occasionally been found. One such from Taunton,† 7¾ inches, is shown in Fig. 451. It was found

* *Arch. Journ.*, vol. xxv. p. 246. I am indebted to the Institute for the use of this cut.

† *Arch. Journ.*, vol. xxxvii. p. 94. Pring, "Brit. and Rom. Taunton," pl. ii.

with palstaves, a socketed celt, rings, and other objects.
The part forming the pin is bent, it would appear intentionally, but for what purpose it is difficult to guess.

Another with a straight pin was found at Chilton Bustle,[*]
Somersetshire. The annular part is divided in the middle,
and is flat and thin. It is shown full size in Fig. 452.

Another object of a similar character, but with the ring
larger (being oval and 4½ inches by 3 inches) and with the
pin part shorter, was found in a barrow between Lewes and
Brighton,[†] with a long pin, to be subsequently mentioned,
and a pair of looped bronze bracelets, like Fig. 482. These
are now in the museum at Alnwick Castle. Another (6
inches, with ring 2 inches in diameter), probably from a
Wiltshire barrow,[‡] is in the collection at Stourhead.

A pin of the same character from the Lake-dwellings of
Savoy has been figured by Rabut.[§]

Another form has a smaller ring at the top, and the pin
beneath is usually curved. Fig. 453, from Wilde,[||] shows
an example of this kind. One of the two pins reported to
have been found with bronze bridles and buckles of "Late
Celtic" character, as well as with a bronze lance-head and
socketed celt, at Hagbourn Hill,[¶] Berks, was of this type.
The other had a flat head.

I have a pin of the same kind (4¼ inches) found at Holt,[**]
Worcestershire. It has, however, a small cross, formed of
five knobs, attached to the front of the ring. It was found
in the bed of the Severn, and was presented to me by Mr.
G. Edwards, C.E. The pins of this character seem to belong
to quite the close of the Bronze Period, if
not indeed to the "Late Celtic."

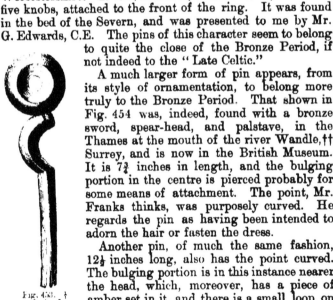

A much larger form of pin appears, from
its style of ornamentation, to belong more
truly to the Bronze Period. That shown in
Fig. 454 was, indeed, found with a bronze
sword, spear-head, and palstave, in the
Thames at the mouth of the river Wandle,[††]
Surrey, and is now in the British Museum.
It is 7¾ inches in length, and the bulging
portion in the centre is pierced probably for
some means of attachment. The point, Mr.
Franks thinks, was purposely curved. He
regards the pin as having been intended to
adorn the hair or fasten the dress.

Another pin, of much the same fashion,
12½ inches long, also has the point curved.
The bulging portion is in this instance nearer
the head, which, moreover, has a piece of
amber set in it, and there is a small loop on

Fig. 453.
Ireland.

Fig. 454.
River Wandle.

* Arch. Journ., vol. ix. p. 106.   † Suss. Arch. Coll., vol. ii. p. 265.
‡ Arch., vol. xliii. p. 469.   § 2ème Mém., " Album," pl. xi. 17. || Fig. 452.
¶ Arch., vol. xvi. p. 348, pl. l.   ** Allies, " Worc.," p. 149, pl. iv. 7.
†† Arch. Journ., vol. ix. p. 8. I am indebted to Mr. Franks for the use of this cut.

the side of the pin, as in Fig. 457, instead of a hole through the bulging part. This specimen was found in a mine near the river Fowey,* at a depth of ten fathoms from the surface, when a new work was begun for searching after tin ore.

The long pin already mentioned as found in a barrow near Lewes † has an expanded head with a boss upon it, and about 4 inches below, an ornamented lozenge-shaped plate, beneath which is a small loop for attachment.

Large pins of the same character have been found in the Lake-dwellings of France, Switzerland, and Italy.

A large bronze pin, 13¼ inches long, found on Salisbury Plain,‡ is described as having a flattened head, ornamented on one side with a pattern. This which is now in the British Museum is, however, of the late Celtic Period.

It is by no means impossible that these larger and heavier pins may at times have served as piercing-tools and even as weapons. The stiletto survives as a ladies' piercing-tool, but no one at the present day would "his quietus make with a bare bodkin;" though there was probably a time when both stiletto and bodkin served a double purpose, and were used, as occasion might require, either as weapons or as tools.

Smaller pins, ornamented at the blunt end, have not unfrequently been found.

A fragment of one discovered by Sir R. Colt Hoare in a barrow at Scratchbury, is engraved in his unpublished plate, and has also been figured by Dr. Thurnam, F.S.A.,§ in his memoir so often quoted. It

Fig. 455.
Scratchbury. ‡

Fig. 456.
Camerton. §

is here reproduced as Fig. 455. Another from a barrow at Camerton,‖ Somerset, has a hollow spheroidal head, with a double perforation. The head and upper part of the stem are decorated with parallel rings and oblique hatching, as may be seen in Fig. 456. In character this pin much resembles some of those from the Swiss Lake-dwellings.

A very similar pin was obtained from a barrow near Firle,¶ Sussex, by Dr. Mantell.

A fine pin, nearly 12 inches long, with a head of this shape, was found near Enniskillen. The upper part of the pin is ornamented with groups

* *Arch.*, vol. xii. p. 414, pl. li. 8.   † *Suss. Arch. Coll.*, vol. ii. p. 260.
‡ *Proc. Soc. Ant.*, 2nd S., vol. iii. p. 469.
§ *Arch.*, vol. xliii. p. 468. I am indebted to the Council of the Soc. Ant. for this and the next cut.
‖ *Proc. Som. Arch. Soc.*, vol. viii. p. 45.
¶ Dr. Thurnam, *ubi sup.* (Horsfield, "Lewes," vol. i. 48, pl. iii. 12).

of five small beadings round it, and between these are spiral ribs, forming many threaded screws alternately right- and left-handed.*

A long pin from Galway,† of which the lower part is twisted into a spiral, has a head with a notch in it, much like that of a modern screw.

The pins with spherical heads, ornamented by circular holes, with concentric circles around them, so common in the Swiss Lake-dwell-

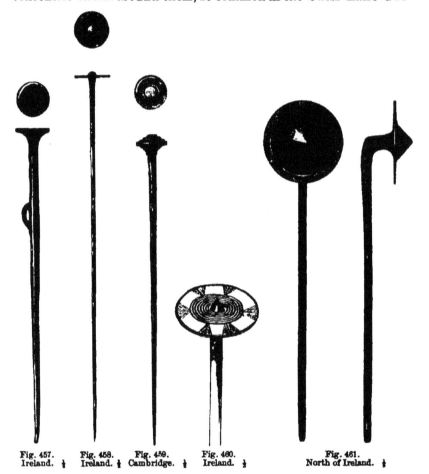

Fig. 457.   Fig. 458.   Fig. 459.   Fig. 460.   Fig. 461.
Ireland. ⅓   Ireland. ⅓ Cambridge. ⅓   Ireland. ⅓   North of Ireland. ⅓

ings, are as yet unknown in Britain. I have, nevertheless, a portion of what appears to be the large spherical head of a pin, which formed part of the hoard found at Dreuil, near Amiens. Instead of holes, however, it has bosses at intervals, with concentric circles round them. In the spaces between are bands of parallel dotted lines.‡

* *Journ. R. Hist. Arch. Assoc. of Ireland*, 4 Sec. vol. v. p. 97.
† *Arch.*, vol. xv. p. 394, pl. xxxiv. 5.   ‡ Like Keller, "Lake-dwellings," pl. xxxiv. 2.

Some of the Swiss pins have knobs of tin, or some other metal than bronze, and even red stones inlaid in the perforations, so that not improbably those which now show merely holes in the metal may have been inlaid with horn or some perishable material.

Pins with flat heads, sometimes of large size, are of not unfrequent occurrence, and appear to belong to the Bronze Age.

An Irish example with a small loop at the side is shown in Fig. 457, from a specimen in my own collection. It has apparently at some time been longer. Some German pins * are provided with side loops in the same manner.

A large pin, 8½ inches, with the upper part beaded, and with a small side loop, was in the hoard found near Amiens, and is preserved in the museum of that town. With it were socketed celts, a sickle, &c.

A pin of the same general form, but without any loop and with a more ornamental head, also from Ireland, is shown in Fig. 458, and an English example, found near Cambridge, in Fig. 459.

One with a plain flat head, and 11¾ inches long, is figured by Wilde (Fig. 446).

Similar pins with flat heads have been found in the Lake-dwellings of Savoy and Switzerland.

The large flat heads are often highly ornamented.

The pin from Ireland, of which the head is shown in Fig. 460,† one-third of the actual size, is 13½ inches long. This cut and Figs. 453, 462, 463, and 465, are kindly lent by the Royal Irish Academy.

The ornamental expanded heads, which usually have a conical projection in the centre, are more frequently turned over so as to be in the same plane as the pins and be visible when stuck into a garment. Fig. 461 is from a specimen of my own found in the North of Ireland.

Fig. 462, from Wilde,‡ shows a small pin of the same kind, found at Keelogue Ford.

Occasionally the head seems disproportionately large to the pin. That of which the highly ornamented head is shown in Fig. 463,§ is only 5¼ inches long, while the head itself is 2¼ inches in diameter.

A grand pin of this kind from Ireland, with the head 4½ inches in diameter, and the pin 10¾ inches long, is in the British Museum. The face of the disc has five concentric circles upon it, with triangles, squares, and ring ornaments between them.

Fig. 462.—Keelogue Ford. ⅓   Fig. 463.—Ireland. ½

---

* Lisch, "Freder. Francisc.," Tab. xxiv. 5, 6.   † "Catal. Mus. R. I. A.," fig. 447.
‡ *Op. cit.*, p. 558, fig. 449; *Journ. Arch. Assoc. of Scot.*, 2nd S., vol. i. p. 194.
§ Wilde, fig. 448.

A Scottish specimen of the same character as Fig. 462 (9 inches), found at Tarves, Aberdeenshire, together with bronze swords, is in the same collection. The head is 1⅜ inches in diameter. Another of the same type from Ireland * is said to have had the cone originally gilt.

The head of another, which was found with a number of bronze swords at Edinburgh,† is shown in Fig. 464. This discovery seems to prove that the pins of this type belong to quite the latter part of the Bronze Period.

Pins with flat heads turned over so as to lie parallel with their stems are of common occurrence in Denmark.‡ They are usually ornamented with concentric ribs, and the heads are sometimes plated with gold. The stems are also often decorated.

Another form of pin has a cup-shaped head, not unlike the termination

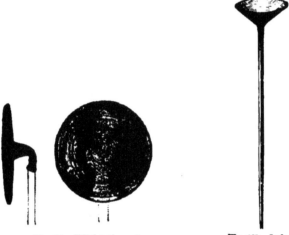

Fig. 464.—Edinburgh.   ½   Fig. 465.—Ireland.   ½

of the large gold clasps, like drawer-handles, so frequently found in Ireland. One of these is shown in Fig. 465, borrowed from Wilde.§

An example of this kind was found in the Heathery Burn Cave. Another pin of this type, 10½ inches long, with the cup-shaped head ⅞ inch in diameter and ⅓ inch deep, with a small cone projecting in the bottom of the cup, was found with a bronze sword and two spear-heads in peat near the Point of Sleat,‖ Skye.

Sir W. Wilde has given figures of numerous other types of pins, but they nearly all belong to a later period than that of which I am treating. That from a brooch at Bowermadden, Caithness, engraved in the *Proceedings of the Society of Antiquaries of Scotland,*¶ is also of later date. Altogether the subject of pins belonging to the Bronze Age in the British Islands is one of

* *Journ. Arch. Assoc. of Ireland,* 2nd S., vol. i. p. 194.
† *Proc. Soc. Ant. Scot.,* N.S. vol. i. p. 322. For the loan of this block I am indebted to the Council of the Society.
‡ Worsaae, " Nord. Olds.," fig. 239.   § "Catal. Mus. R. I. A.," p. 558, fig. 450.
‖ *Proc. Soc. Ant. Scot.,* vol. iii. p. 102.   ¶ Vol. ix. p. 247.

which, in the present state of our knowledge, it is difficult to treat satisfactorily, so few of the more highly developed types having been found in actual association with other bronze relics. In England especially the rarity of bronze pins, as compared, for instance, with their abundance in the Lake-dwellings of Southern Europe, is very striking. As will subsequently be seen, there is nearly as great a scarcity of bracelets and of some other ornaments. It may be that for personal decorations the jet and amber, which during our Bronze Age were so much in fashion for ornaments, suited the native taste better than decorations manufactured from the same metal as that which served for tools and weapons; and that when metal was used gold had the preference. At the same time, for useful articles, such as some kinds of pins, bronze may well have served, and it is to be observed that no pins decorated with gold have as yet been found with bronze weapons in Britain, though they have occurred in other countries.

CHAPTER XVIII.

TORQUES, BRACELETS, RINGS, EAR-RINGS, AND PERSONAL ORNAMENTS.

ALTHOUGH some of the pins described in the last chapter were destined for ornament rather than for use, they cannot as a class be regarded as purely ornamental. The collars and armlets, to which the present chapter is to be devoted, must, I think, be considered as essentially ornaments, though possibly in some cases affording protection to the neck and arms. The modern epaulette was originally intended for the protection of the shoulder, though now, as a rule, little better than an ornament.

The torque, or torc, takes its name from the Latin *torques*, which again is derived *à torquendo*. This word *torques* was applied to a twisted collar of gold or other metal worn around the neck. Among the ancient Gauls gold torques appear to have been abundant, and to have formed an important part of the spoils acquired from them by their Roman conquerors. About 223 B.C.,[*] when Flaminius Nepos gained his victory over the Gauls on the Addua, it is related that instead of the Gauls dedicating, as they had intended, a torque made from the spoils of the Roman soldiers to their god of war, Flaminius erected to Jupiter a golden trophy made from the Gaulish *torques*. The name of the Torquati, a family of the Manlia Gens, was derived from their ancestor, T. Manlius,[†] having in B.C. 361 slain a gigantic Gaul in single combat, whose torque he took from the dead body after cutting off the head, and placed it around his own neck.

On some of the denarii of the Manlia family [‡] the torque forms a circle round the head of Rome on the obverse. Two interesting papers "On the Torc of the Celts," by Dr. Samuel Birch, will be found in the *Archæological Journal.*[§]

Although these gold torques in many instances undoubtedly

---

[*] Florus, lib. ii. c. 4.
[‡] Cohen, " Méd. Cons.," pl. xxvi. 5.
[†] Aulus Gellius, lib. ix. c. 13.
[§] Vol. ii. p. 368; vol. iii. p. 27.

belong to the Bronze Period, they are sufficiently well known to antiquaries to render it needless for me here to enter into any minute.
description of them. The commonest form presents a cruciform
section, so that the twist is that of a four-threaded screw, and at
either end there is a plain, nearly cylindrical bar, turned back so
as to form a kind of hook. I have a fine example of this kind of
torque, found with a bronze anvil (Fig. 217) and other bronze

Fig. 466.—Wedmore. ½

instruments and weapons at Fresné la Mère, Calvados. A similar
but smaller gold torque was found near Boyton, Suffolk,* which is
said to have had the extremities secured together by two small
penannular rings of gold, embracing the two terminal hooks.

One 42 inches long was found on Cader Idris ;† others in
Glamorganshire ;‡ at Pattingham, Staffordshire ;§ and in several
other parts of Britain. Some fine examples of these funicular

* *Arch.*, vol. xxvi. p. 471.   † *Arch.*, vol. xxi. p. 557.
‡ *Op. cit.*, vol. xxvi. p. 464.   § *Op. cit.*, vol. xiv. p. 96.

torques of gold, as well as of other varieties of the same kind of ornament, are in the Museum of the Royal Irish Academy at Dublin.*

The torques formed of bronze are, as a rule, thicker and bulkier in their proportions than those of gold, and the ends are usually left straight or but slightly hooked over so as to interlock. They are never provided with the projecting cylindrical ends already mentioned.

The form most frequently discovered in the British Islands is

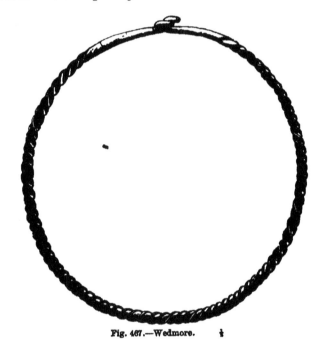

Fig. 467.—Wedmore.   ¼

that known as funicular, one of which is shown in Fig. 466, copied from the *Archæological Association Journal.*†

The original was found with two others at Wedmore, Somersetshire. One of these is of the same type, but of smaller size, and not quite so closely twisted, as shown in Fig. 467; and the other is made of a flat ribbon of metal, ⅜ inch broad, twisted, as shown in Fig. 469, which is copied from the same plate as Figs. 466 and 467.

From another account of these torques,‡ it appears that they were found near Heath House, in the parish of Wedmore, and that with them were two celts and a few amber beads strung on a wire. This latter, to me, sounds doubtful, as the wire is probably a later addition. The weight of

* See Wilde's "Catal.," p. 70, *et seqq.;* and "Vetusta. Monum.," vol. v. pl. xxix.
† Vol. xxi. pl. xii. 2.   ‡ *Arch. Journ.,* vol. vi. p. 81.

the largest is said to be ½ pound, of the second 2 ounces, and of the smallest 1½ ounce.

Another torque of the character of Fig. 466, about 9 inches in diameter, was found with a bracelet, Fig. 481, and a two-looped palstave, Fig. 87, at West Buckland, Somersetshire,* and is in the collection of Mr. W. A. Sanford. It is shown on the scale of one-third in Fig. 468.

A portion of another torque, but of slender make, was found at Pen Pits,† in the same county; and another, somewhat imperfect, near Edington Burtle.‡ With the latter was a portion of a ribbon torque like Fig. 469, two bracelets, some rings, and four palstaves.

Two very fine torques, like Fig. 468, 8¾ inches in diameter, were also found in Somersetshire on the Quantock Hills,§ in 1794. Within each of

Fig. 468.—West Buckland.　⅓

them is said to have been placed a looped palstave, like Fig. 77. The weight of one of the torques is reported to have been nearly 2 pounds.

In the collection of the Rev. E. Duke, of Lake House, near Salisbury, are two fine torques of this kind, one large and heavy, and the other smaller and more slender, which were found near Amesbury. With them were several spiral rings closely resembling Fig. 489.

Two others found with armillæ in Dorsetshire ‖ are now in the British Museum. The larger of these is closely twisted, and about 7½ inches in diameter. The smaller is thicker, and shows a coarser twist, and is about 6¾ inches in diameter. The armillæ are penannular and of rhomboidal section.

* *Arch. Journ.*, vol. xxxvii. p. 107, whence this cut is lent by the Council.
† *Som. Arch. and Nat. Hist. Soc. Proc.*, vol. vii. p. 27.
‡ *Op. cit.*, vol. v. 1854, p. 91.　　　　§ *Arch.*, vol. xiv. p. 94, pl. xxiii.
‖ *Proc. Soc. Ant.*, vol. i. p. 234.

Two small torques, some bronze rings or bracelets, and a palstave are recorded to have been dug up in Woolmer Forest, Hants.* Two spiral rings were found with them.

In the collection of Mr. Durden, at Blandford, are several specimens found at Spetisbury, Dorset. †

I have a thin torque about 6¼ inches in diameter, but unfortunately broken, found in Burwell Fen, Cambridgeshire.

In some instances the plain ends of the torque are left without hooks. Such is the case with the fine collar found, with four looped armlets and a palstave without loop, at Hollingbury Hill,‡ near Brighton, which is now in the British Museum. On each extremity was a spiral ring of

Fig. 469.—Wedmore.   ¼

bronze, considerably larger than the rod forming the torque, and a third ring is shown in the published drawing. The palstave, which is broken in the middle, apparently on purpose, lay within the circle of the torque, which also was broken across the middle. At regular intervals round it lay the four bracelets, which resemble Fig. 482, and vary somewhat in weight.

The third of the torques already mentioned as found at Wedmore is shown in Fig. 469.

It is of a type which occurs more frequently in gold than in bronze, and in the former metal has often been found in Scotland. Several such were discovered under a large stone at Urquhart, Elginshire. Others have been found at Culter, Lanarkshire; § Belhelvie, Aber-

* *Arch. Assoc. Journ.*, vol. vi. p. 88.   † *Arch. Assoc. Journ.*, vol. xxi. p. 232.
‡ *Arch. Journ.*, vol. v. p. 323; *Arch.*, vol. xxix. 372; *Suss. Arch. Coll.*, vol. ii. p. 267.
§ *Arch. Assoc. Journ.*, vol. xvii. p. 211, pl. xxi. 2.

deenshire; Little Lochbroom, Ross-shire; Rannoch, Perthshire; and elsewhere. Some of these are in the Antiquarian Museum at Edinburgh.

There are three or four such in the Museum of the Royal Irish Academy.

A gold torque of this class found at Clonmacnoise,* King's County, has oval balls at each end instead of hooks.

So far as at present known, the funicular torques of bronze are more abundant in the southern and western counties than in the other parts of England. They appear to be unknown both in

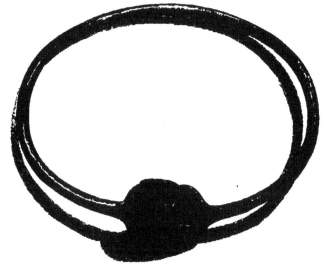

Fig. 470.—Yarnton.   ½

Scotland and Ireland, though torques of Late Celtic patterns occur in those countries.

The inference is that, although socketed celts are rarely if ever found with them, these twisted neck-rings belong to the close of the Bronze Period, and were introduced into Britain from the Continent. The form is, however, rare in the North of France, and the nearest analogues to the English torques with which we are acquainted are to be seen among those from Northern Germany and Denmark.

The Danish form, with broad expanding ends terminating in spirals, and the derivatives from it in which the spirals are represented by solid cast plates with volutes upon them, are nevertheless unknown in Britain, as is also that with the twist alternately to the right and to the left.

* Wilde, " Catal. Mus. R. I. A.," p. 74, fig. 603.

Another form of bronze torque found in Britain is made from a plain piece of wire, hammered out at each end into a broad, nearly quadrangular, plate.

That shown in Fig. 470 lay near the head of a contracted skeleton at Yarnton, four miles from Oxford, at a spot which seems to have been a prehistoric cemetery. I obtained it through the kindness of Professor Rolleston when visiting the place. The ends are ornamented by hammer marking. In a line with the wire forming the torque is a slightly raised flat band perpendicularly fluted; the expanding parts above and below are fluted horizontally. A herald would engrave "azure, a fesse gules" in the same manner, but with the lines much closer together. Two torques of the same character, found at Lumphanan, Aberdeenshire, are in the Antiquarian Museum at Edinburgh.

The form probably belongs to the close of the Bronze Period, if not indeed to the Late Celtic or Early Iron Age.

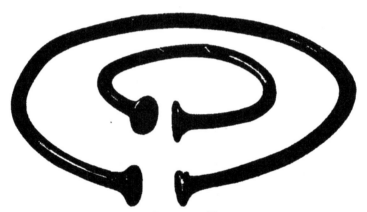

Fig. 471.—Montgomeryshire.   ⅓

A torque about 5 inches in diameter, described as of copper, made of a simple wire, with the ends turned back so as to form hooks, and on each a lenticular button of metal, was found near Winslow, Bucks, * and may also be Late Celtic.

Another form of torque is made from a stout wire expanding into small flat discs at the end, a type which is also common among bracelets both in bronze and gold. A torque of this kind, together with a bracelet, is shown in Fig. 471, kindly lent by the Council of the Society of Antiquaries.

These objects were found with seven others in the parish of Llanrhaiadar-yn-Mochnant, Montgomeryshire.† One of them is said to have had pendants upon it. Several of them were too small to have served as torques for the neck, and were most probably bracelets or anklets. To these penannular ornaments I shall have to refer further on.

* *Arch.*, vol. xi. p. 429, pl. xix. 3.
† *Proc. Soc. Ant.*, 2nd S., vol. iv. p. 467; "Montgom. Coll.," vol. iii. p. 419; vol. iv. p. 247.

The other varieties of torques found in Britain seem decidedly to belong to the Late Celtic rather than to the Bronze Period, so that a brief notice of them will suffice. They are frequently made in two halves, hinged or dowelled together, and are often decorated with a series of ornamental beads.

A collar found in Lochar Moss, Dumfries-shire, is now in the British Museum.* About one-third of it is formed by a solid piece of bronze of flat section, having the face ornamented with a peculiar wavy pattern and the outer rim with cabled lines. The rest consists of fluted melon-like beads with pulley-shaped collars between them. They appear to have been strung on an iron wire.

A portion of another collar found at Perdeswell,† Claines, near Worcester, has the iron wire still preserved. The ornamental beads are flatter, with leaf-shaped projections upon them, and between them are smaller pulley-like beads.

Another, formed in much the same fashion as that from Lochar Moss, was found at Mow-road, Rochdale, Lancashire. ‡ This was in halves, dowelled together with iron pins.

Another, entirely of bronze, is made in two pieces, one part resembling a row of beads, the other engraved like a closely plaited cord, and was found at Embsay, near Skipton, Yorkshire. §

A torque, weighing no less than 3 lbs. 10 ozs. avoirdupois, was found in the parish of Wraxall, Somerset.‖ This also is in halves, with pins to form the joint. It is described as appearing to have been adorned with precious stones. Possibly, like some other objects of Late Celtic manufacture, it may have been inlaid with enamel of different colours.

Bracelets of the same type as the torque and bracelet shown in Fig. 471 have not unfrequently been found in Britain, though, perhaps, they are less common in bronze than in the more precious metal, gold.

They are sometimes slightly hollowed at the expanding ends. One found with the hoard at Marden, Kent,¶ is of this kind. Another plain penannular bracelet tapers off at the ends instead of expanding. This latter is too small for an adult person.

One found, with various other bronze relics, at Ty Mawr, on Holyhead Mountain,** expands at one end and tapers at the other. As is often the case, the inner side of the ring is flatter than the outer.

One, 2⅜ inches by 2 inches inside, expanding at each end, was in the Heathery Burn Cave hoard. Some others were also found there.

In some instances the section of the metal, instead of being rounded, is nearly square. Two such, tapering towards the ends, were found in Dorsetshire,†† with the torques already mentioned, and are now in the British Museum.

* *Arch.*, vol. xxxiv. p. 83, pl. xi.; *Proc. Soc. Ant.*, vol. ii. p. 148; *Arch.*, xxxii. p. 400.
† *Arch.*, vol. xxx. p. 554.
‡ *Arch.*, vol. xxv. p. 595; *Arch. Journ.*, vol. xviii. p. 167.
§ *Arch.*, vol. xxxi. p. 517, pl. xxiii; *Arch. Journ.*, vol. iii. p. 32.
‖ *Arch.*, vol. xxx. p. 521.
¶ *Arch. Assoc. Journ.*, vol. xiv. p. 258, pl. xiii. 2, 3.
** *Arch. Journ.*, vol. x. p. 367; vol. xxiv. p. 254.
†† *Proc. Soc. Ant.*, vol. i. p. 234.

Three plain penannular bracelets were in the hoard of palstaves and socketed celts found at Wallington, Northumberland.

Several have been found in Scotland. Two such bracelets, the one slender and the other thick, were found at Achtertyre, Morayshire,* in company with a socketed celt, a spear-head, Fig. 383, another spear-head,

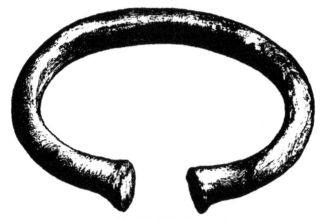

Fig. 472.—Achtertyre.   ⅓

and some fragments of other bracelets and of tin. One of these is shown full-size in Fig. 472.

Another, 2¼ inches in greatest diameter, slightly thickened at the extremities, was found in a peat moss at Conage, Banffshire.†

Other penannular armlets, one of which is shown as Fig. 473, were

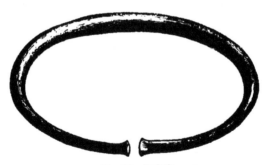

Fig. 473.—Redhill.   ⅓

found with socketed celts at Redhill, Premnay, Aberdeenshire, ‡ and are now in the Antiquarian Museum at Edinburgh; as is another found with burnt bones near Preston Tower, East Lothian.

This very simple penannular form of bracelet is found all over the world, and is indeed the form of necessity adopted wherever it became the fashion to wear thick metal wire round the arm. It was common

* *Proc. Soc. Ant. Scot.*, vol. ix. p. 435.   † *P. S. A. S.*, vol. iv. p. 377.
‡ *P. S. A. S.*, vol. i. p. 138.

among the ancient Assyrians, and several bronze bracelets of this form from Tel Sifr, in South Babylonia, are in the British Museum. The hammered copper bracelets of North America * are usually penannular.

Two very massive penannular armlets, formed of rounded bronze fully ¼ inch in diameter, and weighing about 12 ozs. each, were found with an agate bead and a spindle-whorl in a tumulus near Peninnis Head, in the Scilly Isles.† One of these is shown in Fig. 474.

An imperfect armlet of thick bronze wire was found in a barrow at Wetton, ‡ by the late Mr. Bateman.

Four plain armillæ of bronze found with the spiral ring, Fig. 489, and with a palstave, in Woolmer Forest, Hants. are also in the Bateman Collection. § As already mentioned, two small torques and a celt are said to have been found with them. ‖

Ornamented bracelets, such as have been found in abundance in the

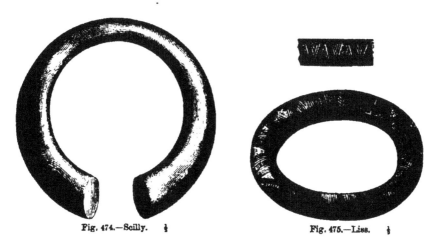

Fig. 474.—Scilly. ½   Fig. 475.—Liss. ½

Swiss Lake-dwellings, and such as are common in most continental countries, are scarce in Britain.

In the British Museum are two bracelets, slightly oval in section, and engraved with parallel lines, chevrons, &c., as will be seen by Fig. 475. They were found at Liss, Hampshire. Though the two ends are brought more closely together than usual in continental examples, the general character of these bracelets is much like that of some French and German specimens. The *patina* upon them closely resembles that on the celt Fig. 17, also found at Liss; so they were probably deposited together.

A curious penannular armlet with flat broad ends, and ornamented with punctured markings, was found with another armlet of smaller diameter, but plain, more massive, and broader, together with the remains

---

* Schoolcraft, "Ethn. Res.," vol. i. p. 92; Squier and Davis, "Anc. Mon. Miss. Vall.," p. 204.

† *Arch. Journ.*, vol. ix. p. 96; *Proc. Soc. Ant.*, 2nd S., vol. v. pp. 406, 422; Borlase, "Nænia Corn.," p. 162.

‡ "Ten Years' Digg.," p. 167.

§ "Catal.," p. 22; *Proc. Soc. Ant.*, vol. ii. p. 83.

‖ *Arch. Assoc. Journ.*, vol. vi. p. 88.

of a skeleton, at Stoke Prior,* Worcestershire. It is now in the British Museum, and is represented in Fig. 476. It may belong to a later period than that of which I am treating, and is possibly Saxon.

Fig. 477, kindly lent by the Council of the Society of Antiquaries of Scotland, shows another form of armlet, made from a bar of nearly semi-

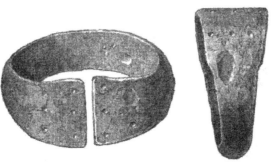

Fig. 476.—Stoke Prior.   ⅓

circular section, bent into a circular form. The original, together with another of the same kind, were found near Stobo Castle,† Peebles-shire, beneath a flat stone, and lying on a large boulder, under which was a collection of small stones, burnt and with apparently calcined bones among them.

Another armlet (3 inches) of the same type was found with an urn

Fig. 477.—Stobo Castle.   ⅓

containing burnt bones in a cairn in the parish of Lanark.‡ A bronze spear-head is stated to have been found with it.

One of the bracelets from the find at Camenz,§ in Saxony, is of nearly the same type.

Two circular armlets, one with the ends slightly apart, were found in Dorsetshire, one in the parish of Milton.‖ I have an imperfect armlet of this kind, found with a palstave, at Winterhay Green, Ilminster, Somerset.

* *Arch. Journ.*, vol. xx. p. 200. The Council of the Institute have kindly lent this figure.

† *Proc. Soc. Ant. Scot.*, vol. ii. p. 277.

‡ *Arch. Assoc. Journ.*, vol. xvii. p. 111, pl. xii. 2; vol. x. p. 8.

§ *Proc. Soc. Ant.*, 2nd S., vol. iii. p. 332.

‖ "Barrow Diggers," p. 77, pl. v. 14, 15.

A penannular armlet of bronze, with compressed oval knobs at the extremities, was found by Mr. F. C. Lukis, with a jet armlet, in the cromlech of *La Roche qui sonne*,* in Guernsey, and is shown in Fig. 478. The scale has been said to be one-third, though from information kindly furnished to me by the Rev. W. C. Lukis, F.S.A., it appears to be one-half.

A somewhat different and more elegantly ornamented armlet from Cornwall † is shown in Fig. 479.

A bronze armilla, made from a flat ribbon of metal, ½ inch broad, and

Fig. 478.—Guernsey. ½

Fig. 479.—Cornwall. ½

ornamented outside with a neatly engraved lozengy pattern, was found with an interment in a barrow at Castern,‡ near Wetton, Staffordshire.

Another, about 1½ inch wide, ornamented with four parallel bands of vertical lines, with chevrons at the end, was found in a barrow at Normanton,§ Wilts, encircling the arm of a skeleton, and is shown in Fig. 480. In this example the ends overlap.

Another, with a series of small longitudinal beads or mouldings upon it, was found near Lake, Wilts, and is in the collection of the Rev. E. Duke. Some plain penannular bracelets from that district are in the same collection.

An armlet of nearly the same character, but narrower, was found in Thor's Cave,‖ near Wetton, Derbyshire. Remains of Late Celtic and of Roman date were found in the same cave.

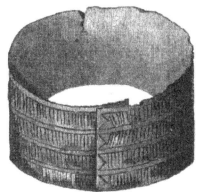

Fig. 480.—Normanton. ½

A fluted bracelet was found with rings and other objects at Edington Burtle, Somersetshire.¶

A bracelet of bronze, of which some of the fragments are represented in Fig. 481, was found with a bronze torque and a two-looped palstave

* *Arch. Assoc. Journ.*, vol. iii. p. 344 (I am indebted to the Council for the use of this cut); *Arch.*, vol. xxxv. p. 247; "Anc. Stone Imp.," p. 417.
† *Proc. Soc. Ant.*, 2nd S., vol. v. pp. 406, 430.
‡ Bateman, "Ten Years' Dig.," p. 167.
§ Hoare's "Anc. Wilts," vol. i. p. 160; *Arch.*, vol. xliii. p. 469, fig. 172. I am indebted to the Council of the Soc. Ant. for the use of this cut.
‖ "Reliquary," vol. vi. p. 211, pl. xx. 1; Dawkins, "Cave Hunting," p. 129.
¶ *Som. Arch. and Nat. Hist. Soc. Proc.*, vol. v. 1854, p. 91.

at West Buckland,* Somersetshire. It is flat on the inside, so that the ornaments appear to have been cast in a mould, though subsequently the more delicate work was added by means of punches or gravers.

Another form of bracelet, probably of earlier date than some of those represented in the previous figures, is of the type shown in Fig. 482. It consists of a long bar of bronze, either circular or subquadrangular in section, doubled over so as to leave a broad loop in the middle, and then curved round so as to form the bracelet, the two ends of the bar being bent over to form a hook, which engages in the central loop. That

Fig. 481.—West Buckland. ½

shown in the figure was formerly in the collection of the late Sir Walter Trevelyan, and is now in the British Museum. As will be seen, the edges are in some parts minutely serrated. The original was discovered with two others, and a ring of the same metal, in a moss at Ham Cross, near Crawley, Sussex.

Four others, forming two pairs, neatly placed round a torque, were found at Hollingbury Hill,† near Brighton, as already described. They are now in the British Museum. I have seen two others of the same kind which were found at Pyecombe, Sussex. They are in the collection

Fig. 482.—Ham Cross. ½

Fig. 483.—Heathery Burn. ½

of Mrs. Dickinson, of Hurstpierpoint. Another was found in a barrow near Brighton,‡ with the long pin already mentioned, and is now at Alnwick Castle. This was slightly ornamented with a kind of herring-bone pattern.

Bracelets constructed on the same principle are sometimes formed of much thinner wire. One from the Heathery Burn Cave,§ already so often mentioned, is shown in Fig. 483.

* Arch. Journ., vol. xxxvii. p. 107. I am indebted to the Institute for the use of this cut. See Figs. 468 and 87.
† Arch. Journ., vol. v. p. 323.
‡ Arch. Assoc. Journ., vol. i. p. 148; Suss. Arch. Coll., vol. ii. p. 260.
§ Proc. Soc. Ant., 2nd S., vol. ii. p. 131. For the use of this cut I am indebted to the Council of the Society.

Another of the same size and character, but made of even thinner wire, was found with a bronze razor, a button, and other antiquities, in the bed of a stream near Llangwyllog Church,* Anglesea. These objects are now in the British Museum. The type is not confined to Britain, for a bracelet clasping in the same manner was found in the Lac du Bourget.†

Penannular bracelets, like Fig. 473, with the ends slightly expanding, have been not unfrequently found in Ireland. One engraved by Wilde ‡ is described as of pure red copper.

In many there are large cup-shaped ends at about right angles to each other. One from Co. Cavan is shown in Fig. 484. I have another of the same type, but much smaller and lighter, from Ballymoney, Co. Antrim.

They much resemble the manillas or ring-money in use on the West Coast of Africa, but are more cup-shaped at the ends. It appears possible

Fig. 484.—Co. Cavan.   ⸸   Fig. 485.—Cowlam.   ⸸

that, like some large Irish rings which will subsequently be described, they are not actually bracelets. The other armillæ engraved by Wilde appear to be of later date than the Bronze Period. The same may be said of the elegant bracelet shown full size in Fig. 485, which is certainly Late Celtic. It was found by Canon Greenwell, F.R.S., on the right arm of a female skeleton in a barrow at Cowlam,§ Yorkshire, and is similar to some found at Arras,‖ in the same county.

Another somewhat plainer bracelet, with a short dowel at one end, fitting into a socket at the other, so as to form an almost invisible joint, was found with a fibula, Fig. 498, on the skeleton of an aged woman in another of the Cowlam¶ barrows, and is shown in Fig. 486.

Another bronze armlet of the same period was found in a barrow in the parish of Crosby Garrett,** Westmoreland. It encircled the right arm of a skeleton, and is penannular, "oval in section, and unornamented, except in having a series of notches along both edges."

* *Arch. Journ.*, vol. xxii. p. 74.
† Perrin, "Etude. préh. sur la Sav.," pl. xviii. 6.
‡ "Catal. Mus. R. I. A.," p. 570, fig. 479.   § "British Barrows," p. 210.
‖ "Cran. Brit.," pl. xii. B 4 ; *Arch.*, vol. xliii. p. 474.
¶ Greenwell's "British Barrows," p. 209.   ** *Op. cit.*, p. 386.

Many bracelets of Late Celtic date have been found at various times in Scotland. Some of these are of very ornate design, and extremely massive; while on others a *repoussé* pattern has been worked upon a plate of thin bronze. Such bracelets hardly come within the scope of the present work, but a few references to engravings of them are subjoined :—

Aboyne, Aberdeenshire (*Arch. Journ.*, vol. xxii. p. 74 ; Wilson's "Preh. Ann. of Scot.," vol. ii. pp. 136, 139).

Alvah, Banffshire (*Proc. Soc. Ant. Scot.*, vol. vi. p. 11, pl. iii. 1).

Muthill, Perthshire, now in the British Museum (*Arch.*, vol. xxviii. p. 435).

Plunton Castle, Kirkcudbright (*Arch. Journ.*, vol. xvi. p. 194 ; *Proc. Soc. Ant. Scot.*, vol. iii. p. 236).

Strathdon, Aberdeenshire (*Proc. Soc. Ant. Scot.*, vol. vi. p. 13, pl. iii. 2).

Fig. 486.—Cowlam.   ½

Among hoards of bronze antiquities belonging to the latter part of the Bronze Period, rings of various sizes are of not unfrequent occurrence. They are usually plain and of circular section, as if formed of a piece of cylindrical wire, though actually cast solid, and do not for the most part seem to require any illustrations. Some also are lozenge-shaped in section.

In the hoard found at Marden,[*] Kent, there were six perfect bronze rings, varying in diameter from $1\frac{1}{8}$ to $1\frac{3}{4}$ inch. In the Heathery Burn Cave were numerous rings of circular section, and varying in thickness from $\frac{1}{2}$ inch to $1\frac{1}{4}$ inch in diameter. Many of these are now in the collection of Canon Greenwell, F.R.S. One, $2\frac{1}{4}$ inches in diameter, was in the hoard found at Westow,[†] Yorkshire, and may have been an armlet. Several stout rings, about 1 inch in diameter, "probably cast in moulds,"

[*] *Arch. Assoc. Journ.*, vol. xiv. p. 258.   [†] *Arch. Assoc. Journ.*, vol. iii. p. 59.

were found with various other antiquities in bronze at Ty Mawr,* Holy-head, and a number of rings of various sizes, from ¾ inch to 1¼ inch in diameter, were found in the deposit at Llangwyllog,† Anglesea. There were also three small rings in the great hoard found at Pant-y-maen,‡ Glancych.

Several rings, some of lozenge-shaped section and of delicate workman-ship, were found in the hoard at Taunton, § with the pin and other objects already mentioned.

Such rings may have served various purposes, but were probably used as means of connection between different straps or accoutrements. Canon Greenwell has called my attention to two separate instances of two rings being found together, in company with a bronze sword, in one case near Medomsley, Durham, and in the other near Rothbury, Northumber-land.

The rings found with remains of chariots at Hamden Hill,‖ near Montacute, Somersetshire, appear to be of Late Celtic date, and to be hollow. A hollow ring, however, 1⅝ inch in diameter, and made from a strip of bronze, fashioned into a tube and left open on the inner side, was found with a socketed celt, a gouge, and other objects of bronze, at Mel-bourn,¶ Cambridgeshire. Many of those from the cemetery at Hallstatt are of this kind, wrought from a thin plate of metal. Some hollow rings from Ireland will subsequently be mentioned.

Fig. 487.—Ireland.   ⅓

Near Trillick,** Co. Tyrone, a pin passing transversely through the body of two rings (see Fig. 496) was found, and with it two large rings about 3¼ inches in diameter, and four smaller, about 2 inches. These latter appear to be hollow, with probably a clay core inside. With these objects a socketed celt and a bronze hammer were found.

Nearly six hundred bronze rings are in the Museum of the Royal Irish Academy.

Some of the Irish rings are cast in pairs, like a figure of 8.†† Others of large size have smaller rings cast upon them. That shown in Fig. 487, borrowed from Wilde,‡‡ is 4¼ inches in diameter, with rings of 1¼ inches diameter upon it. Sir W. Wilde was inclined to regard it as a bangle with two rings by which to suspend it, but this appears to me very doubtful. I have an almost identical example of the form from Bally-money, Co. Antrim.

A gold ring, 4¼ inches in diameter, with a single small ring playing upon it, from the great Clare find, is figured by Wilde.§§ He states that

* *Arch. Journ.*, vol. xxiv. p. 256; *Arch.*, vol. xxvi. p. 483.
† *Arch. Journ.*, vol. xxii. p. 74.   ‡ *Arch. Camb.*, 3rd S., vol. x. p. 224.
§ Pring, "The Brit. and Rom. on the Site of Taunton," p. 50.
‖ *Arch.*, vol. xxi. p. 39.   ¶ *Arch. Journ.*, vol. xi. p. 294.
** *Journ. Hist. and Arch. Assoc. of Ireland*, 3rd S., vol. i. p. 164.
†† "Vallancey," vol. iv. pl. xiv. 8; Wilde, "Catal. Mus. R. I. A.," p. 578, fig. 490.
‡‡ "Catal. Mus. R. I. A.," p. 570, fig. 480.
§§ "Catal. Mus. R. I. A.," p. 46, fig. 573.

" similar articles are occasionally observed sculptured upon the breasts of the statues of ancient Roman generals, the small ring being attached to the dress."

Some few bronze ornaments, which have been thought to be finger rings, have from time to time been found associated with other objects of the same metal, such as armlets, torques, &c.

One found with the armlets and palstaves in Woolmer Forest,* Hants, as already mentioned, is shown in Fig. 488. It has been formed from a small quadrangular bar of metal, cylindrical at the ends, twisted after the manner of an ordinary torque, and subsequently coiled into a spiral ring. Mr. Bateman † describes it as a finger ring. With it was also another twisted bronze ring of the same kind, but of only one coil. It appears doubtful whether these rings were not more of the nature of ornamental beads. It will be remembered that three spiral rings of the same kind, but plain and of about four coils each, were found on the

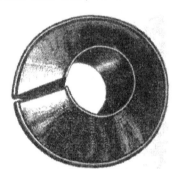

Fig. 488.—Woolmer Forest.   ‡   Fig. 489.—Dumbarton.

extremities of the torque discovered at Hollingbury Hill,‡ Sussex. They were considerably too large to fit on the torque, and were regarded as intended in some way to fasten the garment. Some rings of this kind were found with torques near Amesbury, as already mentioned. A ring of a single coil, but made from a twisted bar like that in the figure, was in the hoard found at Camenz,§ Saxony, in which also were fragments of torques.

I have three small twisted penannular rings of gold which were found with a small torque of the same metal near Carcassonne, Aude. They are of different sizes and weights, but are all too small for the finger or for ear-rings. One of them is indeed too small to pass over the re-curved end of the torque, but the ends may possibly have been pinched together since it was found. I am not aware that any of the rings were ever actually upon the torque, though I have reason to believe they were found with it.

Mr. Franks has recently presented to the British Museum a gold torque from Lincolnshire, which has three banded rings of gold, strung like beads upon it.

* *Proc. Soc. Ant.*, vol. ii. p. 83. The cut is kindly lent by the Council.
† " Catal.," p. 22.   ‡ *Sup.*, p. 378 ; *Arch. Journ.*, vol. v. p. 323.
§ *Proc. Soc. Ant.*, 2nd S., vol. iii. p. 332.

Some small penannular rings found on a gold torque at Boyton have already been mentioned.

The penannular rings so often found in Ireland, and commonly called ring money, may after all be of the nature of beads.

The large hollow penannular ornaments made of thin gold, and nearly triangular in section, seem also to be of the nature of beads or possibly clasps. Straps passed through the narrow notch would require some trouble to take out; but still such beads could be dislodged from their string without its ends being unfastened. The ornament shown in Fig. 489 was found near Dumbarton.*

Others, similar, have been found in Anglesea, Heathery Burn Cave, near Alnwick,† and in other places. They occur also in Ireland.‡ They have frequently been found associated with armlets. Some Egyptian rings of carnelian, ivory, and other materials have similar notches through them. They have, however, been regarded as ear-rings.

Bronze finger rings seem to have been in occasional use.

In a perished urn with burnt bones, found with several others, one containing a barbed flint arrow-head, in the cemetery at Stanlake,§ Oxfordshire, there was a spiral bronze finger ring of the plainest form, the only fragment of metal brought to light during nearly a month's excavations by Mr. Akerman and Mr. Stone. What may have been a finger ring was also found in the Heathery Burn Cave,‖ Durham. It is formed of stout wire, the ends expanding, and slightly overlapping each other, and is ⅞ inch in diameter.

In the hoard of bronze antiquities found near Edington Burtle,¶ Somersetshire, were several small rings; but with one exception they are hardly such as could have served for finger rings. This exceptional ring is penannular, and fluted externally like the bracelet found with it in the same hoard. The form is not unlike that of the gold ring engraved by Wilde ** as his Fig. 609.

Another form of ornament, the ear-ring, appears to have been known in Britain during the Bronze Period. In two of the barrows on the Yorkshire Wolds, explored by Canon Greenwell, F.R.S., female skeletons were found accompanied by such ornaments.

In a barrow at Cowlam,†† "touching the temporal bones, which were stained green by the contact, were two ear-rings of bronze. They have been made by beating the one end of a piece of bronze flat, and forming the other end into a pin-shaped termination. This pin had been passed through the lobe of the ear and then bent round, the other and flat end being bent over it. Thus the ear-ring must have been permanently fixed in the ear." One of these rings is, by Canon Greenwell's kindness, shown

* *Proc. Soc. Ant. Scot.*, vol. iii. p. 24, whence this cut is borrowed.
† *Arch. Journ.*, vol. xiii. p. 295.
‡ "Catal. Mus. R. I. A.," p. 36.
§ *Arch.*, vol. xxxvii. p. 368.
‖ *Proc. Soc. Ant.*, 2nd S., vol. v. p. 426.
¶ *Som. Arch. and Nat. Hist. Soc. Proc.*, vol. v. 1854, p. 91.
** "Catal. Mus. R. I. A.," p. 81.
†† "British Barrows," p. 223.

as Fig. 490, as is one from Goodmanham,* in Fig. 491.   In the latter
case there was a bronze awl, or drill, behind the head ; the ear-ring here
figured was at the right ear, and its fellow, in a more broken condition,

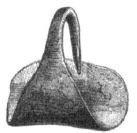   

Fig. 490.—Cowlam.   ⅓   Fig. 491.—Goodmanham.   ⅓

lay under the left shoulder.   The better preserved of the two is somewhat imperfect, and may, I think, have formed a perfect circle when
whole.

Mr. Bateman records finding in a barrow called Stakor Hill,† near

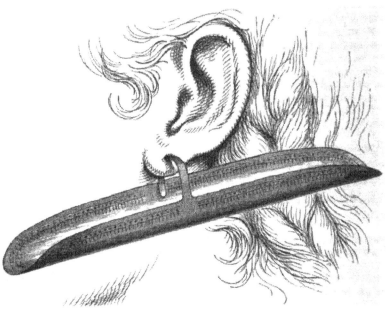

Fig. 492.—Orton.   ⅓

Burton, a female skeleton, "the mastoid bones of which were dyed
green from contact with two small pieces of thin bronze bent in the middle
just sufficiently to clasp the edge or lobe of the ear."   With the skeleton

* "Brit. Barrows," p. 324.   For Fig. 491 I am indebted to the Delegates of the
Clarendon Press.
† "Ten Years' Dig.," p. 80.

was a flint "javelin head," and Mr. Bateman considered the interment to be the oldest he had met with in which metal was present.

By way of illustration, a much longer form of trough-shaped ear-ring may be adduced, though the metal in this instance is gold and not bronze. That shown in Fig. 492 was found with another in a stone cist at Orton, Morayshire.*

It seems possible that a lunette or diadem of gold was buried with these ear-rings.

A pair of circular embossed plates, with a beaded ring on each and a smaller disc above, were found in a tumulus near Lake, Wilts, and have been regarded as ear-rings. They are in the collection of the Rev. E. Duke.

In the Museum of the Royal Irish Academy † is another gold ornament of the same form as Fig. 492. It is, however, smaller, and the lower part is at present flat. Gold penannular rings of torque-like patterns, pointed at each end, and which may have been ear-rings, and not bead-like ornaments, are not uncommon in Ireland and Britain.‡ Rings of nearly the same kind are still in use in Northern Africa. Plain double-pointed penannular ear-rings in bronze are also found, but I am uncertain as to the period to which they should be assigned. Some appear to be of Saxon date.§

I have a pair of ear-rings of circular form from Hallstatt, about 2 inches in diameter, of hollow bronze, made from a thin plate, and with one end pointed which fits into a socket at the other end. Other ear-rings of bronze,‖ from the same cemetery, have a small ring encircling them, to which, in one instance, three small spherical bells are attached.

In the Laibach Museum are some bronze ear-rings of the Early Iron Age, much like those from Goodmanham, but broader.

Ear-rings of the Bronze Period appear to be almost unknown in France. I have, however, specimens found with a hoard of bronze socketed celts, fragments of swords, spear-heads, bracelets, and a variety of other objects at Dreuil, near Amiens, about 1872.

They are two in number, in form like Fig. 490, but rather shorter. One of them is coiled up, and the other has the broad part nearly flat. Each is ornamented with some parallel lines stamped in across the broader part. Several small hollow and some solid rings, circular, semicircular, and flattened in section, were in the same hoard.

Some few objects of bead-like character have from time to time been found in barrows and with other bronze objects. Dr. Thurnam¶ describes a tubular bronze bead, $1\frac{1}{4}$ inch long, found in a barrow in Dorset, and now in Mr. Durden's collection. He thinks the bead mentioned by Sir R. Colt Hoare as found in a barrow near Fovant ** may have been the spheroidal head of the bronze

* *Proc. Soc. Ant. Scot.*, vol. viii. p. 30.
† Wilde, " Catal. Mus. R. I. A.," p. 40, fig. 570.
‡ *Op. cit.*, p. 38.
§ *Arch. Journ.*, vol. xix. p. 88.
‖ Von Sacken, " Grabf. v. Hallst.," Taf. xvii. 4, 6.
¶ *Arch.*, vol. xliii. p. 470.
** " Anc. Wilts," vol. i. p. 243.

pin with which it was found.   Some beads of amber and jet were, however, discovered with it.

A notched bead of tin, like a number of small beads strung together, accompanied a little pin of copper or bronze, most probably an awl, and some conical buttons of bone or ivory, in a barrow on Sutton Verney Down,* in which there had been deposited a burnt body.   Hoare says that "it is the only article of that metal we have ever found in a barrow."

Small beads, or more probably drum-shaped buttons of gold, as suggested by Dr. Thurnam,† have also been found in the Wiltshire barrows.

Beads formed of joints of encrinites, with others formed of burnt clay, as well as a necklace formed of the shells of dentalium, were found in a barrow near Winterbourn Stoke.‡   Glass beads of the notched form have been found with burnt interments, and frequently with bronze instruments in others of the Wiltshire barrows.§   Other beads have spiral ornaments in white upon a blue ground.   A blue glass bead, with three yellow spirals on it, was found with the point of a bronze blade in a cist with burnt bones in a barrow at Eddertoun, Ross-shire.‖   Such beads, known as Clachan Nathaireach,¶ or serpent stones, have been used as charms for diseased cattle and other evils.

Glass beads with the same spiral ornamentation have been found in the cemetery at Hallstatt, and their presence in these graves certainly affords an argument for assigning them to a comparatively late period, or at all events to a time when commerce with the Continent was well established.

Among the objects found at Exning, Suffolk,** are some "curious bullæ" with clay cores, but they appear to belong to a later date.

As will be seen from the list of personal ornaments described in the preceding pages, their forms are but few and their number small in the British Islands, as compared with those of analogous objects found in some continental countries, as, for instance, Scandinavia and Switzerland.   The absence of several forms of torques has already been mentioned; the Danish and North German lunette, or diadem-like bandlets, are also never found in this country, though, perhaps, the crescent-shaped gold plates or "minds" of the Irish antiquaries may represent the same class of ornaments.   Spirals formed by coiling long tapering pieces of wire, such as are common in Scandinavia and throughout Germany, are also unknown, and this circumstance affords an argument against there having been any direct intercourse in very early days between this country and Etruria, where such spiral ornaments abounded. Besides this absence of spirals formed of solid metal, the engraved

* "Anc. Wilts," vol. i. p. 103.   † Arch., vol. xliii. p. 525.
‡ Op. cit., 114. A bead of burnt clay has also been found in a Westmoreland barrow. "Brit. Barrows," p. 55.
§ See Thurnam, Arch., vol. xliii. p. 495.
‖ Proc. Soc. Ant. Scot., vol. v. p. 313, pl. xxi.   ¶ Ibid.
** Arch. Journ., vol. x. p. 3.

spiral ornament which in some countries is characteristic of the Bronze Period may be said to be absolutely unknown in Britain. The nearest approach to it is the ring ornament formed of concentric circles.

The bracelets formed of cylindrical coils of wire are also unknown, as well as those of hollowed bronze with discoidal ends, such as are so common in the Swiss Lake-habitations. Decorated pendants, like those which are found in Switzerland and the South of France, are also wanting. Altogether the bronze ornaments of Britain are neither abundant nor, as a rule, highly artistic; and it would appear that here, at all events, the serviceable qualities of bronze were more highly appreciated than its decorative lustre.

CHAPTER XIX.

CLASPS, BUTTONS, BUCKLES, AND MISCELLANEOUS OBJECTS.

THERE still remain to be noticed a number of objects in bronze, of some of which the precise nature and use are now hardly susceptible of being determined; and of others but so few examples are known that they are best placed in a chapter which, like the present, is intended to treat of miscellaneous articles. It has occasionally been observed of antiquaries that when at a loss to explain the use or destination of some object of bronze or brass, their usual refuge is in the suggestion that it formed some portion of harness, or was what is termed a horse-trapping. To judge from what may be seen on the dray-horses and waggon-horses of the present day, future antiquaries, in examining the relics of the nineteenth century, will have some justification in assigning a vast number of forms of ornamental pendants and tongueless buckles to this comprehensive class of trappings; while a number of curious instruments of brass and other alloys, some of them not unlike complicated dentists' instruments, will probably be given up in despair, though now in most cases susceptible of being recognised by the adept as destined to extract cartridges or their cases from breech-loading guns. If these puzzles await future antiquaries, those of the present day must be pardoned for occasionally being at fault as to the destination of some ancient instrument or ornament, and they may even be forgiven for making suggestions as to probable uses of such objects, provided they do not insist upon possibilities being regarded as strong probabilities, much less as facts.

In Fig. 493 is shown full-size a mysterious object, consisting of a tube with a slight collar at each end, having on one side a long narrow loop of solid metal sub-quadrangular in section, and on the other an elongated oval opening, a part of the side of which has been broken away. It was found with a number of socketed celts, knives, and other articles in the hoard at Reach Fen, Cambridge, already often mentioned. With it was also another smaller object of the same kind, shown in Fig. 494. This, however, has the orifice in the front, and not at the side opposite the loop, the section of which in this case is circular. One end of the tube is plugged up with a bronze rivet. The mouth of the oval opening is rough, and has no lip to it, as in the other case; and within the tube there are remains of wood. I have a broken specimen found at Malton, near Cambridge, of the same character as Fig. 493, but with the loop round in section, and both shorter and stouter. The end of the tube is cast with a flat plate closing the aperture, except for a central hole about ¼ inch in diameter. I have another specimen much like Fig. 493, but the loop is longer and flatter, and beneath it the tube has a long oval opening with a lip around it, as well as a somewhat shorter opening on the opposite side of the tube. The loop also has a deep groove on its inner side extending its whole length. I am not sure where this object was found, but there is little doubt of its being English.

An object like Fig. 493 was found with socketed celts, gouges, and ham-

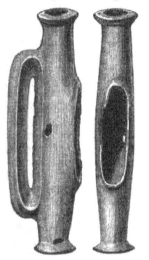

Fig. 493.—Reach Fen. ½   Fig. 494.—Reach Fen. ½   Fig. 495.—Broadward. ½

mers at Roseberry Topping,* Yorkshire, in 1826. With them was a flat quadrangular whetstone (?) and fragments of a flat plate of bronze, the ends hollowed and with crescent-shaped openings or lunettes in them, and with staples for attachment at the corners. There are three rivet-holes on the convex side of the lunettes.

Another object of the same kind was found with a socketed celt, a hollow ring, gouge, &c., at Melbourn,† Cambridge. There were two of these looped tubes found with spear-heads, socketed celts, broken swords, &c., near La Pierre du Villain,‡ Longy, Alderney.

In the great hoard of bronze spear-heads, &c., found at Broadward,§ Shropshire, was a short object of this kind about 1½ inch long, with the loop as large in diameter as the tube and extending the whole length, so

* *Arch. Æliana*, vol. ii. p. 213, pl. iv.; *Arch. Scot.*, vol. iv. p. 55, pl. vii.
† *Arch. Journ.*, vol. xi. p. 294.   ‡ *Arch. Assoc. Journ.*, vol. iii. p. 10.
§ *Arch. Camb.*, 4th S., vol. iii. p. 354. I am indebted to the Council of the Cambrian Arch. Assoc. for the use of this cut.

as to give it the form of the letter D. The orifice of the loop is only ¼ inch long. This specimen is shown in Fig. 495. Another seems to have been found at the same time.

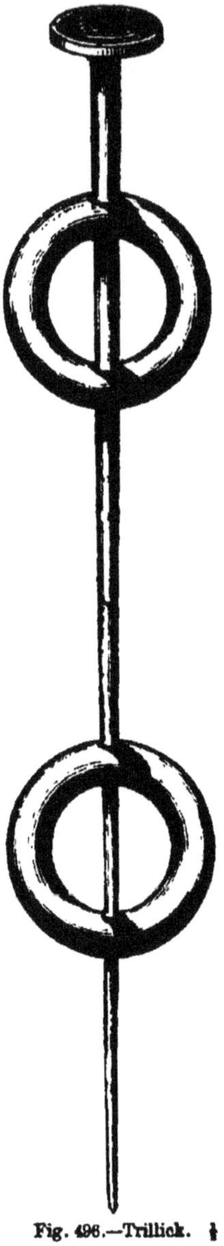

A fragment of another was in the collection of the late Lord Braybrooke.

An example, like Fig. 493, but somewhat broken, was in the deposit of Notre-Dame d'Or, now in the Poitiers Museum.

Another (2¾ inches), almost identical with Fig. 493, was found in a hoard with other objects near Amiens, and is now in the museum of that town.

Another of much the same kind was found at La Parnelle, Manche.*

I have an object from the Seine at Paris, which appears to belong to the same class as the tubes lately described, though without any loop. The tube is in this instance about 3 inches long, with small flanges at each end; and through the middle of it is an oval opening about 1 inch by ⅜ inch, with mouth-pieces standing out on each side of the tube, making the whole length of the oval cross-tube thus formed nearly 1¼ inch. Each mouth-piece has two parallel beads running round it. I am at a loss to assign a purpose to it.

Those with a loop seem to me possibly intended as clasps for leather straps or belts, one end of which passed through the metal loop and was sewn or fastened to the strap so as to form a loop of leather, while a corresponding loop at the other end was inserted into the oval mouth-piece, so that a pin passed down inside the tube would go through it and secure it. This pin need not have been of metal, but of some more perishable material.

The objection to this view is that the side orifice in the tube is not in all cases opposite to the loop, but in one instance at least at right angles to it. A second suggestion is that they were loops in some manner attached to wooden or leather scabbards of swords, which could at any time be detached by withdrawing a pin that passed down the tube. Whatever purpose they served, they do not appear to have been permanently attached to any other article, as in no instance have any rivet-holes been observed in them.

Some of the hollow rings found in Ireland with transverse perforations through them, appear also to have been made for attachment at will to leather or cloth by means of a pin passing through the cross-holes, which at once converted the rings into brooches or buckles of a peculiar kind.

Fig. 496.—Trillick. ¼

This purpose has already been suggested by Mr. T. O'Gorman, in the *Journal of the Royal Historical and Archæological Association of Ireland.*† He there

* *Mém. Soc. Ant. Norm.*, 1827—8, pl. xvii.   † 3rd S., vol. i. p. 164, whence the cut is borrowed.

describes a bronze pin with two thick bronze rings upon it, which was found with two large rings of bronze, four rings of about the same size as those on the pin, a large socketed celt, and a bronze hammer, in what appears to have been a sepulchre near Trillick, Co. Tyrone. These objects are now all in my own collection, and, as will be seen in Fig. 496, there can be no doubt of an efficient form of double buckle being presented by the pin and rings. Whether it was used for fastening a cloak or tunic, as suggested by Mr. O'Gorman, or for some other purpose, I need not stay to examine. I think, however, that the discovery of the pin and perforated rings in juxtaposition throws some light upon the character of other rings with cross perforations, of which many have been found in Ireland. One of these is shown in Fig. 497, borrowed from Wilde.* I have one of precisely the same character, 2¾ inches in diameter, with a cross perforation through the two projecting mouth-pieces, slightly oval, and about the size to receive a common pencil. Vallancey † has figured others, in one of which there is a cross-pin with a small ring at each end, somewhat like a horse's bit.‡ Others, with numerous small loops round the circumference, and with central bosses secured by pins, or occasionally with cross arms within them, appear to be of later date and to have had bands of chain-mail attached. In some of the plain rings, however, there is a portion of a strap of bronze left, which Sir W. Wilde regards as having served to connect the ring-chains, of which he thinks that coats of mail were made. Under any circumstances, these perforated rings seem to come under the category of fastenings or clasps, to which the looped tubes already described may also be referred.

Fig. 497.
Ireland. ½

A perforated ring was in the hoard found at Llangwyllog,§ Anglesea, already mentioned.

Large rings, such as those described in the last chapter, may also have served as connections for bands or straps.

There is, indeed, numismatic evidence that among the Ancient Britons, shortly after the time of Julius Cæsar, rings were employed as connecting links between the different straps forming the harness of war-horses. On a gold coin of Verica,‖ engraved on the title-page of Akerman's "Ancient Coins of Cities and Princes," and now in my own collection, there is on the reverse a warrior on horseback. The engraving of the die is exquisitely minute, and the warrior's saddle is shown to be secured by four girths, and by straps running from it round the chest and the hind-quarters to keep it in position. On the shoulder and the haunches there are rings to which these straps are joined, and from each of these rings another strap runs down to pass below

* "Catal. Mus. R. I. A.," p. 579, fig. 494.   † Vol. iv. pl. xiv.
‡ See Wilde's "Catal.," p. 576 et seqq.
§ Arch. Journ., vol. xxii. p. 74 ; Arch. Camb., 3rd S., vol. xii. p. 97.
‖ Type of Evans, "Anc. Brit. Coins," pl. ii. 9.

the body of the horse. Each ring, therefore, has three straps secured to it, one running forwards, another backwards, and the third downwards. Rings with three loops for straps attached occur among Etruscan Antiquities.[*]

Of brooches proper, with a pin attached by a spring or hinge, and secured by a hasp or catch, none are, I think, known in Britain which can with safety be assigned to an earlier period than the Late Celtic.

Fig. 498.—Cowlam.   ‡

That shown in Fig. 498 was found by Canon Greenwell, F.R.S., in a barrow in the parish of Cowlam,[†] Yorkshire, together with an armlet (Fig. 486) and a necklace of glass beads, on the body of an aged woman. The pin was of iron, which had replaced the original of bronze. I have a somewhat similar brooch from Redmore, near St. Austell, Cornwall, as well as one of longer form and with a larger disc, which was found in a barrow near Bridlington, together with two remarkable buckles formed of penannular rings. These were described by the late Mr. Thomas Wright ‡ (who has figured them) as undoubtedly Roman, but their character is decidedly "Late Celtic." Other brooches of the same character as the figure, found in the Thames, London, and near Avebury, Wilts, are in the British Museum.

Another article in use for fastening or attaching parts of the dress is the button, which claims a high antiquity. I have elsewhere § described some made of stone and jet, in which a V-shaped perforation in the body of the button afforded the means of fastening it to the dress. In the bronze buttons a legitimate loop or shank is found, which is cast in one piece with the button itself.

Fig. 499.
Reach Fen.   ‡

In Fig. 499 are shown three full-size views of one of two bronze buttons from the Reach Fen hoard in my own collection. There is a sharpness and smoothness about their faces which suggests their having been finished by some process of turning or rotary grinding. The centre and raised bands, though similar, are not identical in the two, or it might have been thought that they were cast in a metal mould. Four others were found at the same time.

A button of almost the same size and pattern was found with a razor and other objects at Llangwyllog, Anglesea.‖ One of the same character,

* *Arch. Assoc. Journ.*, vol. xxxvi. p. 110.   † " British Barrows," p. 209.
‡ " Essays on Arch. Sub.," vol. i. p. 25.   § " Anc. Stone Imp.," p. 407.
‖ *Arch. Journ.*, vol. xxii. p. 74; *Arch. Camb.*, 3rd S., vol. xii. p. 97.

but of larger size (1¾ inch), was found with a gouge, socketed celts, &c., at Kensington.* It has a central boss and two raised ridges. Both these buttons are now in the British Museum.

In the Heathery Burn Cave, Durham, was a small button, ¾ inch in diameter, with one loop at the back; and another larger (1¼ inch), with five loops at the back, one in the centre, and the four others at equal distances around it forming four sides of an octagon. This larger button has a series of concentric rings or grooves on the face; the small one has a central pointed boss with one groove around it.

Some curious buttons, like half barrels in shape, were found with a hoard of bronze objects at St. Genouph (Indre et Loire), and are preserved in the Museum at Tours. Numerous buttons of circular form have been found in other parts of France.

Buttons of various sizes and shapes have also been found in abundance in the Swiss Lake-dwellings.

A clay mould, apparently for buttons of this kind, is in the Museo Civico at Modena.

In the cemetery at Hallstatt immense numbers of small button-like objects have been found, some of the warriors' coats having been completely

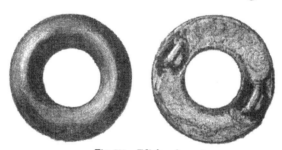

Fig. 500.—Edinburgh. ⅓

studded with them. Some of these are not more than ⅜ inch in diameter, nearly hemispherical, and with a small bar cast across them inside.

A peculiar annular button with two loops at the back, found with bronze swords (see Fig. 353) and a flat-headed pin (Fig. 464) at Edinburgh,† is represented in Fig. 500. The original is now in the Antiquarian Museum at Edinburgh. It has been thought to be the mounting of a belt.

Bronze discs of larger size than any ordinary buttons or clasps are occasionally found. One such, 3¼ inches in diameter, with three concentric circles engraved on one of its faces, was discovered at Castell y Bere, Merionethshire.‡ Another was found at Wolsonbury Hill,§ Sussex. A third, about 5 inches in diameter, with raised concentric rings upon it, is in the Scarborough Museum. One found at Inis Kaltra,‖ Lough Derg, between Clare and Galway, has been figured. It has a hollow conical projection like the umbo of a shield, surrounded by five concentric raised rings, the interval between the second and third being about double that between any other pair. The inner side has grooves corresponding with the

* Proc. Soc. Ant., 2nd S., vol. iii. p. 232.
† Proc. Soc. Ant. Scot., N.S., vol. i., p. 322, whence this cut is borrowed.
‡ Arch. Journ., vol. xi. p. 179.   § Ibid.   ‖ Arch. Journ., vol. ix. p. 200.

external ridges, and across the inside of the hollow umbo is a small bar of metal. The diameter of this ornament is 4¾ inches. It is now in the British Museum. In many respects such discs resemble the so-called *tutuli* of the Scandinavian antiquaries, though the long-pointed form has not been found in the British Islands.

An irregularly rounded flat plate of bronze, about 5 inches by 5½, and 1½ inch thick, apparently hammered out, was found with leaf-shaped

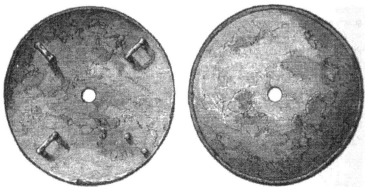

Fig. 501.—Heathery Burn Cave.   ⅔

spear-heads and a sword at Worth,* Devon. I have a round flat plate, about 6¼ inches in diameter and ¼ inch thick, found near Clough, Co. Antrim, which bears deep hammer marks in sets of parallel grooves on both faces. Perhaps such plates were destined to be still further drawn out into sheets for the manufacture of caldrons or other vessels.

In the Heathery Burn Cave, already so often mentioned, were about ten convex plates, with a raised rim round their edge, a small hole in the middle, and four loops cast on at the back. One of these is shown in

Fig. 502.—Heathery Burn Cave.   ⅓

Fig. 501.† With them were found about the same number of broad hoops, of which an example is given in Fig. 502. These are dexterously cast in one piece, with a groove inside corresponding with the raised central ridge on the outside. Their diameter is only about 4¾ inches, while that of the discs is about 5⁵⁄₁₀ inches. It is difficult to see any connection between the two forms, though from the correspondence in their numbers a connection at first sight

seems probable. The hoops have been spoken of as armlets, but I can hardly regard them as such. Most of the specimens are in the collection of Canon Greenwell, F.R.S., though thanks to his kindness I have an example of each; and two hoops and a disc are in the British Museum. Canon Greenwell has two other discs of a somewhat similar character, found with spear-heads and socketed celts near Newark. They are 5½ inches in diameter, with a raised rib round the margin and a central

* *Arch. Journ.*, vol. xxiv. p. 120.
† *Proc. Soc. Ant.*, 2nd S., vol. iii. p. 236. This and the following cut are kindly lent me by the Council of the Society.

hole. The surface, instead of being regularly convex, rises more rapidly towards the centre, so as to make a kind of cone with hollowed sides. There are no loops nor any means of attachment on the interior. It may be that a shank was riveted through the central hole, as was the case with some analogous conical objects from Hallstatt.

Without expressing any definite opinion on the subject, I may call attention to a certain analogy that exists between these hoops and discs, and the hoops and axle ends of Gaulish chariots of the Early Iron Age. The naves of the wheels of the chariot found in the tomb of la Gorge Meillet[*] (Marne) had bronze hoops on either side of the naves, and an ornamented plate at each end of the axle. The hoops, however, are made of plates riveted together, and were not cast in one piece, and the centre of the plates is open, though crossed by an iron pin.

Fragments of what may have been discs of the same kind, with a hole in the centre and four small bosses at intervals around it, were found in the hoard at Stanhope,[†] Durham, which comprised spear-heads, celts, &c., much like those in the Heathery Burn Cave.

Similar large discs with concentric circles upon them, and having loops at the back, have been found in various parts of France, Switzerland, and Italy.[‡]

Another and smaller disc with a central hole, having a short collar round it, is shown in Fig. 503. This is only the rough casting; and at one time I thought it was merely a waste piece or jet from the foundry, as it was discovered with moulds, celts, &c., in the Isle of Harty hoard. Another disc of the same kind was, however, found with the hoard of bronze at Yattendon,[§] Berks, which shows so much finish all over that it would seem to have been adapted for some special purpose, and not to

Fig. 503.—Harty. ¼

have been merely a piece of waste metal. Another disc of the same kind was found in the hoard at Haynes Hill,[||] Kent, and was regarded as part of an utensil. Mr. Franks informs me that an example with a rather longer tube has been found in Brittany. In the Yattendon hoard were also some fragments of thin bronze plate very highly planished on one face, and a hollowed conical piece of bronze, not unlike an extinguisher; but the purpose for which either of these was intended is a mystery.

Returning to bronze objects which appear to be in some manner connected with straps, I may cite some loops or slides of which an example is given in Fig. 504. The original is not in this case English, having formed part of the hoard found at Dreuil, near Amiens. But a specimen of the same size and shape, though rather more convex on the faces, is in Lord Braybrooke's collection at Audley End, and was, I believe, found with other bronze objects, including a hollow ring, in Essex. At first sight such objects might appear to be intended for mouth-pieces of scabbards, but on trial I find that the opening is not wide enough to allow of the passage of a sword blade, much less to admit of a thickness of

* Fourdrignier, "Double Sép. Gaul.," 1878, pl. v. and vi.
† *Arch. Æliana*, vol. i. p. 13, pl. ii. 14.
‡ See Chantre, "Age du Br.," 1ère ptie., p. 156.
§ *Proc. Soc. Ant.*, 2nd S., vol. vii. p. 485.
|| *Arch. Journ.*, vol. xxx. p. 282, fig. 3; *Anthrop. Inst. Journ.*, vol. iii. p. 230.

D D 2

leather or wood in addition. They seem more probably to be slides, such as might have served for receiving the two ends of a leather belt.

In the Dreuil hoard was also a flat kind of ferrule, about 2¼ inches wide and closed at the end, which may have served as a sort of tag or end to a broad strap. There were also socketed celts and knives.

In the same hoard was a loop fluted on one face, like Fig. 505, but with four divisions instead of three, and 2¼ inches wide. The loops shown in Figs. 505 and 506 formed part of a large hoard found near Abergele,* Denbighshire, and described in the *Archæologia*, whence my cuts are copied. There were present in the hoard forty-two loops or slides of this kind, though of various widths, as well as eighteen buttons, a reel-shaped object like Fig. 377, and numerous rings, some of them almost like

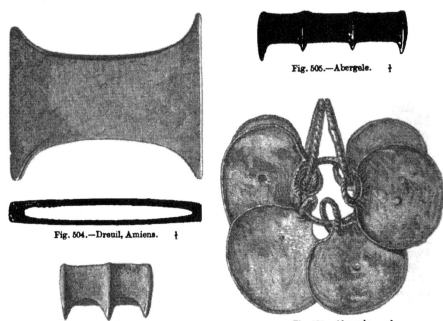

Fig. 505.—Abergele.   ⅓

Fig. 504.—Dreuil, Amiens.   ⅓

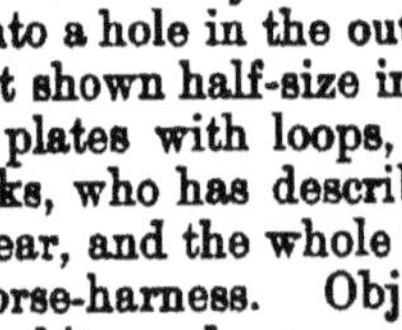

Fig. 506.—Abergele.   ⅓

Fig. 507.—Abergele.   ⅓

buckles in shape. There were also several double rings fitting the one within the other, the inner about 1¼ inch in diameter and the outer about 2¼ inches. They are cast hollow, and on the inner ring is a loop which fits into a hole in the outer ring. In the same hoard was the remarkable object shown half-size in Fig. 507. It consists of three pairs of irregular oval plates with loops, through which is passed a bar of bronze. Mr. Franks, who has described the hoard, says that " the loops show marks of wear, and the whole was probably a jingling ornament to be attached to horse-harness. Objects of the same nature have been found with bridle-bits, and are engraved in Madsen, *Afbildninger*,† and in Worsaae's *Nordiske Oldsager*, Fig. 266."

These examples, however, do not present such close analogies with the

* *Arch.*, vol. xliii. p. 556, pl. xxxvii. figs. 8 and 11.
† Pl. xl. 16; *Samlede Fund*, pl. xvi. 12.

Welsh specimen as do some interlinked rings with flat pendants found at Plonéour,[*] Brittany, with looped palstaves and a flat quadrangular knife. Some other analogous objects are mentioned by M. Chantre,[†] who has also described several *sistrum*-like instruments, to which M. de Mortillet [‡] is inclined to assign an Eastern origin.

Reverting to the Abergele hoard, I may add that Mr. Franks regards it as belonging to the close of the Bronze Period, and conjectures that most of the objects which it comprised formed part of the trappings of a horse.

Bronze bridle-bits, such as have been found in various parts of the Continent,[§] have very rarely been found in Britain, though occasionally discovered in Ireland. In the British Isles they appear for the most part, if not in all cases, to belong to the Late Celtic Period.

Another form of bronze objects of uncertain use is shown in Fig. 508, which is taken from a French and not an English original. This formed part of the Dreuil hoard; and as in so many respects the articles comprised in this deposit present analogies with those found in England, it appeared worth while to call attention to this particular object. It is a kind of semicircular flap, with a hole running through the beaded cylinder at top. What was its purpose I cannot say, though I have a thin gold plate of the same form, but decorated with ring ornaments, that was found at Hallstatt. It may be merely a pendant.

Fig. 508.—Dreuil. ‡

Among other miscellaneous objects of bronze may be mentioned an article of twisted bronze already cited at p. 51. It has a flat tang for insertion into a handle, in which are four rivet-holes. Beyond the handle project two twisted horns, which seem to have nearly or quite met, so as to form a somewhat heart-shaped ring. In the centre opposite the tang is a long slot with a chain of three circular rings attached. The whole covers a space of about 6¼ inches in length by 4¼ inches in breadth. With Sir R. Colt Hoare, "I leave to my learned brother antiquaries to ascertain" what was the ancient use of this singular article, which was found in a barrow at Wilsford,[‖] with a stone hammer, a flanged bronze celt, and other objects in company with an unburnt body.

Portions of three sickle-like objects, with a kind of square tang, through which is a large hole, were found with a palstave and a flat celt and many other bronze antiquities, near Battlefield, Salop.[¶] These measure about 7 inches by 7¼ inches, and their purpose is as much veiled in mystery as that of the Wilsford relic, with which they present a slight analogy.

The flat annular and horseshoe-shaped plates—the one 13 inches in diameter, and the other 2 feet 1 inch long—found with an oblong cup-

* *Arch. Camb.*, 3rd S., vol. vi. p. 137.   † "Age du Bronze," 1ère ptie., p. 188.
‡ *Rev. Anthrop.*, 1875, tome iv. p. 650.
§ See Chantre, "Age du Br.," 1re ptie., p. 152.
‖ "Anc. Wilts," vol. i. p. 209.   ¶ *Proc. Soc. Ant.*, 2nd S., vol. ii. p. 252.

shaped boss on the hill of Benibhrese,* in Lochaber, appear to me to be probably Late Celtic.

Some of the curious spoon-like articles † of bronze occasionally found in all parts of the United Kingdom may also belong to the Late Celtic Period, and most of them probably to quite the close of that period, if not to a later date.

The remarkable bronze rod, about 18 inches long, with small figures of birds and pendent rings upon it, found near Ballymoney,‡ County Antrim, is probably of later date than the Bronze Period: as are also the curious figures of boars and other animals found near Hounslow.§

In concluding this chapter, it may be observed that although I have attempted to give in it some notice of various forms of bronze relics of many of which the use is uncertain, yet that I do not pretend that the list here given comprises all such objects as have been discovered in Britain. In several hoards of bronze there have been found portions of thin plates and fragments of objects the purpose of which is unknown; and I have thought it best not to encumber my pages with notices of mere fragments about which even less is known than about the mysterious articles to the description of which, perhaps, too much space has already been allotted.

---

* *Proc. Soc. Ant. Scot.*, vol. vi. p. 46.

† See *Arch. Journ.*, vol. xxvi. pp. 35 and 52; *Proc. Soc. Ant. Scot.*, vol. v. p. 111; C. R. Smith's " Catal. London Ant.," p. 82; *Arch. Camb.*, 3rd S., vol. viii. p. 208; vol. x. p. 57; " Hor. Fer.," p. 184.

‡ *Trans. Kilkenny Arch. Soc.*, vol. iii. p. 65.   *Annaler for Oldk.*, 1836, p. 175.

§ *Proc. Soc. Ant.*, 2nd S., vol. iii. p. 90.

CHAPTER XX.

OF the various forms of fictile vessels which were in use at the same period as daggers and other weapons formed of bronze, it is not the place here to speak. Much has already been written on the subject, not only in various memoirs which have appeared in the proceedings of our different Antiquarian and Archæological Societies, but also in several standard archæological works. For the pottery found in the tumuli of this country I would more particularly refer to Canon Greenwell's "British Barrows," and to Dr. Thurnam's "Paper on the Barrows of Wiltshire," published in the *Archæologia.** Both these authors agree that none of the pottery from the barrows has been made upon the wheel. The greater part of the fictile ware with which we are acquainted was used for sepulchral purposes, and there appears good reason for supposing that much of it was manufactured expressly for the dead, and not for the living. Still there are a certain number of examples known of what has been termed culinary pottery, some of which have been found in barrows, and some in the remains of dwellings of the Bronze Period. This pottery, unlike the sepulchral, is devoid of ornament, and is well burnt, "plain, strong, and useful," but it is also made by hand. Some of the pottery from the Swiss Lake-dwellings is, however, ornamented in various ways, but the potter's wheel does not seem to have been in use. † And yet, in more than one instance, there have been found in barrows in the South of England weapons of bronze, accompanied by vessels of amber and of shale, which have all the appearance of having been turned in a lathe. Of some of these vessels I have given figures in my "Ancient Stone Implements," ‡ and also stated the particulars of the discoveries. I have also mentioned the discovery of a gold cup in a barrow at Rillaton, Cornwall, which was accom-

---

* Vol. xliii.   † Lubbock, "Preh. Times," 4th ed., p. 223.   ‡ P. 399 *et seqq.*

panied by what appears to have been a bronze dagger.*   As this
vessel is of metal, I have here reproduced the cut as Fig. 509.
It seems to me probable that the same kind of vessel which was
made in the nobler metal may also prove to have been made in
bronze, although as yet no examples have been discovered.   The

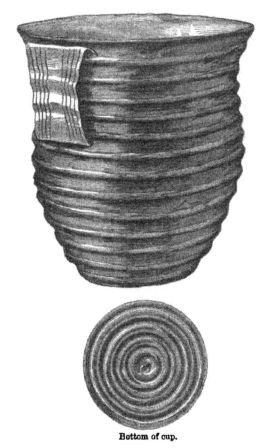

Bottom of cup.

Fig. 509.—Golden Cup: Rillaton. Height, 3¾ inches.

hanging cups of bronze of which many have been found in Scandinavia, and at least one example in Switzerland, are at present
not known to have been discovered within the British Isles.

It was probably not until nearly the close of the Bronze Period
that the art was discovered of hammering out bronze into sufficiently large and thin laminæ for the manufacture of cups and

* Erroneously called a celt by Mr. Kirwan. See Arch. Journ., vol. xxiv. p. 189
whence this cut is borrowed.

vessels. It would be impossible to cast the metal so thin as even that employed for shields, and before ingots or flat plates, like those already mentioned at page 402, could be thus drawn out, an acquaintance with some process of annealing must have been gained. It is a remarkable fact that the same process which has the effect of hardening steel has exactly the contrary effect on copper, and to some extent on bronze. Steel when heated to redness and then dipped in cold water becomes so intensely hard, that tools treated in this manner have to be somewhat tempered, or softened by heat, before they can safely be used; while to soften copper the usual method adopted is to make it red-hot and dip it in cold water. In whatever way the metal was drawn out, some of the large vessels of the transitional period between Bronze and Iron, such as those from Hallstatt, are wonderful examples of skill in working bronze.

Almost the only bronze vessel found in a barrow in England had an iron handle to it, showing that it could not belong to the Bronze Age properly so called. It is, indeed, somewhat doubtful whether it accompanied an interment. In the centre of a low mound near Wetton,[*] Staffordshire, about a foot below the surface, Mr. Bateman found "two very curious vessels," one about four inches high, and of rather globular form, carved in sandstone, and at the distance of a foot from it the other, "a bronze pan or kettle four inches high and six inches in diameter, with a slender iron bow like a bucket handle. It has been first cast and then hammered, and is very slightly marked with horizontal ridges." It was inverted, and above it were traces of decayed wood. There appear to have been some remains of burnt bones near the surface of the ground. This bronze vessel is somewhat like the lower part of an ordinary flower-pot in form. In Mr. Bateman's Catalogue [†] there is a note to the effect that this object is "probably Romano-British," but I have thought it best to cite it.

Several caldrons made of thin bronze plates riveted together have been found in Scotland, in some instances in company with bronze weapons.

In Duddingston Loch,[‡] near Edinburgh, together with swords and spear-heads, were some bronze rings and staples similar in character to those attached to the rim of a large bronze caldron found at Farney,[§] Ulster, but there is no record of any caldrons. Others of these rings are in

* "Ten Years' Dig.," p. 173.   † P. 21.
‡ Wilson, "Preh. Ann.," vol. i. pp. 350, 408.
§ Shirley's "Dominion of Farney;" *Arch. Journ.*, vol. iii. p. 96.

the Antiquarian Museum at Edinburgh, two of which were found with the large caldron here figured (Fig. 510) in the Moss of Kincardine,* near Stirling, in the year 1768. In this case no weapons appear to have been found. At the side is a broad band embossed with circles. This vessel is of large size, being 16 inches high, 16 inches across the mouth, and 25 inches in extreme diameter.

An imperfect caldron, with handles of the same kind, was found at Kilkerran, Ayrshire, with socketed celts and fragments of swords.

Others of these caldrons, but little differing in form from those found with bronze relics, have been accompanied by various tools formed of iron, as, for instance, those found at Cockburnspath, Berwickshire; and in Carlinwark Loch, Kelton, Kirkcudbright. There can, indeed, be little

Fig. 510.—Kincardine Moss.

doubt that such vessels, if belonging to the Bronze Age, are to be assigned to the close rather than to the beginning or even middle of that period.

Several such caldrons have been discovered in Ireland.

That shown in Fig. 511 is about 21 inches in diameter and 12 inches high.† It is composed of a number of pieces of thin bronze, each averaging 3¼ inches broad and decreasing in length near the bottom. "These plates bear the marks of hammering, and are joined at the seams with rivets averaging about half an inch asunder. These rivets have sharp conical heads externally, and some were evidently ornamental, as they exist in places where there are no joinings, and in the circular bottom portion they are large and plain. The upper margin of this vessel is 2¼ inches broad," and corrugated. "Its outside edge next the solid hoop has a double line of perforations in it." It was in a vessel of this kind that part of the great Dowris hoard of bronze antiquities was deposited.

The metal is said by Mr. McAdam, in a paper on "Brazen Caldrons,"

* Wilson, *op. cit.*, vol. i. p. 409. I am indebted to Messrs. Macmillan & Co. for the use of this cut.

† Wilde, "Catal. Mus. R. I. A.," p. 529, fig. 407. This cut has been lent me by the Council of the Academy.

published in the *Ulster Journal of Archæology*,* to be thinner than anything of the kind used in our modern cooking vessels, while the surfaces
are almost as even and level as that of modern sheet brass.

Another caldron from Dowris, more nearly hemispherical, also with
two rings, is in the collection of the Earl of Rosse. A specimen from
Farney has been already mentioned. It resembles Fig. 511.

In the collection of Mr. T. W. U. Robinson, F.S.A., is a remarkably
fine and perfect caldron, closely resembling Fig. 511, found in the parish
of Ballyscullion, Co. Antrim, in June, 1880. The following are its
dimensions :—

Diameter at top	.	.	.	18 inches.
Width of rim	.	.	.	2¾ ,,
Extreme diameter	.	.	.	24 ,,
Height	.	.	.	16 ,,
Outside diameter of rings	.	4¼ ,,

The rings are about ⅜ inch wide and of this section ╫.

Fig. 511.—Ireland.

Although no such vessels have been found in barrows in England, they are not entirely unknown in this country.

A very fine caldron of this character, about 21 inches in extreme
diameter and about 16 inches in height, was dredged up in the Thames
near Battersea, and is now in the British Museum. It is formed of two
tiers of plates above the concave bottom, and has had two rings at the
mouth, one of which, about 5 inches in diameter, remains. The rings are
of this section ╫, which combines great strength with economy of metal.

The expanding rim of the mouth is supported on four small brackets,
pierced so as to leave a saltire ornament in each. The rivet-heads are
about ¼ inch in diameter. From these brackets two strips of thin brass
run down about 3 inches, each ornamented with a fern-leaf pattern.

The bottom of another caldron, from Walthamstow, of about the same
size, is also in the same collection. The metal is remarkably thin.

The two rings of such a caldron, 5¼ inches, of this section ⊢, found
near Ipswich, are in the British Museum. The semi-cylindrical beaded
brackets through which they pass and a part of the rim are still
attached. Another ring was found with a hoard at Meldreth, Cambs.

* Vol. v. p. 82.

In some vessels very large sheets of bronze have been used. That shown in Fig. 512, also from Wilde,[*] is 18½ inches deep, but was formed of three plates only, one for the circular bottom and two for the remainder of the vessel. At the neck is a stout bronze ring, over which the plates are turned. "It originally stood on six feet, each forming an inverted cup." It has suffered much from wear, and has been carefully patched in several places. The metal is very tough and of a rich golden colour. It is composed of—

Copper	88·71
Tin	9·46
Lead	1·66
Iron	Trace
	99·83

Among three bronze vessels from the Dowris find now in the British Museum is one of the form of Fig. 512, 16 inches high.

Fig. 512.—Ireland.

The form is almost identical with some of the bronze urns from the cemetery at Hallstatt, of which several appear to be of Etruscan fabric.

Another vessel of the same character was found in a tumulus in Brittany,[†] and contained burnt bones.

In the collection of Canon Greenwell, F.R.S., is a vessel of hammered bronze of the same character as the figure, but of rather broader proportions, being nearly 17½ inches high and about 16 inches in diameter; at the shoulder the neck contracts to 13 inches. It has the usual two massive handles; and at the bottom is a flat ring with arms across it like a four-spoked wheel, rather more than 9 inches in diameter. The arms are ribbed longitudinally, and the ring has concentric ribs upon it, except at the junction with the arms, where there are cross-ribs. There are five rivets in it, one in the centre and four in the ring opposite each end of the arms. This vessel, which has been patched in more than one place, was found with numerous other bronze objects in the Heathery Burn Cave, already so often mentioned.

A remarkably fine specimen of a vase of this character, found in Capecastle Bog, near Armoy, Co. Antrim, is in the collection of Mr. T. W. U. Robinson, F.S.A. It formerly belonged to Mr. William Gray, of Belfast, who kindly allowed me to engrave it as Fig. 513. Its dimensions are as follows—

Height	17½ inches.
Diameter of mouth	13 ,,
Diameter at shoulder	15½ ,,
Diameter at bottom	7¼ ,,

The weight is 5 lbs. 9 ozs. The plates of which it is formed are carefully riveted together, and are of large size. Some holes which have

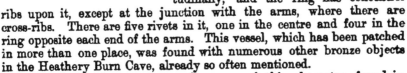

* Catal. Mus. R. I. A., p. 531, fig. 409.   † Rev. Arch., N.S., vol. xxvi. p. 326.

apparently been worn by use have been carefully patched. All the upper part of the vessel above the shoulder is decorated by small raised bosses produced by means of a punch applied on the inside of the vessel, and below the shoulder is a series of triangles embossed in a similar manner forming a kind of vandyke collar round the vessel. This character of ornamentation is very characteristic of the Bronze Period, and though not uncommon on urns formed of burnt clay, has not, I think, been before observed on those made of bronze.

The bottom of the vessel is secured by a ring and cross piece of bronze forming a kind of four-spoked wheel, as shown in the lower figure. The rings for suspension are solid, and hang towards the inside of the vessel.

As will be seen, there is much analogy between this Irish vessel and that from the Heathery Burn Cave last described. The latter, however, is without ornament.

These conical vessels are probably earlier in date than the spheroidal caldrons.

Whether either were actually manufactured in Britain and Ireland is an interesting question. There can, I think, be little doubt that the conical form originated among the Etruscans, whose commerce certainly extended to the northern side of the Alps. *
One of the upright vases

Fig. 513.—Capecastle Bog.

found at Hallstatt † has animal figures upon it almost undoubtedly of Etruscan work, though showing some signs of Eastern influence in their style, and bronze helmets bearing Etruscan inscriptions have been found in Styria. On the other hand, M. Alexandre Bertrand and some other antiquaries are inclined to believe in a more direct commerce with the East along the valley of the Danube or Dnieper. The finding of vessels of the same form in Brittany, England, and Ireland seems to point to a more western course of trade, always assuming that these objects were imported. That some of them

---

* A paper on "Etruscan Commerce with the North," by Dr. Hermann Genthe, will be found in the *Archiv. für Anthrop.*, vol. vi. p. 237.

† Von Sacken, "Das Grabf. v. Hallst.," Taf. xxi. 1.

may have come from abroad appears in the highest degree probable. Not impossibly the *æs importatum* of Cæsar may refer to a continuance of such a trade.   But whether there were no bronze-smiths in the British Isles capable of imitating such products of skill is doubtful.   The bronze shields which are of essentially indigenous character exhibit an amount of dexterity in producing thin plates of bronze quite sufficient for the manufacture of such vessels.   Moreover, the handles of these British and Irish vessels are formed by rings, while those of the vessels from southern countries are loops like the handles of pails or buckets.   The spheroidal caldrons are also of a form and character which appears to be unknown on the Continent, and are therefore, in all probability, of indigenous manufacture.

The careful manner in which some of the vessels are mended affords an argument that such utensils were rare and valuable; but it also shows that the native workmen understood how to make thin plates—unless these were portions of other vessels—and at all events how to rivet plates together.

CHAPTER XXI.

METAL, MOULDS, AND THE METHOD OF MANUFACTURE.

HAVING now passed in review the various forms of weapons, tools, ornaments, and vessels belonging to the Bronze Period of this country, it will be well to consider the nature of the metal of which they are formed, and the various processes by which they were produced and finished ready for use. Some of these processes, as for instance the hammering out of the cutting-edges of tools and weapons, and the production of ornamental designs by means of the hammer and punch, have already been mentioned, and need be but cursorily noticed. The main process, indeed, of which this chapter will treat is that of casting.

Bronze, as already stated, is an alloy of copper and tin, and therefore distinct from brass, which is an alloy of copper and zinc. Many varieties of bronze—or, as it is now more commonly called, gun-metal—are in use at the present day; and one remarkable feature in bronze is that the admixture with copper of the much softer metal tin, in varying proportions, produces an alloy in most if not all cases harder than the original copper; and when the tin is much in excess, as in the metal used for the specula of telescopes, so much harder that, à priori, such a result of the mixture of two soft metals would have been thought impossible. The following table compiled from a paper in *Design and Work*, reprinted in Martineau and Smith's *Hardware Trade Journal*,* gives some of the alloys now in most common use and the purposes to which they are applied :—

Tin.	Copper.	Per cent. of Copper.	
11	108 =	90·76	A common metal for cannon and machine brasses, used also for bronze statues.
11	99 =	90·	Gun-metal proper, used for cannon.
11	96 =	89·72	
11	84 =	88·44	Used for bearings of machinery, frequently called gun-metal.

* April 30, 1879.

Tin.	Copper.	Per cent. of Copper.	
11	72	= 86·75	Rather harder.
11	60	= 84·50	Harder, not malleable.
11	44	= 80·00	Used for cymbals and Chinese gongs.
11	48	= 81·35	Very hard, used for culinary vessels.
11	36	76·69	Bell-metal.
12	36	or 75·00	
11	24	= 68·57	Yellowish, very hard, sonorous.
11	4	= 26·66	Very white, sometimes used for specula with some other slight admixture.

Lord Rosse, however, in casting specula, preferred using copper and tin in their atomic proportions, or 68·21 per cent. of copper and 31·79 of tin.

The addition of tin, while increasing the hardness of copper, also renders it more fusible. In small proportions it but little affects the colour of the copper,* and it is difficult to recognise its presence from the physical characters of the copper, except from that of increased hardness. What appear, therefore, to be copper instruments may, and indeed often do, contain an appreciable admixture of tin, which, however, can only be recognised by analysis.

Besides the superiority of one alloy over another, it appears probable that the method of treatment of the metal may somewhat affect its properties. M. Tresca† found that a gun-metal cast by Messieurs Laveissière, consisting of—

Copper	.	.	.	.	89·47
Tin	.	.	.	.	9·78
Zinc	.	.	.	.	0·66
Lead	.	.	.	.	0·09

was superior in all respects to either the common gun-metal A or the phosphor-bronze B cast at Bourges, the constituents of which were as follows :—

	A	B
Copper	89·87	90·60
Tin	9·45	8·82
Zinc	0·31	0·27
Lead	0·37	0·31
	100·	100·

* Percy's "Metallurgy," vol. i. p. 474 (ed. 1861).
† *Comptes Rendus de l'Ac. des Sc.*, vol. lxxvi. (1873), p. 1232.

The results of both ancient and modern experience as to the proportions in which copper and tin should be mixed, in order to produce a tough and hard though not brittle metal, appear to be nearly the same ; and nine parts of copper to one part of tin may be regarded as the constituents of the most serviceable bronze or gun-metal.

In the following table I have given the results of some of the more recent analyses of bronze antiquities found in the United Kingdom, and have omitted the early analyses of Dr. Pearson[*] in 1796 as being only approximative. I have arranged them so far as practicable in accordance with the different forms of the objects analyzed ; and one feature which is thus brought out tends strongly to confirm the conclusion which has been arrived at from other premises, that certain forms of bronze weapons and other instruments and utensils are of later date than others.

It will be seen, for instance, that in the flat and flanged celts, the palstaves, and even spear-heads, lead, if present at all, exists in but very minute quantity ; whereas in the socketed celts and swords, which are probably later forms, and especially in those from Ireland, this metal occurs in several cases in considerable proportions.

This prevalence of lead is very remarkable in some of the small socketed celts found in very large numbers in Brittany, which from their diminutive size have been regarded as "votive" rather than as destined for actual use. In some of these Professor Pelligot[†] found as much as 28·50 and even 32·50 per cent. of lead, with only 1½ per cent. or a small trace of tin. In others, with a large per-centage of tin, there was from 8 to 16 per cent. of lead. Some of the bronze ornaments of the Early Iron Period also contain a considerable proportion of this metal, which, in the early Roman *as*[‡] and its parts, is found to the extent of from 20 to 30 per cent. Although some such proportion as 9 to 1 appears to have been aimed at, there is great variation in the proportions of the principal ingredients even in cutting tools of the same general character, the tin being sometimes upwards of 18 per cent. and sometimes less than 5 per cent. of the whole.

This variation was no doubt partly due to occasional scarcity of tin ; but, as Dr. W. K. Sullivan has pointed out,[§] there are two

[*] *Phil. Trans.*, 1796, vol. lxxxvi. p. 395.
[†] Chantre, "L'Age du Br.," 1ère ptie., p. 62.
[‡] J. A. Phillips, *Q. J. Chem. Soc.*, vol. iv. p. 266.
[§] O'Curry's "Mann. and Cust. of the Anc. Irish," vol. i. p. ccccxx.

other causes for it : first, the separation of the constituent metals in the fused mass, and the accumulation of the tin in the lower portion of the castings ; and, second, the throwing off of the tin by oxidation when the alloys were re-melted. M. Dusaussoy[*] found that an alloy containing 90·4 per cent. of copper and 9·6 per cent. of tin lost so much of the latter metal by six fusions that it ultimately consisted of 95 per cent. of copper and only 5 per cent. of tin.

With regard to the early sources of the copper and tin used in this country, and in general through Western Europe, it will not be in my power to add much to what has already been published on this subject.

It seems probable that gold, which commonly occurs native and brilliant, was the first metal that attracted the attention of mankind. The next metal to be discovered would, in all probability, be copper, which also occurs native, and has many points of resemblance with gold.

The use of this metal, as I have observed in the Introductory Chapter, no doubt originated in some part of the world where, as on the shore of Lake Superior, it occurs in a pure metallic state. When once it was discovered that copper was fusible by heat, the production of the metal from some of the more metallic-looking ores, such as copper pyrites, would follow ; and in due time, either from association with the metal, or from their colour and weight, some of the other ores, both sulphuretted and non-sulphuretted, would become known.[†]

When once the production of copper in this manner was effected, it is probable that the ores of other metals, such as tin, would also become known, and that tin ores would either

---

[*] O'Curry, op. cit., p. ccccxviii.

[†] For an interesting essay on the sources of bronze, see Prof. Sullivan in the Introduction to O'Curry's " Manners and Customs of the Ancient Irish," p. ccccvii. See also H. H. Howorth, F.S.A., on the " Archæology of Bronze," Trans. Ethnol. Soc., vol. vi. p. 72; Sabatier, " Production de l'or, de l'argent, et du cuivre," &c., 1850 ; Von Bibra, " Die Bronzen und Kupferlegirungen," 1869 ; De Fellenberg, " Bull. de la Soc. des Sc. nat. de Berne," 1860 ; Wocel, " Chemische Analysen anb. Bronze legirungen," in Sitz.-Ber. phil. hist. Classe. Acad. der Wiss. Wien. Bd. xvi. 169 ; " Kelternes, Germanernes og Slavernes Bronzer," in Antiq. Tidskrift., 1852—54, p. 206 ; Morlot, " Les Métaux dans l'Age du Bronze," Mém. Soc. Ant. du Nord, 1866—71, p. 23 ; Wibel, " Die Cultur der Bronze-Zeit Nord und Mittel Europas," 1865 ; Von Cohausen's Review of Wibel, Archiv. für Anth., vol. i. p. 320, vol. iii. p. 37; Lubbock, " Prehistoric Times," p. 59 et seqq.; Zaborowski-Moindron, " L'Ancienneté de l'Homme," 1874 ; Dr. C. F. Wiberg, " Einfluss der Etrusker und Griechen auf die Bronze Cultur," Arch. für Anth., vol. iv. p. 11; Troyon, " Monuments de l'Ant. dans l'Europe barbare," 1868 ; De Rougemont, " L'Age du Bronze," 1866 ; A. Bertrand, " Arch. Celtique et Gauloise," 1876 ; G. De Mortillet, " Origine du Bronze," Revue d'Anthrop., vol. iv. p. 650; Wilson, " Preh. Annals of Scotland," and " Prehistoric Man."

be treated conjointly with the ores of copper, as suggested by
Dr. Wibel, so as at once to produce bronze ; or added to crude
copper, as suggested by Professor Sullivan ; or again, be smelted
by themselves so as to produce metallic tin. At what date it
was generally known that " brass is molten out of the stone "* is,
however, a question difficult to answer.

Native copper and many of its ores occur in Hungary, Norway,
Sweden, Saxony, and Cornwall ; but copper pyrites is far more
generally distributed, and is found in most countries of the world.
So far, therefore, as the existence of this metal is concerned, there
was no necessity for the Britons in Cæsar's time to make use
of imported bronze, especially as tin was found in abundance in
Cornwall, and long before Cæsar's time was exported in considerable
quantities to the Continent. And yet his account may to some
extent be true, as a socketed celt of what is almost undoubtedly
Breton manufacture has been found near Weymouth,† and several
instruments of recognised French types have been found in our
southern counties. Bronze vessels also may have been imported.

Copper and its ores are abundant in Ireland, especially
copper pyrites and gray copper.

Although tin was formerly found in abundance in some parts of
Spain, and also in less quantity in Brittany,‡ there can be but
little doubt that the Cassiterides, with which either directly or
indirectly the Phœnicians traded for tin,§ are rightly identified with
Britain. But, with due deference to Professor Nilsson and other
antiquaries, I must confess that the traces of Phœnician influence
in this country are to my mind at present imperceptible; and it may
well be that their system of commerce or barter was such as
intentionally left the barbarian tribes with whom they traded in
much the same stage of civilisation as that in which they found
them, always assuming that they dealt directly with Britain and
not through the intervention of Gaulish merchants.

The argument, however, that the Phœnician bronze would have
been lead-bronze, because the Phœnicians derived their civilisation and arts from Egypt, and had continual intercourse with
that country, where lead-bronze was early known, appears to me
wanting in cogency. For though the Egyptians may have used

---

* Job, chap. xxviii. v. 2.
† P. 115.
‡ *Comptes Rendus,* 1866, vol. lxii. pp. 223, 346.
§ The doubts raised by the late Sir G. C. Lewis on this point have been dealt with by
Sir John Lubbock, " Preh. Times," p. 63 *et seqq.*

lead-bronzes for statues and ornaments, the Egyptian dagger[*] analyzed by Vauquelin gave copper 85, tin 14, and iron 1 per cent., and showed no trace of lead. Of one point we may be fairly certain, that the discovery of bronze did not originate in the British Isles, but that the knowledge of that useful metal was communicated from abroad, and probably from the neighbouring country, France. When and in what manner that and the other countries of Western and Central Europe derived their knowledge of bronze it is not my intention here to discuss. I will only say that the tendency of the evidence at present gathered is to place the original source of bronze, like that of the Aryan family, in an Asiatic rather than an European centre.

The presence in greater or less proportions of other metals than copper and tin in bronze antiquities may eventually lead to the recognition of the sources from which in each country the principal supplies of metal were obtained. Professor Sullivan, in the book already cited, arrives at the following among other conclusions from the chemical facts at his command :—

1. The northern nations in ancient times used only true bronzes —those formed of copper and tin—of greater or lesser purity according to the kind of ores used.

2. Many of these bronzes contain small quantities of lead, zinc, nickel, cobalt, iron, and silver, derived from the copper from which the bronze was made.

3. Though some bronzes may have been produced directly by melting a mixture of copper and tin ores, the usual mode of making them was by treating fused crude copper with tin-stone.[†] In later times bronze was made by mixing the two metals together.

4. The copper of the ancient bronzes seems to have been smelted in many different localities.

Some analyses of bronze antiquities found in other countries are given in the works indicated below,[‡] in addition to those mentioned on page 418.

---

[*] Von Bibra, *op. cit.*, p. 94.

[†] Dr. Percy, F.R.S., and other practical metallurgists have shown that this view is untenable. See Lubbock, "Prehist. Times," p. 621.

[‡] *Annales for Oldk.*, 1852, p. 249; *Jahrbüch. des Ver. v. Alt.-freund im Rheinl.*, vol. lix. p. 21; Chantre, "Age du Br.," 1ère ptie., p. 62; Perrin, "Et. préh. sur la Savoie," 1870, p. 19; Layard, "Nineveh and Babylon," p. 670.

	Copper.	Tin.	Lead.	Iron.	Nickel.	Cobalt.	Silver.	Zinc.	Sulphur.	Total.	Analyst.
Flat celt, Ireland . .	86·98	12·57					0·37			99·92	B
Flanged celt . . .	90·18	9·82		Trace.						100·00	A
Palstave (Mean) . .	89·33	9·20		0·34					0·24	99·11	A
„ Fife . . .	81·19	18·31	0·75							100·25	D
Socketed celt, Yorkshire	81·15	12·30	2·63	Tr.	0·13		0·07			*96·28	A
Socketed celt, Ireland.	90·69	7·44	1·28	Tr.	Tr.	Tr.			Tr.	99·41	A
„ „ (Mean) .	83·65	11·02	3·20	0·58	0·34					98·79	A
„ „ Wicklow	88·30	10·92	0·10	Tr.					Tr.	99·32	B
„ „ Cavan .	95·64	4·56	0·25				0·02			100·47	B
„ „ Dowris .	85·23	13·11	1·14						0·15	99·63	F
Dagger, Newton, near Cambridge . . .	85·33	14·20	0·29	Tr.	0·27		0·04			†100·13	A
Dagger, Ireland (?) .	99·72								·28	100·	A
„ „ .	87·97	11·35	0·28					Tr.	Tr.	99·60	B
Sword, England (Mean), Chertsey, Br. . .	89·69	9·59		0·33					Tr.	99·61	A
Sword, Scotland . .	88·51	9·30	2·30							100·11	D
„ Ireland (Mean)	91·79	8·17		Tr.					Tr.	99·96	A
„ „ .	87·07	8·52	3·37						Tr.	99·96	B
„ „ (Mean)	85·63	10·03	2·93	0·44						99·03	A
„ „ .	88·63	8·54	2·83							100·00	E
„ „ .	83·50	5·15	8·35	3·00						100·00	E
Spear-head, Ireland .	86·28	12·74	0·07	0·31		0·09				99·49	B
„ „ .	84·64	14·01		Tr.					Tr.	98·65	B
„ „ .	88·42	11·29		Tr.	0·29	0·29				100·29	G
Halberd, Ireland . .	95·85	2·78	0·12	1·32						100·07	B
Shield, Coveney Fen .	87·50	11·62								99·12	C
„ „ .	87·55	11·72			0·40					99·67	C
Trumpet, Dowris . .	79·34	10·87	9·11							99·32	F
Caldron, Scotland . .	92·89	5·15	1·78							99·82	D
„ „ .	84·08	7·19	8·53	0·03						99·83	D
„ Ireland .	88·71	9·46	1·66							99·83	B

A, Mr. J. A. Phillips, see *Quart. Journ. Chem. Soc.*, vol. iv. p. 276.
B, J. W. Mallet, *Trans. R. I. Ac.*, vol. xxii. p. 324.
C, T. H. Henry, F.R.S., *Pub. Camb. Ant. Soc.*, No. xiv. p. 13.
D, Dr. George Wilson, Wilson's "Preh. Ann. of Scot.," vol. i. p. 374.
E, Prof. Davy, „ „ „ „
F, Dr. Donovan, „ „ „ „
G, De Fellenberg.

* In this case oxygen to the extent of 3·83 was present. The bronze had become so friable as to be easily pulverised in a mortar. Mr. J. Arthur Phillips writes about it as follows:—" When a freshly-broken fragment of it is examined under a low magnifying power, it is seen to consist of a metallic net-work enclosing distinct and perfectly formed crystals of cuprite, surrounded by a greyish white substance which is chiefly binoxide of tin. In this alloy the nickel, silver, and iron are evidently accidental impurities, but the lead is no doubt an intentional ingredient." The specific gravity after pulverization is about 7·26 only. † Specific gravity 8·59.

I have here given most of the trustworthy analyses already published, and have only added two new analyses kindly made for me by Mr. J. A. Phillips, F.G.S., of a socketed celt from York-shire and of a small dagger from Newton, near Cambridge.

Those who wish for detailed information as to the composition of the bronze antiquities found in other countries are referred to De Fellenberg's essays and to Von Bibra's comprehensive work.*

The copper which was used by the bronze-founders of old times appears to have been smelted from the ore and run into a shallow concave mould open at top, in which the metal assumed the form of a circular cake, convex below and flat above ; but before becoming sufficiently cold to be quite set into tough metal, these cakes seem as a rule to have been disturbed and broken up into numerous pieces, better adapted for re-melting than the whole cakes would have been. This method of breaking up the solid cakes while hot saved also an infinity of labour ; as to cut such masses into small pieces when cold would, even with modern appliances, be a difficult task ; and with only bronze and stone tools at command would have been nearly impossible. Many of the cakes are, however, interspersed with cavities formed in the metal, and in some cases there seems reason to think that this may have been produced intentionally, so as to render the breaking of the cakes even when cold more readily practicable.

Many of the blocks of metal cast in rough moulds, and known by Italian antiquaries as *æs signatum*, have a similar broken appearance at the ends. Professor Chiericit† has suggested that the moulds in which they were cast were of considerable length, and that from time to time clay and sand were thrown in so as to break the continuity of the metal, which indeed was poured in at intervals, after the insertion of the sand or clay,† to form the break in the mould.

Some pieces of metal which have been regarded as ingots, and which not improbably are really such, have the form of a double-ended axe with a very small shaft hole. They have been discovered with several of the bronze-founders' hoards in France. Dr. V. Gross, of Neuveville, has a fine example of this kind found at Locras, in the Lac de Bienne.‡ It is about 16¼ inches long and 4¾ inches wide at the ends, the hole through the centre being

---

* "Die Bronzen und Kupferlegirungen," 8vo. Erlangen, 1869.
† *Bull. di Paletnol. Ital.*, 1879, p. 159.
‡ Chantre, "Age du Br.," 1ère ptie., p. 36; "Alb.," pl. xxviii.; "Matériaux," vol. xi. pl. i. 1. *Proc. Soc. Ant.* 2nd Ser., vol. viii. p. 250.

about ¼ inch in diameter, and the weight of the ingot, which is of pure copper, is about 6¼ lbs.

Rough lumps of metal have frequently been found with deposits of bronze implements in Britain, these latter being sometimes in a worn-out or broken condition, and apparently brought together as old metal for re-casting. In other deposits the instruments seem new and ready for use, or again they are in an unfinished condition. All the circumstances of these discoveries, however, go to prove that they are in fact the stock-in-trade of the ancient bronze-founders. The jets or waste pieces from the castings, of which I shall subsequently have to speak, are often found mixed with the rude lumps. These lumps have usually the appearance of pure copper, and in many cases have proved to be so on analysis.

Some copper cakes appear, however, to belong to Roman times. They differ in shape from those already described, in being of nearly even thickness, but with the edge inclined as if they had been cast in a small frying-pan. They are from 10 to 13 inches in diameter and about 2 inches thick; and on more than one found in Anglesea[*] there are inscriptions in Roman characters. They weigh from 30 to 50 lbs.

Turning now to the instances of lumps of rough metal being found with bronze weapons and tools, the following may be cited, though other instances are given in the tables at page 462:—

Lanant, Cornwall,[†] heavy lumps of fine copper, found with broken socketed celts, &c.

Kenidjack Cliff, Cornwall,[‡] with palstaves and socketed celts.

St. Hilary, Cornwall,[§] lumps weighing 14 or 15 lbs. each, said to have been found with spear-heads.

Near Worthing, Sussex, several lumps of metal, with palstaves and socketed celts.

Beachey Head,[||] three lumps of raw copper, apparently very pure, with palstaves, socketed celts, &c.

Wick Park, Stogursey, Somerset,[¶] with palstaves, socketed celts, broken swords, spears, &c.

Kingston Hill, Surrey,[**] with socketed celts, fragments of swords, and spear-head.

Beddington, Surrey,[††] with mould, socketed celts, gouge, spear-heads, &c.

Wickham Park, Croydon, Surrey,[‡‡] with palstave, gouge, hammer, &c.

Danesbury, near Welwyn, Herts,[§§] lumps of metal with damaged socketed celts.

[*] *Arch. Camb.*, 4th S., vol. ii. p. 59, vol. viii. p. 210; Pennant's "Tour," vol. i. p. 63; *Arch. Journ.*, vol. xxix. 194; *Proc. Soc. Ant.*, 2nd S., vol. v. p. 286.

[†] *Arch.*, vol. xv. p. 118.
[‡] *Journ. Roy. Inst. Cornw.*, No. xxi.
[§] *Arch.*, vol. xv. p. 120 (Leland).
[||] *Arch.*, vol. xvi. p. 363.
[¶] *Proc. Soc. Ant.*, 2nd Ser., vol. v. p. 427.
[**] *Arch. Journ.*, vol. xxvi. p. 288.
[††] Surrey Arch. Coll., vol. vi.
[‡‡] Anderson's "Croydon," p. 10.
[§§] *Arch. Journ.*, vol. x. p. 248.

Cumberlow, Herts,[*] with palstaves, socketed celts, fragments of swords, &c.

Westwick Row, Hemel Hempsted,[†] several lumps, with socketed celts

Romford, Essex,[‡] lumps of metal in waste pieces and imperfect castings, untrimmed socketed celts, &c.

Fifield, Essex,[§] upwards of 50 lbs. of metal, with socketed celts.

High Roding, Essex,[||] with socketed celts, &c.

Kensington,[¶] with socketed celt, gouge, &c.

Sittingbourne, Kent,[**] with socketed celts, gouges, &c.

Meldreth, Cambs,[††] with socketed celts, chisel, ring of caldron, &c.

Carlton Rode, Norfolk,[‡‡] lumps of metal, with socketed celts, gouges, &c.

Helsdon Hall, Norwich,[§§] pieces of copper, socketed celts, &c.

Earsley Common, York,[||||] several lumps of metal, with nearly a hundred socketed celts.

Martlesham, Suffolk,[¶¶] a large quantity of metal, including some lumps weighing 5 or 6 lbs., with socketed celts, gouge, &c.

West Halton, Lincolnshire,[***] with socketed celts and broken sword.

Roseberry Topping, Yorkshire,[†††] with socketed celts, gouges, hammer &c.

In the Heathery Burn Cave, Durham, and in the Guilsfield find, there was in each case at least one lump of metal.

Besides the cakes of copper, bars of that metal appear to have been hammered into an oblong form, and then cut into lengths of from 4 to 5 inches, weighing each about ¼ lb., and in that state to have served as the raw material for the bronze-founders. Thirteen of these short bars were found at Therfield, near Royston, Herts,[‡‡‡] and Dr. Percy found on analysis that they contained about 98¼ per cent. of copper with a small alloy of tin or antimony, probably the latter. Some fifteen or sixteen "pieces of long triangular brass" are described as having been found with about the same number of celts at Hinton, near Christchurch, Hants.[§§§] These bars "seemed to be pieces of the metal out of which the celts were cast."

In Scotland some "lumps of brass" were found with the swords, spears, &c., in Duddingston Loch.[||||||] Probably other lumps of metal have been found in that country, but they seem to be scarcer in Scotland and Ireland than in England.

Although, as already observed, Spain may have been the principal Western source of tin in early times, and possibly Malacca[¶¶¶] in the East, the trade with Britain for that metal must

[*] *Journ. Anthrop. Inst.*, vol. vi. p. 195. [†] *Penes me*, *Arch. Journ.*, vol. xi. p. 24.
[‡] *Arch. Journ.*, vol. ix. p. 302. [§] *Arch.*, vol. v. p. 116.
[||] In the British Museum. [¶] *Proc. Soc. Ant.*, 2nd Ser., vol. iii. p. 232.
[**] Smith's "Coll. Ant.," vol. i. p. 101. [††] In the British Museum.
[‡‡] *Arch. Journ.*, vol. ii. p. 80. [§§] *Arch.*, vol. v. p. 116.
[||||] *Arch.*, vol. v. p. 114.
[¶¶] *Penes* Capt. Brooke, Ufford Hall, Woodbridge.
[***] *Arch. Journ.*, vol. x. p. 69. [†††] *Arch. Æliana*, vol. ii. p. 213.
[‡‡‡] *Proc. Soc. Ant.*, 2nd S., vol. i. p. 306; *Arch. Journ.*, vol. xviii. p. 86.
[§§§] *Arch.*, vol. v. p. 115.
[||||||] Wilson, "P. A. of Scot.," vol. i. p. 348; *Proc. Soc. Ant. Scot.*, vol. i. p. 132.
[¶¶¶] Crawfurd, *Trans. Eth. Soc.*, vol. iii. p. 350.

have commenced at a very remote epoch. We might expect, therefore, that fragments of tin would be frequently found in the old bronze-founders' hoards. But though lumps of copper have so often been discovered in them, tin is at present conspicuous by its absence. The only instance to which I am able to refer is the discovery at Achtertyre,[*] Morayshire, of four "broken bits of tin," in company with socketed celts, spear-heads, and bracelets. These pieces seem to be fragments of a single bar which was about 6 inches in length, of oval section, and somewhat curved, and in weight about 3 ounces. Though spoken of as tin, the metal is in fact a soft solder composed, according to Dr. Stevenson Macadam, of—

Tin	78·66
Lead	21·34
	100·

This, he points out, is a more fusible alloy than the ordinary plumbers' solder, which consists of 1 of tin to 2 of lead, and fuses at 441 degrees Fahr., as it contains nearly 4 of tin to 1 of lead, and would fuse at 365 degrees. Whether this bar was intended for use as solder, or represents a base tin exported to Scotland from the tin-producing districts, is an interesting question. Professor Daniel Wilson[†] has called attention to the fact that in all the bronze instruments found in Scotland which have been submitted to analysis lead is uniformly present, though in varying proportions. Soldering[‡] is considered to have been entirely unknown in the Bronze Age, and even during the earlier times of the Iron Age; but the art of burning bronze on to bronze was certainly known, and instances of its having been practised are given in preceding pages.

Some fragments of pure metallic tin have from time to time been found on the Continent. A small hammered bar found at the Lake-dwelling of Estavayer,[§] and analyzed by M. de Fellenberg, was free from lead, zinc, iron, and copper.

Besides being found in Cornwall, tin occurs in France,[‖] Saxony, Silesia, Bohemia, Sweden, Spain, and Portugal. It also occurs in Etruria,[¶] and is said to be found in Chorassan.[**]

[*] *Proc. Soc. Ant. Scot.*, vol. ix. p. 435.   [†] "Preh. Ann. of Scot.," vol. i. p. 376.

[‡] Lubbock, "Preh. Times," p. 44; Von Sacken, "Das Grabfeld von Hallstatt," p. 118.   [§] Keller, 3er Bericht, p. 93.

[‖] "Manners and Customs of the Anc. Irish," O'Curry and Sullivan, p. ccccxix.

[¶] "Cong. préh.," Buda-Pest, vol. i. p. 242; *Engineer*, March 26, 1876.

[**] *Arch. für Anth.*, vol. ix. p. 265.

This metal is said by Dionysius[*] to have been struck into coins at Syracuse, but none such are at present known. Among the Ancient Britons,[†] however, tin coins cast for the most part in wooden moulds were in circulation, not in the tin-producing districts, but in Kent and the neighbouring parts of England. Their date is probably within a century of our era, either before or after Christ.

A large ingot of tin, in shape like the letter **H**, was dredged up in Falmouth harbour.[‡] It is 2 feet 11 inches long and about 11 inches wide, and 3 inches thick, and, though a small piece has been cut off at one end, it still weighs 158 lbs. It is shown in Fig. 514. The late Sir Henry James, F.R.S.,[§] has pointed out that the form in which the ingot is cast adapts it for being laid in the keel of a boat, and for being slung on a horse's side, two of them

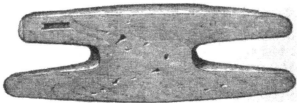

Fig. 514.—Falmouth.

thus forming a proper load for a pack-horse. He has also suggested that this was the form of ingot in which the tin produced in Cornwall was transported to Gaul, and thence carried overland, as described by Diodorus Siculus, to the mouths of the Rhone. Curiously enough this author speaks of the blocks being in the form of astragali, with which this ingot fairly coincides. Other ingots[||] of tin of different form have also been found in Cornwall, but there appears to me hardly sufficient evidence to determine their approximate date, and I therefore content myself with mentioning them. A lump cast in a basin-shaped mould, with two holes in the flat face converging so as to form a V-shaped receptacle for a cord, is in the Blackmore Museum at Salisbury.

What appear to be ingots of copper rather than votive or mortuary tablets have been found in Sardinia,[¶] and in their form present a close analogy with this ingot of tin, though they are of much

[*] Jul. Pollux. "Onom," lib. ix. c. 6, p. 1055.
[†] Evans, "Coins of the Anc. Brit.," p. 123.
[‡] *Arch. Journ.*, vol. xvi. p. 39; whence the cut is borrowed.
[§] *Arch. Journ.*, vol. xxviii. p. 196. See also *Arch. Journ.*, vol. xvi. p. 7, for an interesting paper on Ancient Metallurgy, by the late Prof. J. Phillips.
[||] *Arch. Journ.*, vol. xvi. p. 39.   [¶] Spano, "Paleoetnol. Sarda," p. 26.

smaller dimensions. Both the sides and ends curve inwards, the notch at the ends of some being semicircular. They are counter-marked with a kind of double T.

As to the method of melting the metal but little is known. It seems probable, however, that the crucibles employed must have been vessels of burnt clay provided with handles for moving them; while for pouring out the metal small ladles of earthenware may have been used. At Robenhausen,[*] on Lake Pfäffikon, Switzer-land, small crucibles of a ladle-like form have been found, in some cases with lumps of bronze still in them. Crucibles without handles have been discovered at Unter-Uhldingen,[†] in the Ueber-linger See.

The methods of casting were various. Objects were cast—

1. In a single mould formed of loam, sand, stone, or metal, the upper surface of the casting exhibiting the flat surface of the molten metal, which was left open to the air. In the case of loam or sand castings a pattern or model would be used, which might be an object already in use, or made of the desired form in wood or other soft substance.

2. In double moulds of similar materials. The castings pro-duced in this manner when in unfinished condition show the joints of the moulds. When sand was employed a frame or flask of some kind must have been used to retain the material in place when the upper half of the mould was lifted off the pattern. The loam moulds were pro-bably burnt hard before being used. In many cases cores for producing hollows in the casting were employed in conjunction with these moulds.

3. In what may be termed solid moulds. For this process the model was made of wax, wood, or some combustible material which was encased in a mass of loam, possibly mixed with cow-dung or vegetable matter, which on exposure to heat left the loam or clay in a porous condi-tion. This exposure to fire also burnt out the wax or wood model and left a cavity for the reception of the metal, which was probably poured in while the mould was still hot.

Sir John Lubbock[‡] regards this as the commonest mode of casting during the Bronze Age, but so far as this country is con-

---

* Keller, " Lake-dwellings," Eng. ed., p. 54.   † Op. cit., p. 118.
‡ " Preh. Times," p. 40.

cerned it appears to me to have been very seldom, if ever, in use. Except in highly complicated castings, such as ring within ring, no advantage would be gained by adopting the process, as the same result could usually be obtained by the use of a mould in two halves, while the pattern would then be preserved. In comparing a number of objects together, though, like the six hundred and eighty-eight specimens of celts in the Dublin Museum, no two may appear to have been cast in the same mould, it does not follow that this was actually the case, for allowance must be made for hammering, polishing, and ornamenting, which were subsequent processes, and also for wear at the edge. Even in castings from the same metal mould there will be considerable variations, from differences in the amount of coating used to prevent the hot metal from adhering to mould, and the length stopped off by the core. But of this I shall shortly speak.

The moulds formed of burnt clay have but rarely lasted to our times, though some have been found on the continent of Europe.

One for a perforated axe found among the remains of Lake-dwellings near Laibach, in Carniola, is in the museum of that town. Others will subsequently be mentioned.

The single moulds found within the United Kingdom are all of stone, and are adapted for the production of flat celts, rings, knives, and small chisels. In some cases it is hard to say whether a mould was intended to be used alone or in conjunction with another of the same kind, so as in fact to be only the half of a mould.

The single mould, which I have engraved as Fig. 515, was found near Ballymena, Co. Antrim, and, as will be seen, is for a flat celt of the ordinary form. The material is a micaceous sandstone, which a recent possessor of the mould has thought so well adapted for use as a whetstone, that the mould is in places scored with the marks where apparently a cobbler's awl has been sharpened. A celt cast in such a mould would be flatter on one face than the other, and be blunt at the ends, though much thinner there than in the middle. Before being used it would be submitted to a hammering process, which would render the two faces nearly symmetrical, and at the same time condense the metal and render it harder and fitter for cutting purposes, especially at the edge which was drawn out. In an Irish specimen in my collection there is in one face a deep conical depression, apparently caused by the contraction of the metal in cooling. It was probably necessary to add a little molten metal to the casting while cooling

in order to avoid such defects.   The sides as well as the faces of
these plain celts have usually been wrought with the hammer, and

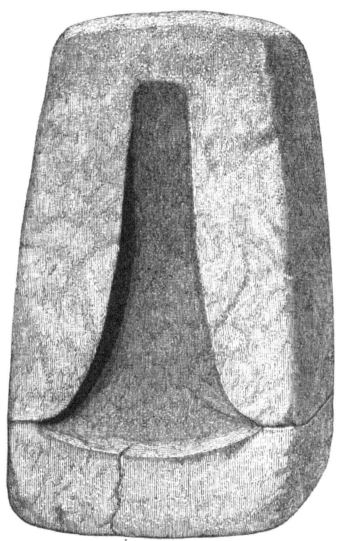

Fig. 515.—Ballymena.   ½

it seems probable that some even of the flanged celts were originally plain castings in an open mould.

Moulds of the same kind have been found, though rarely, in
England.   In a field near Cambo,* near Wallington, Northumber-

* *Arch. Æliana,* vol. iv. p. 107; *Arch. Journ.,* vol. x. p. 2.

land, was found a block of sandstone, having on one face two moulds for flat celts of different sizes, and on the other face another such mould, and also one for a flat ring. It is now in the British Museum.

Stone blocks with moulds cut in them have been found in Scotland.

One with a mould for a large celt in the centre, and near it in one corner of the slab a mould for a very small celt, was found in a cairn near Kintore, Aberdeenshire.*

Another large block, forming the end of a cist, near Kilmartin, Argyleshire,† has nine depressions in it in the form of flat celts, which may have been used as moulds. They are barely an eighth of an inch in depth, and on this account have been thought to be pictorial representations rather than moulds. With a metal so imperfectly fluid as melted bronze, castings could be made thicker than the depth of the moulds, and it is by no means impossible that this stone and another forming part of the same cist may have been intended for the production of castings. The second slab of stone may have served for casting pins.

The stone moulds from Trochrig, near Girvan, Ayrshire,‡ and Alford, Aberdeenshire,§ with depressions of various forms upon them, not improbably belong to a later period than that of which I am treating.

A mould for casting rings, 2¼ inches in diameter, found at Kilmailie, Inverness-shire, is in the Museum at Edinburgh.

One for two flat celts on the one face, and for a larger celt and perhaps a knife on the other, is in the Antiquarian Museum at Edinburgh.||

These moulds are more abundant in Ireland.

One in the Belfast Museum,¶ polyhedral in shape, has moulds upon four of its faces for flat celts of different sizes. In the Bateman Collection is a slab of schistose stone (7 inches by 6 inches) with three such moulds upon it. It was found near Carrickfergus, Co. Antrim.**

On a slab in the Museum of the Royal Irish Academy †† there are moulds for two flat celts, and also for one with a stop-ridge and a loop. It would appear as if the founder must have possessed a second half of this latter mould.

Two moulds formed of stone, and apparently intended for flat or slightly flanged celts, have been found at Bodio in the Lago di Varese.‡‡

Moulds for palstaves and socketed celts have been found both of stone and of bronze, but it will be well to reserve the latter until all the forms of moulds made of stone have been considered. Such celt moulds have always been made in halves.

---

* *Proc. Soc. Ant. Scot.*, vol. ii. p. 33, vol. vi. p. 209.
† *Journ. Ethnol. Soc.*, vol. ii. p. 341; *Proc. Soc. Ant.*, 2nd S., vol. iv. p. 513. *Arch. Assoc. Journ.*, vol. xxxvi. p. 146. Only seven depressions are there described.
‡ *Proc. Soc. Ant. Scot.*, vol. i. p. 45.
§ Ibid., vol. iv. p. 383, and v. p. 109.
|| Ibid., vol. ii. p. 34; Wilson, "Preh. Ann.," vol. i. p. 343, pl. v.
¶ *Arch. Journ.*, vol. iv. p. 335, pl. vi.; Wilde, "Catal. Mus. R. I. A.," p. 392.
** "Catal.," p. 78.   †† Wilde's "Catal.," p. 91, fig. 72.
‡‡ Pegazzoni, "L'uomo preist. nella Prov. di Como," 1878, pl. vi. 18—20.

In Fig. 516 is shown the half of a mould for palstaves, which is now in the Museum of the Royal Irish Academy. The other half is with it. They are formed of sandstone. It is uncertain in what part of Ireland they were found.

Another mould, formed of mica schist, and now in the British Museum, was found in the river Bann, and was intended for short palstaves about 3½ inches long.

The half of a mould for casting palstaves of a somewhat broader form was found near Lough Corrib, Galway,* and is in the Antiquarian Museum at Edinburgh. Another has been engraved by Dunoyer,† who has also figured a mould for a looped palstave, from the Museum of the University of Dublin. A stone mould from Ireland, for palstaves with double

Fig. 516.—Ireland.　⅔　　　　Fig. 517.—Ireland.　⅓

loops, is in the Antiquarian Museum at Edinburgh. As the halves of these stone moulds are rarely made so as to be dowelled together, they are almost always of exactly the same size externally, so as to be readily adjustable into their proper position when tied together for the reception of the metal.

The half of a mould for a small palstave, with transverse edge, is shown full size in Fig. 517. The original is of green schist, and is in the Royal Academy Museum at Dublin. It is remarkable that a mould for so rare a form should have been found. A stone mould for transverse palstaves of the same kind has, however, lately been discovered in the Lac de Bienne ‡ by Dr. V. Gross.

On the Continent stone moulds for ordinary palstaves have been found

* Wilson, "Preh. Ann.," vol. i. p. 358, fig. 46.　　† *Arch. Journ.*, vol. iv. p. 335.
‡ "Les dernières trouvailles du Lac de Bienne," 1879, pl. i. 10; "Matériaux," 1880, pl. i. 10.

in some numbers, especially in the Lake habitations.   In the museum at Geneva are several from the Station of Eaux Vives. The wings as originally cast were vertical to the blades, so that they might be withdrawn from the mould, and they were subsequently hammered over to form the side pockets, as in Fig. 85.

Moulds for looped palstaves have been found in the Lac du Bourget, Savoy.*   One of them is in my own collection.   A broken mould for a palstave was found at Billy (Loir et Cher).†

Others have been found in Hungary.‡

A few stone moulds for casting socketed celts have been found in England.   The half of one, apparently for celts without loops, was found near Milton, Dorsetshire,§ and is now in the Dorchester Museum. It has several holes on the face of the slab, as if for the reception of dowels, on which the other half of the mould would fit.

In another instance a set of moulds has been formed of three slabs of stone, and would produce two varieties of socketed celts, one half of the mould of each being engraved on the two faces of the central slab. It is only this central piece which has been preserved.   It was, I believe, found at Bulford Water, near Salisbury, and not at Chidbury Hill, near Everley, as stated in the "Barrow Diggers." ‖   On one face is the mould for a single-looped socketed celt about 4¼ inches long, of oblong section, with three vertical ribs on the face ; on the other is that for a double-looped celt of the same character, but about 5¼ inches long, also with three vertical ribs.   This mould is formed of some variety of greenstone, and is now in the collection of the Rev. E. Duke, of Lake House, near Salisbury.

Stone moulds for socketed celts, with vertical ribs upon them, have been found in the Lacustrine Station of Eaux Vives, near Geneva.   There are often moulds on each face of the stones.

Others in sandstone for socketed celts have been found in Hungary.¶

Several moulds for such instruments have been discovered in Sweden.** One with diagonal air-passages, like those in Fig. 521, is in the Copenhagen Museum.

Stone moulds for socketed celts have also been found in Scotland. Two pair from the parish of Rosskeen, Ross-shire,†† have been figured by Professor Daniel Wilson.   They are for looped celts rather wide and straight at the edge, about 5 inches long and of hexagonal section. The castings from the one are plain upon the faces ; in those from the other there are three annulets connected by raised ribs, much the same as on one face of the celt from Wigtonshire (Fig. 166).   These moulds had the two halves dowelled together when in use.   On one there appears to be a second mould for a small flat bar.

In Ireland stone moulds for socketed celts are rare, and they appear to

* *Exp. Arch. de la Sav.*, 1878, pl. iv. 187 ; Chantre, "Alb.," pl. lii.

† "Matériaux," vol. x. p. 112.   ‡ "Matériaux," vol. xii. p. 185.

§ "The Barrow Diggers," p. 75, pl. v. 10. It is so badly drawn that it might be taken for a broken mould for a palstave. *Arch.*, vol. xxviii. p. 451.

‖ P. 78.

¶ Hampel, "Cat. de l'Exp. préhist.," 1876, p. 134 ; "Ant. préh. de la Hongrie;" "Matériaux," vol. xii. p. 184.

** Wittlock, "Jord-fynd från Wärend's förhist. Tid.," 1874, p. 68.

†† "Preh. Ann. of Scot.," vol. i. p. 345, figs. 48 and 49. Fig. 61 shows a casting from one of the moulds.

have been for the most part cast in sand or loam. There is, however, in the Museum of the Royal Irish Academy,* the half of a mould of this kind made of mica slate, and much worn by age and exposure, apparently intended for a ribbed socketed celt. It has dowel-holes on the face of the slab.

The mould, or more properly half of a mould, for a tanged knife, with a central rib along the blade, is shown in Fig. 518. It is of close-grained sandstone, and was found near Ballymoney, Co. Antrim. The surface on which the knife has been engraved is ground very smooth, as

Fig. 518.—Ballymoney.   Fig. 519.—Broughshane.

if to fit another half mould. In this other half there was probably little more than grooves for the central rib and tang, as the mould at the edge of the knife would produce a casting fully $\frac{1}{16}$ inch thick, which would require a good deal of hammering out.

Fig. 519 shows the half of a mould for a dagger blade of elegant form. It is of mica slate, and was found near Broughshane, Co. Antrim. It is about 1 inch in thickness; and on the other face are moulds for a small flat chisel with side stops, in total length about $2\frac{5}{8}$ inches, for a flat triangular celt-like tool about $1\frac{1}{4}$ inch long, and an unfinished mould for a segment of a flat ring.

* Wilde, "Catal. Mus. R. I. A.," p. 91, fig. 73.

F F

Stone moulds for daggers have been found in the Italian *terramare.*[*]

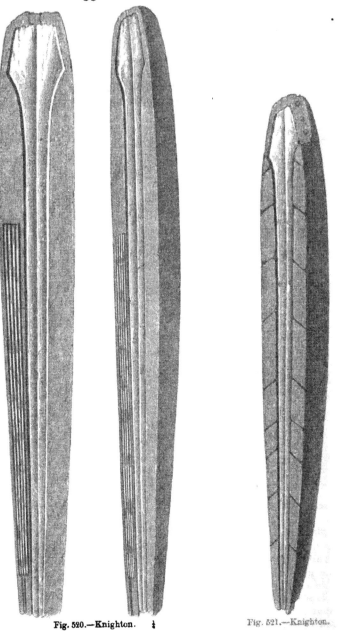

Fig. 520.—Knighton.   ¼   Fig. 521.—Knighton.   ¼

In Figs. 520 and 521 I have reproduced on the scale of one-fourth the engravings of two stone moulds which were found near Knighton,

* Gastaldi, "Nuovi cenni," 1862, Tav. iv. 22.

but in the parish of Hennock, near Chudleigh, Devon, and are published in the *Archæological Journal*.* They are of a light greenish micaceous schist, such as occurs in Cornwall. The large one is 24½ inches in length by 3 inches in its greatest width, the smaller is 21½ inches long and also 3 inches wide. When found the two halves of each mould were in apposition; the longer mould placed vertically, the shorter horizontally. As will be seen, they are for the production of rapier-shaped blades. In the smaller is a series of small channels, to allow of the escape of air during the process of casting. On the larger, by the side of the main mould, is a second, which would produce a slightly tapering casting, ribbed longitudinally on one face and flat on the other. It is difficult to judge of the purpose for which it was intended, but it may possibly have been at once an ornament and a support for the scabbard of the blade.

Some fluted pieces of bronze, such as would be produced from a mould of this kind, are in the museum at Tours, found in a hoard at St. Genouph.

A mould for a short leaf-shaped sword has been found in Ireland.†

A stone mould, formed of green micaceous schist, and found at Maghera, Co. Derry, is in the collection of Canon Greenwell, F.R.S., and is shown in Fig. 522. As will be seen, it is for a spear-head of the ordinary Irish type, with loops on the socket. These, however, were pro-

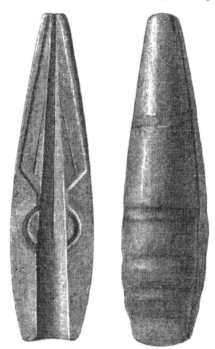

Fig. 522.—Maghera. ½

bably flattened down during the finishing process. The outside of the mould has been neatly rounded, and has shallow grooves in it to assist in keeping the string in place with which the two halves of the mould were bound together when ready for use.

In the same collection is the half of a mould for spear-heads, from Armoy, Co. Antrim. It is much like the figure, but 7⅞ inches long.

I have the half of a mould for a nearly similar spear-head, made of light brown stone, with the sides left square, and not rounded. This is also from the North of Ireland. It is difficult to understand the manner in which the cores for forming the sockets of the spear-heads were supported in the moulds. Possibly small pins of bronze were attached to the

* Vol. ix. p. 185.   † *Mém. des Ant. du Nord*, 1872—77, p. 142.

F F 2

clay core, which kept it in position, but which during the casting process got burnt into the molten metal. I have, however, found no actual traces of such a contrivance. On examining broken spear-heads it will some-times be found that the socket core inside the blade, instead of being simply conical, has lateral projections running into the thicker part of the blade.

A mould for spear-heads of the same kind as Fig. 521, found near Claran Bridge,* in the barony of Dunkellen, Co. Galway, has at the base two pin-holes about 1 inch long and ¼ inch in diameter. Their axes are parallel to that of the socket. These may possibly be connected with the steadying of the core.

A stone mould found at the edge of Lough Ramer, Co. Cavan,† and now in the Museum of the Royal Irish Academy, is quadrangular in section, with moulds for very small lance-heads on three of its faces. On the fourth there are marks of a worn-out mould. The corresponding halves have not been found. Such instances of several half-moulds on a single block of stone are not unfrequent.

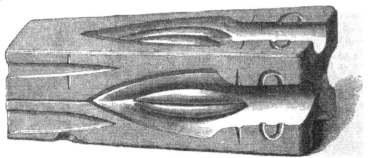

Fig. 523.—Lough Gur.   ⅓

A moiety of a stone mould for casting spear-heads of various sizes, and also pointed objects, "possibly," though not probably, "arrow-heads," was found at Lough Gur,‡ Co. Limerick, and is now in the British Museum. It is a four-sided prism, 6½ inches long and 2½ inches broad at one end of each face, and 1¾ inch at the other. A second similar prism would, it has been observed, give four perfect moulds for casting spear-heads slightly varying in form, but in each case provided with side loops. These loops are as usual semicircular in form on the mould, and were no doubt destined to be flattened in the usual manner by a subsequent process of hammering. There is one special feature in this mould, viz. that at the base of the blade there is a transverse notch in the stone, evidently destined to receive a small pin, which would serve to keep the clay core for the socket in its proper position. There is a similar transverse notch in one of the smaller moulds for the pointed objects. This mould is shown in Fig. 523.

* *Arch.*, vol. xv. p. 349, pl. xxxiv. 1, 2.   † Wilde, "Catal. Mus. R. I. A.," p. 93.
‡ *Arch. Journ.*, vol. xx. p. 170.   The cut is kindly lent by the Council of the Institute.

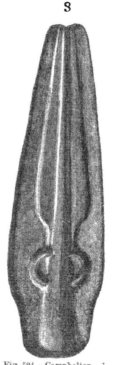

There is a similar notch in a mould for leaf-shaped spear-heads without loops in the Preusker Collection at Dresden. It would seem as if the pin which formed the hole for the rivet was also of use to support the core. Another such mould is in the museum at Modena.

There are similar notches in a stone mould for spear-heads, in one of burnt clay for socketed knives, found at Mœrigen, in the Lake of Bienne, and in one found in the Lake of Varese.*

A small Irish mould for casting broad leaf-shaped lance-heads without loops is in the Antiquarian Museum at Edinburgh.

A mould of much the same character as the Irish examples was found near Campbelton,† in Kintyre, Argyleshire. It is formed of dark serpentine, and one of its halves is shown in Fig. 524. On the same spot were found two polished stone celts and another stone mould for spear-heads, in two portions, also of serpentine, shown in Figs. 525 and 526, both sides being cut for moulds, one for a looped spear-head and the other for one without loops. Dr. Arthur Mitchell, who has described this find, says that in this second mould the two halves are not alike,

Fig. 524.—Campbelton. ⅓

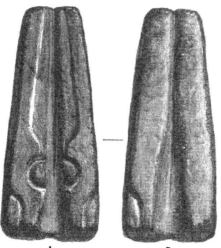

Fig. 525.—Campbelton. ⅓

Fig. 526.—Campbelton. ⅓

* Ranchet e Regazzoni, *Atti della Soc. Ital. de sc. nat.*, vol. xxi.
† *Proc. Soc. Ant. Scot.*, vol. vi. p. 48, pl. vi. I am indebted to the Council for the use of these four blocks.

as in the one first described. In this case one-half has the shape of the spear-head deeply cut into the stone, so as to include the whole thickness of the edge of the spear, and the other side has simply the midrib alone cut on it, and the rest of that side of the mould is gently bevelled towards the edges, the result of which simple plan is that when the two sides are laid together a perfect mould is made, the two sides of the casting being almost exactly alike, less labour being thus required than in forming an outline exactly alike on both sides of the stone mould, and the result being equally satisfactory.

An English, or rather Welsh, quadrangular mould, much like that from Lough Gur, was found between Bodwrdin * and Tre Ddafydd, Anglesea. It is formed of hone-stone 9¼ inches long, with the sides tapering from 2 inches to 1½ inch. It is adapted for casting looped spear-heads of two sizes, and what has been regarded as a double-looped celt. The fourth side has a conical groove, and may be the complement of another more defined mould, as is the case with Fig. 525B. It has been thought to have been for a spike-like javelin. What has been regarded as the mould for double-looped celts seems also to be the shallow half of a mould for spear-heads. In the museum at Clermont Ferrand † there is an analogous stone mould for palstaves of three types and a point or ferrule.

Of other stone moulds, I may mention one for casting buckles of a kind like those from Polden Hill, which was found at Camelford, Cornwall.‡ This is not improbably of Late Celtic date.

I have a flat oval slab of compact grit, about 2 inches thick, having on one face a mould for a thin oval plate of metal about 5 inches by 4½ inches, and on the other a mould for a rather thicker oval plate, about 6 inches by 4½ inches. It was found near Nantlle, Carnarvon, and was given me by Mr. R. D. Darbishire, F.S.A. I am uncertain as to the period to which it ought to be assigned.

Of foreign moulds of stone besides those already cited, I may mention some for double-ended hatchets and for flat celts which have been found in the Island of Sardinia.§

A number of moulds formed of stone, principally mica-schist, were found by Dr. Schliemann ‖ during his excavations on the presumed site of Troy. They were for casting flat celts, tanged spear-heads or daggers, and various other forms. Several of the blocks had moulds on both sides and ends, and served for casting as many as a dozen different objects.

The moulds made of bronze which have been found in this country are for palstaves, socketed celts, and gouges only. They appear to be more abundant in England than in any of the neighbouring parts of Europe. At one time the whole school of English

* *Arch. Journ.*, vol. iii. p. 257, vol. vi. p. 385 ; Lindenschmit, "A. u. h. V.," vol. ii. Heft. xii. Taf. i. 5.
† *Arch. Journ.*, vol. xviii. p. 166.
‡ *Proc. Soc. Ant.*, vol. iv. p. 148. § Spano, " Paleoetnol. Sard.," p. 27.
‖ " Troy and its Remains," pp. 82, 110, 139, 173, 261, &c.

antiquaries regarded the moulds for socketed celts as cases or sheaths specially prepared to hold such instruments.* To Vallancey, I think, belongs the credit of being the first to recognise their true character. In writing about the half of a bronze mould for palstaves found in Ireland, he observes,† "Dr. Borlase and Mr. Lort had seen brass cases of these instruments, which fitted them as exactly as if they had been the molds in which the instruments were cast. I cannot conceive why these gentlemen hesitate

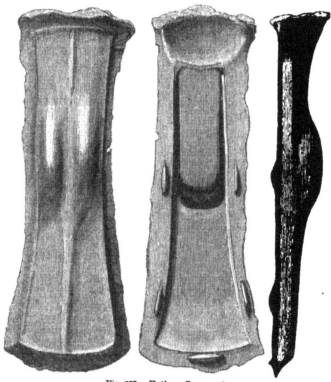

Fig. 527.—Hotham Carr.   ½

to call them molds, as a certain proof that they were manufactured in Ireland, where the Romans came not, either as friends or foes, the molds are found in our bogs ; they are of brass also, mixed with a greater quantity of iron, or in some manner tempered much harder than the instruments." I am not sure that the latter remark as to the comparative hardness of the moulds holds good in all cases, otherwise the correctness of the opinion expressed by Vallancey, now about a hundred years ago, is undeniable.

* See *Arch.*, vol. v. p. 108 *et seqq.*   † "Collectanea," vol. iv. p. 59.

In Fig. 527 are given three views of one half of a complete mould for palstaves, which was found with a hoard of bronze objects, including seven palstaves without loops, at Hotham Carr, in Yorkshire, E.R. It is in the collection of Canon Greenwell, F.R.S. Among the palstaves which were found with it only one was in an undamaged condition. As will be seen from the figure, there are projections or dowels on the face of this half of the mould which fit into corresponding depressions in the counterpart, so as to

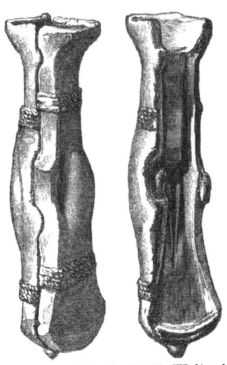

Fig. 528.—Wiltshire. ½   Fig. 529.—Wiltshire. ½

steady the two halves when brought together and keep them in proper position. At the top is a cup-shaped cavity for the reception of the metal. Any portion of the casting which occupied this part of the mould was broken off from the palstave when it was cool, and was kept for re-melting. Such waste pieces, or jets, from the moulds are of common occurrence in the old founders' hoards, and some will be subsequently noticed.

Another mould for simple palstaves was found in Danesfield, near Bangor,* in 1800. It is for a blade rather wider at the edge and narrower in the shank than that produced by the Yorkshire mould. With it was found another mould for a looped palstave of about the same size.   One half of each pair of moulds is in the British Museum, and the other half in Lord Braybrooke's collection at Audley End.   The half of a bronze mould for a simple palstave, with a shield-shaped ornament below the stop-ridge, was found in Ireland.† One of the same kind was lately in the collection of Mr. Stevenson of Lisburn.

In the British Museum is another mould for looped palstaves, which is shown in Figs. 528 and 529, for the use of which I am indebted to the Council of the Society of Antiquaries.‡ The original was found in Wiltshire. It is remarkable as bearing on each of its halves bands evidently cast from actual twine which has been upon the model; but the bands on the two

* *Arch. Journ.*, vol. vi. p. 386, vol. xviii. p. 166 ; *Arch. Camb.*, 3rd S., vol. ii. p. 128.
† Vallancey, "Coll.," vol. iv. p. 59, pl. x. 10.   ‡ *Proc. Soc. Ant.*, vol. iii. p. 158.

halves do not coincide, being on the one placed higher than on the other. The sides are also joggled together in a singular manner. As to the bands of cording, it may be that the model of the first half of the mould was formed of clay, which when dry, in order to prevent its being broken, was tied on to the palstave on which it had been shaped, and was thus moulded in clay or loam; and that afterwards, when the second half of the mould had to be cast by a similar process, the model for it was tied on to the half-mould already formed, the binding being in contact with the side of the band already in relief upon the back and sides of the half-mould.

Several palstave moulds formed of bronze have been found in different countries in Europe.

The half of one, found in the Saône, for looped palstaves, is in the museum at Lyons.*

General A. Pitt Rivers, F.R.S., has one from the neighbourhood of Macon.†

M. Charles Seidler, of Nantes, has another.

Another from the hoard of Notre-Dame d'Or, Vienne, is in the museum at Poitiers.

M. Forel has another found in the Lake-dwellings at Morges.‡

A palstave mould of bronze, found near Medingen, is in the museum at Hanover.§ The half of one found at Polsen, near Merseburg,‖ is in that of Berlin.

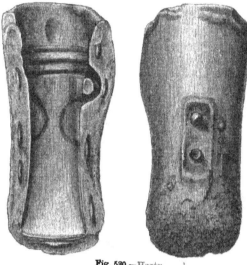

Fig. 530.—Harty.

Another bronze mould from the neighbourhood of Grünberg,¶ is in the museum at Darmstadt.

There are several bronze moulds of this character in the Museum of Northern Antiquities at Copenhagen.

In Figs. 530 and 531 are engraved the halves of two moulds for casting socketed celts of different sizes and patterns, which were found with a number of other relics in the Isle of Harty, Sheppey, and are now in my own collection. I have already given an account of this discovery elsewhere; ** but as it throws so

* Chantre, "Album," pl. i.; "Age du Br.," 1ère. ptie., p. 26.
† *Proc. Soc. Ant.*, 2nd S., vol. v. p. 433.
‡ Keller, 3er Bericht, p. 109, pl. vii. 43; Troyon, "Hab. Lac.," pl. x. 15.
§ Lindenschmit, "Alt. u. h. V." vol. ii. Heft. xii. Taf. i. 3.
‖ Bastian und A. Voss, "Die Bronze-schwerter des K. Mus. zu Berlin," Taf. xiv. 9.
¶ Lindenschmit, *ubi sup.*, Taf. i. 4.
** *Proc. Soc. Ant.*, 2nd S., vol. v. p. 408; "Cong. préh.," Stockholm vol. i. p. 445.

much light upon the whole process of casting as practised towards the close of the Bronze Period, it will be desirable to give a somewhat detailed account of the entire find and its teachings in this place.

The hoard, which may very fairly be described as the stock-in-trade of an ancient bronze-founder, consisted of the following articles—

Both halves of the mould, Fig. 530.

5 celts cast in this mould and a fragment.

Both halves of the mould, Fig. 531.

1 celt cast in it.

One-half of a smaller mould with a portion of a lead lining adhering to it, as kindly determined for me by Dr. J. Percy, F.R.S.

3 celts, more or less worn out, apparently cast in it.

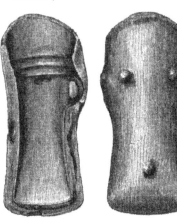

Fig. 531.—Harty. ½

2 large celts from different moulds.

2 small socketed celts from other and different moulds.

Both halves of a gouge mould, Fig. 532.

2 gouges, both from one mould, but it is doubtful whether they are from this. See Fig. 205.

2 pointed tools, Fig. 220.

1 double-edged knife, Fig. 253.

1 single-edged knife, Fig. 260.

1 perforated disc, Fig. 503.

1 ferrule, Fig. 377.

1 part of a curved bracelet-like object of doubtful use, with small hole near the end.

1 hammer or anvil, Fig. 211.

1 small hammer, Fig. 212.

2 pieces of rough copper.

1 whetstone, Fig. 540.

Of the largest mould itself, Fig. 530, not much need be said. The dowels on the face of one of the halves have been much injured by oxidation, so that the two parts of the mould do not now fit so well together as they did originally. On the outside of each valve are two projecting pins intended to hold the cord in position, by which the two parts of the mould were held together when in use.

As will be seen, the mould itself is somewhat bell-mouthed. Of the ornamental "flanches" on the celt, I have already given the history at page 108. The instruments cast from this mould, and present in the hoard, are five in number, four in fairly perfect condition, and one broken in two in the middle. Though cast in the same mould, no two are absolutely alike. Not only do they vary in width at their edges—the natural result of one having been more freely hammered out than another—but in the upper part, to which very little has been done in the way of hammering or grinding since the celt left the mould, there are striking differences. As will be seen, the mould is calculated to produce three parallel mouldings round the mouth of each celt; but in one of the castings only two of these mouldings are present; in another there are three, and there is metal enough beyond to represent half the width of another moulding. In two others the length is equivalent to nearly another moulding, so that the celts appear to have four mouldings round their mouths; and in the fifth celt there is a collar of plain metal extending $\frac{3}{8}$ inch beyond the three bands (see Fig. 113.) On comparing this instrument with that first described, the difference in the length above the loop is upwards of $\frac{1}{2}$ inch. This difference can only be accounted for by a difference in the arrangement of the mould and core at the time of casting. On comparing the interior of one celt with that of another, it is evident that the core was not produced in any mould or core-box, as the small projecting ribs of metal left as usual to help in steadying the haft vary in number and position. In the case of the celt broken in two in the middle, the core has been placed so much out of the centre that there is a large hole in the casting where there was not room for the metal to run. The system adopted appears, therefore, to have been much as follows.

First, the mould was tied together in proper position, and loam or clay was rammed into it so as tightly to fill the upper part. The mould was, secondly, taken apart—and the clay removed and probably left to become nearly dry. Thirdly, the lower part of the clay was then trimmed to form the core, a shoulder being left which would form the mould for the top of the celt. The upper part of the clay would be left untouched, beyond having two channels cut in it to allow of the passage of the melted metal. Fourthly, the mould would be tied together again with the prepared core inside, the untrimmed part of which would form a guide for its due position in the mould. Fifthly, the mould would then be placed vertically, probably by being stuck into sand, and the melted metal would be poured down the channels. When cool the runners thus formed would be broken off, and the fractured surfaces would be hammered or ground. The knife found with the hoard was probably used for cutting the channels and trimming the core. If such a process as that which I have described were in use, it is evident that the chances would be much against the shoulders of the clay core being always cut at exactly the same place, and we have at once a reason for the variation here observed.

There is another cause for slight variations in the sharpness of the mouldings and the other details of the castings. In order to prevent the molten bronze from adhering to the bronze mould, the latter must have been smeared over with something by way of protection, so as to form a thin film between the metal of the mould and that of the casting. Modern founders, when casting pewter in brass, or even iron, moulds,* "anoint" the latter with red ochre and white of egg, or smoke the inside of the mould; and our plumbers prevent solder from amalgamating with lead by using lamp-black and size, or even by rubbing it with a dock-leaf. No doubt the ancient founders had some equally simple method, such as brushing the mould over with a very thin coat of marl. Turning now to the second mould, Fig. 531, it will be seen that just below the mouldings there is accidentally present a sharply defined small recess; the impression, however, of this recess on the celt cast in this mould is not nearly so sharp, probably in consequence of the mould having been smeared as lately suggested. It will also be noticed that though there is a double band of mouldings in the mould, there is but one and a fraction on the celt itself, which is shown in Fig. 114.

The outside of this mould is provided with three knobs to keep the binding cord from slipping off. The other and smallest half-mould has a single projection in the middle, like an imperfectly formed loop. The three celts which were apparently cast in this mould show great uniformity at their upper ends, and to the reason for this I think the lead adhering to the mould furnishes a clue. It is evident that if, in preparing the cores, instead of beginning by having the mould empty and ramming clay into it,

* Holtzappfel, "Turning and Mech. Manip.," vol. i. p. 321; *Arch. Journ.*, vol. iv. p. 337.

which was subsequently to be trimmed, the founder placed a celt in the mould, its socket would act as a core-box or mould for a clay core which would require no further trimming so far as the part of forming the socket was concerned. On opening out the mould this core could be withdrawn from the socket of the model celt, and when dry would be ready for use. Perhaps in the celts with long and not highly tapering sockets there would be a difficulty in getting out the clay unbroken, and the process would not be found to answer; but in the case of the small celts there would probably be less difficulty. In this mould I think we have the remains of a celt formed of lead, an instrument which would be utterly useless as a cutting tool, but which might well have been made and kept as a core-box. The very fact of its being made of another metal would prevent its being confounded with the other castings and being bartered away; while in the first instance a casting in lead might have been made on a wooden core, which could probably be trimmed to the exact shape required more readily than one of clay. I have elsewhere* called attention to the fact that wooden moulds were in use among the Ancient Britons for the casting of coins formed of tin. Several socketed celts made of lead have from time to time been found, though not in association with bronze-founders' hoards, and have been a great puzzle to antiquaries. One found at Alnwick,† near Sleaford, Lincolnshire, was thought to have come from a barrow. One found with bronze celts in the Morbihan, is in the collection of the Rev. Canon Greenwell, F.R.S., but it is doubtful whether it was used as a core-box. The use which I have suggested for them is at all events one that is possible, but we must wait for further discoveries before accepting it as the only cause for their existence.

A mould for sword hilts found in Italy,‡ and now in the museum at Munich, is formed by three pieces of bronze, even the core by which the cavity in them was produced being formed of that metal.

But that the cores were frequently if not always made of clay, and not, as has been sometimes supposed, of metal, is proved by the numbers of socketed celts which from time to time have been found with the cores still in them, though this, it is true, has been the case in France rather than in England. In the great hoard of socketed celts found near Plénée Jugon, in Brittany, the majority

* "Anc. British Coins," p. 124.
† *Proc. Geol. and Polyt. Soc. of Yorkshire*, 1866, p. 439.
‡ Lindenschmit, "Alt. u. h. Vorz.," Heft. i. Taf. ii. 10, 11, 12.

were as they had come from the mould, with the clay cores still in them, burnt as hard as brick by the heat of the metal. I have already mentioned this fact in describing the tool from the Harty hoard, which appears to have been used for extracting the cores. I have also described the anvil, if such it be, and the hammer, Figs. 211 and 212, by means of which, probably, the edges of the celts were drawn out and hardened. I will now add that the celt, Fig. 114, is too long and too broad at the edge for that part of it to enter into the mould in which it was cast. This shows how much its edge was drawn out by hammering. The final sharpening was no doubt effected by the whetstone, Fig. 540.

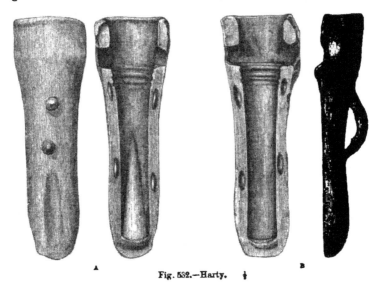

Fig. 532.—Harty. ⅓

The other mould from this hoard is almost unique of its kind. Two views of each of its halves are given in Fig. 532. Originally there was a loop on the back of each half, but from one this has in old times been broken off. The arrangement for carrying the core is different from what it seems to have been in the other moulds. There is in the upper part of the mould when put together a transverse hole, which would produce what may be termed trunnions on the clay core, and assist materially in holding it in proper position during the process of casting. From the upper surfaces of the gouges found with the mould, it appears that there were two channels cut for the runners of metal, one at the middle of each half of the mould, so as to alternate with the joint of the mould through which the air could escape during the casting process.

What appears to be part of a mould for gouges was found in the hoard of Notre-Dame d'Or, and is now in the museum at Poitiers.

I must now return to the other examples of moulds for socketed celts which have been found in this country.

One, with external loops on each half, like that on Fig. 532B, was found with looped palstaves, socketed celts, and broken dagger or sword blades, at Wilmington,* Sussex, and is now in the museum at Lewes. All these objects, as is the case in many other hoards, had been deposited in a vessel of coarse pottery.

Another mould, found with eleven celts and fragments of weapons at Eaton,† near Norwich, has smaller and broader loops near the top. On each side of the face of one half, a little distance from the actual mould, and roughly following its contour, is a shallow groove, into which fits a corresponding ridge on the counterpart. The outer face of each half is ornamented with two slightly curved vertical ribs, one on each side of the loop, and joined at the base by a transverse rib. It is for casting celts about 4¼ inches long, and of the ordinary form.

Another mould, for celts with an octagonal neck, was found on the Quantock Hills,‡ Somersetshire (and not in Yorkshire), and is now in the British Museum. The halves are adjusted to each other by a rib and groove, as on that last mentioned, and the back is ornamented with a peculiar raised figure with three vertical lines and a straight transverse line at the top, and two lines at the bottom running up to the central vertical line so as to form on each side of it an angle of about 120°. At the junction there is a ring ornament, and two others near the angles formed with the side lines. This mould has a transverse hole at the top like that in the gouge-mould already mentioned.

Another mould, also in the British Museum,§ is for celts with three vertical ribs on the face. This likewise has a transverse and nearly square hole at the top, and also recesses in each half-mould, so as to give four points of support to the core between which the channels for the runners might be cut. On the outside, near the top, is a loop, and near the bottom two projecting pins to retain the string. This appears to be the mould from Yorkshire belonging to Mr. Warburton, figured by Stukeley.∥

The half of another mould for celts, of nearly the same character, was found in the Heathery Burn Cave,¶ already so often mentioned, and is shown in Fig. 533, for the use of which I am indebted to the Council of the Society of Antiquaries.

Another mould was found in the fen at Washingborough,** near Lincoln. Another, from Cleveland,†† found with chisels, gouges, &c., is in the Bateman Collection.

A part of another was found in a hoard at Beddington, Surrey,‡‡ and a

---

* Suss. Arch. Coll., vol. xiv. p. 171; Arch. Journ., vol. xx. p. 192.

† Arch., vol. xxii. p. 424; Arch. Journ., vol. vi. p. 387; "Arch. Inst.," Norwich vol., p. xxvi. I have assumed that the mould described in these passages is one and the same.

‡ Arch., vol. v. pl. vii.; Arch. Journ., vol. iv. p. 336, pl. iii. 5, 6, 7, 8.
§ Arch. Journ., vol. iv. pl. ii. 5, 6, 7, 8.   ∥ "Itin. Cur.," pl. xcvi, 2nd ed.
¶ Proc. Soc. Ant., 2nd S., vol. ii. p. 132; Arch. Journ., vol. xix. p. 358.
** Arch. Journ., vol. xviii. p. 166.   †† Ibid.
‡‡ "Surrey Arch. Soc. Coll.," vol. vi.

fragment of another at Wickham Park, Croydon. This latter is now in the British Museum.

A bronze mould for socketed celts, found at Eikrath, was in the collection of the late Dr. Hugo Gärthe, of Cologne. Upon the outside there are six ribs with ring ornaments at the ends, diverging from a loop in the centre.

A bronze mould for socketed celts, ornamented with V-shaped lines, and found at Gnadenfeld,[*] in Upper Silesia, is in the Berlin Museum.

Another bronze mould with an external loop, also for socketed celts, was found in Gotland,[†] and is in the Stockholm Museum.

A magnificent mould for socketed celts was found in the Cotentin[‡] in 1827. It has broad loops outside either half, with three processes from it running up and down the mould.

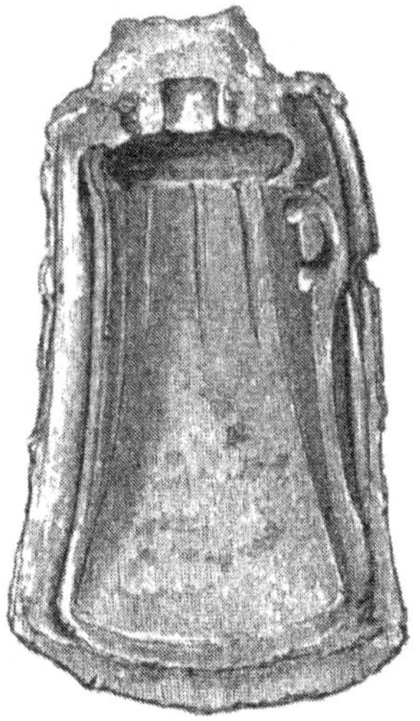

A bronze mould for spear-heads was exhibited in Paris in 1878. A part of another was in the Larnaud hoard, and is now in the museum at St. Germain.

There were some fragments of bronze moulds in the great Bologna hoard.

Fig. 533.—Heathery Burn. ¼

The process of casting bronze instruments in loam, clay, or sand must have been much the same as that in use at the present day; but it was very rarely that the mould consisted of more or less than two pieces. On a great many bronze instruments the joint of the mould is still visible; and in some of the large hoards, such as those which have been found in the North of France, we see the castings just as they came from the moulds, except that the runners have been broken off. For socketed celts there were usually two runners of metal; for palstaves sometimes two, and sometimes only one nearly the full width of the upper part. It is not uncommon to find castings which show that the two halves of the mould or the flasks have slipped sideways, so that they were not in proper position when the casting was made.

I have a palstave from a large hoard found near Tours, in which the lateral displacement of the mould is as much as a quarter of an inch, so that there is what geologists might term a "fault" in the casting. The metal which has been in contact with what was the face of the mould is smooth, and appears to have been cast against

* Bastian und A. Voss, " Die Bronze-schwerter des K. Mus.," p. 76.
† Ulfsparre, "Svenska Fornsaker," pl. viii. 93.
‡ Mém. Soc. Ant. Norm., 1827-8, pl. xviii.

clay. A considerable variety of patterns was in use by the founder to whom this hoard belonged, and they appear to have been of metal and not of wood, some of the palstaves having been apparently cast from tools already shortened by wear.

That castings were occasionally made even from tools already mounted in their handles is proved by the Swiss hatchet, Fig. 185.

Some portions of moulds formed of burnt clay were found with broken palstaves, socketed celts, gouges, knives, spear-heads, daggers, swords, lumps of metal, runners, &c., at Questembert, Brittany, and are in the museum at Vannes.

Part of a mould for spear-heads formed of burnt clay was found in the Lac du Bourget ;[*] but the most interesting discoveries are those which have been made by Dr. V. Gross at the station of Mœrigen,[†] on the Lake of Bienne. He there found a considerable amount of the plant of an ancient bronze-founder, all of whose moulds, however, were either in stone or burnt clay, and not formed of metal. The stone moulds appear to have been principally used for the plainer articles, such as knives, sickles, pins, &c., while for articles with irregular surfaces, or requiring cores, clay was preferred. Of clay moulds Dr. Gross recognises two types : one formed in a single piece, which could serve but once, and which was broken in extracting the casting ; and the other, which was composed of two or more pieces, and which could be used over and over again. Of the first kind there were two examples—one for a socketed chisel and the other for a socketed knife. The form of the mould for a chisel is nearly cylindrical, with a funnel-shaped opening at one end, at the bottom of which are two holes leading into the interior of the mould. The clay between these two holes forms part of a conical core. Such a mould would give the idea of its having been formed on a model of wax on the system known as that of *cire perdue ;* but this appears not to have been really the case, for on examination the mould itself appears to have been originally formed of two halves, or valves, formed of fine clay, which had been well burnt, and these when put together had been surrounded by an external envelope of coarse clay, which held them and the core they enclosed in their proper position. The core itself seems to have been T-shaped, the ends of the transverse line being triangular and fitting into corresponding recesses in the valves of the mould.

[*] Chantre, " Alb.," pl. liv. 5.   [†] Keller, 7ter Bericht, p. 16, Taf. xvii.

The best-preserved mould of the second kind was one for a socketed hammer, which was also provided with a core of the same kind. It seems to me, however, that the distinction drawn by Dr. Gross between the two classes of moulds does not really exist, as by enveloping such a mould as that for the hammer in a mass of clay it would be transferred from the second class to the first.

Clay moulds for socketed-celts have been found in Hungary.*

In some Scandinavian examples† of what appear to have been ceremonial axes there is merely a thin coating of bronze cast over a clay core, but no such specimens have as yet been found in Britain. That bronze so thin could have been cast shows wonderful skill in the founder.

The heads and runners, jets or waste pieces, from the castings were reserved for being re-melted, and are frequently found in the

Fig. 534.—Stogursey. ½   Fig. 535.—Stogursey. ½   Fig. 536.—Stogursey. ½

bronze-founders' hoards. They are of course of various sizes, but are usually conical masses, showing the shape of the cup or funnel into which the metal was poured, and having one, two, or more processes from them showing the course of the metal into the mould.

Figs. 534, 535 and 536, all from the same hoard, found at Stogursey,‡ Somersetshire, will give a fair idea of the general character of these waste pieces, or jets. They are shown with their flat face downwards, or in the reverse position to what they occupied when in the molten state, and exhibit one, two, and four runners from them respectively. No less than fifteen of these objects were found with this deposit—six with one runner, three with two, and six with four.

Jets of metal, for the most part with two runners, were found with the Westow hoard,§ Yorkshire, those of Marden,‖ Kent; of Kensington;¶

* "Matériaux," vol. xii. p. 184.
† "Aarböger for Nord. Oldk.," 1866, p. 124.
‡ Proc. Soc. Ant., 2nd S., vol. v. p. 409.
§ Arch. Journ., vol. vi. p. 382; Arch. Assoc. Journ., vol. iii. pp. 10 and 58.
‖ Arch. Assoc. Journ., vol. xiv. p. 258.
¶ Proc. Soc. Ant., 2nd S., vol. iii. p. 232.

and of Hounslow. Those from the two latter deposits are in the British Museum.

Another waste piece, 1¾ inch long, with two runners, was found in the Heathery Burn Cave,* and is shown in Fig. 537.

A very symmetrical jet, circular, with four irregularly conical runners proceeding from it, was in the hoard found at Lanant,† Cornwall, and is now in the Museum of the Society of Antiquaries.

Another oval head (2 inches long), with four runners from it, has much the appearance of a sword pommel. It was found with socketed celts on Kenidjack Cliff,‡ Cornwall.

A perforated disc, with a collar round the central hole (Fig. 503), which at one time § I regarded as a waste piece from a casting, I have now reason to think was prepared for some special purpose, as at least one object of this class has been found with the runners removed, and in a finished condition. See page 403.

Fig. 537.
Heathery Burn.

The conical lump of metal found with the hoard at Marden,‖ Kent, and described as "a very rare species of fibula," may be the head of metal from a casting.

Some conical funnels of burnt clay, found in the Lake-dwellings near Laibach, have been regarded as having served to receive the metal in the casting process.

Runners of the same character as those already described have been found in different countries, including Denmark¶ and Sweden.**

We must now briefly consider the processes to which the castings were subjected before being finally brought into use. Where the objects had sockets cast over clay cores, those cores had to be removed, probably by means of pointed tools, such as that already described under Fig. 220. Where they were solid they seem in most cases to have undergone a considerable amount of hammering, which both rendered the metal more compact, and to a certain extent removed the asperities resulting from the joints in the mould. With edged tools and weapons, whether socketed or not, the edges especially were drawn down by means of the hammer.

These hammers, as has already been shown, were occasionally themselves of bronze, and so also were some of the anvils. It is, however, probable that in most cases both hammers and anvils were stones, either natural pebbles and flat slabs, or occasionally wrought into special shapes. In South Africa at the present day the iron assegais are wrought with hammers and anvils of stone. Judging from the unfinished condition of the tools and weapons in some

* *Proc. Soc. Ant.*, 2nd S., vol. ii. p. 132. I am indebted to the Council for the use of this cut ; *Arch. Journ.*, vol. xix. p. 358.

† *Arch.*, vol. xv. p. 118, pl. ii.   ‡ *Journ. Roy. Inst. of Cornwall*, No. xxi. fig. 4.
§ " Petit Album," pl. xxv. 6.   ‖ *Arch. Assoc. Journ.*, vol. xiv. p. 260.
¶ Worsaae, " Nord. Olds.," figs. 213, 214.   ** Montelius, " La Suède préh.," fig. 40.

of the old bronze-founders' hoards, and from large deposits of socketed celts having been found with the clay cores still in them, it seems not improbable that the founders often bartered away their castings nearly in the state in which they came from the moulds, with only the runners broken off, and that those who acquired them finished their manufacture themselves. Possibly a hammering process upon the surface of the socketed spear-heads and celts would so loosen the cores that they would fall out or could be extracted with merely a pointed stick.

After the hammering, the surface of most weapons and of some tools was further polished, probably by friction with sand, or with a rubbing-stone of grit. I have elsewhere described some of the stone rubbers which appear to have been in use in conjunction with sand, for the purpose of grinding and polishing the faces of different forms of perforated stone axes, which in Britain at all

Fig. 538.—Kirby Moorside.

Fig. 539.—Hove.

events belonged to the period when bronze was known. It is, therefore, probable that similar rubbers were employed for grinding and polishing the faces of bronze weapons; and the rubber shown in Fig. 538 appears to have been destined for this purpose. It was found with several socketed celts at Keldholm, near Kirby Moorside, North Riding of Yorkshire, and is now in Canon Greenwell's collection. The material seems to be trap.

No doubt many other such rubbing-stones must exist, and it is possible that some of those which I have regarded as used for the grinding and polishing of weapons of stone may have served for those of bronze. Whetstones of various kinds have from time to time been discovered in company with bronze instruments. Near Little Wenlock,[*] Staffordshire, some spear-heads, a socketed celt, and part of a dagger were found in 1835, and with them are recorded to have been three or four small whetstones. In the Dowris hoard[†] also some rubbers of stone with convex, concave, and

flat surfaces were present.   In my "Ancient Stone Implements"*
I have given an account of a number of whetstones found at
various places in company with bronze relics, not unfrequently
with interments in barrows, and I need not here repeat the
details.   I reproduce, however, in Fig. 539 a whetstone found
in a barrow at Hove, near Brighton,† with the remains of a
skeleton, a stone axe-head, an amber cup, and a small bronze
dagger.

Another whetstone, shown in Fig. 540, was found with the
hoard in the Isle of Harty, and no doubt was employed by the
ancient bronze-founder for finishing off the edges of the socketed
celts and gouges in which he dealt.   It is made from a sort of
ragstone.

The decoration of the surfaces of bronze implements by sunk, and
in some cases by raised lines appears to have been
effected, not as a rule by any method of engraving,
but by means of punches, as already described in
Chapter III.   I have in that chapter accidentally
omitted to mention two decorated bronze celts which
have been figured and described by Mr. Llewellynn
Jewitt, F.S.A.‡   They were both found at a place called
Highlow, in the High Peak of Derbyshire, about two
miles from Hathersage, and are in the possession of the
Duke of Devonshire.   There seems some reason to
believe§ that the celts were found in a barrow accompanied by burnt bones and pottery.   One of them
(6¾ inches) is flat and ornamented with lines of slightly
impressed chevrons running along it.   The other (6½
inches) is flanged and ornamented with a similar herring-
bone pattern, which in this instance ends in a row of
triangles near the edge of the celt.   In some few cases the patterns
may have been engraved, and I find on trial that there is no difficulty in engraving such parallel lines as are frequently seen on
dagger blades by means of a flake of flint.   Such an instrument
suffers but little by wear, and by means of a ruler, either straight
or curved, there is no difficulty in engraving lines of the required
character in the bronze, though the lines are hardly so smooth as
if made with a chisel-edged punch.

Fig. 540.
Harty.   ½

* Chap. xi. p. 235 *et seqq.*
† *Suss. Arch. Coll.*, vol. ix. p. 120, whence this cut is borrowed; *Arch. Journ.*,
vol. xiii. p. 184, vol. xv. p. 90.   ‡ "Reliquary," vol. iv. p. 63.
§ Pennington, " Barrows and Bone Caves of Derbyshire," 1877, p. 51.

Notches which would assist in the breaking off of superfluous pieces of metal, such as the runners in the moulds, can readily be made with flint flakes used as saws.

For smoothing the surface of bronze instruments flint scraping-tools are not so efficient, as they are liable to "chatter" and to leave an uneven and scratched surface, much inferior to one produced by friction with a gritty rubber.

There remains little more to be said with regard to the manufacture of the ancient bronze tools and weapons. It may, however, be observed that the processes of hammering-out and sharpening the edges were employed not only by those who first made the instruments, but also by the subsequent possessors. Many tools, such for instance as palstaves, like Fig. 65, were no doubt originally much longer in the blade than they are at present, and have in the course of use either been broken and again drawn down and sharpened, or have been actually worn away and "stumped up" by constant repetition of these processes. The recurved ends of the lunate cutting edges of many such instruments are also due to repeated hammering-out. In some instances the broken part of one instrument has been converted into another form—as, for example, a fragment of a broken sword into a knife or dagger, or a palstave that has lost its cutting end, into a hammer.

CHAPTER XXII.

CHRONOLOGY AND ORIGIN OF BRONZE.

HAVING now passed in review the various forms of instruments, arms, and ornaments belonging to the Bronze Period of Great Britain, it will be well to attempt some chronological arrangement of the different types, and to examine the means at our command for fixing the approximate date and duration of the Period as well as the sources from which the knowledge of bronze in this country was derived.

The sequence and extent of variation in the types of an instrument or weapon destined to serve some given purpose are of course important factors in any theoretical calculation of the length of time such an instrument was in use. For if the type has remained one and the same during the whole period of the use of the instrument, it affords no evidence as to the length of its duration; whereas, if it has varied, and the sequence of its variations can be traced, their nature and extent may afford some means of judging of the length of time probably necessary for the development of the succession of forms. Or where an instrument has been so well adapted for its particular ends that no material modification in its form was likely to take place in it, so long as its use was limited to its original purpose, yet the springing from it of what may be termed collateral types of instruments specialized for other though analogous purposes may also be indicative of the original form having remained in use during a lengthened period of time.

The extremely numerous variations which may be observed in socketed celts afford conclusive evidence of that instrument having been employed in this country during a long series of years; and the collateral varieties, such as socketed chisels and gouges, as well as the more distantly related socketed hammers, give corroborative testimony to the same effect.

Improvements in the method of working metals will often react on the forms of tools and weapons, but here again the chronological element exists, as old processes and old forms are slow to die, especially among a people of no very high material civilisation. The discovery, for instance, of the art of producing hollow sockets in bronze castings by the use of cores of loam or clay, though it materially modified the form of many instruments, did not cause the entire extinction of the older forms without sockets, the use of which in some cases went on side by side with that of the instruments of more novel invention; and this fact tends to prove that bronze must have long been in use for tools with tangs instead of sockets, before the process of coring was known. Indeed, as I have elsewhere* pointed out, the Bronze Period of Britain is susceptible of division into an earlier and later stage, the former mainly characterized by instruments which were let into their hafts or handles, and the latter by those which received their handles in sockets. As will subsequently be seen, it may be divided even into three more or less distinct stages.

A division into two stages has been suggested for the Scandinavian Bronze Age. M. Gabriel de Mortillet has in like manner divided the Bronze Period of France and Switzerland into an earlier and later stage—the one distinguished by flanged celts, which came into use at the close of the Stone Period (his Epoque *robenhausienne*), and the other by palstaves and socketed celts, which he regards as belonging to the close of the Bronze Period. To these two stages he has applied the terms *morgien* and *larnaudien*, derived from the Lake-dwelling of Morges, in the Lake of Geneva, and from the large founder's hoard discovered at Larnaud (Jura). Curiously enough he regards the flat celts as being even more recent in date than the socketed, forgetful that the form with flanges at the sides can hardly by any possibility have been an original type, as such flanges must either have been produced by hammering the sides of flat celts, or must have been cast in a mould consisting of two halves, which certainly cannot have been so early a form of mould as a simple recess in stone, sand, or clay, adapted for casting a nearly flat plate of metal like a wedge-shaped celt.

Such flat celts, as has already been mentioned, have been found with interments in barrows associated with what were apparently lance-heads of flint, and maces and battle-axes of stone; and their nearest allies, those with but slight flanges—the result of ham-

* *Proc. Soc. Ant.*, 2nd S., vol. v. p. 412.

mering the sides—have also been found under similar circumstances.

The knife-daggers, as described in Chapter X., and the awls or prickers, are the only other bronze instruments which in this country can challenge a similar antiquity; and none of these, as a rule, are found in those deposits of bronze objects to which the name of "hoards" has been given.

As M. Gabriel de Mortillet and others have pointed out, these hoards are of more than one character. In certain cases they seem to have been the treasured property of some individual who would appear to have buried his valued tools or weapons during troublous times, and never to have been able to disinter them. In other cases the hoards were probably the property of a trader, as they consist of objects ready for use and in considerable numbers; and in others, again, they appear to have been the stock-in-trade of some bronze-founder of ancient times, as they comprise worn out and broken tools and weapons, lumps of rough metal, and even the moulds in which the accumulation of bronze was destined to be recast.

Mr. Worsaae has suggested that some of these hoards may be of a votive character and have been deposited in the ground as precious offerings to the gods. I am not, however, aware of any of our British hoards being of such a character that they can safely be regarded as votive.

As to the other three kinds of hoards, the small group from Wallingford* (No. 60 in the following table), consisting of a socketed celt, gouge, and knife, and a tanged chisel and razor, may be taken as a good instance of a private deposit. That of Stibbard † (No. 8), consisting of seventy palstaves and ten spear-heads, some of them rough from the mould, would appear to have belonged to a merchant; and the Harty hoard (No. 105), described in the last chapter, affords a typical example of the stock-in-trade of a bronze-founder.

In some other cases, deposits, especially when consisting exclusively of ornaments, may possibly be of a sepulchral character.

The value of the evidence afforded by hoards, especially by those of the first and second kinds lately mentioned, is great and unquestionable in determining the synchronism of various forms of instruments—as, for instance, of plain and looped palstaves with socketed celts. In the case of the bronze-founders' hoards of

* Page 128.   † Page 84.

old metal, it is of course possible that the fragments contained may belong to various periods. Nevertheless the objects, as a rule, appear to be such as were in use at the time, and which, being worn out or broken, were collected by the bronze-founder for the purpose of re-melting. In order to make them at once more portable and more ready for placing in the crucible, he generally broke the larger and longer articles into fragments, broken spear-heads, swords, &c., being frequently present in the hoards, as well as the jets or waste pieces of metal broken off from castings. In some instances fragments of various instruments have been inserted in the sockets of others, so as to diminish the space occupied by the whole.

As will subsequently be seen, by far the greater number of the undoubted bronze-founders' hoards belong to a time when socketed celts were already in use, and therefore to the close rather than the beginning of our Bronze Period.

M. Ernest Chantre has divided the principal hoards of the Bronze Age discovered in France into three principal categories, to which he has applied the terms "*Trésors*," "*Fonderies*," and "*Stations*." The first, as a rule, comprise articles which have never been in use, and are, in fact, of the same character as the hoards which I have classed under the head of "Personal" or "Merchants." The principal *trésors*, those of Réallon, Ribiers, Beaurières, Manson, Frouard, are characterized by the presence of socketed instruments; and in two instances—those of La Ferté-Hauterive, and Vaudrevanges, Rhenish Prussia—either an ingot or a mould of metal was present. I should, therefore, have classed these two among the "*fonderies*."

M. Chantre has, however, in the main, restricted this term to hoards consisting principally of broken objects, and of these *fonderies* he has examined some fifty in France. In the southern part of that country these hoards are by no means so constantly characterized by the presence of socketed celts and other socketed instruments as in Britain. In the north of France, however, the socketed forms are more frequent in the hoards.

The *stations* are considered to represent habitations of the Bronze Age of the same character as the Lake-dwellings, but fixed on *terra firma* instead of on piles or artificial islands. Some of the hoards placed under this head appear from the presence of moulds and lumps of metal to be those of founders.

Hoards of broken objects of bronze have been found in other parts of Europe, but it seems needless to do more than mention the fact. I may, however, refer to the hoards of Camenz and Grossenhain, in Saxony,* of which I gave an account to the Society of Antiquaries some fifteen years ago.

In the following lists I have divided the principal hoards discovered in the United Kingdom into two main categories, the one, in which socketed celts, gouges, or other tools were absent; the other, in which they were present in greater or less abundance. This is perhaps the simplest method of arriving at what may be regarded as a fairly trustworthy chronological division. Some of the results of an examination of the lists will subsequently be discussed. In the first list I have given the precedence to those hoards in which flat or flanged celts were present. Second, I have placed those in which there were palstaves. Third, those in which ornaments were found; and last, those mainly characterized by swords and spear-heads, or spear-heads and ferrules, but in which both palstaves and socketed celts were absent.

In the second list I have placed at the head the hoards in which socketed celts, sometimes accompanied by palstaves, were found associated with swords or spears, while mere tools, such as gouges and hammers, were absent. Next come a few cases in which socketed celts occurred either in company with ornaments or alone. Then follow the hoards in which chisels, gouges, or hammers were found, but no lumps of metal were present. After these are placed the bronze-founders' hoards, in which lumps of metal and the jets or waste pieces from castings were found, including one or two Scotch and Irish hoards; and, finally, those in which moulds were present.

In each case I have attempted to distinguish whether a hoard was personal or belonged to a merchant or founder, by adding the letters P, M, or F. Where two of these letters occur, the hoard seems to come under either category. It is possible that some of those characterized by a P may be sepulchral.

Appended to the tabulated lists is a more detailed account, mentioning some of the principal features in each case, and giving references to the works in which the discoveries are recorded. Of course this is to a great extent a repetition of what has been recorded in previous pages. It must be observed that the numbers given in the lists do not always refer to entire objects but frequently to fragments only. Where the numbers are unknown the presence of the objects is shown by an *x*.

* *Proc. Soc. Ant.*, 2nd S., vol. iii. p. 328

LIST I.	1. Arreton Down P.M.	2. Plymstock P.M.	3. Battlefield M.	4. Postlingford Hall M.	5. Rhoesneeney M.F.	6. Broxton P.	7. Sherford M.	8. Stibbard M.	9. Quantock Hills P.	10. Hollingbury Hill P.	11. Edington Burtle P.M.	12. Woolmer Forest P.	13. West Buckland P.	14. Blackmoor M.F.	15. Fulbourn Common P.P.	16. Pant-y-maen M.F.	17. Wicken Fen F.P.	18. Corbie Moss P.	19. Weymouth P.	20. Whittingham P.	21. Worth M.	22. Stoke Ferry M.P.	23. Brechin M.	24. Duddingston Loch M.	25. Point of Sleat P.	26. River Wandle P.	27. Tarves P.	28. Maentwrog M.F.	29. Bloody Pool M.F.	30. Broadward M.	
METAL																															M
JETS																															J
MOULDS																															Mo
MISCELLAN.		4							2		4					1					4										Mi
CALDRONS																					4										O
RINGS								3	6	2		3		3																	R
CLASPS																											2				Cl
BUTTONS																															Bu
BRACELETS								4	3	4	1																				Br
TORQUES								2	1	1	2	1																			T
PINS																								1	2						P
TRUMPETS																															Tr
FERRULES	1													1	2	4	1												6	4	F
SPEAR-HEADS						1	10							26	1	13	2	1		3	2	4	4	2	1			1		87	Sp
TANGED SP.	9	1																													TS
SCABBARDS														2		1	1					1						1			Sc
SWORDS														27	2	4	5	1	1	2	2	4	4	1		8				4	S
RAPIERS																												8			R
DAGGERS	2	3				1																									D
HALBERDS	1																					1									H
RAZORS																															R
KNIVES																															K
SICKLES									4																						S
HAMMERS																															H
AWLS																															A
GOUGES																															G
CHISELS	1					1																									Ch
SOCK. CELTS																															SC
PALSTAVES		4			6	2	6	70	2	1	4	1	2													1					FO
FLANGED CTS.	4	16	4	19	3																										FC

LIST II.

	31	32	33	34	35	36	37	38	39	40	41	42	43	44	45	46	47	48	49	50	51	52	53	54	55	56	57	
METAL																												M
JETS																												J
MOULDS																												Mo
MISCELLAN.			2				4	4		4		2	4	4								6		2				Mi
CALDRONS																												C
RINGS									2													4					1	R
CLASPS																											1	Cl
BUTTONS																												Bu
BRACELETS	3																											Br
TORQUES											3									1								T
PINS										2										1								P
TRUMPETS																												Tr
FERRULES	1	1	1																									F
SPEAR-HEADS	4	4	2			1	7	16	2	4	4	1		4	2	6	1	2				28	2	2	4	4		Sp
TANGED SP.																												TS
SCABBARDS																							1					Sc
SWORDS		6				2	2	20	1	2	4												4					S
RAPIERS	1	2			1																							R
DAGGERS										1																		D
HALBERDS																												H
RAZORS										3																		R
KNIVES		1								1												5				1	1	K
SICKLES																						2						S
HAMMERS																							1		1			H
AWLS																												A
GOUGES																						6		1	1	1	1	G
CHISELS																						3						Ch
SOCK. CELTS	4	7	16	2	4	1	6	41	7	4	1	3	1	4	6	4	2	1	2	4	31	2	4	1	1	4		SC
PALSTAVES	1	8	1	4	1																		3	12				P
FLANGED CTS.																							1					FC

No.	Hoard	Metal
31.	Mawgan	P.M.
32.	Wallington	M.
33.	Nottingham	M.F.
34.	Nettleham	M.
35.	Haxey	?
36.	Ambleside	P.M.
37.	Bilton	M.F.
38.	Alnwick Castle	M.P.
39.	Flixborough	M.F.
40.	Shenstone	F.M.
41.	Wrekin Tenement	P.M.
42.	Llandyssilio	P.
43.	Dunbar	M.F.
44.	Little Wenlock	P.P
45.	Winmarleigh	P.
46.	Newark	M.
47.	Hagbourn Hill	M.P.
48.	Ty Mawr	P.
49.	Wedmore	M.
50.	Wymington	M.
51.	Roepham	F.
52.	Yattendon	M.P
53.	Taunton	P.P
54.	Beacon Hill	M.P
55.	Ebnall	M.P
56.	Exning	P.P
57.	Melbourn	P.P

LIST II. (*continued.*)

		METAL	JETS	MOULDS	MISCELLAN.	CALDRONS	RINGS	CLASPS	BUTTONS	BRACELETS	TORQUES	PINS	TRUMPETS	FERRULES	SPEAR-HEADS	TANGED SP.	SCABBARDS	SWORDS	RAPIERS	DAGGERS	HALBERDS	RAZORS	KNIVES	SICKLES	HAMMERS	AWLS	GOUGES	CHISELS	SOCK. CELTS	PALSTAVES	FLANGED CTS.
58.	Stanhope	F.?			2										5			1					1			1	1		4		
59.	Thornton	P.													1							1			1	1	1	2	2		
60.	Wallingford	P.M.																										1		4		
61.	Whittlesea	P.											1					1												2		
62.	Barrington	P.																	1				1									
63.	Porkington	P.						3		2	1		1										1				1		1			
64.	Trillick	P.M.						5																2								
65.	Bo Island	P.	15	5			1				1		1		3	3		9									1		25	2	1
66.	Llangwyllog	F.	10	13	2									2	4		16	4				1	2			1	3	1	16	5	
67.	Meldreth	F.	4					3							21			6									1		4	2	
68.	Houndow	F.	8	5											13			5									2		4	2	1
69.	Hundred of Hoo	F.	8	5							1				5		1	4					1				2	1	4	3	
70.	Guilsfield	F.M.	3												1													3	2	1	
71.	Stogursey	F.M.																										3			
72.	Chrishall	F.		1				1																			6				
73.	Romford	F.	1												1			1		1							1				
74.	Cumberlow	F.																							1		4		47	1	
75.	Beachy Head	F.														2				1									2	2		
76.	Oxford	F.?																											3			
77.	Westow	F.M.																													2	
78.	Carlton Rode	F.																			1							1		12	2	
79.	Kenidjack Cliff	F.		1					2							1			1					1					2	11	1	
80.	Helsdon Hall	F.																						1			1			21	1	
81.	Worthing	F.M.	3		3	3	5	8	2	6					7			2	1	4		5	5		1	3	6	2	9	29	1
82.	Reach Fen	F.	5		5	4		8							8	1	1	8				1			1	2	2	1	9	5	
83.	Haynes Hill	F.	9																								2				
84.	Allhallows	F.														1												1				

LIST II. (continued.)

Category	Abbr.
METAL	M
JETS	J
MOULDS	Mo
MISCELLAN.	Mi
CALDRONS	C
RINGS	R
CLASPS	Cl
BUTTONS	Bu
BRACELETS	Br
TORQUES	T
PINS	P
TRUMPETS	Tr
FERRULES	F
SPEAR-HEADS	Sp
TANGED SP.	Ts
SCABBARDS	Sc
SWORDS	S
RAPIERS	R
DAGGERS	D
HALBERDS	H
RAZORS	R
KNIVES	K
SICKLES	Si
HAMMERS	H
AWLS	A
GOUGES	G
CHISELS	Ch
SOCK. CELTS	SC
PALSTAVES	P
FLANGED CTS.	FC

Hoards:

85.	St. Hilary	F.
86.	Alderney	F.M.
87.	Kingston Hill	F.
88.	Sittingbourn	F.
89.	Martlesham	F.
90.	Lanant	F.
91.	West Halton	F.
92.	Burwell Fen	F.M.
93.	Marden	F.
94.	Kensington	F.
95.	Roseberry Topping	F.
96.	Danesbury	F.
97.	Earsley Common	F.
98.	High Roding	F.M.
99.	Panfield	F.?
100.	Westwick Row	P.
101.	Aehtertyre	F.
102.	Dowris	M.F.
103.	Hotham Carr	F.?
104.	Beddington	F.
105.	Harty	F.
106.	Heathery Burn	F.
107.	Wickham Park	F.
108.	Wilmington	F.
109.	Cleveland	F.
110.	Eaton	F.

LISTS OF HOARDS.

LIST I.

Locality.	Remarks.	Reference.
1. Arreton Down, Isle of Wight.	Flanged celts, some ornamented, tanged spear-heads, ferrule to one, halberd? one socketed dagger.	*Arch.*, vol. xxxvi. p. 326.
2. Plymstock, Devon.	Flanged celts, straight chisel.	*Arch. Journ.*, vol. xxvi. p. 346; *Trans. Devon. Assoc.*, vol. iv. p. 304.
3. Battlefield, Shrewsbury.	Mostly melted. Flat celts, palstaves, curved objects.	*Proc. Soc. Ant.*, 2nd S., vol. ii. p. 251.
4. Postlingford Hall, Clare, Suffolk.	Flanged celts, some ornamented.	*Arch.*, vol. xxxi. p. 496; *Proc. Soc. Ant.*, vol. i. p. 83.
5. Rhosnesney, Wrexham, Denbighshire.	Palstaves, all from one mould; castings for a dagger and for flanged celts of narrow form.	*Arch. Camb.*, 4th S., vol. vi. p. 72.
6. Broxton, Cheshire.	Tanged chisel; socketed spear-head.	*Penes* Sir P. de M. G. Egerton, F.R.S.
7. Sherford, Taunton, Somerset.	One palstave, a defective casting.	Pring, "British and Roman Taunton," p. 76.
8. Stibbard, near Fakenham, Norfolk.	Castings for small palstaves and spear-heads.	*Arch. Inst.*, Norwich vol. p. xxvi.
9. Quantock Hills, Somerset.	Each palstave laid within a torque.	*Arch.*, vol. xiv. p. 94.
10. Hollingbury Hill, Brighton, Sussex.	Palstave laid within a torque, bracelets around.	*Arch. Journ.*, vol. v. p. 323; *Arch.*, vol. xxix. p. 372, &c.
11. Edington Burtle, Somerset.	One casting for a flat sickle; ribbed bracelet and ring.	*Som. Arch. and Nat. Hist. Proc.*, vol. v. (1854) pt. ii. p. 91.
12. Woolmer Forest, Hants.	There appears some doubt about the small torques.	*Arch. Assoc. Journ.*, vol. vi. p. 88; *Bateman's Catal.*, p. 22.
13. West Buckland, Somerset.	Two-looped palstave.	*Arch. Journ.*, vol. xxxvii. p. 107.
14. Blackmoor, Hants.	Fragments of swords and sheaths, large and small spear-heads.	White's "Selborne," Bell's ed., 1877, vol. ii. p. 381.
15. Fulbourn Common, Cambs.	Swords broken, leaf-shaped spear-heads, broad-ended ferrules.	*Arch.*, vol. xix. p. 56.
16. Pant-y-maen, Cardiganshire.	Swords and leaf-shaped spear-heads, broken or damaged.	*Arch. Camb.*, 3rd S., vol. x. p. 221.
17. Wicken Fen, Cambs.	Nearly all fragmentary; fragments perhaps of two swords.	In British Museum.
18. Corsbie Moss, Legerwood, Berwickshire.	Sword perfect.	*Proc. Soc. Ant.*, vol. iii. p. 121.
19. Weymouth, Dorset.	Both sword and spear-head nearly perfect.	*Penes Auct.*
20. Thrunton Farm, Whittingham, Northumberland.	Spear-heads, leaf-shaped, and with lunate openings; all objects unbroken.	*Proc. Soc. Ant.*, 2nd S., vol. v. p. 429.
21. Worth, Washfield, Devon.	Sword and leaf-shaped spear-heads, perfect.	*Arch. Journ.*, vol. xxiv. p. 120.

Locality.	Remarks.	References.
22. Stoke Ferry, Norfolk.	Swords and leaf-shaped spear-heads broken, halberd.	ones Auct.; Proc. Soc. Ant., 2nd S., vol. v. p. 425.
23. Brechin, Forfarshire.	Swords, &c., unbroken.	Arch. Journ., vol. xiii. p. 203; Proc. Soc. Ant. Scot., vol. i. pp. 181 and 224.
24. Duddingston Loch, Edinburgh.	Swords, spear-heads, &c., in fragments; caldron.	Proc. Soc. Ant. Scot., vol. i. p. 132; Wilson, "Preh. Ann. of Scot.," vol. i. p. 348.
25. Point of Sleat, Isle of Skye.	Sword, spear-head, and pin, perfect.	Proc. Soc. Ant. Scot., vol. iii. p. 102.
26. River Wandle, Surrey.	All objects nearly perfect.	Arch. Journ., vol. ix. p. 7.
27. Tarves, Aberdeenshire.	Objects mostly perfect.	Horæ ferales, p. 161.
28. Cwm Moch, Maentwrog, Merionethshire.	Objects unbroken; loops at base of blade of spear-head.	Arch., vol. xvi. p. 365.
29. Bloody Pool, South Brent, Devon.	Spear-heads mostly barbed; all objects broken.	Arch. Journ., vol. xii. p. 84; xviii. p. 160.
30. Broadward, Leintwardine, Herefordshire.	Spear-heads, leaf-shaped, with perforations in blade, and barbed.	Arch. Camb., 4th S., vol. iii. p. 345; iv. 202.

LIST II.

31. Mawgan, Cornwall.	Rapier in high preservation.	Arch., vol. xvii., p. 337.
32. Wallington, Northumberland.		In Sir C. Trevelyan's Collection.
33. Nottingham.	Fragments of swords, and possibly of scabbard-tip.	Proc. Soc. Ant., 2nd S., vol. i. p. 332.
34. Nettleham, Lincolnshire.	Socketed celts of peculiar types.	Arch. Journ., vol. xviii. p. 159.
35. Haxey, Lincolnshire.		Penes Canon Greenwell, F.R.S.
36. Ambleside, Westmoreland.	Swords described as broad-swords, and sharp-pointed swords.	Arch., vol. v. p. 115.
37. Bilton, Yorkshire.	Swords broken, one spear-head ornamented.	Arch. Assoc. Journ., vol. v. p. 349.
38. Alnwick Castle, Northumberland.	Found in 1726.	Arch., vol. v. p. 113.
39. Flixborough, Lincolnshire.	Sword broken. Possibly palstaves.	Arch. Journ., vol. xxix. p. 194.
40. Greensborough Farm, Shenstone, Staffordshire.	Swords apparently perfect.	Arch., vol. xxi. p. 548.
41. Wrekin Tenement, Shrewsbury.	One celt, a few swords, about 150 spear-heads and fragments.	Arch., vol. xxvi. p. 464.
42. Llandysilio, Denbighshire.	See p. 119.	Penes Canon Greenwell, F.R.S.
43. Dunbar, Haddingtonshire.	Uninjured.	Proc. Soc. Ant. Scot., vol. x. p. 440.
44. Little Wenlock, Shropshire.	Spear-heads mostly broken, whetstones with them. Possibly the same hoard as No. 41.	Hartshorne, "Salop. Ant.," p. 96; Arch. Journ., vol. viii. p. 197.

H H

Locality.	Remarks.	Reference.
45. Winmarleigh, Garstang, Lancashire.	One spear-head, large, and with lunate openings; all found in "a cist or box."	*Arch. Journ.*, vol. xviii. p. 158.
46. Near Newark, Nottinghamshire.	Two large discs in hoard.	*Penes* Canon Greenwell, F.R.S.
47. Hagbourn Hill, Berks.	Bridle-bits and late Celtic buckles, said to have been found; coins also?	*Arch.*, vol. xvi. p. 348.
48. Ty Mawr, Holyhead.	Said to have been found in a box.	*Arch.*, vol. xxvi. p. 483.
49. Heath House, Wedmore, Somerset.	Amber beads found at same time; possibly palstaves and not socketed celts.	*Arch. Journ.* vol. vi. p. 81.
50. Wymington, Beds.	About sixty celts found.	Specimens *penes Auct.*
51. Reepham, Norfolk.	Found about 1747.	*Arch.*, vol. v. p. 114.
52. Yattendon, Berks.	Swords in fragments, tanged chisels and knives, two socketed knives, *flat* celt much worn.	*Proc. Soc. Ant.*, 2nd S., vol. vii. p. 480.
53. Taunton, Somerset.	Flat sickles, looped pin.	*Arch. Journ.*, vol. xxxvii. p. 94.
54. Beacon Hill, Charnwood Forest, Leicestershire.	Leaf-shaped spear-heads.	*Proc. Soc. Ant.*, vol. iv. p. 323.
55. Ebnall, Oswestry, Salop.	Two punches?	*Arch. Journ.*, vol. xxii. p. 167.
56. Exning, Suffolk.	Mostly perfect?	*Arch. Journ.*, vol. x. p. 3: vol. ix., p. 303.
57. Melbourn, Cambs.	Sword broken, a clasp.	*Arch. Journ.*, vol. xi. p. 294.
58. Stanhope, Durham.	Leaf-shaped spears, fragment of sword, broken hammer, &c.	*Arch. Æliana*, vol. i. p. 13.
59. Thorndon, Suffolk.	All entire. Most of these are figured on previous pages.	*Arch. Journ.*, vol. x. p. 3.
60. Wallingford, Berks.	Entire; mostly here figured.	*Penes Auct.*
61. Whittlesea, Cambridgeshire.	Entire; one celt with loop on face.	In Wisbech Museum.
62. Barrington, Cambs.	Perfect.	*Penes Auct.*
63. Porkington, Shropshire.	Point broken off sword.	*Arch. Journ.*, vol. vii. p. 195.
64. Trillick, Tyrone.	Perfect; two rings with cross perforations for the pin.	*Journ. Hist. and Arch. Assoc. of Irel.*, 3rd S., vol. i. p. 164.
65. Bo Island, Fermanagh.	Sword and hammer broken.	*Penes Auct.*
66. Llangwyllog, Anglesea.	Connected with the other hoards by the razor and buttons.	*Arch. Journ.*, vol. xxii. p. 74.
67. Meldreth, Cambs.	Most of the objects broken; socketed chisel, flat lunate knife with opening in middle, caldron ring.	In British Museum.
68. Hounslow, Middlesex.	One *flat* celt, swords in fragments.	*Proc. Soc. Ant.*, 2nd S., vol. iii. p. 90; vol. v. p. 428.
69. Hundred of Hoo, Kent.	Most of the objects broken. See p. 95.	*Arch. Cant.*, vol. xi. p. 123.

Locality.	Remarks.	Reference.
70. Guilsfield, Montgomeryshire.	Objects for the most part broken, spear-heads with lunate openings.	*Proc. Soc. Ant.*, 2nd S., vol. ii. p. 251; *Arch. Camb.*, 3rd S., vol. x. p. 214; *Montg. Coll.*, vol. iii. p. 437.
71. Wick Park, Stogursey, Somerset.	Swords broken, numerous fragments of other forms.	*Proc. Soc. Ant.*, 2nd S., vol. v. p. 427.
72. Chrishall, Essex.	Portion of socketed knife.	Neville's "Sep. Exp.," p. 3.
73. Romford, Essex.	Swords broken, socketed chisel, celts not trimmed.	*Arch. Journ.*, vol. ix. p. 302.
74. Cumberlow, Baldock, Herts.	Swords in fragments.	*Journ. Anth. Inst.*, vol. vi. p. 195.
75. Beachy Head, Eastbourne, Sussex.	Fragment of sword, four gold bracelets.	*Arch.*, vol. xvi. p. 363.
76. Burgesses' Meadow, Oxford.	An ingot 9¾ inches long.	In Ashmolean Museum.
77. Westow, Yorkshire.	Seventeen fragments included among the celts; one chisel socketed, two tanged.	*Arch. Journ.*, vol. vi. p. 381; *Arch. Assoc. Journ.*, vol. iii. p. 58.
78. Carlton Rode, Norfolk.	One tanged gouge, tanged and socketed chisels.	Smith's "Coll. Ant.," vol. i. 105; *Arch. Journ.*, vol. ii. 80; *Arch. Assoc. Journ.*, vol. i. p. 51; *Arch.*, vol. xxxi. p. 494.
79. Kenidjack Cliff, Cornwall.	Large oval jet.	*Journ. Roy. Inst. of Corn.*, No. xxi.
80. Helsdon Hall, Norfolk.	Found before 1759.	*Arch.*, vol. v. p. 116.
81. Worthing, Sussex.	Found in an earthern vessel.	Specimens *penes Auct.*
82. Reach Fen, Cambs.	Fragments of swords and many broken objects.	*Arch. Assoc. Journ.*, vol. xxxvi., p. 56.
83. Haynes Hill, Saltwood, Kent.	Objects nearly all broken.	*Arch. Journ.*, vol. xxx. p. 279; *Journ. Anth. Inst.*, vol. iii. p. 230.
84. Allhallows, Hoo, Kent.	Objects mostly broken, flat knife. See p. 214.	*Arch. Cant.*, vol. xi. p. 124.
85. St. Hilary, Cornwall.	Swords in fragments; weight altogether about 80 lbs.	*Arch.*, vol. xv. p. 120.
86. Longy Common, Alderney.	Socketed sickle, objects mostly broken.	*Arch. Assoc. Journ.*, vol. iii. p. 9.
87 Kingston Hill, Coombe, Surrey.	Objects all fragmentary.	*Arch. Journ.*, vol. xxvi. p. 288.
88. Sittingbourne, Kent.	In two urns; broken sword and rings in one urn, celts, &c., in the other.	Smith's "Coll. Ant.," vol. i. p. 101; *Arch. Journ.*, vol. ii. p. 81.
89. Martlesham, Suffolk.	Fragments of swords, socketed knife.	*Penes* Capt. Brooke.
90. Lanant, Cornwall.	Fragments of swords; pieces of gold in one celt.	*Arch.*, vol. xv. p. 118.
91. West Halton, Lincolnshire.	Fragment of sword.	*Arch. Journ.*, vol. x. p. 69.
92. Burwell Fen, Cambs.	The ring penannular and of triangular section.	*Penes Auct.*
93. Marden, Kent.	Found in an earthen vessel, mostly broken.	*Arch. Assoc. Journ.*, vol. xiv. p. 257.
94. Kensington, Middlesex.	Knives broken.	*Proc. Soc. Ant.*, 2nd S., vol. iii. p. 232.

Locality.	Remarks.	References.
95. Roseberry Topping, Yorkshire.	Mostly broken.	*Arch. Æliana*, vol. ii. p. 213 ; *Arch. Scotica*, vol. v. p. 55.
96. Danesbury, Welwyn, Herts.	Mostly imperfect.	*Arch. Journ.*, vol. x. p. 248.
97. Earsley Common, Yorkshire.	Nearly 100 celts found in 1735.	*Arch.*, vol. v. p. 114.
98. High Roding, Essex.	Some figured in previous pages.	In British Museum.
99. Panfield, Essex.	Possibly other forms found at same time.	*Proc. Soc. Ant.*, 2nd S., vol. v. p. 428.
100. Westwick Row, Hemel Hempsted, Herts.	One celt broken.	*Penes Auct.*
101. Achtertyre, Morayshire.	With tin. See p. 425.	*Proc. Soc. Ant. Scot.*, vol. ix. p. 435.
102. Dowris, Parsonstown, King's County.	With caldrons, trumpets, bells, &c. See p. 361.	Wilde, "Catal. Mus. R. I. A.," pp. 360, 613, 626 ; *Proc. R. I. Ac.*, vol. iv. pp. 237, 423.
103. Hotham Carr, Yorkshire.	Palstaves almost all damaged.	*Penes* Canon Greenwell, F.R.S.
104. Beddington, Surrey.	Many fragments, mould broken.	*Surrey Arch. Soc. Coll.*, vol. vi. ; Anderson's "Croydon," p. 10.
105. Isle of Harty, Kent.	See p. 441.	*Penes Auct.*
106. Heathery Burn Cave, Durham.	Socketed knife, large collars and discs. See p. 119, &c.	*Arch. Journ.*, vol. xix. p. 358 ; *Proc. Soc. Ant.*, 2nd S., vol. ii. p. 127.
107. Wickham Park, Croydon, Surrey.	Mould broken, other objects mostly fragmentary ; list partly compiled from Anderson, and partly from originals.	Anderson's "Croydon," p. 10 ; British Museum.
108. Wilmington, Sussex.	In an urn, mostly broken or worn.	*Suss. Arch. Coll.*, vol. xiv. p. 171 ; *Arch. Journ.*, vol. xx. p. 192 ; *Proc. Soc. Ant.*, 2nd S., vol. v. p. 423.
109. Cleveland, Yorkshire.	Said to be in the Bateman Collection. Possibly the same hoard as No. 95.	*Arch. Journ.*, vol. xviii. p. 166.
110. Eaton, Norfolk.	Spear-heads apparently broken.	*Arch.*, vol. xxii. p. 424 ; *Arch. Journ.*, vol. vi. p. 387 ; *Arch. Inst.*, Norwich vol. p. xxvi.

Turning now to the lists, the following observations may be made, though they must be accepted as liable to revision under the light of future discoveries :—

1. That flat celts and knife-daggers, such as have been frequently found in barrows, rarely occur in hoards, only two instances being recorded of the occurrence of flat celts.

2. That flanged celts and palstaves are occasionally found together, while the latter are frequently associated with socketed celts.

3. That socketed weapons are of rare occurrence in association with flanged celts, though a socketed dagger and a ferrule for a tanged spear-head or dagger were present in the Arreton Down hoard.

4. That such tanged spear-heads or daggers are never found in company with socketed celts.

5. That torques are more frequently associated with palstaves than with socketed celts, and are mainly confined to our western counties.

6. That there are several instances of swords and scabbards, and spear-heads and ferrules being found together without either palstaves or socketed celts being with them.

7. That swords, or their fragments, are not found with flanged celts.

8. That socketed celts are often found with swords and spear-heads, or with the latter alone.

9. That socketed celts are often accompanied by gouges, and somewhat less frequently by hammers and chisels, though even where such tools occur, spear-heads are generally present.

10. That caldrons, or the rings belonging to them, have been discovered with socketed celts, both in England and Ireland.

11. That where metal moulds are found in hoards they are usually those for socketed celts.

12. That where lumps of copper or rough metal occur in hoards, socketed celts are, as a rule, found with them.

The general inferences are much the same as have already been indicated in former chapters, viz., that two of the earliest forms of bronze weapons discovered in the British Isles are the flat and the slightly flanged celts, and the thin knife-daggers. That these are succeeded by the more distinctly flanged celts, and the tanged spear-heads, with which probably some of the thick dagger-blades found in barrows are contemporary. That subsequently the celts with a stop-ridge and the palstave form came in and remained in use to the close of the Bronze Period, though to a great extent supplanted by the socketed celt which, as has already been shown, was probably evolved from one of the forms of the palstave ; and it may here be remarked that flanged celts with a stop-ridge seem rarely, if ever, to occur in the hoards. That the socketed chisels, gouges, hammers, and knives are contemporary with the socketed celts, as are also socketed spear-heads and swords.   That hoards in which palstaves only, and not socketed celts, are present rarely belonged to ancient bronze-founders ; but that the deposits which these artificers have left behind them almost all denote a period when the art of coring, and thereby producing socketed tools and weapons, was already well known.

From this latter circumstance, and the comparative abundance of bronze-founders' hoards, it may reasonably be inferred that in this country they belong for the most part to the close of the Bronze Period.   To how recent a date bronze remained in use for cutting purposes is a question difficult of accurate solution.   There are, indeed, two instances in which socketed celts are reported to have been discovered in company with ancient British coins, but in neither case is the evidence altogether satisfactory.   Two unin-scribed silver coins, of the type of my Plate F, No. 2*, are stated to have been found with a human skeleton and a bronze celt at Cann, near Shaftesbury, in 1849 ; but I believe that this state-ment would, if it were now capable of being sifted, resolve itself into the fact of the two coins, the celt, and some bones having been found near together by the same workman, without their being actually in association together.   The type of the coins, though probably among the earliest in the British silver series, is one which was derived from gold coins struck some considerable time after the introduction of a gold coinage into this country, and probably belongs to the first century B.C.   If such coins were in contemporary use with socketed celts, it is strange that none of the gold coins of earlier date have ever been found associated with bronze instruments.

It is true that in the account given in the *Archæologia*† of the antiquities discovered on Hagbourn Hill, Berks, it is stated that at the bottom of a pit about four feet from the surface of the ground was a further circular excavation, in which, together with bronze bridle-bits and buckles of Late Celtic patterns, were socketed celts, and a spear-head of bronze, and, in addition, some coins. These, however, were not seen by the writer of the account, but he was informed " that one of them was silver and the other gold, the latter of which was rather large and flat, and perhaps one of the lower empire."   Looking at the Late Celtic character of some of the objects it seems possible that Ancient British coins might have been found with them ; but, on the other hand, it is evident that the particulars given of the find were all derived from the

* Evans's " Coins of the Anc. Britons," p. 102.   † Vol. xvi. p. 348.

workmen who dug up the objects, and not from personal observation; and it is possible that not only were the coins described not actually found with the bronze celts and spear-heads, but that these latter were not discovered in actual association with the Late Celtic bridle-bits. I have, however, provisionally accepted the account of their being found together, relying to some extent on the Abergele* hoard, in which some buckles allied in form to those from Hagbourn Hill were present, associated with slides such as have been elsewhere found with socketed celts.

Whatever may be the real state of the case in these discoveries, there is every probability of a transition having gradually taken place in this country, from the employment of bronze for cutting tools and weapons of offence to the use of iron or steel for such instruments; in other words, from a Bronze Age to an Iron Age, such as that to which the term "Late Celtic" has been applied.

That this transition must have been effected, at all events in the South of Britain, prior to the Roman invasion, is shown, as has already been pointed out, by the circumstance that the Early Iron swords found in France belong in all probability to a period not later than the fourth or fifth century B.C., while the southern parts of Britain had, long before Cæsar's time, been peopled by Belgic immigrants, who either brought the knowledge of iron with them or must have received it after their arrival from their kinsmen on the continent, with whom they were in constant intercourse. In the more northern parts of Britain and in Scotland an acquaintance with iron was probably first made at a somewhat more recent period; but in the Late Celtic interments in Yorkshire no coins are present, and the iron and other objects found exhibit no traces of Roman influence. Moreover, the Roman historians, who have recorded many of the manners and customs of the northern Britons, do not in any way hint at their weapons being formed of bronze.

In Ireland, perhaps, which was less accessible from the continent than Britain, the introduction of iron may have taken place considerably after the time when it was known in the sister country; but there appears to have been a sufficient intercourse between Scotland and the north of Ireland at an early period for the knowledge of so useful a metal, when once gained, to have been quickly communicated from one country to the other.

* *Supra*, p. 405; *Arch.*, vol. xliii. p. 556.

On the whole I think we may fairly conclude that in the southern parts of Britain iron must have been in use not later than the fourth or fifth century B.C., and that by the second or third century B.C. the employment of bronze for cutting instruments had there practically ceased. These dates are of course approximate only, but will at all events serve to give some idea of the latest date to which bronze weapons and tools found in England may with some degree of safety be assigned.

As to the time at which such weapons and tools were here first in use, we have even less means of judging than we have as to when they fell into desuetude. It is, however, evident that the Bronze Period of the British Isles must have extended over a long period of years, probably embracing many centuries. The numerous bronze-founders' hoards, containing fragments of tools and weapons of so many various forms, testify to the art of bronze-founding having been practised for a lengthened period; and yet in all of these the socketed celt occurs, or some other socketed instruments, which we know to have been contemporary with it, are present. It is true that the socketed celt was not originally developed in this country, but was introduced from abroad; and, as has already been pointed out, was derived from a form of palstave which is of rare occurrence in Britain. Yet the length of time requisite for the modification of the flat form of celt to that with flanges, of this latter again to that with the flanges produced into wings, and finally the transition into the palstave with the wings hammered over so as to form sockets on each side of the blade, must itself have been of very great duration.* The development of the forms of palstave common to Britain and the opposite shores of the Continent must also have demanded a long lapse of years, and most of the stages in its evolution can be traced in this country. We have the flat celt, the flanged celt, and the flanged celt with a stop-ridge; and we can trace the modification of form from one stage to another until the characteristic palstave is reached, in which the stop-ridge is as it were formed in the actual body of the blade. And it is to be observed that this form of palstave had already been developed at the time represented by the earliest of the ordinary bronze-founders' hoards, in which, moreover, the flanged celts, either with or without a stop-ridge, are hardly ever present.

* See also Col. A. Lane Fox's "Primitive Warfare, Sect. III.," in *Journ. R. U. Service Inst.*, vol. xiii.

The Bronze Age of Britain may, therefore, be regarded as an aggregate of three stages : the first, that characterized by the flat or slightly flanged celts, and the knife-daggers frequently found in barrows associated with instruments and weapons formed of stone ; the second, that characterized by the more heavy dagger-blades and the flanged celts and tanged spear-heads or daggers, such as those from Arreton Down ; and the third, by palstaves and socketed celts and the many forms of tools and weapons, of which fragments are so constantly present in the hoards of the ancient bronze-founders. It is in this third stage that the bronze sword and the true socketed spear-head first make their advent.   The number of these hoards, and the varieties in the forms of these swords and spear-heads, as well as in the socketed celts and other tools, would, I think, justify us in assigning a minimum duration of some four or five centuries to this last stage.   The other two stages together must probably have extended over at least an equal lapse of time ; so that for the total duration of the Bronze Period in Britain we cannot greatly err in attributing eight or ten centuries. This would place the beginning of the Period some 1,200 or 1,400 years B.C.—a date which in many respects would seem to fit in with what we know as to the use of bronze in the southern parts of Europe.*

Although I have thus attempted to assign a definite chronology to our Bronze Age, I do so with all reserve, as any such attempt is founded upon what are at best imperfect data, and each of the stages I have mentioned may have been of far longer duration than I have suggested, though it is not likely that any of them should have been materially shorter.

There is, it must be acknowledged, the difficulty which I have already mentioned, as to the absence of nearly all traces of the later stages of the Bronze Period in the graves and barrows that have been examined in Britain.†   The reason of this absence has still to be discovered ; but it may perhaps have been the case that during this time the method or fashion of interring the dead underwent some change, and the practice of placing weapons and ornaments with the bodies of departed friends and relatives fell into disuse.   Among the bronze-using occupants of the Yorkshire Wolds, whose burial-places have been explored by Canon Green-well, the interments by inhumation were much in excess over those

* The Bronze Period of Switzerland has by some been calculated to have begun not less than 3,000 years B.C.—Zaborowski Moindron, " L'Anc. de l'homme," 1874, p. 208.
† See Greenwell's " British Barrows," p. 44 *et seqq.*

which took place after cremation, but in other parts of England the proportions are reversed. Out of fourteen instances * in which bronze articles were associated with an interment, it was only in two that the body had been burnt ; or taking the whole number of burials, viz. 301 by inhumation and 78 after cremation, bronze articles were found with 4 per cent. of the burials of the former kind and only 2½ per cent. with those of the latter. This seems to point to a tendency towards departing from the old custom of burying weapons with the dead for use in a future life. And, indeed, if the custom of burning the dead became general, the inducement to place such objects among mere dust and ashes would be but small. An urn or a small recess in the ground would suffice to contain the mightiest warrior, and his weapons would be out of place beside the little calcined heap which was left by the purifying fire. Even the practice of raising mounds or barrows over the interments may have ceased, and "when the funeral pyre was out and the last valediction over, men took a lasting adieu of their interred friends."

It has been suggested that the absence of the later bronze forms with interments is due to a superstitious reverence for the older forms, so that the habit of burying the flat wedge-shaped axe † and the dagger with the dead continued down to the later Age of Bronze ; but I cannot accept this view.

In Scandinavia‡ interments with which bronze swords and other weapons are associated, have frequently been discovered ; and in some instances in which coffins, hollowed out in trunks of trees, have been used, even the clothing has been preserved. In this country also coffins of the same kind have occasionally been discovered, but the bronze objects which have been placed in them are of the same character as those which are found in the barrows of the district, and never comprise socketed weapons or swords. Stone weapons are also occasionally present. Remains of clothing made of skins and of woven woollen fabric have also been found. The best-known instance of the discovery of the latter was in a barrow at Scale House,§ near Rylston, Yorkshire, examined by Canon Greenwell, who has recorded other instances of these tree-burials. Neither bronze nor stone were in this instance present.

It is not, however, my intention to dilate upon the burial customs of our Bronze Age, as they have already been so fully

* "British Barrows," p. 19.   † Dawkins's "Early Man in Britain," p. 348.
‡ See Worsaae in *Arch. Journ.*, vol. xxiii. p. 30.
§ "British Barrows," pp. 32, 375. See also *Reliquary*, vol. vi. p. 1.

discussed by Canon Greenwell, Dr. Thurnam, Sir John Lubbock, and others.

It will now be desirable to say something as to the sources from which the use of bronze in this country was derived, though on this subject also much has already been written.

The four principal views held by different authors have thus been summarized by Colonel A. Lane Fox, now General Pitt Rivers :—*

1. That bronze was spread from a common centre by an intruding and conquering race, or by the migration of tribes.

2. That the inhabitants of each separate region in which bronze is known to have been used discovered the art independently, and made their own implements of it.

3. That the art was discovered and the implements fabricated on one spot, and the implements disseminated from that place by means of commerce.

4. That the art of making bronze was diffused from a common centre, but that the implements were constructed in the countries in which they were found.

For a full discussion of these hypotheses I must refer the reader to General Pitt Rivers' Paper, but I shall here make use of some of the information which he has collected, premising that in my opinion there is a certain amount of truth embodied in each of these opinions.

The first view, of an intruding and conquering race having introduced the use of bronze into their country, has been held by most of the Scandinavian antiquaries, and Professor Boyd Dawkins seems to regard a Celtic invasion and conquest of the Iberic peoples in Britain as having been the means by which the knowledge of bronze was extended from Gaul to these islands. The osteological evidence in favour of the bronze-using Britons having as a rule been of a different race from the stone-using people of our Neolithic times is strongly corroborative of such a view ; as is also the change which is to be noted in the burial customs of the two periods. Such an immigration or conquest must, however, have taken place at a very early period if we accept Sir John Lubbock's† view, that between B.C. 1500 and B.C. 1200 the Phœnicians were already acquainted with the mineral fields of Britain, a period at which it must not be forgotten the use of bronze had long been known in Egypt. Although it is true that

* "Primitive Warfare, Sect. III. ;" *Journ. R. U. S. Inst.*, vol. xiii.
† "Preh. Times," p. 73.

at present we have no satisfactory proof of any Phœnician influence on the people of our Bronze Age, yet if at so early a period there was an export of tin from this country, the search for that metal and the means employed for its production would almost of necessity tend to an acquaintance with copper also, even supposing, what is improbable, that those who traded for tin in order to manufacture bronze with it kept the knowledge of this latter alloy from those with whom they had commercial relations, or that the natives of Britain were not already acquainted with more metals than tin when the trade first began. But to this subject I shall recur. It may be observed by the way that the date assigned for this Phœnician intercourse corresponds in a remarkable manner with the date assigned for the earliest instances of the use of bronze in Britain, which was suggested on other grounds.

The second view of the independent discovery of bronze in different regions has little or nothing to support it so far as the different countries of Europe are concerned, though there is a possibility that the discovery of copper and of the method of alloying it with tin, so as to produce bronze, may have been made independently in America. But it may even there be the case that the knowledge of bronze was imported from Asia.* In Europe, however, when once the use of the metal was known, there were certain types of weapons and implements developed in different countries which in a certain sense may be regarded as instances of independent discoveries.

The third view, that the art was discovered at some single spot at which subsequently implements were manufactured and disseminated by commerce must, at least to a limited extent, be true. Wherever the discovery of bronze may have been made, there is ample evidence of its use having spread over the greater part of Europe if not of Asia; and at first the spread of bronze weapons and tools was in all probability by commerce. Even subsequently there were local centres, such as Etruria, from which the manufactured products were exported into neighbouring countries, as well as to those lying to the north of the Alps. Some even of the bronze vases found in Ireland, though themselves not of Etruscan manufacture, bear marks of Etruscan influences in their form and character. In each country in Europe there may have been one or more localities in which the manufacture of bronze objects was

* Worsaae, in "Aarb. for Nord. Oldk.," 1879, p. 327.

principally carried on, though it may now be impossible to identify the spots. Such large hoards of unfinished castings as those of Plénée Jugon, and other places in Brittany, prove that district, for instance, to have been at one time a kind of manufacturing centre. Indeed, a socketed celt of Breton type, unused, and still retaining the burnt clay core, has been found on our southern coast.

The process of casting, as practised by the ancient bronze-founders, was, moreover, one requiring a great amount of skill; and though there appear to have been wandering founders, who, like the bell-founders of mediæval times, could practise their art at any spot where their services were required, yet there were probably fixed foundries also, where the process of manufacture could be more economically carried on, and where successive generations passed through some sort of apprenticeship to learn the art and mystery of the trade.

The fourth opinion, that the use of bronze spread from some single centre, though implements were manufactured in greater or less abundance in each country where the use of bronze prevailed, is one that must commend itself to all archæologists. It does not, of course, follow that in any given district the bronze tools and weapons were all of home manufacture, and none of them imported. There is, on the contrary, evidence to be found in most countries that some, at least, of the bronze instruments found there are of foreign manufacture, and introduced either by commerce or by the foreign travel of individuals.

Where the original centre was placed, from which the European use of bronze was propagated, is an enigma still under discussion, and one which will not readily be solved. Appearances at present seem to point to its having been situate in Western Asia ;* but the whole question of the origin and development of the Bronze civilisation has been so recently discussed by my friend Professor Boyd Dawkins, in his "Early Man in Britain," that it appears needless here to repeat the opinions of which he has given so good an abstract. Suffice it to say, that it has been proposed to regard the bronze antiquities of Europe as belonging generally to three provinces,† the boundaries of which, however, cannot be very accurately defined. These provinces are—the Uralian, comprising Russia, Siberia, and Finland ; the Danubian, which consists of the

* See A. Bertrand in *Rev. Arch.*, vol. xxvi. p. 363.
† See Chantre, "Age du Bronze," 2ème ptie. p. 281.

Hungarian, Scandinavian, and Britannic sub-divisions or regions; and the Mediterranean, composed of the Italo-Greek and Franco-Swiss sub-divisions.

I must confess that I do not attach such high importance to this classification as at first sight it would seem to merit; for on a close examination it appears to me to involve several serious incongruities. Take, for instance, the Danubian province, and it will be found that the differences in type of bronze instruments belonging to the Hungarian region, when compared with those of the British, are on the whole greater than the difference presented when they are compared with the types of the Italian region, which, however, is made to belong to another province. There is, moreover, a difficulty in synchronizing the antiquities belonging to different provinces or regions, so as to be sure that any comparisons between them are of real value. Taking, for example, the Uralian province, it will at once be seen that though in Finland some Scandinavian types occur, such as swords and palstaves, yet the great majority of the bronze antiquities belonging to it, so far as at present known, consist of socketed celts, often with two loops; of daggers, with their hafts cast in one piece with the blade; and of perforated axes, sometimes with the representations of the heads of animals; in fact, of objects which evidently belong to a very late stage in the evolution of bronze, and which, as Mr. Worsaae has pointed out, not improbably show traces of Chinese influence. Such objects can hardly be satisfactorily compared with those of a province in which the whole development of bronze instruments, from the flat celt and small knife, to the socketed celt and the skilfully cast spear-head and sword, can be traced.

All things considered, I think it will be better and safer to content ourselves for the present with less extensive provinces; and, so far as these are concerned, the sub-divisions already enumerated may be accepted, and are quite sufficiently large, if, indeed, they are not too extensive. In the Britannic province, a part of France is included by M. Chantre, and there are certainly close analogies between many of the types of the south of England and those of the north and north-west of France. For the purpose of the present work, though accepting M. Chantre's boundary in the main, I shall, however, restrict the Britannic province to the British Isles.

On a general examination of our British types it is satisfactory to see how complete a series of links in the chain of development of the bronze industry is here to be found, though many of them bear undoubted marks of foreign influence, and prove that though some of the types were of native growth, yet that others were originally imported. On general grounds, I have assigned an antiquity of 1,200 or 1,400 years B.C. to the introduction of the use of bronze into this country, but it is a question whether this antiquity will meet all the necessities of the case; for we can hardly imagine the Phœnicians, or those who traded with them, landing in Britain and spontaneously discovering tin. On the contrary, it must have been from a knowledge that the inhabitants of Britain were already producers of this valuable metal that the commerce with them originated; and the probable reason that tin was sought for by the native Britons was in order to mix it with copper, a metal which occurs native in the same district as the tin. If, therefore, the Phœnician intercourse, direct or indirect, commenced about 1500 B.C., the knowledge of the use of tin, and probably also of copper, dates back in Britain to a still earlier epoch.

A comparison of the various British types of tools and weapons with those of Continental countries has been frequently instituted in the preceding pages, but it will be well here to recapitulate some of the principal facts. We have in Britain the flat form of celt in some abundance, though none of the specimens exhibit traces of being direct imitations of hatchets formed of stone, as would probably have been the case in any country where the use of metal for such instruments originated. And yet many of our British flat celts exhibit a certain degree of originality, inasmuch as they are decorated with hammer- or punch-marks in a manner peculiar to this country, and others in a fashion but rarely seen abroad. We can trace the development of the flanged celt from the flat variety, through specimens with almost imperceptible flanges, the result merely of hammering the sides, to those with the flanges produced in the casting. At the same time, the flanges are never so fully developed as in some of the French examples.

The development of a stop-ridge between the flanges, which eventually culminated in the ordinary palstave form, can probably be better observed in the British series than in that of any other country. At the same time, the origin of the other form of palstave—that without a definite stop-ridge, and with semicircular wings bent over so as to form a kind of side-pocket—can best be traced on the Continent, and especially in the south of France. It was from this form of palstave that the socketed celt was developed, and although this development seems to have taken place abroad, possibly in Western Germany, the form was introduced into Britain at an early period of its existence, as is proved by the semicircular projections and curved "flanches" so common on the faces of the socketed celts of this country.

Our knife-daggers may originally have been of foreign introduction, but evidently belong to a time when metal was scarce, and like the flat and slightly-flanged celts have often been found associated with stone implements. The dagger-blades of stouter make, which seem to have succeeded them, show analogies with French, Italian, and German examples; but similar blades, with a tang such as those from the Arreton Down hoard, seem to be almost peculiar to Britain. The fact, however, that the socketed blade found with them has its analogues both in Switzerland and Egypt suggests the probability of the tanged form being also of foreign, and possibly Mediterranean origin; indeed, a specimen is reported to have been found in Italy.

Our halberd blades with the three rivets are nearly allied to those of northern Germany; and the type appears never to be found in France, though I have met with a solitary example in Southern Spain, and the form is not unknown in Italy, there being one from the province of Mantua in the British Museum. Socketed chisels, hammers, and gouges were probably derived from a foreign source; but tanged chisels, though not absolutely wanting in the North of France, are more abundant in the British Isles than elsewhere. Long narrow chisels with tangs were, however, present in the great Bologna hoard.

Bronze socketed sickles are almost peculiar to the British Isles, though they have occasionally been found in the North of France. The flat form, from which they must have been developed, is of rare occurrence, though not unknown in Britain. Its origin is to be sought in the South of Europe, though the British examples more closely resemble German and Danish forms than those of any other country. Tanged single-edged knives are almost unknown in our islands, though so abundant in the Swiss Lake-dwellings and in the South of France. Double-edged knives with a socket are, however, almost peculiar to Britain and Ireland, though they are found in small numbers in the North of France. The tanged razor may also be regarded as one of our specialities, though not unknown in Italy. Most of the foreign varieties have a ring for suspension at the end of the tang, a peculiarity almost unknown in Britain.

Bronze swords, no doubt, originated on the Continent ; and as such long thin blades required great skill in casting, it seems probable that their manufacture was to some extent localized at particular spots, and that they formed an important article of commerce. The same type has been discovered in countries wide apart, and many of those found in Scandinavia are now regarded as being of foreign origin.   Still there are some British types which are rarely or never found abroad, and the discovery of moulds proves conclusively that both leaf-shaped and rapier-shaped blades were cast in these islands.   The latter kind of blades are, indeed, almost exclusively confined to Britain and the north of France.   Bronze scabbard-ends, as distinct from mere chapes, seem also to be confined to the same tract of country.

When we turn to the spear-heads of these islands we find that though the leaf-shaped form prevails over the greater part of Europe, yet that those with loops at the side of the socket and with loops at the base of the blade are common in the British Isles, while they are extremely rare in France, and almost unknown elsewhere.   The same may be said of the type with the small eyelet-holes in the blade, and of those with barbs.   Those with crescent-shaped openings in the blades are also almost unknown elsewhere, though one example has been found in Russia.   Our bronze shields with numerous concentric rings are also specially British.

Among ornaments formed of bronze, there are few, if any, that we can claim as our own.   Our torques seem more nearly connected with those of the Rhine district than of any other part of Europe. Our bracelets, which are not common, hardly present any special peculiarities, and brooches we have none.

Our spheroidal caldrons seem to be of native type, but with them are vases which almost undoubtedly show an Etruscan influence in their origin.

We have here then, I think, sufficient proof that Britain, though not unaffected by foreign influences, and in fact deriving many of the types of its tools and weapons from foreign sources, was, nevertheless, a local centre in which the Bronze civilisation received a special and high development ; and where, had extraneous influences been entirely absent after the time when the knowledge of Bronze was first introduced, the evolution of forms would probably

I I

have differed in but few particulars from that which is now exhibited by the prevailing types found in this country.

If we compare these British types with those of the other regions which together make up the so-called Danubian province, we shall at once be struck, not by the analogies presented, but by the marked difference in the general *facies*.

Taking Scandinavia to begin with, and Mr. Worsaae's types as giving the characteristics of that region, what do we find? The perforated axe-hammers and axes of bronze are here entirely wanting; the tanged swords and the majority of those with decorated hilts are also unknown. There is hardly a type of dagger common to this country and Scandinavia. The saws, knives, and razors are of quite another character, but there is a resemblance in the sickles to a rare British type. The flat and flanged celts of the two regions are of nearly the same kind, and in one rare instance there is a similar decoration on a reputedly Danish and on an Irish celt. The palstaves, however, are of an entirely different character, with the exception of the form with semicircular wings, which is not essentially British. The socketed celts are nearly all unlike those of this country; and though the leaf-shaped spear-heads present close analogies, the looped and eyed kinds are absent. The shields are of a different character from ours. The *tutuli* and diadems are here unknown. There is but one form of torque common to this country and Denmark. Brooches, combs, and small hanging vases are never met with in Britain; and the spiral, whether formed of wire or engraved as an ornament, is conspicuous by its absence.

If we take the Hungarian region, we are driven to much the same conclusions. The perforated axes and pick-axes, principally formed of copper, the semicircular sickles, the spiral ornaments, the swords with engraved hilts of bronze, and several forms of minor importance are absent in Britain, while the socketed celts and the majority of the palstaves are of markedly different types, though that with the semicircular wings hammered over is of common occurrence in Hungary.

In Northern Germany the types of bronze may be regarded as intermediate between those of Hungary and Scandinavia, though in some few respects presenting closer analogies with those of Britain, with which, as will subsequently be seen, there may have been some commercial intercourse. The connection between British and German types is, however, but small, and on the whole I think that the evidence here brought forward is sufficient to prove that the British Isles can hardly be properly classified as forming part of any Danubian province of bronze.

The connection between France and Britain during the Bronze Period cannot be denied, and in many respects there is an identity of character between the bronze antiquities of the North of France and those of the South of England. The North of France cannot, however, at any time since the first discovery of bronze, have been absolutely shut out from all communication with the South and East. The East must always have been affected by the habits of those who occupied what is now Western Germany; and the South can hardly have been exempt from the influence of Italy, if not, indeed, of other Mediterranean countries. I am inclined to think that these external influences acted also on the bronze industry of Britain, not so much directly as indirectly, and that some of the types in this country may be traced to an Italian or German origin as readily as to a French.

It is, I think, a fact that as close a resemblance in type, so far as regards our earliest bronze instruments, may be found among Italian examples as among French. Many of the slightly flanged celts of Italy can hardly be distinguished from those of Britain, except by the faces of the latter being more frequently decorated; and there is also a great similarity between the dagger-blades of the two countries. In the later forms, such as palstaves and socketed celts, the difference between British and Italian examples is sufficiently striking. May it not be the case that at the time when first the commerce between Britain and the Mediterranean countries originated, always assuming that such a commerce took place, the flanged celt was the most advanced type of hatchet known by those who came hither to trade, and the palstave and socketed form were subsequently developed? At a later period it was the German influence that was felt in Britain, rather than the Italian, for our socketed celts appear, as already stated, to have had the cradle of their family in Western Germany; and the few flat sickles that have been found in Britain, as well as the more numerous torques, show a closer connection in type with those of Germany than with those of France or any other country. Whether this introduction of what appear to be North German types can in any way be attributed to commercial relations between the two countries, and especially to a trade in amber, is worth consideration. The abundance of amber ornaments in some of the graves of our Bronze Period shows how much that substance was in use

At the same time, the eastern shores of England might have furnished it in sufficient quantity to supply the demand, without having recourse to foreign sources.   I have known amber thrown up on the beach so far south as Deal.

A curious feature in the comparison of the later bronze antiquities of Britain and those of France, is the marked absence of many of the forms which abound in the remains of the Lake-dwellings of Savoy, as well as in those of Switzerland. A glance through " Rabut's Album "* or " Keller's Lake-dwellings," will at once show how few of the specimens there figured could pass as having been discovered in the British Isles.   The large proportion of ornaments to tools and weapons is also striking.   There is, indeed, as M. Chantre has pointed out, a closer connection between the bronze antiquities of the South of France and those of Switzerland and Northern Italy, than with those of Northern France.

Even the character of the ornaments is in many cases essentially different.   The hollowed form of bronze bracelet, made from a thin plate bent in such a manner as to show a semicircular section, is entirely wanting in Britain, and is very rarely found in the North of France.

Enough has, however, now been said in favour of regarding Britain as one of those centres into which a knowledge of the use of bronze was introduced at a comparatively early date, and where a special development of the bronze industry arose, extending over a lengthened period, and modified from time to time by foreign influences.   On the transition from bronze to iron, it is not necessary here further to enlarge.   I have, in treating of the different forms of tools and weapons, pointed out those which I considered to belong to the close of the Bronze Period ; and it is probable that these forms for some time continued in use, side by side with those made of the more serviceable metal, iron, which ultimately drove bronze from the field, except for ornamental purposes or for those uses for which a fusible metal was best adapted.   It seems probable that, as was the case in Mediterranean countries, some of the socketed weapons, such as spear-heads, which were more easily cast than forged, may for some time have been made of bronze in preference to iron ; but at present our knowledge of any transitional period is slight, and this question would be best treated of in a work on the Late Celtic or Early Iron Period of Britain.

* "Habitations Lacustres de la Savoie," 1864, 1867, 1869.

Among the ornaments in use in this country during the Bronze Period, are some, the history of which, if it could be traced, might throw light upon the foreign intercourse of that time, for glass and ivory were probably not of native production.* Glass beads have occasionally been found in barrows of the Bronze Age, nearly always in our southern counties, and with burnt interments. They are usually small tubes of opaque glass of a light blue or green colour, with the outer surface divided into rounded segments, so as to give the appearance of a number of spheroidal beads side by side. I am not aware of any having been discovered with interments of the Bronze Age on the Continent, but it seems probable that such beads have been found, and they may eventually assist in marking out the lines of ancient commerce with this country. A few larger beads, with spiral serpent-like ornaments upon them, have likewise been found; but these, also, I am unable to compare with any Continental examples. The finding of glass, however, in tombs belonging to the early portion of our Bronze Age is suggestive of some method of intercourse, direct or indirect, with Mediterranean countries. The small quoit-like pendants, formed of a greenish vitrified material, which have been found in Sussex† with burnt interments of the Bronze Age, closely resemble Egyptian porcelain, and their presence in this country corroborates this suggestion.

The discovery of beads made in sets like those of glass, of a bracelet, buttons, pins, and hooks, all, in Dr. Thurnam's opinion, formed of ivory, gives indications in the same direction; for though billiard balls have been manufactured from Scottish mammoth ivory of the Pleistocene Period, the fossil tusks found in Britain are, as a rule, too much decomposed to be any longer of service, and in this respect differ materially from the fossil mammoth tusks of Siberia, which still furnish so much of our table cutlery with handles.

For the jet and amber ornaments of the Bronze Period we have not, of necessity, to go so far afield as for glass. Abundance of jet is to be obtained in our own country, and the usual type of jet necklace,‡ with a series of flat plates, seems to be essentially British. Some of the amber plates found at Hallstatt are, how-

* See Thurnam in *Arch.*, vol. xliii. p. 494.
† *Arch.*, vol. xliii. p. 497.
‡ See "Ancient Stone Impts.," p. 411. I may take this opportunity of correcting the statement that the Assynt necklace is inlaid with gold. It is merely engraved with various patterns, in which micaceous grains of sand got lodged and were mistaken for gold.

ever, of the same form, and perforated in the same manner, so that possibly these jet necklaces may have been made in imitation of foreign prototypes in amber. How far the amber ornaments of the Bronze Period in Britain were of native production we have no good means of judging; but the circumstance just mentioned is suggestive of Hallstatt and Britain having been supplied from a common source, which may have been on the shores of the Baltic. On the other hand, our amber ornaments differ, as a rule, from those of Scandinavia, and, as already remarked, our eastern coast would furnish an ample supply of the raw material without seeking it abroad. It must,. however, be remembered that some of the forms of our bronze instruments show traces of German influence, and that in Strabo's time both amber and ivory were among the articles exported from Celtic Gaul to Britain. The remarkable amber cup from the Hove barrow, near Brighton, I have described elsewhere.*

It remains for me to say a few words as to the general condition of the inhabitants of Britain during the Bronze Age; but on this subject, apart from the light thrown upon it by the tools, weapons, and ornaments which I have been describing, and by the contents of the graves of the period, we have in this country but little to guide us. Such a complete insight into the material civilisation of the period as that afforded by the Lake-dwellings of Switzerland, Savoy, and Northern Italy is nowhere vouchsafed to us in Britain. The Irish crannoges, which, in many respects, present close analogies with the pile-buildings, have remained in use until mediæval times, and in no instance has the destruction of a settlement by fire contributed to preserve for the instruction of future ages the household goods of the population. The nearest approach to a Lake-dwelling in England is that examined in Barton Mere,† Suffolk, where, however, the results were comparatively meagre. A single spear-head was found, apparently of the type of Fig. 406, and the remains of various animals used for food, including the urus and the hare, which latter in Cæsar's time the Britons did not eat.

The information to be gained from the burial customs and the contents of the graves has already been gathered by the late Dr. Thurnam and by Canon Greenwell, as well as by other antiquaries, and I cannot do better than refer to the forty-third volume of

* " Ancient Stone Impts.," p. 402.
† Dawkins's " Early Man in Britain," p. 352; *Quart. Journ. Suff. Inst.*, vol. i. p. 31.

the "Archæologia," and to "British Barrows."[*] I may, however, shortly depict some of the principal features of the external conditions of the bronze-using population of these islands, taken as a whole, for no doubt the customs and condition of the people were by no means uniform throughout the whole extent of the country at any given moment of time.

As to their dwellings, we seem to have no positive information, but they probably were of much the same character as those of the Swiss Lake population, except that for the most part they were placed upon the dry land, and not on platforms above the water. Their clothing was sometimes of skins, sometimes of woollen cloth, and probably of linen also, as they were acquainted with the arts of spinning and weaving. Of domesticated animals they possessed the dog, ox, sheep, goat, pig, and finally the horse. They hunted the red deer, the roe, the wild boar, the hare, and possibly some other animals. For the chase and for warfare their arrows were tipped with flint, and not with bronze; and some other stone instruments, such as scrapers, remained in use until the end of the period. At the beginning, as has already often been stated, the axe, the knife-dagger, and the awl were the only articles of bronze in use. For obtaining fire, a nodule of pyrites and a flake of flint sufficed. Some cereals were cultivated, as is shown by the bronze sickles. Pottery they had of various forms, some apparently made expressly for sepulchral purposes; but they were unacquainted with the potter's wheel. Some vessels of amber and shale, turned in the lathe, may have been imported from abroad. Ornaments were worn in less profusion than in Switzerland; but the torque for the neck, the bracelet, the ear-ring, the pin for the dress and for the hair, were all in use, though brooches were unknown. Necklaces, or gorgets, formed of amber, jet, and bone beads were not uncommon; and the ornaments of glass and ivory, such as those lately mentioned, were probably obtained by foreign commerce. Gold, also, was often used for decorating the person, though coins, and apparently even the metal silver, were unknown. They appear to have been accomplished workers and carvers of wood and horn, and there were among them artificers who inlaid wood and amber with minute gold pins almost or quite as skilfully as the French workmen of the last century, who wrought on tortoise-shell. In casting

---

[*] See also Rolleston's App. to "British Barrows;" Lubbock's "Prehist. Times;" Dawkins's "Early Man in Britain," &c., &c.

and hammering out bronze they attained consummate skill, and their spear-heads and wrought shields could not be surpassed at the present day.   The general equipment of the warrior in the shape of swords, daggers, halberds, spears, &c., and the tools of the workman, such as hatchets, chisels, gouges, hammers, &c., have, however, all been dealt with at large in previous pages. They contrast with the arms and instruments of the preceding Neolithic Age more by their greater degree of perfection than by their absolute number and variety.   The material progress from one stage of civilisation to the other was no doubt great, but the interval between the two does not approach that which exists between Palæolithic man of the old River-drifts and Neolithic man of the present configuration of the surface of Western Europe.

So far as the general interest attaching to the Bronze Period is concerned, it may readily be conceded that it falls short of that with which either of the two stages of the Stone Period which preceded it must be regarded.   The existence of numerous tribes of men who are, or were until lately, in the same stage of culture as the occupants of Europe during the Neolithic Age, affords various points of comparison between ancient and modern savages which are of the highest interest, while there exists at the present day not a single community in which the phases of the Bronze culture can be observed.   The Palæolithic Age has, moreover, a charm of mysterious eld attaching to it as connected with the antiquity of the human race which is peculiarly its own.

The Bronze Age, nevertheless, from its close propinquity to the period of written history, is of the highest importance to those who would trace back the course of human progress to its earliest phases ; and though in this country many of the minute details of the picture cannot be filled in, yet, taken as a whole, the broad lines of the development of this stage of civilisation may be as well traced in Britain as in any other country.   It has been a pleasure to me to gather the information on which this work is based ; and I close these pages with the consolatory thought that, dry as may be their contents, they may prove of some value as a hoard of collected facts for other seekers after truth.

FINIS.

GENERAL INDEX.

A

Achilles, shield of, 12; spear of, 18, 242
Addua, Gauls defeated on the, 374
Æs importatum, 414, 419; *signatum*, 422
Æschylus quoted, 11
Æsculapius, temple of, 18
Æstii, the, iron scarce among, 19
Æthiopians, bronze rare among, 17
African axe of iron, 149; ironworkers, 181; swords, 306; trumpet, 359
Agamemnon, breast-plate of, 12
Agatharchides quoted, 8
Akerman, J. Y., F.S.A., cited, 391, 399
Alban necropolis, 341
Alcinous, walls of palace of, bronze-plated, 11
Algonquins, fusing of copper among the, 3
Alloys, various, of copper and tin, 22, 178, 265, 352, 415, 476
Amber, beads, 135, 189, 244, 366, 394, 487; buttons or studs, 217; cup with interment, 243, 486; hilts or pommels, 228, 229; ornaments, 373, 483, 485, 487; trade in, 483, 486
American tomahawks, 162
Amulets, celts used as, 134
Analysis of metal of caldron, 412; celts, 417, 421; Indian celts, 40; chisels, Mexican and Peruvian, 166; shield, 346; solder, 425; trumpets, 360, 363; various bronzes, 415 to 422
Anderson, Mr. Joseph, quoted, 239, 290
Anvils, 180 to 183, 375, 451
Ariantes, Scythian king, 318
Armillæ and Armlets. *See* Bracelets
Arreton Down type of spear-head, 257, 480
Arrow-heads, 216, 318, 323; flint, 39, 42, 167, 190, 223, 226, 236, 318, 391, 487
Arundelian marbles, 14
Aryan name for copper, 10
Asiatic origin of bronze, 2, 276, 420, 477
Assyrians, early use of iron among, 9; wore pen-annular bracelets, 383
Asteropæus, breast-plate of, 13
Ausonius quoted, 29
Awls, 188 to 191; double-pointed, 190; tanged, 189, 190; handled, 191; with interments, 189, 190, 191; 225, 241, 319, 392, 457
Axes, 14, 41, 147 to 156, 161, 162; African modern iron, 149; ceremonial, 450; Egyptian, 147; Hungarian, 147, 161, 482; clay mould for, 428; of copper, 265; perforated, 161, 478, 482; stone, 190, 226
Axe-hammers, of stone, 217, 224, 225, 243
Axe-shaped socketed celts, 142
Aymara Indians, 148
Aymard, M., collection, 215
Aztec chisel, 166

B

Banks, Sir J., quoted, 34, 155
Banks, Rev. S., collection, 78, 133
Barnwell, Rev. E. L., quoted, 55, 77
Barthélemy, Abbé, quoted, 20

Bateman collection, *see* Museums, Sheffield; Mr., quoted, 42, 44, 151, 190, 225, 227, 228, 383, 390, 392, 393, 402, 409
Battle-axe of Menelaus, 14. *See* Axes
Bayonet-like blades, 255, 256
Beads, 393; agate, 383; amber, 135, 189, 244, 366, 487; bone, 487; bronze, 381, 394; dentalium shells, 394; fluted, 381; glass, 134, 366, 394, 485; gold, 391, 394; ivory, 485; jet, 118, 158, 366, 394, 487; joints of encrinite, 394; pen-annular, 385, 391; pottery, 366; pulley-shaped, 381; tin, 394; with leaf-shaped projections, 381; with spiral ornaments, 394, 485
Beck, Rev. James, F.S.A., collection, 60, 84, 87
Beck, Dr. L., quoted, 15
Beger quoted, 28, 29
Bell or rattle of bronze, 364
Bell collection in the Ant. Mus., Edinburgh, 105
Bell-metal, 416
Bells to ear-rings, 393
BENIIIE, its meaning, 7
Bertrand, M. Alexandre, quoted, 300, 413
Birch, Dr. S., F.S.A., quoted, 9, 147, 374
Birds on rod, 406
Blackett, Sir Edward, collection, 351
Blackmore Museum. - *See* Museums, Salisbury
Blades, bayonet-like, 255, 256; curved, 264; difficulty of determining character of, 258, 260; lance-shaped, perforated, 213; of dissimilar character, in the same interment, 241; tanged, 211, 244
Blaeuw's Atlas, 162
Bloxam, Mr. M. H., F.S.A., collection, 75, 179
Boars found at Hounslow, 406
Bodkin obsolete as weapon, 369
Bone, instruments of, 189, 285, 366; of Horus, 8; of Typhon, 6, 8; plates for sword-hilt, 296; pommels for dagger-hilts, 228; rings, 51
Borlase, Dr., quoted, 30, 32, 439
Bourgeois, the Abbé, 160
Bouterolle. *See* Chapes
Boynton, Mr. T., collection, 327
Bracelets, 381 to 388; 90, 96, 135, 136, 155, 198, 333, 377; American, 383; Assyrian, 383; beaded, 385; circular, 384; gold, 94, 180, 209, 283, 285; jet, 385; Late Celtic, 385 to 388; looped, 76, 368, 378, 384, 386, 387; penannular, 381, 382; Scottish, 388, 400; with interments, 135, 385, 387
Bracer of chlorite slate, 223
Brackenridge, Rev. G. W., collection, 67
Brackstone, Mr., collection, 93, 131, 132
Braybrooke, Lord, collection, 211, 398, 403, 440
Brent, Mr. John, F.S.A., 88, 114
Bridle-bits, 144, 322, 368, 404, 405, 470
Bristles, possible early use of, 191
Britain, condition of its inhabitants in the Bronze Age, 486
Britannic province of bronze antiquities, 478
British types of instruments mostly indigenous, 24, 481

INDEX,

GEOGRAPHICAL AND TOPOGRAPHICAL.

See also " Hoards " and " Museums " in General Index.

Bo Island, 180, 292, 466
Enniskillen, 324, 369

GALWAY.

Galway, 370
Athenry, 320, 345
Athleague, Bog of Aughrane, 207
Claran Bridge, Dunkellen, 436
Headford, 314
Keelogue Ford, 142, 306, 371
Lough Corrib, 431

KILKENNY.

Piltown, Iverk, 306

KERRY.

Aghadoe, 293
Chute Hall, Tralee, 358
Derrynane, 360
Killarney, 361

KING'S COUNTY.

King's County, 61
Boyne River, near Edenderry, 155
Clonmacnoise, 379
Dowris, 176, 179, 211, 220, 293, 335, 360, 361, 410, 411, 412, 452, 468

LEITRIM.

Ballinamore, 236

LIMERICK.

Limerick, 361
Ballynamona, 352
Lough Gur, 313, 436

LONDONDERRY.

Londonderry, 141, 176, 215, 251
Balteragh, 207
Garvagh, 200
Lissane, 252
Maghera, 330, 435
Magherafelt, 244
Newtown Limavady, 268, 291
Portglenone, 361

LONGFORD.

Longford, 81
Carlea, 141
Lanesborough, 101

LOUTH.

Greenmount, Castle Bellingham, 63

MAYO.

Ballina, 141

MEATH.

Meath, 140
Athboy, 140
Dunshaughlin, 141
  " Crannoge at, 236
Kells, 207
Trim, 67

MONAGHAN.

Monaghan, 220, 256
Farney, 409
Lisletrim Bog, 295

SLIGO.

Colloony, 246
Kilrea, 247

TIPPERARY.

Tipperary, 63, 253, 272
Burrisokane, 171
Clonmel, 323
Cloonmore, Templemore, 305
Cullen, 293, 296
Rathkennan Bog, 251
Roscrea, 266

TYRONE.

Arboe, 142
Ballygawley, 201, 268
Ballynascreen, 212
Dungannon, 358
Galbally, 252
Terman, 324
Trillick, 61. 102, 140, 141, 180, 389, 399, 466

WESTMEATH.

Westmeath, 88, 100, 259
Athlone, 201, 314
Mullingar, 176

WEXFORD.

Slieve Kileta Hill, 266

FRANCE.

Gaul, 300, 426
France, 41, 83, 94, 95, 114, 119, 142, 281, 287, 207, 301, 369, 401, 403, 425, 480
France, North of, 19, 81, 116, 304, 379, 448, 480, 481, 483
France, North-west of, 81, 115
  " South of, 57, 85, 131, 153, 234, 479, 484
Brittany, 117, 124, 135, 181, 223, 403, 412, 417, 419, 477
Normandy, 43, 79; 91

AIN.

Cormoz, 300, 301

AISNE.

Aisne, 250

ALLIER.

Ferté Hauterive, La, 458
Gannat, 20

AUDE.

Carcassonne, 390
Cascastel, 122

BOUCHES DU RHONE.

Bounias, Cave of, 223

CANTAL.

Aliès, 287
Mons, St. Flour, 307

CALVADOS.

Escoville, 86
Frosné la Mère, 180, 183, 189, 209, 375

COTE D'OR.

Alise Ste. Reine, 293, 315, 341
Auxonne, 356
Cosne, 300
Magny Lambert, 300

COTES DU NORD.

Lamballe, 116
Moussaye, Plénée-Jugon, 115, 116, 445, 477

DOUBS.

Doubs, 43, 172
Besançon, 293

DROME.

Beaurières, 458
Marsanne, 307

EURE.

Bernay, 77, 78, 81
Evreux, 52
Gasny, 77
Les Andelys, 79

EURE ET LOIRE.

Lutz, 122

Lightning Source UK Ltd.
Milton Keynes UK
UKOW05f0912290915

259471UK00011B/386/P